Frommer's®

Peru

ition

by Neil Edward Schlecht

WILEY

John Wiley & Sons, Inc.

Published by:

JOHN WILEY & SONS, INC.

Copyright © 2013 John Wiley & Sons Ltd, The Atrium, Southern Gate, Chichester, West Sussex PO19 8SQ, UK

Telephone (+44) 1243 779777

Email (for orders and customer service enquiries): cs-books@wiley.co.uk. Visit our Home Page on www.wiley.com

Publisher: Kelly Regan
Production Manager: Daniel Mersey
Editor: Mark Henshall with Andrea Kahn
Project Editor: Hannah Clement
Cartography: Guy Ruggiero
Photo Editor: Cherie Cincilla, Richard H. Fox
Front cover photo: Market scene in Pisac valley in Cuzco © Pilar Susana Olivares Novoa
Back Cover photo: Machu Pichu Peru: Llamas amongst ruins © Llukee / Alamy Images

British Library Cataloguing in Publication Data

A catalogue record for this book is available from the British Library

ISBN 978-1-118-28754-5 (pbk), ISBN 978-1-118-33362-4 (ebk), ISBN 978-1-118-33476-8 (ebk), ISBN 978-1-118-33135-4 (ebk)

Typeset by Wiley Indianapolis Composition Services

Printed and bound in the United States of America

5 4 3 2 1

CONTENTS

5 SUGGESTED ITINERARIES 64

6 LIMA 76

7 THE CENTRAL COAST & HIGHLANDS 126

8 CUSCO 163

9 MACHU PICCHU & THE SACRED VALLEY 214

10 SOUTHERN PERU 265

11 AMAZONIA 319

12 NORTHERN PERU 356

13 PLANNING YOUR TRIP TO PERU 428

14 USEFUL TERMS & PHRASES 452

Index 462

LIST OF MAPS

ABOUT THE AUTHOR

Neil Edward Schlecht first trekked to Machu Picchu in 1983 during a junior year abroad in Quito, Ecuador, and he has continued making regular pilgrimages to Peru ever since. He is the author and coauthor of more than a dozen travel guides (including *Frommer's Barcelona Day by Day*, *Buenos Aires Day by Day*, and *Peru Day by Day*) and has written articles on travel, art, wine, and tennis for the *Irish Times*, *Galeria Antiqvaria*, CNN.com, and USOpen.org. After long stints in Spain and Brazil, he currently resides in Litchfield County, Connecticut.

HOW TO CONTACT US

In researching this book, we discovered many wonderful places—hotels, restaurants, shops, and more. We're sure you'll find others. Please tell us about them, so we can share the information with your fellow travelers in upcoming editions. If you were disappointed with a recommendation, we'd love to know that, too. Please write to:

Frommer's Peru, 6th Edition
John Wiley & Sons, Inc. • 111 River St. • Hoboken, NJ 07030-5774

ADVISORY & DISCLAIMER

Travel information can change quickly and unexpectedly, and we strongly advise you to confirm important details locally before traveling, including information on visas, health and safety, traffic and transport, accommodation, shopping and eating out. We also encourage you to stay alert while traveling and to remain aware of your surroundings. Avoid civil disturbances, and keep a close eye on cameras, purses, wallets and other valuables.

While we have endeavored to ensure that the information contained within this guide is accurate and up-to-date at the time of publication, we make no representations or warranties with respect to the accuracy or completeness of the contents of this work and specifically disclaim all warranties, including without limitation warranties of fitness for a particular purpose. We accept no responsibility or liability for any inaccuracy or errors or omissions, or for any inconvenience, loss, damage, costs or expenses of any nature whatsoever incurred or suffered by anyone as a result of any advice or information contained in this guide.

The inclusion of a company, organization or Website in this guide as a service provider and/or potential source of further information does not mean that we endorse them or the information they provide. Be aware that information provided through some Websites may be unreliable and can change without notice. Neither the publisher or author shall be liable for any damages arising herefrom.

FROMMER'S STAR RATINGS, ICONS & ABBREVIATIONS

Every hotel, restaurant, and attraction listing in this guide has been ranked for quality, value, service, amenities, and special features using a **star-rating system.** In country, state, and regional guides, we also rate towns and regions to help you narrow down your choices and budget your time accordingly. Hotels and restaurants are rated on a scale of zero (recommended) to three stars (exceptional). Attractions, shopping, nightlife, towns, and regions are rated according to the following scale: zero stars (recommended), one star (highly recommended), two stars (very highly recommended), and three stars (must-see).

In addition to the star-rating system, we also use **eight feature icons** that point you to the great deals, in-the-know advice, and unique experiences that separate travelers from tourists. Throughout the book, look for:

special finds—those places only insiders know about

fun facts—details that make travelers more informed and their trips more fun

kids—best bets for kids and advice for the whole family

special moments—those experiences that memories are made of

overrated—places or experiences not worth your time or money

insider tips—great ways to save time and money

great values—where to get the best deals

Warning—traveler's advisories are usually in effect

The following abbreviations are used for credit cards:

AE	American Express	DISC	Discover	V	Visa
DC	Diners Club	MC	MasterCard		

TRAVEL RESOURCES AT FROMMERS.COM

Frommer's travel resources don't end with this guide. Frommer's website, **www. frommers.com,** has travel information on more than 4,000 destinations. We update features regularly, giving you access to the most current trip-planning information and the best airfare, lodging, and car-rental bargains. You can also listen to podcasts, connect with other Frommers.com members through our active-reader forums, share your travel photos, read blogs from guidebook editors and fellow travelers, and much more.

THE BEST OF PERU

Peru may be inseparable from Machu Picchu and the legacy of the Inca Empire, but a scratch beneath the surface reveals a fascinating and dynamic country that preserves its Andean traditions. Cosmopolitan types dive into Lima's world-class dining, while travelers in Gore-Tex outdoor gear gather at pubs around Cusco's 500-year-old Plaza de Armas in anticipation of ruins treks. Canoe excursions set out from remote Amazon ecolodges in search of piranha and pink dolphins. In Sacred Valley markets, artisans haggle over handwoven alpaca textiles. And the religious quickly turns to profane as highland processions explode into wild celebrations with surreal masks and dangerous-looking scissor dancers.

SIGHTSEEING **Cusco** revels in its Andean traditions, with exquisite Inca stonemasonry on nearly every street. Take a train though the **Sacred Valley** to the Inca town of **Ollantaytambo** and legendary **Machu Picchu.** Float on **Lake Titicaca,** the world's highest navigable lake; board a small plane to get a birds-eye view of the **Nasca Lines;** and wander the alleyways of **Arequipa**'s Santa Catalina convent, carved out of white volcanic stone. The fast-paced capital **Lima** has revitalized its colonial quarter to go along with its sophisticated nightlife and shopping.

EATING & DRINKING The word's out: contemporary Peruvian cuisine is one of the world's most surprising and sophisticated. Get a heaping plate of tuna, sliced into Asian-inflected *tiradito* right off the boat, or savor **ceviche** at a hip, open-air restaurant. The highlands are famed for what the Incas ate: 300 varieties of potatoes and grains like **quinoa.** There are exotic tropical fruits from the Amazon and *ají* **peppers** that spice up all kinds of dishes. Taste a coca or passion-fruit sour—mixologists' takes on the classic **pisco sour** (invented in Lima).

NATURE Peru's natural diversity is astounding: bold **Andes** mountains running down the middle of the country, a 3,220-km (2,000-mile) **Pacific coast,** and the dense **Amazon basin** rainforest, which covers nearly two-thirds of Peru. Whether you're into extreme sports, birding, or photography, you'll find national parks with snowcapped volcanoes, towering desert sand dunes, and spine-tingling sights like brightly colored macaws gathering daily at mineral licks in **Tambopata.**

HISTORY Peru wears its complex web of pre-Columbian cultures and Spanish colonialism on its handwoven sleeve. From Inca ruins such as the mammoth **Sacsayhuamán** fortress overlooking Cusco and pre-Inca archaeological sites like **Chan Chan** to pastel-colored colonial mansions

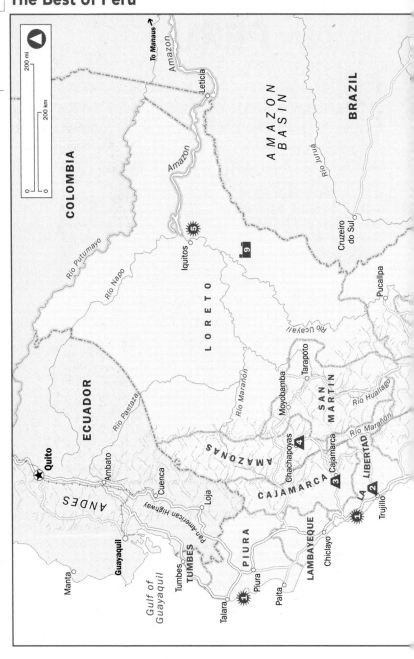

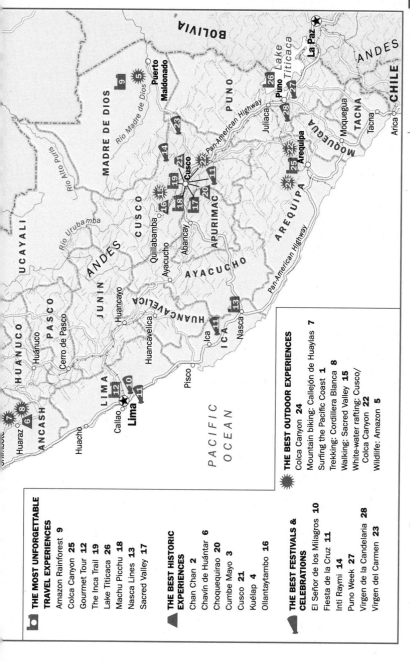

THE MOST UNFORGETTABLE TRAVEL EXPERIENCES

Amazon Rainforest **9**
Colca Canyon **25**
Gourmet Tour **12**
The Inca Trail **19**
Lake Titicaca **26**
Machu Picchu **18**
Nasca Lines **13**
Sacred Valley **17**

THE BEST HISTORIC EXPERIENCES

Chan Chan **2**
Chavín de Huántar **6**
Choquequirao **20**
Cumbe Mayo **3**
Cusco **21**
Kuélap **4**
Ollantaytambo **16**

THE BEST FESTIVALS & CELEBRATIONS

El Señor de los Milagros **10**
Fiesta de la Cruz **11**
Inti Raymi **14**
Puno Week **27**
Virgen de la Candelaria **28**
Virgen del Carmen **23**

THE BEST OUTDOOR EXPERIENCES

Colca Canyon **24**
Mountain biking: Callejón de Huaylas **7**
Surfing the Pacific Coast **1**
Trekking: Cordillera Blanca **8**
Walking: Sacred Valley **15**
White-water rafting: Cusco/Colca Canyon **22**
Wildlife: Amazon **5**

in **Trujillo** and the great royal tombs and treasures of the **Lord of Sipán,** you don't have to look far for a thrilling history lesson.

THE most unforgettable TRAVEL EXPERIENCES

- **Checking off a gourmet tour:** Peruvian cuisine—wonderfully diverse, creative, and accomplished—is finally getting its due. Trying ceviche is a must, but go beyond that and delve into restaurants focusing on the finest regional cuisines in Peru: Arequipeña, Chiclayana, and Cusqueña. See p. 265.

- **Soaring over the Nasca Lines:** One of South America's great enigmas, these designs, etched into the desert between 300 B.C. and A.D. 700 can only be appreciated from the air. Decide whether they're signs from the gods, astronomical calendars, or even extraterrestrial airports. Small-craft overflights dip and glide as you pick out mysterious figures such as "the Astronaut." See p. 146.

- **Marveling at Machu Picchu:** Cradled by the Andes and swathed in clouds, the ruins of the legendary "lost city of the Incas" are one of the world's most spectacular sites. Despite its enormous popularity, the site remains a thrilling experience, especially at sunrise, when rays of light creep over the mountaintops. See p. 238.

- **Hiking the Inca Trail (Cusco):** An arduous 4-day trek to Machu Picchu leads across astonishing Andean mountain passes and through some of the greatest attractions in Peru, including dozens of Inca ruins, dense cloud forest, and breathtaking mountain scenery. The trek has a superlative payoff: a sunrise arrival at the glorious ruins of Machu Picchu, shrouded in mist at your feet. See p. 238.

- **Worshiping the stars (Sacred Valley):** On a clear night, it's not hard to perceive the Incas' worship of the natural world, in which the moon was a deity. If your visit coincides with a full moon in that gargantuan sky and you identify the Southern Cross, you'll be talking about it back home for months. See p. 253.

- **Floating on Lake Titicaca:** To locals, the world's highest navigable body of water is a mysterious and sacred place. Get an anthropology lesson by staying with a local family on two inhabited natural islands, Amantaní and Taquile. Adventure seekers can even kayak on the lake's placid waters. See p. 266.

- **Watching condors soar (Colca Canyon):** Witness the flight of giant Andean condors, majestic birds with wingspans of up to 3.5m (11 ft.), over the world's second-deepest canyon. Each morning the condors suddenly appear, slowly circle, and gradually gain altitude with each pass until they soar silently above your head and journey down the river. See p. 308.

- **Plunging deep into the jungle:** Peru's massive tracts of Amazon-basin rainforest are a humid world unto themselves. Take an antique riverboat cruise, stay at a rustic jungle lodge and teeter on a canopy walk, or lose yourself with a private guide, making camp and catching dinner along the way. See p. 319.

THE most unforgettable CITY EXPERIENCES

- **Raising an eyebrow at the Larco Herrera (Lima):** Peru's great museums are almost all in Lima, and this archaeology collection includes 45,000 pieces of pre-Columbian art from the Moche dynasty (A.D. 200–700). Pornographic ceramics, with massive phalluses in compromising positions, in the Moche Sala Erótica may give you a jolt. See p. 89.

o **Partying in Barranco (Lima):** Though a suburb of Lima, seaside Barranco feels like an independent village, worlds removed from the chaotic capital. Artsy and easygoing during the day, at night its restaurants, bars, and nightclubs explode with energy. See p. 92.

o **Discovering a city of churches (Ayacucho):** For decades this colonial gem of a small highland city was prisoner to a homegrown guerrilla movement, precluding most visitors from relishing its collection of 33 colonial-era churches. Newly safe, Ayacucho erupts during Easter and Carnaval celebrations. See p. 153.

o **Getting lost at Santa Catalina (Arequipa):** The 1579 white-stone Santa Catalina Convent is an intricate architectural ensemble, with cobblestone streets, passageways, plazas, and cloisters, where 200 sequestered nuns once lived. A sunny afternoon here is like being transported to a small 16th-century Andalusian village. It's even more atmospheric on candlelit night visits. See p. 290.

o **Bar hopping in Cusco:** Though Cusco's historic quarter retains a strong Andean vibe, it's also a dynamic international city, and its pubs and nightclubs thump with a lively mix of locals and travelers from across the globe. When the evening lights glow amber in the Plaza de Armas, the action begins to heat up. See p. 194.

o **Venturing out on the river (Iquitos):** This humid Amazon city is distinguished by rubber-baron mansions covered in colorful Portuguese glazed tiles along the riverfront, as well as wild wooden houses on stilts in the often-flooded shantytown district of Belén, where locals get around by canoe. See p. 337.

THE most unforgettable
FOOD & DRINK EXPERIENCES

o **Dining with a celebrity chef:** Gastón Acurio, Peru's most famous chef, is a global ambassador for Peruvian cuisine. See what the fuss is about at any of his restaurants, from the original, Astrid y Gastón, and trendy La Mar in Lima, to Chicha, his take on regional cuisine in Arequipa and Cusco (p. 184). See p. 99 and 100.

o **Slurping ceviche:** A staple of Peruvian coastal cuisine, ceviche has taken the world by storm. A tantalizing dish of raw fish and shellfish marinated in lime or lemon juice and hot chili peppers, it's wonderfully refreshing and spicy. It's traditional for lunch, and best at a seaside *cevichería.* See p. 103.

o **Savoring a pisco sour:** Peru's national drink is a delicious concoction made from white-grape brandy, made frothy when mixed with egg whites, lemon juice, sugar, and bitters. Cold and complex, it's the closest thing to a Peruvian margarita. Look for trendy variations, such as the coca sour (pisco macerated in coca leaves), or those made with *maracuyá* (passion fruit) or any number of tropical fruit juices, such as *lúcuma.* See p. 140.

o **Sampling chifa & nikkei:** Large Chinese and Japanese immigrant populations have greatly influenced modern Peruvian cooking. Go upscale with raw fish at Toshiro's (p. 100), or try what's become a Peruvian staple: *Chifa,* a local variant of Chinese. See p. 98.

o **Barbecuing Peruvian-style:** *Pachamanca*—cooking over hot stones in a hole in the ground—is the local version of a barbecue get-together. On weekends in the Andes countryside, families gather around smoky subterranean grills, cooking up pork, beef, potatoes, and vegetables. If you don't stumble on one, you can get *pacha-manca*-style dishes in traditional *quinta* restaurants. See p. 234.

o **Going native with jungle cuisine:** In the Amazon, stay away from endangered animals like sea turtle (usually offered in a soup); caiman; and even *paiche,* an Amazon-size local fish that until recently was considered fair game. Instead, try *patarashca,* a steamed river fish wrapped in banana leaves; *juanes,* a kind of rice *tamale*; and *timbuche,* a thick soup made with local fish. See p. 319.

THE best WAYS TO SEE PERU LIKE A LOCAL

o **Visiting Surquillo food market (Lima):** It's not the fanciest market, but if you want to get a feel for where Lima's top chefs and local families shop for fresh produce, seafood, and meats, don't miss this lively, redolent market at the edge of Miraflores, a fascinating food-shopping and cultural experience. See p. 108.

o **Fishing for piranha (N. Amazon):** Head deep into the jungle and head out on the Amazon or its tributaries in a dugout canoe to fish for piranha. Most are surprisingly small, but their famous teeth are ferocious looking. Have the lodge cook fry 'em up for you that night. See p. 350.

o **Using local transport:** Take *motocarros* (motorcycle rickshaws), *combis,* and *colectivos* (private vans that pick up passengers along the road), even if you have to squeeze in and sit across from a woman with a baby goat on her lap. Hear locals speaking Quechua on their cell phones and experience how most Peruvians get around. See p. 431.

o **Singing protest songs 'til the sun comes up:** A true Peruvian cultural musical highlight is visiting an authentic *peña,* a small, informal club featuring musicians and patrons singing *música folclórica.* The best are in Lima, but one of my favorites is **Peña Usha Usha** in Cajamarca. See p. 395.

o **Trying *chicha* & *cuy*:** *Chicha,* home-brewed beer made from fermented maize, is served at modest taverns or homes flying the *chicha* flag—a long pole with a red flag or balloon letting people know there's *chicha* inside. Served lukewarm in plastic tumblers, it's not to many foreigners' liking. Equally hard to swallow is *cuy,* or guinea pig, an inexplicable local delicacy with more teeth and bones than meat. See p. 25.

o **Self-medicating with *mate de coca*:** Coca-leaf tea, a legal local beverage and centuries-old tradition, gives you a break when dealing with the high altitude of the Andes—which can make your head spin and your body reel. Rural highlanders chew coca leaves, as the Incas did, but you can get nearly the same relief from coca tea. See p. 164.

o **Trippin' jungle style:** Imitate the ancient ways of Amazon tribes and shamans by participating in an *ayahuasca* ceremony. The natural hallucinogenic potion, made of herbs, roots, and other plants, messes with your mind. But for locals, it's a deeply respected ritual. See p. 352.

THE best FAMILY EXPERIENCES

o **Seeing a riot of marine life (Islas Ballestas):** Take an island cruise around the Paracas National Reserve for up-close views of an amazing roster of protected species, including huge colonies of sea lions, endangered turtles, Humboldt penguins, red-footed boobies, pelicans, and red-footed cormorants. The islands are considered Peru's Galápagos. See p. 132.

o **Puzzling over the Nasca Lines:** Imagine a giant drawing book etched into the desert sands—that's what the Nasca Lines look like from the window of a small plane. Point out mysterious figures like "the Astronaut" and see if your kids believe in extraterrestrials. See p. 146.

o **Surfing big sand (Ica):** Sands in the peculiar, arid landscape of the southern desert rise to the highest dunes in South America. Jump onboard a fast-growing extreme sport: surfing the dunes on sand boards. The biggest are at Cerro Blanco near Nasca, but the prettiest spot is Huacachina Lagoon outside of Ica. See p. 141.

o **Appreciating Inca masonry (Cusco):** Monumental Inca walls, constructed of giant granite blocks so well carved that they fit together without mortar like jigsaw puzzle pieces, dominate historic Cusco. Down alleyways lined with polygonal stones, kids can pick out the famous 12-angled stone and a series of stones that forms the shape of a large puma. See p. 173.

o **Sliding and hiding at Sacsayhuamán (Cusco):** Among the Incas' greatest ruins, these zigzagged defensive walls—with some blocks weighing as much as 300 tons—are an unexpected delight for kids. Some large stones have time-worn grooves, which children have discovered make great slides. And nearby is a stone funhouse of claustrophobia-inducing tunnels. See p. 179.

o **Getting wide-eyed at Machu Picchu:** Even small children are speechless faced with the wonder of Machu Picchu. See the sun come rising over the Andes at dawn, while older kids can climb to the top of steep Huayna Picchu for unrivaled birds-eye views of the ruins. See p. 238.

o **Hopping on an Andean train:** The train to Machu Picchu from Cusco is a thrilling journey through the sacred Urubamba Valley, filled with anticipation, while the train south to Lake Titicaca is full of transfixing highland scenery, also with a giant payoff at the end. But for true thrillseekers, there's nothing like el Tren Macho, the world's highest train, from Lima to Huancayo. See p. 152.

o **Taking a boat to floating Islands (Titicaca):** Although kids will wonder how people can live on man-made islands fashioned out of squishy reeds, the more fascinating inhabited islands are Taquile and Amantaní, where staying with a family is a cultural lesson they're unlikely to forget. See p. 270.

o **Zipping along the treetops (Amazon):** Although Peru's Amazon isn't quite a Costa Rican playground, there is a zipline in the northern Amazon, and a handful of lodges in both major sections of the Amazon basin have delicate canopy walks above the trees, giving you a keen perspective on the dense rainforest. See p. 352.

THE best OUTDOOR EXPERIENCES

o **Bagging South America's highest peaks (Cordillera Blanca):** For expert climbers, the Cordillera Blanca is a mountaineering mecca. From May to September, fit and acclimated climbers can notch several 6,000m (20,000-ft.) summits in the Parque Nacional Huascarán in just a couple of weeks. Huascarán, at 6,768m (22,205 ft.), is the big one, the tallest tropical mountain in the world. See p. 404.

o **Walking in the serene Sacred Valley:** You don't have to join the crowds on the strenuous 4-day Inca Trail to Machu Picchu. Ollantaytambo and Yucay are the best bases for easy walks in the pretty countryside of the Urubamba Valley. The trek from the Inca site Moray to the ancient Salineras salt mines is particularly beautiful. See p. 237.

o **Running big-time white water:** Just beyond Cusco are some excellent river runs, ranging from mild to world-class; novices can do 1-day trips to get their feet (and more) wet, while more experienced rafters can take multi-day trips. The area around the Colca Canyon is even better for extremely technical white-water rafting. See p. 221.

o **Plunging into the world's second-deepest canyon (Colca):** Trek deep into the canyon, from the Cruz del Cóndor lookout, or explore the beautiful valley's agricultural terraces and colonial villages on horseback or mountain bike. Nothing wrong with hewing close to the edge of the river and walking from one village to another, either; end the day in luxurious hot springs. See p. 312.

o **Spotting elusive birds & wildlife (Amazon):** Peru's southern Amazon rainforest, one of the most biologically diverse on the planet, is terrific for viewing wildlife and more than 1,000 species of birds—including the sight of thousands of macaws and parrots feeding at a clay lick. Keep your eyes peeled for more elusive wildlife, such as caimans and river otters. See p. 333.

o **Surfing the waves (Pacific Coast):** Wave connoisseurs are sweet on Peru's long Pacific coastline and a great variety of left and right reef breaks, point breaks, and big-time waves. Northern Peru, best from October to March, is the top choice of most, and surfers hang out in the easygoing fishing villages of Huanchaco and Máncora. See p. 59.

o **Spinning on big-time single track (Callejón de Huaylas):** For splendid mountain biking, hit the Cordillera Blanca, where hundreds of mountain and valley horse trails lace lush fields and push past picturesque Andean villages and alpine lakes. Hard-core peddlers can test their lung capacity climbing to 5,000m (16,400-ft.) mountain passes. See p. 57.

THE best HISTORIC EXPERIENCES

o **Witnessing a clash of cultures (Cusco):** The one-time Inca capital is a living museum of Peruvian history, with Spanish colonial churches and mansions constructed atop Inca granite walls. Most fascinating mash-up: The Temple of the Sun and the church of Santo Domingo. Streets still have Quechua names dating to Inca times, such as Saqracalle ("Where the demons dwell"). See p. 169.

o **Measuring perfection (Ollantaytambo):** Ollanta's fortress ruins have some of the Incas' finest stonemasonry, including 200 stone steps straight to the top. Other engineering genius is the grid of 15th-century *canchas,* or city blocks, that form the old town. Canals ripple alongside the stone streets, carrying water down from the mountains. See p. 230.

o **Trekking to really remote ruins (Kuélap/Choquequirao):** Notch bragging rights by making arduous journeys to ruins you'll have virtually to yourself. Kuélap is a complex of 400 round buildings surrounded by a massive defensive wall, while Choquequirao, an Inca site still only 30% uncovered, takes 4 or 5 days on foot to get there and back. Both are thought of as the new Machu Picchu. See p. 384.

o **Marveling at a millennial aqueduct (Cumbe Mayo):** Amid strange rock formations is a pre-Inca aqueduct constructed around 1000 B.C., likely the oldest man-made structure in South America. The 8km (5-mile) canal is carved from volcanic stone in perfect lines to collect and redirect water on its way to the Pacific Ocean. See p. 392.

- **Imagining Chan Chan:** The capital of the Chimú Empire, Chan Chan (c. A.D. 1300) is the largest adobe complex of pre-Columbian America. Wandering among its nine royal palaces, especially the peculiar friezes of Tschudi Palace, will set your mind spinning on the Chimús' scope and sophistication. See p. 363.

THE best FESTIVALS & CELEBRATIONS

- **Crossing cultures at Fiesta de la Cruz:** The Festival of the Cross isn't as solemnly Catholic as it sounds. Best in Lima, Cusco, and Ica, the festival features vibrant cross processions as well as folk music and dance, the highlight being the famed and daring "scissors dancers," who long ago performed on top of churches. See p. 35.

- **Hitting a purple patch at El Señor de los Milagros (Lima):** Prince would love this highly religious procession—the largest procession in South America—with tens of thousands of reverent followers clad in bright purple. The Lord of Miracles lasts an entire day and venerates a painting of Jesus Christ, created by an Angolan slave and a lone survivor of the devastating 1746 earthquake. See p. 88.

- **Worshiping the sun at Inti Raymi (Cusco):** One of the continent's most spectacular pageants, the Festival of the Sun celebrates the winter solstice, honoring the Inca sun god with colorful Andean parades, music, and dance. The event envelops Cusco and transforms the Sacsayhuamán ruins overlooking the city into a majestic stage. See p. 181.

- **Going wild at Virgen del Carmen (Paucartambo):** The minuscule, remote Andean colonial village of Paucartambo hosts one of Peru's wildest festivals. The 3 days of dance, drinking, and frightening costumes pack in thousands, who camp all over town and then wind up (only temporarily, one hopes) at the cemetery. See p. 211.

- **Getting all folksy at Virgen de la Candelaria (Puno):** Candlemas (or Virgen de la Candelaria), spread over 2 weeks, is one of the greatest folk religious festivals in South America, an explosion of music, dance, and some of the most fantastical costumes and masks seen anywhere. See p. 272.

- **Celebrating Puno Week (Puno):** Marking the region's Amerindian roots, a massive procession from Lake Titicaca into town pays homage to the legend of the first Inca emperor emerging from Titicaca's waters to establish the Inca Empire. From there it deviates into dance, music, and drunken oblivion. See p. 272.

THE best PLACES TO GET AWAY FROM IT ALL

- **Staying at exclusive Isla Suasi (Lake Titicaca):** Revel in exclusivity at this eco-resort on its own tiny island in the blue expanse of Titicaca. The sunsets are surreal, and your companions on hikes are rare resident vicuñas. See p. 278.

- **Marveling at Colca Valley:** Vargas Llosa's "Valley of Wonders" has everything from giant Andean condors circling overhead and snowcapped volcanoes to narrow gorges, and 14 frozen-in-time colonial villages. Collagua and Cabana natives are descendants of pre-Inca ethnic communities, identified by distinctive embroidered and sequined hats. See p. 308.

○ **Diversifying in Tambopata and Manu:** Naturalists can really lose themselves in Peru's Southern Amazon: **Tambopata** is blessed with more species of birds than any place of similar size, including its famous macaw clay lick; and remote **Manu,** as close as you'll come to virgin rainforest anywhere, has the highest bird, mammal, and plant diversity of any park on the planet. See p. 320.

○ **Being spoilt at Huascarán National Park:** A goldmine for trekkers and climbers, the longest tropical mountain range in the world features 200 alpine lakes, 600 glaciers, and incomparable mountain vistas. A UNESCO Biosphere Reserve and World Heritage Trust site, the park contains nearly the whole of the celebrated Cordillera Blanca. See p. 44.

○ **Protecting at Pacaya-Samiria National Reserve:** The largest protected area in Peru and one of the best-conserved in the world, this reserve of pristine rainforest and wetlands contains some of the Amazon's greatest wildlife, including pink dolphins, macaws, black caimans, spider monkeys, and giant river turtles. See p. 44.

○ **Getting funky at Máncora:** Long popular with surfing addicts and bohemian travelers who passed through and never left, this funky northern coastal town is now gaining a reputation for more than its waves and bars. New hotels and restaurants are luring a whole new breed of sophisticated traveler. See p. 398.

THE best MARKETS & SHOPPING

○ **Loading up at Miraflores (Lima):** The upscale Miraflores neighborhood is full of shops stocked to the rafters with handicrafts, silver jewelry, and antiques from around Peru. For one-stop shopping, *artesanía* minimalls have the country's widest selection of ceramics, textiles, and art. See p. 106.

○ **Spending studio time at Barrio de San Blas (Cusco):** Cusco's most flavorful shopping zone is the picturesque neighborhood of San Blas, which rises into the hills and bursts with the workshops of artists and artisans, art galleries and ceramics shops. Duck into studios and see artists at work. See p. 172.

○ **Getting busy at Mercado de Artesanía (Pisac):** Though the country's most popular market, this lively institution—awash in colorful Andean textiles, including rugs, sweaters, and ponchos—still cannot be missed. It takes over the central plaza and spills across adjoining streets. See p. 217.

○ **Hanging high at Chinchero's handicrafts market:** Less known than Pisac's market, but more authentic and with higher-quality artisanal goods. Sellers from remote mountain populations still wear traditional garments. But be warned: the altitude is as dizzying as the textiles. See p. 225.

○ **Going local at Isla Taquile, Lake Titicaca:** Taquile islanders are famous for their dress and exquisite handwoven textiles. Travelers can pick up very fine embroidered waistbands and wool stocking caps in Peru, including some that are normally reserved for community authorities. See p. 276.

- **Donning alpaca in Arequipa:** Arequipa is the top spot for great designs in alpaca, vicuña, and wool sweaters, ponchos, and *chullos* (hats with earflaps). Visit alpaca boutiques inhabiting the old cloisters of the La Compañía church or the stalls of the general handicrafts market in what used to be the old town jail. See p. 294.
- **Taking in Barrio Belén (Iquitos):** The wildly colorful (and odiferous) market in this waterfront neighborhood, where many houses sit on stilts above the river, spreads over long blocks and sells everything under the Amazon sun. Keep an eye out for unusual Amazon fish and fruits, and exotic jungle meats. See p. 343.

PERU IN DEPTH

Peru has a habit of turning virtually every visitor into an amateur archaeologist or outdoors enthusiast. Intriguing ruins, the legacies of the Incas and even more ancient pre-Columbian cultures, fire the imagination, and outstanding museum collections of ceramics, textiles, and remarkably preserved mummies weave a complex tale of some of the world's most advanced cultures. Dense tracts of Amazonian rainforest and forbidding Andes summits are known to only a select few adventurers. And yet—Machu Picchu's immense popularity notwithstanding—with so many sites still being excavated, and ruins almost continually discovered in remote jungle regions, Peru still has the rare feeling of a country in the 21st century that hasn't been exhaustively explored.

The third-largest country in South America (after Brazil and Argentina), Peru has grown immensely as a travel destination over the past decade—though it still seems comparatively undervalued, given all it has to offer. With spectacular Andes mountains and highland culture, a swath of Amazon rainforest second only to Brazil, one of the richest arrays of wildlife in the world, and some of the Americas' greatest ruins of pre-Columbian cultures, Peru deserves to be experienced by so many more people.

When the Spanish conquistador Francisco Pizarro and his fortune-hunting cronies descended on Peru in 1528, they found not only vast riches, but also a highly sophisticated culture. The Spaniards soon overpowered the awed and politically weakened Inca Empire, but they didn't discover the Incas' greatest secret: The imperial city of Machu Picchu, today acclaimed as the pinnacle achievement of the continent's pre-Columbian societies.

Most people still know Peru only as the land of the Incas. Yet today it is a land of dynamic, cosmopolitan cities with world-class restaurants; indeed, Peru's tantalizing regional cuisines have taken many parts of the world by storm, on the shoulders of a few celebrity chef-ambassadors. Mountain bikers and surfers, ice climbers and mountaineers, birders and naturalists are flocking to Peru's vast jungle, desert, coast, and mountains.

While it embraces its traditions and storied pre-Columbian past, Peru is undeniably a country on the move. Just a couple of decades removed from military dictatorships, extreme poverty, and homegrown terrorism, Peruvians are proud of their nation's new incarnation as a stable democracy with enviable economic growth. The novelist Mario Vargas Llosa, winner of the 2010 Nobel Prize for Literature, has extolled his country's economic and social progress: "I do not remember—and I'm 75 years old—a time when Peru has had such a good image abroad."

Peru's fascinating history is in evidence everywhere: in mortarless Inca stones that serve as foundations for colonial churches; open graves with bits and pieces of ancient textiles; and in traditional dress, foods, and festivals, as well as strongly held Andean customs and beliefs. Visitors to Peru will discover a country and a people rooted in a glorious past but looking forward to a future of new possibilities.

PERU TODAY

Peru's recent history of suffering—two decades of political mayhem and corruption, hyperinflation, surprise attacks from homegrown Maoist "Shining Path" terrorists, cocaine trafficking, and violent street crime—is well documented. Throughout the 1980s and early '90s, Peruvians fled the capital and the countryside, fearful of attack; few travelers were brave enough to plan vacations in the troubled nation.

Though Peru is rich in artifacts and culture, it remains poor and a society dominated by elites. Although a third of the population lives at or below the poverty line, in recent years the level of extreme poverty has dropped considerably, to 7.6%. The horrendous violence of two decades ago has now almost completely abated, and outside of areas deep in the jungle, there are no areas where visitors should not feel welcome to travel. Rumors of a Shining Path revival have not been borne out, even though at least two major attacks in the last decade, including a bombing near the U.S. embassy in Lima, have been attributed to the group.

The disgraced and now ailing former president Alberto Fujimori, who fled the country to live in exile in Japan, was arrested in Chile in 2005 attempting to return to Peru in a surprise bid to run for president. Extradited to Peru and jailed, Fujimori was convicted on charges of ordering the murders of suspected Shining Path guerrillas and their collaborators by death squad (he remains in a jail in Lima, sentenced to 25 years for his role in ordering death squads, along with three other concurrent sentences, including for abuse of power, bribery, and illegal wiretapping of phones). The trial marked the first time in Peruvian history that a former president has been tried for crimes committed during his administration.

DATELINE

Pre-Columbian

20 000–10 000 B.C. The earliest settlers, most likely migrants from Asia, arrive.

1000 B.C.–900 B.C Establishment of Chavín de Huántar.

700 B.C. Rise of Paracas culture in the southern desert.

300 B.C.–A.D. 700 Nasca Lines created.

A.D. 200 Consolidation of Moche dynasty in northern Peru.

CA. 300 Burial of Lord of Sipán.

1150 Construction of Chan Chan begins.

Colonial Era & Independence

1200 Manco Cápac becomes the first Inca (emperor) and founds Inca Empire.

1438 Reign of the Inca Pachacútec; Sacsayhuamán and Machu Picchu built.

1460–65 Inca conquest of southern desert coast; empire extends to Ecuador.

1527 Inca civil war.

1532 Atahualpa defeats brother to gain control of the Inca Empire. Pizarro captures Atahualpa.

continues

With the 2001 election of Alejandro Toledo, the country's first president of native Indian origin, many Peruvians believed that the country had finally turned a corner and that the 21st century would bring stability, progress, and prosperity. Although the economy initially grew at an impressive rate, the road to a safer and more stable Peru ran into more than a few bumps along the way. Like previous governments, Toledo's administration was plagued by instability, abuse of power, and poor management, opening the door for former president Alan García, who returned from exile abroad and improbably captured the 2006 presidential election. García positioned himself as a centrist, seeking to put a clamp on inflation and aggressively pursuing free-market policies. Most notably, he pushed aggressively for a free-trade agreement with the United States, a treaty entered into force in 2009 (Peru is seeking similar agreements with Mexico and Canada). The Peruvian economy recorded a robust growth rate of 9.2% in 2008, a 15-year high and one of the most impressive in the world.

But Peru's political realities continue to be unique, if not surreal. The former army officer Ollanta Humala was elected in 2011, defeating Keiko Fujimori, the right-wing daughter of former (and you'll recall, jailed) Alberto Fujimori. Humala, previously a firebrand and outspoken nationalist, battled Shining Path guerrillas, led a military uprising against Fujimori in 2000, and is saddled with a controversial family (including a brother currently in jail for kidnapping and killing police officers). But he has positioned himself as a nonideological reformer in the model of Brazil's transformative former president Luiz Inacio Lula da Silva, a one-time leftist labor union leader who oversaw Brazil's rise to global economic prominence. Like Lula, Humala argues that he is poised to cement Peru's economic and social transformation into a modern, stable democratic nation.

The Peruvian economy has continued to expand, dropping off only slightly to a 6.9% growth rate in 2011, while many of the world's economies were still struggling to find their way out of recession. Although much of that growth has been stimulated by foreign investment in mining and other sectors, from which few Peruvians benefit, there is a growing sense of optimism. Tourism growth has averaged 10% annually, with record-setting numbers of travelers (1 million plus) embarking on ecotourism in

1533 Spaniards assassinate Atahualpa; Cusco sacked and burned by Spaniards.	1824 Peru defeats Spain and becomes the last colony in Latin America to gain its independence.
1535 Francisco Pizarro establishes Lima and names it capital of the Viceroyalty of Peru.	1849–74 Chinese workers (100,000) arrive in Peru as menial laborers.
1541 Pizarro killed in Lima.	1870s Rubber boom in the Peruvian Amazon.
1572 Tupac Amaru, the last Inca emperor, captured and executed.	1879–83 Chile defeats Peru and Bolivia in the War of the Pacific; Peru loses southern territory to Chile.
1780 Tupac Amaru II leads failed revolt against Spanish.	**20th Century**
1821 General José de San Martín captures Lima and proclaims Peru's independence.	1948 Coup d'état installs military government.

WATCH YOUR language

The term *cholo* is often used to describe Peruvians of color and obvious Amerindian descent, usually those who have migrated from the highlands to the city. It is frequently employed as a derogatory and racist term by the Limeño population of European descent, but former President Alejandro Toledo claimed the term for himself and all *mestizos* (those of mixed race) of Peru, in an attempt to demonstrate pride in their common culture and to take the sting out of the term. Afro-Peruvians are more commonly called *morenos*(as) or *negros*(as). Using any of these terms can potentially be a complicated and charged matter for foreigners, especially those who have little experience in the country or fluency in the language. At any rate, it's best for gringos (foreigners; almost always not a derogatory term) simply to steer clear of such linguistic territory. It's better to refrain from making distinctions among races and colors than to risk offending someone.

Peru's protected natural areas, and a dizzying number of swank new hotels (both Peruvian and internationally owned) springing up across the country, including in far-flung places like the banks of Lake Titicaca, Colca Canyon, and the formerly ramshackle, hippie beach destination Máncora. Peru is poised to become the second-largest coffee producer in South America, and is projected to register one of the highest growth rates and lowest inflation rates in the Americas, just behind the region's juggernaut, Brazil. The capital Lima, experiencing a real-estate boom, has undertaken construction of an underground subway system, and the city will host Rock in Rio, a major international music festival, in 2014. Mario Vargas Llosa, Peru's most famous novelist (and former presidential candidate), won the Nobel Prize for Literature in 2010, becoming the first Peruvian to do so, and also for the first time, a Peruvian film, *The Milk of Sorrow,* was nominated for an Academy Award for Best Foreign Film. The acclaimed Afro-Peruvian singer Susana Baca was named Peru's

1963 Peru returns to civilian rule; Fernando Belaúnde Terry becomes President.

1968 Civilian government ousted in coup led by General Juan Velasco Alvarado.

1969 Large-scale land reform and nationalization programs initiated.

1970 Disastrous landslide kills 20,000 in Yungay (Ancash).

1975 Velasco ousted in coup.

1980 Peru returns to civilian rule with re-election of Fernando Belaúnde.

Maoist terrorist organization, Sendero Luminoso (Shining Path), and a smaller group, Tupac Amaru (MRTA), launch armed guerrilla struggle.

1982 Debt crisis; deaths and "disappearances" escalate following military crackdown on guerrillas and drug traffickers.

1985 Alan García wins presidency, promises to rid Peru of military and police "old guard." Belaúnde first elected president to turn over power to a constitutionally elected successor since 1945.

continues

Minister of Culture in 2011 (becoming the first black minister in Peru's history), and major international pop stars like Bono of U2 have descended on Cusco, Machu Picchu, and Tambopata National Reserve, validating Peru's rising profile.

Though there's an incipient national swagger that's been sorely missing for decades, based on the prospects of prosperity for some and renewed growth of a middle class, in Peru the divide between rich and poor, coastal elites and indigenous highlanders, and modern and traditional, continues to loom large. Without a doubt, a newly confident Peru is more welcoming than ever for visitors. All those unfortunate years of corrupt politicians, lawlessness, and economic disarray may have clouded but never eclipsed the beauty and complexity of this fascinating Andean nation.

THE MAKING OF PERU

Peru is littered with archaeological discoveries of many civilizations, from highland to coast. Two decades ago, a *National Geographic* team discovered Juanita the Ice Maiden, an Inca princess sacrificed on Mount Ampato more than 500 years ago. (Her frozen corpse is now exhibited in Arequipa's Museo Santuarios Andinos; see p. 292.) Only in the last decade, archaeologists unearthed more than 2,000 extraordinarily well-preserved mummies from one of Peru's largest Inca burial sites, found under a shantytown on the outskirts of Lima. Researchers describe Caral, a site in central Peru, believed to date to 2600 B.C., as the oldest city in the Americas, and archaeologists recently celebrated the discovery of a 4,000-year-old temple on the northern coast.

First inhabited as many as 20,000 years ago, Peru was the cradle of several of the most ancient and sophisticated pre-Columbian civilizations in the Americas. The Chavín, Paracas, Nasca, Huari, Moche, and Incas, among others, form a long line of complicated, occasionally overlapping, and frequently warring cultures stretching back to 2000 B.C. Before the Incas, two other civilizations, the Chavín and the Huari-Tiahuanaco, achieved pan-Andean empires. Most of what is known about pre-Columbian cultures is based on the unearthing of temples and tombs because none possessed a written language. Further complicating matters is the fact that, as one

1988 Hyperinflation and bankruptcy rock Peru. Shining Path's guerrilla bombing and assassination campaign intensifies.

1990 Human rights groups estimate as many as 10,000 political murders (including thousands of *campesinos*) in Peru. Alberto Fujimori, son of Japanese immigrants, runs on anticorruption platform and defeats Mario Vargas Llosa, Peru's best-known novelist.

1992 Fujimori dissolves Congress, suspends the constitution, and imposes censorship. Shining Path

leader Abimael Guzmán arrested and sentenced to life in prison.

1994 6,000 Shining Path guerrillas surrender to authorities.

1996 Tupac Amaru guerrillas seize 490 hostages at the residence of the Japanese ambassador. The American Lori Berenson convicted of treason by a secret military court and sentenced to life in prison for plotting with Tupac Amaru Revolutionary Movement.

1997 Peruvian special forces launch an attack and free hostages held

culture succeeded a previous one, it imposed its values and social structure on the vanquished but also assimilated features useful to it, making distinction among some early cultures exceedingly difficult.

Prehistory (20 000 B.C.–6000 B.C.)

Early societies were located mainly in the coastal areas and highlands. Many fell victim to warfare, cyclical floods, extended drought, and earthquakes. Evidence of pivotal pre-Columbian cultures—including ruined temples; spectacular collections of ceramics, masks, and jewelry; and tombs found with well-preserved mummies—is everywhere in Peru, and some sites are only now being excavated and combed for clues.

The first inhabitants are thought by most historians to have crossed the Bering Strait in Asia during the last ice age, worked their way across the Americas, and settled in the region around 20 000 B.C. (although this migratory pattern has been disputed by some scholars). They were nomadic hunter-gatherers who lived along the central and northern coasts. The Pikimachay cave, which dates to 12 000 B.C., is the oldest known inhabited site in Peru. The earliest human remains, discovered near Huánaco in highland Peru, are from around 7000 B.C. Early Peruvians were responsible for cave paintings at Toquepala (Tacna, 7000 B.C.) and houses in Chillca (Lima, 5000 B.C.). Experts say that recent analysis of findings at the coastal site Caral, in the Supe Valley, demonstrates the existence of the earliest complex civilization in the Americas. The city was inhabited as many as 4,700 years ago, 1,000 years earlier than once believed.

Pre-Inca Cultures (100 B.C.–A.D. 1100)

A long line of equally advanced cultures preceded the relatively short-lived Inca Empire. Over several thousand years, civilizations up and down the south Pacific coast and deep in the highlands developed ingenious irrigation systems, created sophisticated pottery and weaving techniques, and built great pyramids, temples, fortresses, and cities of adobe. Early peoples constructed mysterious cylindrical towers and the even more enigmatic Nasca Lines, giant drawings of animals and symbols

at the Japanese ambassador's residence. El Niño—the worst of the century—causes severe drought in Peru.

Modern Times

2000 Fujimori re-elected by landslide to a third 5-year term. His chief of intelligence, Vladimiro Montesinos, caught on videotape bribing an opposition politician. Fujimori resigns, goes into exile in Japan.

2001 Montesinos captured in Venezuela. Plane carrying American missionaries shot down by Peruvian military. Alejandro Toledo becomes Peru's first president of native Indian origin. Massive earthquake rocks Arequipa and southern Peru.

2002 Peru seeks to extradite former president Fujimori from Japan.

2003 Toledo declares state of emergency. Interpol issues arrest warrant for Fujimori and Congress requests Fujimori's extradition from Japan.

continues

Center of the World

The word Inca means "Children of the Sun," while Cusco is literally "navel," a reference no doubt to its central place in the continent-spanning Inca Empire.

somehow etched into the desert plains for eternity.

Over the course of nearly 15 centuries, pre-Inca cultures settled principally along the Peruvian coast and highlands. Around 6000 B.C., the Chinchero people along the southern desert coast mummified their dead, long before the ancient Egyptians had thought of it. By the 1st century B.C., during what is known as the Formative, or Initial, period, Andean society had designed sophisticated irrigation canals and produced the first textiles and decorative ceramics. Another important advance was the specialization of labor, aided in large part by the development of a hierarchical society.

The earliest known Peruvian civilization was the **Chavín culture** (1200–400 B.C.), a theocracy that worshiped a feline, jaguar-like god and settled in present-day Huántar, Ancash (central Peru). Over 8 centuries, the Chavín, who never developed into a military or mercantilistic empire, unified groups of peoples across Peru. The most spectacular remnant of this culture, known for its advances in stone carving, pottery, weaving, and metallurgy, is the Chavín de Huántar temple, 40km (25 miles) east of Huaraz (see p. 407). The ceremonial center, a place of pilgrimage, contained wondrous examples of religious carving, such as the Tello Obelisk and the Raimondi Stella. The temple demonstrates evidence of sophisticated engineering and division of labor.

A subsequent society, the **Paracas** culture (700 B.C.–A.D. 200), took hold along the southern coast. It is renowned today for its superior textile weaving, considered perhaps the finest example of pre-Columbian textiles in the Americas. The Paracas peoples were sophisticated enough to dare to practice trepanation, a form of brain surgery that consisted of drilling holes in the skull to cure various ailments and correct cranial deformation. You can see fine examples of Paracas textiles and ceramics at the Julio C. Tello Museum in Paracas (see p. 132).

2005 Fujimori arrested in Chile; jailed next year in Peru (where he remains).

2006 Former President Alán García elected President after return from exile.

2007 7.9 earthquake devastates southern desert coast (Pisco and Ica).

2010 Mudslides in Sacred Valley strand 2,000 tourists at Machu Picchu and kill 5. Mario Vargas

Llosa becomes first Peruvian to be awarded Nobel Prize for Literature. Lori Bensen released from prison after 15 years.

2011 Ollanta Humala is elected President. The Afro-Peruvian singer Susana Baca is named Minister of Culture, becoming Peru's first black minister in more than 200 years.

The Classical period (A.D. 200–1100) was one of significant social and technological development. Likely descendants of the Paracas, the Moche and Nasca cultures are among the best studied in pre-Columbian Peru. The **Moche** (or **Mochica**) civilization (A.D. 200–700), one of the first true urban societies, dominated the valleys of the north coast near Trujillo and conquered a number of smaller groups in building their widespread empire. The Moche were a highly organized hierarchical civilization that created extraordinary adobe platform complexes, such as the Temples of the Sun and Moon near Trujillo (the former was the largest man-made structure of its day in the Americas), and the burial site of Sipán, near Chiclayo, where the remains and riches of the famous Lord of Sipán, a religious and military authority, were unearthed in remarkably preserved royal tombs (remarkably brought to life, as it were, at the Museo Tumbas Reales in Lambayeque; see p. 378). Moche pottery, produced from molds, contains vital clues to their way of life, down to very explicit sexual representations. Its frank depictions of phalluses, labia, and nontraditional bedroom practices might strike some visitors as pre-Columbian pornography. The best spot to view the extraordinary (in all senses of the word) ceramics of the Moche is the Rafael Larco Herrera Museum in Lima; see p. 89.

The **Nasca** culture (A.D. 300–800) established itself along the coastal desert south of Lima. Nasca engineers created outstanding underground aqueducts, which permitted agriculture in one of the most arid regions on Earth, and its artisans introduced polychrome techniques in pottery. But the civilization is internationally known for the enigmatic **Nasca Lines** (see p. 146), geometric and animal symbols etched indelibly into the desert, elements of an agricultural and astronomical calendar that are so vast that they can only really be appreciated from the window of an airplane.

The **Huari** (also spelled **Wari**) culture (A.D. 600–1100), an urban society that was the first in Peru to pursue explicitly expansionist goals through military conquest, settled the south-central *sierra* near Ayacucho (there's an excellent archaeological site outside the city; see p. 153). Along with the **Tiahuanaco** people, with whom they shared a central god figure, the Huari came to dominate the Andes, with an empire spreading all the way to Chile and Bolivia. Both cultures achieved superior agricultural technology, in the form of canal irrigation and terraces.

Separate regional cultures, the best known of which is the **Chimú** culture (A.D. 700), developed and thrived over the next 4 centuries. The Chimú, adroit metallurgists and architects, built the monumental citadel of Chan Chan (see p. 363), a compound of royal palaces and the largest adobe city in the world, near the northern coastal city Trujillo. The Chimú were the dominant culture in Peru before the arrival and expansion of the Incas, and they initially represented a great northern and coastal rivalry to the Incas. Other cultures that thrived during the same period were the **Chachapoyas,** who constructed the impressive Kuélap fortress in the northern highlands; the **Ica** (or **Chincha**), south of Lima; and the *altiplano* (high plains) groups that built the finely crafted *chullpa* towers near Puno and Lake Titicaca. The Sicán (or Lambayeque) culture, which built great temple sites and buried its dead with extraordinary riches, fell to the Chimú near the end of the 14th century. The Chimú themselves were, in turn, conquered by the Incas.

The Inca Empire (1200–1532)

Though Peru is likely to be forever synonymous with the Incas, who built the spectacular city of Machu Picchu high in the Andes and countless other great palaces and temples, the society was merely the last in a long line of pre-Columbian cultures. The

Inca Empire (1200–1532) was relatively short-lived, but it remains the best documented of all Peruvian civilizations. Though the height of its power lasted for little more than a century, the Inca Empire extended throughout the Andes, all the way from present-day Colombia down to Chile—a stretch of more than 5,635km (3,500 miles). At its apex, the Inca Empire's reach was longer than even that of the Romans.

The Incas were a naturalistic and ritualistic people who worshiped the sun god Inti and the earth goddess Pachamama, as well as the moon, thunder, lightning, and the rainbow, all regarded as deities. The Inca emperors were believed to be direct descendants of the sun god. The bold Andes Mountains were at least as important in their system of beliefs: The dwelling places of respected spirits, the 7,000m (22,960-ft.) peaks were the sites of human sacrifices. The Incas founded Cusco, the sacred city and capital of the Inca Empire (which they called Tahuantinsuyo, or Land of Four Quarters). The ruling sovereign was properly called the Inca, but today the term also refers to the people and the empire.

The Incas' Andean dominance was achieved through formidable organization and a highly developed economic system. The Incas rapidly expanded their empire first through political alliances and absorption, and then by swift military conquest. Though the Incas imposed their social structure and way of life, they also assimilated useful skills and practices, even granting administrative positions to defeated nobles of the Chimú and other cultures. The Incas thus succeeded in achieving political and religious unification across most of their domain.

The Incas recorded an astounding level of achievement. They never developed a system of writing, but they kept extraordinary records with an accounting system of knots on strings, called *quipus.* They laid a vast network of roadways, nearly 32,200km (20,000 miles) in total across the difficult territory of the Andes, connecting cities, farming communities, and religious sites. A network of runners, called *chasquis,* operated on the roads, relaying messages and even transporting foodstuffs from the coast to the Andes. *Tambos,* or way stations (such as Tambo Colorado near Paracas; see p. 134), dotted the highways, serving as inspection points and shelters for relay runners. The Inca Trail was a sacred highway, connecting the settlements in the Urubamba Valley to the ceremonial center, Machu Picchu.

The Incas' agricultural techniques were exceedingly skilled and efficient, with advanced irrigation systems and soil conservation. The Incas were also extraordinary architects and unparalleled stonemasons. Inca ruins reveal splendid landscaping and

Chakana, the Inca Cross

The ever-present Inca cross, the **Chakana** (consisting of four symmetrical sides of three steps each and a hole in the middle) is the very symbol of Inca civilization and its complex cosmology. Represented in it are three levels of existence or worlds (*Hana Pacha,* the higher world of the *apus,* or gods; *Kay Pacha,* the middle world of man's everyday existence; and *Ucu Pacha,* the lower world inhabited by spirits of the dead and ancestors). The hole in the center of the cross is both the axis through which a shaman might travel to other worlds and states of consciousness, and representative of Cusco, the center of the Incan empire. Some believe the Chakana to be a compass or calendar. The familiar motif of three steps is seen repeatedly in Inca constructions, from Machu Picchu to the Temple of the Sun in Cusco.

graceful construction of perfectly cut stones and terraces on inaccessible sites with extraordinary views of valleys and mountains.

A rigid hierarchy and division of labor ruled Inca society. At the top, just below the Inca sovereign (who was also the chief military and religious figure and considered a descendant of the sun), was the ruling elite: nobles and priests. Tens of thousands of manual laborers provided the massive manpower necessary to construct temples and palaces throughout the empire. The Inca kept chosen maidens, or Virgins of the Sun (*acllas*), who serviced him and Inca nobles.

Extraordinarily tight community organization was replicated across the empire. At the heart of the structure was the Inca's clan, the *panaca*, composed of relatives and descendants. Spanish conquistadors chronicled a dynasty that extended to 12 rulers, from **Manco Cápac,** the empire's founder in 1200 who was said to have risen out of Lake Titicaca, to **Atahualpa,** whose murder in Cajamarca by Spanish conquerors spelled the end of the great power.

The Inca **Pachacútec** ruled from 1438 to 1463, and he is considered the great builder of Inca civilization. Under his rule, Cusco was rebuilt, and some of the most brilliant examples of Inca architecture were erected, including Cusco's Qoricancha (Temple of the Sun; see p. 175), the Ollantaytambo and Sacsayhuamán fortresses (see p. 179), and, of course, the famed religious retreat Machu Picchu. Pachacútec also initiated the empire's expansion. It was Pachacútec's successor, **Tupac Yupanqui** (1463–93), however, who achieved dominance from Ecuador to Chile. A great conqueror, he defeated his Chimú rivals in northern Peru.

After the death of the Inca **Huayna Cápac** in 1525, civil war ensued, brought on by the empire splitting between his two sons, Atahualpa and Huáscar. The Spaniards, arriving in northern Peru in 1532, found a severely weakened empire—a pivotal reason the Incas so swiftly succumbed to a small band of invading Spaniards. Another key was the Spaniards' superior military technology. Against cannons and cavalry, the Incas' slings, battle-axes, and cotton-padded armor stood little chance. But their defeat remains puzzling to most visitors to Peru, not to mention many scholars.

Spanish Conquest & Colonialism (1532–CA 1800)

Columbus and his cohorts landed in the Americas in 1492, and by the 1520s, the Spanish conquistadors had reached South America. Francisco Pizarro led an expedition along Peru's coast in 1528. Impressed with the riches of the Inca Empire, he returned to Spain and succeeded in raising money and recruiting men for a return expedition. In 1532, Pizarro made his return to Peru over land from Ecuador. After founding the first Spanish city in Peru, San Miguel de Piura, near the Ecuadorian border, he advanced upon the northern highland city of Cajamarca, an Inca stronghold. There, a small number of Spanish troops—about 180 men and 30 horses—cunningly captured the Inca emperor Atahualpa. The emperor promised to pay a king's ransom of gold and silver for his release, offering to fill his cell several times over, but the Spaniards, having received warning of an advancing Inca army, executed the emperor in 1533. It was a catastrophic blow to an already weakened empire. (You can visit "El Cuarto de Rescate," the ransom room, in Cajamarca; see p. 389.)

Pizarro and his men massacred the Inca army, estimated at between 5,000 and 6,000 warriors. The Spaniards installed a puppet Inca, Tupac Huallpa, the brother of Huáscar, who had died while Atahualpa was being held. They then marched on Cusco, capturing the capital city on November 15, 1533, and emptying the Sun Temple of its golden treasures. After the death of Tupac Huallpa en route, a new puppet was appointed, Manco Inca.

Two years later Pizarro founded the coastal city of Lima, which became the capital of the new colony, the Viceroyalty of Peru. (For a taste of Lima's colonial riches, stroll the historic quarter of Lima Centro; see p. 84.) The Spanish crown appointed Spanish-born viceroys the rulers of Peru, but Spaniards battled among themselves for control of Peru's riches, and the remaining Incas continued to battle the conquistadors. A great siege was laid to Cusco in 1536, with Manco Inca and his brothers directing the rebellion from the fortress Sacsayhuamán (see p. 179). Pizarro was assassinated in 1541, and the indigenous insurrection ended with the beheading of Manco Inca, who had escaped to Vilcabamba, deep in the jungle, in 1544. Inca Tupac Amaru led a rebellion in 1572 but also failed and was killed.

Over the next two centuries, Lima gained in power and prestige at the expense of the old Inca capital and became the foremost colonial city of the Andean nations. The Peruvian viceroyalty stretched all the way from Panama to Tierra del Fuego. Cusco focused on cultural pursuits and became the epicenter of the Cusco School of painting (Escuela Cusqueña), which incorporated indigenous elements into Spanish styles, in the 16th and 17th centuries.

Independent Peru (1821–1942)

By the 19th century, grumbling over high taxes and burdensome Spanish controls grew in Peru, as it did in most colonies in the Americas. After liberating Chile and Argentina, José de San Martín set his sights north on Lima in 1821 and declared it an independent nation the same year. Simón Bolívar, the other hero of independence on the continent, came from the other direction. His successful campaigns in Venezuela and Colombia led him south to Ecuador and finally Peru. Peru won its independence from Spain after crucial battles in late 1824. Though Peru mounted its first civilian government, defeat by Chile in the War of the Pacific (1879–83) left Peru in a dire economic position.

Several military regimes ensued, and Peru finally returned to civilian rule in 1895. Land-owning elites dominated this new "Aristocratic Republic." In 1911, the Yale historian Hiram Bingham happened upon the ruins of the imperial city Machu Picchu—a discovery that would begin to unravel the greatness of the Incas and forever associate Peru with the last of its pre-Columbian civilizations.

Peru launched war with Ecuador over a border dispute—just one of several long-running border conflicts—in 1941. Though the 1942 Treaty of Río de Janeiro granted the area north of the River Marañón to Peru, Ecuador would continue to claim the territory until the end of the 20th century.

Present-Day Peru (1945–Present Day)

Peru's modern political history has been largely a turbulent mix of military dictatorships, coups d'état, and disastrous civilian governments, engendering a near-continual cycle of instability. Particularly in the 1980s and 1990s, Peru became notorious for government corruption at the highest levels—leading to the exile of two recent presidents—and widespread domestic terrorism fears.

Peru shook off two decades of dictatorship in 1945 after a free election (the first in many decades) of José Luis Bustamante y Rivero. Bustamante served for just 3 years. General Manuel A. Odría led a coup and installed a military regime in 1948. In 1963, Peru returned to civilian rule, with Fernando Belaúnde Terry as president. The armed forces overthrew Belaúnde in 1968, but the new military regime (contrary to other right-leaning dictatorships in Latin America) expanded the role of the state, nationalized a number of industries, and instituted agrarian reform. The land-reform initiatives failed miserably. Reelected in 1980, Belaúnde and his successor, Alan García (1985–90), faced, and were largely unsuccessful in dealing with, hyperinflation, massive debt, nationwide strikes, and two homegrown guerrilla movements—the Maoist Sendero Luminoso (Shining Path) and the Tupac Amaru Revolutionary Movement (MRTA)—that destabilized Peru with violent terror campaigns throughout the late 1980s and early 1990s. Peruvians fled the capital and the countryside, fearful of attack; few travelers were brave enough to plan vacations in the troubled nation. Meanwhile, Peru's role on the production end of the international cocaine trade grew exponentially.

García refused to pay Peru's external debt (which prompted both the IMF and World Bank to cut off support) and then fled into exile after being charged with embezzling millions. With the economy in ruins and the government in chaos, Alberto Fujimori, the son of Japanese immigrants, defeated the Peruvian novelist Mario Vargas Llosa and became president in 1990. In 1992, Fujimori's government arrested key members of both the MRTA and the Shining Path (catapulting the president to unprecedented popularity). His administration turned authoritarian, however, shutting down Congress in 1992, suspending the constitution, and decreeing an emergency government that he effectively ruled as dictator. There was a massive abuse of power on the part of the police and military, who engaged in systematic repression that led to kidnappings and killings of suspected terrorists. Many were overt political targetings of innocents.

Austerity measures got Peru on the right track economically, with reforms leading to widespread privatizations, annual growth of 7%, and a drop in inflation from more than 10,000% annually to about 20. Many Peruvians reluctantly accepted Fujimori's overturn of democracy. Having pushed to get the constitution amended so that he could run for successive terms, Fujimori was reelected in 1995. Fujimori resigned the presidency in late 2000 and escaped into exile in Japan after a corruption scandal involving his shadowy intelligence chief, Vladimiro Montesinos. Videotape of Montesinos bribing a congressman and subsequent investigations (including a daily barrage of secret videotapes broadcast on national television) revealed a government so thoroughly corrupt that it was itself involved in the narcotics trade that it was ostensibly stamping out. Fujimori had funneled at least $12 million to private offshore accounts. Montesinos escaped to Venezuela, where he was harbored by the government until found and returned to Peru for imprisonment.

Alejandro Toledo, a political newcomer from a poor Indian family, won the 2001 election and became Peru's first president of the 21st century. A shoeshine boy and son of peasants who went to Harvard and Stanford, became a World Bank economist, and ultimately wrestled the top office from a corrupt leader was the very embodiment of the dream of social mobility—in a country where there is little upward movement by non-whites. Toledo offered an encouraging symbol of hope to both Peruvians and the international community. Yet, like previous governments, Toledo's administration was plagued by instability, abuse of power, and poor management.

Fujimori was arrested in Chile in 2005 attempting to return to Peru in a surprise bid to run for president. Extradited to Peru and jailed in 2006, Fujimori stood trial on charges of ordering the murders of suspected Shining Path guerrillas and their collaborators by death squad (he remains in a jail in Lima, sentenced to 25 years for his role in ordering death squads, along with three other concurrent sentences, including for abuse of power, bribery, and illegal wiretapping of phones). The trial marked the

EATING & drinking

Peruvian cuisine is among the finest and most diverse cuisines found in Latin America and, indeed, the world. It is one of the most important contributors to the wave of Pan-Latino restaurants gaining popularity across the globe. As knowledge of Peruvian food spreads, more and more travelers are even making focused gastronomic pilgrimages to Peru—for many travelers, the cuisine will rank among the highlights of their visit.

Peruvian cooking differs significantly by region, and subcategories mirror exactly the country's geographical variety: coastal, highlands, and tropical. The common denominator among them is a blend of indigenous and Spanish (or broader European) influences, which has evolved over the past 4 centuries. Traditional Peruvian coastal cooking is often referred to as comida criolla, and it's found across Peru. The other main types of cuisine are andino, or Andean (highlands), and novo andino (creative or haute twists on and updates of traditional highlander cooking). Several celebrity chefs, including Gastón Acurio and Pedro Miguel Schiaffino, are leading the charge of contemporary Peruvian cuisine, often offering their creative takes on traditional dishes.

Coastal preparations concentrate on seafood and shellfish, as might be expected. The star dish, and the most exported example of Peruvian cuisine, is ceviche, a classic preparation of raw fish and shellfish marinated (not cooked) in lime or lemon juice and hot chili peppers, served with raw onion, sweet potato, and toasted corn. Ceviche has been around since the time of some of Peru's earliest civilizations, although a traditional Andean argument over whether Peruvians or Ecuadorians should be credited with creating it persists. Cevicherías, traditionally open only for lunch, usually serve several types of ceviche as well as a good roster of other seafood. Tiradito is finely sliced fish marinated with lime juice and ají peppers, essentially Peruvian sashimi or carpaccio. Other coastal favorites include escabeche (a tasty fish concoction served with peppers, eggs, olives, onions, and prawns), conchitas (scallops), and corvina (sea bass). Land-based favorites are cabrito (roast kid) and ají de gallina (a tangy creamed chicken and chili dish).

Highlanders favor a more substantial style of cooking. Corn and potatoes were staples of the Incas and other mountain civilizations before them. Meat, served with rice and potatoes, is a mainstay of the diet, as is trout (trucha). Lomo saltado, strips of beef mixed with onions, tomatoes, peppers, and french-fried potatoes and served with rice, seems to be on every menu. Rocoto relleno, a hot bell pepper stuffed with vegetables and meat, and papa rellena, a potato stuffed with veggies and then fried, are just as common (but are occasionally extremely spicy). Soups are excellent.

In the countryside, you might see people in the fields digging small cooking holes in the ground. They are preparing pachamanca, a roast cooked over stones. It's the Peruvian version of a picnic; on weekends, you'll often see

first time in Peruvian history that a former president had been tried for crimes committed during his administration.

Peru had been engaged in a longstanding dispute with Yale University in the United States over the possession of thousands of valuable pre-Columbian artifacts removed from Peru during the archaeological expeditions of Hiram Bingham, the Yale professor credited with rediscovering Machu Picchu in 1911 and publicizing it to the world. Peru claimed it had merely loaned the artifacts to Yale and even sought the

families outside Cusco and other places stirring smoking fires in the ground while the kids play soccer nearby. *Cuy* (guinea pig) is considered a delicacy in many parts of Peru, including the *sierra*, but its elevated status was never much apparent to me. It comes roasted or fried, with head and feet upturned on the plate.

In the Amazon jungle regions, most people fish for their food and their diets consist almost entirely of fish such as river trout and *paiche* (a huge river fish, now considered endangered). Restaurants feature both of these, with accompaniments including *yuca* (a root), *palmitos* (palm hearts) and *chonta* (palm-heart salad), bananas and plantains, and rice *tamales* known as *juanes*. Common menu items such as chicken and game are complemented by exotic fare such as caiman, wild boar, turtle, monkey, and piranha fish—but even though some locals eat some items that are endangered and illegal to serve in restaurants, it doesn't mean that you should. (See p. 38 for more information.)

In addition to Peruvian cooking, visitors will find plenty of international restaurants, including a particularly Peruvian variation, *chifas* (restaurants serving Peruvian-influenced Chinese food, developed by the large immigrant Chinese population), a mainstay among many non-Chinese Peruvians. *Chifas* are nearly as common as restaurants serving *pollo a la brasa* (spit-roasted chicken), which are everywhere in Peru.

Drinking is less of an event in Peru. While Peruvian wines from the coastal desert south and local beers are improving, they still can't really compare with superior examples found elsewhere on the continent (Chile and Argentina, predominantly). Most wines in better restaurants come from these three countries, along with Spain. Yet one indigenous drink stands out: *pisco*, a powerful white-grape brandy. The pisco sour (a cocktail mixed with pisco, egg whites, lemon juice, sugar, and bitters) is effectively Peru's margarita: tasty, refreshing, and ubiquitous. New takes on the pisco sour have sprung up at sophisticated mixology bars: *maracuyá* (passion fruit) sours, coca sours (made with macerated coca leaves), and other sours highlighting indigenous tropical fruits, such as *lúcuma*. Pisco is also taken straight.

Peruvians everywhere (but especially in the highlands) drink *chicha*, a tangy, fermented brew made from maize and inherited from the Incas. Often served warm in huge plastic tumblers, it is unlikely to please the palates of most foreign visitors, although it's certainly worth a try if you come upon a small, informal place with the *chicha* flag (often a red balloon) flying in a rural village (it means something akin to "get your fresh *chicha* here"). *Chicha morada*, on the other hand, is nothing to be afraid of. It is a delicious but sweet nonalcoholic beverage, deep purple in color, prepared with blue corn and served chilled, the perfect accompaniment to ceviche. *Masato* is a beer made from *yuca*, typical of the Amazon region.

intervention of U.S. President Barack Obama in the matter. In 2010, Yale finally stopped asserting its claim and agreed to return the bulk of the artifacts, long held in the Peabody Museum in New Haven, Connecticut, by the end of 2012 in anticipation of the creation of a new museum in Cusco (on which Yale will advise).

Peru's 30 million people are predominantly *mestizo* (of mixed Spanish and indigenous heritage) and Andean Indian, but the population is a true melting pot of ethnic groups. Significant minority groups of Afro-Peruvians (descendants of African slaves, living mainly in the coastal area south of Lima), immigrant Japanese and Chinese populations among the largest in South America, and smaller groups of European immigrants, including Italians and Germans, help make up Peru's population of 28 million. In the early days of the colony, Peruvian-born offspring of Spaniards were called *criollos,* though that term today refers mainly to coastal residents and Peruvian cuisine.

After Bolivia and Guatemala, Peru has the largest population by percentage of Amerindians in Latin America. Perhaps half the country lives in the *sierra,* or highlands, and most of these people, commonly called *campesinos* (peasants), live in either small villages or rural areas. Descendants of Peru's many Andean indigenous groups in remote rural areas continue to speak the native languages Quechua (made an official language in 1975) and Aymara or other Amerindian tongues, and for the most part, they adhere to traditional regional dress. However, massive peasant migration to cities from rural highland villages has contributed to a dramatic weakening of indigenous traditions and culture across Peru.

Peruvians are a predominantly Roman Catholic people (more than 90% claim to be Catholic), although Protestant evangelical churches have been winning converts, a fact that is worrisome to the Catholic Church. Animistic religious practices (worship of deities representing nature), inherited from the Incas and others, have been incorporated into the daily lives of many Peruvians and can be seen in festivals and small individual rituals such as offerings of food and beverages to Pachamama, or Mother Earth.

Dining Customs

Among the more interesting dining customs—beyond the eating of guinea pig—is the lovely habit of offering a sip of beer or *chicha* before the meal to Pachamama, or Mother Earth. Many Peruvians still ritualistically thank the earth for its bounty, and they show their appreciation by spilling just a bit before raising the drink to their own mouths.

Restaurants range from the rustic and incredibly inexpensive to polished places with impeccable service and international menus. Set three-course meals are referred to by a variety of terms: *menú del día, menú económico, menú ejecutivo, menú de la casa,* and *menú turístico.* They are all essentially the same thing and can sometimes be had for as little as S/15. In general, you should ask about the preparation of many Peruvian dishes because many are quite spicy. Informal eateries serving Peruvian cooking are frequently called *picanterías* and *chicherías.*

Fixed-price lunch deals are referred to as *menús del día* (or simply *menú*). The majority of restaurants include taxes and services in their prices, and your bill will reflect the menu prices. Others (including some upscale restaurants), however, separate taxes and services, and the bill can get pretty byzantine, especially when it comes to imported wine. You might see a subtotal, followed by a 10% service charge, a 20% "selectivo" wine tax, and a 19% IGV (general sales tax). It's crazy. Fortunately, the restaurants that do this are rare.

 Peruvian Cooking Sites

For additional information on Peruvian cooking, check out **www.cocinaperuana.com**, which features a history of Peruvian cuisine, a glossary, recipes, and a guide to restaurants in Peru. A good food blog dedicated to Peruvian restaurants and cooking is **http://www.perufood.blogspot.com**.

Note: Some upscale restaurants will place a couple of small plates of cheese, sausage, olives, or other tidbits on your table to nibble on as you wait for your meal. In almost all cases, you will be charged for these items, called a *cubierto,* or cover. Usually, it'll add S/5 to S/20 to your bill. If you don't touch the stuff, in theory you shouldn't have to pay for it because you didn't order it, but many restaurants automatically tack on the charge—and few are the customers who don't consider the *cubierto* part of the cost of eating out.

Dining hours are not much different from typical mealtimes in cities in North America or Great Britain, except that dinner *(cena)* is generally eaten after 8pm in restaurants. Peruvians do not eat nearly as late as Spaniards. Although lunch *(almuerzo)* is the main meal of the day, for most visitors, it generally is not the grand midday affair it is in Spain, unless you are dining at an outdoor *quinta,* where most locals linger over lunch for a couple of hours.

If you invite a Peruvian to have a drink or to dine with you, it is expected that you will pay (the Spanish verb *invitar* literally connotes this as an invitation). Do not suggest that a Peruvian acquaintance join you in what will certainly be an expensive restaurant or cafe for him or her, and then pony up only half the tab.

Music

There is evidence of music in Peru dating back 10,000 years, and musical historians have identified more than 1,000 genres of music in the country. Traditional instruments include *pututos* (trumpets made from seashells) and many other wind instruments crafted from cane, bone, horns, and precious metals, as well as a wide range of percussion instruments. Exposure to Western cultures has introduced new instruments such as the harp, violin, and guitar to Peruvian music. But Peruvian music can still be identified by its distinctive instruments, and there are many besides the basics of highland music.

The **cajón** is a classic percussion instrument, typical in *música criolla* and *música negra,* as well as marinera. A simple wooden box with a sound hole in the back, the cajón is played by a musician who sits on top and pounds the front like a bongo. The cajón has been introduced into flamenco music by none other than the legendary flamenco guitarist Paco de Lucía. Another popular instrument is the **zampoña,** which belongs to the panpipe family and varies greatly in size. The zampoña is never absent at festivals in southern Peru, particularly Puno.

For additional information on Peruvian music, see the section below, "Peru in Pop Culture."

Dance

Dances associated with Afro-Peruvian music include lively and sensual **festejo** dances, in which participants respond to the striking of the cajón, one of Afro-Peruvian music's essential instruments. The **alcatraz** is an extremely erotic dance. Females enter the dance floor with tissue on their posteriors. The men, meanwhile, dance with lit candles. The not-so-subtle goal on the dance floor is for the man to light the woman's tissue (and thus become her partner).

Peruvian tourism authorities produce a guide to festivities, music, and folk art, and it features a diagram of native dances in Peru. Especially up and down the coast, and in the central corridor of the Andes, the map is a bewildering maze of numbers indicating the indigenous dances practiced in given regions. Two dances, though, have become synonymous with Peru, the huayno and marinera.

The **huayno** is the essential dance in the Andes, with pre-Columbian origins fused with Western influences. Couples dancing the huayno perform sharp turns, hops, and taplike *zapateos* to keep time. Huayno music is played on quena, charango, harp, and violin. The **marinera,** a sleek, sexy, and complex dance of highly coordinated choreography, is derivative of other folkloric dances in Peru, dating back to the 19th century. There are regional variations of the dance, which differ most from the south coast to the northern highlands. Dancers keep time with a handkerchief in one hand. Marinera music in Lima is performed by guitar and cajón, while a marching band is de rigueur in the north. Marinera festivals are held across Peru, but the most celebrated one is in Trujillo in January.

One of the most attention-getting dances in Peru, though, is that performed by **scissors dancers.** Their *danza de las tijeras* is an exercise in athleticism and balance. Dancers perform gymnastic leaps and daring stunts to the sounds of harp and violin. The main instrument played to accompany the dance is the pair of scissors, made up of two independent sheets of metal around 25 centimeters (10 inches) long. The best places to see scissors dancers are Ayacucho, Arequipa, and Lima.

Textiles

Woven textiles have to be considered among the great traditional arts of Peru. Peru has one of the most ancient and richest weaving traditions in the world; for more than 5,000 years, Peruvian artisans have used fine natural fibers for hand weaving, and the wool produced by alpacas, llamas, and vicuñas is some of the finest in the world, rarer even than cashmere. The most ancient textiles that have been found in Peru come from the Huaca Prieta temple in Chicama and are more than 4,000 years old. In pre-Columbian times, handwoven textiles, which required extraordinary patience and skill, were prized and extremely valuable; distinctive textiles were indicators of social status and power. They were traded as commodities. Paracas, Huari, and Inca weavings are among the most sophisticated and artful ever produced in Peru. The Paracas designs were stunningly intricate, with detailed animals, human figures, and deities against dark backgrounds. Huari weaving features abstract figures and bold graphics. The Incas favored more minimalist designs, without embroidery. The finest Inca textiles were typically part of ritualistic ceremonies—many were burned as offerings to spirits.

Whereas pre-Columbian civilizations in Peru had no written language, textiles were loaded with symbolic images that serve as indelible clues to the cultures and beliefs of textile artists. Worship of nature and spiritual clues are frequently represented by motifs in textiles. Many of the finest textiles unearthed were sacred and elaborately embroidered blankets that enveloped mummies in burial sites. Found in tombs in the arid coastal desert, one of the world's driest climates, the textiles are remarkably preserved in many cases.

Contemporary Peruvian artisans continue the traditions, sophisticated designs, and techniques of intricate weaving inherited from pre-Columbian civilizations, often employing the very same instruments used hundreds of years ago and still favoring natural dyes. The drop spindle (weaving done with a stick and spinning wooden wheel), for example, is still used in many regions, and it's not uncommon to see women and young girls spinning the wheel as they tend to animals in the fields. Excellent-quality woven items, the best of which are much more than mere souvenirs, include typical Andean *chullo* wool or alpaca hats with earflaps, ponchos, scarves, sweaters, and blankets.

PERU IN POP CULTURE
Books & Literature

The classic work on Inca history and the Spanish conquistadors is *The Conquest of the Incas* (Harvest Books, 2003) by John Hemming, a very readable narrative of the fall of a short-lived but uniquely accomplished empire. *Lost City of the Incas* (Phoenix Press, 2003) is the travelogue and still-amazing story of Hiram Bingham, the Yale academic who brought the "lost city" to the world's attention in 1911. Bingham's book makes for a very interesting read, especially after so many years of speculation and theory about the site. Also available by Bingham is *Inca Land: Explorations in the Highlands of Peru* (National Geographic, 2003, although originally published in 1922), detailing four expeditions into the Peruvian Andes.

The Incas and their Ancestors (Thames and Hudson, 2001), by Michael Moseley, is a good account of the Inca Empire and, importantly, its lesser-known predecessors. For most readers, it serves as a good introduction to Peru's archaeology and the sites they will visit, although some people find that it reads too much like a textbook. Illustrations include black-and-white photographs of Inca drawings and a few color photos. A terrific story of a recent archaeological find is *Discovering the Ice Maiden: My Adventures on Ampato* (National Geographic Society, 1998) by Johan Reinhard. The account of Reinhard's discovery of a mummified Inca princess sacrificed 500 years ago on a volcano summit in southern Peru details the team's search and its race to save what is considered one of the most important archaeological discoveries in recent decades. The book contains excellent color photographs of the maiden who can now be viewed in Arequipa. Reinhard's *The Ice Maiden: Inca Mummies, Mountain Gods, and Sacred Sites in the Andes* (National Geographic, 2005) is a memoir of archaeological adventures and the impact of his discovery of Juanita (both on him personally and the interpretation of Peruvian history).

The Peru Reader: History, Culture, Politics (Duke University Press, 1995), edited by Orin Starn, is one of the finest primers on Peru's recent history and political culture. It includes essays by several distinguished voices, including Mario Vargas Llosa.

The Madness of Things Peruvian, Democracy Under Siege, by Alvaro Vargas Llosa (Transaction Publishers, 1994) isn't easy to find, and it only chronicles up to the mid-'90s, but it is a well-rendered analysis of the failings of Peruvian democracy. Robin Kirk's *The Monkey's Paw: New Chronicles from Peru* (University of Massachusetts Press, 1997) is a story of the impact of social and economic upheaval in Peru on marginalized peoples, with the homegrown guerrilla movements taking center stage.

Naturalists and birders might want to pick up *A Field Guide to the Birds of Peru* (Ibis Pub Co., 2001) by James F. Clements, although it is perhaps not the comprehensive field guide that a country as biologically diverse as Peru deserves. Many serious birders prefer *A Guide to the Birds of Colombia* (Princeton University Press, 1986) by Steven Hilty and William Brown, probably the definitive regional guide (and covering many of the birds also found in Peru). Also of interest is *A Parrot Without a Name: The Search for the Last Unknown Birds on Earth* (University of Texas Press, 1991) by Don Stap, an account of John O'Neill and LSU scientists documenting new species in the jungles of Peru.

Peru: The Ecotravellers' Wildlife Guide (Academic Press, 2000) by biologists David Pearson and Les Beletsky, is a 500-page handbook survey of Peruvian flora and fauna, including information about conservation, habitats, national parks, and reserves. It's a good introduction for readers ready to explore the Peruvian outdoors, from the

Andes to the Amazon and other repositories of Peru's magnificent animal and plant life. The book is nicely illustrated and useful for identification purposes.

Peter Frost's *Exploring Cusco* (Nuevas Imágenes, 1999) is one of the best-detailed local guides, with excellent historical information and frank commentary by the author, a long-time Cusco resident, on the ancient Inca capital, the Sacred Valley, and, of course, Machu Picchu. *Peru & Bolivia: Backpacking and Trekking* (Bradt Publications, 1999) by Hilary Bradt, is a trusty guide, now in its third decade, of classic treks in Peru and Bolivia. Although it's in its seventh edition, with several new walks and treks added, some readers find it outdated. Still, it's a good all-around guide for trekkers and walkers.

The Cloud Forest: A Chronicle of the South American Wilderness (Ingram, 1996) is a travelogue by Peter Matthiessen, who trekked some 10,000 miles through South America, including the Amazon and Machu Picchu. Matthiessen found larger-than-life characters and ancient trails deep in the jungle, experiences that led to the author's fictional novel *At Play in the Fields of the Lord* (Vintage Books, 1991). Set in the unnamed Peruvian jungle, it's a thriller about the travails of the missionary Martin Quarrier and an outsider, Lewis Moon, a mercenary who takes a much different tack while immersing himself in a foreign culture. Both are displaced outsiders whose lives have an irreversible impact on native Amerindian communities deep in the Amazon.

Another good travelogue on Peru is *The White Rock* (Overlook, 2003) by Hugh Thomson, an absorbing account of Thomson's 20 years traveling throughout the Andes of Peru, Bolivia, and Ecuador in search of lost Inca cities.

The towering figure in contemporary Peruvian fiction is **Mario Vargas Llosa,** Peru's most famous novelist and a perennial candidate for the Nobel Prize, who was nearly elected the country's president back in 1990. It's difficult to choose from among his oeuvre of thoroughly praised works; *Aunt Julia and the Scriptwriter* (Penguin, 1995) is one of his most popular works, but it's without the heft of others, such as *The Real Life of Alejandro Mayta* (Noonday Press, 1998), a dense meditation on Peruvian and South American revolutionary politics that blurs the lines between truth and fiction, or *Death in the Andes* (Penguin, 1997), a deep penetration into the contemporary psyche and politics of Peru. Another side of the author is evident in the small erotic gem *In Praise of the Stepmother* (Penguin, 1991), a surprising and beautifully illustrated book. His powerful book *The Feast of the Goat* (Farrar Straus & Giroux, 2001), about the Dominican dictator Rafael Trujillo, made the year-end best lists of many critics in 2001. Vargas Llosa might be a difficult and "heavy" writer, but he is an unusually engaging one.

Alonso Cueto is one of the next generation's most ballyhooed novelists; he won several international awards for *La Hora Azul* (*The Blue Hour;* Editorial Anagrama, 2005). *El Susurro de la Mujer Ballena* (*The Whisper of the Whale Woman;* Planeta, 2007) is his latest.

César Vallejo, born in Peru in 1892, is one of the great poets of Latin America and the Spanish language. *Complete Posthumous Poetry* (University of California Press, 1980), in translation, and *Trilce* (Wesleyan University Press, 2000), a bilingual publication, are the best places to start with this great poet. Vallejo wrote some of the poems in *Trilce,* a wildly creative and innovative avant-garde work that today is considered a masterpiece of modernism, while in prison. Vallejo later fled to Europe and immersed himself in the Spanish Civil War.

Film

Peru's film industry trails far behind those of its neighbors Argentina and Brazil, though a recent Oscar nomination may begin to change that. In a historic achievement for Peruvian film *La Teta Asustada* ("The Milk of Sorrow") by Claudia Llosa, was nominated for an Academy Award for Best Foreign Language Film in 2010 (it also received the Golden Bear award at the Berlin International Film Festival in 2009). Less exalted but also reaching an international audience was *Máncora* (Maya Entertainment Group, 2009), a sexy Peruvian road movie set in part in the Pacific surfing resort along the northern coast, which debuted at the Sundance Film Festival in 2009.

The best-known films about or featuring Peru are still foreign. Two recent documentaries try to untangle the lasting impact of disgraced former president Alberto Fujimori. *The Fall of Fujimori: When Democracy and Terrorism Collide* (Stardust Productions, 2006) is a portrait of the eccentric ex-President and his controversial war against guerrilla movements in Peru. *State of Fear* (Skylight Pictures, 2006), based on the findings of the Peruvian Truth Commission, chronicles the 2-decade-long reign of terror by Shining Path. It doesn't shy away from documenting the abuses of the government in fighting terrorism.

Touching the Void (IFC Films, 2004), available on DVD, is the harrowing dramatic reenactment (based on the book by Joe Simpson) of a climber's disastrous and near-fatal accident climbing in the Andes mountains near Huaraz. It is gripping, but may derail any mountaineering plans you had.

The Dancer Upstairs (Fox Searchlight, 2003), a drama directed by John Malkovich and starring Javier Bardem, is a political thriller loosely based on the hunt for Abimael Guzman, the Shining Path leader, and the complicated story of the American Lori Benson, implicated and imprisoned as a terrorist collaborator in Peru (though the movie is set in an unnamed South American nation). *The Motorcycle Diaries* (MCA Home Video, 2005), an excellent 2004 film by Walter Salles about the young Che Guevara, is, in large part, a travelogue of Argentina, Chile, Colombia, and Venezuela, but Machu Picchu plays a scene-stealing role.

Peter Matthiessen's novel *At Play in the Fields of the Lord* (1991) was later made by Hector Babenco into an occasionally pretty but silly movie starring John Lithgow, Daryl Hannah, and Tom Beringer with a bowl-cut and face paint, and relocated from the Amazon basin of Peru to Brazil.

Music

Many travelers may be at least superficially familiar with the dominant strains of Peruvian music. Anyone who has traveled in Europe, South America, or even Asia is likely to have seen and heard roving bands of street musicians decked out in high-lander garb (ponchos and *chullo* hats) playing the *música folclórica* that emanates from high in the Andes mountains. Known for its use of the **quena** (pan flute), played like a recorder, **charango** (from the lute family), and mandolin, the distinctive sounds of this Peruvian music—similar to that heard in other Andean countries, such as Bolivia and Ecuador—were widely sampled in the Simon and Garfunkel song "El Cóndor Pasa." That song was based on a melody by a Peruvian composer, Daniel Alomía Robles, who himself had appropriated a traditional Quechua *huayno* folk melody.

I'd point adventurous ears with an interest in ethnomusicology toward a handful of Andean *música folclórica* recordings released by the Smithsonian Folkways Series.

"Mountain Music of Peru," a two-volume series released in the early 1990s, includes recordings, celebratory and religious in nature, that were made in mountain villages in the 1960s. As such, they are raw and lack studio polish. Smithsonian also issues other volumes covering the traditional regional music of Peru, from "Cajamarca and the Colca Valley" (Vol. 3) to "The Region of Ayacucho" (Vol. 6). Though its song selections aren't specifically Peruvian, listeners may also enjoy the "Rough Guide to the Music of the Andes" compilation.

Just as there is a notable divide in Peruvian cuisine, with radically different takes in the *sierra* (mountains) and *costa* (coast), so, too, is Peruvian music divided along these lines. In coastal areas, principally Lima and communities just south, such as El Carmen, the most distinctive music came from the Afro-Peruvian population, descendants of slaves. Black Peruvians created a unique mix of African rhythms and Spanish and other European influences, called *música criolla*. Percussion is fundamental, in addition to strings and vocals, but the music is frequently bluesier than its jazz-inflected Afro counterparts that developed in Brazil and Cuba. A great place to start exploring is the compilation, selected by David Byrne and released on his Luaka Bop label, "Afro-Peruvian Classics: The Soul of Black Peru," featuring the influential singers and groups Eva Ayllón, Susana Baca, Perú Negro, Chabuca Granda, Nicomedes Santa Cruz, and others. Those same stars (but no repeat songs) are also featured on "The Rough Guide to Afro Peru."

Chicha is a relatively new addition to the list of musical genres. A hybrid of sorts of the huayno (see above) and Colombian *cumbia*, *chicha* is an extremely popular urban dance, especially among the working class. It has spread rapidly across Peru and throughout Latin America.

The current Minister of Culture, Susana Baca, has reached an audience of American and international ears through her recordings on the Luaka Bop label. Look for her eponymous album or "Ecos de Sombra." Both are superb. In Peru, Eva Ayllón is even more of a megastar. A good recording available worldwide is "Eva! Leyenda Peruana." Another long-time female Afro-Peruvian performer is Chabuca Granda; a greatest hits collection of her work is called "Latinoamericana." Perú Negro's albums "Sangre de un Don" and "Jogorio," recorded after the death of the group's founder Ronaldo Campos in 2001, are both widely available.

A taste of Peruvian music serves either as great preparation for a trip to Peru or as a fond souvenir after the fact. But nothing equals grooving to live Peruvian coastal *música criolla* in a nightclub, at a stylish Lima jazz bar, or *peña*—a one-time social club now frequented by locals and tourists for live music—or hearing highlands' *música folclórica* during an Andean festival or stumbling upon it in a town square. The renaissance of Peru's indigenous musical forms is a hugely welcome development in this culturally rich country.

WHEN TO GO

Peak travel season for foreigners is, in great part, determined by the weather. Peru experiences two very distinct seasons, wet and dry—terms that are much more relevant than "summer" and "winter." Peru's high season for travel coincides with the driest months: May through October, with by far the greatest number of visitors in July and August. May and September are particularly fine months to visit much of the country. Airlines and hotels also consider the period from mid-December through mid-January as peak season.

From June to September (winter in the Southern Hemisphere) in the highlands, days are clear and often spectacularly sunny, with chilly or downright cold nights, especially at high elevations. For trekking in the mountains, including the Inca Trail, these are by far the best months. This is also the best time of the year to visit the Amazon basin: Mosquitoes are fewer, and many fauna stay close to the rivers (although some people prefer to travel in the jungle during the wet season, when higher water levels allow for more river penetration). Note that Peruvians travel in huge numbers around July 28, the national holiday, and finding accommodations in popular destinations around this time can be difficult.

Climate

Generally, May through October is the dry season; November through April is the rainy season, and the wettest months are January through April. In mountain areas, roads and trek paths can become impassable. Peru's climate, though, is markedly different among its three regions. The coast is predominantly arid and mild, the Andean region is temperate to cold, and the eastern lowlands are tropically warm and humid.

On the desert **coast,** summer (Dec–Apr) is hot and dry, with temperatures reaching 77°F to 95°F (25°C–35°C) or more along the north coast. In winter (May–Oct), temperatures are much milder, though with high humidity. Much of the coast, including Lima, is shrouded in a gray mist called *garúa.* Only extreme northern beaches are warm enough for swimming.

In the **highlands** from May to October, rain is scarce. Daytime temperatures reach a warm 68°F to 77°F (20°C–25°C), and nights are often quite cold (near freezing), especially in June and July. Rainfall is very abundant from December to March, when temperatures are slightly milder—64°F to 68°F (18°C–20°C), dropping only to 59°F (15°C) at night. The wettest months are January and February. Most mornings are dry, but clouds move in during the afternoon and produce heavy downpours.

Although the Amazon **jungle** is consistently humid and tropical, with significant rainfall year-round, it, too, experiences two clearly different seasons. During the dry season (May–Oct), temperatures reach 86°F to 100°F (30°C–38°C) during the day. From November to April, there are frequent rain showers (which last only a few hours at a time), causing the rivers to swell; temperatures are similarly steamy.

Lima's Average Temperatures & Precipitation

	JAN	FEB	MAR	APR	MAY	JUNE	JULY	AUG	SEPT	OCT	NOV	DEC
AVG. HIGH (°F)	77	79	79	75	70	66	63	63	63	66	68	73
AVG. HIGH (°C)	25	26	26	24	21	19	17	17	17	19	20	23
AVG. LOW (°F)	66	68	66	65	61	59	57	56	56	57	61	63
AVG. LOW (°C)	19	20	19	18	16	15	14	13	13	14	16	17
WET DAYS	1	0	0	0	1	1	1	2	1	0	0	0

Cusco's Average Temperatures & Precipitation

	JAN	FEB	MAR	APR	MAY	JUNE	JULY	AUG	SEPT	OCT	NOV	DEC
AVG. HIGH (°F)	66	66	67	68	68	67	67	68	68	70	69	68
AVG. HIGH (°C)	19	19	19	20	20	19	19	20	20	21	21	20
AVG. LOW (°F)	44	44	44	41	37	34	34	34	39	42	43	43
AVG. LOW (°C)	7	7	7	5	3	1	1	1	4	6	6	6
WET DAYS	12	11	10	6	4	3	4	3	2	2	1	5

CURRENT WEATHER CONDITIONS The best place to head online for a detailed weather forecast is **www.go2peru.com/weather_peru.htm** or www.wunder ground.com/global/PR.html.

WHEN YOU'LL FIND BARGAINS The cheapest time to fly to Peru is usually during the off season: from late October to mid-December and from mid-January through April. Though that coincides with the rainy season in the highlands and jungle, it's the peak of summer along the coast, and many Peruvians holiday in coastal resorts December through February. Remember that weekday flights are often cheaper than weekend fares.

Rates generally increase in June, then hit their peak in high travel seasons between July and September, and in December for the run-up to Christmas and New Year. July and August are also when most Europeans take their holidays, so besides higher prices, there are more crowds and more limited availability of the best hotel rooms.

You can avoid crowds, to some extent, by planning trips for October through April, though you should be mindful of the trade-off in weather conditions. In general, the shoulder seasons (April to June, late September through October) are the best combination of fewer crowds and relatively lower prices. Be mindful of major Peruvian holidays, particularly at places like Cusco and Machu Picchu, which are also major destinations for Peruvians as well as international travelers.

Calendar of Events

For additional information on major festivals, see www.infoperu.com.pe/en/informacion_fest.php. For additional information about regional festivals, see individual destination chapters. Also check http://events.frommers.com, where you'll find a searchable, up-to-the-minute roster of what's happening in cities all over the world.

JANUARY

Entrega de Varas, Cusco. Community elders (*yayas*) designate the highest authorities of their villages in this pre-Columbian festival, which is celebrated with *chicha* (fermented maize beer) and *llonque* (sugar-cane alcohol); elders give the mayor the *vara* (a staff, or scepter) as a symbol of his position of authority. January 1.

Fiesta de la Santa Tierra, Lake Titicaca. The main festival on Isla Amantaní sees the population split in two—half at the Temple of Pachamama and the other half at the Temple of Pachatata—symbolizing the islanders' ancient dualistic belief system. Third Thursday in January.

Marinera Dance Festival, Trujillo. One of the stateliest dances in Peru, the flirtatious marinera involves a couple, each partner with a handkerchief in his or her right hand. The man wears a wide-brimmed hat and poncho, and the woman wears a lace Moche dress. For 10 days, the festival, which draws couples from

all over the country, is held in the Gran Chimú soccer stadium. There are also float processions throughout the city and dancing in the Plaza de Armas. January 20 to January 30.

FEBRUARY

Virgen de la Candelaria (Candlemas), Puno. Puno lives up to its billing as Folk Capital of the Americas with this festival, which gathers more than 200 musicians and dance troupes. On the festival's main day, February 2, the Virgen is led through the city in a colorful procession of priests and pagans carefully maintaining the hierarchy. Especially thrilling is the dance of the demons, or *la diablada*. Dancers in wild costumes and masks blow panpipes and make offerings to the earth goddess Pachamama. February 1 to February 14.

Carnaval. Lively pre-Lenten festivities. (Look out for balloons filled with water—or worse.) Cajamarca is reputed to have the best and wildest parties; Puno and Cusco are also good. The weekend before Ash Wednesday.

MARCH

Festival Internacional de la Vendimia (Wine Festival), Ica. A celebration of the grape harvest and the region's wine and pisco brandy, with fairs, beauty contests, floats, and musical festivals, including Afro-Peruvian dance. Second week of March.

Las Cruces de Porcón, Porcón. Near Cajamarca, a dawn procession of massive decorated wooden crosses through the valley of Porcón re-creates the entry of Christ into Jerusalem. The main day of the festival, Palm Sunday, presents four separate ceremonies. Ultimately, the crosses are decorated with mirrors (symbolizing the souls of the dead), and locals hang metal bells to announce the arrival of the crosses to the community. Mid-March to first week of April.

Lord of the Earthquakes, Cusco. Representing a 17th-century painting of Christ on the cross that is said to have saved the city from a devastating earthquake, the image of the Lord of Earthquakes (*El Señor de los Temblores*) is carried through the streets of Cusco in a reverential procession, much like the Incas once paraded the mummies of their chieftains and high priests. Easter Monday, late March or early April.

Semana Santa. Handsome and spectacularly reverent processions mark Easter week. The finest are in Cusco and Ayacucho. Late March/early April.

APRIL

Peruvian Paso Horse Festival, Pachacámac. The Peruvian Paso horse, one of the world's most beautiful breeds, is celebrated with the most important annual national competition at the Mamacona stables near Pachacámac, 30km (19 miles) south of Lima. April 15 to April 20.

MAY

Fiesta de la Cruz. The Festival of the Cross features folk music and dance, including "scissors dancers," and processions in which communities decorate crosses and prepare them for the procession to neighboring churches. The *danzantes de tijeras* (scissors dancers) re-create old times, when they performed on top of church bell towers. Today the objective is still to outdo one another

with daring feats. Celebrations are especially lively in Lima, Cusco, and Ica. May 2 and 3.

Qoyllur Rit'i, Quispicanchis, near Cusco. A massive indigenous pilgrimage marks this ritual, which is tied to the fertility of the land and the worship of Apus, the spirits of the mountains. It forms part of the greatest festival of native Indian nations in the hemisphere: Qoyllur Rit'i. The main ceremony is held at the foot of Mount Ausangate, with 10,000 pilgrims climbing to the snowline along with dancers in full costume representing mythical characters. Others head to the summit, in search of the Snow Star, and take huge blocks of ice back down on their backs—holy water for irrigation purposes. First week in May.

Fiesta de Mayo, Huaraz. Also known as *El Señor de la Soledad,* this festival is celebrated with traditional dances, ski races, and a lantern procession. May 2 to May 10.

JUNE

Corpus Christi, Cusco. A procession of saints and virgins arrives at the Catedral to "greet" the body of Christ. Members of nearby churches also take their patron saints in a procession. An overnight vigil is followed by a new procession around the Plaza de Armas, with images of five virgins clad in embroidered tunics and the images of four saints: Sebastian, Blas, Joseph, and the Apostle Santiago (St. James). Early June.

Virgen del Carmen, Paucartambo. In a remote highland village 4 hours from Cusco, thousands come to honor the Virgen del Carmen, or Mamacha Carmen, patron saint of the *mestizo* population, with 4 days of splendidly festive music and dance, as well as some of the wildest costumes in Peru. Dancers even perform daring moves on rooftops. The festival ends in the cemetery in a show of respect for the souls of the dead. Pisac also celebrates the Virgen del Carmen festival, almost as colorfully. June 15 to June 18.

Semana del Andinismo, Huaraz and Callejón de Huaylas. For outdoors fanatics, this celebration of outdoor adventure includes opportunities to partake in trekking, skiing, mountain biking, rafting, rock climbing, and hang-gliding—and plenty of parties to accompany them. Mid- to late June.

Inti Raymi, Cusco. The Inca Festival of the Sun—the mother of all pre-Columbian festivals—celebrates the winter solstice and honors the sun god with traditional pageantry, parades, and dances. One of the most vibrant and exciting of all Andean festivals, it draws thousands of visitors who fill Cusco's hotels. The principal event takes place at the Sacsayhuamán ruins and includes the sacrifice of a pair of llamas. General celebrations last several days. June 24.

San Juan, Cusco and Iquitos. The feast day of St. John the Baptist, a symbol of fertility and sensuality, is the most important date on the festival calendar in the entire Peruvian jungle. John the Baptist has taken on a major symbolic significance because of the importance of water as a vital element in the entire Amazon region. Events include fiestas with lots of music and regional cuisine. In Iquitos, don't miss the aphrodisiac potions with suggestive names. June 24 in Cusco; June 25 in Iquitos.

San Pedro/San Pablo, near fishing villages in Lima and Chiclayo. The patron saints of fishermen and farmers, Saint Peter and Saint Paul, are honored at this festival; figures of the saints are carried with incense, prayers, and hymns down to the sea and are taken by launch around the bay to bless the waters. June 29.

JULY

Fiesta de Santiago, Isla Taquile. This celebration of St. James is a festive and very traditional pageant of color, with exuberant dances and women in layered, multicolored skirts. July 25 and August 1 and 2.

Fiestas Patrias. A series of patriotic parties mark Peru's independence from Spain in 1821. Official parades and functions are augmented by cockfighting, bullfighting, and Peruvian Paso horse exhibitions in other towns. The best celebrations are in Cusco, Puno, Isla Taquile, and Lima. July 28 and 29.

AUGUST

Santa Rosa de Lima, Lima. Major devotional processions honor the patron saint of Lima. August 30.

SEPTEMBER

International Spring Festival, Trujillo. Trujillo celebrates the festival of spring with marinera dance, decorated streets and houses, floats, and schoolchildren dancing in the streets—led, of course, by the pageant beauty queen. Last week in September.

OCTOBER

El Señor de los Milagros, Lima. The Lord of Miracles is the largest procession in South America, and it dates from colonial times. Lasting nearly 24 hours and involving tens of thousands of purple-clad participants, it celebrates a Christ image (painted by an Angolan slave) that survived the 1746 earthquake and has since become the most venerated image in the capital. October 18.

NOVEMBER

Todos Santos & Día de los Muertos. Peruvians salute the dead by visiting cemeteries carrying flowers and food. Families hold candlelit vigils in the cemetery until dawn. The holiday is most vibrantly celebrated in the highlands. November 1 and 2.

Puno Week, Puno. A major procession from the shores of the lake to the town stadium celebrates Manco Cápac, who, according to legend, rose from the waters of Lake Titicaca to establish the Inca Empire. Dances and music take over Puno, with events often taking a turn for the inebriated. Spectacular "Day of the Dead" celebrations coincide with Puno Week. First week of November.

DECEMBER

Santuranticuy Fair, Cusco. One of the largest arts-and-crafts fairs in Peru—literally, "saints for sale"—is held in the Plaza de Armas. Artisans lay out blankets around the square, as in traditional Andean markets, and sell figurines and Nativity scenes as well as ceramics, carvings, pottery, and *retablos* (altars). Vendors sell hot rum punch called *ponche.* December 24.

Public Holidays

National public holidays in Peru include New Year's Day (Jan 1), Three Kings Day (Jan 6), Maundy Thursday and Good Friday (Easter week, Mar or Apr), Labor Day (May 1), Fiestas Patrias (July 28–29), Battle of Angamos (Oct 8), All Saints' Day (Nov 1), Feast of the Immaculate Conception (Dec 8), and Christmas (Dec 24–25).

RESPONSIBLE TOURISM

Sustainable, responsible tourism means conscientious travel. It means being careful with the environments you explore and respecting the communities you visit. Two overlapping components of sustainable travel are ecotourism and ethical tourism. Peru is a major ecotourism destination, and many of the companies organizing good, sustainable travel initiatives can be found in chapter 4, "The Best Special Interest Trips." See also chapter 3 "Peru's Natural World."

Traveling "green" and seeking sustainable tourism options is a concern in almost every part of the world today. Peru, with its majestic large expanses of nature, including the Amazon basin that covers two-thirds of the country, is a place where environmentally and culturally conscientious travel is not something to think about—it's the reality of the present and future. Although one could argue that any trip that includes an airplane flight or rental car can't be truly green, you can go on holiday and still contribute positively to the environment; all travelers can take certain steps toward responsible travel. Choose forward-looking companies that embrace responsible development practices, helping preserve destinations for the future by working alongside local people. An increasing number of sustainable tourism initiatives can help you plan a family trip and leave as small a "footprint" as possible on the places you visit.

The **International Ecotourism Society (TIES)** defines ecotourism as responsible travel to natural areas that conserves the environment and improves the well-being of local people. TIES suggests that ecotourists follow these principles:

- Minimize environmental impact.
- Build environmental and cultural awareness and respect.
- Provide positive experiences for both visitors and hosts.
- Provide direct financial benefits for conservation and for local people.
- Raise sensitivity to host countries' political, environmental, and social climates.
- Support international human rights and labor agreements.

You can find some eco-friendly travel tips, statistics, and touring companies and associations—listed by destination under "Travel Choice"—at the **TIES** website, www.ecotourism.org.

While much of the focus of ecotourism is about reducing impacts on the natural environment, ethical tourism concentrates on ways to preserve and enhance local economies and communities, regardless of location. You can embrace ethical tourism by staying at locally owned hotels or shopping at stores that employ local workers and sell locally produced goods. In Peru, it's a great idea to pick up artisanry such as textiles and ceramics from shops that ensure that the very artisans are well compensated for their labors. Many times those artisans are residents of poor, rural communities and "fair trade" shops are increasingly seen. Many highlight the names of artisans and their home communities on their wares.

Volunteer travel has become increasingly popular among those who want to venture beyond the standard group-tour experience to learn languages, interact with locals, and make a positive difference while on vacation in Peru. Volunteer options are listed under "Volunteer & Study Programs," in chapter 4.

Deforestation is the main threat to Peru's fragile ecosystem. Farming has virtually wiped out most of the region's rainforests, and logging is a major threat. Such destruction has been devastating to many species, including man himself, in the form of displaced indigenous tribes, and has led to drinking-water shortages, flash flooding, and mudslides. Though environmental awareness is growing, solving the region's huge environmental problems, including not just deforestation but the effects of overpopulation and industrial pollution, clearly remains an uphill struggle.

Peru has 72 million hectares (178 million acres) of natural-growth forests—70% in the Amazon jungle region—that comprise nearly 60% of the national territory. Peru has done a slightly better job of setting aside tracts of rainforest as national park reserves and regulating industry than have some other Latin American and Asian countries. The Manu Biosphere Reserve, the Tambopata National Reserve, and the Pacaya-Samiria National Reserve are three of the largest protected rainforest areas in the world, and the government regulates entry of tour groups. Peru augmented the Bahuaja-Sonene National Park, which was created in 1996, by 809,000 hectares (nearly 2 million acres) in 2001. INRENA, Peru's Institute for Natural Resource Management, enforces logging regulations and reseeds Peru's Amazon forests, and, in 2008, President García created the country's first Ministry of the Environment. A handful of Peruvian and international environmental and conservation groups, such as ProNaturaleza and Conservation International are active in Peru, working on reforestation and sustainable forestry projects.

Yet Peru is losing nearly 300,000 hectares (740,000 acres) of rainforest annually. The primary threats to Peru's tropical forests are deforestation caused by agricultural expansion, cattle ranching, logging, oil extraction and spills, mining, illegal coca farming, and colonization initiatives. Deforestation has shrunk territories belonging to indigenous peoples and wiped out more than 90% of the population. (There were once some six million people, 2,000 tribes and/or ethnic groups, and innumerable languages in the Amazon basin; today the indigenous population is less than two million.) Jungle ecotourism has exploded in Peru, and rainforest regions are now much more accessible than they once were, with more lodges and eco-options than ever. Many are taking leading roles in sustainable tourism even as they introduce protected regions to more travelers.

Besides sustainable travel to Peru's wilderness, national parks and reserves, and threatened areas, there are everyday things you can do to minimize the impact—and especially the carbon footprint—of your travels. Remove chargers from cell phones, PSPs, laptops, and anything else that draws from the mains, once the gadget is fully charged. Turning off all hotel room lights (plus the TV and air-conditioning) can have a massive effect; it really is time all hotels had room card central power switches.

Green trips also extend to where you eat and stay. Vegetarian foods tend to have a much smaller impact on the environment because they eschew energy- and resource-intensive meat production. Most hotels now offer you the choice to use your towels for more than 1 night before they are re-laundered—laundry makes up around 40% of an average hotel's energy use.

One matter that travelers should watch out for in jungle areas are restaurants that serve "bush meats" and endangered species. *Paiche*, a huge white freshwater river fish found in the Amazon and its tributaries, is now endangered and is illegal in restaurants, as are caiman, *lagarto* (alligator), and *motelo* (turtle, often listed on menus as *sopa de motelo,* served in its shell, or *muchangue,* turtle eggs). The fact that these are illegally hunted, and thus prohibited for sale of any kind, seems to matter little. Some experts also suggest that even ordering *chonta* or *palmitos* (hearts of palm) is inadvisable, as the amount it takes from 20-year-old trees for a large salad is very hard to sustain. Ethical travelers at a minimum should not order any of those dishes and perhaps choose not to patronize a restaurant that deals in illegal, endangered species. However, not every exotic animal should be considered off-limits to diners. Alpaca, *cuy* (guinea pig), and piranha are perfectly fine to eat if you're a moderately adventurous carnivore.

In some markets in jungle towns, like the famed **Mercado de Belén** in Iquitos in the northern Amazon, all kinds of endangered animals, both alive and butchered, are offered for sale—including land and river turtles, monkeys, caiman, and more. Some foreigners understandably think that the humane thing to do would be to purchase the live, usually mistreated and malnourished, animals and take them to an animal refuge, such as **Pilpintuwasi Butterfly Farm.** Officials there, however, say that this is emphatically the wrong approach—no matter how well meaning. It is participating in illegal commerce and only encourages the sellers to continue to sell endangered species at the market. The best way to protest is not to purchase them, and even better is to report their presence to a local environmental protection agency (which can be frustrating and ineffectual, but a small step that must be taken repeatedly if any progress on these issues is to be made).

Among Peruvian hotel chains, one stands out as a model for the industry. Although **Inkaterra** operates just four hotels and lodges—two in Aguas Calientes at the base of Machu Picchu and two in Tambopata, in Southern Amazonia—it is a leader among green, sustainable tourism initiatives. The group, which began with a research center for scientists in the Amazon, takes environmental issues seriously: Its properties are carbon neutral, and it operates a not-for-profit environmental organization, which actively monitors environmental deterioration in the Peruvian rainforest. The chairman of the group sits on the board of Conservation International. Other hotel groups, and particularly those operating ecolodges in the Amazon, are following suit, being careful to ensure that a healthy percentage of jobs and benefits stay local and that the lodges' imprint on their fragile environment is minimal. In a country like Peru, with such a large tract of virgin rainforest and developmental needs, maintaining a balance between income generation/tourism and sustainable development is a huge ongoing challenge.

A source for environmentally sensitive hotels is **It's a Green Green World** (www.itsagreengreenworld.com), which lists green and eco-friendly places to stay, mostly ecolodges in the Amazon. **Responsible Travel** (www.responsibletravel.com, www.responsiblevacation.com in the U.S.) is one among a growing number of environmentally aware travel agents, with dozens of green Peru trips offered. **Vision on Sustainable Tourism** (www.tourism-vision.com) is another excellent news hub. Carbon offsetting (not uncontroversial) can be arranged through, among others, **Climate Care** (www.climatecare.org).

For flexible **volunteering** opportunities that you can build into your Peru itinerary, see "Volunteer & Study Programs," p. 61. In addition to the resources listed above, see www.frommers.com/planning/ for more tips on responsible travel.

PERU'S NATURAL WORLD

3

"**P**eru" is derived from a word in Quechua signifying "land of abundance," a remarkably apt name to describe this diverse country. There is little question that, in its distinct costa, sierra, and selva (coast, highlands, and jungle) regions, Peru is blessed with an enormous variety of wilderness and some of the world's greatest and most diverse plant and animal species. It has been reported that Peru contains 84 of the known 103 biosystems in the world; more than 400 species of mammals and 300 species of reptiles; 50,000 plant species (among them the world's highest count of orchids, more than 3,000 kinds); and nearly 2,000 bird species, about 10% of the world's total. With desert sands, dense Amazon rainforest canopy, stunning Andean peaks, and the world's deepest canyons, Peru is a country that begs travelers to get outdoors.

ECOSYSTEMS

Peruvians are fond of pointing out that their country consists of three distinct geological components: coast, *sierra* (highlands), and *selva* (jungle). Although the largest cities are situated along the coast, the Amazon rainforest (which makes up nearly two-thirds of Peru) and the bold Andes mountain range dominate the country. The Pacific coastal region is a narrow strip that runs from one end of the country to the other (a distance of some 2,200km/1,400 miles) and is made up almost entirely of desert. The Andes, South America's longest mountain range, is the most significant topographical feature of the Peruvian landscape. The mountain ranges in the center of Peru, north of Lima, are among the highest in South America. Within Huascarán National Park, the Cordillera Blanca stretches 200km (124 miles) and contains a dozen peaks more than 5,000m (16,400 ft.) tall; the highest is Huascarán, at 6,768m (22,205 ft.). In the extreme south of Peru, near Puno and Lake Titicaca, the Andes yield to the *altiplano* (the arid high plains), with altitudes of 3,300 meters (11,000 ft.). The *selva* ranges from cloud forest in the south to low-lying flatlands in the north. Although more than 60% of Peru is Amazon rainforest, only about 5% of the country's human inhabitants reside there. Massive Lake Titicaca, shared with Bolivia, is the largest lake in South America and the world's highest navigable body of water (at 3,830m/12,566 ft.).

FLORA & FAUNA

Peru is extraordinarily rich in biodiversity. Nearly two-thirds of Peru is jungle, and many naturalists and biologists believe that Peru's Amazon rainforest holds the greatest diversity in the world. Peru is home to more than 400 species of mammals (of which about 70 are endemic and about 100 are threatened or endangered), 2,000 species of fish, 1,800 birds, and more than 50,000 plants (including 3,000 species of orchids). Incredibly, the country counts 84 of 103 existing ecosystems and 28 of the 32 climates on the planet among its remarkable statistics. Recent studies have shown that a region just south of Iquitos has the highest concentration of mammals anywhere in the world. Peru's other significant fauna are the great Andean condors, found principally in Colca Canyon, near Arequipa, and the rich marine life of the Paracas National Reserve and Islas Ballestas (Peru's version of the Galápagos Islands), home to communities of endangered Humboldt penguins and sea turtles, sea lions, red-footed boobies, and flamingoes. Coastal Peru south of Lima is also home to one of the greatest population densities of dolphins in the world, with one-third of the world's species identified.

In the Andes mountains and altiplano region, perhaps the most emblematic creatures are the four species of camelids, both domesticated and wild, that roam at high elevations. Highland birds are led by the Andean condor, with its magnificent wingspan.

The Humboldt current brings cold Pacific waters to the Peruvian coast, facilitating a rich habitat for marine life, especially seabirds and marine mammals (33 species). At Paracas National Reserve alone, there are 200-plus species of birds, including vast high-density colonies.

The tropical rainforest east of the Andes, which occupies more than 60% of Peru, is one of the world's richest habitats, with tremendous plant and animal life. The jungle is home to 32 species of primates, several types of great jungle cats, rare large mammals like giant otters and pink river dolphins, an array of reptiles, amphibians and fish, and more than 1,000 species of birds. Macaw clay licks, where thousands of parrots and macaws gather to feed off the minerals, are one of the world's great nature sights. Peru counts more than 1,800 species of birds within its borders, the second highest number of any country. Dedicated birders find Manu National Park and Tambopata National Reserve among the world's greatest birding destinations.

Actual wildlife viewing differs greatly, of course, from perusing rosters of species. Most casual visitors and even many dedicated naturalists may never see a rare jungle cat like the jaguar. However, anyone on a dedicated lodge tour or river cruise in the Amazon with a good guide or visiting other parts of Peru celebrated for their wildlife (such as Paracas National Reserve or Colca Canyon) will be exposed to an impressive display of nature. Whether you go to Peru to check 100 species off your lifetime bird list, or just to get a taste of what ecotourism is all about, you'll be surrounded by a rich and varied collection of flora and fauna. The information below is only a very selective and limited introduction to the incredible wealth found in Peru's rainforests, highlands, and coastal regions.

ENVIRONMENTAL THREATS

The vast Amazon basin that pertains to Peru holds a phenomenal wealth of flora and fauna but a dwindling human presence. Indigenous Amazonian tribes have been greatly reduced by centuries of disease, deforestation, and assimilation. There were once some six million people, 2,000 tribes and/or ethnic groups, and innumerable languages in the Amazon basin; today the indigenous population is less than two million. Still, many traditions and languages have yet to be extinguished, especially deep in the jungle—though most visitors are unlikely to come into contact with groups of unadulterated, non-Spanish-speaking native peoples.

Peru is losing nearly 300,000 hectares (740,000 acres) of rainforest annually. The primary threats to Peru's tropical forests are deforestation caused by agricultural expansion, cattle ranching, logging, oil extraction and spills, mining, illegal coca farming, and colonization initiatives. Deforestation has shrunk territories belonging to indigenous peoples and wiped out more than 90% of the population.

Peru has 72 million hectares (178 million acres) of natural-growth forests—70% in the Amazon jungle region—that comprise nearly 60% of the national territory. Peru has done a slightly better job of setting aside tracts of rainforest as national park reserves and regulating industry than have some other Latin American and Asian countries. The Manu Biosphere Reserve, the Tambopata National Reserve, and the Pacaya-Samiria National Reserve are three of the largest protected rainforest areas in the world, and the government regulates entry of tour groups. Peru augmented the Bahuaja-Sonene National Park, which was created in 1996, by 809,000 hectares (nearly 2 million acres) in 2001. INRENA, Peru's Institute for Natural Resource Management, enforces logging regulations and reseeds Peru's Amazon forests, and in 2008, President García created the country's first Ministry of the Environment. A handful of Peruvian and international environmental and conservation groups, such as ProNaturaleza and Conservation International are active in Peru, working on reforestation and sustainable forestry projects.

Jungle ecotourism has exploded in Peru, and rainforest regions are now much more accessible than they once were, with more lodges and eco-options than ever. Many are taking leading roles in sustainable tourism even as they introduce protected regions to more travelers.

NATIONAL PARKS & RESERVES

Peru's extraordinary natural environment features a wealth of protected areas, wildlife reserves, and archaeological zones. Dozens of national parks and nature preserves make up a bit more than 10% of Peru. The majority of these national parks and nature reserves are undeveloped tropical forests, with few services or facilities available for tourism. Others, however, offer easier access to their wealth of natural wonders. The discussion below is not a complete listing of all of Peru's national parks and protected areas. Rather, it details the ones that are the most accessible and most rewarding for visitors, including several of the largest and most biodiverse on the planet.

Many of them require visitors' permits, for a small fee. If you go with an organized tour, the tour operators almost always take care of the bureaucratic details and include the fees in their package price. See the listings of specialty tour operators in chapter 4.

Peru's protected natural areas go by several names in Spanish, according to distinct legal statutes and protections: *parques nacionales* (national parks), *reserves nacionales* (national reserves), *sanctuarios nacionales/históricos* (national or historic sanctuaries), and *zonas reservadas* (reserve zones), among others.

Manu National Park & Biosphere Reserve

Manu is probably the most famous national park in Peru. Covering nearly a million hectares (nearly 2½ million acres), Manu National Park & Biosphere Reserve is the second-largest protected area in the country and one of the largest in South America. It is also thought to be the most biodiverse zone on Earth. Created in 1973, the park reserve is on the eastern slopes of the Andes within the Amazon basin and comprises an extraordinary variety of habitats, including tropical lowland forest, mountain forest, and grasslands. The reserve zone contains the lower Manu River, the Río Alto Madre de Dios, and a number of beautiful oxbow lakes. About 1,000 bird species—about a quarter of all birds known in South America and 10% of all species in the world—and more than 200 species of mammals have been identified. Also found in the park are at least 13 endangered wildlife species, including black caimans, giant river otters, and ocelots. Botanists have claimed that Manu has a greater number of plant species than any other protected area on Earth.

Manu is superb for observing wildlife, but trips to Manu are lengthy and costly. Most trips bus travelers in and fly them out by light aircraft. There are very few lodges within the designated reserve and cultural zones, and access to the reserve zone is by organized tour. Independent visits are possible in the cultural zone only.

Tambopata National Reserve

The Tambopata National Reserve is more accessible and less restrictive than Manu. The park is made up principally of lowland forest along the Tambopata River. A number of lodges are in and around the reserve, accessible from Puerto Maldonado. The lodges offer shorter stays but usually include naturalist-led expeditions to remote areas. Independent travel with a guide can also be arranged in Puerto Maldonado. Although Manu is more celebrated and probably more pristine, with greater species diversity, the flora and fauna that can be observed by most visitors at Tambopata are remarkably similar.

 Giant Otters

One of the most fascinating creatures that visitors have a chance of spotting in the southeastern Amazon basin in Peru is the giant otter *(Pteronura brasiliensis)*, the largest of the 13 otter species in the world. Hunted for its pelt, it has landed on the World Conservation Union ignominious Red List of Endangered Species and has probably been eliminated in Argentina and Uruguay. It has recovered in Peru, but fewer than a couple of hundred probably exist.

Giant otters today are primarily "hunted" by tourists and photographers. The large and very active animals are found in lakes and rivers of tropical lowlands, where they can rather easily be observed. Conservationists are concerned that otters in Manu and Tambopata, among other places, have suffered from human interference in the form of tourist canoes, which leads to long-term changes in behavior and decreases in reproduction. Less invasive observation towers and viewing platforms have been constructed in Cochas Otorongo and Salvador in the Manu Biosphere Reserve. The Giant Otter Project of the Frankfurt Zoological Society (www.giantotterperu.org) is overseeing monitoring and protection of the species in the Pacaya-Samiria National Reserve and the Manu and Bahuaja-Sonene national parks in southeastern Peru.

Huascarán National Park

Home to a chain of snowcapped mountains that comprise the longest tropical range in the world, the 161km (100-mile) Cordillera Blanca in the central Andes, Huascarán is a mecca for climbers and a host of outdoor and adventure travelers. Its scenery and offerings—mountain climbing, trekking, horseback riding, white-water rafting, fishing, and mountain biking, among others—are perhaps unequaled in the Americas. With 200 alpine lakes, 600 glaciers, spectacular mountain vistas, and nearby ancient pre-Columbian ruins, though, Huascarán is also a magnet for travelers who want to appreciate the scenery with just their eyes, not necessarily their legs and lungs.

Named for the highest peak in Peru, the park's altitude ranges from 2,500m to 6,768m (8,202 ft.–22,205 ft.) and includes more than two dozen snowcapped peaks above 6,000m (19,700 ft.). Huascarán is the second-highest park in the South American Andes. Climbing and trekking opportunities range from expert to moderate, with the latter easily managed by anyone in good shape. Arrangements for manageable 2-day walks and 2-week camping hikes crisscrossing the formidable passes of the Cordillera can be easily arranged in Huaraz and Caraz.

For independent treks in the park, a permit must be obtained from the park office in Huaraz. Some locals and foreign visitors have complained that the national park is not being managed as well as it might be, and that trash has accumulated along the major trails.

Machu Picchu Historical Sanctuary

Machu Picchu is much more than the famous Inca ruins carved into a mountainside. The Machu Picchu Historical Sanctuary, named a UNESCO natural and cultural World Heritage Site in 1983, is a designated archaeological zone and 33,000-hectare (81,545-acre) preserve. International concern over environmental damage to Machu Picchu and the Inca Trail led the Peruvian government to introduce more stringent measures to protect the zone's natural heritage, including limits on the number of people allowed on the trail. Proposals that would severely compromise the natural environment, such as the building of cable cars to the ruins, have been defeated, at least for now.

International environmental and conservation groups, such as World Parks Endowment, have been lobbying the Peruvian government to create a large Inca National Park and expand the protected area around Machu Picchu into the neighboring Vilcanota and Vilcabamba mountains, which would establish a major protected area.

Pacaya-Samiria National Reserve

The largest natural reserve in Peru, Pacaya-Samiria is one of the Amazon's (and the world's) richest wildlife habitats. Covering more than 2 million hectares (5 million acres) of pristine rainforest and wetlands in the north-central Amazon region (about 322km/200 miles south of Iquitos), the reserve is difficult to penetrate during the rainy season (Dec–Mar). The reserve is full of rivers and lakes, and it boasts some of the Amazon's most abundant species of flora and fauna.

Pacaya-Samiria is considerably less accessible than the jungle farther north and is much less visited than Manu or Tambopata. Several tour operators now organize river cruises, canoe trips, and camping expeditions, and a couple of native communities are promoting camping trips and immersion experiences. A permit from INRENA, the Peruvian parks authority, is required to enter the preserve.

Paracas National Reserve

South of Lima, in the department of Ica on the southern coast, this peninsula is blessed with an abundance of marine wildlife and seabirds. About two-thirds of the 335,000-hectare (827,800-acre) reserve is ocean; the desert landscape is barren and rather absent of most plant life. The Ballestas Islands, contained within the nature reserve, are rich in bird and sea lion life, and present excellent and very accessible opportunities for viewing wildlife up close.

SAFETY & ETIQUETTE IN NATURAL PERU

Although many outdoor travel itineraries in Peru require no special medications or vaccinations, there are special considerations for jungle travel. Additionally, acclimatization to the high altitude of the Andes is essential for anyone seeking to do trekking or climbing in the mountains.

For tropical travel in Peru, the Centers for Disease Control and Prevention recommends vaccinations against yellow fever, hepatitis A or immunoglobulin (IG), hepatitis B, typhoid, and booster doses for tetanus-diphtheria and measles, as well as pills for malaria. For more detailed information, see "Health," in "Fast Facts" in chapter 13.

Most tours and activities are extremely safe, but there are risks involved in any adventure activity. The risks involved in mountain climbing, ice climbing, and white-water rafting are considerable. Know and respect your own physical limits and skills (or lack thereof) before undertaking any high-risk activity.

Be prepared for extremes in temperature and rainfall, and wide fluctuations in weather. A sunny morning hike can quickly become a cold and wet ordeal, so it's a good idea to carry some form of rain gear when hiking in the rainforest, bring sufficient protection against the cold at high altitudes, and have a dry change of clothing waiting at the end of the trail. Be sure to bring plenty of sunscreen, no matter where you travel. See "What to bring," below, for more suggestions.

If you do any trekking or camping, exercise caution with the native species that live in natural habitats. Don't go poking under rocks or fallen branches: Snake bites are very rare, but don't do anything to increase the odds. If you do encounter a snake, stay calm, don't make any sudden movements, and *do not* try to handle it. The chance of getting bitten by a venomous snake is small; however, if you're bitten, wash out the bite and surrounding area very thoroughly (don't go Hollywood and try to suck out the venom). Because the bite might cause swelling, remove your jewelry. If symptoms persist, seek medical attention; the best way to demonstrate to a doctor what kind of snake bit you, of course, is to hand over the dead snake—certainly not always possible. Also beware of centipedes, scorpions, and spiders, including tarantulas, brown recluses, and black widows. If you are bitten by a dog or another creature, such as a bat, there is a risk of rabies. Wash out the wound thoroughly with soap and water, and seek medical attention. For a detailed "disease risk analysis" and other precautions, take a look at **Travel Medicine**'s website at **www.travmed.com**.

Avoid swimming in jungle rivers unless a guide or local operator can vouch for their safety. Although white-water sections and stretches in mountainous areas are generally pretty safe, many rivers in the Amazon basin are home to contingents of crocodile and caiman populations.

WHAT TO bring

Outdoor and adventure travel in Peru requires some special gear, and it's a good idea to come prepared; you're more likely to find a better selection of equipment, apparel, and other outdoor gear at home than you are in Peru. You can rent some equipment, such as crampons for ice climbing, but you'd be wise to bring most nontechnical items with you.

The most basic items for travelers to Peru who are doing any sort of light adventure, such as trekking or jungle lodge stays, are (already broken-in and preferably waterproof) **hiking boots** (it's not a bad idea to take them in a carry-on or wear them on the plane, to avoid their loss), outdoor apparel such as **fleece pullovers,** and a **daypack.**

Essential gear for almost all travelers to Peru includes
- a sun hat
- sunscreen
- cold-weather and water-repellent clothing
- light trekking shoes or boots
- several pairs of thick socks

Additional items for light adventure include
- good backpacking or climbing boots
- a base layer (thermal underwear or wicking-quality shirt)

- malarial pills (if traveling to jungle regions)
- insect repellent
- a pocketknife
- toilet paper
- a flashlight or headlamp
- a mosquito net
- a sleeping bag
- diarrhea medicine
- energy bars or other trail snack foods
- sports sandals or comfortable slides for post-climbing and trekking, or for river and wet-weather wear
- a water bottle or other portable hydration system
- a good internal-frame backpack

Stuff to bring for hard-core adventure travel includes
- food supplies and cooking equipment
- a filter and/or water-purification tablets
- a first-aid kit
- a compass and whistle
- a tent, camping stove, and cookware
- adequate fuel
- topographical maps of trails

Bugs and bug bites (and blisters) will probably be your greatest health concerns in the Peruvian wilderness. For the most part, bugs are merely an inconvenience, although mosquitoes can carry malaria or dengue (see "Health" in "Fast Facts" in chapter 13 for more information). Strong repellent and proper clothing will minimize both the danger and the inconvenience. On beaches, you might be bitten by sand fleas. These nearly invisible insects leave an irritating welt. Try not to scratch because this can lead to open sores and infections.

However, in all probability, Peru's bounteous nature needs to be protected from visitors more than visitors need to be protected from it. A fundamental component of enjoying nature is leaving the natural environment undisturbed. The responsible outdoor traveler's maxim is: Take nothing but memories (and photos); leave nothing but footprints. Do not cut or uproot plants or flowers. Pack out everything you pack in, and *never* litter. Leave places the way you found them. If you see garbage lying around in protected areas, pack it out, along with your own trash. Don't scratch your name or any other graffiti on trees or ancient monuments. On trails, bury your excrement as far as possible from the trail. Over the years, too many insensitive trekkers along the Inca Trail, among other spots, did not follow this common-sense advice and did so much damage that international organizations, such as UNESCO, worried about the trail's survival.

To support local communities and appreciate what you have the rare opportunity to experience, it's a great idea to use (and adequately tip or pay) local guides and porters, and support locally owned businesses and artisans.

THE BEST
SPECIAL-
INTEREST TRIPS

4

Peru is perhaps the most diverse and best-equipped out-doors destination in South America. It's the rare visitor from abroad who arrives in Peru with the intention of staying clean and dry in pressed slacks and loafers; most gringos who set foot beyond Lima are outfitted in fleece pullovers, hiking boots, daypacks, and water-repellent gear, with plans for active travel. Beyond the great out-doors, other active trips focus on culinary Peru—the diverse national cuisine is one of the world's finest, even if until recently it flew under the radar of many foodie types—volunteering, and language classes.

Ecotourism and outdoors travel are the bulk of special-interest travel to Peru. Amazingly, though, given its natural abundance, Peru is still rela-tively new to the ecotourism game. Its infrastructure to receive large groups of ecotourists is not quite as developed as that of some other countries, such as Costa Rica—though the gap is closing fast. Tour opera-tors, guides, and agencies, both local and international, are increasingly specializing in outdoor and active travel. The oldest jungle lodges in the Peruvian Amazon have been around for more than three decades. Ecolodges, climbing and rafting expeditions, and birding and hiking trips all cater to environmentally aware and responsible travelers with deep interests in nature and seeing "the real Peru."

In the minds of many nonspecialists, getting outdoors in Peru is still limited to easily reached day hikes in the valleys, jungle treks and lodges, and strenuous treks along ancient Inca trails. Of course, you can also go hard-core, plunging deep into the jungle or mountains on thrilling, multi-day outdoors trips experiencing the best of natural Peru. Everything from soft adventure and easy walks to extreme sports is available and easily arranged either on your own (for the former) or with top-notch agencies and guides.

Whether you want to make active and outdoor travel the sole focus of your trip or treat it as just an add-on, there are many different ways to approach it. This chapter lays out your options, from tour operators who run multi-activity package tours (and frequently include stays at ecolodges) to the best spots in Peru to get outdoors (with listings of tour operators, guides, and outfitters that specialize in each). You'll also find educational and volunteer travel options for those with the time and desire to work toward the maintenance and preservation of Peru's natural wonders and gain a more in-depth understanding of Peru's resources, culture, and people.

ORGANIZED ADVENTURE TRIPS

Because most travelers have limited time and resources, organized ecotourism or adventure travel packages, arranged by tour operators abroad or in Peru, are popular ways of combining cultural and outdoor activities. Birding, horseback riding, rafting, and hiking can be teamed with visits to destinations such as Cusco, the Sacred Valley and Machu Picchu, or Arequipa and Lake Titicaca.

Traveling with a group has several advantages over traveling independently. Accommodations and transportation are arranged, and most (if not all) of your meals are included in the cost of a package. If your tour operator has experience and a decent track record, you should proceed to each of your destinations quickly without the snags and long delays that you might face if traveling on your own. You'll also have the opportunity to meet like-minded travelers who are interested in nature and active sports. Some group trekking trips include *porteros* or *arrieros* (porters or muleteers) who carry extra equipment. On some luxury treks of the Inca Trail and other, alternative trails, porters will even carry your backpack, so all you have to be concerned with is getting yourself up and over the mountain passes.

 Inca Trail Regulations

Trekkers once could set off on the Inca Trail on their own (as I once did), but new regulations imposed by the Peruvian government to limit environmental degradation and damage to the trail itself now require all trekkers to go with officially sanctioned groups, guides, and porters. See the "Inca Trail Regulations" box and "Inca Trail Agencies," both in chapter 9, for more information.

In the best cases of organized outdoors travel, group size is kept small (10–15 people), and tours are escorted by knowledgeable guides who are either naturalists or biologists. Be sure to inquire about difficulty levels when you're choosing a tour. While most companies offer "soft adventure" packages (which travelers in decent but not supremely athletic shape can handle), others focus on more hard-core activities geared toward extremely fit and seasoned adventure travelers.

U.S. & INTERNATIONAL ADVENTURE TOUR OPERATORS

These agencies and operators specialize in well-organized and coordinated tours that cover your entire stay. Many travelers prefer to have everything arranged and confirmed before arriving in Peru—a good idea for first-timers and during high season (especially for travel to Cusco and its immediate environs, including the Inca Trail). Many of these operators provide great service but are not cheap; 10-day tours generally cost upwards of $2,500 or more per person, and do not include airfare to Peru.

Abercrombie & Kent ★★ (www.abercrombiekent.com; ✆ **800/554-7016**) calls itself the "original luxury travel company." It runs an extensive lineup of high-end luxury trips, all of which are well managed and pampered, with stays in many of the finest hotels available. The tours aren't cheap, but if you want to go in style, A&K is the way to go. Group size is generally limited to 16 people. More than a dozen Peru itineraries are available, including to the Amazon, Colca Canyon, and Lake Titicaca (as well as combo trips with the Galápagos); check the website for occasional discounts on selected tours and dates.

Adventure Life ★ (www.adventure-life.com; ✆ 800/344-6118), based in Missoula, Montana, and specializing in Central and South America, has an interesting roster of often rugged Peru trips, frequently with a community focus, including a 10-day multi-sport tour (mountain biking, hiking, rafting, jungle tour, and Machu Picchu), rainforest ecolodge tours, and a 10-day "Cachiccata Trek: The Inca Trail Less Traveled," as well as plenty of tour extensions. One Peru trip is specifically designed to raise money (40% of trip cost) for the organization's nonprofit fund (which aims to give back to local communities).

Adventure Specialists ★ (www.adventurespecialists.org; ✆ 719/783-2076) travels only to the Copper Canyon (Mexico), Colorado, and Peru. In Peru, it specializes in treks, horse trips, and archaeology expeditions, as well as wildlife and birding adventures by dugout canoe in the Manu Biosphere Reserve. The founder is one of the archaeologists credited with the November 2003 rediscovery of Llactapata, a "lost" Inca city.

Amazonia Expeditions (www.perujungle.com or www.peruandes.com; ✆ 800/ 262-9669) has offered good-value, personalized, and flexible ecotourism trips to the Peruvian jungle and the Andes since 1981. Trips of up to 7 days are all-inclusive (even laundry and tips are included). Jungle trips are to the Tahauyo Lodge (4 hr. from Iquitos), Tahuayo River Amazon Research Center, and the Tamshiyacu-Tahuayo Reserve (they are the only licensed tour operator to the latter), and have access to the longest canopy zipline in the Peruvian Amazon. The two different websites focus on the group's jungle adventures and Inca ruins/Andes treks respectively.

Andean Treks ★★ (www.andeantreks.com; ✆ 617/924-1974) is a personalized, high-quality Latin American adventure-tour operator that focuses on trekking in the Andes and exploring the jungle throughout Peru. The Massachusetts-based group's roster of reasonably priced trips for all levels includes cloud forest treks, llama trekking, trips to Manu and Tambopata, and highlands treks that combine whitewater rafting or Amazon lodge stays. Trips range from easy to hard-core.

Backroads ★ (www.backroads.com; ✆ 800/462-2848) is a luxury-tour company that offers upscale, light-adventure trips around the globe, and it has several tours of Peru on its menu. It specializes in walking, hiking, and biking (and family) tours from Cusco to Machu Picchu, some of which incorporate stays at the Mountain Lodges of Peru (p. 256). Service is personalized and the guides are top-notch.

Butterfield & Robinson ★ (www.butterfield.com; ✆ 866/551-9090 or 800/ 6781-1477 in Europe) is a top upscale tour company that promotes biking and walking trips. You'll stay at some of the country's finest hotels and will get full van support for any light adventure trips. To Peru, it offers 7- and 8-day "Peru Walking" tours (one a private family trip). Trips are top-of-the-line (with commensurate pricing).

GorpTravel (www.gorp.com; ✆ 877/440-GORP [4677]), a self-styled "Guide to Outdoor Travel," is a wholesaler with a vast range of options for adventure and more general travel throughout Peru and the world offered by outfitters across the globe. It recently offered more than 150 outdoor-oriented vacations to Peru (including a "Peru Top 20" list). A few are basic highlights trips, while others are cultural and language vacations or specialist adventures for very active and adventurous sorts.

International Expeditions (www.internationalexpeditions.com; © 800/234-9620) features luxurious Peruvian Amazon River cruises, as well as guided trips to Cusco and Machu Picchu. Visitors help with reforestation projects and participate in conservation programs and tree planting with local naturalists.

Journeys International ★★ (www.journeys.travel; © 800/255-8735), based in Ann Arbor, Michigan, offers small-group (4–12 people) natural history tours guided by naturalists. Trips include the 9-day "Amazon & Andes Odyssey," which includes the Tambopata National Reserve along with Cusco, Machu Picchu, and the Sacred Valley; special Amazon and Inca trips for families, and even unusual trips such as the folkloric, 12-day "Andes Villages and Paucartambo festival."

Mountain Travel Sobek ★★★ (www.mtsobek.com; © 888/831-7526 or 0808/234-2243 in the U.K.) offers seven itineraries to Peru, including the 8-day "Andean Explorer," with day hikes and rafting. Options for mountaineers and committed trekkers include 13 days of strenuous trekking in Cordillera Blanca (mostly camping); a shorter 5-day (but still hard-core) trekking option in the same area; a challenging 15-day rafting trip along the Tambopata River (half camping, half inns); and a new, 5-day Amazon River luxury cruise. A unique trip is the off-the-beaten path "Ausangate Inn-to-Inn," as well as a Machu Picchu trek with stays at the cool inns owned and operated by **Mountain Lodges of Peru** (see below). Trips are helpfully rated for difficulty. The company was named one of *National Geographic Adventure*'s "Best Outfitters on Earth."

Overseas Adventure Travel ★ (www.oattravel.com; © 800/955-1925) offers natural history and "soft adventure" itineraries, with optional add-on excursions. Tours are limited to 16 people and are guided by naturalists. All accommodations are in small hotels, lodges, or tent camps. The 11-day "Real Affordable Peru" includes rafting on the Urubamba and a *curandero* healing ceremony. The 16-day "Machu Picchu & Galápagos" tour features a good bit of walking. Amazon River cruises and rainforest trips are also featured.

Southwind Adventures ★ (www.southwindadventures.com; © 800/377-9463) is a Colorado-based South American specialist, planning distinctive and high-end adventure trips with a cultural emphasis in South America. Among them are about a half-dozen Peruvian trips, from mountain biking to specialty tours such as the unique "Urubamba Weaver's Trek." Custom trips include a Grand Andean Traverse trekking expedition, with possibilities for bird-watching, rafting, and family adventure.

Tropical Nature Travel ★★★ (www.tropicalnaturetravel.com; © 877/827-8350) is known as one of the most sophisticated conservation groups organizing travel to jungle wildlife lodges in Manu and Tambopata. In tandem with its local conservation partner, InkaNatura, it operates four lodges, including Manu Wildlife Center, Cock of the Rock Lodge, Sandoval Lake Lodge, and the new Heath River Wildlife Center; and its Amazon jungle trips can't be beaten. The outfit has expanded its itineraries to include trekking, rafting, and archaeology culture trips to places such as Chachapoyas and Colca Canyon.

Wilderness Travel ★★★ (www.wildernesstravel.com; © 800/368-2794) is a Berkeley-based outfitter specializing in cultural, wildlife, and hiking group tours that are arranged with tiered pricing (the cost of the trip varies according to group size). There are 13 different adventurous tours to Peru, including a 17-day Trekking in the Cordillera Blanca, Choquequirao trail to Machu Picchu, and a unique "Peru Festivals Trek." Wilderness Travel also offers softer, luxury treks to Machu Picchu with stays at the cool inns owned and operated by **Mountain Lodges of Peru** (see below). Trips are helpfully graded according to difficulty.

4

THE BEST SPECIAL-INTEREST TRIPS

Adventure Tour Operators

Wildland Adventures ★★★ (www.wildland.com; © 800/345-4453), based in Seattle, is one of the top international outdoor-tour companies with operations in Peru. It offers excellent special-interest trekking and rainforest expedition programs, with customizing options. There are lodge-based programs, primarily in the jungle; river cruises into Pacaya-Samiria; trekking expeditions, such as the Machu Picchu Mountain lodges trek; and trips for active families (that include hiking and biking). Wildland's programs are well designed, guides are very professional, and the organization is focused on authentic travel experiences—all reasons *National Geographic Adventure* named it one of the "Best Outfitters on Earth."

In addition to these companies, many extremely well-regarded environmental organizations regularly offer organized trips to Peru. **The Nature Conservancy** ★★ (www.nature.org/greenliving/greenshopping/travel/index.htm; © 800/628-6860) offers "conservation journeys" with members; the trips change from year to year, but past trips to Peru have included a riverboat Amazon voyage that visits the Nature Conservancy project in the Pacaya-Samiria National Reserve. The **Smithsonian Institution** ★★ (www.si.edu; © 877/338-8687) offers "Smithsonian Journeys," study tours for members, which have included a river cruise of the northern Amazon and a long (and expensive) trip down the Amazon from Belém, Brazil, to Pevas, Peru. The **National Audubon Society** (getoutside.audubon.org/audubon-travel-nature-odysseys; © 800/967-7425) also offers "Nature Odysseys," which focus on birding and natural history arranged through carefully selected travel partners. An excellent resource for information on ecotravel is **Sacred Earth** (www.sacredearth.com), a loose consortium of "ethnobotanists" and ecotravelers that publishes an e-zine and has links to a half-dozen featured trips and workshops to Peru, including Manu camping journeys and shamanistic "Listening to the Plants" tours of the northern Amazon.

PERU-BASED AGENCIES & TOUR OPERATORS

Many tour companies based in the United States and elsewhere subcontract portions of their tours to established Peruvian companies on the ground in Lima, Cusco, and across the country. Though it's often simpler to go with international tour companies, in some cases, independent travelers can benefit by organizing their tours directly with local agencies. Prices on the ground can be cheaper than contracting a tour from abroad, but there are risks of not getting what you want when you want it. Also, the world of subcontracting can be byzantine, and even Peruvian travel agencies hire out adventure and outdoor specialists.

Local agencies offering adventure options abound, especially in Cusco, Arequipa, Huaraz, and Iquitos. These agencies can arrange everything from white-water rafting to day treks to horseback riding. Some tours might be held only when there are enough interested people or on fixed dates, so it's worthwhile to contact a few of the companies before you leave for Peru to find out what they might be doing when you arrive. See the sections on local tour and adventure agencies in each of the destination chapters; for travel in the Sacred Valley, Amazon basin, Lake Titicaca, Colca Canyon, and the Huaraz area, these are pretty much indispensable unless you contract with an international operator prior to your trip.

Class Adventure Travel (CAT) ★ (www.cat-travel.com; © 877/240-4770 in the U.S. and Canada, 0207/0906-1259 in the U.K.) is a fine all-purpose agency with offices in Lima and Cusco (it also has offices in Bolivia, Chile, and Argentina). In addition to professionally organizing virtually any kind of travel detail in Peru, its adventure offerings include rafting, trekking, and jungle tours.

Explorandes Peru ★★ (www.explorandes.com; ✆ **01/715-2323**) has been doing trekking and river expeditions in Peru for nearly 3 decades, and has regional offices in Lima, Cusco, Huaraz, and Puno. One of the top high-end agencies for treks and mountaineering in Peru, it's reasonably priced and especially good for forming very small private groups. It offers a number of soft adventure trips (with stays in hotels and full- and half-day river trips) and an even more impressive lineup of real adventure, including cool, unique trips such as llama trekking to Chavín, a festival trek, rafting on the Apurímac River, treks on southern peaks around Cusco, and hard-core trekking in the Cordillera Blanca and Huayhuash. Amazon extensions are available.

Mountain Lodges of Peru ★★★ (www.mountainlodgesofperu.com; ✆ **877/491-5261** in the U.S. and Canada, **0800/014-8886** in the U.K., or **01/421-7777**), a Peruvian trekking company, has built a series of small, spectacular lodges on private lands in the Vilcabamba mountain range west of the Sacred Valley. The sleek inns have whirlpools, fireplaces, and nice dining rooms. The company offers its own 6-day treks to Machu Picchu and also contracts with a handful of international adventure tour operators, including **Backroads, Mountain Travel Sobek, Wildland,** and **Wilderness Travel** (see above).

Peru Expeditions ★ (www.peru-expeditions.com; ✆ **01/447-2057**) is a Lima-based company run by Rafael Belmonte, a dedicated cyclist. His company runs all kinds of cool trips across Peru, including treks, four-wheel-drive vehicle tours, and mountain biking, as well as Andean festivities tours, and more standard tours to destinations such as Arequipa, Cusco, and Colca Canyon.

Peru for Less ★★ (www.peruforless.com; ✆ **877/269-0309** in the U.S. and Canada or **203/002-0571** in the U.K.), originally based in Texas and now headquartered in Lima, lives up to its plainspoken name, promising some of the lowest prices among major agencies in Peru. It has a great roster of affordable Peru tour packages, such as "Historical Peru," which visits Lima, Paracas, Nasca, Arequipa, Cusco, and Machu Picchu, and very competent teams on the ground. It has recently branched out with alternative trekking tours in the Cusco region, including small-group treks to Choquequirao and Vilcabamba and a dozen more. Tours include guides, hotels, all visits and transfers, plus daily breakfast.

SAS Travel Peru ★ (www.sastravelperu.com; ✆ **084/249-194**), based in Cusco, is one of the most popular agencies organizing outdoor travel for backpackers and budget-minded travelers. Its roster includes the Inca Trail, a number of short treks in the Cusco area, and a couple of longer, more challenging mountain treks lasting up to a week. Jungle treks are to Manu and Tambopata. SAS also offers white-water rafting, paragliding, climbing, mountain biking, and horseback riding.

OUTDOOR ACTIVITIES A TO Z

The listings in this section describe the best places to practice particular sports and activities and include the top tour operators and outfitters. If you want to focus on only one active sport during your trip to Peru, these companies are your best bets for quality equipment and knowledgeable service—but almost all of them will allow you to combine one activity with another or engage in general cultural sightseeing.

Balloning & Paragliding

In the mid-1970s, two foreigners constructed a balloon out of cotton and reed in an effort to prove that ancient cultures could have used balloons to design the mysterious Nasca Line drawings in the southern desert sands. But that didn't spark a wild interest in ballooning and hang-gliding or paragliding in Peru. So many parts of the country would be glorious to fly silently over: the Sacred Valley, the Nasca Lines, the valleys of the Callejón de Huaylas, the magnificent pre-Columbian ruins, and the great canyons near Arequipa. The only outfitter (sporadically) operating balloon flights in Peru is a U.S.-owned company, **Aero Sports Club of the Sacred Valley,** Av. de la Cultura 220, Ste. 36, Cusco (www.globosperu.com; ℂ 084/232-352). It offers flights in the Urubamba Valley, though on an inconsistent basis. If you're interested, contact the company before your trip to Peru (and have other backup plans). Flights are generally May through August only, but often you'll find the website saying simply "Sorry, at this time we are not taking reservations. Check back." In other words, don't plan your trip around hot-air ballooning.

Paragliding over the cliffs of Lima's Costa Verde is an up-and-coming urban adventure. Outfitters operating daily beginner courses and tandem flights, thermal currents permitting: **AeroXtreme** (www.aeroxtreme.com; ℂ 01/242-5125); **Fly Adventure** (www.flyadventure.net; ℂ 01/650-8147); and **Peru Fly** (www.perufly.com; ℂ 01/9930-86795).

Birding

Peru is one of the greatest countries on Earth for birders. The bird population in Peru is, incredibly, about 10% of the world's total. With nearly 2,000 species of resident and migrant birds identified throughout Peru, great bird-watching sites abound.

Manu Biosphere Reserve, believed to have the highest concentration of bird life on the planet, is legendary among birders. It boasts more than 1,000 species of birds. Cocks-of-the-rock, quetzals, toucanets, tanagers, and seven species of colorful macaws await patient birders. Some visitors have spotted as many as 500 species in relatively short visits to Manu. For specialists, the **Manu Wildlife Center** has the best reputation among birders, although **Pantiacolla Lodge** is highly recommended, too.

The **Tambopata National Reserve** is also extraordinary for birding and more accessible than Manu. The reserve, about a third the size of Costa Rica, claims more species of birds (around 600) and butterflies (more than 1,200) than any place of similar size. Both Tambopata and Manu are famous for their *collpas,* or salt licks, where hundreds of macaws, parrots, and other birds appear daily to feed. Nearer to Puerto Maldonado, good birding areas include the Sandoval and Valencia lakes, but they cannot compare to either of the major reserves. **Explorer's Inn** is renowned as one of the top birding lodges in South America.

In the northern Amazon, the **Pacaya-Samiria National Reserve** is home to more than 500 species of birds. The northern Amazon doesn't have quite the reputation that the varied cloud forests leading to Manu and the rest of the southeastern jungle do, although there is excellent birding in and around the protected Machu Picchu Sanctuary.

A handful of jungle lodges and river-cruise operators offer specialized birding options, but none is as complete as the trips offered by the specialist tour operators below. **Inkaterra Machu Picchu Pueblo Hotel** (p. 262) organizes birding tours and has more than 100 species of birds on its property in Aguas Calientes.

A portal with good information on birding in Peru is **Peru Birding Routes** (www.perubirdingroutes.com), with articles about birding, bird-watching routes, multimedia and photo guides, conservation information, and birding forums. Birding sites worth visiting are **Ornifolks,** a network of birding enthusiasts (www.ornifolks.org), and **WorldTwitch** (www.worldtwitch.com), which has links to field guides, birding lodges, tour operators, and organizations throughout Peru, as well as the Americas and the Caribbean.

Although Peru is one of the top birding destinations in the world, specialists complain about the lack of an essential field guide. See "Peru in Pop Culture" in chapter 2, for books about birding in Peru.

TOUR OPERATORS

Birding Peru (www.birdingperu.com) is a Peru-based tour operator that links to birding trips offered by major outfitters to all regions of the country, including the highlands, coasts, and rainforest, and provides good general information on birding throughout Peru.

Field Guides ★★ (fieldguides.com; ☎ 800/728-4953) is an Austin, Texas-based specialty birding travel operator with trips worldwide. It features eight birding trips to Peru, including the Manu Biosphere Reserve, Tambopata, Machu Picchu and the eastern slope of the Andes, the Amazon, and a 12-day tour of the endemic-rich region of northern Peru. Group size is limited to 14 participants.

Kolibri Expeditions ★ (www.kolibriexpeditions.com; ☎ 01/273-7246), based in Lima, offers dozens of birding tours across Peru and South America, including condor-watching trips. Most are no-frills, budget camping trips, but the outfit now also offers a few pampered, high-end trips (such as the "Marvelous Spatuletail Tours").

 Butterflies

Peru has become famous among bird-watchers, but naturalists who are fans of butterflies are in for an equal treat. Peru has the greatest diversity of butterflies in the world and the largest number of species: 3,700 (more than those found in all of subequatorial Africa).

Manu Expeditions ★★★ (www.birding-in-peru.com; ☎ 084/225-990) has a specialty service focused on birding expeditions throughout Peru and South America. The company is run by Barry Walker, a renowned birder and local guide who's also the British Consul in Cusco. The outfitter's roster of 15 birding trips is among the most complete in Peru, and they even offer what might be perfect for many couples: "Cusco and Machu Picchu for Birders and non-Birding Partners."

Tanager Tours ★ (www.tanagertours.com; ☎ 01/9858-36609) is a Dutch-owned specialist bird-watching tour operator based in Trujillo. It organizes birding trips to Manu, Puerto Maldonado, and many other spots in Peru.

Wings ★ (wingsbirds.com; ☎ 866/547-9868 in the U.S. and Canada or 520/320-9868) is a specialty bird-watching travel operator with 3 decades of experience in the field. It promotes three trips to Peru, including an 18-day trip to Machu Picchu and the Manu Biosphere Reserve and one to the north and Andes in search of the long-whiskered owlet. Group size is usually between 6 and 18 people.

Horseback Riding

Lovers of horseback riding will find several areas in Peru to pursue their interest, as well as hotels and operators that can arrange everything from a couple of hours in a saddle to 2-week trips on horseback. The best areas for treks on horseback are the Colca Canyon, near Arequipa, and the Callejón de Huaylas, the valley near the peaks of the Cordillera Blanca; a couple of local and international tour operators offer horse trekking in those areas. Otherwise, your options are mostly limited to a few country hotels in Cajamarca, the Sacred Valley, and Colca Valley.

In the area around Pisco, horseback riding is available in Ica at **Hotel Las Dunas Resort Ica-Peru** (p. 143). For riding on the outskirts of Cusco, the **Casa Andina** hotel group (www.casa-andina.com) arranges excellent day-long trips, available for walking between the ruins (Sacsayhuamán, Q'enko, Puca Pucara, and Tambomachay) just beyond Cusco and in the countryside. In the Sacred Valley, check out **Sonesta Posadas del Inca** (p. 230) and **Sol y Luna Lodge & Spa** (p. 228); in Ollantaytambo, you can usually arrange horseback riding along valley trails by asking around the main square. The **Las Casitas del Colca** (p. 317) has horses for treks in the Colca Valley and Canyon; local agencies in Arequipa that arrange horseback treks through the Colca Canyon include **Colca Trek (Carlos Zarate Adventures)** (www.colcatrek.com; ✆ **054/263-107**) and **Peru Trekking** (✆ **054/223-404**). In Huaraz, try **Andino Club Hotel** (p. 414) or **Monttrek** (below), which arranges good horseback mountain and valley treks. A number of country hotels just outside Cajamarca have horses for riding, including **Hotel & Spa Laguna Seca, Hotel Posada del Puruay,** and **Hostal Portada del Sol Hacienda;** see chapter 12 for details.

TOUR OPERATORS

Adventure Specialists (www.adventurespecialists.org; ✆ **719/630-2086**) organizes horse-supported Machu Picchu treks, including the unique 8-day "Machu Picchu Pony Express."

Manu Expeditions ★★★ (www.manuexpeditions.com; ✆ **084/225-990**) operates plenty of bird-watching and canoe trips in the jungle, but they also organize horseback riding from the Manu Wildlife Center, as well as horseback riding adventures along the Inca Trail and to Machu Picchu and 1- and 2-day riding programs in the Sacred Valley, suitable for novices and families.

Monttrek (✆ **043/421-124**), based in Huaraz, offers horseback riding and other adventure sports in the area around the Cordillera Blanca.

Perol Chico ★★ (www.perolchico.com; ✆ **51/9503-14066**) in Urubamba operates a ranch and is one of the top horseback-riding agencies in Peru, offering full riding vacations with Peruvian Paso horses and stays at the ranch, as well as 1- and 2-day rides (and up to 12-day horseback adventures in the Sacred Valley).

Sol y Luna Lodge & Spa (p. 228) in Urubamba also organizes horseback-riding programs that range from a half-day trip to 14-day trips in the Sacred Valley on Peruvian Paso horses.

Southwind Adventures (www.southwindadventures.com; ✆ **800/377-9463**) offers horse-packing among its roster of adventure trips in Peru.

Jungle Lodges & Tours

Nearly two-thirds of Peru is rainforest, and options for exploring it are myriad, from jungle lodges to independently guided treks, to river cruises. The most important issue is choosing which major jungle destination fits best with your interest, time, and budget. Nearly all the international and Peruvian tour operators and wholesalers that do outdoor and adventure travel—for that matter, almost all agencies that handle travel to Peru—have some sort of jungle packages available. Some, of course, are more immersion-oriented than others. You can do a jungle add-on to a trip to Cusco

WHICH JUNGLE? COMPARING piranhas & MONKEYS

Choosing where to go in the Peruvian jungle is complicated. To begin, you need to define how much time and money you can spend, how you want to get there, and how much immersion—expeditions range from light to hard-core—you're interested in once there.

Cusco is the best base for excursions to the southern jungle, while ecolodges and cruise trips in the northern jungle are accessible from Iquitos, to which most visitors fly. For many, the relative proximity of the southern Amazon basin to Cusco and the Sacred Valley makes a jungle experience in that part of the country all the more appealing.

Of the major jungle regions, the Manu Biosphere Reserve is the least touched by man. It is the most inaccessible zone and, therefore, also the most expensive for expeditions. Most visits require close to a week. But Manu also provides perhaps the best opportunities for viewing Amazon wildlife (especially birds). The

Tambopata National Reserve also offers excellent jungle experiences and wildlife, including easy access to the splendid macaw clay lick, with less expenditure of time and money.

Peru's northeastern jungle near Iquitos has suffered the most penetration by man and tour operators, having been accessible to travelers for much longer than other parts of the Peruvian jungle. For travelers, though, the region is more convenient, with many more expeditions and lodges operating there, and prices are generally more affordable. Note, however, that the chances of phenomenal large mammal sightings—which are remote anywhere—are even slimmer in the northern Amazon. Travelers with limited time and budgets often fly to Iquitos (by far the most interesting jungle city in Peru) and hop on an inexpensive jungle lodge tour from there, although similarly reasonably priced tours are available from Puerto Maldonado in the south.

or a full-scale jungle trek and cruise lasting 2 weeks or more. See the earlier tour operators listed in "U.S. and International Adventure Tour Operators" and the individual lodges and companies in chapter 11.

Mountain Biking

Compared to other adventure sports, mountain biking is still in its infancy in Peru, although fat-tire options are growing fast. **Colca Valley, Huaraz** and the **Callejón de Huaylas,** and the **Sacred Valley** are the major areas for off-road cycling. The **Manu jungle** is also good for hard-core biking. Several tour companies in those places rent bikes, and the quality of the equipment is continually being upgraded. If you plan to do a lot of biking and are very attached to your rig, bring your own. See individual destination chapters for rental listings.

My favorite mountain-biking spots are horse and mountain trails in the spectacular Callejón de Huaylas, which provide the kind of amazing climbing found in the Rockies of the western United States and mountain views that are second to none. Mountain bikers, along with other adventure-sports fans, descend on Huaraz and the valley every June for its celebrated **Semana del Andinismo.** The Colca Valley is also an outstanding region for hard-core mountain biking, though there are fewer tour outfitters targeting the area. For gentler (but not necessarily so) but also incredibly scenic trail riding, while not straying far from Peru's top sights, you can't beat the Sacred Valley.

TOUR OPERATORS & OUTFITTERS

In Huaraz and the Callejón de Huaylas, the top two agencies for mountain biking, with excellent equipment and single-track routes, are **Mountain Bike Adventures ★★★** (www.chakinaniperu.com; ✆ **043/424-259**), run by the seasoned Julio Olaza, and **Pony Expeditions ★★** (www.ponyexpeditions.com; ✆ **043/391-642**), run by Alberto Cafferata. **Monttrek** (✆ **043/421-124**) also offers organized mountain-biking tours.

Peru Bike ★ (www.perubike.com; ✆ **01/260-8225**), based in Lima, has a great schedule of Andes mountain-biking trips across Peru, including Huascarán and Lake Titicaca loops and cool day trips, on GT bikes. **Peru Expeditions ★** (www.peru-expeditions.com; ✆ **01/447-2057**), based in Lima, is run by a former top cyclist and runs mountain-biking trips in the Sacred Valley to Machu Picchu.

In Cusco, **Peru Discovery ★★** (www.perudiscovery.com/English; ✆ **054/637-155**) is the top specialist, with a half-dozen bike trips that include hard-core excursions to the southern Amazon as well as Cusco and the Sacred Valley. Several local outfitters offer 1- to 5-day organized mountain-biking excursions for novices and experienced single-trackers, including: **Amazonas Explorer ★** (www.amazonas-explorer.com; ✆ **084/252-846**), with half- and full-day Inca site and city rides, as well as more adventurous multi-day cycling tours; **Apumayo Expediciones ★** (www.apumayo.com; ✆ **084/9847-66732**), offering half- and full-day rides in Cusco and the Sacred Valley; **Eric Adventures ★★** (www.ericadventures.com; ✆ **877/867-9682** in the U.S. and Canada **800-098-8514** in the U.K., or **084/272-862**), with several good mountain biking itineraries across Peru; and **Instinct Travel** (www.instinct-travel.com; ✆ **084/233-451**).

In the Sacred Valley, **Eco Montana** (www.ecomontana.com), run by the mountain biker Omar Zarzar, rents good mountain bikes and organizes extended as well as shorter cyclotourism rides around Urubamba, with top equipment. **Manu Adventures** (www.manuadventures.com; ✆ **084/261-640**) and **Manu Nature Tours** (www.manuperu.com; ✆ **084/252-721**) offer mountain-biking add-ons to rainforest lodge stays and jungle treks. In Arequipa, **Colca Trek** (www.colcatrek.com; ✆ **054/263-107**) and **Peru Trekking** (✆ **054/223-404**) feature mountain biking in the Colca Canyon.

River Cruises

River cruises along the Amazon and its tributaries are one of the best ways to experience the Peruvian jungle. Cruises give travelers the option of floating luxury and good meals, as well as the ability to stop in and see several different environments and river and jungle communities. The huge and remote **Pacaya-Samiria National Reserve** is one of the best and most up-and-coming zones for cruises into pristine jungle and wetlands; see chapter 11 for details. Iquitos-based **Jungle Expeditions ★** (www.junglex.com; ✆ **065/262-340**) and **Green Tracks Amazon Tours & Cruises** (www.amazontours.net; ✆ **800/892-1035** in the U.S. and Canada) offer a variety of river cruises in the northern Amazon, and **International Expeditions ★** (www.ietravel.com; ✆ **800/234-9620**) is one of the most experienced tour operators organizing luxurious river cruises from the United States. But by far the coolest thing going in Amazon cruises is the luxo **Aqua Expeditions ★★★** (www.aquaexpeditions.com; ✆ **866/603-3687** in the U.S. and Canada or **01/434-5544**), which offers a duo of sleek, modern, and very stylish ships (the *Aqua* and *Aria*) with an haute-cuisine menu created by a famous Peruvian chef (Pedro Miguel Sciaffino) that's far from your typical boat or cruise fare. In all respects, this clearly isn't your grandfather's cruise. A new company in Iquitos, **AmazonEco** (www.historic-amazon-boats.com; ✆ **01/6523-1913**), associated with the handsome new hotel Casa Morey (p. 348), has launched voyages on antique steam boats from the late 19th and early 20th centuries along the Maranon and Samiria Rivers, into the Pacaya-Samiria National Reserve.

Surfing

Though it remains somewhat under the general public's radar, Peru has recently become one of the world's top surfing destinations among surfing aficionados. It has 2,000km (1,200 miles) of Pacific coastline and huge possibilities for left and right reef breaks, point breaks, and monster waves, and boarders can hit the surf year-round. Northern beaches, especially Puerto Chicama north of Trujillo, and Cabo Blanco and other spots near Máncora, even farther north, draw surfers to some of the gnarliest waves in South America. There are also good surfing beaches south of Lima, though they aren't as spectacular as in the north, where the waters are also much warmer. The north is better from October to March, while the surfing in the south is good April through December and tops in May. The best surfing site, with webcams and reports on water conditions and the best beaches up and down Peru, is **www.peruazul.com**. Check out **www.wannasurf.com/spot/South_America/Peru** for basic surfing information and maps, as well as **Wave Hunters** (below) for good information and surf tours to Peru. Local surfing outfitters in the main destinations handle lessons and board rentals.

TOUR OPERATORS

Pure Vacations (www.purevacations.com/south-america/peru/; ✆ **(44) 0845/229-0045**), based in the U.K., has organized surf travel since the 1990s and combines northern Peru with Ecuador for 14-day surf trips.

Wave Hunters (www.wavehunters.com/peru-surfing/peru.asp; ✆ **760/494-7392**), a California-based organization, offers a surfeit of good information on Peru's coastline and celebrated waves, as well as different, inexpensive small-group surfing tours in central and northern Peru, including stays at Pico Alto International Surf Camp in Punta Hermosa. They work with a local group called **Octopus Surf Tours** in northern Peru.

Trekking & Mountain Climbing

Peru is one of the world's great trekking and mountain-climbing destinations, and its mountains and gorgeous valleys, ideal for everything from hard-core climbs to 6,000m (19,700-ft.) peaks to gentle walks through green valleys, are one of the country's calling cards. Experienced mountaineers, ice climbers, trekkers, and regular old athletic types and hikers beeline to Peru to experience the grandeur of the great Cordillera Blanca, the volcanoes and canyons around Arequipa, and, of course, the Andes mountains in and around Cusco. The most celebrated trek, of course, is the Inca Trail to Machu Picchu—truly one of the world's most rewarding treks, provided that the crowds don't get you down in high season. Many agencies in Cusco offer guided treks to Machu Picchu; so do larger international operators, some of whom are now offering newer alternatives to the Inca Trail. See chapter 9 for additional information on recommended tour operators.

Trekking circuits of varying degrees of difficulty lace the valleys and mountain ridges of Peru's *sierra*. Yet only a few have become popular, commercial trekking routes. Independent trekkers who like to blaze their own trail (metaphorically speaking—you should always stick to existing trails) have a surfeit of options in Peru for uncrowded treks.

The best months for climbing are during the dry season, between May and September (June–Aug is perhaps best). In Huaraz, the Semana de Andinismo, held annually in June, attracts mountain climbers from around the world.

One of the best independent resources for hiking and climbing information in Peru is the **South American Explorers** clubhouses in Lima and Cusco (www.saexplorers. org; ✆ **01/445-3306** in Lima, or **084/245-484** in Cusco). You have to become a member first ($50 per year) for full access to their trail reports and other information, but if you're serious about trails and climbs in Peru, it's money well spent. You can join via the website or on the spot at a clubhouse.

TOUR OPERATORS

There are numerous candidates to organize trekking tours of Peru from abroad, whether you're interested in light day hikes, inn-to-inn trekking, or serious, high-altitude multi-day camping treks through the Andes. See "U.S. & International Adventure Tour Operators," earlier in this chapter, for complete listings. Among the best are **Adventure Specialists, Andean Treks, Mountain Travel Sobek, Southwind Adventures, Wilderness Travel,** and **Wildland Adventures.** All have plenty of options, good guides, and high levels of professionalism. One of the top Peruvian operators with a national reach is **Explorandes;** it and all the agencies authorized to lead Inca Trail treks offer many options in Cusco and across Peru. Other full-purpose travel agencies, such as **Peru for Less,** are also jumping in to offer their clients a series of alternative treks in the Cusco highlands and elsewhere.

The local agencies listed in chapters 9 and 12 are the best places to turn if you want to organize some trekking or climbing once on the ground in Peru. There are also excellent local agencies specializing in experienced mountain-climbing expeditions in Arequipa, Huaraz, and Caraz. The best groups arrange a large number of area climbs and have equipment rental. Several have a 24-hour mountain-rescue service.

White-Water Rafting

Peru, home to the origin of the mighty Amazon and great canyon rivers, has some stunning opportunities for white-water rafting. Whether you're a total novice or a world-class river runner, Peru has fantastic white water suited to your abilities. The rivers flowing through the **Colca** and **Cotahuasi canyons,** other rivers nearer to Arequipa, and the Andean rivers of the **Urubamba Valley** stand out. A good adventurous experience is rafting in the Amazon jungle on the **Tambopata River.** There's also good white water on the **Río Santa** in the Callejón de Huaylas.

If you're just experimenting with river rafting, stick to Class II and III rivers. If you already know your way around a raft and a paddle, there are plenty of Class IV and V sections to run. Hard-core runners come to Peru for some fantastic, multi-day rafting trips to Class V and even Class VI rivers in remote canyons. The best months for rafting are May through September, when water levels are low. (During the rainy season, canyon rivers can be extremely dangerous.)

TOUR OPERATORS

A half-dozen agencies in Arequipa, Cusco, and the Sacred Valley organize a range of local white-water opportunities. See chapter 9 for more information. Specialists include **Amazonas Explorer ★★★** (www.amazonas-explorer.com; ✆ **084/252-846**), which offers white-water rafting tours that can be combined with Inca Trail treks. Trips, which feature small groups, can be booked from abroad. Among its Peru trips are rafting on the Río Apurímac, inflatable canoeing on the source of the Amazon (combined with trekking the Inca Trail), rainforest rafting, and extreme Class IV to VI in Cotahuasi, the world's deepest canyon. **SwissRaft Peru ★★★** (www.swissraft-peru.com; ✆ **084/264-124**), based in Cusco, organizes 1-day rafting trips year-round on the Apurímac, Cusipata, and Chuquicahuana, as well as 4-day trips on the Apurímac. **Eric Adventures ★★** (www.ericadventures.com; ✆ **877/867-9682** in the U.S. and Canada **800-098-8514** in the U.K., or **084/272-862**) is more of an adventure generalist, but offers a full roster of rafting and kayaking trips on rivers in the Sacred Valley, southern Amazon, and Colca, as well as kayaking on Lake Titicaca.

VOLUNTEER & STUDY PROGRAMS

Study and volunteer programs, including Spanish-language programs, are often a great way to travel in and experience a country with greater depth than most independent and package travel allows. Cultural immersion and integration with locals are the aims of many such programs, leading to a richer and more unique experience for many travelers.

Volunteering, in particular, often leads to greater culture sensitivity and cross-cultural learning experiences. Especially in a developing country such as Peru, volunteers see up-close the realities of the lack of running water and electricity, the relative absence of luxuries, and simple, home-cooked foods—not to mention local customs and traditions. And, at least for a short time, volunteers get the rewarding opportunity to lend their abilities and sweat toward addressing some of the challenges Peruvians face. Such aspects of Peruvian life might be considerably more difficult to apprehend if staying in nice hotels and dining at upscale restaurants.

Most volunteer organizations are not-for-profit entities that charge participants to go abroad (to cover administrative and other costs), so volunteering isn't usually a way to get a free vacation.

Some international relief organizations, such as **Doctors Without Borders** (www.doctorswithoutborders.org) and **CARE** (www.care.org), accept volunteers to work crises and relief efforts.

Culinary Vacations & Cooking Classes

Peru's sophisticated, diverse cuisine has attracted a great deal of worldwide attention in the past decade, and gastronomic tourism is beginning to take hold in Peru. Two companies offer food-centric vacations. **A Taste of Peru ★** (www.atasteofperu.com; ✆ **01/247-5208**) is run by a young Peruvian woman named Penélope Alzamora, who studied culinary arts in the U.S. She offers half- and full-day culinary experiences, as well as 8-day customized foodie trips to many parts of Peru, taking in food markets and restaurants in Lima and Cusco, and participants attend pisco tastings and ceviche demonstrations.

Pica Peru ★ (www.peruculinaryvacations.com; ✆ **866/440-2561**), based in Denver, Colorado, is run by Kazia Jankowski, a food writer and author of the *Moon Peru* travel guide. Her company offers 1-day culinary excursions as well as multi-day tours that include cooking classes, beginning in Lima restaurants and then traveling to Cusco and the Sacred Valley, or instead venturing to the north coast and the surfing capital Máncora. Trips last 9 to 10 days, with a maximum of eight travelers, and include four cooking classes.

Aracari ★★ (www.aracari.com; ✆ **312/239-8726** in the U.S. or **511/651-2424** in Peru), an upscale Peruvian agency that designs excellent custom tours, offers a "Peru for Art Lovers and Foodies" trip and creates personalized culinary tours with exclusive visits to private houses and haciendas offered for private luncheons and cocktails, as well as cooking classes, visits to food markets, and dining at some of the finest restaurants in Peru.

Research Opportunities

Earthwatch Institute ★★ (www.earthwatch.org; ✆ **800/776-0188**) has a unique mission: It sends travelers out to work in the field alongside scientists involved in archaeology and environmental conservation. There are several Peru research and education trips: You can join a 13-day excavation of a pre-Inca site, assist with research on Peruvian macaws, or document the biology of Andean rivers. But the trips are not all work; they're a way to see a fascinating slice of the country from an insider's—academic or conservationist—perspective.

Mundo Azul ★ (www.mundoazul.org; ✆ **01/99410-4206**), based in Lima, takes volunteers on environmental conservation and sustainable development programs along the coast (marine biology research) and in the Amazon basin (threatened species). Trips off the coast south of Lima to view and photographically document the large population of playful dolphins may be the most fun you can have doing an environmentally conscious volunteer program.

Spanish-Language Programs

International Partners for Study Abroad (www.studyabroadinternational.com; ✆ **602/765-1205**) lists a number of Spanish-study programs in Lima as well as Cusco. **GorpTravel** (www.gorp.com; ✆ **877/440-GORP [4677]**) occasionally lists Spanish-study programs of short duration in Peru and other South American countries; follow the "Learning Vacations" link on the website for options.

The best local language schools are located in Cusco, Lima, and Arequipa. Many foreigners choose to go to Cusco to study Spanish for extended periods; several Cusco programs, offering both short- and long-term study programs, often with home stays, are listed in chapter 8. One particular standout school in Cusco is the **Amigos Spanish School,** Zaguan del Cielo B-23 (www.spanishcusco.com; ✆ **084/242-292**); it's a nonprofit school that assists disadvantaged children through its Amigos Foundation. In Lima, **El Sol Escuela de Español,** Grimaldo de Solar 469, Miraflores (http://elsol.idiomasperu.com; ✆ **800/381-1806**) marries language classes to cooking workshops, dance classes, and other activities. Other schools to try in Lima are the **Instituto Cultural Peruano Norteamericano,** Angamos Oeste 160, Miraflores (www.icpna.edu.pe; ✆ **01/241-1940**) and **Instituto de Idiomas,** Camino Real 1037, San Isidro (✆ **01/442-8761**). In **Arequipa,** classes are on offer via the **Centro de Intercambio Cultural,** Cercado Urbanización Universitaria (www.ceicaperu.com; ✆ **054/221-165**); **Centro de Idiomas UNSA,** San Agustín 106 (✆ **054/247-524**); and **Centro Cultural Peruano Norteamericano,** Melgar 209 (✆ **054/801-022**).

Volunteer Programs

Cross-Cultural Solutions ★★★ (www.crossculturalsolutions.org; ✆ **800/380-4777**), with offices in New Rochelle, New York, and Brighton, U.K., offers week-long volunteer programs in Peru (in Lima's Villa El Salvador shantytown and Ayacucho, formerly a stronghold of the guerilla organization the Shining Path). The "Volunteer Abroad" section lists a number of opportunities for volunteering in Peru, including teaching and environmental research. **Projects Abroad ★★** (www.projects-abroad. org; *𝓒* **888/839-3535**), with headquarters in New York and a local field office in Urubamba (in the Sacred Valley), organizes several unique volunteer and internship opportunities in Peru, including Inca restoration projects (such as the Sacsayhuamán ruins on the outskirts of Cusco), rainforest conservation, teaching, and nursing. **Pro-World ★** (www.proworldvolunteers.org; *𝓒* **877/429-6753** in the U.S. and Canada, or **018/6559-6289** in the U.K.) has its headquarters in Bellingham, Washington, and it offers work, study, and internship programs in Peru in the fields of health, environmental conservation, and social and economic development based in Cusco and Urubamba. The organization has built schools, irrigation systems, and fish farms. **World Leadership School ★★** (www.worldleadershipschool.com; *𝓒* **888/831-8109**) is a Colorado-based organization that operates 3- to 4-week programs, concentrating on infrastructure and natural disaster prevention in El Carmen on the desert coast; cultural preservation in Ollantaytambo in the Sacred Valley; and climate change and ecosystem preservation in Puerto Maldonado, the gateway to the southern Amazon jungle.

Other volunteer programs include **Habitat for Humanity ★★★** (www.habitat. org; *𝓒* **800/422-4828**), with a base in Arequipa (Comité Nacional Hábitat para la Humanidad Perú; *𝓒* **054/422-724**), and **Volunteers for Peace** (www.vfp.org; *𝓒* **802/259-2759**), based in Vermont.

SUGGESTED ITINERARIES

You want to get the most out of your trip to Peru in the time that you have available. Here are some ideas for structuring your travels. Unless you have a solid month to spend, you probably won't get to see as much of Peru as you'd wish, at least on a first trip. Peru is deceptively large, and at least as important are the considerable geographic and transportation barriers that complicate zipping around the country. Some regions require difficult travel by land, with no air access. It's ill-advised to try to do too much in too short a period; in addition to travel distances and transportation routes, you've got to take into account other factors—such as jet lag and acclimatization to high altitude—that require most visitors to slow down. Of course, slowing down is never a bad thing, so feel free to trim the itinerary, too—particularly since several of the itineraries are go, go, go—and add days in a particularly relaxing place, such as the Sacred Valley or Colca.

REGIONS IN BRIEF

Peru shares borders with Ecuador and Colombia to the north, Brazil and Bolivia to the east, and Chile to the south. It lies just below the Equator and is the third-largest country in South America—larger than France and Spain combined, covering an area of nearly 1,300,000 sq. km (500,000 sq. miles). Peruvians will tell you that their country comprises three distinct geological components: coast, *sierra* (highlands), and *selva* (jungle). The capital, Lima, and most major cities are on the coast, but the Amazon rainforest, which makes up nearly two-thirds of Peru, and the bold Andes mountain range dominate its topography.

THE CENTRAL COAST & HIGHLANDS The Pacific coastal region is a narrow strip that runs from one end of the country to the other (a distance of some 2,200km/1,400 miles) and is almost entirely desert. Lima, the capital, lies about halfway down the coast. To the south, in one of the driest areas on Earth, are Pisco, Ica, and Nasca, the cradle of several of Peru's most important ancient civilizations, as well as the famously mysterious Nasca Lines and the Ballestas Islands, promoted locally as "Peru's Galápagos" for their diverse indigenous fauna. The area is especially prone to earthquakes, such as the devastating one that struck the region in August 2007. Inland and tucked high in the central Andes, Ayacucho is one of Peru's most fascinating cities, known for its colonial churches and artisanship but less felicitously associated with the Shining Path terrorist group.

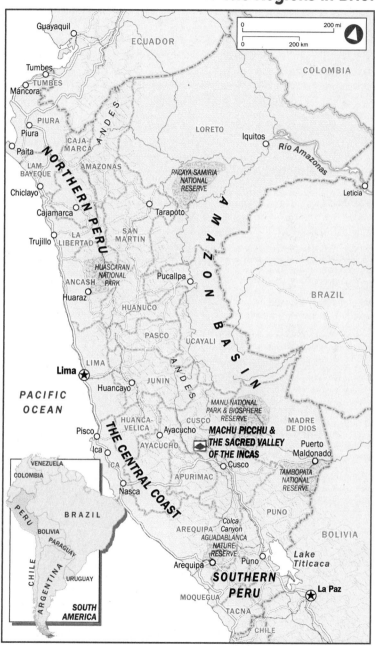

CUSCO & THE SACRED VALLEY   The dramatic Andes mountains in south-central Peru contain the country's most famous sights, including the former Inca capital of Cusco and scenic highland villages that run the length of the beautiful Sacred Valley. Cusco sits at an elevation of some 3,400m (11,000 ft.). The valley is dotted with singularly impressive Inca ruins, of which Machu Picchu (and the Inca Trail leading to it) is undoubtedly the star. Indigenous culture is particularly strong in the region.

SOUTHERN PERU   Massive Lake Titicaca, shared with Bolivia, is the largest lake in South America and the world's highest navigable body of water (at 3,830m/12,566 ft.). Indigenous peoples inhabit ancient villages on islands (some of them man-made) in the middle of this huge body of water. Puno, at the edge of Lake Titicaca, is a rough-and-tumble town that hosts some of Peru's liveliest folkloric festivals. The elegant colonial city of Arequipa is one of Peru's most gorgeously situated, at the base of towering volcanoes. Nearby is Colca Canyon, twice as deep as the Grand Canyon and site of perhaps the best place in all South America to get an up-close view of the regal Andean condor.

AMAZONIA   Although about 60% of Peru is Amazon rainforest, only about 5% of the country's human inhabitants reside there. One of the world's most dazzling arrays of wildlife—more than 1,700 species of birds (more than the population found in the continental U.S.) and 2,000 species of fish—make it their home. For the visitor, there are two primary jungle destinations. The northern jungle, of which Iquitos is the principal gateway (but accessible only by plane or boat), is the most explored and has the most facilities. Much less trafficked and more controlled is the Madre de Dios department in the south, which contains Manu Biosphere Reserve, Puerto Maldonado, and Tambopata National Reserve. These can be reached by land or air from Cusco.

NORTHERN PERU   Peru's north encompasses desert, coast, and the country's highest mountains, but it is much less visited than the south—even though it possesses some of the country's most outstanding archaeological sites. Trujillo, Chiclayo, and Cajamarca (a lovely small city in the highlands) are the main cities of interest. Near Trujillo and Chiclayo are Chan Chan, Túcume, and Sipán, extraordinary (if today enigmatic) adobe cities, pyramids, and royal tombs and treasures that predate the Incas. A couple of Peru's finest archaeological museums are near Chiclayo.

   The mountain ranges dominate the center of Peru, north of Lima. Within Huascarán National Park, the Cordillera Blanca stretches 200km (124 miles) and contains a dozen peaks more than 5,000m (16,400 ft.) tall; the highest is Huascarán, at 6,768m (22,205 ft.). The region is a favorite of trekkers and outdoor-adventure travelers who come to Peru with white-water rafting, ice climbing, and other sports in mind. The main jumping-off point for these activities is the town of Huaraz. In valleys east of the capital is the important archaeological site Chavín de Huántar.

Peru's UNESCO World Heritage Sites

- Cusco city (designated in 1983)
- Machu Picchu Historic Sanctuary (1983)
- Archaeological Site of Chavín (1985)
- Huascarán National Park (1985)
- Manu National Park (1987)
- Chan Chan Archaeological Zone (1988)
- Río Abiseo National Park (1990)
- Historic Center of Lima (1991)
- Nasca Lines (1994)
- Historic Center of Arequipa (2000)

Also in northern Peru are unassuming beach towns where the waves attract surfers from across the globe; Máncora (a growing beach resort), Órganos, and Punta Sal are among the most popular along a 25km (15-mile) stretch of coast. They are attracting increasingly international visitors and Peruvian city-dwellers with chic new hotels and second homes.

THE BEST OF PERU IN 2 WEEKS

This 2-week itinerary will allow you to experience the greatest of southern Peru, from its historic colonial cities to its natural wonders. First on everyone's list, of course, are the lively ancient Inca capital Cusco and that empire's legendary lost city, Machu Picchu. But in a relatively short amount of time you can also delve into dense Amazonian jungle; Lake Titicaca, the world's highest navigable body of water; and one of the world's deepest canyons, Colca. (Keep in mind, though, this is a very full itinerary, and you may need to cut either the jungle or Colca Canyon.) You wouldn't be the first to find it irresistible to linger in Cusco and the Sacred Valley (especially if you want to hike the Inca Trail or do another highland trek).

Day 1: Touch Down in Lima

All international flights arrive into the capital, Lima, and even though most people are headed elsewhere, you may want or find yourself obligated to spend at least a day in Lima. Make the most of it by touring the revitalized **colonial quarter** of Lima Centro (p. 84), or perhaps visiting one of the country's outstanding museums, such as the **Museo Rafael Larco Herrera** archaeology museum (p. 89), and hitting either a great *cevichería* or a cutting-edge *novo andino* restaurant.

Then move on your way to Peru's most famous Inca attractions. (If you're able to get an overnight flight that puts you into Lima early in the morning, you may want to consider an immediate connection to Cusco to save time and avoid the hassles of Lima, buying yourself an extra day elsewhere.)

Days 2 & 3: Cusco, Inca Capital

Although your goal might be to hit Cusco running, the city's daunting altitude, more than 3,400m (11,000 ft.), prohibits that. Spend a couple of days seeing the old Inca capital at a relaxed pace, making sure to hang out around the **Plaza de Armas** and visit **La Catedral (Cathedral), Convento de Santa Catalina (Santa Catalina Convent),** and **Qoricancha (Temple of the Sun).** Cusco is one of the best places in Peru to shop, eat, and party, so make sure to squeeze those vital activities in with sightseeing.

Day 4: The Stuff of Legend: Machu Picchu

Though Machu Picchu really deserves an overnight stay, if you're trying to see the best of Peru in 2 weeks, you can't afford the time. So take the morning train from Cusco to Machu Picchu **(Aguas Calientes),** South America's number-one attraction. Spend the middle part of the day exploring the **ruins** here (p. 238) and then head back to Cusco on the train.

Day 5: Back in Cusco

If you weren't able to catch an archaeology museum in Lima, or even if you did, check out the beautifully designed **Museo de Arte Precolombino (MAP;**

p. 173). Enjoy some of the lively cafes, bars, and restaurants of Cusco; you'll find plenty while strolling around the **Barrio de San Blas** (p. 172). If you have time and plenty of energy, catch a cab (or walk up) to the fantastic Inca ruins overlooking the city, **Sacsayhuamán** (p. 179).

Days 6–8: Into the Jungle

Take an early-morning, half-hour flight from Cusco to **Puerto Maldonado,** the gateway to the southern Peruvian Amazon jungle of **Tambopata National Reserve** (p. 328). Board a boat for a 2-day, 1-night trip to one of the jungle lodges along the Río Madre de Dios. (If you have time and the Amazon is high on your list, a 3-day, 2-night adventure, either within 1 hour of Puerto Maldonado or 4 to 5 hours away along the Río Tambopata, is even better.) On the third day, head back to Puerto Maldonado and then catch a return flight to Cusco. Spend the night in Cusco; see chapter 8 for options.

Day 9: The Train to Titicaca

From Cusco, take the extraordinarily scenic train south to **Puno** and **Lake Titicaca** (if you want to visit some of the Inca ruins en route, take one of the premium tour bus services that make a day of the journey). Spend the night in Puno and rest up (and get accustomed to the even higher altitude) for the next day's boat trip out on the lake (p. 270).

Day 10: Lake Titicaca & Isla Taquile

While an overnight trip that allows you to spend a night with a family either on Isla Taquile or Amantaní is the best way to experience the people and customs of Titicaca, you can also do a 1-day trip that lets you visit the **Uros floating islands** and an afternoon stop to see the fascinating island culture of **Isla Taquile** (p. 276). (For anyone with an extra couple of days, an unforgettable Titicaca experience is the **Suasi Island** ecolodge; p. 278.)

Day 11: Elegant Arequipa

Catch an early-morning flight from Juliaca (the nearest airport, an hour from Puno) to Arequipa, the elegant southern city known as "La Ciudad Blanca" for its beautiful colonial buildings made of *sillar,* or white volcanic stone. Stay close to the pretty **Plaza de Armas** and spend the afternoon at the wondrous **Monasterio de Santa Catalina** (p. 290), one of the finest examples of colonial religious architecture in the Americas.

Days 12 & 13: Colca Valley

From Arequipa, set off on a 2-day, 1-night exploration of **Colca Valley,** the finest spot in South America to observe giant Andean condors, which soar overhead at **Cruz del Cóndor** (p. 312), at the edge of Colca Canyon. On the first day, explore some of the historic and picturesque villages of the valley and relax at the **La Calera** thermal baths just outside Chivay (p. 311), and spend the night at a rustic hotel in the valley before setting out early the next morning for the condor spectacle. Return that evening to Arequipa.

Day 14: Final Morning in Arequipa, then Home

Arequipa is Peru's top spot for fine alpaca goods. Spend the morning shopping for sweaters, shawls, and scarves before flying to **Lima,** where you'll catch your flight back home.

The Best of Peru in 2 Weeks

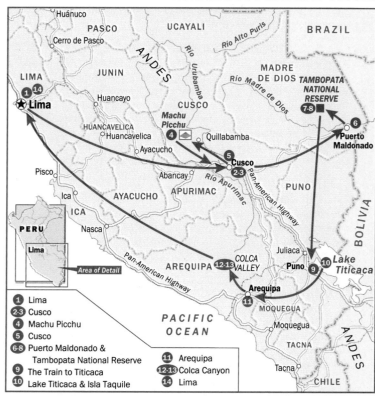

1 Lima
2-3 Cusco
4 Machu Picchu
5 Cusco
6-8 Puerto Maldonado &
   Tambopata National Reserve
9 The Train to Titicaca
10 Lake Titicaca & Isla Taquile
11 Arequipa
12-13 Colca Canyon
14 Lima

CUSCO HIGHLANDS IN 1 WEEK

With a single week in Peru, it's best to concentrate on a manageable regional trip. For first-timers, there's one place almost everyone has absolutely got to see: Machu Picchu. I certainly have no problem with that; it's perhaps the top sight in South America. In one week, you can experience Cusco, the Inca capital that's become a dynamic travelers' hub; the empire's once-thought-lost imperial city; and the serene Urubamba Valley that the Incas held sacred.

Day 1: Through Cusco to the Sacred Valley

All international flights arrive in Lima, but try to arrange it so that an overnight flight gets you there very early in the morning, with time enough to get an 8am or 9am flight to Cusco (note that flights are occasionally delayed by weather in Cusco, though, so the earlier the flight, the better). With only a week in Peru, there's little need to linger in Lima unless you want a day to take it easy and see the colonial quarter of Lima Centro and have lunch at a *cevichería*.

Because the altitude in Cusco (more than 3,400m/11,000 ft.) is so daunting, head first to the lower Sacred Valley and save the capital city for the end of your trip. Relax at a country hotel in the Sacred Valley (most can arrange a pickup at Cusco airport); see p. 228 for options.

Day 2: Pisac's Market & Inca Ruins

If possible, schedule your trip so that Day 2 is a market day (Tuesday, Thursday, or, best of all, Sunday). Take a *combi* or taxi to Pisac and check out the lively **artisans' market** in the Plaza de Armas. Have lunch at **Ulrike's Café** (p. 219) right on the main square. After lunch visit the great **Inca ruins** (p. 218) looming above town; either hike up to them (this may be very challenging for those who've just arrived) or take a taxi. Pisac's ruins will give you a taste of what you're about to see in Ollantaytambo and Machu Picchu. Head a little farther along in the valley (again by taxi or combi) to a rustic country hotel near **Urubamba** or **Yucay,** where you'll have dinner and spend the night.

Day 3: On to Ollantaytambo

Wake early and take a combi or taxi to **Ollantaytambo** (p. 230) to explore the spectacular **Fortress Ruins** (p. 232) before the busloads arrive. Then grab lunch at **Café Mayu** (p. 234) by the train station and wander the Inca **Old Town** (p. 233). Energetic travelers can climb the path up to old Inca granaries for great views of Ollanta and the valley. Or take a taxi back towards Urubamba and hike along the river to **Salineras de Maras** (p. 223), the ancient salt mines, or catch a combi and then taxi to **Moray,** an enigmatic Inca agricultural site.

If you don't mind moving around, you could transfer to a hotel in Ollanta to enjoy it at night when there are few tourists (and be there early for the train the next morning to Machu Picchu). Otherwise head back to your hotel in the valley around Urubamba.

Day 4: What You Came For: Machu Picchu

Catch an early-morning train from Ollantaytambo to **Aguas Calientes** (p. 259). Catch the bus up to the ruins and spend the day exploring the site (hiking up to the **Huayna Picchu peak** for panoramic views if you're in shape; p. 247). Have lunch at the Machu Picchu Sanctuary Lodge next to the ruins and stay until late in the afternoon, after the large tour groups have left. Spend the night either next to the ruins (if you've got very deep pockets) or back down in Aguas Calientes (which is actually more fun). Hit the bars along the railroad tracks to share stories with some of the backpackers who've survived the Inca Trail.

Days 5 & 6: Colonial Cusco

Sticking to the area near the Plaza de Armas, visit the **Cathedral** (p. 169) and the **Santa Catalina Convent** (p. 175) in the morning. After lunch, see the stunning **Qoricancha (Temple of the Sun;** p. 175), the site that best illustrates Cusco's clash of Inca and Spanish cultures. Take a walk along the **Calles Loreto** and **Hatunrumiyoc** to see some more magnificent Inca stonework. In Plaza Nazarenas, check out the beautifully designed **Museo de Arte Precolombino (MAP;** p. 173) and some of the upscale alpaca goods shops on the square. Then stop at **MAP Café** (p. 184), the chic restaurant in the museum's courtyard, or **Limo,** for sushi and superb views of the Plaza de Armas (p. 186),

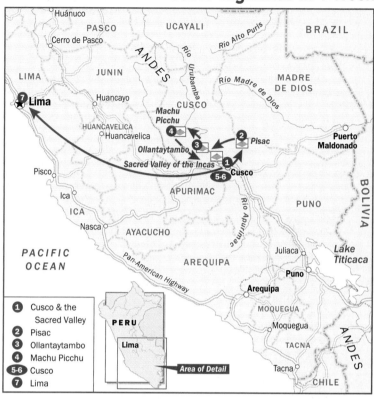

- **1** Cusco & the Sacred Valley
- **2** Pisac
- **3** Ollantaytambo
- **4** Machu Picchu
- **5-6** Cusco
- **7** Lima

for a celebratory dinner. End the evening with a pisco sour at one of the lively cafes or bars near the Plaza de Armas afterward.

The next morning, pop into a few alpaca and silver jewelry shops around the Plaza de Armas and Plaza Nazarenas. Hike up to the hilly **San Blas** (p. 172) neighborhood, site of dozens of cool shops and art galleries and do some shopping for handicrafts, souvenirs, and art. Have a relaxing lunch at **Jack's Café Bar** (p. 189), a popular gringo hangout. After lunch, catch a cab (or walk) up to **Sacsayhuamán** (p. 179), the fantastic ruins overlooking the city. For dinner, try **Cicciolina** (p. 185) or **Chicha,** a star chef's take on local Cusqueña cuisine (p. 184). Later, get a taste of Cusco's hopping nightlife at one of the pubs or nightclubs around the Plaza de Armas.

Day 7: To Lima & Home

Have a final stroll around Cusco before catching a flight to Lima. You'll probably have an evening flight back home, so you may have enough time for a ceviche lunch in Lima and, if you're ambitious, a short tour of colonial **Lima Centro** (p. 84) in the late afternoon.

OUTDOOR ADVENTURES IN PERU

Few places pack the kind of outdoor bounty and natural beauty into their borders the way Peru does. This itinerary is designed for high-octane thrill seekers, to take in some of Peru's most scenic natural areas as well as give a taste of some unusual ways to tackle the outdoors. For a pure adrenaline rush, it's hard to beat incredible Andean treks, white-water rafting, mountain biking at insane altitudes, and board surfing on towering sand dunes. This itinerary omits some obvious outdoors choices, including the Amazon basin and Andes peaks near Huaraz (which are so great and time consuming to experience fully that travelers keenly interested in either should perhaps concentrate on a week's or longer adventure trip to either destination, eschewing other outdoors destinations).

Days 1 & 2: Nasca's Famed Sands

To get a look at Nasca's famous **Nasca Lines** (p. 146) etched in the desert floor, and also an incredible view of the craggy, interminable desert, catch a mid-morning overflight at Nasca airport. In the afternoon, head out to the highest sand dunes in the Americas and try one of the newest extreme sports in Peru, **sandboarding.** Cerro Blanco, just 8km (5 miles) from Nasca, is the destination of choice for sandboarders (p. 142). The next day head out to **San Fernando** (p. 142) for an all-day dune-buggy adventure to a desert oasis of sea lions, penguins, and maybe even condors on the coast (Casa Andina Nasca can arrange a trip).

Days 3–6: Colca Canyon

Spend the afternoon wandering the old quarter of Arequipa, which is ringed by three volcanoes, and check out the spectacular **Santa Catalina** monastery. The next morning, head by bus to Colca Canyon (3 hr.), where you'll spend the next couple of days. Check into one of the country lodges and go for an afternoon **horseback ride** and cap off the day lounging in stone **hot springs pools** overlooking the river at Colca Lodge (p. 317). The next morning get an early start to witness the goosebump-inducing flight of giant Andean condors at **Cruz del Cóndor** (p. 312). In the afternoon, go **mountain biking;** a great ride is starting from Patapampa, at 4,877m (16,000 ft.) and rocketing down single-track paths used by local llama herders to Chimay. The next day, hike down 1,000 m (3,200 ft.) into the canyon to the **Sangalle Oasis**—minimum 7 hours (p. 314).

Alternative Outdoors: One-Stop Shopping

Hard-core adventurers might want to focus all their time and do a variety of activities in one area. Huaraz and the great Cordillera Blanca have limitless outdoors possibilities, including lengthy and arduous multi-day treks through some of the planet's most astounding scenery, with views of Peru's highest peaks and emerald lagoons. You could also throw in ice climbing, mountain biking, river rafting, and rock climbing and easily come up with 2 weeks or more of concentrated outdoors adrenaline without ever leaving the Cordillera Blanca and Callejón de Huaylas. A great 5-day trek like the Santa Cruz trail might only be the beginning of your adventures.

Outdoor Adventures in Peru

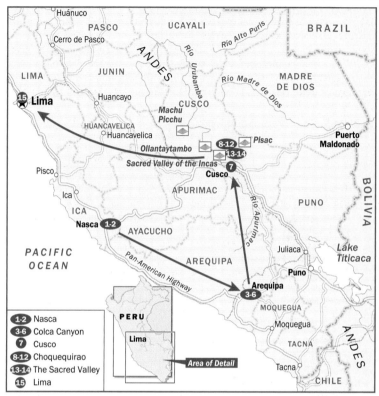

Key to map:
- **1-2** Nasca
- **3-6** Colca Canyon
- **7** Cusco
- **8-12** Choquequirao
- **13-14** The Sacred Valley
- **15** Lima

Day 7: A Breather in Cusco

Fly back through Lima and on to Cusco. In the afternoon, hike up through the San Blas neighborhood to the grand **Sacsayhuamán ruins** (p. 179), one of the Incas' finest monuments, on what is essentially a rest day.

Days 8–12: Trek to Choquequirao

An alternative to the Inca Trail, embark on this 4-day trek to **Choquequirao** (p. 256), spectacular but rarely visited Inca ruins high above the Apurímac River. The route descends to a campsite next to the river only to climb 1,219 vertical meters (4,000 ft.) the next day. (Choquequirao is just one of several stunning multi-day treks in the Cusco highlands; if you've never been to Peru before, you may want to opt for the granddaddy of them all, the Inca Trail, which takes you right to the foot of Machu Picchu.) White-water fanatics might prefer to trade a 4-day rafting trip for the trek to Choquequirao.

Days 13 & 14: The Sacred Valley

After your trek down from Choquequirao, come back to earth in the serene Sacred Valley of the Incas. Here you can do one day's **white-water rafting** on the Urubamba River, or, if you'd prefer to keep your hiking boots on, do a day hike and walk from the Inca site of Moray down to the **Salineras salt mines** (p. 223; 3 hr.).

Day 15: Above the Fray in Lima

Although there's adventure enough in Lima just dodging murderous traffic, there's one last opportunity for outdoors adventure before your flight out. If you're lucky you'll have a chance to catch a thermal current and get up in the air in a **paraglider,** soaring out over Miraflores and the Costa Verde (p. 95).

UNDISCOVERED PERU

With Cusco and Machu Picchu at the forefront, Peru's tried-and-true gringo trail through the southern Andes attracts the majority of visitors. Some get off the beaten track by doing alternative ruins treks in the area around Cusco, but you can get even farther off the gringo trail. If this is a return trip to Peru, or you simply have an aversion to going where everybody else does, why not venture inland to other highlands cities and north to locations of great, if often difficult to decipher, archaeological sites?

Days 1 & 2: Ayacucho

Fly to Ayacucho from Lima. For decades, this long-suffering city, essentially occupied by homegrown terrorist groups, was cut off from the rest of Peru. Newly welcoming, Ayacucho is a feast of **colonial churches and manor houses** (p. 156) cradled in the Andes. It also throws the most spectacular Easter festivities in the country. Just beyond Ayacucho are the 1,400-year-old ruins of the **Huari** culture and the town of **Quinua,** famous for staging the epic battle for Peruvian independence, and its artisans, the finest in Peru.

Days 3 & 4: Cajamarca

Return by air to Lima and then fly north to Cajamarca. Spend a day exploring the city's lively street market and impressive colonial core, including **Conjunto Monumental de Belén** and **El Cuarto de Rescate** (p. 389). The next day, head out to the evocative rock formations of **Cumbe Mayo** (p. 392) and drop in on the thermal baths at **Baños del Inca** (p. 390).

Days 5 & 6: Kuélap

Travel by land to Chachapoyas, an arduous, nearly all-day journey. The next morning, catch a combi to the **Kuélap ruins** (p. 384). These magnificent and extremely remote ruins are more than 300 years older than Machu Picchu and in some ways nearly its equal. They are without doubt much less touristy. If you make it here, you may have the fortress ruins of some 400 buildings all to yourself. Spend the night at the site or in a nearby lodge.

Days 7 & 8: Chiclayo

Travel by bus to Chiclayo, one of the most important commercial cities of the north. Although this busy city is rather unimpressive aesthetically, it, along with Trujillo, lies at the epicenter of northern Peru's archaeology. Visit the fascinating **Mercado Modelo** and then head out to the countryside to the **Museo**

Tumbas Reales de Sipán (p. 378), which contains the spectacular funereal chamber and treasures of the Lord of Sipán, and the **Museo Nacional Sicán** (p. 379). Then explore **Túcume** (p. 380), a complex of 26 adobe pyramids.

Days 9 & 10: Trujillo & Huanchaco

Fly from Chiclayo to Trujillo and spend a half-day touring the city's handsome colonial core, one of the finest in Peru. In the afternoon, visit the **Huacas de Moche** (p. 366), enormous adobe pyramids dating to A.D. 500. The next day, explore the various sites of **Chan Chan** (p. 363), the huge Chimú complex on the outskirts of Trujillo. In the afternoon, relax and eat some ceviche in the tranquil fishing village and summer and weekend resort **Huanchaco.** Return to Lima the next morning.

LIMA

Founded in 1535, Lima was the Spanish Crown's "City of Kings," the richest and most important city in the Americas and considered to be the most beautiful colonial settlement in the region. Lima was home to some of the Americas' finest baroque and Renaissance churches, palaces, and mansions, as well as the continent's first university. Today's modern capital, with a population of more than eight million—about one-third of Peru's population—sprawling and chaotic Lima thoroughly dominates Peru's political and commercial life. Although many travelers used to give it short shrift, Lima is newly welcoming to visitors. The historic *centro* is being spruced up, and spread across the capital are the country's most creative restaurants, finest museums, and most vibrant nightlife. Limeño cuisine is the subject of growing international buzz, and foodies bent on a gastronomic tour of Peru are flocking to Lima's diverse restaurant scene.

HISTORY   Peculiar in a modern capital, evidence of pre-Columbian culture exists throughout the city, with the remains of adobe pyramids next to high-rises. Founded by the conquistador Francisco Pizarro and for two centuries the headquarters of the Spanish Inquisition, the city's colonial wealth and importance are on view throughout Lima Centro.

SIGHTSEEING   Concentrate on colonial *casonas* and baroque churches in the historic center, as well as Peru's finest collection of archaeology museums. Then see a gentler side of the city in outer suburbs such as Barranco, a former fishing village along the coast.

EATING & DRINKING   Lima is not just the dining capital of Peru but the best eating city in South America. From *cevicherías* serving the city's signature dish and neighborhood huariques (holes-in-the-wall) to celebrity chefs and Japanese and Chinese fusion cuisines, Lima's got it all. It also has Peru's best pisco bars; the pisco sour was born here, after all.

ARTS & CULTURE   The city's impressive art and archaeology museums serve as perfect introductions to the rich history and culture you'll encounter elsewhere in Peru; not to be missed are Rafael Larco Herrera Museum, the world's largest private collection of pre-Columbian art, and Museo de la Nación, which traces the history of Peru's ancient civilizations.

SHOPPING   Lima is Peru's shopping mecca, with superb regional handicrafts from across the country, ranging from excellent handmade textiles and colonial-style artwork to altarpieces from Ayacucho. Most head straight to the big markets in Miraflores, but a better experience is browsing small boutiques and galleries run by collectors and connoisseurs, especially in Barranco.

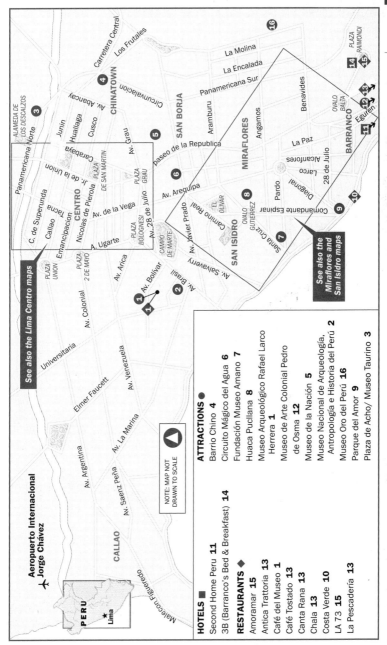

Aeropuerto Internacional Jorge Chávez

NOTE: MAP NOT DRAWN TO SCALE

PERU

Lima

See also the Lima Centro maps

See also the Miraflores and San Isidro maps

CHINATOWN

CENTRO

SAN BORJA

SAN ISIDRO

MIRAFLORES

BARRANCO

CALLAO

La Molina

La Encalada

Panamericana Sur

Aramburu

Benavides

Angamos

La Paz

Larco

Alcanfores

28 de Julio

Pardo

Diagonal

Comandante Espinar

Santa Cruz

OVALO GUTIERREZ

EL OLIVAR

Camino Real

Av. Javier Prado

Av. Arequipa

Av. Salaverry

CAMPO DE MARTE

PLAZA BOLOGNESI

A. Ugarte

Av. 28 de Julio

Nicolas de Piérola

Emancipación

Av. de la Vega

Jr. de la Union

Carabaya

Lampa

Av. Abancay

Av. Grau

Cusco

Huallaga

Junin

Panamericana Norte

Los Frutales

Carretera Central

Circunvalacion

Paseo de la Republica

PLAZA DE SAN MARTIN

PLAZA GRAU

PLAZA 2 DE MAYO

PLAZA UNION

Tacna

Callao

C. de Superunda

ALAMEDA DE LOS DESCALZOS

Av. Colonial

Universitaria

Elmer Faucett

Av. Venezuela

Av. La Marina

Av. Argentina

Av. Saenz Peña

Malecon Figueredo

Av. Arica

Av. Brasil

Av. Bolivar

OVALO BALTA

PLAZA RAIMONDI

Eguren

HOTELS ■
Second Home Peru **11**
3B (Barranco's Bed & Breakfast) **14**

RESTAURANTS ◆
Amoramar **15**
Antica Trattoria **13**
Café del Museo **1**
Café Tostado **13**
Canta Rana **13**
Chala **13**
Costa Verde **10**
LA 73 **15**
La Pescadería **13**

ATTRACTIONS ●
Barrio Chino **4**
Circuito Mágico del Agua **6**
Fundación Museo Amano **7**
Huaca Pucllana **8**
Museo Arqueológico Rafael Larco Herrera **1**
Museo de Arte Colonial Pedro de Osma **12**
Museo de la Nación **5**
Museo Nacional de Arqueología, Antropología e Historia del Perú **2**
Museo Oro del Perú **16**
Parque del Amor **9**
Plaza de Acho/ Museo Taurino **3**

THE BEST TRAVEL EXPERIENCES IN LIMA

o **Delving into a pre-Columbian past.** Lima's first-class museums are a great intro-duction to Peru's complex ancient civilizations, from the Moche to the Chimú. But an unexpected tie to the past are the ancient adobe pyramids (such as Huaca Pucllana) plunked down in residential neighborhoods. South of Lima are the ruins of Pachacámac, which date to the first century. See p. 94.

o **Strolling colonial Lima.** Newly safe and spruced-up Lima Centro is home to many of Peru's best colonial and republican-era palaces and mansions, baroque and Renaissance churches. Strolling through the historic quarter makes plain the city's great early importance. See p. 84.

o **Savoring ceviche.** Peru's signature dish is a tantalizing plate of raw fish and shell-fish marinated in lime or lemon juice and *ajíes*, or chili peppers. A plate of tangy ceviche served at an informal neighborhood restaurant—a huarique to locals—is an unforgettable Limeño experience. See p. 103.

o **Kicking back in Barranco.** This easygoing former seaside village with colorfully painted old houses is the place to go to get away when you're feeling overwhelmed by Lima's big-city chaos. Famous for its happening nightlife, increasingly it's home to boutique hotels and terrific restaurants. See p. 92.

o **Rocking a peña.** Lima's vibrant *criollo* music culture is on display at its peñas, lively music clubs where folkloric and Afro-Peruvian music and dance, emphasiz-ing both percussion and audience participation, go deep into the night. You've got to hit at least one in Lima. See p. 110.

ESSENTIALS

Getting There

BY PLANE   Lima is the gateway for most international arrivals to Peru; see "Get-ting There & Getting Around" in chapter 13, "Planning Your Trip to Peru," for more detailed information. All flights from North America and Europe arrive at Lima's **Aeropuerto Internacional Jorge Chávez** (www.lap.com.pe; ✆ 01/595-0666), located 16km (10 miles) west of the city center. Lima is connected by air with all major cities in Peru; there are regular flights to Ayacucho, Cusco, Puerto Maldonado, Juliaca, Arequipa, Tacna, Cajamarca, Chiclayo, Trujillo, Pucallpa, Iquitos, Tarapoto, and Piura. The major domestic airlines are **LAN** (www.lan.com; ✆ 212/582-3250 in the U.S., or **01/213-8200**), **LC Busre** (www.lcperu.pe; ✆ 01/619-1313), **Peruvian Airlines** (www.peruvianairlines.pe; ✆ 01/716-6000), **Star Perú** (www.starperu.com; ✆ 01/705-9000), and **Taca** (www.taca.com; ✆ 01/511-8222).

The airport has a tourist information booth (in the international terminal only), two 24-hour currency-exchange windows, three banks, ATMs, a post office, and car-rental desks, including **Avis** (www.avis.com; ✆ **01/575-1637,** ext. 4155), **Budget** (www.budget.com; ✆ **01/575-1674**), and **Hertz** (www.hertz.com; ✆ **01/575-1390**). The tourist information booth can help with hotel reservations. The arrival and departure terminals can be very congested, especially when a number of flights arrive at once, and early in the morning when many flights depart Lima for Cusco. Be very mindful of your luggage and other belongings at all times. To get through large groups of travelers and relatives all hovering about, you might need to forget about being polite and simply push your way through the crowd.

Remember to reconfirm your flight at least 48 hours in advance and arrive at the airport with ample time before your flight. *Flights are frequently overbooked,* and passengers who have not reconfirmed their flights or who arrive later than (usually) 45 minutes before scheduled departure risk being bumped from the flight. Flights to Cusco are especially popular; make your reservations as far in advance as possible. Also check to be sure that you will have enough time to make your connecting flight if coming from overseas, and that you haven't been sold a charter flight inadvertently (American Airlines did this to me, and I was forced to stay over a day in Lima until I could get a regular flight the next day).

 Rent a Phone

Lima's Jorge Chávez International Airport is the best place to rent a cell phone for use in Peru. Young female representatives of **Peru Rent-a-Cell** (✆ **01/517-1856**) lurk about in the arrivals terminal offering inexpensive cell phone use (just $10 for the phone, up to a month, and incoming calls are free).

To get from the airport to Lima—either downtown or to suburbs such as Miraflores, San Isidro, and Barranco (the sites of most tourist hotels)—you can take a taxi or private bus. When you exit with your luggage, you will immediately be besieged with taxi offers; the ones nearest the door are invariably the most expensive. **Taxis** (who have plenty of representatives hawking their services) inside the security area at the international arrivals terminal charge S/40–S/45 to Miraflores (about 30 minutes to 1 hour from the airport) and S/30–S/35 to downtown Lima (Lima Centro)—though they'll almost certainly begin by asking for more.

The **Urbanito Airport shuttle service** (✆ **01/814-6932** or **01/517-1893**) delivers passengers to the doors of their hotels. Stop by the desk in the international terminal for information about buses to downtown ($6), and Miraflores and San Isidro ($8), which leave every half-hour or so. The shuttle stops at the hotel of each passenger; at peak hours, if there are many passengers, this might not be the fastest way from the airport. Unless you're alone, it's also probably not the cheapest. Call a day ahead to arrange a pickup for your return to the airport. Private **limousine taxis** (*taxis ejecutivos,* or *remises*) also have desks in the airport; their fares are about $45 one-way. One to try is **MitsuTaxi** (✆ **01/261-7788**).

BY BUS Lima is connected by bus to neighboring countries and all major cities in Peru. No central bus terminal exists, however; the multitude of bus companies serving various regions of the country all have terminals in Lima, making bus arrivals and departures exceedingly confusing for most travelers. Many terminals are located downtown, although several companies have their bases in the suburbs. Most bus terminals have nasty reputations for thievery and general unpleasantness; your best bet is to grab your things and hop into a cab pronto. Of the dozens of bus companies servicing the capital and points around the country, the largest with frequent service in and out of Lima are **Ormeño** (www.grupo-ormeno.com.pe; ✆ 01/472-5000), Av. Javier Prado Este 1059, San Isidro; Av. Carlos Zavala 177 (✆ 01/427-5679); **Cruz del Sur,** Av. Javier Prado Este 1101, La Victoria (www.cruzdelsur.com.pe; ✆ 01/311-5050), and Jirón Quilca (www.cruzdelsur.com.pe; ✆ 01/424-1005); **Transportes Civa,** Av. Paseo de la República 575 (www.civa.com.pe; ✆ 01/418-1111); and **Oltursa,** Av. Aramburú 1160, San Isidro (www.oltursa.com.pe; ✆ 01/708-5000).

BY TRAIN   For information on one of South America's most spectacular (but infrequent) rail journeys, from Lima to Huancayo in the central highlands, see "Highest Railroad in the World" box on p. 152.

Visitor Information

A 24-hour tourist information booth, **iPerú** (✆ **01/574-8000**), operates in the international terminal at the Jorge Chávez International Airport. The most helpful **iPerú** office is in Miraflores, at the **Larcomar** shopping mall, Módulo 10, Av. Malecón de la Reserva 610 (✆ **01/445-9400**), open Monday through Friday from 11am to 1pm and 2 to 8pm. Another office is in San Isidro at Jorge Basadre 610 (✆ **01/421-1627**), open Monday through Friday from 8:30am to 6:30pm. The **Oficina de Información Turística** in Lima Centro is at Pasaje Los Escribanos 145, just off the Plaza de Armas, in Lima Centro (✆ **01/427-6080**); it's open Monday through Saturday from 9am to 6pm.

One of the best private agencies for arrangements and city tours, as well as general information, is **Fertur Perú,** Jr. Junín 211 (www.fertur-travel.com; ✆ **01/427-2626**), with an office in the Hotel España and a branch at Calle Schell 485 in Miraflores (✆ **01/445-1760**). Another excellent spot for information and advice, particularly on outdoor and adventure travel in Peru, such as trekking, mountaineering, and rafting, is the office of **South American Explorers,** Piura 135, Miraflores (www.saexplorers.org; ✆ **01/445-3306**). The organization is legendary among veteran South American travelers, and it's not a bad idea to become a member ($50) before traveling so that you can take advantage of its resources (you can also join on the spot). The clubhouse in Lima maintains a library of maps, books, trail information, trip reports, and storage facilities. It's open Monday through Friday from 9:30am to 5pm (Wed until 8pm), and Saturday from 9:30am to 1pm. There are also clubhouses in Cusco and Quito, Ecuador.

City Layout

Lima is an exceedingly diffuse city, so it's complicated to get around. The city center, known as Lima Centro, abuts the Río Rímac and the Rímac district across the river. The city beyond central Lima is a warren of ill-defined neighborhoods; most visitors are likely to set foot in only San Isidro, Miraflores, and Barranco, which hug the coast and the circuit of urban beaches leading to the so-called "Costa Verde." Major thoroughfares leading from the city center to outer neighborhoods are Avenida Benavides (to Callao); Avenida Brasil (to Pueblo Libre); Avenida Arequipa, Avenida Tacna, and Avenida Garcilaso de la Vega (to San Isidro and Miraflores); Paseo de la República (also known as Vía Expresa) and Avenida Panamá (to Miraflores and Barranco); and Avenida Panamericana Sur (to San Borja and south of Lima).

Neighborhoods in Brief

Lima Centro   Lima Centro is the historic heart of the city, where the Spaniards built the country's capital in colonial fashion. It has repeatedly suffered from earthquakes, fires, and neglect, so although it was once the continent's most important colonial city, stunning examples of the original town are less prevalent than one might expect. Much of Lima Centro is dirty, unsafe, crowded, and chaotic, although city officials are finally getting to much-needed restoration of the remaining historic buildings and have drastically upgraded police presence in the city center (making it just about as safe as anywhere in the city during the day). The great majority of visitors stay in outer suburbs rather than Lima Centro; most hotels are small *hostales* (inns) aimed at budget travelers and backpackers. The absolute heart of the Lima Centro is the Plaza de Armas, site of La Catedral (cathedral) and government palaces, and nearly all the colonial mansions and churches of interest are within walking distance of the square. Several of Lima's top museums are in **Pueblo Libre,** a couple of kilometers southwest of Lima Centro, while **San Borja,** a couple of kilometers directly south of Lima Centro, holds two of the finest collections in all of Peru.

Miraflores & San Isidro San Isidro and Miraflores, the city's most exclusive residential and commercial neighborhoods, are farther south (5–8km/3–5 miles) toward the coast. These districts are now the commercial heart of the city, having usurped that title from Lima Centro some years ago. San Isidro holds many of the city's top luxury hotels and a slew of offices and shopping malls. Miraflores is the focus of most travelers' visits to Lima; it contains the greatest number and variety of hotels, bars, and restaurants, as well as shopping outlets. A number of the city's finest hotels are along the *malecón* (boulevard) in Miraflores. Although San Isidro and Miraflores are middle-class neighborhoods, both are congested and not entirely free of crime.

Barranco Barranco, several kilometers farther out along the ocean, is a tranquil former seaside village that is the city's coolest and most relaxed district, now known primarily for its nightlife. It is where you'll find many of Lima's best restaurants and especially bars, and live-music spots, frequented by Limeños and visitors alike. Though there are only a few boutique hotels and hostels in Barranco, increasingly it's becoming a cool place to stay, especially for young people. The next district along the beach is **Chorrillos,** a residential neighborhood known primarily for its *Pantanos de Villa,* or swamps that are rich with flora and fauna.

Getting Around

Navigating Lima is a complicated and time-consuming task, made difficult by the city's sprawling character (many of the best hotels and restaurants are far from downtown, spread among three or more residential neighborhoods), heavy traffic and pollution, and a chaotic network of confusing and crowded *colectivos* and unregulated taxis.

BY TAXI Taxis hailed on the street are a reasonable and relatively quick way to get around in Lima. However, taxis are wholly unregulated by the government: All anyone has to do to become a taxi driver is get his hands on a vehicle—of any size and condition, although most are tiny Daewoo "Ticos"—and plunk a cheap TAXI sticker inside the windshield. Then he is free to charge whatever he thinks he can get—with no meters, no laws, and nobody to answer to except the free market. One has to counsel visitors to be a bit wary of taking taxis in Lima, even though I personally have never had problems greater than a dispute over a fare. (If you're not fluent in Spanish, and even if you are but you have an obviously non-Peruvian appearance, be prepared to negotiate fares.) Limeños tell enough stories of theft and even the occasional violent crime in unregistered cabs to make hailing one on the street inadvisable for older visitors or for those with little command of Spanish or experience traveling in Latin America. If you hail a taxi on the street, taxi drivers themselves have told me, try to pick out older drivers; many contend that young punks are almost wholly responsible for taxi crime. If the issue of getting into quasi-official cabs makes you nervous, by all means call a registered company from your hotel or restaurant—especially at night (even though the fare can be twice as much).

Registered, reputable taxi companies—the safest option—include **Taxi Amigo** (© 01/349-0177), **Taxi Line** (© 01/330-2795), **Taxi Móvil** (© 01/422-6890), and **Taxi Seguro** (© 01/275-2020). Whether you call or hail a taxi, you'll need to establish a price beforehand—so be prepared to bargain. Most fares range from S/8 to S/15. From Miraflores or San Isidro to downtown, expect to pay S/15; and from Miraflores to Barranco, S/12. Note that when you hail a taxi on the street, the fare requested will surely be a bit higher; it makes sense to try to haggle.

BY BUS   The big news in public transportation has been the 2010 inauguration of the modern, clean, and very efficient **Metropolitano Bus** (www.metropolitano.com. pe; © 01/203-9000), which travels along the Vía Expresa and Paseo de la República, connecting Lima Centro to Miraflores, Barranco, and as far south along the coast as Chorrillos. It is most convenient for traveling to Lima Centro, Miraflores, and Barranco, although the single, straight line of stops will still leave you a long walk or short taxi ride from many destinations (six new routes are planned for the future). Fares are S/1.50, deducted from a minimum fare card of S/5. The buses run daily from 6am to 9:50pm. The major stops are: Lima Centro: Tacna and Jr. de la Unión; San Isidro: Javier Prado, Canaval y Moreyra, and Aramburú; Miraflores: Angamos, Ricardo Palma, Benavides and 28 de Julio; and Barranco: Balta and Bulevar.

Other than the Metropolitano, *micros,* colectivos, and *combis* (all names for varying sizes of buses that make both regular and unscheduled stops) are very inexpensive means of transportation in the city, but are very confusing for most visitors and not recommended.   Micros and combis are very inexpensive means of transportation in the city (see the "*Combi* or Carro? Getting Around in and out of Town" box in Chapter 13 for more info). Routes are more or less identified by signs with street names placed in the windshield, making many trips confusing for those unfamiliar with Lima. Some do nothing more than race up and down long avenues (for example, the bus labeled TODO AREQUIPA travels the length of Avenida Arequipa). For assistance, ask a local for help; most Limeños know the incredibly complex bus system surprisingly well. Although they sometimes seem to hurtle down the street, because they make so many stops, trips from the outer suburbs to downtown can be quite slow. Most micros and combis cost S/3, and slightly more after midnight and on Sunday and holidays. When you want to get off, shout *baja* (getting off) or *esquina* (at the corner). From Lima Centro to Miraflores, look for buses with signs in the windows indicating LARCO–SCHELL–MIRAFLORES (or some combination thereof). From Miraflores to downtown Lima, you should hop on a bus headed along WILSON/TACNA. Buses to Barranco have signs that read CHORILLOS/HUAYLAS.

BY FOOT   Lima can be navigated by foot only a neighborhood at a time (and even then, congestion and pollution strongly discourage much walking). Lima Centro and Barranco are best seen by foot, and, although large, Miraflores is also walkable. Between neighborhoods, however, a taxi is essential.

BY CAR   For getting around Lima or the immediate region, this is not even a consideration.

FAST FACTS

American Express   Av. Santa Cruz 621, Miraflores (© 01/710-3900), open Monday to Friday 9am to 5pm; Jr. Rio de Janeiro 216, Miraflores (© 610-6000); same hours.

ATMs/Banks   Peruvian and international banks with currency-exchange bureaus and ATMs are plentiful throughout Lima Centro, especially in the outer neighborhoods such as

Miraflores, San Isidro, and Barranco, which are full of shopping centers, hotels, and restaurants. Money-changers (sometimes in smocks with obvious "$" insignias) patrol the main streets off Parque Central in Miraflores and central Lima with calculators and dollars in hand.

Doctors & Hospitals

The U.S. and British embassies (see "Embassies & Consulates," below) provide lists of English-speaking doctors, dentists, and other healthcare personnel in Lima. An organization called **Doctor Más** (✆ **01/444-9377**) sends English-speaking doctors to hotels for emergencies and prescriptions. For dentists, you might also try contacting the **International Academy of Integrated Dentistry,** Centauro 177, Urbanización Los Granados, Monterrico, Surco (✆ **01/435-2153**). English-speaking medical personnel and 24-hour emergency services are available at the following hospitals and clinics: **Clínica Anglo-Americana,** Alfredo Salazar, Block 3, San Isidro (✆ **01/712-3000**); **Clínica San Borja,** Guardia Civil 337, San Borja (✆ **01/475-4000**); **Maison de Santé,** Calle Miguel Adgouin 208 (✆ **01/619-610**), near the Palacio de Justicia (✆ **01/428-3000,** emergency **01/427-2941**); and **Clínica Ricardo Palma,** Av. Javier Prado Este 1066, San Isidro (✆ **01/224-2224**). For an ambulance, call **Alerta Médica,** at ✆ **01/470-5000,** or **San Cristóbal,** at ✆ **01/440-0200.**

Embassies & Consulates

U.S., Avenida La Encalada, Block 17, Surco (✆ **01/434-3000**); **Australia,** Víctor A. Belaúnde 147/Vía Principal 155, office 1301, San Isidro (✆ **01/222-8281**); **Canada,** Calle Bolognesi 228, Miraflores (✆ **01/319-3200**); **U.K.** and **New Zealand,** Av. Jose Larco 1301, Miraflores (✆ **01/617-3000**).

Emergencies

In case of an emergency, call the 24-hour **traveler's hotline** (✆ **01/574-8000**) or the **tourist police,** or POLTUR (✆ **01/460-1060** in Lima, or **01/460-0965**). The **INDECOPI** 24-hour hotline can also assist in contacting police to report a crime (✆ **01/224-7888** in Lima, **01/224-8600,** or toll-free **0800/42579** from any private phone).The general **police** emergency number is ✆ **105;** for **fire,** dial ✆ **116**.

Internet Access

Internet *cabinas* (booths) are everywhere in Lima. Rates are about S/2 to S/3 per hour, and most are open daily from 9am to 10pm or later. Try **Telnet,** Jr. Camaná 315; **Internet Pardo,** Av. José Pardo 620; **Cybersandeg,** Jr. de la Unión 853, Of. 112; **Wamnet,** corner of Diez Canseco and Alcanfores, Mezzanine, Miraflores; or **C@bin@s de Internet,** Diez Canseco 380, Miraflores.

Mail & Postage

Lima's main post office (*Central de Correos*) is on the Plaza de Armas at Camaná 195 (✆ **01/427-0370**) in central Lima. The Miraflores branch is at Petit Thouars 5201 (✆ **01/445-0697**); the San Isidro branch is at Calle Las Palmeras 205 (✆ **01/422-0981**). A **DHL/Western Union** office is at Nicolás de Piérola 808 (✆ **01/424-5820**).

Newspapers & Magazines

In Lima, you will find copies (although rarely same-day publications) of the *International Herald Tribune* and the *Miami Herald,* as well as *Time, Newsweek,* and other special-interest publications. Top-flight hotels sometimes offer free daily fax summations of the *New York Times* to their guests. Among local publications, look for *Rumbos,* a glossy Peruvian travel magazine in English and Spanish with excellent photography. *El Comercio* and *La República* are two of the best daily Spanish newspapers.

Pharmacies

Two huge, multiservice pharmacies (*farmacias*) open 24 hours a day are **Farmacia Deza,** Av. Conquistadores 1140, San Isidro (✆ **01/440-3798**); and **Pharmax,** Av. Salaverry 3100, San Isidro, in the Centro Comercio El Polo (✆ **01/264-2282**). A chain with a number of storefronts across Lima is **Superfarma,** at Av. Benavides 2849 (✆ **01/222-1575**) and Avenida Armendariz, Miraflores (✆ **01/446-3333**). These and other pharmacies have 24-hour delivery service. For additional locations, consult the Yellow Pages under "Farmacias" and "Boticas."

Police

The **Policía Nacional de Turismo (National Tourism Police)** has staff members that speak English and are specifically trained to handle the needs of foreign visitors. The main office in Lima is at Av. Javier

Prado Este 2465, 5th Floor, San Borja (next to the Museo de la Nación); the 24-hour tourist police line is (℃) **01/574-8000.** Also see "Emergencies" above.

Safety Lima is calmer and apparently safer than anytime I can remember, but in Lima Centro and the city's residential and hotel areas, the risk of street crime remains. Although carjackings, assaults, and armed robberies are not routine, they're not unheard of either. Armed attacks at ATMs have also occurred. Use ATMs during the day, with other people present. Most thefts occur on public transportation, such as buses and combis. There have been several reports of thieves who've boarded buses in and out of Lima to cities both north and south of the capital, relieving passengers at gunpoint of their valuables. Be very careful with your belongings; leave your passport and other valuables in the hotel safe, and use a money belt. Public street markets are also frequented by thieves, as are parks (especially at night) and the beaches in and around Lima. Although the large-scale terrorist activities of the local groups Sendero Luminoso and MRTA were largely stamped out in the early 1990s, there have been reports of a possible resurgence. Neither group, however, is currently active in any of the areas covered in this book.

Telephone Lima's area code is 01. It need not be dialed when making local calls within Lima, but it must be dialed when calling Lima from another city. Telephone booths are found throughout the city; the principal Telefónica del Perú office, where you can make long-distance and international calls, is on Plaza San Martín (Carabaya 937) in Lima Centro ((℃) **01/224-9355**). It's open Monday through Saturday from 8am to 6pm and Sunday 8am to 1pm.

EXPLORING LIMA

Many visitors to Lima are merely on their way to other places in Peru, and few spend more than a couple of days in the capital. But because nearly all transport goes through Lima, most people take advantage of layovers to see what distinguishes the city: its colonial old quarter—once the finest in the Americas—and several of the finest museums in Peru, all of which serve as magnificent introductions to Peruvian history and culture.

Much of the historic center has suffered from sad neglect; the municipal government is committed to restoring the aesthetic value, but, with limited funds, it faces a daunting task. Today central Lima has a noticeable police presence and is considerably safer than it was just a few years ago. A full day in Lima Centro should suffice; depending on your interests, you could spend several days traipsing through Lima's many museum collections, many of which are dispersed in otherwise unremarkable neighborhoods. But for those with a couple of extra days in the city, when Lima's traffic and grit get to you, head to the artsy coastal neighborhood, Barranco, home to Lima's best nightlife and the site of a handful of excellent small museums. It will likely greatly improve your impressions of the capital.

Lima Centro: Colonial Lima

Lima's grand **Plaza de Armas ★** (also called the **Plaza Mayor,** or **Main Square**), the original center of the city and the site where Francisco Pizarro founded the city in 1535, is essentially a modern reconstruction. The disastrous 1746 earthquake that initiated the city's decline leveled most of the 16th- and 17th-century buildings in the old center. The plaza has witnessed everything from bullfights to Inquisition-related executions. The oldest surviving element of the square is the central bronze fountain, which

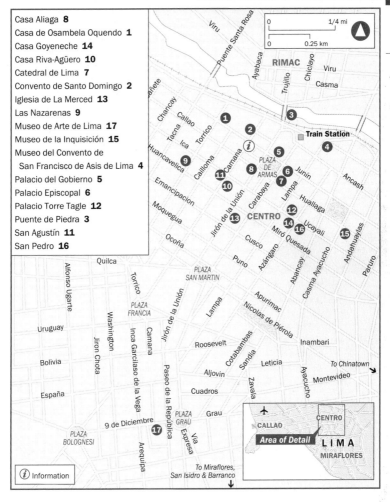

Casa Aliaga **8**
Casa de Osambela Oquendo **1**
Casa Goyeneche **14**
Casa Riva-Agüero **10**
Catedral de Lima **7**
Convento de Santo Domingo **2**
Iglesia de La Merced **13**
Las Nazarenas **9**
Museo de Arte de Lima **17**
Museo de la Inquisición **15**
Museo del Convento de
  San Francisco de Asis de Lima **4**
Palacio del Gobierno **5**
Palacio Episcopal **6**
Palacio Torre Tagle **12**
Puente de Piedra **3**
San Agustín **11**
San Pedro **16**

(i) Information

dates from 1651. Today the square, although perhaps not the most beautiful or languid in South America, is still rather distinguished beneath a surface level of grime and bustle (and it has been named a UNESCO World Heritage Site). The major palaces and cathedral are mostly harmonious in architectural style and color. (The facades are a mix of natural stone and a once-bold yellow color now dulled by smog and mist.) On the north side of the square is the early-20th-century **Palacio del Gobierno (Presidential Palace),** where a changing of the guard takes place daily at noon; free guided visits of the palace are offered Monday through Friday from 10am to 12:30pm. The **Municipalidad de Lima (City Hall)** is on the west side of the plaza. Across the square is **La Catedral (Cathedral),** rebuilt after the earthquake, making it by far the oldest building on the square, and, next to the cathedral, the **Palacio Episcopal (Archbishop's Palace),** distinguished by an extraordinary wooden balcony.

A block north of the Plaza de Armas, behind the Presidential Palace, is the Río Rímac and a 17th-century Roman-style bridge, the **Puente de Piedra** (literally, "stone bridge"). It leads to the once-fashionable **Rímac** district, today considerably less chic—some would say downright dangerous—although it is the location of a few of Lima's best *peñas,* or live *criollo* (Creole/coastal) music clubs. The **Plaza de Acho bullring,** once the largest in the world, and the decent **Museo Taurino (Bullfighting Museum)** are near the river at Hualgayoc 332 (🕻 01/482-3360). The museum is open Monday through Friday from 9am to 3pm, and Saturday from 9am to 2pm, and admission is S/6. The ring is in full swing during the Fiestas Patrias (national holidays) at the end of July; the regular season runs October through December.

Five blocks southwest of Plaza de Armas is Lima Centro's other grand square, **Plaza San Martín.** Inaugurated in 1921, this stately square with handsome gardens was recently renovated. At its center is a large monument to the South American liberator, José de San Martín.

Lima's **Barrio Chino,** the largest Chinese community in South America (200,000 plus), is the best place to get a taste of the Peruvian twist on traditional Chinese cooking in the neighborhood's *chifas.* For recommendations, see the "Peruvian *Chifas*" box on p. 98. The official boundary of Chinatown is the large gate on Jirón Ucayali.

THE TOP ATTRACTIONS

Catedral de Lima ★ CATHEDRAL   Lima's baroque cathedral, an enlargement of an earlier one from 1555, was completed in 1625. It suffered damage in earthquakes in 1687 and was decimated by the big one in 1746. The present building, again damaged by tremors in 1940, is an 18th-century reconstruction of the early plans. Twin yellow towers sandwich an elaborate stone facade. Inside are several notable Churrigueresque (Spanish baroque) altars and carved wooden choir stalls, but the cathedral is best known for the chapel where Francisco Pizarro lies and a small **Museo de Arte Religioso (Museum of Religious Art)** housed in the rear of the church.

Immediately to the right after you enter the church is a chapel decorated in magnificent Venetian mosaics and marble. In case you don't know whose earthly remains are inside the tomb, letters in mosaic tiles over the arch of the chapel spell out FRANCISCO PIZARRO. The founder of Lima and killer of the Incas' emperor was himself assassinated in the Plaza de Armas in 1541, but his remains weren't brought to the cathedral until 1985. (They were discovered in a crypt in 1977.) Look closely at the mosaic on the far wall, which depicts his coat of arms, Atahualpa reaching into his coffer to cough up a ransom in the hopes of attaining his release, and other symbols of Pizarro's life. The museum has a few fabulous painted-glass mirrors from Cusco, a collection of unsigned paintings, and a seated sculpture of Jesus, with his chin resting pensively on his hand; it's as bloody a figure of Christ as you're likely to see. Allow about an hour for a visit.

Plaza de Armas. www.arzobispadodelima.org. 🕻 **01/427-5980.** Admission to cathedral and museum S/10 adults, S/5 students. Guides available in English and Spanish (voluntary tip). Mon–Sat 9am–4:30pm.

Museo de la Inquisición 🏛   MUSEUM   This magnificent mansion across the street from the House of Congress once belonged to the family considered the founders of Lima, but it became the tribunal for the notorious Spanish Inquisition. Today it is a museum that soberly addresses religious intolerance from the Middle Ages through colonial times. The handsomely restored house itself is worth a visit because it's a fine peek at the elegant rooms of a prominent 16th-century colonial home (including the intricately carved ceiling of the Tribunal room). But its unfortunate history is plainly evident in the catacombs, which served as prison cells; on view are several instruments of torture. At least 32 Peruvians died here during the Inquisition, which persisted until 1820. The guided tour lasts about an hour.

Plaza Bolívar (Junín 548). www.congreso.gob.pe/museo.htm. © **01/427-5980.** Free admission. Guided tours in English, Spanish, French, and Portuguese. Daily 9am–5pm.

Museo del Convento de San Francisco de Asis de Lima ★★ CONVENT/MUSEUM   Probably the most spectacular of Lima's colonial-era churches, the Convent of Saint Francis is a strikingly restored, yellow-and-white 17th-century complex that survived the massive earthquake in 1746. The facade is a favorite of thousands of pigeons, who rest on rows of ridges that rise up the towers—so much so that, from a distance, it looks like black spots add an unexpectedly funky flavor to the baroque church. Cloisters and interiors are lined with beautiful *azulejos* (glazed ceramic tiles) from Seville; carved *mudéjar* (Moorish-style) ceilings are overhead. The mandatory guided tour takes visitors past the cloisters to a fine museum of religious art, with beautifully carved saints and a series of portraits of the apostles by the studio of Francisco Zurbarán, the famed Spanish painter. For many, though, the most fascinating component of the visit is the descent into the catacombs, which were dug beginning in 1546 as a burial ground for priests and others. (As many as 75,000 bodies were interred here before the main cemetery was built.) File past loads of bones—it's unknown how many levels down they go—and see a round well lined with perfectly laid skulls and femurs. Also of great interest are the church, outfitted with an impressive neoclassical altar, and a fantastic 17th-century library with 20,000 books, many of which date to the first years after Lima's foundation. A breathtaking carved Moorish ceiling over a staircase is a reconstruction of the original from 1625. Allow 1½ hours to see it all, including waiting time for an English-language tour.

Ancash s/n (Plaza de San Francisco). www.museocatacumbas.com. © **01/426-7377.** Admission S/7 adults, S/3.50 students. Guides available in English and Spanish. Daily 9:30am–5:30pm.

COLONIAL CHURCH ROUNDUP ★★

Lima Centro has a number of fine colonial-era churches worth visiting. Most are open Monday through Saturday for visits, and most have free admission.

Directly south of La Catedral on Azángaro at Ucayali, **San Pedro ★** (© **01/428-3017**), a Jesuit church that dates to 1638, is perhaps the best-preserved example of early colonial religious architecture in the city. The exterior is simple and rather austere, but the interior is rich with gilded altars and balconies. The bold main altar, with columns and balconies and sculpted figures, is particularly impressive. There are also some beautiful 17th- and 18th-century baroque *retablos* (altars) of carved wood and gold leaf. A small museum of colonial art is to the right of the entrance of the church, which is open Monday through Saturday from 7am to noon and 5 to 8pm; admission is free.

Iglesia de La Merced, Jr. de la Unión at Miró Quesada (© **01/427-8199**), 2 blocks southwest of the Plaza de Armas, was erected on the site of Lima's first Mass in 1534. The 18th-century church has a striking carved baroque colonial facade.

Inside, the sacristy, embellished with Moorish tiles, and the main altar are excellent examples of the period. The church also possesses a nice collection of colonial art. Yet it is perhaps most notable for the devoted followers of Padre Urraca, a 17th-century priest; they come daily in droves to pay their respects, praying and touching the large silver cross dedicated to him in the nave on the right, and leaving many mementos of their veneration. The church is open Monday through Saturday from 8am to noon and 4 to 8pm.

Practically destroyed during an 1895 revolution, **San Agustín,** at the corner of Jr. Ica and Jr. Camaná (© **01/427-7548**), is distinguished by a spectacular Churrigue-resque facade, one of the best of its kind in Peru, dating to the early 18th century. San Agustín's official hours are daily from 8 to 11am and 4:30 to 7pm, but, in practice, it's frequently closed. The **Convento de Santo Domingo,** at the corner of Conde de Superunda and Camaná, toward the River Rímac (© **01/427-6793**), draws many Peruvians to visit the tombs of Santa Rosa de Lima and San Martín de Porras. It is perhaps of less interest to foreign visitors, although it does have a very nice main cloister. It's open Monday through Saturday from 9am to 12:30pm and 3 to 6pm; admission is S/3.

Las Nazarenas, at the corner of Huancavelica and Avenida Tacna on the north-west edge of the colonial center (© **01/423-5718**), has a remarkable history. It was constructed in the 18th century around a locally famous painting of Christ by an Angolan slave. Known as "El Señor de los Milagros," the image, painted on the wall of a simple abode (many slaves lived in this area on the fringes of the city), survived the massive 1655 earthquake, even though everything around it crumbled. People began to flock to the painting, and soon the Catholic Church constructed a house of worship for it. Behind the altar, on the still-standing wall, is an oil replica, which is paraded through the streets on a 1-ton silver litter during the El Señor de los Milagros festival; this is one of Lima's largest festivals and is held on October 18, 19, and 28 and November 1. Everyone wears purple during the procession. Las Nazarenas is open Monday through Saturday from 6:30am to noon and 5 to 8:30pm.

COLONIAL PALACE ROUNDUP ★

The historic quarter of Lima, the old administrative capital of Spain's South American colonies, once boasted many of the finest mansions in the hemisphere. Repeated devastation by earthquakes and more recent public and private inability to maintain many of the superb surviving *casas coloniales*, however, has left Lima with only a handful of houses open to the public.

Casa Riva-Agüero, Camaná 459 (ira.pucp.edu.pe; © **01/626-6600**), is an impressive 18th-century mansion with a beautiful green-and-red courtyard that now belongs to the Catholic University of Peru. It has a small folk-art museum in the restored and furnished interior. The house is open Monday through Friday from 10am to 5pm and 2 to 7:30pm; admission is S/2. **Casa Aliaga ★★,** Jr. de la Unión 224 (casadealiaga.com; © **01/427-7736**), is the oldest surviving house in Lima, dating from 1535. It is also one of Lima's finest mansions, with an extraordinary inner patio and elegant salons, and it continues to be owned and lived in by descendants of the original family. The house is open Monday through Friday from 9am to 5pm (by advance reservation, reservas@casadealiaga.com); admission is S/30. It can also be visited as part of a city tour (S/75) conducted exclusively by **Lima Tours** (www.limatours.com.pe; © **01/619-6900**). A worthy alternative if you don't want to spring for a guided tour is **Casa de Osambela Oquendo,** Conde de Superunda 298

A "MAGIC" water PARK ★

Lima Centro's newest attraction, the colorful fountains of the **Circuito Mágico del Agua** waterpark, are a great place to take the kids and beat the heat. The best time to visit the 13 fountains shooting into the sky and a tunnel kids will love to carouse beneath is at night, when the spectacle of colorful effects and dancing waters set to music is delightful (shows at 7:15, 8:15, and 9:30pm). The centerpiece, the Magic Fountain, propels a stream 76 meters (250 ft.) into the air, a Guinness record. The waterpark (http://www.parquedela reserva.com.pe/en/circuit.php; ✆ **01/ 427-1993**) is located at Parque de la Reserva (Av. Petit Thouars at Jr. Madre de Dios), in the Santa Beatriz district. It's open Wednesday through Sunday, 3–10:30pm, and admission is S/4, free for children under 4.

(✆ **01/428-7919**). The tallest house in colonial Lima, today it belongs to the Ministry of Education. Although it's still not officially open for visits, the caretaker will usually show visitors around, including up four levels to the baby-blue cupola-mirador for views over the city. (The original owner built the house so he could see all the way to the port.) Next door is a 1770 house in a lamentable state; squatters inhabit it. The Osambela house has a spectacular patio, 40 bedrooms, and eight wooden balconies to the street, a sure sign of the owner's great wealth. It's open daily from 9am to 5pm; admission is free, but tips are accepted.

A couple of blocks east of the Plaza de Armas at Ucayali 363 is **Palacio Torre Tagle ★**, the most famous palace in Lima and one of the most handsome in Peru. Today the early-18th-century palace, built by a marquis who was treasurer of the Royal Spanish fleet, belongs to the Peruvian Ministry of Foreign Affairs and, sadly, can no longer be visited by the public (though it may be worth inquiring at the Ministry, next door at Ucayali 318). Its exterior, with a gorgeous baroque stone doorway and carved dark-wood balconies, is very much worth a look (and you might get a peek inside the courtyard if a group of dark suits enters or leaves when you're passing by). Across the street from Torre Tagle, **Casa Goyeneche** (also called **Casa de Rada**) is another impressive 18th-century mansion, with distinct French influences; it's also not open to the public (although you might be able to manage a peek at the patio). Those with a specific interest in colonial architecture might also want to have a look at the facades of **Casa Negreiros,** Jr. Azángaro 532; **Casa de las Trece Monedas,** Jr. Ancash 536; **Casa Barbieri,** Jirón Callao at Rufino Torrico; **Casa de Pilatos,** Jr. Ancash 390; and **Casa la Riva,** Jr. Ica 426.

THE TOP MUSEUMS

To locate the following museums, see the "Lima at a Glance" map on p. 77.

Museo Arqueológico Rafael Larco Herrera ★★★ MUSEUM Founded in 1926, this museum has the largest private collection of pre-Columbian art in the world. It concentrates on the Moche Dynasty, especially on its refined ceramics, with an estimated 45,000 pieces—including incredibly fine textiles, jewelry, and stonework from several other ancient cultures—all housed in an 18th-century colonial building. Rafael Larco Hoyle is considered the founder of Peruvian archaeology (he named the museum after his father); he wrote the seminal study *Los Mochicas* in

1938, although he succeeded in publishing only six chapters. (The rest has now been posthumously published.)

The Moche (A.D. 200–700), who lived along the northern coast in the large area near present-day Trujillo and Cajamarca, are credited with achieving one of the greatest artistic expressions of ancient Peru. The collection might be overwhelming to visitors who know little about the Moche, but one soon learns that the pottery gives clues to all elements of their society: diseases, curing practices, architecture, transportation, dance, agriculture, music, and religion. The Moche are also celebrated in the modern world for their erotic ceramics. The Sala Erótica here is removed from the general collection, like the porn section in a video store. It's outdoors, downstairs, and across the garden. The Moche depicted sex in realistic, humorous, moralistic, religious, and—above all—explicit terms; the most common and even a few deviant practices are represented. If you're traveling with kids, expect giggles or questions about the ancient Peruvians' mighty phalluses. Plan on spending 2 hours to see it all.

An excellent and attractive on-site restaurant, **Café del Museo ★** (under the auspices of Peru's celebrity chef Gastón Acurio) makes a great lunch or an early dinner spot, so you might want to plan your visit around dining there.

Av. Bolívar 1515, Pueblo Libre. www.museolarco.org. Ⓒ **01/461-1312.** Admission S/30 adults, S/25 seniors, S/15 students. Private guides available in English and Spanish (tip basis, minimum S/10). Daily 9am–10pm (until 6pm Dec 26 and Jan 1). Take a taxi or the "Todo Brasil" colectivo to Avenida Brasil, and then another to Avenida Bolívar. If you're coming from the Museo Nacional de Arqueología, Antropología e Historia del Perú (p. 90), walk along the blue path.

Museo de la Nación ★★ ☺ MUSEUM Peru's ancient history is exceedingly complicated—not to mention new territory for most visitors to the country. Indeed, Peru's pre-Columbian civilizations were among the most sophisticated of their times; when Egypt was building pyramids, people in Peru were constructing great cities. Lima's National Museum, the city's biggest and one of the most important in Peru, guides visitors through the highlights of overlapping and conquering cultures and their achievements, seen not only in architecture (including scale models of most major ruins in Peru), but also in highly advanced ceramics and textiles. The exhibits, spread over three rambling floors, are ordered chronologically—very helpful for getting a grip on these many cultures dispersed across Peru. They trace the art and history of the earliest inhabitants to the Inca Empire, the last before colonization by the Spaniards. In case you aren't able to make it to the archaeology-rich north of Peru, pay special attention to the facsimile of the Lord of Sipán discovery, one of the most important in the world in recent years. For the most part, explanations accompanying the exhibits are in both Spanish and English. Allow 2 to 3 hours for your visit.

Av. Javier Prado Este 2465, San Borja. Ⓒ **01/476-9878.** Admission S/9 adults, S/3 seniors, S/1 students. Tues–Sun 9am–6pm. Guides in several languages can be contracted. You can get here by colectivo along Av. Prado from Av. Arequipa, but it is much simpler to take a taxi from Lima Centro or Miraflores/San Isidro.

Museo Nacional de Arqueología, Antropología e Historia del Perú ★
MUSEUM With such a mouthful of an official name, you might expect the National Museum of Archaeology, Anthropology, and History to be the Peruvian equivalent of New York City's Metropolitan Museum of Art. It's not (especially because much of the museum's huge collection remains in storage), but it's a worthwhile and enjoyable museum that covers Peruvian civilization from prehistoric times

ALL THAT glitters ISN'T NECESSARILY GOLD

The privately held **Museo Oro del Perú (Gold Museum),** for decades the most visited museum in Peru, was part of a must-see museum triumvirate in Lima only a few years ago. But that was before the National Institute of Culture and the Tourism Protection Bureau declared just about everything in the museum—some 7,000 or more pieces—to be fake. The massive collection, mainly consisting of supposed pre-Columbian gold, was assembled by one man, Miguel Mujica Gallo—who, perhaps fortunately, died just days before the investigation into his collection was launched. Although the museum was expensive and poorly organized, all that glittering gold—augmented by hundreds (if not thousands) of ceremonial objects, tapestries, masks, ancient weapons,

clothing, several mummies, and military weaponry from medieval Europe to ancient Japan—certainly caught many a visitor's eye over the years. Though the museum contends that everything on display is authentic, it's pretty difficult to recommend visiting a collection with such a fraudulent history. The museum is located at Av. Alonso de Molina 1100, Monterrico (www.museoroperu.com.pe; © 01/345-1292; daily 11:30am–7pm; admission S/33 for adults, S/16 for students). A taxi is the most direct way here; coming by colectivo involves taking at least two buses along Arequipa to Avenida Angamos, changing to one marked UNIVERSIDAD DE LIMA, and asking the driver to let you off at the Museo de Oro.

to the colonial and republican periods. There are ceramics, carved stone figures and obelisks, metalwork and jewelry, and lovely textiles. On view are early ceramics from 2800 B.C. in the central Andes, the great granite Tello Obelisk from the Chavín period, burial tombs, and mummies in the fetal position wrapped in burial blankets. There's also a selection of erotic ceramics from the Moche culture, but it's not nearly as extensive as that of the Museo Arqueológico Rafael Larco Herrera (p. 89). Individual rooms are dedicated to the Nasca, Paracas, Moche, and Chimú cultures. Toward the end of the exhibit, which wanders around the central courtyard of the handsome 19th-century Quinta de los Libertadores mansion (once lived in by South American independence heroes San Martín and Bolívar), is a large-scale model of Machu Picchu with buttons allowing visitors to identify key sectors of the complex. Basic descriptions throughout the museum are mostly in Spanish, although some are also in English. Allow about an hour for your visit. From the museum, you can follow a walking path along a painted blue line to the Rafael Larco Herrera Museum. It's about a mile away, or 20 minutes straight into traffic on Antonio de Sucre.

Plaza Bolívar s/n, Pueblo Libre. museonacional.perucultural.org.pe. © 01/463-5070. Admission S/12 adults, S/3.50 seniors and students. Private guides available in English and Spanish (tip basis, minimum S/10). Tues–Sat 9am–5pm; Sun 10am–4pm. Take a taxi here, or take the "Todo Brasil" colectivo to Avenida Vivanco, and then take a 15-min. walk.

OTHER MUSEUMS
To locate Fundación Museo Amano and Museo de Arte Colonial Pedro de Osma, see the "Lima at a Glance" map, on p. 77.

Although a residential neighborhood and not immediately thought of as having many tourist sights, apart from the small but excellent Museo de Arte Colonial Pedro de Osma (p. 92), the charming seaside district of Barranco is still one of the highlights of Lima. Its serenity and laid-back artiness is a welcome contrast to the untidy and seedy character of the rest of the city, and a stroll around the tranquil side streets of brightly colored bungalows is the best way to restore your sanity. It's little wonder that artists and writers have long been drawn to Barranco. Beneath the poetically named wooden footbridge Puente de los Suspiros (Bridge of Sighs) is a gentle passageway, La Bajada de Baños, which leads to a sea lookout and is lined with lovely, squat single-family houses, spindly trees, and stout cacti. During the daytime, the barrio is mellow and tropical-feeling, with sultry breezes coming in from the sea, but at night the area is transformed into Lima's hedonistic hot spot, with locals and visitors flocking to the discos and watering holes here—much to the dismay of local residents who don't own a bar or restaurant.

Fundación Museo Amano 🎁 MUSEUM   This nicely designed museum features a collection of artifacts belonging to a single collector, representing some of Peru's most important civilizations, including the Chimú and the Nasca. The textiles and ceramics are among the best displayed in Lima, and the collection really shows the strength of Chancay weaving (a culture from the northern coast), which you might not see a whole lot of elsewhere. You really have to want to see the collection, though (and qualify, as restrictive as that sounds); it's open for limited hours and only by previous appointment to small groups. Allow about an hour or more.

Calle Retiro 160, Miraflores. www.fundacionmuseoamano.org.pe. ✆ **01/441-2909.** Free admission (donations encouraged). Mon–Fri 3–5pm by appointment (guided tour in Spanish). Take a taxi to the 11th block of Av. Angamos Oeste/Av. Santa Cruz.

Museo de Arte de Lima (MALI) ★ MUSEUM   Just south of Lima Centro's colonial core and Plaza San Agustín, in Parque de Lima, this newly refurbished museum in the handsome 19th-century Palacio de Exposiciones is now well worth a visit. It holds the country's finest collection of contemporary Peruvian art, fine colonial and republican-era art and furnishings, and pre-Columbian textiles and ceramics.

Paseo Colón 125. www.mali.pe. ✆ **01/204-0000.** Admission S/12 adults, S/4 students and seniors. Tues–Fri and Sun 10am–8pm, Sat 10am–5pm.

Museo de Arte Colonial Pedro de Osma ★★ MUSEUM   This private museum, located in a historic, ornate Barranco mansion (Palacio de Osma), focuses on colonial Peruvian art from areas that were among the most distinguished cultural centers of the day, including Cusco, Arequipa, and Ayacucho. The house is extraordinary, and the collection of religious art, including polychrome sculptures, *retablos* (altarpieces), and paintings from the Cusco school, is exceptional for a small, private museum. Out back, across the gardens, is a separate building with a collection of 16th- to 19th-century silver. Plan on spending an hour here.

Pedro de Osma 421, Barranco. www.museopedrodeosma.org. ©**01/467-0141.** Admission S/20 adults, S/10 students (guided tours in Spanish and English, included in admission). Tues–Sun 10am–6pm. By colectivo from Av. Tacna to Barranco.

Organized Tours

Lima is a large, sprawling, and confusing city, so if you want to make quick work of a visit, an organized tour of the major sights might be the best option. Standard city tours are offered by innumerable agencies. Among the most dependable is **Lima Tours,** Belén 1040 (www.limatours.com.pe; © **01/619-6900**), which is the only organized tour with access to the Casa Aliaga, one of the most historic colonial mansions in Lima. A standard half-day tour of Lima Centro costs S/75. Lima Tours also offers visits to Pachacámac as part of its "Lima Arqueológica" tours, as well as highlights packages across Peru.

Peruvision, Jr. Chiclayo 444, Miraflores (www.peruvision.com; © 01/447-7710), offers daylong sightseeing tours of Lima, including a choice of excursions for S/250, as well as 2-hour tours for S/70. **Contacto Lima** (contactolima@tsi.com.pe; © 01/224-3854) offers half-day city tours of "colonial and modern Lima," full-day tours, museum tours, and trail riding on Peruvian pacing horses, as well as tours to Nasca and Paracas, south of Lima. **Fertur Perú ★,** Jr. Junín 211 (www.fertur-travel.com; © 01/427-2626), with an office in the Hotel España (and a branch at Calle Schell 485 in Miraflores), is a highly professional outfit, run by a Peruvian-American couple, with reasonably priced city tours and 4-day packages to sights across Peru. **Class Adventure Travel (CAT) ★,** Grimaldo del Solar 463, Miraflores (www.cattravel.com; © 01/444-2220), is an excellent all-purpose agency run by a knowledgeable and friendly Dutch couple; it offers a 3-day city tour and travel arrangements around Peru.

Free short **walking tours** of Lima are frequently offered by the Municipalidad de Lima (Town Hall). For the latest schedule, call © **01/427-4848** or **01/427-6080,** ext. 222.

Mirabus (www.mirabusperu.com; © **01/476-4213**) is a double-decker bus that leaves from Parque Kennedy and offers several tours, from Lima Centro to a night tour and even a dinner buffet tour and visits outside of town to Pachacámac and Puerto del Callo. Tours range from S/8 for a downtown colonial tour to S/150 for the dinner bus. Although it sounds a bit uncomfortably close to those stag or bachelorette bus parties where everyone drinks his or her way across town, **El Bus Parrandero,** Av. Benavides 330, Of. 101, Miraflores (www.elbusparrandero.com;

 Me Ama, No Me Ama, Me Ama . . .

A curious park along the ocean at the edge of Miraflores, much beloved by Limeños looking to score, is the **Parque del Amor** (literally, "Love Park"), designed by the Peruvian artist Victor Delfín with a nod to Antoni Gaudí's Parque Güell in Barcelona, Spain. It features good views of the sea (when it's not shrouded in heavy fog), benches swathed in broken-tile mosaics, and, most amusingly, a giant, rather grotesque statue of a couple making out—which is pretty much what everyone does nearby. Benches are inscribed with sentimental murmurs of love, such as *vuelve mi palomita.* If it's Valentines Day, stand back.

ARCHAEOLOGICAL sites IN LIMA ★

Lima is hardly the epicenter of pre-Columbian Peru, and few visitors have more than the museums featuring ancient Peruvian cultures on their minds when they hit the capital. Surprisingly, there are a handful of *huacas*—adobe pyramids—that date to around A.D. 500 and earlier interspersed among the modern constructions of the city. The archaeological sites are junior examples of those found in northern Peru, near Chiclayo and Trujillo. If you're not headed north, Lima's huacas, which have small museums attached, are worth a visit.

In San Isidro is **Huaca Huallamarca** (also called Pan de Azúcar, or "Sugar Loaf"), at the corner of Avenida Nicolás de Rivera and Avenida El Rosario. The perhaps overzealously restored adobe temple of the Maranga Lima culture has several platforms and is frequently illuminated for special presentations. It's open Tuesday through Sunday from 9am to 5pm; admission is S/5 for adults and S/3 for students. Also in San Isidro is the **Huaca Juliana,** a pre-Inca mound dating to A.D. 400. It's at Calle Belén at Pezet and keeps the same hours as Huallamarca; admission is free. **Huaca Pucllana ★★** is a sacred pyramid, built during the 4th century and still undergoing excavation, in Miraflores at the corner of calles General Borgoño (Block 8) and Tarapacá, near Avenida Arequipa (http://pucllana.perucultural.org.pe; ✆ **01/445-8695**). It has a small park, a terrific restaurant (p. 100), and an *artesanía* gallery. From the pyramid's top, you can see the roofs of this busy residential and business district. It's open Wednesday through Monday from 9am to 4pm; admission is S/7 and S/3 for students.

Unfortunately, a few of these sites occasionally do not keep consistent hours, so you might find yourself staring through a chain-link fence if there's no one on hand to let you in.

✆ **01/445-4755**), is a colorful party bus promoting gregarious evening tours of Lima, with unlimited drinks, snacks, and live music. Tours are given Monday through Saturday from 8 to 11pm, departing from Larcomar shopping mall; the party ride costs S/90. Perfect if you've got your heart set on reliving (or continuing) your college days while you're in Lima.

Outdoor Activities & Spectator Sports

BEACHES   Although Lima is perched on the Pacific coast, Río de Janeiro it's not. Still, several beaches in Miraflores and Barranco are frequented by locals, especially surfers, in the summer months. The beaches are unfit for swimming, however: The waters are heavily polluted and plagued by very strong currents. Worse, they're stalking grounds for thieves. Although the beaches aren't that appealing in and of themselves, they might serve those with an interest in people-watching: The sands are very much frequented by Limeños in the summer (Dec–Mar). Much nicer and cleaner beaches are located immediately south of Lima (see "Side Trips from Lima," later).

BICYCLING & JOGGING   Given Lima's chaotic traffic, jogging is best confined to parks. Probably the best area is the bicycling and jogging paths along the *malecón* in Miraflores, near the Marriott and Miraflores Park hotels. Contact the **Club de Bicicleta de Montaña (Mountain Bike Club),** Calle César Ortega s/n (✆ **01/872-4021**), which has information about routes near Lima and places to rent mountain bikes.

BULLFIGHTING Bullfighting, less of a national craze here than in Spain or Mexico, is held in July and in the main season from October to December at the 18th-century **Plaza de Acho,** Jr. Hualgayoc 332, in Rímac (✆ **01/315-5000** or **01/481-1467**), the third-oldest ring in the world. Events are held Sunday afternoon. The *fiestas taurinas* bring matadors from Spain and take place at the same time as the Señor de los Milagros in October. Tickets, which range from about S/60 to S/300 for a single event (depending on whether seats are in the shade), can be obtained at the box office at the bullring. They can also be purchased at **Farmacia Deza,** Av. Conquistadores 1140, San Isidro (✆ **01/440-3798**), or by phone from **Teleticket** (✆ **01/242-2823**). Inquire about advance tickets by sending an e-mail to plazadeacho@peru.com.

GOLF Golf courses in Lima aren't open to nonmembers. Your best bet for golf is to stay at one of the exclusive hotels with golf privileges at the elite Lima Golf Club in San Isidro: **Country Club Lima Hotel** (p. 119) and **Sonesta Hotel El Olívar Lima** (p. 122).

PARAGLIDING A sport that has quite literally taken off in Lima is paragliding (*parapente*). Look along the cliffs of the Costa Verde in Miraflores and points south and on propitious days, you're likely to spot a paraglider soaring high above (as high as 200 to 500m above ground). No experience is required; novices can team up for a tandem ride with an instructor for a good introduction to the thrill of motorless soaring. Companies to contact include: **Aeroextreme Paragliding School** (www. aeroxtreme.com); **Fly Adventure** (www.flyadventure.net); and **PeruFly** (www.peru fly.com). Most flights meet in Parque del Amor in Miraflores and take off from a small *parapuerto* (little more than a small piece of park grass) just north.

PERUVIAN PACING HORSES Peruvian Paso horses (*caballos de paso),* which have a unique four-beat lateral gait, are considered by many to be the world's smoothest riding horse and also one of the showiest of all horse breeds. If you're already a fan of the breed, or just a fan of horses in general, seeing them on their home turf could be exciting. There are *concursos* (show events) scheduled at different times of the year; there's a big one in April (free admission). Information about exhibitions is available from the **Asociación Nacional de Caballos Peruanos de Paso,** Bellavista 549, Miraflores (✆ **01/444-6920** or **01/447-6331**).

SOCCER Important league and national *fútbol* (soccer) matches are held at the venerable 50-year-old **Estadio Nacional,** Paseo de la República, Blocks 7–9, located just 5 minutes from the city center. Popular teams include Alianza Lima, Alianza Atlético, Universitario (known as "La U"), and Sporting Cristal. Tickets (S/10–S/75) for most matches can be purchased the same day at the stadium or from **Teleticket** (✆ **01/242-2823**).

SURFING Although several beaches in Miraflores and Barranco are popular with surfers in summer and are fine for beginners, the best beaches in southern Peru— Punta Hermosa, Punta Rocas (highly recommended), Cerro Azul, and Pico Alto (which is supposed to have the biggest waves)—are beyond Lima. Surfing in southern Peru is best from April through December (and at its peak in May); surfers who hit the waves year-round usually do it in wet suits. Check out **www.wannasurf.com/ spot/South_America/Peru/Lima** for specialist information, including a chart of southern beaches that specifies skill level and breaks. Information, equipment, boards (for sale only), and accessories are available at **O'Neills,** Av. Santa Cruz 851,

Miraflores (📞 **01/242-4486**); and **Focus,** Leonardo DaVinci 208, San Borja (📞 **01/ 475-8459**).

Especially for Kids

At first glance, busy Lima may not seem like the most kid-friendly city. The best breaks from sightseeing are the **Circuito Mágico del Agua** (p. 89), a waterpark with colored fountains and a nightly light show; and the **Miraflores malecón,** or boulevard (p. 81), where you're likely to spot paragliders taking off for tandem flights above the coastline. Older kids might enjoy some of Lima's more offbeat attractions, such as the ancient (4th century A.D.) adobe pyramid **Huaca Pucllana** (p. 94); **Museo Arqueológico Rafael Larco Herrera** (p. 89), the world's greatest collection of pre-Columbian ceramics (though you might wish to exercise discretion when faced with showing the children the Sala Erótica's explicit forms); and the catacombs at **Convento de San Francisco** (p. 87), with neat stacks of thousands of human bones that kids will either find creepy or cool, or perhaps both. For those enamored of horses, check out the **Peruvian Paso horses** (p. 95) and shows of this unique, prancing breed (information from **Asociación Nacional de Caballos Peruanos de Paso).** If the city becomes overwhelming, do as many Limeños do and head to the more easygoing seaside districts **Barranco** and **Chorrillos** (p. 92).

WHERE TO EAT

Lima is the most cosmopolitan dining city in all of Peru, and perhaps the greatest food city in South America, with restaurants of all budgets and a wide range of cuisines—from upscale seafood restaurants and *comida criolla* (coastal Peruvian cooking), to Chinese and plenty of Italian, French, and other international restaurants. Lima is also the top spot in the country to sample truly creative gastronomy, as well as the dish Peru is perhaps best known for: ceviche. Although there are more restaurants classified as "very expensive" than anywhere else in Peru, diners coming from North American and European capitals should recognize that while not inexpensive, Lima's top restaurants are the equal of many top dining capitals and comparatively much less expensive than high-end restaurants in New York, London, Paris, or Rome.

Sometimes entire streets and neighborhoods specialize in a single type of food. In Lima Centro, you can visit the *chifas* of Chinatown, and in Miraflores, a pedestrian street off Parque Central (Boulevard San Remo) is referred to as "Little Italy" for its scores of lookalike pizzerias and Italian restaurants, which draw scores of tourists looking for cheap eats and plentiful beer. Museum goers-slash-foodies can kill two birds with one stone at the Museo Arqueológico Rafael Larco Herrera, which now features a handsome restaurant, **Café del Museo** (p. 90), with a menu by Gastón Acurio, the celebrated chef and man behind the restaurants Astrid y Gastón, Cebichería La Mar, and T'anta.

Restaurants here, predictably, are most crowded in the early evening, especially Thursday through Saturday. In the business districts of Miraflores and San Isidro, lunch can also get quite busy—at least in the nicer restaurants that are popular with local and international businessmen. To locate restaurants in Lima Centro, Miraflores, and San Isidro, see the maps "Lima Centro Hotels & Restaurants" (p. 115), "Miraflores Hotels & Restaurants" (p. 117), and "San Isidro Hotels & Restaurants" (p. 121).

Lima Centro

MODERATE

El Fayke Piurano ★ 📷 ✔ CEVICHE/SEAFOOD If you tire of all the hip, upscale takes on traditional *cevicherías* in Lima, check out this local favorite, a very simple and small but colorful place with vibrant paintings on the walls. It's the best *cevichería* in Lima Centro, known among insiders for ceviche, *tiradito,* and *arroz con mariscos* (seafood rice), frequently seasoned with a healthy amount of *ají* (hot peppers). Portions are big—I mean massive—and prices are quite a bit lower than what you'll find in Miraflores, San Isidro, and Barranco, and you're unlikely to be sitting next to someone from your hometown.

Jr. Huancavelica 165. www.cevicheria-faykepiurano.com. ✆ **01/428-6697.** Reservations recommended. Main courses S/18–S/36. AE, DC, MC, V. Daily 10am–6pm.

El Rincón Que No Conoces ★★ 📷 ✔ CREOLE/PERUVIAN Although stuck in a bit of a no-man's land—at the edge of Lima Centro—this authentic, amiable, old-school Peruvian *criollo* restaurant, helmed by Teresa Izquierdo Gonzáles, a 70-something institution of a chef, is worth the trek. Doña Teresa has been cooking here for 3 decades, and her neighborhood eatery may have gotten a little more polished and popular (it's even welcomed Food Network's Rachel Ray through its doors), but it hasn't deviated from its mission: classic Creole cooking. A good place to start is with a *causa* (a yellow potato torta stuffed with chicken, shrimp, or tuna), or perhaps a *palta rellena* (stuffed avocado). A similarly classic main dish is the *tacu-tacu* (rice and beans) with *asado a la tira* (short ribs). The menu is long, portions are large, and you can hardly take a wrong turn. To sample a variety of Creole cooking, check out Wednesday's great-value, all-you-can-eat buffet (including pisco sour) for S/40. With a name like "The Corner Joint You've Never Heard of," one might expect this to be a modest little hut with no sign out front. Instead, it's a cozy two-story restaurant with high ceilings and a warm atmosphere—reflective of the woman in the kitchen.

Bernardo Alcedo 363, alt. cuadra 20 de Petit Thouars, Lince. www.elrinconquenoconoces.pe. ✆ **01/471-2171.** Reservations recommended. Main courses S/20–S/35. No credit cards. Tues–Sun noon–5pm and 7:30pm–midnight.

El 550 Barra Peruana ★★ 📷 PERUVIAN This chef-driven outpost is a true find for good eats when visiting Lima's colonial center. The chef-owner, Israel Laura, studied in Barcelona and takes pride in putting out an affordable menu of excellent Peruvian dishes in this homey but colorful and good-looking place, decorated with pop-art posters and fiery red walls. You might start off with the *salto de tigre,* slices of fresh fish in *leche de tigre,* accompanied by yucca chips, or the terrific ceviche 550. Main courses are evenly divided between fish and meat. Laura's shellfish risotto (or paella chola) is excellent, as is the classic *seco a la norteña* (a lamb dish) and mixed grill that he calls *orgía a lo pobre* ("poor man's orgy"). If you're in the mood for a cocktail, the bar turns out some nice libations. The chef's newest restaurant in Miraflores (www.el550.com/miraflores; 550 Kriollo Gurmet, on Av. 2 de Mayo 385) is a more elaborate and more upscale take on Peruvian standards, but equally appealing.

Jr. Cañete 550. www.el550.com. ✆ **01/425-0706.** Reservations recommended. Main courses S/22–S/30. AE, DC, MC, V. Daily 11am–5pm and Thurs–Sat 7:30pm–midnight.

L'Eau Vive 📷 FRENCH/PERUVIAN If you're feeling obscenely rich in this developing country, you'll do a tiny bit of good and feel better by eating here. Run by

Chinatown (Barrio Chino), southeast of the Plaza de Armas and next to the Mercado Central (beyond the Chinese arch on Jirón Ucayali), is a good place to sample the Peruvian take on Chinese food. These *chifas*, inexpensive restaurants with similar menus, are everywhere in the small but dense neighborhood. Among those worth visiting (generally open daily 9am–10pm or later) are **Wa Lok ★★**, Jr. Paruro 864 (*©* **01/427-2750**), probably the best known in the neighborhood; and **Salón China**, Jr. Ucayali 727 (*©* **01/428-8350**), which serves a good lunch buffet for S/30.

a French order of nuns, the restaurant donates proceeds to charity. In a colonial palace 2 blocks from the Plaza de Armas, it features several large dining rooms with high ceilings. If you come for the cheap lunch *menú,* though, you'll have to sit in the simpler front rooms. The "a la carte" dining rooms are considerably more elegant. The lunch menu is a deal, and at night you get a pious show free with dinner: The nuns sing "Ave Maria" promptly at 9:30pm. The French menu includes items such as prawn bisque, trout baked in cognac, and grilled meats; it also incorporates some international dishes from around the globe—chiefly, the many countries from which the order's nuns come. The restaurant's heyday was clearly a few years ago, but this is still an old favorite you can feel good about patronizing, even if it's not the finest meal you can have in Lima.

Ucayali 370. *©* **01/427-5612.** Reservations recommended on Fri–Sat nights. Main courses S/12– S/45. AE, MC, V. Mon–Sat 12:30–3pm and 7:30–9:30pm.

Los Escribanos PERUVIAN   On one of Lima Centro's more appealing streets, a tiny pedestrian passageway near the Plaza de Armas, this unassumingly elegant two-story eatery has an attractive terrace with outdoor tables. Popular with local businessmen and travelers who trickle out of the tourism information office next door, it offers particularly good deals at lunch (with bargain *platos únicos* and a fixed-price menu that's served until 9pm). The evening menu lists plenty of *criollo* and seafood plates from the Peruvian coast, including gourmet dishes with pre-Columbian influences. At lunch, though, most people sit down to more standard fare, such as grilled trout and fettuccine Alfredo, served with a salad and beverage.

Pasaje Nicolás de Ribera El Viejo (Los Escribanos) 137–141. *©* **01/428-1005.** Reservations recommended on Fri–Sat nights. Main courses S/12–S/30. MC, V. Mon–Thurs 8am–9pm; Fri–Sat 8am–midnight.

INEXPENSIVE

Cocolat Café BISTRO   A good and quick spot for lunch or dinner is this simple little bistro on the popular pedestrian passageway, near the Plaza de Armas, that's lined with restaurants. It serves sandwiches, salads, and sides such as empanadas; the midday menu is a particularly good deal for an appetizer and main course. Top it off with a great selection of homemade chocolates and good coffee, and you might just want to linger for a while on the sidewalk terrace. It's also a good spot for breakfast.

Pasaje Nicolás de Ribera El Viejo (Los Escribanos) 121. *©* **01/427-4471.** Reservations not accepted. Main courses S/9–S/15. No credit cards. Mon–Sat 8am–6:30pm.

VERY EXPENSIVE

Astrid y Gastón ★★★ INTERNATIONAL/PERUVIAN   Hidden discreetly behind a nonchalant facade (though one of an antique colonial house), on a busy side street leading to Parque Kennedy, is this warm and chic modern colonial dining room and cozy bar. It continues to be among my favorite restaurants in Lima (and it's the only Peruvian restaurant on the list of the World's 50 Best Restaurants), even though it now has some high-end challengers. Gastón Acurio has been Peru's celebrity chef for at least a decade, with a burgeoning empire of fine-dining restaurants not only in Lima but also a handful of other cities in both North and South America and a cooking show on TV. His signature restaurant in the capital is warm and elegant, with high white peaked ceilings and orange walls decorated with colorful modern art. In back is an open kitchen and a secluded wine-salon dining room. The place is sophisticated and hip but also low-key. The menu might be called *criollo*-Mediterranean: Peruvian with a light touch. Try spicy roasted kid or the excellent fish called *noble robado*, served in miso sauce with crunchy oysters. The list of desserts—the work of Astrid, the other half of the husband–wife team—is nearly as long as the main course menu, and they are spectacular. Fans of Acurio should check out **La Mar Cebichería** (p. 100) and his latest Lima restaurant, **Panchita** (Av. Dos de Mayo 298, Miraflores; ℂ 01/447-8272), his take on traditional anticuchos, or kebabs.

Cantuarias 175, Miraflores. www.astridygaston.com. ℂ**01/242-4422.** Reservations required. Main courses S/38–S/79. AE, DC, MC, V. Mon–Sat 12:30–3:30pm and 7:30pm–midnight.

Brujas de Cachiche ★ CRIOLLO   The "Witches of Cachiche" celebrates 2,000 years of local culture with a menu that's a tour of the "magical" cuisines of pre-Columbian Peru. The chef even uses ancient recipes and ingredients. The extensive menu includes classic Peruvian dishes, such as *ají de gallina,* but concentrates on fresh fish and shellfish and fine cuts of meat with interesting twists and unusual accompaniments. Brujas de Cachiche sole is prepared with Asian and *criollo* spices, and served with peas and bell peppers sautéed in soybean sauce. A steak in pisco-butter sauce comes with braised mushrooms. Among the excellent desserts, several continue the indigenous theme, such as *mazamorra morada* (purple corn pudding and dried fruit). The restaurant, in a sprawling old house with several warmly decorated dining rooms, is popular both night and day with well-heeled Limeños, expat businessmen and foreign government officials, and tourists; it's exclusive and it's expensive, but it's worth the splurge. A lunch buffet is served Tuesday through Friday and Sunday from 11am to 4pm, and gastronomic festivals are frequent.

Jr. Bolognesi 460, Miraflores. www.brujasdecachiche.com.pe. ℂ**01/447-1883.** Reservations recommended. Main courses S/32–S/65. AE, DC, MC, V. Mon–Sat 1pm–midnight; Sun noon–5pm.

Fiesta Chiclayo Gourmet ★★ NORTHERN PERUVIAN   I'm sure few visitors probably know much, if anything, about the cuisine of Chiclayo, a city in northern Peru, but it's famous among Peruvians for its unique contributions to their nation's kitchen. And the name of the restaurant probably doesn't entice foreigners much, conjuring a Cancun bar with wet T-shirt contests, but this gourmet restaurant in rather laid-back digs for an upscale Miraflores restaurant serves some of the best hearty fare in the capital; in fact, it's the favorite restaurant of a Limeño friend who's quite the gourmand. The surroundings are pretty simple, even if the food is not. Try the charcoal-grilled ceviche, *tacu-tacu con medallones de mero* (rice and beans with medallions of grouper), or the Chiclayana specialties baby goat and *arroz con pato* (rice with duck). Be warned that this can be fairly heavy food; you may need a siesta after a visit to Fiesta.

Av. Reducto 1278, Miraflores. www.restaurantfiestagourmet.com. ℭ **01/242-9009.** Reservations recommended. Main courses S/39–S/65. AE, DC, MC, V. Daily 12:30–5pm and 8–11pm.

La Mar Cebichería ★★ CEVICHE/SEAFOOD   The restaurant everyone in Lima seems to be lining up to get in—no reservations are accepted, so get there early or sneak in late in the afternoon—is this upscale *cevichería,* courtesy of hot chef Gastón Acurio. Fashionable, stylishly designed, and moderately priced, it represents the best of traditional Limeño cooking, but with an edge. Some ceviche purists will tell you that you don't need to go to a hip, expensive spot for ceviche, and while it's true the most authentic ceviche spots are no-frills neighborhood joints, there's nothing wrong with jazzing up the formula in my book. The airy, plant-filled space has a chic, modern touch, with an angular, poured concrete facade, bamboo roof, turquoise chairs, and cement floors. The fish—choose from a couple of dozen types of ceviche, as well as rice-based seafood dishes and whole fish—is always fresh and carefully prepared. The restaurant even features a cool cocktail bar with great pisco-based drinks, like the "Cholopolitan," that would surely be a hit late into the night were it to stay open. But owing to *cevichería* tradition, it's strictly a daytime affair.

Av. La Mar 770, Miraflores. www.lamarcebicheria.com. ℭ **01/421-3365.** Reservations not accepted. Main courses S/29–S/69. AE, DC, MC, V. Mon–Fri noon–5pm; Sat–Sun noon–5:30pm.

Restaurant Huaca Pucllana ★★ NOUVEAU PERUVIAN   Located in an unparalleled setting—within the compound of a 1,500-year-old adobe pyramid built by the original inhabitants of Lima—is one of the city's greatest dining surprises. This beautiful and serene upscale restaurant, with knockout views of the pyramid and secluded in the midst of Lima's chaotic jumble, makes for a remarkable night out. The low hump of adobe bricks and excavation walkways are illuminated at night, and diners can take a tour of the construction and digs after dinner. The restaurant is handsomely designed in a rustic colonial style; you can dine indoors or out, but the best spot is surely the covered terrace. The menu is creative Peruvian, with fusion touches spicing up classic *criollo* cooking. Excellent appetizers include *humitas verdes* (*tamales*) and *causitas pucllana* (balls of mashed potato with shrimp and avocado). Main courses are focused on meats, such as rack of lamb, but I had an excellent marinated grouper with an interesting Asian twist. Desserts are worth saving room for; the napoleon, with chocolate mousse and passion fruit sorbet between chocolate cookies, is heavenly.

General Borgoño, Block 8 (Huaca Pucllana), Miraflores. www.resthuacapucllana.com. ℭ **01/445-4042.** Reservations recommended. Main courses S/32–S/65. AE, DC, MC, V. Mon–Sat noon–4pm and 7:30pm–midnight; Sun 12:30–4pm.

Toshiro's ★★★ JAPANESE-PERUVIAN/SEAFOOD   A big reason behind the rise of Lima's incredible coastal cuisine is the influence of Japanese cooking. If you want to go to the very roots of that contribution, you might as well start at one of the first and still one of the best. Chef Toshiro Konishi came to Peru three decades ago, with Nobu, who went on to create a sushi empire stretching from New York to London, and let the interest in Japanese and Peruvian cooking catch up to him. The restaurant looks like a traditional sushi bar and is probably the finest place to sample authentic Japanese fusion (Nikkei) cuisine in Lima. The flavors and textures are extraordinary. Sushi fanatics should just sit at the bar and let the chefs lead the way. Japan may be famed for the quality of its fresh fish, but the Peruvian Atlantic can't be far behind.

Av. Conquistadores 450, San Isidro. www.toshiros.com. © **01/221-7243.** Reservations required. Main courses S/32–S/70. AE, DC, MC, V. Mon–Sat noon–3pm and 7–11pm.

EXPENSIVE

El Mercado ★★★ SEAFOOD/CRIOLLO   One of the hottest restaurants in town is this cool seafood grill by superstar/hipster chef Rafael Osterling (the man behind Rafael). With an indoor–outdoor, industrial-chic aesthetic and long bar backed up by a grill, it throbs with energy and delightful preparations from superb ceviches to delectable designer sandwiches. From the outside, it looks like some hip architect's small museum: two cubes rising above a sleek wood wall. Inside it's equal parts loft, garden, and raucous bar. Serving lunch only, it is positively mobbed daily— and doesn't take reservations, so come right when it opens, be prepared to wait, or grab a seat at the long bar (where you can watch everything being made and the wood grill in action; it's the best seat in the house). An inexpensive long might be a tasty combination of sandwiches with diverse ingredients and flavors, but the superb grilled ceviche and tiraditos are hard to resist. The long menu also features rice, pasta *chifa* (Peruvian Chinese), and Asian-inflected fish dishes. You may just have to return.

Hipólito Unánue 203, Miraflores. www.rafaelosterling.com. © **01/221-1322.** Reservations not accepted. Entrees S/22–S/55. AE, DC, MC, V. Tues–Sun 12:30–5pm.

Pescados Capitales ★★ CEVICHE/SEAFOOD   With an easygoing, hip style that's similar to Cebichería La Mar's, this upscale ceviche and seafood restaurant is popular with Lima's *gente bella* (beautiful people). The name is a sly riff on the phrase for "original sin" (*pescado*, or fish, being just one letter removed from *pecado*, or sin); the dishes have names like "ire," "envy," and "avarice," and the menu declares that a few larger dishes are for the "vain or gluttonous." The restaurant has a large open-air terrace where overflow crowds sip pisco sours and beers on weekend afternoons, and a big, airy, and busy dining room under a high bamboo and glass roof. A terrific starter is Lujuria Freudiana (grilled baby squid), while the ceviche capital is a yummy mix of sole, salmon, and tuna.

Av. La Mar 1370, Miraflores. www.pescadoscapitales.com. ©**01/421-8808.** Reservations recommended. Main courses S/28–S/52. AE, DC, MC, V. Daily 12:30–5pm and Mon–Sat 7–11pm.

MODERATE

Antico Ristorante Italiano di Porto Rotondo ★ ITALIAN   A pretty yellow colonial house with an inviting library-like club bar off to one side, Porto Rotondo is a sophisticated retreat in the midst of Miraflores's hustle and bustle. Inside you'll find deep red walls, black-and-white tile floors, and large mirrors. The menu focuses on classic and well-prepared Italian dishes: ravioli, risotto, gnocchi, and *osso buco,* as well as fresh fish. Some nights, there are many more people sitting at the bar than around the dining tables in the next room.

Recavarren 265, Miraflores. © **01/447-9575.** Reservations recommended. Main courses S/25–S/40. MC, V. Daily noon–4pm and 8pm–midnight.

Dánica ★★ ITALIAN/MEDITERRANEAN/PERUVIAN   This favorite of residents of San Isidro and Miraflores Limeños, by Vanessa Siragusa, a young female chef, is what might be called a gourmet neighborhood eatery. The interior is casual, looking more like a cozy bistro than a fine-dining destination, and though you can get Italian comfort food, Vanessa Siragusa also turns out some very creative and elaborate fusion dishes. If there's one dish (besides the scrumptious desserts) to highlight, it might be the stir-fried beef risotto, a cross between Peru's mainstay *lomo saltado* and Italian risotto (though the *raviolis de asado,* or roast meat ravioli with mustard sauce, comes in a close second). But in keeping with the neighborhood theme, it's one of the friendliest (not to mention, best-value) restaurants in town—there's little doubt why friends of mine return nearly every week to visit Dánica. Siragusa has opened a second location in Miraflores, Av. Armendariz 524 (✆ **01/ 445-8743**).

Av. Emilio Cavenecia 170, San Isidro. www.danica.pe. ✆ **01/421-1891.** Reservations recommended. Main courses S/22–S/40. AE, DC, MC, V. Mon–Sat 12:30pm–midnight; Sun 12:30–10pm.

Segundo Muelle ★ ☺ CEVICHE/SEAFOOD   At the top of most people's lists of favorite Peruvian dishes is ceviche, and you won't have trouble finding a *cevichería* anywhere along the coast. Often you have to choose between either upscale or down-and-dirty versions. This informal lunch-only place in Miraflores, across from the cheesy Parque del Amor and oceanfront *malecón,* is one of the most reasonable options in Lima for excellent fresh fish and ceviche plates without any fuss. Choose between a simple, almost cafeteria-style interior and an upstairs outdoor deck with sea views. If you're new to ceviche, you can't go wrong with the *mixto* (white fish, octopus, prawns, snails, scallops, and squid). A long list of other fish dishes is offered, including sole, salmon, and seafood pastas. Top off your meal with *chicha morada,* a purple corn beverage made with pineapple and lemon—it's sweet and delicious. Kids' plates are available for S/15. Another branch is in San Isidro at Av. Conquistadores 490.

Av. Carnaval y Moreyra 605, San Isidro. www.segundomuelle.com. ✆ **01/241-5040.** Reservations not accepted. Main courses S/20–S/40. MC, V. Daily noon–5pm.

Sophie Bistró ★★ 🍴 🍂 PERUVIAN BISTRO/TAPAS   This understated but handsome neighborhood joint is a welcome counterpoint to several of Lima's scenester restaurants. A casually elegant corner spot with real flair, it has banquettes, chandeliers, and a handsome long bar—perfect for a relaxed, lingering dinner. Start with an excellent cocktail and move on to a menu of fresh fish, a long list of tapas with interesting twists, and interpretations of iconic dishes from both north and south Peru. Dishes are Peruvian given an international spin. If it's a variety of flavors you crave, this is the perfect spot to assemble a dinner of tapas and appetizers and share. With high quality, excellent presentation, and cool surroundings, Sophie represents excellent QPR (quality/price ratio).

Cl. Juan Moore 176, Miraflores. www.sophiebistro.com. ✆ **01/628-1229.** Reservations recommended. Entrees S/16–S/39. AE, DC, MC, V. Daily noon–5pm and Mon–Sat 7–11pm.

T'anta ★★ ☺ CAFE/PERUVIAN   Like a Peruvian Dean & Deluca (an upscale deli/market in New York City), T'anta ("bread" in Quechua) serves delicious, casual eats in its cafe or prepared foods to go. It has a complete menu, with a full range of creative snack foods and small meals, including classic Peruvian dishes. From fresh salads and panini to Peruvian sandwiches called *sánguches* and homemade pastas and terrific desserts, this stylish but informal place, the brainchild of Astrid (the dessert wizard of Astrid y Gastón fame) hits the spot no matter what you're in the mood for, or when. It's very chic and modern, with poured concrete and an angled glass wall.

CEVICHERÍAS: EATING LIKE A PERUVIAN

You can't really go to Peru—especially Lima—without sitting down for an irresistibly fresh plate of ceviche (also written cebiche), the tantalizing plate of raw fish and shellfish that's marinated in lime or lemon juice and chili peppers and served with toasted corn, sweet potato, and raw onion. The citrus juices "cook" the fish, so it's not really raw the way sushi is. Plenty of restaurants of all stripes—from lowly neighborhood joints to snooty fine-dining spots popular with government bureaucrats and visiting businessmen—offer ceviche, but you really have to go to an authentic *cevichería* for the true experience. In addition to **Segundo Muelle** (p. 102) and **Canta Rana** (p. 105), another worth checking out is **Punta Sal,** Malecón Cisneros, block 3, at the corner of Trípoli in Miraflores (© **01/242-4524**), one of a small chain of informal *cevicherías* pretty similar to Segundo Muelle. Hip takes on the *cevichería* include Gastón Acurio's **La Mar Cebichería** (p. 100) and **Pescados Capitales** (p. 101). Peruvians view ceviche as a daytime dish, and most *cevicherías* aren't even open for dinner (the high acidity makes for difficult nighttime digestion for many); for the full experience, go at lunchtime and order a classic pisco sour to start, followed by *chicha morada* (or, if you're feeling kinky, a bottle of curiously neon-yellow Inka Cola).

With its full list of cool cocktails (such as the *maricucha* or *aguaymanto* sour), it's also a great spot for drinks. You may come for a coffee or a cocktail, but I guarantee that you'll end up at least having dessert. One dessert that had me coming back for more was the *tartita de maracuyá* (passion-fruit tart). There are now three other locations, including in Lima Centro on Pasaje Nicolás de Rivera del Viejo 142 and Pancho Fierro 115 in San Isidro.

Av. 28 de Julio 888, Miraflores. © **01/447-8377.** Reservations not accepted. Main courses S/19–S/44. AE, DC, MC, V. Daily 8am–midnight.

INEXPENSIVE

Café Café CAFE/COFFEE   A tried-and-true people-watching spot with a menu of 100-plus drinks and dozens of gourmet coffees, this agreeable two-story cafe, located just off the main park in Miraflores, is also ideal for a quick lunch or simple dinner. The predominantly young crowd drops by not only to meet up with friends and hang out at the outdoor tables, but also to sample inexpensive pizzas, salads, or one of the 26 sandwiches. For folks in need of a real meal, there are also larger plates, including a fish of the day. It's also a good spot to have a quick and inexpensive breakfast or a late-night snack after hitting bars. This spot is just one of several branches in town.

Mártir Olaya 250, Miraflores. © **01/445-1165.** Main courses S/12–S/34. AE, DC, MC, V. Sun–Thurs 8am–1am, Fri–Sat 8am–3am.

Barranco

To locate the following restaurants, see the "Lima at a Glance" map on p. 77.

VERY EXPENSIVE

Costa Verde SEAFOOD   Any time a restaurant in Peru lists its prices in dollars, you know it's not going to be cheap. Costa Verde, perched on a promontory jutting out into the ocean along the "green coast" south of Miraflores, is probably as expensive a meal as you'll have in Peru, but it's also good enough to draw a decent number of Limeños celebrating special occasions. It draws a bigger share of foreigners, as evidenced by the touristy little national flags the hostess places on everyone's table. The big-time seafood buffet is what makes everyone's eyes bulge. There's a daily lunch buffet and also a huge gourmet dinner buffet ($60 a head), which the restaurant claims is registered in the *Guinness Book of Records*. The regular menu seems not to have changed in more than 3 decades of business, but you can't really argue with sea bass with wild mushrooms and morel sauce with scallop mousse, or basil and ricotta gnocchi with river shrimp in saffron sauce. Sit in the glass-enclosed atrium—although it's rather devoid of character, you'll get to hear the sound of waves crashing against the shore. Then again, that could be the sound of your bank account groaning.

Circuito de Playas (Playa Barranquito), Barranco. ℅ **01/227-1244.** Reservations recommended. Main courses $15–$40. AE, DC, MC, V. Daily noon–11pm.

EXPENSIVE

Amoramar ★★ SEAFOOD/CRIOLLO   Fashionable and deserving of the hype, this hip and modern open-air spot in the delightful backyard of a 1900 Barranco mansion (home to an art gallery) looks something like an upscale Scandinavian biergarten. It's sleek, stylish, and very popular with Lima's beautiful people (and family gatherings for lunch on Saturdays and Sundays). Two restaurateurs with big success at other well-regarded Lima restaurants, La Gloria and Pescados Capitales (p. 101), joined forces to create this Barranco favorite. The classic coastal seafood dishes, some with creative twists, are—along with the setting—the big draw. Standout items include the *pasta negra a lo macho* (black squid pasta), ceviches, and *arroces* (rice dishes). But the menu also features dishes not seen on every upscale seafood restaurant, including many with Asian and Mediterranean twists. Two dishes my wife and I recently tried, *tacu tacu al pesto con salmón* (pesto-*criollo* rice and beans with salmon) and *arroz con pato crujiente* (rice with crispy duck) were both very tasty.

García y García 175. www.amoramar.com. ℅**01/651-1111.** Main courses S/27–S/59. AE, DC, MC, V. Mon–Sat noon–3:30pm and 7:30–midnight; Sun noon–6pm.

Chala ★ FUSION/PERUVIAN   This sleek restaurant and lounge down by the "bridge of sighs" in Barranco was one of my new faves in Lima a couple of years ago; although it now has a new chef and might not be the revelation it once was, it's still very good. The restaurant serves imaginative fare it calls *"costa fusion,"* meaning adaptations of Peruvian coastal and Limeño dishes with Mediterranean and Asian influences. While the chic, colorful interior is coolly international, the gorgeous long deck outdoors, under an old wooden ceiling, tall trees, and squawking birds, has a great tropical, and sexy, feel. Start by sipping a *maracuyá* (passion-fruit) sour and munching on banana chips, before moving on to an extremely fresh salad with mushrooms, avocado, and tomatoes. A tasty entree, identified by the esoteric name "Oleaje Espirituoso," is a terrific dish of grouper served on a bed of zucchini gnocchi and a crème of *huacatay* (a local herb).

Bajada de Baños 343, Barranco. www.chala.com.pe. ℅ **01/252-8515.** Reservations recommended. Main courses S/28–S/55. AE, DC, MC, V. Mon–Sat noon–4pm and 7pm–midnight; Sun noon–4pm.

MODERATE

Antica Trattoria ★ 🍴 ☺ ITALIAN   This charming and laid-back Italian restaurant perfectly suits the surrounding neighborhood, which has large doses of both qualities. It has a number of small, separate dining rooms decorated with a warm, rustic and minimalist masculinity: stucco walls, dark wood-beamed ceilings, country-style wood tables, and simple, solid chairs. The house specialty is gourmet pizza from the wood-fired ovens, but the menu has several tempting ideas to lure you away from pizza, such as homemade pastas and *osso buco,* or delicious *lomo fino a la tagliata* (beef buried under a mound of arugula). The relaxed environment makes this a great date place, as well as the perfect spot for dinner before stepping out to one of Barranco's live music or dance clubs.

San Martín 201, Barranco. ✆**01/247-5752.** Reservations recommended. Main courses S/19–S/42. AE, DC, MC, V. Daily noon–midnight.

Canta Rana ★ 🍴 CEVICHE/SEAFOOD   A relaxed and informal place (in local lingo, a huarique) that looks almost like the interior of a garage and is immensely popular with locals, "the Singing Frog" is the very definition of a neighborhood *cevichería.* You might not guess it from the outside, but it's one of the best spots in town for ceviche and fresh seafood in a classic coastal manner. The menu lists 15 types of sea bass, including one stuffed with langoustines, as well as infinite varieties of ceviche. The traditional ceviche (big enough for two) is served on a flat plate with heaps of purple onions, some *choclo* (maize), and a wedge of *camote* (sweet potato). The best way to wash it down is with a chilled pitcher of *chicha morada.* The shacklike interior is decorated with simple wood tables, and the walls are festooned with *fútbol* (soccer) paraphernalia. For a high dose of local color and excellent seafood, Canta Rana's a perfect lunch spot.

Génova 101, Barranco. ✆ **01/247-7274.** Reservations recommended. Main courses S/18–S/40. AE, MC, V. Tues–Sat 11am–11pm; Sun–Mon 11am–6pm.

La Pescadería ★★ ☺ CEVICHE/SEAFOOD   The latest entry in the upscale-*cevichería*-by-a-famous-chef category—for which the city seems to have an insatiable appetite—enters pretty much at the top. Rather than aiming to be a chic, new-school take on a traditional Limeño lunch-only eatery, this initiative by Pedro Miguel Schiaffino wears tradition on its sleeve. A fun conversion of a beautiful old house on Barranco's main drag, it's a lively family-and-friends joint: informal and not in the least intimidating, as some of Schiaffino's competition is. Parents with young kids make up a good part of the dining crowd. With high ceilings, gorgeous tile floors, and a busy bar and small foodstuffs shop, it feels classic (although, unlike a tradition-bound *cevichería,* it's open for dinner, too, except on Sundays). The menu isn't innovative, but the ceviches, tiraditos, causas, chupes, and other fresh seafood are excellent across the board, and prices are pretty accessible. The only item on the menu that might break the bank is the lobster.

Av. Grau 689, Barranco. www.lapescaderia.pe. ✆ **01/453-5855.** Reservations recommended. Main courses S/24–S/40 (lobster, S/90). AE, DC, MC, V. Mon–Sat noon–4pm and 8–11pm; Sun noon–6pm.

LA 73 ★★ 🍴 PERUVIAN FUSION   This welcoming neighborhood bistro is comfortable and relaxed, the kind of place you might drop by a couple of times a week if you lived in the 'hood, but it's more ambitious than that, as its full name, La 73 Paradero Gourmet, reveals. A hidden gem, it's a creative take on the unassuming corner restaurant and surprisingly stylish and hip, with subway tiles and pop-art posters. Salads, several of which have an Asian accent, such as the tuna tartare salad, are tasty starters, and the standard menu and daily chalkboard specials include a number of unusual preparations, such as the blue cheese quinoa with beef tenderloin. Everyone's favorite dessert is the churros con chocolate. LA 73 has quickly become a favorite of visitors as well as barrio regulars for after-work cocktails, lunches on the outdoor patio, and home-cooked favorites for dinner, and it's not hard to see why.

Av. El Sol Oeste 175. www.restaurantela73.com. ℂ **01/247-0780.** Main courses S/22–S/42. AE, DC, MC, V. Tues–Sat 11am–11pm; Sun–Mon 11am–6pm.

INEXPENSIVE

Café Tostado 🍴 HOME COOKING/PERUVIAN   It's hard to call this amazingly authentic little lunch (and early dinner, I suppose) spot a restaurant, even. It's something akin to a country eating club in the midst of the big city, an extraordinarily rustic dining hall that looks like the kind of place a bunch of Argentine gauchos would chow down after a long morning working the herds on the pampas. But it's popular with Limeños of all stripes, from laborers, retired guys, business folks in stylish suits, and hipsters, who gather at communal tables and choose one of two dishes on offer. There's no menu, just the daily dish. Tuesday, for example, is hearty pastas, such as tallarines with homemade pesto. The cook, Pepe, who's found every day stirring myriad pots and pans at the open kitchen in back, is best known for his rabbit a la orange (served only by advance order). No alcohol or beer is served; just sodas and water. For some visitors to Lima, this may be a stretch; others will be pleased to find something wholly unique and local in an increasingly homogenized world.

Nicolás de Pierola 232, Barranco. ℂ **01/247-7133.** Reservations recommended. Main courses S/10–S/25. No credit cards. Daily 11am–7pm.

SHOPPING

The Peruvian capital has the greatest variety of shopping in the country, from tiny boutiques to handicraft and antiques shops. Although shopping at markets in *sierra* villages and buying direct from artisans in the highlands or on the islands of Lake Titicaca are superior cultural experiences, don't discount the fact that, unless you ship the loot home, you'll most likely have to lug it back to Lima. In Lima, you can find traditional handicrafts from across Peru; prices are not usually that much higher, and the selection might be even better than in the regions where the items are made. One exception is fine alpaca goods, which are better purchased in the areas around Cusco, Titicaca, and Arequipa, both in terms of price and selection.

Miraflores is where most shoppers congregate, although there are also several outlets in Lima Centro and elsewhere in the city, although Barranco is growing as a shopping destination. Most shops are open daily from 9:30am to 12:30pm and 3 to 8pm.

Antiques & Jewelry

Look for silver jewelry and antiques along Avenida La Paz in Miraflores. In particular, there's a little pedestrian-only passageway at Av. La Paz 646 that's lined with well-stocked antiques shops, many with nice religious art, including **La Línea del Tiempo ★** (ℂ **01/241-5461**) and **SAS Antiquedades** (ℂ **01/241-1092**). Other Miraflores antiques shops include **El Almacén de Arte,** Francia 339 (ℂ **01/445-6264**), and **Porta 735,** Porta 735 (ℂ **01/447-6158**). A shop I particularly like is **La Casa Azul ★**, Alfonso Ugarte 150 (ℂ **01/446-6380**), which specializes in colonial furniture, religious art, and other fantastic decorative pieces. The friendly owners can help arrange shipping and assist with getting export approval for especially valuable pieces.

Ilaria ★★, Av. Larco 1325, Miraflores (www.ilariainternational.com; ☎ **01/444-2347**) is the granddaddy of Peruvian jewelry stores; with 24 shops across the country, it's tops in terms of design in elegant silver art objects, jewelry, and decorative items. Many designs are based on traditional, antique Peruvian designs. Additional *platerías* and *joyerías* (silver and jewelry shops) worth a visit are **El Tupo,** La Paz 553, Miraflores (☎ **01/444-1511**) and in downtown Lima, **Joyería Gold/Gems Perú,** Pasaje Santa Rosa 119 (☎ **01/426-7267**), which stocks Colombian emeralds and fashionable, inexpensive Italian steel jewelry. **Esther Ventura ★**, Malecón Almirante Grau 1157, Chorrillos (www.esterventura.com; ☎ **01/467-1180**), a creative local jewelry designer, has a studio on the boardwalk in Chorrillos, south along the coast from Barranco. Her fine silver jewelry is based on pre-Incan and original designs.

Handicrafts & Textiles

Miraflores is home to the lion's share of Lima's well-stocked shops, which overflow with handicrafts from around Peru, including weavings, ceramics, and silver. A terrific shop with carefully chosen, unique items of artisanship is **Killari ★★**, Alcanfores 699 (☎ **01/447-8684**). Several dozen large souvenir and handicrafts shops are clustered on and around Avenida Ricardo Palma (a good one is **Artesanías Miraflores,** no. 205) and Avenida Petit Thouars (try **Artesanía Expo Inti,** no. 5495). **Indigo ★**, Av. El Bosque no. 260, San Isidro (www.galeriaindigo.com.pe; ☎ **01/440-3099**) is one of Lima's top handicrafts and gift stores, with thoughtfully selected original designs from most regions across Peru. You'll find items here that you won't find in the big, multi-booth markets. **Kuntur Wasi ★★**, Ocharan 182, Miraflores (☎ **01/9809-2056**) is a beautiful shop run by the owners, seasoned collectors with a shop brimming with some of the highest-quality *arte* popular from around Peru. Handicrafts shops elsewhere in Miraflores include **Agua y Tierra,** Diez Canseco 298 (☎ **01/445-6980**), and **Silvania Prints,** Diez Canseco 378 (☎ **01/242-0667**).

For fine alpaca goods, head to **Kuna ★★**, Av. Larco 671, Miraflores (☎ **01/447-1623**), one of the most original and highest-quality purveyors of all things alpaca, with excellent contemporary designs for men and women. Other locations include Larcomar mall and the Larco Herrera museum. Other alpaca shops include **Alpaca Mon Repos ★**, Centro Comercial Camino Real (☎ **01/221-5331**); **Alpaca Peru,** Diez Canseco 315 (☎ **01/241-4175**); and **All Alpaca,** Av. Schell 375 (☎ **01/427-4704**).

For artisan furniture and decorative art objects skillfully handcrafted from wood, don't miss **Artesanos Don Bosco ★★★**, Av. San Martín 135 (www.artesanosdonbosco.com; ☎ **01/265-8480**), which recently opened a storefront/gallery in Barranco in a beautiful 19th-century casona. A nonprofit organization begun by an Italian priest in the Andes near Huaraz, in north-central Peru, these artisans (trained in poor, remote highlands communities) create extraordinary, unique pieces, with a tongue-and-groove technique and many with curved forms. Each piece is the work, start to finish, of a single artisan. The organization operates a charity promoting development efforts among indigenous communities throughout the Americas.

One of the largest shops, which stocks a huge range of Peruvian handicrafts from all over the country, is **Peru Artcrafts ★**, in the Larcomar shopping mall, Malecón de la Reserva 610 (☎ **01/446-5429**). Although it's considerably more expensive than other shops (all prices are in dollars), it's perhaps the best for last-minute and one-stop shopping. A giant *artesanía* market with dozens of stalls is the **Mercado**

Indio ★, Avenida Petit Thouars 5245 (at General Vidal), Miraflores. (In fact, almost all of Avenida Petit Thouars, from Ricardo Palma to Vidal, is lined with well-stocked handicrafts shops.) For most visitors to Lima, this is one-stop shopping for Peruvian handcrafts, arts, gifts, and souvenirs from around the country. Another good spot for handicrafts from around Peru, in Lima Centro, is the **Santo Domingo** *artesanía* **arcades,** across the street from the Santo Domingo convent on Conde de Superunda and Camaná.

In Barranco, the finest upscale purveyor of crafts and home furnishings is **Dédalo ★★★**, Saenz Peña 295 (✆ 01/477-0562). If you arrive here around mid-day and hungry, you'll be happy to find a little cafe out back in the garden, serving salads, sandwiches, and *tamales*. A superb selection of folk art and handcrafts from across Peru can be found at **Las Pallas ★★★**, Cajamarca 212 (✆ 01/477-4629); the owner, a British woman named Mari Solari, has been collecting Peruvian folk art for 3 decades and displays it all in several rooms of her fine Barranco house. For fine *retablos* and artisanship typical of Ayacucho (which produces some of Peru's most notable pieces), visit the **Museo-Galería Popular de Ayacucho,** Av. Pedro de Osma 116, Barranco (✆ 01/247-0599).

Markets & Malls

Lima Centro's crowded **Mercado Central (Central Market),** open daily from 8am to 5pm, is south of the Plaza Mayor, at the edge of Chinatown. You'll find just about everything there, but you should take your wits and leave your valuables at home. The **Feria Artesanal** (Artisans' Market, occasionally called the Mercado Indio, or Indian Market, but not to be confused with the Mercado Indio in Miraflores) has a wide variety of handicrafts of varying quality, but at lower prices than most tourist-oriented shops in Lima Centro or Miraflores (quality might also be a bit lower than at those shops). Haggling is a good idea. The large market is located at Avenida de la Marina (blocks 6–10) in Pueblo Libre and is open daily from noon to 8pm. Small handicrafts markets, open late to catch bar and post-dinner crowds, are situated in the main squares in both Miraflores and Barranco.

My favorite market in Lima is the fascinating and diverse **Mercado de Surquillo ★★** (Avenida Paseo de la Republica at Ricardo Palma, Miraflores/Surquillo), where Limeños and many of the top chefs in town go to get fresh produce, seafood, meats, and a wide array of kitchen implements. It's a terrific food-shopping and cultural experience.

The **Jockey Plaza Shopping Center** (✆ 01/437-4100) is a modern American-style shopping mall—the newest, biggest, and best in Lima—with department stores, restaurants, movie theaters, a supermarket, and some 200 exclusive shops. It's next to the Jockey Club of Peru at Hipódromo de Monterrico, at the intersection of Javier Prado and Avenida Panamericana Sur in Surco. It's open daily from 11am to 9pm. **Centro Comercial Larcomar ★★** (✆ 01/445-7776) in Miraflores along the *malecón* and Parque Salazar (near the Marriott hotel), is one of the swankest malls in Lima, with a slew of restaurants, movie theaters, and upscale shops overlooking the ocean. It's open daily from 10am to 8pm and is a weekend destination for many Limeños.

ENTERTAINMENT & NIGHTLIFE

Bars & Pubs

MIRAFLORES **Bar Huaringas ★★★**, Bolognesi 472 (www.brujasdecachiche. com.pe; ✆ 01/447-1133), the elegant upstairs at the restaurant Brujas de Cachiche (p. 99), is one of the top spots in the country for a pisco sour, the national cocktail. The list of piscos is impressive, and the mixologists pour perfect variations on pisco sours, beginning with a coca or maracuyá sour. **Scena ★**, Francisca de Paula 226 (www.scena.com.pe; ✆ 01/445-9688) is a sleek modern restaurant with a good wine selection and lively bar scene; DJs spin tunes here in the evenings. **Art Déco Lounge ★★**, Manuel Bonilla 227 (www.artdecolima.com; ✆ 01/242-3969), a handsome conversion of an older home in Miraflores, takes its colorful and detailed Deco interiors very seriously, as it does the menu of cocktails and nicely selected wine list. **La Esquina Winebar,** Berlín 920 (www.laesquina.com.pe; ✆ 01/242-2456) is a nice little wine bar/restaurant, in a city that has very few of them. There's a new second location in Barranco, at Jr. Centenario 165 (✆ 01/248-7387). **O'Murphy's Irish Pub,** Shell 627 (✆ 01/242-1212), is a long-time favorite drinking hole with a small menu of pub grub. Expect a pool table, darts, Guinness on tap, and Brits and Irishmen hoisting it. They also host live music on Thursday. **Son de Cuba,** Bulevar San Ramón 277 (✆ 01/445-1444), is on the pedestrian street called "Little Italy" by locals, but the club focuses on Caribbean rhythms and drinks Tuesday through Sunday.

BARRANCO The delightful area around the Puente de los Suspiros in Barranco has some of the coolest watering holes in Lima. My favorite is **Santos ★★**, Jr. Zepita 203 (✆ 01/247-4609), a hip joint with an inventive decor, easygoing vibe and slender balcony with views out to the ocean; the place is packed on weekend nights. Right across the bridge is the slick upscale bar and restaurant, **Picas ★**, Bajada de Baños 340 (www.picas.com.pe; ✆ 01/252-8095), serving great (if pricey) cocktails to a well-dressed crowd. Nearby, **La Posada del Mirador,** Pasaje La Ermita 104 (✆ 01/477-1120) occupies an old house overlooking the ocean, in a verdant setting with indoor and outdoor garden seating. **Posada del Angel,** Av. Pedro de Osma 164 (and 222; ✆ 01/247-0341), is a baroque cafe-bar with two locations on the same street and occasional live jazz and folk music. **Ayahuasca ★★,** Prolongación San Martín 130 (✆ 9810-44745), is one of Barranco's hottest—and biggest—nightspots, a stylish and usually packed bar in a stately colonial mansion with swank furnishings, art exhibits, and great cocktails, including an impressive array of pisco sours. For a real taste of old-school Peru, stop by the legendary **Bodega Juanito ★★**, Av. Grau 274 (✆ 01/994-96176), a former apothecary that sports a plain, if charmingly retro (aka Soviet Union) look, with fluorescent lighting, industrial fans, and walls littered with theater and film posters. There's a peculiar rule that men not accompanied by women have to retreat to the back room to down their pitchers of beer. Juanito's is a long-time hangout for Barranco's artists and intellectuals, who smoke, drink, and devour the fantastic, locally famous ham sandwiches. An old train car parked just off the main park is actually a cocktail bar; **Expreso Virgen de Guadalupe,** Av. Prolongación San Martín 15 (✆ 01/252-8907) is a charming 1920s *vagón* with gorgeous wood, stained-glass windows, and live piano music, specialty coffees, and cocktails. It's perfect if you're trying to escape some of the noisier joints in Barranco—like **Amnesia,** Bulevar

Sánchez Carrión 153, just off the municipal square (℡ 01/477-9577). It's open only Thursday through Saturday. **El Ekeko,** Av. Grau 266 (℡ 01/247-3148), once an atmospheric neighborhood bar with occasional live music, has become a rowdy sports bar full of *fútbol*-watching and beer-swilling patrons.

LIMA CENTRO   There are two good pubs downtown owned by the same folks. One is **Rincón Cervecero,** a German-style bier hall, at Jr. de la Unión 1045 (www.rincon cervecero.com.pe; ℡ 01/428-1422). The other, **Estadio Fútbol Club,** Av. Nicolás de Piérola 926 (www.estadio.com.pe; ℡ 01/428-8866), is strictly for *fútbol* fans: It's a three-level bar (and disco on weekends) that amounts to a museum of the sport, and with dozens of big-screen TVs, it can get pretty rowdy when a big Peruvian or international game is on. Just beyond Lima Centro, in Pueblo Libre, is **Antigua Taberna Queirolo ★,** Av. San Martín 1090 (at Av. Vivanco) (antiguatabernaqueirolo.com; ℡ 01/460-0441), a local institution. The atmospheric pisco bar and winery, with a long marble-topped bar, is one of the oldest in Peru, now into its second century. Taste one of the house piscos, accompanied by good snacks (*piqueos*) and more substantial Peruvian specialties such as *rocoto relleno* (stuffed hot pepper).

Live Music Clubs

MIRAFLORES   Satchmo ★, Av. La Paz 538 (℡ 01/444-4957), is a sophisticated joint with a variable roster of live bands, including jazz combos—as the name would indicate. It's a good date spot. Cover charges range from S/20 to S/50. Another great spot for live jazz (as well as bossa nova and Afro-Peruvian evenings) is **Jazz Zone ★★,** Av. La Paz 656, Pasaje El Suche (www.jazzzoneperu.com; ℡ 01/241-8139); covers from S/10 to S/35. **Crocodilo Verde ★,** Francisca de Paula 226 (www.crocodilo verde.com; ℡ 01/445-7583), has jazz on Wednesday and a variable program of live music on weekends, with cover charges ranging from S/10 to S/30.

BARRANCO   My vote for best live-music club in Lima is **La Noche ★★,** Bolognesi 307 (www.lanoche.com.pe; ℡ 01/477-1012). Despite its prosaic name, this sprawling multilevel club feels like a swank tree house, with a great stage and sound system and good bands every night that run the gamut of styles (although it's frequently jazz), plus a hip mixed Limeño and international crowd. Monday night jam sessions (no cover charge) are particularly good; otherwise, cover charges range from S/5 to S/40. There's also a La Noche outpost in Lima Centro, at the corner of Jirón Camaná and Jirón Quilca. **La Estación de Barranco ★,** Pedro de Osma 112 (www. laestaciondebarranco.com; ℡ 01/247-0344) is another nice place, housed in an old train station, with live music Tuesday through Saturday and a slightly more mature crowd (both locals and tourists); the music on tap is often *criolla*. The classic upstairs bar **La Taberna de Barranco ★,** Av. Grau 268 (no phone), schedules both live rock and pop for the youngsters (often early shows beginning at 9pm), and occasional peña and Afro-Peruvian shows late on weekends for a more sophisticated crowd. **Bar Mochileros ★,** Av. Pedro de Osma 135 (℡ 01/247-1225), is a cool pub that hops with exotic cocktails and young people spilling out into the courtyard; there's occasional live rock, from punk to electronica, on weekends.

Peñas

The classic Limeño night outing is a *peña*, a performance at a *criollo* music club that quite often inspires rousing vocal and dance participation. A visit to Lima really isn't complete until you've seen one.

MIRAFLORES **Caballero de Fina Estampa** ★, Av. del Ejército 800 (© **01/441-0552**), named for one of the most famous Peruvian songs of all time, is one of the city's chicest peñas, with a large colonial salon and balconies. The cover charge is S/50. **Sachún,** Av. del Ejército 657 (© **01/441-4465**), is favored by tourists and middle-class Limeños who aren't shy about participating with their feet and vocal cords. The cover charge ranges from S/25 to S/50.

BARRANCO **De Rompe y Raja** ★, Manuel Segura 127 (www.derompeyraja.pe; © **01/247-3271**), is a favorite of locals that's open Thursday to Saturday nights. Look for the popular Matices Negros, an Afro-Peruvian dance trio. The cover is usually around S/35. **Peña del Carajo!** ★, Calle Catalino Miranda 158 (www.delcarajo.com.pe; © **01/247-7023**), is another cool peña with good live music, percussion, and dance shows Tuesday through Saturday starting at 10pm. Covers range from S/20 to S/40. **La Candelaria,** Bolognesi 292 (www.lacandelariaperu.com; © **01/247-1314**), is a comfortable club celebrating Peruvian folklore. It's open Friday and Saturday from 9pm onward; the cover is normally S/30. **Don Porfirio** ★★, Manuel Segura 115 (© **01/477-3119**), is a bit more downscale than most peñas and preferred by locals, an amiable, hidden-away spot invites participation in its good-quality music-and-dance shows. Cover is generally S/20. **Las Guitarras,** Manuel Segura 295 (© **01/479-1874**), is where locals go to play an active part in their peña. A cool spot, it's open Friday and Saturday only, with no cover charge and no credit cards accepted.

LIMA CENTRO **Brisas del Titicaca** ★★★, Jr. Walkulski 168, the first block of Avenida Brasil, near Plaza Bolognesi (www.brisasdeltiticaca.com; © **01/332-1901**), is a cultural institution featuring *noches folclóricas*—indigenous music-and-dance shows—that are some of the finest in Lima. Shows are Tuesday and Wednesday at 8pm, Thursday at 9:15pm, and Friday and Saturday at 10:15pm. You can even catch a dance show with lunch, Friday and Saturday from noon to 6pm. Covers range from S/30 to S/70.

Dance Clubs

Many of Lima's discos are predominantly young and wild affairs. Cover charges range from S/15 to S/50. The main drags in Barranco, Avenida Grau and Pasaje Sánchez Carrión (a pedestrian alley off the main square), are lined with raucous clubs that go late into the evening and annoy Barranco residents. Two very chic and popular discotheques, **Gótica** ★★ (www.gotica.com.pe; © **01/445-6343**) and **Aura** ★★ (www.aura.com.pe; © **01/242-5516**) face each other in the Larcomar shopping center, Malecón de la Reserva 610, Miraflores and feature interconnected open-air terraces, great sea views and dance music ranging from electronica to the Latin specialty, *pachanga*. Also check out **Deja-Vu,** Av. Grau 294 (© **01/247-6989**); the decor is based on TV commercials, and "waitress shows" tease horny patrons. It's a dancefest from Monday to Saturday; the music trips from techno to trance. **Café Bar Kitsch,** Bolognesi 743, Barranco (© **01/242-3325**), is one of Lima's hottest bars—literally, sometimes it turns into a sweatbox—with over-the-top decor and recorded tunes that range from 1970s and 1980s pop to Latin and techno. The 2010 opening of **Crobar Lima** ★★, Playa Barranquito s/n, Barranco (www.crobar.com; no phone), the latest in the line of an international chain of high-energy nightclubs (others are in Buenos Aires, Beijing, Miami, and Chicago) with guest DJs and throbbing all-night dance tunes, was big news in Lima.

Theater & the Performing Arts

Lima's **Teatro Municipal,** the pride of the local performing-arts scene and the primary locale for theater, ballet, opera, and symphony performances, burned to the ground more than a decade ago. Since then, the National Symphony Orchestra and the National Ballet Company have performed at the **Museo de la Nación,** Avenida Javier Prado (✆ 01/476-9875). The 1940s-era **Teatro Segura,** Huancavelica 265 (✆ 01/426-7206) has picked up some of the slack for opera and music concerts. Frequent cultural events, including films and music recitals, are held every week at the **Centro Cultural Ricardo Palma,** Larco Herrera 770, Miraflores (✆ 01/446-3959), and the **British Council,** Calle Alberto Lynch 110, San Isidro (✆ 01/221-7552). The **Instituto Cultural Peruano Norteamericano,** at the corner of Angamos and Arequipa in Miraflores (✆ 01/446-0381), hosts theater, jazz, classical, and folk music. See the daily newspaper *El Comercio* (www.elcomercioperu.com.pe) for updated lists of live performing-arts events in Lima (in Spanish only).

Lima has a good theater scene, although, as one might expect, nearly all plays are in Spanish. Two of Lima's best theaters are **Teatro Canout,** Av. Petit Thouars 4550, Miraflores (✆ 01/422-5373), and **Teatro Auditorio Miraflores,** Av. Larco 1036, Miraflores (✆ 01/447-9378). Tickets are available at the box offices.

Gay & Lesbian

Although Peru as a whole remains fervently Catholic and many gay and lesbian Peruvians feel constricted in the expression of their lifestyle, Lima is the most progressive city in the country, with the most facilities and resources for gays and lesbians, including a significant number of nightclubs. Among the most popular are **Gitano 2050,** Berlín 231, Miraflores (no phone), probably the best-known gay disco in the city, with two cruising balconies overlooking the dance floor; **Downtown Vale Todo ★,** Pasaje los Pinos 160, Miraflores (✆ 01/444-6433), has closed down a couple of times but is again popular with go-go boys, and it puts on occasional shows with strippers; and **La Cueva,** Av. Aviación 2514, San Borja (✆ 01/224-3731), a lively disco with an eclectic soundtrack and large dance floor. A gay-oriented combination sauna/gym/bar/video lounge is **Baños Tivoli,** Av. Petit Thouars s/n, San Isidro (✆ 01/222-1705). All are generally open Wednesday through Saturday (Gitano 2050 and Sauna Tivoli are open Sun as well); cover charges range from S/15 to S/40. Visit **lima.queercity.info** for more information on gay Lima and gay Peru, including all the latest bars, discos, and saunas (bathhouses).

Cinema

Most foreign movies in Lima are shown in their original language with subtitles. Commercial movie houses worth checking out include **Multicines Larcomar,** Malecón de la Reserva 610, Miraflores (✆ 01/446-7336); **Multicines Starvisión El Pacífico,** Av. José Pardo 121, near the roundabout at Parque Central, Miraflores (✆ 01/445-6990); **Cinemark Perú Jockey Plaza,** Av. Javier Prado 4200 (✆ 01/435-9262). Art and classic films are shown at the **Filmoteca de Lima** in the Lima Museo de Arte, Paseo Colón 125, Lima Cercado (✆ 01/423-4732), and **El Cinematógrafo,** Pérez Roca 196, Barranco (✆ 01/477-1961). Most theaters in the suburbs cost more than the ones in Lima Centro, but they're more modern and better equipped. Several have matinee prices and discounts on Tuesday. For a list of films *subtituladas* (with subtitles), consult the Friday edition of *El Comercio*. The term *doblada* means "dubbed." Tickets run from S/12 to S/20.

Casinos

Peruvians are big on casinos, and many of the larger upscale hotels in Lima have casinos attached. Some of the better ones are the Stellaris Casino at the **JW Marriott Hotel** (p. 115); **Grand Hotel Miraflores,** Av. 28 de Julio 151, Miraflores (✆ 01/447-9641); **Country Club Lima Hotel** (p. 119); and **Sheraton Hotel & Casino,** Paseo de la República 170, Centro (✆ **01/433-3320**). Most casinos are open Monday through Thursday from 5pm to 2am, and Friday through Saturday from 5pm to 5am.

WHERE TO STAY

Lima Centro has a handful of hotels and budget inns, but most people head out to the residential neighborhoods of Miraflores and, to a growing extent, Barranco. San Isidro is the prime business district of Lima and full of hotels primarily, if not exclusively, designed for business travelers. These *barrios* (San Isidro in particular) have less in the way of official sights, but they are more convenient for dining, nightlife, and shopping, and probably safer, if not necessarily much quieter.

Hotel rates in Lima are the highest in the country, especially at the top end. There are plenty of midrange and budget choices, although comparatively few have the charm of affordable *hostales* in other cities. Particularly at the top echelon, hotels tack on taxes and service charges to quoted rates, whereas most moderate and less-expensive inns quote rates that already include all taxes and service charges. Be on the lookout for any hotel that tries to charge you the 19% IGV (sales tax) on the basic room rate in addition to a 10% service charge, though; foreigners and nonresidents with the passport to prove it are exempt from the IGV (but not the service charge). Most *hostales* in Lima—unlike in Cusco, Arequipa, and a few other highland towns—do feature 24-hour hot water.

Lima Centro
INEXPENSIVE

Hotel España ✔ Near the Convento de San Francisco and just 4 blocks from the Plaza de Armas, this extremely popular budget *hostal* has a funky flair and communal atmosphere. If you're looking to hook up with backpackers from around the globe and set off to explore Peru, you can't do better than Hotel España. It occupies a rambling colonial building chock-full of paintings, ceramics, faux Roman busts, plants, and even the occasional mummy. A maze of rooms, most with shared bathrooms and some with odd numbers, is located up a winding staircase. The rooms themselves are simple, with concrete floors but brightly colored walls; they're well-kept, but with cheesy bedspreads. The leafy rooftop garden terrace, with views of San Francisco, is a good place to hang out and trade travel tales. Security is said to be a little lax, so store your stuff in the lockers. Hot water goes to the early bird. The place can be noisy and even a little nuts, but that's part of its charm.

Azángaro 105, Lima. www.hotelespanaperu.com. ✆/fax **01/428-5546.** 30 units. $12 double without bathroom; $18 with bathroom. No credit cards. **Amenities:** Cafeteria. *In room:* No phone.

La Posada del Parque Hostal   Monica Moreno runs this safe and welcoming guesthouse, which occupies a lovely 1920s *casona* on what has to be one of the most peaceful streets near the center of Lima—it's a long cul-de-sac lined with gardens and other stately homes. Her house, in the Santa Beatriz district, is full of Peruvian popular art and offers unusual amenities at an economical rate, such as Internet access, satellite TV, and homemade pizzas and beer upon request. Monica is more than willing to help travelers with all their needs. The rooms are fairly mediocre though, it has to be said, and breakfast is pretty chintzy. Competition at the budget and midrange level is strong in other, better-equipped areas of the city (such as Barranco), for prices that aren't that much higher.

Parque Hernán Velarde 60, Santa Beatriz, Lima. www.incacountry.com/posadadelparque. ✆ **01/433-2412.** Fax 01/332-6927. 9 units. $45–$48 double. MC, V. Rates include continental breakfast. **Amenities:** Wi-Fi (in lobby, free). *In room:* TV, no phone.

Miraflores

VERY EXPENSIVE

Miraflores Park Hotel ★★★   The exceedingly elegant Miraflores Park Hotel, an Orient-Express property, bathes business executives and upscale tourists in unsurpassed luxury and excellent ocean views. It hugs the *malecón,* the park-lined avenue that traces the Lima coastline. From the cozy, library-like lobby and handsome restaurant to the elegant, plush rooms (including marble and granite bathrooms most New Yorkers would give their left arms to have), the hotel is a distinguished address from head to foot. All rooms are suites with comfortable king-size beds and sitting areas, and they're more European Old World than the stark contemporary style found in competitors like Casa Andina and the Westin. The rooftop pool isn't large, but it affords great coastal views. If you can opt for or upgrade to a room with ocean views, your stay will be greatly enhanced. Special promotional rates are often available online.

Av. Malecón de la Reserva 1035, Miraflores, Lima. www.mira-park.com. ✆ **01/610-4000.** Fax 01/242-3393. 81 units. $370–$720 deluxe double; from $795 and up suite. AE, DC, MC, V. **Amenities:** 2 restaurants; bar; cafe; concierge; exercise room; small outdoor rooftop pool; spa; squash court; smoke-free rooms; 24-hour room service. *In room:* A/C, TV/DVD, fridge, Wi-Fi ($15/day).

EXPENSIVE

Casa Andina Private Collection Miraflores ★★ ☺   Casa Andina, the continually growing Peruvian hotel chain, took over this high-rise hotel, which had been Lima's first five-star hotel but was then abandoned for a number of years, and completely gutted it, turning it into its showcase property. The result is a favorite of business travelers: It has all the amenities and services of the city's top luxury business hotels, but without the exorbitant prices of many of its competitors. But it's also great for leisure travelers and families, and is considerably less expensive than most big-city, five-star hotels. The well-designed accommodations are sleeker and more luxurious than at most of the group's other hotels, and many feature nice views over the city. The sleek, modern restaurant is quite good, and the spa and indoor heated swimming pool are excellent bonuses. Look online for discounts.

La Paz 463, Miraflores, Lima. www.casa-andina.com. ✆ **866/220-4434** toll-free in the U.S., **08/082-343-805** in the U.K., or **01/213-9739.** Fax 01/445-4775. 148 units. $319–$359 double; $419–$669 and up suite. Rates include breakfast buffet. AE, DC, MC, V. **Amenities:** 2 restaurants;

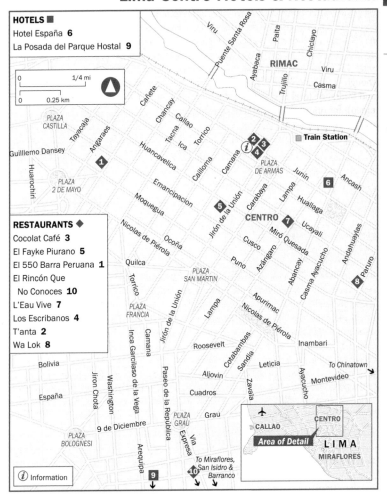

HOTELS ■
Hotel España **6**
La Posada del Parque Hostal **9**

0 | 1/4 mi
0 | 0.25 km

PLAZA CASTILLA
Guilllemo Dansey
PLAZA 2 DE MAYO
Huarochiri
Tayacaja
Angaraes
Cañete
Chancay
Callao
Tacna
Ica
Torrico
Huancavelica
Cailloma
Camana
Emancipacion
Moquegua
Jirón de la Unión
Nicolas de Piérola
Ocoña
Quilca
Torrico
PLAZA FRANCIA
Inca Garcilaso de la Vega
Washington
Camana
Jirón de la Unión
Paseo de la República
Bolivia
España
Jiron Chota
9 de Diciembre
PLAZA BOLOGNESI
Arequipa

Viru
Puente Santa Rosa
Paita
Chiclayo
Ayabaca
RIMAC
Viru
Trujillo
Casma

Junín
Ancash
■ **Train Station**
PLAZA DE ARMAS
Carabaya
Lampa
Huallaga
CENTRO
Cusco
Miró Quesada
Ucayali
Azángaro
Puno
Abancay
Casma Ayacucho
Andahuaylas
Paruro
PLAZA SAN MARTIN
Apurímac
Nicolas de Piérola
Lampa
Roosevelt
Cotabambas
Sandia
Leticia
Inambari
Aljovin
Zavala
Ayacucho
To Chinatown →
Montevideo
Cuadros
Grau
PLAZA GRAU
Via Expresa
✈ CALLAO
Area of Detail
CENTRO
L I M A
MIRAFLORES
To Miraflores, San Isidro & Barranco

🛈 Information

RESTAURANTS ◆
Cocolat Café **3**
El Fayke Piurano **5**
El 550 Barra Peruana **1**
El Rincón Que No Conoces **10**
L'Eau Vive **7**
Los Escribanos **4**
T'anta **2**
Wa Lok **8**

bar; concierge; gym; heated indoor swimming pool; spa; smoke-free rooms. *In room:* A/C, TV, fridge, Wi-Fi (free).

JW Marriott Hotel Lima ★ This upscale business traveler's hotel isn't as luxurious as the exclusive Swissôtel, but it's more affordable, making it a very good value given the overall quality and dependability of the Marriott chain. It's a gleaming, ultramodern 25-story high-rise building hugging the coast and parks along the *malecón,* replete with glitzy ground-floor shops and a much-frequented casino. It seems to serve mostly short- and long-term business travelers from North and South

America, but it's perfectly fine for leisure travelers and families. Children can be easily entertained at the outdoor pool or on the tennis court. Rooms are very well equipped and comfortable, with nice bathrooms, if without a whole lot of individual character. Inexpensive weekend rates are frequently available, making the Marriott one of the best high-end values in Lima.

Av. Malecón de la Reserva 615, Miraflores, Lima. www.marriott.com/hotels/travel/limdt-jw-marriott-hotel-lima. © **800/490-5816** in the U.S. and Canada, or **01/217-7000**. Fax 01/217-7100. 300 units. $320–$378 double; $448–$468 suite. AE, DC, MC, V. Valet parking. **Amenities:** 2 restaurants; cafe; concierge; health club; outdoor pool; sauna. *In room:* A/C, TV, fridge, hair dryer, Wi-Fi.

Sonesta Posada del Inca Miraflores   The Miraflores branch of a chain with a handful of hotels across Peru, this small hotel has an excellent location and is efficient and professionally run. Centrally located just 2 blocks from Parque Central (Parque Kennedy), it's within easy walking distance of Miraflores's many nightclubs, restaurants, and shops. The ocher-and-deep-green rooms are pretty basic and aren't huge, but they come with comfortable beds and good-size bathrooms.

Alcanfores 329, Miraflores, Lima. www.sonesta.com/miraflores. © **800/SONESTA (766-3782)** or **01/241-7688**. Fax 01/447-1164. 28 units. $263 double. Rates include breakfast buffet. AE, DC, MC, V. Free parking. **Amenities:** 24-hr. cafe and bar; concierge; fitness center (½ block from hotel); smoke-free rooms. *In room:* A/C, TV, fridge.

MODERATE

Casa Andina Classic Miraflores San Antonio ★ ♥   Well located, and well executed, like all Casa Andina properties, this midsize hotel—one of three the chain operates in the capital—has ample bedrooms that are cheerfully decorated, with brightly striped bedspreads and sunburned yellow walls. Marble bathrooms are large, and the breakfast buffet is a winner. Casa Andina is perfect for the traveler who seeks comfort, good value, and no unpleasant surprises. A second Casa Andina Classic is located nearby, at Av. Petit Thouars 5444.

Av. 28 de Julio 1088, Miraflores, Lima. www.casa-andina.com. © **866/220-4434** toll-free in the U.S., **08/082-343-805** in the U.K., or **01/213-9739**. Fax 01/445-4775. 49 units. $109–$129 double. Rates include breakfast buffet. AE, DC, MC, V. **Amenities:** Babysitting; concierge; room service; smoke-free rooms. *In room:* A/C, TV, fridge, Wi-Fi (free).

Casa Andina Select Miraflores ★★ ☺   Splitting the difference between its flagship Private Collection and more basic Classic hotels, this new (2012) addition to the Casa Andina portfolio, in the heart of Miraflores, is a midrange winner. The staff's attention to detail gets very high marks. Sophisticated, but just shy of being flat-out luxurious, the new 11-story construction features a spa, sun terrace, and ample, well-equipped and warmly decorated, contemporary rooms, with hardwood floors and black-and-white photographs of Peruvian scenes. Bedding is excellent. For both business and leisure travelers seeking excellent services, usually associated with a larger hotel, but easier-on-the-wallet prices than some big luxury hotels, this is an excellent choice.

Schell 452, Miraflores, Lima. www.casa-andina.com. © **866/220-4434** toll-free in the U.S., **08/082-343-805** in the U.K., or **01/213-9739**. Fax 01/445-4775. 155 units. $169–$199 double; $219 suite. Rates include breakfast buffet. AE, DC, MC, V. **Amenities:** Restaurant; bar; concierge; gym; heated swimming pool; spa; smoke-free rooms. *In room:* A/C, TV, fridge, Wi-Fi (free).

Hotel Antigua Miraflores ★ 🛄   This charming 1923 mansion, full of authentic Peruvian touches and color, calls itself "a hidden treasure in the heart of Miraflores." As many return visitors know, that's not just hype. The hotel, which just added 30

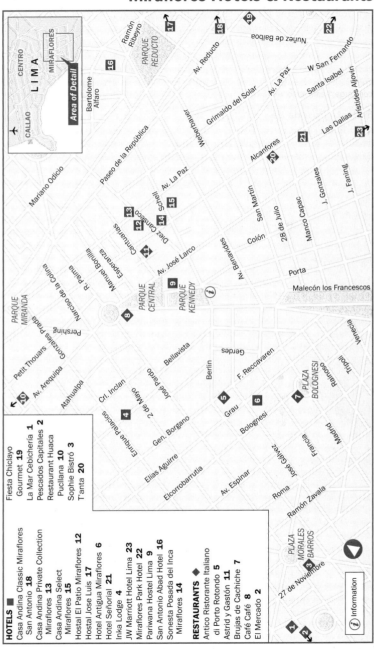

HOTELS ■

Casa Andina Classic Miraflores
San Antonio **18**
Casa Andina Private Collection
Miraflores **13**
Casa Andina Select
Miraflores **15**
Hostal El Patio Miraflores **12**
Hostal Jose Luis **17**
Hotel Antigua Miraflores **6**
Hotel Señorial **21**
Inka Lodge **4**
JW Marriott Hotel Lima **23**
Miraflores Park Hotel **22**
Pariwana Hostel Lima **9**
San Antonio Abad Hotel **16**
Sonesta Posada del Inca
Miraflores **14**

RESTAURANTS ◆

Antico Ristorante Italiano
di Porto Rotondo **5**
Astrid y Gastón **11**
Brujas de Cachiche **7**
Café Café **8**
El Mercado **2**

Fiesta Chiclayo
Gourmet **19**
La Mar Cebichería **1**
Pescados Capitales **2**
Restaurant Huaca
Pucllana **10**
Sophie Bistró **3**
T'anta **20**

ⓘ Information

new rooms and has been recently renovated, takes hospitality seriously. The staff is exceptionally helpful and friendly. The quaint house is lined with colonial Peruvian art, and built around a leafy courtyard. Rooms, traditionally decorated, range from huge suites with large Jacuzzis and kitchenettes to comfortable double rooms with handcrafted furniture and good-quality beds. Some of the older rooms are a bit dated. Bathrooms are well equipped, with colonial tiles, brass fixtures, and bathtubs. The public rooms look more like an art gallery than a hotel lobby (paintings are for sale).

Av. Grau 350, Miraflores, Lima. www.peru-hotels-inns.com. ☏ **01/201-2060.** Fax 01/201-2070. 65 units. $99–$135 double. Rates include breakfast selections and airport pickup (2-night stay required). AE, DC, MC, V. Free parking. **Amenities:** Restaurant; bar; small gym; Jacuzzi. *In room:* A/C, TV, fridge, Wi-Fi (free).

Hotel Señorial   Just 3 blocks from Larcomar mall, this conveniently located and homey midsize hotel is built around an attractive garden courtyard and offers a host of amenities, including a solarium with Jacuzzi, restaurant, and bar (where they serve their very own pisco), Wi-Fi, and a substantial breakfast. Rooms are clean and pretty nice for the price.

José Gonzáles 567. www.senorial.com. ☏ **01/444-5755.** 62 units. $72 double. Rates include breakfast. AE, DC, MC, V. **Amenities:** Restaurant; bar. *In room:* A/C, TV, fridge, Wi-Fi (free).

INEXPENSIVE

Hostal El Patio Miraflores 🏨   Set back from the street, behind an iron gate and built around a flower-filled Andalusian-style patio, this friendly, good-value inn has real personality. It's an unexpected but welcome respite from the grime and chaos of Lima. The comfortable, if not luxurious, rooms in the rambling colonial mansion feature good natural light and are cozy and brightly colored. Though a relatively small hotel, it's run very efficiently, and the staff goes out of its way to help visitors find their way in Lima. If you pay in cash, you get about a 10% discount.

Calle Ernesto Diez Canseco 341, Miraflores, Lima. www.hostalelpatio.net. ☏ **01/444-2107.** Fax 01/444-1663. 25 units. S/156–S/186 double; S/231 suite. Rates include continental breakfast. AE, DC, MC, V. *In room:* A/C, TV, fridge, Wi-Fi (free).

Hostal Jose Luis 🏊   This youth-hostel-like B&B—which keeps itself hidden away by not posting a sign out front—has operated on word of mouth for more than 2 decades. Now with new owners and renovated, it's deceptively large, with a capacity for nearly 60 guests; it's one of the least expensive places in Miraflores. It's secluded in a quiet residential part of the district, a 10-minute walk from Parque Central and its hubbub of nightlife and shops. A definite family feeling here, with cooking and laundry facilities. The common rooms are busy with furnishings and patterned wallpaper, and rooms are very clean and comfortable for the price. They all have private bathrooms.

Francisco de Paula Ugarriza 727, Miraflores, Lima. www.gulivers.com/4253. ☏ **01/444-1015.** Fax 01/446-7177. 20 units. $30–$50 double. Rates include continental breakfast. No credit cards. **Amenities:** Kitchen. *In room:* No phone, Wi-Fi (free).

Inka Lodge   A modern and well-run small *hostal* with good facilities, such as a roof terrace, computers with Internet access, kitchen use, and storage lockers. Rooms aren't large, but they're tastefully decorated for the price, and the location, on a quiet street just 5 blocks from Parque Kennedy in the heart of Miraflores, is safe and convenient. Choose from doubles with shared bathrooms or rooms for three or more, or dorm rooms with bunk beds. Bathrooms are well maintained. Thoughtful touches, many of which are uncommon among budget *hostales,* include free bottled water and round-the-clock coffee.

Elias Aguirre 278, Miraflores, Lima. inkalodge.com. © **01/242-6989.** 7 units. $30 double with shared bathroom; $15 per person in shared dorm rooms. Rates include taxes and continental breakfast. MC, V. **Amenities:** High-speed Internet (in lobby); kitchen use; storage lockers. *In room:* A/C, TV, no phone.

Pariwana Hostel Lima 🗡 Related to the terrific hostel of the same name in Cusco (p. 205), this Lima incarnation boasts a convenient location facing Parque Kennedy, but isn't lucky enough to have the digs of its sister property (a lovely colonial manor house). Then again, Lima can hardly compete with Cusco on aesthetic grounds, either. Still, this is a good choice for students and backpackers (and single women, for whom there are sex-segregated dorm rooms) who are looking more for inexpensive digs and bonhomie than anything else (including quiet, as the place is long on both fun and noise). There are lots of group activities, a bar/restaurant, games, breakfast until 1pm and more. Rooms aren't quite as sparkling as in Cusco, but with rooftop terrace, locker and storage services, and cheap meals (not to mention drinks), that may not matter much for a couple of nights, as the price is right.

Av. Larco 189, Miraflores, Lima. www.pariwana-hostel.com. © **01/242-4350.** 60 units. S/95 double with shared bathroom; S/110 double with bathroom; S/29–S/38 per person in dorm room with shared bathroom. Rates include breakfast. No credit cards. **Amenities:** Restaurant/bar; lockers; TV room. *In room:* No phone, Wi-Fi (free).

San Antonio Abad Hotel ★ 🗡 Named for a saint, this clean and very friendly neighborhood hotel aims high. Its goal is to be welcoming and comfortable, and on those grounds it succeeds. The colonial building, near the commercial center of Miraflores and several parks, has a garden terrace, fireplace, and sitting room. Rooms, which are simply decorated but ample, have private bathrooms with round-the-clock hot water. Because of street noise (ever present in Lima), you might ask for a room with an interior courtyard view. The free airport pickup is unusual at this price level.

Av. Ramón Ribeyro 301, Miraflores, Lima. www.hotelsanantonioabad.com. © **01/447-5475.** Fax 01/446-4208. 24 units. $75 double. Rates include breakfast buffet and airport pickup. AE, DC, MC, V. Free parking. **Amenities:** Restaurant; bar. *In room:* A/C, TV, fridge, hair dryer on request.

San Isidro

VERY EXPENSIVE

Country Club Lima Hotel ★★★ ☺ This grand and sprawling hacienda-style hotel, built in 1927, is a character-filled place to rest your head. For pure elegance, nothing in Lima can touch it. Despite the trappings, the hotel is cozy and low-key. Rooms—all of which are suites, with separate work areas—are luxurious, with antiques and old-world appeal. Many of the huge, stunning marble bathrooms have large Jacuzzis and separate showers. It is ideal for just about anyone, including families, but especially perfect for stressed-out business travelers who've seen one too many blandly elegant hotels. Public rooms are refined, with chandeliers and wood-beam ceilings. Afternoon tea is served to the accompaniment of live piano music, and the English Bar is great for one of Lima's best pisco sours. Appropriately enough, it's next to a golf course and tennis club (guest privileges included). The hotel is actually pretty fairly priced for this elevated luxury and service, especially if you're able to get a corporate rate or special offer on the hotel website.

Los Eucaliptos 590, San Isidro, Lima. www.hotelcountry.com. © **800/745-8883** in the U.S. and Canada, or **01/611-9000.** Fax 01/611-9002. 75 units. $440–$615 double; $490–$1,650 suite. AE, DC, MC, V. Valet parking. **Amenities:** 3 restaurants; bar; concierge; fitness center; access to nearby Lima Golf Club; outdoor pool; spa; tennis court. *In room:* A/C, TV, fridge, Wi-Fi.

Swissôtel Lima ★★   One of Lima's most sophisticated properties is this sparkling high-rise hotel. It takes its pedigree as part of the international Swissôtel chain very seriously. The lobby is awash in fine carpets, corridors are curiously lined with giant neoclassical columns, restaurants serve Swiss and Italian as well as Peruvian fare, and service is, of course, eminently efficient. Rooms are spacious and well-appointed. Executive rooms include a work desk, two telephone lines, a coffee machine, a private executive lounge/boardroom, and cocktails (!). Rooms don't have a ton of personality, unlike the public spaces, but they're very well equipped. For business facilities, this property rivals Casa Andina Private Collection, the Westin, and Miraflores Park Hotel. Value rates and packages are often available.

Vía Central 150 (Centro Empresarial Real), San Isidro, Lima. www.swissotel.com. © **01/421-4400.** Fax 01/421-4422. 244 units. $219–$550 double; $650 and up suite. AE, DC, MC, V. Valet parking. **Amenities:** 3 restaurants; cafeteria; bar/lounge; concierge; fitness center; small heated outdoor pool; sauna; spa. *In room:* A/C, TV.

The Westin Lima Hotel & Convention Center ★★★   Lima's newest luxury hotel, in Peru's tallest building, certainly makes a statement. Perhaps more notable for the swank public spaces and dramatic cityscape views from the floor-to-ceiling windows of rooms than the rooms themselves (though these are spacious and have outstanding bathrooms), this Starwood property is where to head if you're craving an urbane stay with every service imaginable. Designed by the renowned Lima architect Bernardo Fort-Brescia, who designed the Tambo del Inka in the Sacred Valley, the spa and indoor pool are aptly described by the name of the former: heavenly. Some may find the soaring lobby, with abundant use of massive murals, shiny glass and metal, and colorful light effects, to be a bit over the top. The quality of the beds is absolutely first-rate, and service is extremely professional across the board. For business travelers, it's tough to improve upon. Some advance purchase prices online make this pricey hotel relatively affordable.

Las Begonias 450, San Isidro, Lima. www.starwoodhotels.com. © **01/ 201-5000.** Fax 01/242-3393. 81 units. $229–$680 deluxe double; from $399–$930 and up suite. AE, DC, MC, V. **Amenities:** 2 restaurants; 2 bars; concierge; gym; spa; heated indoor pool. *In room:* A/C, TV/DVD, fridge, Wi-Fi ($10/day).

EXPENSIVE

Libertador Lima Hotel ★   Smack in the middle of the San Isidro financial district, the Libertador—which overlooks the private Lima Golf Club—is relatively unassuming and tranquil, especially considering the more imposing and flashier hotels nearby. Still, that's its charm. It doesn't try too hard, but it gets the job done for guests who are both business travelers and tourists. Part of a five-member, well-run Peruvian chain of upscale hotels, this midsize offering is handsomely decorated with modern art, Kilim rugs, and bold colors, eschewing the typical blandness of business hotels. It also has a nice top-floor restaurant and bar with good views. It's quite a good value, especially if you can get an upgrade to a junior suite or reserve online.

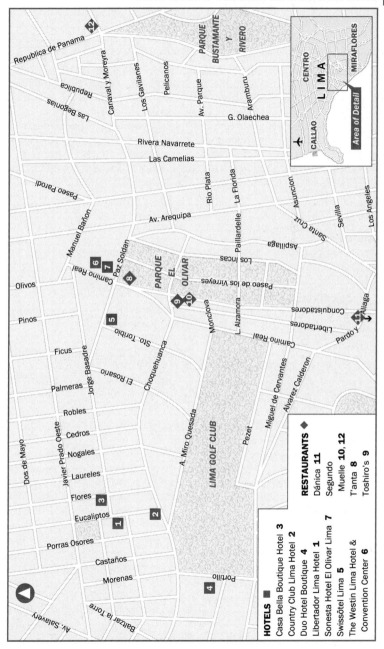

HOTELS
Casa Bella Boutique Hotel **3**
Country Club Lima Hotel **2**
Duo Hotel Boutique **4**
Libertador Lima Hotel **1**
Sonesta Hotel El Olivar Lima **7**
Swissôtel Lima **5**
The Westin Lima Hotel &
Convention Center **6**

RESTAURANTS ◆
Dánica **11**
Segundo
Muelle **10, 12**
T'anta **8**
Toshiro's **9**

Los Eucaliptos 550, San Isidro, Lima. www.libertador.com.pe. ℓ **877/778-2281** in the U.S. and Canada, or **01/518-6500.** Fax 01/518-6290. 43 units. $130–$190 double; $285 suite. AE, DC, MC, V. Valet parking. **Amenities:** Restaurant; bar; concierge; gym; Jacuzzi; sauna. *In room:* A/C, TV, fridge.

Sonesta Hotel El Olívar Lima ★   The Sonesta chain's top-of-the-line property, aimed squarely at visiting business travelers, is named for the historic Olive Grove Park, which it faces. This seven-story hotel is well located for its clientele, in a peaceful section of the San Isidro business district of the city. The rooms, a step up from the more rustic decor in the chain's Posadas del Inca, are quite large, with boldly colored fabrics and beige marble bathrooms. Service is friendly and efficient, and the amenities outdo those of most hotels in the city. The recently revamped restaurant is winning accolades in the Peruvian press, and is an excellent spot for lunch or dinner.

Pancho Fierro 194, San Isidro, Lima. www.sonesta.com/lima. ℓ **800/SONESTA (766-3782)** or **01/712-6000.** Fax 01/712-6099. 134 units. $176–$533 double; $289–$676 suite. Rates include breakfast buffet. Children 7 and under stay free in parents' room. AE, DC, MC, V. Free parking. **Amenities:** 2 restaurants; cafe; cocktail lounge; bar; concierge; fitness center w/rooftop outdoor pool; Jacuzzi; sauna; Wi-Fi in public areas. *In room:* A/C, TV/DVD, fridge.

MODERATE

Casa Bella Boutique Hotel ★ 🍴   A very pleasant midrange choice in an area better known for its business-oriented luxury hotels, this safe and homey, exceptionally clean inn, 1 block from the swank Country Club, offers private and quiet rooms that do a good job at making you feel like you're staying in someone's home. The spacious and airy rooms are attractively decorated, with comfy beds, and several have backyard garden views. Whether for a few days or a longer stay, Casa Bella is tough to beat for the price. There's now a second location in Miraflores, Av. De La Aviación 565 (ℓ **01/241-1446**), which is in fact more conveniently located for dining, shopping, and attractions, not to mention access to the park along the coast.

Las Flores 459 San Isidro. www.casabellaperu.net. ℓ **720/648-3451** in the U.S., or **01/421-7354.** 12 units. $89 double; $95–$175 suite. Rates include continental breakfast. MC, V. Free parking. **Amenities:** Kitchen. *In room:* Wi-Fi (free)

Duo Hotel Boutique ★★ 🛍   Many hotels misuse the term boutique, equating it simply with small. This is truly a boutique hotel, and unique in Lima: A smart, small hotel in a lovely town house on one of Lima's most tranquil streets, in San Isidro. If you despair of the capital's noise and chaos, this is the place for you. Were I a businessman traveling to Lima for frequent or extended stays, this would be my home. Sure, there are fancier and more prestigious hotels with more services and facilities, but none has the intimate, relaxing neighborhood feel of this charming new hotel. It's the kind of place that's perfect to unwind at after a long day—of either meetings or sightseeing. Bonuses are a nice bistro restaurant and backyard with small swimming pool. The cleanly decorated contemporary rooms have excellent bedding, and the high-ceilinged lobby is one I'd bet many guests would like to have as a living room, so comfortable is the feel of this place. Forgot your laptop? The hotel will lend you one.

Valle Riestra 576, San Isidro, Lima. www.duohotelperu.com. ℓ **01/628-3245**. Fax 01/628-8175. 20 units. $140–$150 double; $165–$175 suite. Rates include breakfast buffet. AE, DC, MC, V. Free parking. **Amenities:** Restaurant; outdoor pool; concierge; 24-hour room service. *In room:* A/C, TV/DVD, fridge, Wi-Fi (free).

Barranco

MODERATE

Second Home Peru ★★★ 🛏 Lilian Delfín runs this unique inn in the coast-hugging home of her father, the artist Victor Delfín (whose studio and living quarters are apart from the main house). And it keeps getting better: Lilian has added three new rooms, several with expansive ocean views. The 1913 home overflows with artistic flavor. Though it overlooks the ocean and rooms are spacious and handsome, the rambling two-story house is probably not for everyone. But many will find it a magical home away from home in Lima. My large room had a beautiful wood floor and beams, a huge picture window framing the misty gray Pacific, deep claw-foot tub, and luxurious linens. Lilian often takes guests to visit her father's studio, where a giant puma-head fountain spouts water into the swimming pool (open to guests). And you get to have breakfast at the Gaudiesque, neo-medieval kitchen. If you're headed to Cusco, check out Lilian's brother's **Second Home Cusco** (p. 206).

Domeyer 366, Barranco, Lima. www.secondhomeperu.com. ℂ **01/247-5522.** Fax 01/247-1042. 8 units. $105–$125 double; $120 suite. Rates include continental breakfast. AE, DC, MC, V. Free parking. **Amenities:** Kitchen; outdoor pool. *In room:* A/C, TV, Wi-Fi (free).

3B (Barranco's Bed & Breakfast) ★★ 🍃 A big cut above the *hostales* that have begun to populate Barranco, this place may call itself a B&B, but it's really a smart and terrific-value boutique hotel, with stylish contemporary rooms and public spaces (including a kitchen and airy lounge, with a rooftop terrace and additional 3rd-floor accommodations to come). Rooms aren't overly large or plush, but they're immaculate and decorated with colorful art and photographs, and have excellent modern bathrooms. With plenty of unexpected amenities, exceptional and friendly service, and a good location in Barranco, this popular inn is a winner and welcome upgrade even from Lima's middle-of-the-road midprice options. Look online for promotional rates that make it even more of a bargain.

Jr. Centenario 130 (between blocks 9/10 Av. Grau). www.3bhostal.com. ℂ **01/247-6915.** 16 units. $88 double. Rates include breakfast. AE, DC, MC, V. **Amenities:** Kitchen; lounge; rooftop terrace. *In room:* A/C, TV, Wi-Fi (free).

SIDE TRIPS FROM LIMA

Most visitors to Lima, having seen the highlights of the colonial center and a few museums, head out on long-distance buses and planes to Cusco and Machu Picchu, Nasca, Arequipa, and north to the jungle. However, if you have time for an excursion or two closer to the Peruvian capital, consider the pre-Columbian ruins at Pachacámac or the attractive beaches south of Lima.

Pachacámac

31km (19 miles) S of Lima

The finest ruins within easy reach of Lima, **Pachacámac,** in the Lurín Valley, was inhabited by several pre-Columbian cultures before the Incas. The extensive site, a sacred city and holy place of pilgrimage, includes plazas, adobe-brick palaces, and pyramidal temples, some of which have been rebuilt by the Peruvian government. It makes for an interesting visit, especially if you're not planning on heading north to the archaeological sites near Chiclayo and Trujillo.

The earliest constructions here date to the 1st century, although the site reached its apex during the Huari (or Wari) culture (10th century). Pilgrims came here to pay homage to the feared oracle and creator-god, Pachacámac, who was believed to be responsible for earthquakes and matters of state such as war. The Incas conquered the site in the 15th century, and it was one of the most important shrines in the Americas during their rule, although its ceremonial importance began to wane soon afterward. However, two of the most important structures on-site, the Temple of the Sun and the Acllahuasi (or Mamacuña) palace (where "chosen maidens" served the Inca), both date to the Inca occupation. Hernán Pizarro and his gold-hungry troops arrived in 1533 but were disappointed to find a paucity of riches. On the premises is a small museum of pre-Columbian artifacts, including textiles and the dual-personage carved wooden idol of Pachacámac, god of fire and son of the sun god.

The site (pachacamac.perucultural.org.pe; ℂ **01/430-0168**), which occupies a low hill, is large; allow at least a few hours to visit by foot (the visit from Lima can be completed in a half-day). English-speaking guides are usually available for hire at the entrance if you don't arrive with a guide-led group. The site's open Tuesday to Saturday 9am to 4:30pm. Admission is S/6 for adults, S/3 for students, and S/1 for children.

GETTING THERE   Pachacámac is about 45 minutes from Lima by car or bus. Combis (with signs reading PACHACAMAC/LURIN) leave from Avenida Abancay and the corner of Ayacucho and Montevideo in Lima Centro. The most convenient way to visit—cheaper than hiring a taxi, unless there are several of you—is by a half-day organized tour, offered by Lima Vision, Lima Tours, and other companies; see "Organized Tours," earlier in this chapter. Most tours cost between S/75 and S/125 per person, including transportation and guide. Taxis charge about S/40 one-way from Miraflores.

The Southern Beaches

30–70km (19–43 miles) S of Lima

The best beaches easily accessible from Lima line the coast south of the city. Popular spots along the shadeless, arid desert landscape are El Silencio, Punta Hermosa (a good place for ceviche and fresh fish in any number of rustic seafood restaurants), Punta Negra, Santa María, and Pucusana. Probably the best bet is Pucusana, a small fishing village, although it's the farthest beach from Lima. The attractive beaches are very popular with Limeños during the summer months; on weekends, the southern coast is a long line of caravans of sun-seekers.

Note: Even though you can swim in the ocean at this distance from the capital, the currents are very strong, and great caution should be exercised. You should also be careful with your possessions because thieves frequent these beaches. Finally, be forewarned that the beaches are only moderately attractive.

A little farther south along the Panamericana Sur, at km. 97.5, is the trendy recreational area called **Asia** (www.asiasurplaza.com), an entertainment-oriented boulevard packed with fashionable shops, restaurants, bars, and discos, all within easy reach of the beaches Playa Blanca, La Isla, and Las Brisas.

GETTING THERE   Unless you have wheels, the best way to tour the beaches south of Lima is to hop on a combi, like Limeños do. Those marked "San Bartolo" (another one of the beaches) leave from Angamos and Panamericana Sur in Lima; others at

Jirón Montevideo and Jirón Ayacucho in Lima Centro will also get you to the beaches. You'll have to tell the driver where you want to get off (or hop off wherever a number of fellow bus travelers do), and then walk a mile or less down to the beach.

The ride costs S/5 and takes anywhere from 45 minutes to 2 hours. The beaches and their markers are as follows: El Silencio, Km 42; Punta Hermosa, Km 44; Punta Rocas, Km 45; Punta Negra, Km 46; San Bartolo, Km 52; Santa María, Km 55; and Pucusana, Km 65.

THE CENTRAL COAST & HIGHLANDS

7

South of Lima along the coast, the hot and extraordinarily dry desert province of Ica—one of the most arid places on Earth—contains one of Peru's most peculiar sights: The Nasca Lines, huge pre-Columbian drawings scratched into the desert and the source of many questions and wild theories about Peru's ancient past. The Paracas and Nasca cultures that took root here (roughly 1300 B.C.–A.D. 700) were two of Peru's most advanced, acclaimed today for their exquisite textile weavings and ceramics considered among the finest produced by pre-Columbian Peru. Despite its turbulent history, newly welcoming and peaceful Ayacucho, tucked in the central highlands, has the country's finest collection of colonial-era churches, and it's also the epicenter of Peru's most celebrated folk art.

HISTORY The region forms part of the oldest geological strata in the country; fossils date back as far as the Tertiary or Quaternary eras. The enigmatic Nasca Lines are the most obvious evidence of pre-Columbian cultures. Besides that head-scratching site are others tied to the ancient cultures that once settled and irrigated these desert lands, including remarkable stone aqueducts—evidence of advanced engineering—and an evocative burial ground.

THINGS TO DO There's little to compare to the strange allure of flying over the **Nasca Lines** in a small plane. Explore unique marine life on the **Paracas National Reserve** and the **Ballestas Islands;** visit homespun **pisco wineries** near Ica; and 33 colonial churches and manor houses in **Ayacucho.**

EATING & DRINKING The country's famous cocktail, the **pisco sour,** is made with the white-grape brandy that shares its name with the town. The region's wineries (near Ica) make Peru's best wines and, of course, pisco. Pair it with **ceviche** and **fresh seafood** from the coastal waters in open-air restaurants or swank new hotel restaurants in Paracas.

NATURE The **Ballestas Islands** have been likened to Ecuador's Galápagos Islands for their unusual flora and fauna, including thousands of sea lions, flamingos, and endangered Humboldt penguins. The maritime sanctuary encompasses the desert sands and beaches of the **Paracas Peninsula** and a lovely bay with curious rock formations. **Huacachina**

Lagoon is a beautiful green-and-blue oasis in the midst of the monochrome desert and South America's highest sand dunes.

ACTIVE PURSUITS   Desert enthusiasts will be thrilled: Take to the region's newest sport, **sandboarding** on massive sand dunes, or roll across the desert in an *arenero* (**4x4 dune buggy**).

THE BEST TRAVEL EXPERIENCES IN THE CENTRAL COAST & HIGHLANDS

- **Plunging into Peru's marine-life sanctuary:** Get up close and personal with Humboldt penguins, flamingos, and barking sea lions. (Pay no attention to the bird guano drenched sections of the islands!) See p. 131.
- **Tasting pisco at the source:** This complex white-grape brandy belongs to Peru, and don't let Chileans tell you otherwise. Sip it straight, in a pisco sour (or newfangled coca or maracuyá sour), or crack open a bottle on a winery tour. See p. 140.

7

Pisco & the Reserva Nacional de Paracas

THE CENTRAL COAST & HIGHLANDS

Paracas, Ica, and Nasca are all within striking distance of Lima, but for those with limited time, a visit to the region could complicate moving on to other places in Peru. With no flights available from Lima, you'll need to travel overland along the desert coast to get to the department of Ica, and by land again if you're headed to any of the other major destinations in Peru—in all likelihood, adding a couple of days to your trip. (For many travelers, that will mean returning to the capital and catching a flight.) The vast Carretera Panamericana (Pan-American Hwy.), a two-lane strip of asphalt that extends the length of Peru from the Ecuadorian border all the way down to Chile, slices through this section of the desert lowlands, and bus travel is direct, if not always visually stimulating. Many visitors move on by bus from Nasca to Arequipa or Lake Titicaca. Although Ayacucho is a long and winding Andean bus ride from Lima or Ica, you can now easily fly there in just an hour from the capital (but not yet from Cusco or other cities).

o **Gliding over the dunes:** There are two great ways to experience the desert's sand dunes, the highest in South America: either sandboarding, which is like surfing, but on hot sand; or rumbling across the dunes in an *arenero* (dune buggy). See p. 142.

o **Marveling at the Nasca Lines:** You'll lose your mind—but hopefully not your lunch—flying over these giant, mysterious desert drawings in the craggy sands below. It's not hard to see why the crazy theories popped up. See p. 146.

o **Experiencing Easter in Ayacucho:** One of Peru's great spectacles is a fiercely reverent and mystical display that takes over this otherwise quiet and quaint colonial town of 33 churches. See p. 153.

PISCO & THE RESERVA NACIONAL DE PARACAS ★★

260km (162 miles) S of Lima; 75km (47 miles) NW of Ica; 205km (127 miles) NW of Nasca

This dusty, unremarkable town that will sound familiar to anyone who's had a pisco sour in a Peruvian bar or restaurant (and you'll probably wonder why'd they name a cocktail after this town). The first town of any size to the south of Lima, Pisco is also the first settlement beyond the beaches and ruins outside the capital that draws the attention of travelers. Yet that interest has little to do with the (rather lacking) attributes of the town and almost everything to do with the natural attractions in abundance at the nearby Ballestas Islands and Paracas National Reserve, just 22km (14 miles) from the center of Pisco. A few kilometers west of the Pan-American Highway, Pisco is a small port and fishing village of very modest interest (beyond the Moorish-inspired Municipal Palace) that sometimes serves as a base for those wanting to visit Paracas Peninsula and Bay without paying the higher prices commanded by the resort.

In this seismic and often-devastated area, Pisco was perhaps the hardest hit town by the 2007 earthquake that leveled much of the region. As much as 85% of central Pisco—where most homes were constructed of adobe—was destroyed, including nearly 20,000 homes and the city's San Clemente Church, where more than 130

Pisco

people died while attending Mass. More modern buildings mostly survived, though the five-story Hotel Embassy in Pisco collapsed, killing 15 guests and employees.

Essentials
GETTING THERE
There are frequent buses up and down the coast from Lima to Arequipa, with stops in between. From Lima, frequent buses normally take between 3 and 4 hours to reach Pisco. However, because the town is not directly on the Carretera Panamericana, not all coastal buses stop there. Be sure to confirm that the bus won't merely leave you on the side of the road en route to Ica (which would result in the hassle of getting a *combi* to town). **Ormeño,** Av. Carlos Zavala 177, Lima (www.grupo-ormeno.com.pe; **01/472-5000**) and **Cruz del Sur,** Avenida Paseo de la República, Lima (www.cruzdelsur.com.pe; ✆ **01/311-5050**) travel from Lima to Pisco and to Ica, Nasca, and Arequipa. **Transportes Soyuz** (www.soyuz.com.pe; ✆ **01/265-0501**) connects Pisco with Ica as well as Lima; you'll find an office in Lima at Av. México 331, La Victoria, and in Pisco (✆ **056/531-014**) at Av. Ernesto R. Diez Canseco 41. Bus terminals are located right in the center of town, on or just off the Plaza de Armas. Frequent *colectivos* travel to Ica from Pisco.

PARACAS culture

Paracas might be best known for its great natural coastal beauty and wildlife, but the region is no less recognized (especially among archaeologists and historians) as the home of several advanced cultures that thrived in Peru before the Incas. The so-called *hombre de Santo Domingo* (Santo Domingo man), whose remains date to 7000 B.C., was found on the west shore of the Bay of Paracas.

Little was known about the Paracas culture, an ancient Amerindian civilization founded along the south-central coast more than 3,000 years ago, until 1925, when the Peruvian archaeologist Julio C. Tello discovered extraordinary burial sites, now referred to as the Paracas Necropolis, concealed by the desert sand dunes on the isthmus of the Península de Paracas. The arid climate and layers of sand had done wonders to protect extraordinary embroidered textiles—largely found within burial sites—that today are recognized as the finest representatives of pre-Columbian Peruvian woven art. The Paracas culture produced textiles of unrivaled color, technique, and design. The most exquisite examples of funereal textiles are found at Lima's Museo de la Nación (p. 90), but there are also fine pieces in Ica at the Museo Regional (p. 139) and at the Museo de Sitio Julio C. Tello within the Paracas National Reserve (p. 131).

Also found at the sites were skulls that reveal fascinating information about the Paracas social structure and notions of physical beauty. The Paracas employed methods to alter the shape of the skull,

elongating it with weights and boards, to connote social status. Many of the skulls found in the Paracas Necropolis have stretched and sloped craniums. The Paracas people also practiced a crude form of brain surgery called trepanation. Like medieval physicians, who believed bloodletting aimed at the forehead was a cure-all, Paracas doctors surgically drilled holes in the skull to treat both physical trauma and, it seems, psychological disorders. The formation of scar tissue indicates that many of the patients actually survived the operations, although, of course, it's impossible to say how their physical or behavioral problems were affected.

The Paracas culture flourished from roughly 1300 B.C. to A.D. 200, but scholars are most knowledgeable about the late period of development, from 300 B.C. to A.D. 200. At the Paracas Necropolis, researchers discovered more than 400 funerary bundles, each consisting of a mummified priest or nobleman swathed in brilliantly woven and embroidered funeral tapestries. The large and exceptionally detailed, colorful weavings feature repetitive motifs of birds, fish, and other animals, revealing a keen sense of textile design and artistry.

Little is known about the disappearance of the Paracas culture around A.D. 200. Farther south along the coast, the Nasca culture reigned for about 5 centuries, itself eventually succeeded by the Huari and then Ica cultures, the last of which succumbed to the expanding Inca Empire by the 15th century.

GETTING AROUND

The best way to get around Pisco itself is on foot because anything of interest—hotels, restaurants, the cathedral—is only minutes from the Plaza de Armas. Taxis are readily available and cheap for any trip within the city (S/3–S/4). For transport to the Paracas National Reserve and other areas of interest, the best idea is often to hire a taxi (about S/25). The most efficient way to see the highlights of the area is with a tour company, especially because there is no public transportation on the peninsula or within the reserve.

BY BUS   Combis to the Ballestas Islands and Paracas National Reserve (marked EL CHACO–PARACAS) depart from the Pisco market on Fermín Tangus every half-hour at a rate of S/3.

BY BOAT   Boat tours of the Paracas Bay and Ballestas Islands are available right on the El Chaco waterfront (S/50–S/75 per person) or by arranging an organized tour.

ORGANIZED TOURS

The following companies all offer packages to the Ballestas Islands and Paracas National Reserve (as well as tours to Tambo Colorado and Nasca): **Zarcillo Connections,** Callao 137 (www.zarcilloconnections.com; ℰ **056/536-636**); **Ballestas Travel Service,** San Francisco 249 (ℰ **056/533-095**); and, near Ica, **Huacachina Tours,** Av. La Angostura 355, L-47, in front of the Hotel Las Dunas (www.huacachina tours.com; ℰ **056/256-582**).

VISITOR INFORMATION

The **Municipality of Pisco office** at the Plaza de Armas (ℰ **056/532-525**) might be able to provide some rudimentary tourist information; a better bet is one of the travel agencies offering tours to Paracas and other places in the region. See "Organized Tours" in "Getting Around," above.

FAST FACTS

Banco de Crédito, Pérez Figuerola 162 (ℰ **056/532-954**), has a Visa-compatible ATM. You'll also find *cambistas,* or money exchangers, hovering around the Plaza de Armas. If you need medical attention, go to **Hospital Antonio Skrabonja Antoncich (ESSALUD),** San Francisco 322 (ℰ **056/532-784**) or **San Juan de Dios,** Av. San Juan de Dios 350 (ℰ **056/532-332**). In an emergency, you can reach the **police** at the Plaza de Armas, Calle San Francisco (ℰ **056/532-165**). The **post office** is at Av. Federico Uranga 211, Independencia (ℰ **056/220-208**). There's a **Telefónica del Perú** office at Bolognesi 298.

Exploring the Area

RESERVA NACIONAL DE PARACAS NATURE RESERVE ★★

Established in 1975, the Paracas National Reserve is the primary marine conservation center in Peru. Comprising the Paracas Bay and Peninsula (the Ballestas Islands technically are just outside the Reserve, but in practice generally considered part), it's a place of spectacular wildlife, strange desert vistas, and gorgeous unpopulated beaches. The 14,504-sq.-km (5,600-sq.-mile) reserve is about two-thirds ocean, so don't come expecting to see a zoo-like array of plants and animals at every turn—except on the Islas Ballestas, where several thousand sea lions, in addition to many other species, lie about in plain view.

What is not water in the Paracas National Reserve is hot and dry land, with no transportation to speak of except for independently hired taxis. For this reason, most tourists tend to visit the reserve as part of an organized tour. However, adventurous travelers with plenty of water, sunscreen, and stamina can get to know the peninsula and its rich marine birdlife on their own, camping far from other humans. Safety has become a concern in recent years, though, so camping alone is not a good idea.

Dirt roads crisscross the Paracas Peninsula, and a paved road goes around it, out toward Punta Pejerrey, near the Candelabro (see "Islas Ballestas," below). The dirt roads are the most interesting, reaching minuscule fishing villages such as attractive **Lagunillas** and a cliff-top lookout point, **Mirador de los Lobos,** with views of the ocean and lots of sea lions. Sadly, the August 2007 earthquake destroyed the famous **Cathedral** rock and cave formation, one of the National Reserve's great attractions.

To hike around the peninsula, it's about 21km (13 miles) round-trip to the lookout point (5km/3 miles from the Tello Museum to Lagunillas). Begin at a turnoff left of the paved road beyond the museum. The beach of **La Mina,** within walking distance of Lagunillas, is one of the most beautiful on the peninsula, and very popular in summer. There are few facilities of any kind on the peninsula. You are allowed to camp on the beautiful beaches (where you might see no other humans, just pelicans and other birds), and there are a couple of seafood restaurants in Lagunillas—**Tía Fela's** is the best place around for fresh fish.

Museo de Sitio Julio C. Tello MUSEUM   Named for the Peruvian archaeologist credited with uncovering many of the mysteries of the ancient Paracas culture, the Julio Tello Site Museum is located just past the entrance to the Paracas National Reserve, 5km (3 miles) from Paracas beach. The museum suffered considerable damage from the 2007 earthquake and, while open, is still in the process of being renovated. It contains a small but instructive exhibit of ceramics and textiles that depict the evolution of the Paracas culture. The Paracas were experts at mummifying their dead; in the mummies, you can see the peculiar practices of cranial deformation and cranial trepanation, or brain surgery. The Paracas also admired trophy heads, and warriors often attached the heads of defeated foes to their armor to instill fear into their opponents.

Near the museum is the **Paracas Necropolis** (100 B.C.–A.D. 300), comprising the archaeological sites of Cabezas Largas and Cerro Colorado. First explored in the 1920s, it is the oldest discovered site in the region. Tello uncovered Paracas burial sites containing superb funerary cloths, skulls, and other artifacts—all key elements in his groundbreaking studies of the Paracas culture. However, there is very little to see today at the sites. About 270m (886 ft.) toward the bay is a viewing tower, constructed to allow viewings of the dozens (or hundreds) of flamingos often gathered on the beach (usually July–Nov only).

Carretera Pisco, Km 27, Puerto San Martín, Paracas. © **056/620-436.** Admission S/10 adults, S/5 students and seniors, S/3 children 9 and under. Daily 9am–5pm.

Islas Ballestas ★★

The primary focus of a visit to the reserve is a boat tour of the Islas Ballestas (pronounced "*Ees*-lahs Bah-*yes*-tahs"). Although the islands can't really live up to locals' touting of them as the "Peruvian Galápagos," they do afford tantalizing close-up views of the habitat's rich roster of protected species, including huge colonies of barking sea lions, endangered turtles and Humboldt penguins, red-footed boobies, pelicans, and

A Birder's Boon

The Ballestas Islands are smack in the middle of the Humboldt Current, which flows 3,220km (2,000 miles) from Antarctica along the Pacific coastline. In the warm, shallow waters along the Peruvian coast, the current makes abundant growth of phytoplankton possible, which stimulates an ecological food chain that culminates in the largest concentration of birds on Earth.

Paracas National Reserve

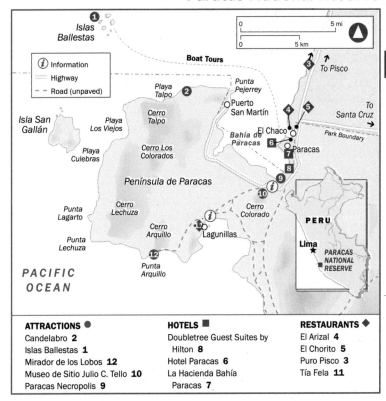

ATTRACTIONS ●
Candelabro **2**
Islas Ballestas **1**
Mirador de los Lobos **12**
Museo de Sitio Julio C. Tello **10**
Paracas Necropolis **9**

HOTELS ■
Doubletree Guest Suites by
  Hilton **8**
Hotel Paracas **6**
La Hacienda Bahía
  Paracas **7**

RESTAURANTS ◆
El Arizal **4**
El Chorito **5**
Puro Pisco **3**
Tía Fela **11**

red-footed cormorants. During the summer months (Jan–Mar), baby sea lions are born, and the community becomes even more populous and noisy. The wall-like, cantilevered islands are literally covered with birds; 110 migratory and resident seabirds have been documented, and the bay is a stopover point in the Alaska-Patagonia migration route. Packs of dolphins are occasionally seen slicing through the water; less frequently, humpback whales and soaring Andean condors can also be glimpsed.

The islands are often referred to by locals as *las islas guaneras* because they are covered in bird droppings. (*Guano* is the Quechua word for excrement.) The nitrogen-rich *guano* is harvested every 10 years and made into fertilizer. (A factory can be seen on the first island.) No humans other than the *guano* collectors—no doubt a contender for worst job title in the world—are allowed on the islands, and all the species in the reserve are protected by law. In practice, however, there are no specially assigned police officers or boats available to enforce protection.

En route to the islands, boats pass the famous **Candelabro,** a giant candelabra-like drawing etched into a cliff overlooking the bay. The huge etching, 126m long and 72m wide (413×236 ft.), looks as though it could be a cousin to the Nasca Lines, and it is similarly shrouded in mystery. Some believe that it's a ritualistic symbol of the Paracas or Nasca cultures, while others contend that it dates only to the 18th or 19th

Organized Tours

Most people visit the Paracas National Reserve and Ballestas Islands as part of organized tours ($15–$25 per person, with guides, transportation, and entrance fees all included in the price) from one of the dozen operators on the main street. Those who prefer to visit the reserve on their own must pay an entrance fee upon entering the reserve (S/5 for adults and students 14 and older; free for children 13 and under). You can enter the reserve without a guide, but it's highly recommended that you contract one in order to get the most out of a visit. Much that is unique about the area—its climate and conditions, and its migratory wildlife—is not always immediately obvious.

century, when it served as a protective symbol and navigational guide for fishermen and sailors.

Most organized tours take visitors from the San Andrés port to the El Balneario resort, a beach playground for upscale residents of Lima, and then on to Playa El Chaco, where boats leave for 1-hour tours of the Ballestas. You can also independently contract an island boat tour here from one of the 13 operators on the main street. Tours run to about S/40 per person, and each boat has an English- or French-speaking guide on board. Most start early in the morning, between 7 and 8am. Visitors are not allowed to set foot on the islands, although boats get close enough for good viewing. Sweaters and windbreakers, hats, and sunscreen are essential.

TAMBO COLORADO RUINS ★

An Inca fortress and probably the best-preserved ancient architectural complex on the central coast, this outpost is thought to have been an administration checkpoint for Andean coastal migration. It was probably also where the Inca chieftain and his minions stayed for periods as he traveled back and forth between the Inca capital, Cusco, and coastal settlements. Unlike other archaeological sites, where the characteristic vibrant colors have long faded, here at least some of the original red, white, and yellow walls are still preserved. (The name of the complex, *Colorado,* refers to the red color of the walls.) Also unique in the Inca canon, the structures here were constructed not of neatly cut stone, but of materials that could be used for long-term construction, given the lack of rain on the desert coast.

The complex contains a central plaza, storehouses, living quarters, and military installations. If you're headed to Cusco, you can be assured of seeing more impressive Inca sites, but Tambo Colorado is rewarding for archaeology fans and Inca completists. The site is quite removed from Pisco—about 45km (28 miles) northeast of town. It lies about 5km (3 miles) outside the town of Humay, to which you can take a bus, but service is highly erratic. If you are intent on seeing Tambo Colorado, it's advisable to either go with an organized guided tour or hire a taxi, which will take you out to the site, wait for you, and return you to Pisco for about S/120. The site is open daily from 9am to 5pm; admission is S/5.

Where to Eat

Pisco and Paracas are hardly dining capitals, and most restaurants are simple affairs. The majority of visitors to Paracas National Reserve, if staying at one of the nicer options, tend to dine at their hotels; the **Doubletree**, **Hotel Paracas,** and **La**

Hacienda Bahía Paracas all have good restaurants. There are several popular and informal seafood eateries at **Playa El Chaco** waterfront in Paracas, where launches for the Islas Ballestas depart.

Café Chali ★ PERUVIAN   On a side street off the Plaza de Armas in Pisco, this homey spot serves a variety of affordable meals that could almost be termed gourmet, and in large portions. Try classic Peruvian dishes like *papas a la huacaína* and excellent ceviche, or lighter fare that includes sandwiches and salads. The owner makes his own desserts daily.

Av. San Martin 198, Pisco. ℂ **01/9810-43734**. Main courses S/12–S/24. MC, V. Daily noon–10pm.

El Arizal ★ CEVICHE/SEAFOOD   One of many seafood restaurants along the malecón in El Chaco, fronting the Bay of Paracas, this simple and popular, family-run place deserves a visit because the seafood is consistently fresh and prices manageable. Good options include the *arroz con mariscos* (seafood rice) and ceviche *mixto*. Other seafood options include mussels and crab.

Malecón de El Chaco, s/n. No phone. Main courses S/14–S/30. MC, V. Daily 8am–5pm.

El Chorito CEVICHE/SEAFOOD   Set back a block from the waterfront in El Chaco, this contemporary-looking restaurant is one of the better seafood places on the bay's main drag, perfect for a lunch of ceviche and grilled fish.

Av. Paracas, s/n, Paracas. ℂ **056/545-054**. Main courses S/7–S/28. AE, MC, V. Daily noon–9pm.

Puro Pisco ★★ SEAFOOD/PERUVIAN   The name sounds like you should expect to taste through a lineup of pisco spirits—which you can do if you wish—but this gourmet restaurant with bay views, a recent and most welcome addition to the region's dining scene, is mostly a specialist in fresh seafood and shellfish, featuring a catch of the day. Try the ceviche, octopus, or black rice with squid, or one of the classic dishes, such as *lomo saltado*.

Av. Genaro Medrano 460 (Bahía de San Andrés), Pisco. www.puropisco.net. ℂ **056/542-384**. Reservations recommended. Main courses S/15–S/35. MC, V. Daily 8am–5pm.

Tía Fela CEVICHE/SEAFOOD   Out on the Paracas Peninsula in the fishing village of Lagunillas, where there is a host of simple seafood restaurants especially popular with tourists and locals on weekends, Tía Fela is the best of the lot. A relaxed spot with great views, it's dependable for the area's go-to menu items, ceviche and fresh grilled fish.

Playa de Lagunillas s/n. No phone. Main courses S/8–S/22. No credit cards. Daily 9am–9pm.

The Desert Quakes

This region along the southern desert coast, where the South American Plate collides with the Nazca Plate, is also one of the most seismically active regions of the world. The most recent tragedy struck in August 2007 when a massive earthquake, which registered 7.9 on the Richter scale, devastated much of Pisco and Ica, killing more than 500 people and leaving nearly 100,000 homeless. The hardest hit parts of the region are still being rebuilt (especially after yet another, though less damaging, earthquake in early 2012). For more info on the aftermath of the 2007 earthquake, see p. 137.

Where to Stay

EXPENSIVE

Doubletree Guest Suites by Hilton ★★ ☺

This large, contemporary waterfront resort on Santo Domingo beach and next to the entrance to the nature reserve was the first of the three big hotels to open in Paracas. With starkly modern furnishings, excellent views of Paracas Bay, a massive 8,000-square-foot pool (quite the Limeño family scene during weekends and vacation time), and a bundle of outdoor activities, including a kids' club and nautical sports, this makes an ideal getaway for families. Rooms are spacious, chic, and crisp, and have terraces or balconies that overlook either the bay or the main pool and gardens (it's hard to beat the former). Once happily ensconced here, most guests choose to eat most or all meals at the hotel, either in the main restaurant or at the pool snack bar.

Urb. Santo Domingo, Paracas National Reserve, Pisco. doubletree1.hilton.com. © **01/617-1000.** Fax 01/444-2171. 120 units. $179–$279 double. AE, DC, MC, V. **Amenities:** Restaurant; bar; fitness center; outdoor pool; spa. *In room:* A/C, TV, fridge, Wi-Fi (free).

Hotel Paracas ★★★ ☺

Now an upscale Starwood Luxury Collection property, this large Mediterranean-style hotel on the bay has been wholly transformed and is the swankest and priciest place to stay in the region. Its cool aesthetic is the work of famed Lima architect Fernando Fort-Brescia, who has a way with pools (he also designed the stunning Tambo del Inka resort in the Sacred Valley). Airy and sophisticated, with great views of the water, it features an extraordinary infinity pool, cool lounge bar and deck, as well as a remodeled restaurant and a new spa with water circuit. Rooms in the two-story, whitewashed villas are spiffier, too, furnished with bamboo appointments, and they have either bay or garden views, and all have small terraces (the most luxo suites have private plunge pools). With features including a children's playground, water-skiing, kayaks, and paddleboats, it's an especially good option for families. The hotel organizes its own Ballestas Islands visits, and it can arrange private-plane trips to the Nasca Lines as well. The hotel serves good lunch buffets, open to nonguests.

Av. Paracas s/n, Paracas National Reserve, Pisco. www.starwoodhotels.com. © **056/581-333.** Fax 01/446-5079 in Lima. 120 units. $225–$465 double; $625 suites. AE, DC, MC, V. **Amenities:** 2 restaurants; 2 bars; fitness center; 3 outdoor pools; spa. *In room:* A/C, TV, fridge, Wi-Fi (free).

La Hacienda Bahía Paracas ★★ ☺

Another indication of Paracas's growing popularity at the high end is the arrival of this lovely new hotel, upscale but a shade more down to earth than its competitors at the top rung. Perched on the edge of the Bahía de Paracas, and curving around a large, palm tree-lined pool with excellent bay views, this cozy, contemporary hotel employs traditional Peruvian architecture materials like huarango wood and local stone in its warm and spacious rooms, as well as glowing amber lanterns outside, to replicate the feel of a coastal hacienda (make sure you request a room with a bay view, as some overlook the parking lot, which would be a tremendous disappointment). It features a small spa, fireplace lounge, museum of pre-Columbian

More *Luxe* in Paracas

Hotel groups both Peruvian and international are seriously banking on Paracas becoming a top luxury destination; competition will increase at the top end with the new 100-room **Aranwa Paracas Resort & Spa** (www.aranwahotels.com/paracas.php), slated to open nearby in late 2013.

7

Pisco & the Reserva Nacional de Paracas

THE CENTRAL COAST & HIGHLANDS

EARTHQUAKE aftershocks

The massive 7.9 earthquake that rocked Pisco and Ica in late 2007 destroyed the famous Cathedral rock formation in the Paracas National Reserve, leveled major churches—Ica's Señor de Luren and Pisco's San Clemente—and severely damaged invaluable pre-Hispanic artifacts, including mummies and ceramics, in museums in Ica and Pisco. More than 37,000 homes were destroyed, half of them in Pisco. Officials estimated that 85% of central Pisco, where most homes in the region were constructed of adobe and incapable of withstanding the tremors, was destroyed.

While aid flooded in from around the world, and Peru sent in its military to keep the peace and try to get the most drastically affected communities back on their feet, it will take years for them to recover, and many who lost their homes may never be able to rebuild.

textiles and ceramics, and a restaurant with a handsome thatched-roof terrace overlooking the bay.

Urb. Santo Domingo, Paracas National Reserve, Pisco. www.hoteleslahacienda.com/paracas. © **051/213-1000.** Fax 01/213-1020 in Lima. 60 units. $260–$320 double. AE, DC, MC, V. **Amenities:** Restaurant; bar and lounge; outdoor pool; spa; tennis court; on-site museum. *In room:* A/C, TV, fridge, Wi-Fi (free).

INEXPENSIVE

Hostal Posada Hispana 🔥   This small, colonial-style hotel just 1½ blocks from the Plaza de Armas is managed by a Spaniard, a long-time resident of Peru, and his Peruvian wife. Popular and a good-value inn for those traveling on a budget, it's quite nicely decorated for the price, with loft spaces and private bathrooms. The friendly *hostal* has a backyard garden and also operates a charming little restaurant, with a bamboo-and-thatched roof, that serves paella, pizzas, and common Peruvian dishes.

Bolognesi 222, Pisco. www.posadahispana.com. ©/fax **056/536-363.** 24 units. $30 double. Rates include taxes. No credit cards. **Amenities:** Restaurant; bar. *In room:* TV, Wi-Fi.

Hostal Villa Manuelita ★ 🔥   One of the nicest spots in the lackluster Pisco hotel scene is this centrally located colonial house, which is colorfully and nicely restored. The century-old house is just a half-block from the main square, and it offers spacious, handsomely decorated rooms that are very good value. The house features a large living room and a Spanish-style central courtyard with a fountain—definitely a step up from most inexpensive accommodations.

San Francisco 227, Pisco. www.villamanuelitahostal.com. ©/fax **056/535-218.** 16 units. $30 double. Rates include taxes. No credit cards. **Amenities:** Restaurant/pizzeria; bar. *In room:* TV, fridge.

ICA

300km (186 miles) S of Lima; 75km (47 miles) SE of Pisco; 130km (81 miles) NW of Nasca

Surrounded by sand dunes, Ica is a bustling colonial town with stifling heat and a collection of attractive churches and notable colonial mansions. Yet most of the principal attractions are located beyond the city. Ica is known primarily for its bodegas, wineries that produce a range of wines and pisco, the white-grape brandy that is the essential ingredient in the national drink, the ubiquitous pisco sour (served as a welcome drink at bars, hotels, and restaurants throughout Peru). Also welcome to travelers in the unrelentingly dry, sandy pampas of the department is Huacachina Lagoon, an unexpected oasis amid palm trees and dunes on the outskirts of Ica. In Ica proper is a small collection of interesting colonial mansions and churches, as well as the surprisingly excellent Museo Regional, with some splendid exhibits on the area's rich archaeological finds.

Ica was first settled as early as 10,000 years ago and then inhabited by a succession of advanced cultures, including the Paracas, Nasca, Wari, and Ica civilizations. The Inca Pachacútec incorporated the Ica, Nasca, and Chincha valley territories in the 15th century, but by the mid-16th century, the Spaniards had arrived, and Jerónimo Luis de Cabrera founded the Villa de Valverde del Valle de Ica, which grew in importance as a commercial center focusing on wine and cotton production.

Years later, Ica is still recovering from the great 2007 earthquake. The city's beloved Señor de Luren church was leveled, and a frightening number of residents lost their homes.

Essentials

GETTING THERE   There are frequent buses from Lima to Ica (4 hr.), which drop passengers in the center of town. Frequent service also connects Ica to Nasca (2 hr.) and Pisco (45 min.). **Cruz del Sur,** Avenida Paseo de la República, Lima (www. cruzdelsur.com.pe; ✆ 01/311-5050), and **Ormeño,** Av. Carlos Zavala 177, Lima (www.grupo-ormeno.com.pe; ✆ 01/472-5000), both travel between Lima, Pisco, Nasca, and Arequipa. **Transportes Soyuz,** Av. México 331 (La Victoria), Lima (www.soyuz.com.pe; ✆ 01/265-0501), connects Ica with Lima and Pisco, and is the fastest and best service (with the most frequent departures) from either city. Bus terminals in Ica are located in the center of town on or just off Jirón Lambayeque, a couple of blocks west of the Plaza de Armas.

GETTING AROUND   Ica is quite spread out, and getting around town will most likely involve taking inexpensive taxis, which flood the streets. (Most trips around town cost less than S/8.) Taxis are especially useful in visiting the wineries located outside of town. There are also *ciclotaxis,* or bicycle rickshaws, which are cheaper still but less secure. Some visitors enjoy taking them out to Huacachina.

You can arrange Nasca Lines overflights from Ica, although it's considerably more common (not to mention much, much cheaper) to organize them in Nasca. If you want to do it from Ica, contact **AeroCondor** (www.aerocondor.com.pe; ✆ 01/421-3105). For additional flight information, call the **Aeródromo de Ica,** Carretera Panamericana Sur, Km 299 (✆ 056/256-230).

ORGANIZED TOURS   For organized tours, contact **Huacachina Tours,** Av. La Angostura 355, L-47, in front of the Hotel Las Dunas (www.huacachinatours.com; ✆ 056/256-582); or **Pelican Travel & Service,** Jr. Independencia 156 and Jr. Lima 121 (✆ 056/225-211).

VISITOR INFORMATION   The **tourist information office** is located at Av. Grau 150 (✆ 056/227-287), and the **tourism police** can be found on the Plaza de Armas (✆ 056/227-673).

FAST FACTS   **Banco de Crédito,** Av. Grau 109, at the corner of Callao (✆ 056/233-711), has an ATM. You'll also find money exchangers on the Plaza de Armas. For medical attention, go to **Hospital Félix Torrealva Gutiérrez,** Bolívar 1065 (✆ 056/234-798), or **Hospital de Apoyo,** Camino a Huacachina s/n (✆ 056/235-231 or 056/235-101 for emergencies). If you need the **police,** its

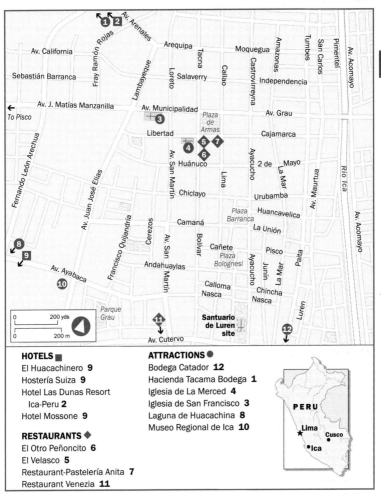

HOTELS ■
El Huacachinero **9**
Hostería Suiza **9**
Hotel Las Dunas Resort
  Ica-Peru **2**
Hotel Mossone **9**

RESTAURANTS ◆
El Otro Peñoncito **6**
El Velasco **5**
Restaurant-Pastelería Anita **7**
Restaurant Venezia **11**

ATTRACTIONS ●
Bodega Catador **12**
Hacienda Tacama Bodega **1**
Iglesia de La Merced **4**
Iglesia de San Francisco **3**
Laguna de Huacachina **8**
Museo Regional de Ica **10**

PERU
Lima ★
Cusco
●Ica

headquarters are located at Lambayeque, block 1 (✆ **056/224-553**). You'll find a
post office at San Martín 156 (✆ **056/234-549**) and a **Telefónica del Perú** office
at Jr. Huanuco 289 (✆ **056/217-247**).

Exploring the Area

Museo Regional de Ica ★ 🎒   MUSEUM   Ica's Regional Museum, founded
in 1946 and frequently hailed as one of the best small museums in the country,
houses a very good collection of intricate Paracas textiles, Nasca ceramics, mummies,
fossils, deformed skulls, and trophy heads, as well as colonial and republican art. The
well-organized collection also includes important pieces from the Huari, Ica, Chincha, and Inca civilizations, giving visitors an excellent primer on the region's rich

history and archaeology. You'll find *quipus,* knotted strings used by the Incas, who, in lieu of a writing system, made and maintained calculations, records, and historical notes with them; and a large-scale model (1/500) of the Nasca Lines behind the museum. Allow about 45 minutes for a visit.

Jirón Ayabaca, Block 8 s/n. ⓒ **056/234-383.** Admission S/12 adults, S/6 students. Mon–Sat 8am–7pm; Sun 9am–1pm. The museum is about a mile, or a 20-min. walk, from Ica's Plaza de Armas; you can also take bus 17 from the plaza to reach it.

BODEGAS (WINERIES)

Dispersed throughout the Ica countryside are some 85 traditional artisanal wineries that produce pisco and still table wines. Several of the larger bodegas welcome visits; these can be interesting because pisco is such a unique Peruvian product, but they're unlikely to be the most fascinating winery tours you'll experience in your lifetime (certainly don't go expecting something on the order of Argentina or Chile). They don't usually draw big crowds, so visits can be a little homespun and even haphazard. If you don't have your own transportation, the best way to visit the following bodegas is either to take a taxi or check with one of the travel agencies in town (see "Organized Tours," above) about organized tours. Tours given on the premises of the wineries are usually in Spanish only.

Harvest time, from late February to April, is by far the best time to visit. At other times, the bodegas can be very quiet; it might be difficult finding someone to give a tour, but you might also have the chance to sit down for a drink with the owner.

Bodega Catador   Located in the Subtanjalla district 7km (4⅓ miles) from Ica, this old bodega, resuscitated in 1970, offers free tours and tastings. It has a small wine museum, and a restaurant and tavern that often have live music. (The winery curiously calls this a "discothèque.") A small Centro Turístico displays photographs and videos of the production process.

Fondo Tres Esquinas 102 (Ctra. Panamericana Sur, Km 296), Subtanjalla, Ica. ⓒ **056/403-295** or **056/403-427.** Free admission. Daily 8am–6pm.

Bodegas Vista Alegre   Just 3km (1¾ miles) north of the center of Ica in the La Tinguiña district, this winery is one of the oldest and largest in Peru. It was a Jesuit hacienda until the late 18th century; in 1857, the winery was established by the Picasso brothers, and it's now well known for its pisco production. Although it's

Pisco Sour

The pisco sours that groups of tourists get served as welcome drinks at restaurants and hotels across the country are often light and frothy—pale imitations of the more potent and tart pisco sours that are the real thing. However, there's been a real revival of interest in this classic Peruvian drink, and in addition to the traditional cocktail, mixologists have come up with delectable variations such as coca sours, maracuyá sours, and lucumá sours, taking advantage of Peru's indigenous plants and fruits. Here's the recipe for an authentic pisco sour:

    2 oz. pisco
    1 oz. lime juice
    1/4 oz. simple syrup
    1/2 egg white
    1 dash Angostura bitters

Shake with ice and strain into glass; garnish with bitters on the creamy top.

possible to walk from Ica (Avenida Grau from the Plaza de Armas, over the Ica River), it's not advisable, as numerous burglaries have been reported along the route.

Camino a La Tinguiña Km 2, Ica. www.vistaalegre.com.pe. ©**056/232-919.** Free admission. Mon–Fri 9am–2pm.

Hacienda Tacama Bodega ★   About 10km (6¼ miles) northeast of Ica, housed in a 16th-century colonial hacienda, this winery, one of the largest and best known producers in the region, exports its pisco and table wines—some of the finest in Peru—to a number of countries. The Olaechea family has owned the winery since 1889. Despite the farm building's age—it's one of the oldest in the valley—the bodega uses modern technology, which has been updated since suffering earthquake damage in 2007. The vineyard is still irrigated, incredibly, by the amazing Achirana irrigation canal built by the Incas.

Av. Camino Real, s/n (Camino a La Tinguiña), Ica. ©**056/228-395.** Free admission. Daily 9am–5pm.

Ocucaje ★   About 35km (22 miles) south of Ica, on the grounds of a colonial hacienda, this remote traditional winery, which dates to the 16th century, is where the locally famous Vino Fond de Cave was born. The winery and its on-site resort suffered significant damage in the August 2007 earthquake.

Av. Principal s/n. www.ocucaje.com. ©**01/251-4571.** S/15 per person for tour. Mon–Fri 9am–noon and 2–5pm; Sat 9am–noon.

COLONIAL CHURCHES & MANSIONS

Ica has several colonial churches and mansions of note, even though many have been felled by earthquakes over the years. **Iglesia de La Merced** (also called **La Catedral**), on the southwest corner of the Plaza de Armas, is a late-19th-century colonial church with a handsomely carved altar. **Iglesia de San Jerónimo,** Cajamarca 262, is primarily of interest for its altar mural. **Iglesia de San Francisco,** though constructed in 1950, is notable for its stained glass; it's at Avenida Municipalidad, at Avenida San Martín. The most important church to worshipers, the neoclassical **Templo del Santuario de Luren,** Calle Ayacucho at Piura, was sadly destroyed by the 2007 earthquake that struck the region.

Among the most attractive of Ica's *casonas,* or colonial mansions, are the **Casona del Marqués de Torre** (today the Banco Continental), on the first block of Calle Libertad; **Casa Mendiola,** on Calle Bolívar; **Casona Alvarado,** a Greco-Roman imitation at Cajamarca 178; and **Casona Colonial El Portón,** Calle Loreto 223.

OUTDOOR ACTIVITIES

Laguna de Huacachina ★ ☺   NATURE   If you stumble upon this gentle oasis in the middle of the desert, surrounded by massive sand dunes and palm trees and ringed by a boardwalk, you might think it's a mirage. Only 5km (3 miles) southwest of the center of Ica, Huacachina (pronounced "Wah-kah-*chee*-nah") Lagoon is a good place to relax (although the water can be pretty murky, full of algae) if you're suffering from the heat, and there's a small resort village with a few hotels and restaurants. Locals contend that the sulfur-rich waters of the lagoon have curative medicinal properties (Huacachina was once an important resort in the 1920s, but today it's largely the domain of backpackers who come to hang out and drink at inexpensive inns and surf the dunes or paddleboat across the lagoon). Regular buses to Huacachina depart from the Plaza de Armas in Ica. Better yet, you can take an inexpensive and quick taxi; it's best to request one from your hotel and establish the price beforehand (rates run to about S/15).

Oasis: San Fernando

Desert dunes and nature worshippers might consider a trek to San Fernando, a little-known and less-visited coastal oasis. As Peru's coastal-desert sand dunes have gotten more popular with extreme sports types, a few agencies and hoteliers have begun to offer 4x4 excursions to this spot—which seems like more of a desert mirage even than Huacachina. Hop aboard an *arenero* (dune buggy) and bound across waves of desert sands until you arrive at a pretty beach and colonies of sea lions, seals, penguins, and maybe even some Andean condors circling overhead. It's an all-day excursion, and you'll get hot and pretty dirty, but it's a thrill ride devoid of tourists. **Casa Andina Classic Nasca** (p. 151) organizes visits, and you might also check with the local agencies **Mystery Peru** (p. 148) and **Alegría Tours** (p. 145).

Sandboarding ★ ☺ OUTDOOR ADVENTURE   In the sand dune-laden desert landscapes in southern Peru, surfing the dunes on sand boards and rumbling across the sands in *areneros* (dune buggies) are popular sports. The largest sand dunes in South America, reaching a height of 2,000m (6,560 ft.), are just 8km (5 miles) from Nasca, and there are also really high dunes around the Huacachina Lagoon outside of Ica.

Sandboarding, a cross between downhill skiing and snowboarding on grainy stuff rather than white powder, is fairly easy to get a handle on (or that's what they tell me). You can really build up some speed, and accomplished boarders can maneuver almost like they would on the slopes. It can be very hot, though, and tough going, because there aren't any lifts to transport you back up the dune. After a few spills, you'll be covered in sand. Accidents can occur, so it's best to get some instruction from a local or the outfit renting the boards.

Adrenaline-fueled adventure trips in buggies are available through local tours (information is available at the **Hotel Paracas;** p. 136) or at the 210m (690-ft.) dunes around the Huacachina Lagoon outside of Ica, where a restaurant and the **Hostal Rocha** rent sand boards (about S/5 an hour; ☎ **056/222-256**).

Where to Eat

Despite its considerable size for the region, Ica offers little in the way of fine dining. Most locals and visitors tend to gravitate toward the Plaza de Armas and the handful of sandwich shops, rotisserie-chicken places, and informal restaurants there.

El Otro Peñoncito PERUVIAN   A long-time family-owned and art-filled restaurant offers a hugely varied menu of *criollo* (Creole) specialties (including the house dish, stuffed *pollo a la Iqueña*) and basic chicken, meat, and fish dishes, including some vegetarian plates.

Bolívar 255. ☎ **056/233-921.** Main courses S/12–S/26. MC, V. Daily 7am–11pm.

El Velasco PERUVIAN   A popular cafeteria-style restaurant and bakery, around since the 1930s, this agreeable place serves both Peruvian and international dishes at very affordable prices, but it's better known for its generous selection of baked goods, desserts, and coffee.

Libertad 137. ☎ **056/218-182.** Main courses S/10–S/25. MC, V. Daily 8am–10pm.

Restaurant-Pastelería Anita ★ PERUVIAN   Fairly upscale for Ica, this long-time cafeteria-style restaurant features a pretty good set-menu lunch menu, as well as a long list of sandwiches, plus pastries and sweets for breakfast or a pick-me-up.

Libertad 133. ℰ **056/218-582.** Main courses S/10–S/30. MC, V. Daily 8am–11pm.

Restaurant Venezia ★ ITALIAN   With a history dating back to the arrival in Ica of an Italian immigrant in 1956, this amiable, still family-run restaurant in its sixth decade serves a good selection of Italian dishes, including homemade pastas, Neapolitan-style pizzas (even a gluten-free version!), and meats, such as *scallopine al vino, milanesa,* and *cordon bleu.* For dessert, it's got to be ice cream (in the '60s, the restaurant was called Bar Restaurant Heladería Venecia).

Av. San Martin 1229. www.restaurantvenezia.com. ℰ **056/210-372.** Main courses S/12–S/34. MC, V. Tues–Sun 11am–3pm and 6–11pm.

Where to Stay
EXPENSIVE
Hotel Mossone   A famous luxury resort hotel back in the 1920s, this century-old mansion at the Huacachina Lagoon is a fancy, colonial-style hotel that hasn't made much effort to keep up with the times. It slipped into neglect for a few decades and still feels a bit dilapidated, with the central patio—along with its lagoon location—its best feature. Rooms are dank and in need of updating, though the restaurant, featuring a relaxing deck overlooking the oasis, is an enjoyable place to relax. Most who choose the Mossone have their hearts set on staying at the lagoon and doing some sandboarding, but even to them it is likely to seem overpriced for what it is. El Huacachinero (below) is probably a better choice.

Balneario de Huacachina, Ica. reservas@derramajae.org.pe. ℰ **056/236-136.** Fax 056/236-137. 43 units. $86 double. Rates include taxes. AE, DC, MC, V. **Amenities:** Restaurant; bar; outdoor pool. *In room:* TV.

Hotel Las Dunas Resort Ica-Peru ★ ☺   On the outskirts of Ica is this sprawling complex of white Mediterranean-style villas with pretty landscaped grounds, three swimming pools, and good sports opportunities, including horseback riding, golf, tennis, *frontón* (something like a cross between paddle tennis and jai alai), sandboarding, and volleyball. In terms of services and amenities, if not necessarily character, it's a step up from the other top hotel in the area, the Mossone (above). Rooms are surprisingly large and nicely furnished, and most have garden views. A nice little bonus is the planetarium that provides a good introduction to the Nasca Lines (admission S/20).

Av. La Angostura 400, Ica. www.lasdunashotel.com. ℰ/fax **056/256-224** or **01/213-5000** for reservations. 106 units. $113–$184 double. Rates include taxes. AE, DC, MC, V. **Amenities:** Restaurant; cafeteria; bar; small gym; 2 outdoor pools; sauna. *In room:* A/C, TV, fridge.

INEXPENSIVE
El Huacachinero ★ 🌮   A convivial, cute little *hostal,* this is probably the best choice for staying right on the lagoon, and is understandably popular with backpackers. Rooms, well maintained and comfortable for the price, are built around an attractive outdoor pool with a sun terrace and bar. The hotel focuses on dune experiences, operating its own "green buggy" services and sandboarding trips, and the resident parrots are either entertaining or annoying, depending on your tolerance.

Avenida Perotti, Balneario de Huacachina, Ica. www.elhuacachinero.com. ℰ **056/217-435.** Fax 056/256-814. 24 units. S/120 double. No credit cards. **Amenities:** Cafeteria; bar. *In room:* TV, mini-bar, Wi-Fi.

Hostería Suiza ★   Also at the edge of the Huacachina Lagoon, and operated by the family that once ran the elegant Hotel Mossone (above), this friendly, homey, and very comfortable *hostal* is pretty good value. Rooms, some of which overlook the lagoon, are very clean and attractive, and the bright tiled bathrooms are also quite nice. The outdoor pool and flower-filled gardens are a nice bonus at this price, at the high end of the budget range. The inn also operates desert sand buggy excursions, which are perfect for adventurous kids.

Balneario de Huacachina, Ica. www.hosteriasuiza.com.pe. © **056/238-762.** Fax 056/219-516. 22 units. $50 double. Rates include taxes. AE, DC, MC, V. **Amenities:** Restaurant; bar; outdoor pool. *In room:* No phone.

NASCA ★

443km (275 miles) S of Lima

Nasca (also spelled Nazca) would just be a dusty little desert town of little interest were it not for the peculiar presence of massive, mysterious drawings—the famed Nasca Lines—etched into the sands of the pampas more than a millennium ago. Ancient peoples created a vast tapestry of "geoglyphs" (trapezoids and triangles, 70-odd animal and plant figures, and more than 10,000 lines) that have baffled observers for decades. They are so large, with some figures reaching dimensions of 300m (1,000 ft.), that they can be appreciated only from the air. Over the years, theorists have posited that they were signs from the gods, agricultural and astronomical calendars, or even extraterrestrial airports. Some believe that the drawers of the lines must themselves have had the ability to fly, perhaps in hot-air balloons, over the designs below. The wildest theories, contending that they were created by extraterrestrials, prompted the old book and movie *The Chariots of the Gods,* but have been discredited by all but fringe-dwelling true believers.

Both the town and the drawings are named for the Nasca culture (300 B.C.–A.D. 700), which succeeded the Paracas civilization along the southern desert coast. Little was known about the Nasca until the beginning of the 20th century. Today the Nasca are renowned for their exquisitely stylized pottery, among the finest of pre-Columbian Peru. The small town of Nasca was devastated by a monstrous earthquake in 1996 and has struggled to get back on its feet. Most constructions in town were adobe, which crumbled and were replaced by hastily built concrete houses. The new construction adds to the dusty frontier feel of the town.

The surrounding desert is a strange, eerie place. What you see flying over the Nasca Lines is an unending expanse of craggy, dusty, origami-like folds in the sands, like deep wrinkles in a wizened face. While nothing in the region equals the impact of a flight over the Lines, the town has a couple of good museums and two archaeological sites that evoke the Nasca culture that flourished in the area.

Essentials

GETTING THERE   From Lima, **Cruz del Sur** buses (www.cruzdelsur.com.pe; © **01/311-5050**) pass through Nasca on the way to Arequipa; the trip to Nasca takes 6 to 7 hours. **Ormeño** (www.grupo-ormeno.com.pe; © **01/472-5000**) makes the trip from Lima as well as Cusco (24-plus hr.) and Arequipa (10 hr.), and, like Cruz del Sur, returns to Lima. **Expreso Wari** (www.expresowari.com.pe; © **01/423-6640**) also makes the long journey between Cusco and Nasca (20–22 hr.).

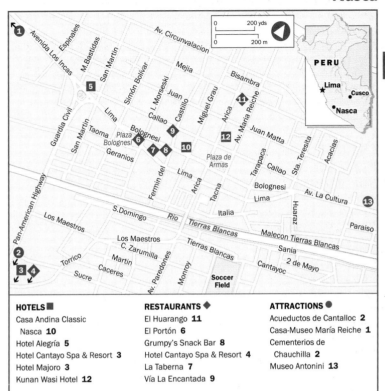

HOTELS ■

Casa Andina Classic
  Nasca **10**
Hotel Alegría **5**
Hotel Cantayo Spa & Resort **3**
Hotel Majoro **3**
Kunan Wasi Hotel **12**

RESTAURANTS ◆

El Huarango **11**
El Portón **6**
Grumpy's Snack Bar **8**
Hotel Cantayo Spa & Resort **4**
La Taberna **7**
Vía La Encantada **9**

ATTRACTIONS ●

Acueductos de Cantalloc **2**
Casa-Museo María Reiche **1**
Cementerios de
  Chauchilla **2**
Museo Antonini **13**

GETTING AROUND   Downtown Nasca can be easily covered by foot, which is fine for most restaurants and Museo Antonini. However, virtually all other sights require either private transportation (taxi) or going through a local agency on organized visits (often the cheapest and most efficient route unless you're with several people who can share the cost). See organized tours, below. A taxi to the Aerodrome is about S/5. To far-flung destinations such as Cahuachi and Chauchilla, you should hire a taxi for round-trip transportation including wait time (you might also be able to negotiate a full day for around S/100-S/120).

ORGANIZED TOURS   The following agencies are the best of those offering city and regional packages and information on the area (as well as Nasca Lines packages): **Alegría Tours,** Jr. Lima 168 (www.alegriatoursperu.com; ℭ **056/523-431**); and **Nanasca Tours,** Lima 160 (ℭ **034/522-917**). **Mystery Perú,** Ignacio Morsesky 126 (www.mysteryperu.com; ℭ **056/522-379**) goes beyond the standard Nasca Lines tours, offering longer (1-hr.) and helicopter flights over the Lines, dune buggy trips, and combo trips to the Cahuachi and Estaquería temples.

VISITOR INFORMATION   The **tourist information office** (ℭ **056/522-418**), Callao 783 (Plaza de Armas) in the Municipal building, offers maps, hotel and tourism packages, and guide information. It's open Monday to Friday from 9am to 3pm. Tourist information can also be obtained from one of the travel agencies in town, such as **Alegría Tours,** although they are primarily interested in selling tour packages.

FAST FACTS **Banco de Crédito** (© 056/522-445), at Avenidas Grau and Lima, has an ATM with the Visa logo, as does **Banco de la Nación** (no phone), Lima 431. For medical attention, go to **EsSalud,** María Reiche 308 (© **056/522-438**), or **Hospital de Apoyo,** Callao s/n (at Morsesky; © **056/522-586**). The **police** (© 056/ 522-442) are on Los Incas, next to the roundabout on Lima and Panamericana, near the Ormeño station. The **post office** is at Fermín de Castillo 379, between Callao and Bolognesi. The **Telefónica del Perú** office (© **056/523-045**) is at Lima 545.

Exploring the Area

For flights over the Nasca Lines, it's often simplest to go to the airport and purchase tickets directly from one of the charter airlines there. Visitors who want to see more than just the Lines would probably benefit from arranging a group tour with one of the Nasca travel agencies (see p. 145), because the major archaeological sites are scattered about the valley and complicated to get to.

NASCA LINES ★★★

The unique Nasca Lines remain one of the great enigmas of the South American continent. The San José Desert, bisected by the great Pan-American Highway that runs the length of Peru, is spectacularly marked by 70 giant plant and animal figures, as well as a warren of mysterious geometric lines, carved into the barren surface. Throughout the Nasca Valley, an area of nearly 1,000 sq. km (390 sq. miles), there are at least 10,000 lines and 300 different figures. Most are found alongside a 48km (30-mile) stretch of the Pan-American Highway. Some of the biggest and best-known figures are about 21km (13 miles) north of Nasca. Most experts believe they were constructed by the Nasca (pre-Inca) culture between 300 B.C. and A.D. 700, although predecessor and successor cultures—the Paracas and Huari—might have also contributed to the desert canvas. The lines were discovered in the 1920s when commercial airlines began flights over the Peruvian desert. From the sky, they appeared to be some sort of primitive landing strips.

As enigmatic as they are, the Nasca Lines are not some sort of desert-sands Rorschach inkblot; the figures are real and easily identifiable from the air. With the naked eye from the window of an airplane, you'll spot the outlines of a parrot, hummingbird, spider, condor, dog, whale, monkey with a tail wound like a top, giant spirals, huge trapezoids, and, perhaps oddest of all, a cartoonish anthropomorphic figure with its hand raised to the sky that has come to be known as the "Astronaut." Some figures

 A Serious Map

Travelers who are serious about exploring the Nasca Lines should consider picking up the Instituto Geográfico Nacional's extremely detailed topographical map, available from IGN (www.ign.gob.pe) or from the South American Explorers (www.saexplorers.org). It's much more detailed than what we offer here, or the cartoonish drawings you'll get at an agency in Nasca.

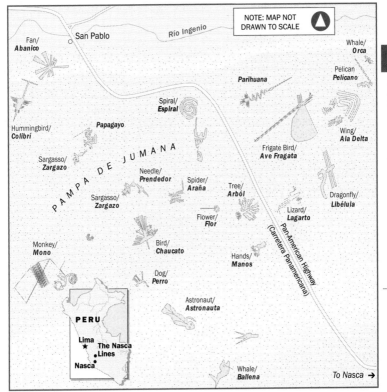

are as much as 300m (1,000 ft.) long, while some lines are 30m (100 ft.) wide and stretch more than 9.5km (6 miles).

Questions have long confounded observers. Who constructed these huge figures and lines? And, of course, why? Apparently, over many generations, the Nasca people removed hard stones turned dark by the sun to "draw" the lines in the fine, lighter-colored sand. The incredibly dry desert conditions—it rains only about 50 centimeters a year, on average—preserved the lines and figures for more than 1,000 years. Why the lines were constructed is more difficult to answer, especially considering that the authors were unable to see their work in its entirety without any sort of aerial perspective. The scientist who dedicated her life to study of the Lines was a German mathematician, María Reiche. For 5 decades, she lived austerely in the Peruvian desert and walked alone among the Lines, taking painstaking measurements and making drawings of the site. She concluded that the Lines formed a giant astronomical calendar, crucial to calculating planting and harvest times. According to this theory, the Nasca were able to predict the arrival of rains, a valuable commodity in such a barren territory. Other theories abound, though. Nasca is a seismic zone, with 300 fault lines beneath the surface and hundreds of subterranean canals; an American scientist, David Johnson, proposed that the trapezoids held clues to subterranean

Cahuachi, an ancient adobe complex west of the Nasca Lines—said by some to be twice as large as Chan Chan, the massive city of the Chimú along the north coast—was the most important ceremonial and administrative center belonging to the Nasca culture. The ruins, in poor condition and, in large part, buried under sand, are still undergoing excavation. Because of ongoing work, only a handful of temples and pyramids may be visited, and only by guided tour. (The major agencies in Nasca usually offer the site as part of a group tour for around $35–$45 per person.) Also on the premises is **El Estaquería,** a construction of rows of huarango trees that probably marked important grave sites. The ruins are 30km (19 miles) from Nasca. The director of the Antonini Museum in Nasca has unearthed a spectacular collection of painted textiles, made with seven different dyes, at Cahuachi that he hopes to eventually exhibit in a new museum in Nasca. Many of the finest examples of Nasca ceramics in existence were also discovered at Cahuachi.

water sources. Some suggest that the Lines not only led to water sources, but that they also were pilgrimage routes, part of the Nasca's ritual worship of water. Notions of extraterrestrials and the Nasca's ability themselves to fly over the Lines have been dismissed by most serious observers.

An observation tower *(mirador)* stands beside the Pan-American Highway (about 19km/12 miles north of Nasca), but it allows only a vague and partial view of three figures: the hands, lizard, and tree. The view from the tower (S/3 adults, S/2 students) is vastly inferior to the multiple bird's-eye views one gets on the overflight, but it's the best you'll be able to do if you can't take the stomach-turning dips and dives of the light-craft flights. (Only 10 min. into one recent flight, the four French travelers onboard with me were all tossing their *petits déjeuners* into the white plastic bags that had been thoughtfully provided.)

A half-dozen small charter airlines offer flights over the Lines from the small airport in Nasca. Flights (35–45 min.) cost $75 to $130, while those originating in Ica run to about $150 to $180. Pilots give very basic descriptions of the figures as they fly overhead. The small aircraft seat between three and five passengers.

If you're interested in seeing the Lines only and you don't have time for the town of Nasca or the surrounding area, by far the most convenient—although certainly not the cheapest—way to see the Lines is as part of a 1-day round-trip package from Lima with **Mystery Peru,** Ignacio Morsesky 126, Nasca (www.mysteryperu.com; ✆ **056/522-379**), including pickup and drop-off in Lima and lunch ($325 per person). Unfortunately, there are no independent flights from Lima to Nasca (or from any other city to Nasca), so you'll have to get there by bus—a 7-hour ride.

For the best visibility, try to go in the morning or late afternoon, but be prepared for conditions that frequently delay flights and occasionally make taking off impossible.

Companies operating Nasca Lines overflights from Nasca's Aeródromo de Nasca, Carretera Panamericana Sur, Km 447 (✆ **056/523-665**) include **Aerodiana** (www.aerodiana.com.pe; ✆ **01/444-3075**); **AeroIca** (www.aeroica.net; ✆ **01/445-0859**); and **Aeroparacas** (www.aeroparacas.com; ✆ **01/265-8073**). Your best bet for arranging an overflight is with one of the Nasca agencies or directly at the airport; Mystery Peru in particular has quite a number of overflight options, including a special in-depth 1-hour flight for $190. Alegría Tours (p. 145) and Mystery Peru both permit advance online reservations and purchases, in some cases with discounts.

OTHER NOTABLE SIGHTS NEAR NASCA

Acueductos de Cantalloc RUINS About 4km (2½ miles) southwest of Nasca are very well-preserved stone aqueducts, part of a sophisticated subterranean system constructed by the Nasca to irrigate the fields in the pampas. There are 35 beautifully built Inca or pre-Inca aqueducts, or *puquios*, with surface air vents that form spirals descending to the water current. The canals, many S-shaped to slow the flow of water, still function and are used by local farmers. Nearby, Los Paredones, the ruins of an Inca trade center, is in poor shape, requiring a fertile imagination to conjure the activity that once reigned here.

Ctra. Puquio–Cusco. Admission $4. Daily 8am–5pm. Take a taxi (about S/25 round-trip, incl. waiting time) or go with an organized tour group ($15–$18 per person).

Casa-Museo María Reiche MUSEUM The German mathematician María Reiche was the foremost expert on the Nasca Lines, earning her the nickname "Dame of the Desert." She dedicated most of her adult life to studying them, debunking the loonier theories about their purposes, and doing more than even the Peruvian government to publicize the Lines' existence. Reiche died in 1998 at the age of 95. Today the simple room where she worked and lived, which her tomb has been placed next to, has been converted into a small museum paying tribute to Reiche's life and the Lines, complete with maps, models, plans, and photos. The Casa-Museo (also variously referred to as Museo de Sitio María Reiche Newman and Museo Regional María Reiche) is located in the district called San Pablo, between Ica and Nasca. Allow a half-hour to tour the museum.

Caserío la Pascana, Ctra. Panamericana Sur, Km 420 (27km/17 miles from Nasca), San Pablo. ℂ **056/234-383** or **056/522-428.** Admission S/5. Mon–Fri 9am–7pm; Sat 8:30am–6:30pm; Sun 9am–1pm. By taxi (about S/45 round-trip).

Nasca Culture

The Nasca civilization is best known for its artistry on a grand scale: those massive and monstrously baffling line drawings on the desert floor of the coastal pampas. But among scholars, the culture is acclaimed for producing the most sophisticated ceramicists of pre-Columbian Peru and ingenious engineers who irrigated their desert fields with hydraulic systems and aqueducts that carried underground water.

The Nasca succeeded the Paracas in the desert region south of present-day Lima. Whereas the Paracas were extraordinary weavers and designers of textiles, the Nasca culture distinguished itself with highly artistic pottery. Its glazed ceramics featured vivid but earthy colors and symbolic motifs, and mineral-based pigments ensured lasting colors. Many of the stylized figures and lines on Nasca pottery closely echo the Nasca Lines, reinforcing theories about the latter's authorship.

Cementerios de Chauchilla ★ 📷 RUINS   About 30km (19 miles) south of Nasca is an extensive valley of tombs from the Inca-Chincha period (A.D. 1000–1400). It is a necropolis rather than a mere cemetery: Thousands of graves have been uncovered in the area. Only 12 underground tombs are exposed for visitors, although they present a rich picture of the ancient culture of the desert valley. One tomb holds only children, and others are populated with the remains of adults with thick, Rasta-like dreadlocks. The cemetery has been open to the public since only 1997, and only in the past year were the tombs covered with thatched roofs, which is why many skulls appear whitewashed from the blazing desert sun. The desert's very dry conditions helped preserve the mummies over the centuries. Fragments of textiles, feathers, and even bone are scattered about the site, clues to the cemetery's discovery by *huaqueros* (grave robbers) and how underfunded this project remains. Allow about 3 to 4 hours for travel time and viewing the necropolis.

Chauchilla (30km/18 miles from Nasca). Admission S/5. Daily 8am–5pm. Getting to Chauchilla is complicated, as there is no public transportation to the site; taxi (about S/90 round-trip, incl. waiting time) and tour group ($25 per person) are the only options.

Museo Antonini ★ ☺ MUSEUM   This excellent private archaeology museum, a labor of love inaugurated by an Italian foundation in 1999, addresses local Nasca culture with excellent exhibits that detail the process as well as the results of archaeological excavations in the area. On view are fine ceramics, trophy heads worn by warriors after beheadings to inspire fear among enemies, musical instruments, and a few well-preserved mummies. In the gardens out back are the Bisambra aqueduct, an ancient Nasca stone irrigation canal, reproductions of tombs, and scale models of the Nasca Lines. The director hopes one day soon to be able to open a new museum in Nasca to show off the world's greatest collection of painted textiles—made with seven different types of vegetable dyes—all uncovered from the huge adobe city of Cahuachi nearby. Plan to spend about an hour here.

Av. de la Cultura 600 (Bisambra), a 10-min. walk from the Plaza de Armas. ℂ **056/523-444.** Admission S/15. Daily 9am–7pm.

Where to Eat

Dining choices are a bit less limited in Nasca than in other parts of the region. Most travelers come just to view the Nasca Lines, staying just one night, and they tend to eat at their hotels. Hotels with pretty good restaurants include **Casa Andina Classic Nasca** and **Hotel Alegría.**

El Huarango ★ PERUVIAN   One of the better restaurants in Nasca, this charming place—look up, it's on the third floor—is popular with both locals and travelers for its rooftop garden terrace. Dishes are largely coastal Peruvian favorites, such as *ají de gallina* (chicken in a spicy cream sauce), served in ample portions.

Jr. Arica 602. ℂ **056/522-141.** Main courses S/14–S/30. MC, V. Mon–Sat 11am–5pm.

El Portón ★ PERUVIAN/INTERNATIONAL   With its breezy, colonial-style decor, this traditional restaurant is dependable for international standards, such as pastas, lasagna, and pizzas, as well as *criollo* dishes like *seco de cabrito* (goat stew).

Av. Ignacio Morseski 120 (at Av. Lima). ℂ **056/523-490.** Main courses S/14–S/25. MC, V. Daily 11am–10pm.

Grumpy's Snack Bar ☺ SNACK BAR   A simple little place with bamboo walls and a name that's sure to appeal to kids, here you'll find a large menu of good snacks, including pizzas, salads and burgers, and fruit juices, perfect for a light lunch—because you don't want a really full stomach before your overflight of the Nasca Lines.

Jr. Bolognesi 182. No phone. Main courses S/8–S/18. AE, DC, MC, V. Daily 11am–10pm.

Hotel Cantayo Spa & Resort ★★ INTERNATIONAL   The most elegant restaurant in Nasca and one of the only options for an unusual taste of fine dining along the southern desert coast, this is the place to seek out when you're in need of hard-to-find organic vegetables and salads, gourmet Italian dishes, lightly prepared grilled fish, and a rarely seen Andean specialty for lunch: *pachamanca,* a barbecue of potatoes, meat, and vegetables roasted in an underground pit. If you're pining for a good bottle of wine or imported cheeses, this is the place to splurge.

Ctra. Puquio–Cusco (4km/2½ miles southwest of Nasca). ✆ **056/522-283.** Main courses S/21–S/60. AE, DC, MC, V. Daily 11am–10pm.

La Taberna ☺ INTERNATIONAL   This local and traveler's long-time favorite—testified to by the graffiti scrawlings of hundreds of international visitors on the walls—serves a wide variety of dishes, including Peruvian specialties like *lomo saltado* and ceviche. Vegetarians will be happy with salads and pastas, as well as paella-style *fideua.* There's usually live music in the evenings.

Jr. Lima 321. ✆ **056/806-783.** Main courses S/14–S/25. MC, V. Daily 9am–4pm and 6–11pm.

Vía La Encantada ★ PERUVIAN/INTERNATIONAL   This spiffy bi-level restaurant is dependable for international standards, such as pastas, lasagna, and pizzas, as well as good salads and *criollo* dishes like *seco de cabrito* (goat stew). If you opt for an early dinner, this is a good place to catch sunset on the balcony with a pisco sour in hand. It's also a good spot the next morning for a full American breakfast.

Jr. Bolognesi 282. hotellaencantada.com.pe. ✆ **056/522-930.** Main courses S/14–S/25. MC, V. Daily 7am–midnight.

Where to Stay
EXPENSIVE
Hotel Cantayo Spa & Resort ★ 🏨   Located next to the Cantalloc Aqueduct, this mission-style hacienda has been converted into a sprawling spa hotel. Rustic and peaceful, it features sweeping panoramic mountain views, large rooms adorned with Balinese and Tibetan touches, a huge swimming pool, extensive gardens, and a jogging track. The Italian owners have positioned it as a relaxing refuge, which takes its cues from the region's more spiritual and mystical attractions, offering a menu of exoticism: tai chi, yoga, Japanese meditation, and not only massages and facials but also Watsu treatments. If you consider yourself more grounded than that, you can indulge in horseback riding and long walks around the property. That said, some guests might feel a bit marooned out in the countryside. The hotel's restaurant is the best in Nasca and worth a visit even if you aren't staying here.

Carretera Puquio–Cusco, Nasca. www.hotelcantayo.com. ✆ **056/522-264** or **056/522-283** for reservations. Fax 056/522-283. 40 units. $190 double; $270 executive suite. Rates include breakfast. AE, DC, MC, V. **Amenities:** Restaurant; Jacuzzi; 2 outdoor pools; spa. *In room:* A/C, TV.

MODERATE
Casa Andina Classic Nasca ★★ 🍴   Though there are no other chains in Nasca, Casa Andina, a still-growing group of Peruvian hotels, is making sure it's got all the top tourist spots in the country covered. This charming hotel, appreciated by families and

more upscale travelers (for whom there are few good options in Nasca), follows the company's midsize, midrange, and always consistent formula. Located downtown, right on the pedestrian mall that's one block from the main square, it is the largest hotel in Nasca. Rooms—built along a sunny, open-air interior corridor—are ample and nicely decorated, with colorful interiors and nice, clean bathrooms. The outdoor pool isn't large, but it features a large and cheery, bougainvillea-filled patio.

Jr. Bolognesi 367, Nasca. www.casa-andina.com. © **866/220-4434** toll-free in the U.S., **08/082-343-805** in the U.K., or **01/213-9739.** Fax 056/521-067. 60 units. $89–$119 double. Rates include breakfast buffet. AE, DC, MC, V. **Amenities:** Restaurant; outdoor pool. *In room:* A/C, TV, Wi-Fi (free), hair dryer upon request.

Hotel Majoro ★ 🎁 ☺   This rustic old hacienda features simple rooms around courtyards and tranquil, extensive gardens full of bougainvillea. The owners recently pumped much-needed investment and life into the place, though it retains the feel of an elegant country house, with horse stables and open space. The common areas have been completely transformed and are now warm and inviting. Accommodations are spacious, clean, and charming where they were once dumpy. The two large, garden-like pools are terrific places to relax and let the kids run around. It's set in Majoro, a few kilometers along a dusty road beyond the airport. Check online for promotions, as the hotel advertises some good package deals that include Nasca Lines overflights and other excursions.

Ctra. Panamericana Sur, Km 452 (Majoro) Nasca. www.hotelmajoro.com. © **056/522-481.** Fax 056/522-750. 39 units. $100–$135 double. $145–$185 suites. Rates include breakfast. AE, DC, MC, V. **Amenities:** Restaurant; bar; 2 outdoor pools. *In room:* TV.

INEXPENSIVE

Hotel Alegría ★   The down-to-earth and traveler-friendly Alegría, with a white-washed Andalusian look, is the most popular inexpensive hotel in town, and a good place to meet up with others exploring this region of Peru. Rooms are basic, but the nice leafy patio garden and small pool are excellent bonuses for a hotel at this price point (although you could stay at the Casa Andina Classic for not much more, if you get a deal). It operates a good travel agency and has loads of facilities and services, including free Internet access for guests, bus-station pickup, and luggage storage. Some of the new chalet-style rooms have air-conditioning.

Highest Railroad in the World

Lima is the starting point of the **Ferrocarril Central Andino** (www.ferrocarrilcentral.com.pe; © **01/226-6363**), the highest railway in the world, which runs from Lima to Huancayo in the central highlands (up to 4,781m/15,686 ft.). Unfortunately, the line has a problematic history (enough to discourage most reasonable travelers from planning their trips to Peru around it): The so-called "Tren Macho" was shut down for most of the 1980s and 1990s. It is again operating after long periods of inactivity, however. The incredibly scenic, 12-hour passenger train, which crosses 58 bridges and passes through 69 tunnels, runs once a month between July and November and costs from S/165 to S/300 for a round-trip). Trains leave Lima from the **Estación Central de Desamparados,** Jr. Ancash 201, just behind the Government Palace. Check for updates before you arrive in Peru.

Lima 168, Nasca. www.hotelalegria.net. ©/fax **056/522-497.** 48 units. $60 double. Rates include breakfast and prearranged pickup from bus stop. DC, MC, V. **Amenities:** Restaurant; bar; outdoor pool; Wi-Fi (free); free parking. *In room:* A/C in some units, TV, minibar.

Kunan Wasi Hotel ★ 🍴   A block from the Plaza de Armas, this exceedingly friendly and well-equipped place is a sparkling clean, if slightly spartan, small hotel with excellent services. The cool, gleaming surfaces of the marble bathrooms and brightly colored rooms are a nice antidote to the dusty, hot, monochrome desert. The owner is extremely helpful and willing to help make travel arrangements. For the budget traveler, it's tough to do better.

Arica 419, Nasca. www.kunanwasihotel.com. © **056/524-069.** Fax 056/521-067. 20 units. $40 double. Rates include continental breakfast. AE, DC, MC, V. **Amenities:** Wi-Fi (free). *In room:* TV, minibar.

AYACUCHO: GEM IN THE CENTRAL HIGHLANDS ★★

585km (364 miles) SE of Lima; 337km (209 miles) NE of Pisco; 590km (367 miles) W of Cusco

Hijacked in the 1980s by Shining Path terrorists who claimed the city as their base, cutting it off from Peru and the rest of the world for 2 decades, Ayacucho is at last devoid of bloody conflict and begging to be discovered. High in the central Andes, with more of its Spanish colonial architecture intact than almost any other city in Peru, the city claims the crown as the epicenter of Peruvian *artesanía* (popular art). The renowned *retablos* (see box below), ceramic churches, and whimsical red-clay figurines one sees all over Peru (and in Latin American shops from Austin to Amsterdam) are all produced locally.

Locals are fond of claiming that the most critical developments in Peruvian history are all tied to Ayacucho. As the site of the earliest-known human presence in Peru (nearby Pikimachay) and the one-time capital of the powerful Huari culture (200–100 B.C.), Ayacucho is, in fact, a place where crucial battles for the soul of Peru have taken place. The Chanca people bravely resisted the aggressively expanding Inca Empire, and the bloody Battle of Ayacucho against Spanish forces in 1824 launched the country's independence.

Given its history, it's not surprising that Ayacucho means "City of Blood" or "City of the Dead." Yet Ayacucho has much more to offer than its notoriety: Visitors will find a welcoming and spectacularly serene city seemingly cleansed of its violent past. It's so easygoing and unassuming that it's almost inconceivable that it could have been held hostage for so long by terrorists intent on rending Peruvian society. As it continues to distance itself from the guerrilla violence of the 1980s and early 1990s, Ayacucho is keen to attract travelers to its nearly three dozen colonial churches within blocks of the Plaza Mayor and famously spectacular Easter week festival and carnival celebrations.

Essentials

GETTING THERE

BY PLANE   By far the best way to get to Ayacucho is to fly from Lima on **LC Busre** (www.lcbusre.com.pe; © **01/619-1313**) or **Star Perú** (www.starperu.com; © **01/705-9000**) which fly daily; the flight is 1 hour and costs about $99 one-way. The **Alfredo Mendívil Duarte** airport (© **066/812-418**) is 4km (2½ miles) east of downtown on Av. del Ejército 950. Taxis, which charge S/8 to downtown, await arriving flights.

BY BUS Executive service buses from Lima via Pisco take about 8 hours on a very demanding road through the mountains; contact **Ormeño** (www.grupo-ormeno.com. pe; ☎ 01/472-5000) or **Cruz del Sur** (www.cruzdelsur.com.pe; ☎ 01/311-5050). Executive buses are infinitely preferable to regular service; note that they travel at night only on the direct return to Lima. There is no central bus terminal in Ayacucho; **Cruz del Sur** is located on Av. Mariscal Cáceres 1264 (☎ 066/812-813), and **Ormeño** is at Jr. Libertad 257 (☎ 066/812-495).

GETTING AROUND

The best way to get around Ayacucho itself is on foot because most places of interest—hotels, restaurants, the cathedral—are only minutes from the Plaza Mayor. Taxis and mototaxis are readily available and cheap for any trip within the city; taxis charge S/3 to S/4, and mototaxis charge S/2. A taxi to the Barrio de Santa Ana is a good idea, but if you want the driver to wait while you visit the *artesanía* galleries, negotiate a price beforehand. For transport to **Quinua** and other outlying attractions, colectivos depart from the *paradero* (bus stop) at the corner of Jirón Salvador Cavero and Jirón Ciro Alegría in the eastern part of Ayacucho (Urbanización Santa Bertha).

ORGANIZED TOURS

For guided tours and transportation in the area, contact **Wari Tours,** Portal Independencia 70 (☎ 066/311-415).

VISITOR INFORMATION

A small **iPerú** tourist counter greets arriving planes at the airport every morning from 6:30 to 8:30am. The **iPerú** office at Portal Municipal 48 (Plaza Mayor; ☎ 066/818-305) is extremely helpful and is open Monday through Saturday from 8:30am to 7:30pm, and Sunday from 8:30am to 2:30pm.

FAST FACTS

Banco de Crédito (☎ 066/522-445) Portal Unión 27 (Plaza Mayor), has a Visa-compatible ATM. You'll also find money-changers hanging around the Plaza Mayor. Several pharmacies line Jirón 28 de Julio, including **Farmacia del Pino,** Jr. 28 de Julio 123 (☎ 066/312-080). For emergencies, contact the **National Tourism Police** at Jr. 2 de Mayo 100 (at Jirón Arequipa; ☎ 066/312-055). The 24-hour **National Police** office is at Jr. 28 de Julio 325 (☎ 066/312-332). The main hospital is **Hospital Regional de Ayacucho,** Av. Independencia 355 (☎ 066/312-180). The **post office** is at Jr. Asamblea 295 (☎ 066/312-224).

Exploring the City

Ayacucho's pretty and placid **Plaza Mayor ★★** (also called the **Plaza de Armas**), the epitome of a highland town square and the heart of the city, is lined by grand 16th- to 18th-century homes with stone arches and colonial red-tile roofs. It is one of the best surviving examples of colonial architecture in Peru. Eight walkways radiate out from the center in the form of a star, and you'll probably find yourself crisscrossing the square several times a day. The plaza's lovely gardens and soaring views of the cathedral and surrounding mountains make it a perfect place to occupy an iron bench and watch locals get their pictures made around the Monument to Antonio José de Sucre in the center.

ATTRACTIONS ●
Casona Chacón **7**
Casona Cristóbal Castilla y Zamora **15**
Casona del Boza y Solís **11**
Casona Olano **19**
Casona Ruíz de Ochoa **20**
Catedral de Ayacucho **12**
Museo Arqueológico Hipólito Unanue **1**
Museo de la Memoria **3**
San Francisco de Asís **23**
Santa Clara de Asís **24**
Templo de la Compañía de Jesús **16**
Templo de San Cristóbal **25**
Templo de Santa María Magdalena **4**
Templo de Santa Teresa **26**
Templo de Santo Domingo **6**
Templo del Arco **2**
Templo y Convento de La Merced **21**

HOTELS ■
Hostal La Florida **14**
Hostal Marquez de Valdelirios **27**
Hotel Santa Rosa **10**
Hotel Tres Máscaras **22**
Via Via Ayacucho **9**

RESTAURANTS ◆
Antonino **13**
Café Bar New York **18**
El Monasterio **18**
La Casona **5**
Sandra **17**
Wallpa Sua **8**

On the south side of the plaza (Portal Municipal 49) is the Basílica Menor, or **Catedral de Ayacucho** ★, ordered built by King Philip in 1612 and completed in 1672. Beyond an ornate stone facade and two bell towers are three naves, an elaborately carved pulpit, silver and gold-leaf altars, and a collection of colonial-era religious paintings. The cathedral is open to visitors Monday through Saturday from 5 to 7pm, and Sunday from 9am to 5pm; admission is free.

The Plaza Mayor is lined with notable 16th- and 17th-century colonial houses, which belonged to the most powerful citizens of Ayacucho, including: **Casona Cristóbal Castilla y Zamora,** Portal Municipal 50 (✆ **066/312-230;** Mon–Fri 8am–4pm), with a beautiful courtyard and now home to the Universidad Nacional de Huamanga, founded in 1677; and **Casona del Boza y Solís,** Portal Constitución 15 (✆ **066/312-229;** Mon–Fri 8am–noon and 2–6pm). A block west of the Plaza de Armas is **Casona Ruíz de Ochoa** (better known as **Casona Jáuregui**), Jr. 2 de Mayo 210 (✆ **066/314-299;** Mon–Fri 8am–5pm), a handsomely restored, bright yellow 18th-century house with stone arches and blue doors, balconies, and shutters across from Templo de La Merced. Look for the carved eagles on the massive portal. Two other colonial *casonas*, now owned by banks and off-limits to visitors, are worth a look from the street: **Casona Olano,** Jr. 28 de Julio 175, one of the most distinguished examples of 16th-century colonial architecture in the city; and **Casona Chacón,** Portal Unión 28.

At the northern edge of downtown are two museums that are well worth a visit for an understanding of Ayacucho's ancient and more recent history. The **Museo de la Memoria** ★★, Prolongación Libertad 1229 (www.anfasep.org; ✆ **066/317-170;** admission S/3; Mon–Fri 9am–1pm and 3–6pm) is a small but affecting museum chronicling Ayacucho's disastrous period of conflict and dirty war. Ayacucho was witness to two decades (1980–2000) of Sendero Luminoso (Shining Path) terrorism and overzealous armed forces attempts to eradicate their presence, which resulted in the disappearance and murder of about 70,000 people, most of them peasants (and about half of those in the Ayacucho area). There are photographs of the disappeared, clothing articles from those taken prisoner, and a facsimile of a torture chamber. The exterior of the museum is blanketed in a mural proclaiming "Never again," while the Parque de Memoria out front contains a sculpture depicting the wounds of violence.

Museo Arqueológico Hipólito Unanue ★, Av. Independencia 502 (Centro Cultural Simón Bolívar) (✆ **066/312-056;** admission S/3; Tues–Sun 9am–5pm) is a nicely designed museum that focuses on the ancient cultures of the Ayacucho area, including the Huari and Chancas. On view are some excellent ceramics, a trio of tiny mummies, and a room full of a half-dozen, massive stone sculptures taken from the Huari site outside Ayacucho. An unexpected treat lies in front of the museum: a botanical garden of varied types of cacti.

COLONIAL CHURCHES

Anyone with an interest in colonial churches will be in heaven in Ayacucho, which overflows with 33 examples, dating back as far as 1540, in a relatively small downtown area. In fact, Ayacucho is one of the few Peruvian cities that retains a significant colonial architectural core. Most churches can be visited only early in the morning or during Mass hours on Sunday (except where noted below).

North of the Plaza Mayor, and perhaps the most visually striking of the collection, is the finely sculpted **Templo de Santo Domingo** ★ (1548), Jirón 9 de Diciembre

Ayacucho plays host to some of the most spectacular popular festivals in Peru. The week-long Easter celebration, **Semana Santa ★★★**, features nightly candlelit processions and daily fairs. It culminates in a stunning and emotional procession on Easter Sunday that makes its way around the Plaza Mayor. The procession is marked by the annual appearance of a massive (15×8m/ 49×26-ft. high) throne made entirely of white wax and carried by 200 people. Note that all hotels and *hostales* in Ayacucho are booked months in advance for Easter week, although you might find additional lodging offered in private homes.

Carnaval Ayacuchano is an authentic Quechua carnival celebration, one of the most colorful in the country. For 3 days in February or March, dancing and festivities take over the streets of Ayacucho, including the official proclamation of the *Ño Carnavalon,* or giant papier-mâché figure of the Rey Momo. The celebration also includes the unveiling of political songs, elaborate masks, and the Festival del Puchero, a typical Carnaval Ayacuchano dish served on Tuesday of Holy Week. In rural areas, carnival celebrations are starkly traditional, marked by manifestations such as ancient fertility rites.

The **Bajada de los Reyes Magos (the arrival of the Three Kings)** on January 6 and **La Virgen de la Candelaria** on February 2 are two other notable festivals, though they're not nearly as popular as Carnaval and Semana Santa. For more information on festivals in Ayacucho, contact **iPerú** (www.promperu. gob.pe; (🖀 **066/318-305**).

at Jirón Bellido, the city's second convent. Its unique facade is marked by rustic earth-colored bricks, two towers framing a row of spikes, and three Romanesque arches at the ground level. Inside is a magnificent carved, gold-leaf main altar that holds la Virgen del Rosario.

The majority of churches are south and west of the Plaza Mayor. In any direction you walk in Ayacucho, however, there are lasting examples of religious architecture marking Ayacucho's colonial importance. Little except for an exterior wall and an original squat bell tower remains of **Templo de San Cristóbal,** Jirón 28 de Julio at Jirón 2 de Mayo, the first church in Ayacucho (not open to the public). It dates to 1540, the year of the Spanish founding of the city, making it one of the oldest churches in South America. Built of brick and adobe, it was quite evidently a simple and rustic design. **Templo de la Compañía de Jesús** (1605), Jirón 28 de Julio between Jirón Lima and Jirón San Martín, founded as a Jesuit school and church, is an imposing baroque brick structure a half-block west of the Plaza Mayor. Its massive towers were added in the 18th century. **Templo y Convento de La Merced** (begun 1540), Jirón 2 de Mayo at Jirón San Martín, the second church and first convent in Ayacucho, is well worth a visit.

Templo de Santa Teresa ★ (1703), Jr. 28 de Julio s/n, faces a pretty, serene plaza across from San Cristóbal. Visitors must first enter the convent, to the right of the church, and ask permission to visit the church (it remains a convent of 20 cloistered Carmelite nuns, who sell sweets and other items through a closed window), which is entered around the corner from the plaza. The main altar is a fabulously chunky example of gold-leaf carving. **Santa Clara de Asís** (1568), Jirón Grau at Nazareno, the first monastery in Ayacucho and the second in Peru, features the largest tower in the city. Inside are good examples of *mudéjar* (Moorish-style) woodcarving and an interesting sculpture of the Immaculate Conception on the main altar.

Other colonial churches of interest to completists are **San Francisco de Asís** (1552), Jirón 28 de Julio at Jirón Vivanco, the only church besides the cathedral to have three naves; the baroque **Templo de Santa María Magdalena** (1588), Jirón Sol at Avenida Mariscal Cáceres, founded by the Dominican order but a three-time victim of fire; and the small and sweet snow-white **Templo del Arco,** a postcard-perfect example of a simple South American colonial church, on Plazoleta María Parado de Bellido (near the **Mercado Artesanal** in the El Arco district, north of the Plaza Mayor).

Where to Eat

Down-to-earth Ayacucho is a great place to sample traditional Quechua specialties. It's also known for its artisanal wheat bread. In addition to the restaurants below, a good spot for breakfast is **Sandra,** Jr. 28 de Julio 183 (no phone), a little cafe and *juguería* (juice bar). It serves a huge *café con leche,* massive *jarras* of fresh juices, *tamales,* salads, and sandwiches on herb-crusted pita bread. Within the courtyard of the Centro Cultural, Jr. 28 de Julio 178, there are a couple of cafes for light meals, snacks, coffee, dessert, and breakfast; check out **Café Bar New York** (© **066/313-079**), which has seats outdoors overlooking the patio.

MODERATE

La Casona ★ PERUVIAN   Though brightly lit, this comfortable restaurant, as popular with locals as it is with visitors to Ayacucho, is a nice spot to sample a varied and good-value menu of Andean *criollo* cooking. Built around a pleasant, plant-filled courtyard, the restaurant features grilled meats, roast chicken, trout, and a host of *platos tradicionales,* or regional specialties, such as *chancho al horno con qapchi* (oven-baked pork). A nice appetizer is the huge avocado stuffed with chicken—a meal in itself. Most dishes come with either golden potatoes or salad.

Jr. Bellido 463.© **066/312-733.** Reservations recommended Fri–Sat. Main courses S/10–S/25. MC, V. Daily 7am–10pm.

Wallpa Sua ★ PERUVIAN   This bustling restaurant with multiple dining rooms and a massive grill and rotisserie is hugely popular with Ayacuchanos, who flood the place for delectable spit-roasted chicken and grilled meats. The chicken is as good as advertised by locals; the quarter bird with fries and salad is a steal for S/10.

Garcilaso de la Vega 240.© **066/313-905.** Main courses S/10–S/28. No credit cards. Daily 11am–10pm.

INEXPENSIVE

Antonino ★ PIZZA/ITALIAN   A dimly lit local favorite for its extensive roster of pizzas and pastas, both pretty authentic, with good cocktails to boot. In the front room is a pizza oven and chef knocking out homemade pastas; the dining room tucked away in back is where locals on dates tend to hide.

Jr. Cusco 144.© **066/315-738.** Main courses S/6–S/15. MC, V. Daily 5–10pm.

El Monasterio 🌶 PERUVIAN   Occupying a corner of the Centro Cultural courtyard, with outdoor tables, this restaurant is essentially a *pollería*—a simple restaurant serving roasted chicken—in a slightly upscale location. There are other things on the menu, but I never once saw anyone order anything but the chicken. And with good reason: it's flavorful and plentiful, and it's a steal. For just a couple of bucks, you can

AYACUCHO'S renowned RETABLOS

Ayacucho has a long tradition of finely crafted *artesanía*, and the city and environs are said to produce 40 different specialized crafts. Perhaps most famous and emblematic of Ayacucho are the *retablos*, wooden boxes that open to show off two or three levels of busy scenes populated by dozens of laboriously hand-carved and hand-painted figures. A tradition brought by Spaniards and first produced in Peru during early colonial times in the 16th century, they were then known as Cajones de San Marcos or San Antonio, and they served as portable altars that devotees of St. Mark or St. Anthony carried with them on their travels through the Andes. The *retablos* were often used in efforts to convert indigenous peoples to Catholicism. Although the scenes depicted were once strictly religious, today they represent quotidian scenes of life in the *sierra*, from weddings to harvest scenes

and popular festivals (although Nativity scenes remain very popular).

The doors and exterior usually feature brightly painted flowers, and the *retablos* range from miniature versions with tiny figurines to others that are 1.8m (6 ft.) tall and hold 100 or more figures inside. *Retablos* are so identifiable with Ayacucho that enormous ones are displayed at the airport (more than 3m/10 ft. tall) at the luggage turnstile, and newspaper kiosks around the Plaza Mayor are decorated like oversize *retablos*.

Other handicrafts that are indigenous to the region are red-clay ceramics, including humorous depictions of groups of musicians and small bulls, and model churches; tightly woven and brightly colored *tejidos*, or textiles; carved alabaster, or *piedra de Huamanga*; figures of saints; crucifixes; chess sets; and art naïf *tablas de Sarhua*.

get a quarter of a roasted chicken, french fries, and salad. The other items on the menu are mainly the usual Andean suspects, such as *lomo saltado* (strips of beef with fried potatoes, onions, and tomatoes over rice).

Jr. 28 de Julio 178 (in Centro Cultural). ✆ **066/313-905.** Reservations not accepted. Main courses S/9–S/20. No credit cards. Daily 11am–11pm.

Shopping

For food shopping, and the cultural experience that good Peruvian markets provide, don't miss **Mercado 12 de Abril ★**, Jr. 28 de Julio (between Chorro and San Juan de Dios) (✆ **066/836-166;** daily 7am–4pm). Ayacucho's popular food market is bustling with all manner of food and juice kiosks and produce and meat vendors.

One spot in town to shop for the famous *retablos,* ceramic churches, and other typical *artesanía* of the Ayacucho region is the **Mercado Artesanal Shosaku Nagase,** Plazoleta María Parado de Bellido (5 blocks north of the Plaza Mayor; no phone). At this sprawling facility, the government operates training programs for those wanting to work in the production of handicrafts, and there are two buildings of stalls selling local works. It was once full of artisans, but the selection has diminished in recent years.

Barrio Santa Ana ★, some 10 blocks southwest of the Plaza Mayor, is the old heart of Ayacucho's Quechua culture and *artesanía.* Around the main square, Plazuela de Santa Ana, are several family-run galleries. At several, you can watch textiles and rugs being created. Some rugs are highly valued and have been exhibited internationally. Sadly, the area on recent visits has seemed a little depressed and devoid of the activity it once displayed. Try Alejandro Gallardo's **Galería Latina,** Plazuela de Santa Ana 105 (✆ **066/528-315**); **Alfonso Sulca Chávez,** Plazuela de Santa Ana 83 (✆ **066/312-990**); and **Galería Arte Popular de Fortunato Fernández,** Plazuela de Santa Ana 63–64 (✆ **066/313-192**). **Galería Wari,** Mariscal Cáceres 302 (✆ **066/312-529**), is the studio and home of Gregorio Sulca, a celebrated textile and plastic artist who has exhibited his sophisticated rugs, paintings, and other pieces based on deep research into the Quechua culture in Germany and the U.S. If he's around and you speak Spanish, it's worth engaging him in conversation for an explanation of some fundamental Quechua philosophy and the historical and theoretical underpinnings of his (expensive) work.

The finest handicrafts shopping, however, is found at the source of most of the typical regional *artesanía.* The tiny pueblo **Quinua** (see box, p. 161) is where most of the ceramic churches and *retablos* are made by local artisans, and it is a fascinating Quechua village. Prices are cheaper than in Ayacucho and much cheaper than in Lima or Cusco; the selection also is much better.

Where to Stay

Given its years in the hinterlands of the tourism circuit, it's not surprising that Ayacucho isn't exactly overflowing with good hotel choices. Still, there's a large, if uninspiring, hotel that caters mostly to business travelers and a small selection of easygoing, family-run *hostales.*

MODERATE

Hotel Santa Rosa ★   While the colonial character is in the magnificent arcaded courtyards and exterior—the rooms could use a serious update in style, starting with the bedspreads—this is still a recommended place to stay. It's got Wi-Fi, a good central location, and the courtyard is a splendid place for breakfast on a sunny morning.

Jr. Lima 166. www.hotel-santarosa.com. ✆ **066/312-083.** 38 units. S/130 double. Price includes breakfast. No credit cards. **Amenities:** Restaurant; bar. *In room:* A/C, Wi-Fi (free).

Via Via Ayacucho ★★ 🛅   Despite a superb location right on the gorgeous main square, this new Belgian/Dutch traveler's *hostal* rates as a find; few people seem to know about it, but don't expect that to be the case for long. Although a great place to meet up with adventurous fellow travelers, most of them young, it's actually a pretty stylish boutique hotel, with stunning views and nicely equipped rooms named for regions of the world. There's a nice restaurant/cafe and a rooftop sun terrace.

Portal Constitución 4 (Plaza de Armas). www.viaviacafe.com/en/ayacucho/hotel. ✆ **066/312-834.** 14 units. S/120–S/130 double; S/1595 suite. Price includes breakfast. No credit cards. **Amenities:** Restaurant; bar/cafe. *In room:* A/C, TV, Wi-Fi (free).

INEXPENSIVE

Hostal La Florida 🍴   A relaxed and friendly, family-run small *hostal* just 3 blocks from the main square, this is one of the better spots in town. It's secure and quiet, and rooms on the top floor across the small, leafy courtyard have excellent views of the surrounding rooftops and mountains. En-suite bathrooms are small but clean, and—a rarity at this cheap price—rooms have cable TV. There's a cute little cafe next door, a good spot for breakfast and other informal meals.

Jr. Cusco 310, Ayacucho. ✆ **066/812-565.** 12 units. S/65 double. No credit cards. **Amenities:** Cafe. *In room:* TV.

Tours of Huari & Quinua

If you'd rather visit Huari and Quinua with a more convenient, organized tour rather than on your own (which, given spotty transportation, especially from Huari to Quinua, can be trying), try **Wari** **Tours** (Jr. Lima 138; www.waritours.com; ✆ **066/311-415**); or **Urpillay Tours** (Portal Constitución 4; www.ayacuchoviajes. com; ✆ **066/315-074**). Group and private tours range from S/35–S/150.

Hostal Marquez de Valdelirios 🎁   This *hostal,* housed in a handsome colonial house, is an offbeat find. On a peaceful, well-manicured boulevard just a few blocks north of the busy downtown (a 10-min. walk from the Plaza Mayor), it feels like a retreat. On the outside, it looks almost high design, with artfully placed blue flowerpots against the stark white stucco walls and deep wood exterior. Rooms, which are all on the interior, are comfortably outfitted, if not overly large. They might not live up to the promise of the exterior, but for the bargain price, they're more than comfortable. Breakfast is served on the sunny terrace.

Alameda Valdelirios 720, Ayacucho. ✆ **066/318-944.** 14 units. S/75 double. Rates include breakfast. No credit cards. **Amenities:** Bar. *In room:* TV.

Hotel Tres Máscaras ★   One of the best deals in town is this exceedingly friendly *hostal* built around a plant-filled courtyard with soothing distant views of the mountains. Rooms are very comfortable and clean for the price, making this fresh-air retreat a true bargain for budget travelers.

Jr. Tres Máscaras 194. ✆ **066/312-921.** 14 units. S/50 double. No credit cards. **Amenities:** Bar.

A Side Trip to Quinua & Huari ★★

Although Ayacucho is well known throughout the country as the popular arts capital of Peru, most of the famous *artesanía* originate from Quinua, a lovely and gentle *sierra* town located 37km (23 miles) northeast of Ayacucho. If you'd prefer to buy at the source, preferably from the artisan who crafted the work rather than from a mere salesperson, Quinua is tops in Peru. The red-tile roof of nearly every house in town is topped with a ceramic church of the kind foreigners are more likely to buy and display on a table or bookshelf. The churches serve as roof-bound protectors against evil spirits.

A beautiful stone passageway leads up to the main cobblestone plaza, populated by whitewashed buildings and the village church. Even though local artisans export their ceramic churches and figures of musicians around the world, Quinua is still the kind of place where little girls whisper and point at visiting gringos.

Local Quechua artisans have become very adept at commercializing and marketing their artisanship. Traditionally, all the ceramic pieces were unpainted or in earth tones. Increasingly, artisans have introduced pastels and bright colors, and the two traditional church towers have gradually begun to bend outward fancifully. But classic pieces are still produced. A few of the best-known local ceramicists, including Mamerto Sánchez, have now moved their studios to more profitable environs such as Lima, cutting out the middle man. There are touristy stalls near the main road and a couple of shops, but for the best shopping, you'll need to venture up the stairs to the heart of the village. The peaceful back streets behind the Plazuela de Armas, especially Jirón Sucre and Jirón San Martín, are where to find the best popular art galleries, and it's not unusual to find pottery firing and hand painting taking place.

Galería Familia Sánchez ★, Jr. San Martín 151 (*€* **066/810-212**), is the studio and gallery of Mamerto Sánchez's son. Walter follows in his father's footsteps, and his studio produces some of the best ceramic pieces and churches in Quinua. Across the street is **Galería Ayllu,** Jr. San Martín s/n (no phone). A number of other galleries, including **Artesanía Anclla** and **Artesanía El Quinuino,** are clustered on Jirón San Martín. A medium-size church costs between S/50 and S/90. Antique *retablos* and churches are difficult to find; your best bet is with antiques dealers in Lima or Cusco.

After you've had your fill of *artesanía,* hike up the hill to **La Pampa,** an expansive plain with stunning panoramic views of the surrounding mountains (especially in the sweet light of late afternoon). Quinua is embedded in most Peruvians' memories as the site of the battle for independence from Spain, and the plain is crowned by a large white obelisk commemorating the 1824 Battle of Ayacucho. The walk up from town takes about 30 minutes.

A few restaurants and *hostales* can accommodate you if you want to linger or spend the night in peaceful Quinua. You won't have much to do besides visit *artesanía* galleries, but you'd be hard-pressed to find a simpler, prettier, and more authentic *sierra* town. The small **Hostal Las Américas,** Jr. San Martín s/n, above Artesanía Anclla (*€* **066/965-7721;** S/30 double), has comfortable-enough rooms in the house of one of the best-known local artisans.

On the way to Quinua, 22km (13 miles) north of Ayacucho, is the **Complejo arqueológico de Huari** (also spelled **Wari**) **★**, one of the oldest urban walled centers in the Americas (dating to around A.D. 600). The Huari culture, perhaps the first centrally governed "nation" in the Andes, was one of the most important in early Peru; its empire stretched north to Cajamarca and south to Cusco. The massive (300-hectare/750-acre) ruins, though badly deteriorated, are of thick, 10m-high (33-ft.) stone walls, houses, tunnels, and flat ceremonial areas, and well worth a visit for anyone with an interest in pre-Inca archaeology. The gorgeous desert-like High Andes setting is covered in bright green cacti, and the serene views of the mountains are breathtaking. Archaeologists have theorized that Huari urban planning and their system of religious, political, and military organization served as a model for the Incas. The city, which contained three levels of underground burial chambers, once had as many as 50,000 inhabitants; it was abandoned around A.D. 800. On-site are a visitor center and small museum **(Museo de Sitio Wari)** exhibiting photographs, dioramas, and artifacts discovered at the complex. The ruins are open Tuesday through Sunday from 9am to 5pm; admission is S/3.

To get to Quinua and Huari, take a colectivo at the corner of Jirón Salvador Cavero and Jirón Ciro Alegría in the east part of Ayacucho (Urbanización Santa Bertha). The trip (S/3) takes about an hour, and vans return hourly. Going on your own, and stopping off at Huari en route or on the way back to Ayacucho is easily done, but wait times for a colectivo to pass by and pick you up can occasionally be excruciating.

CUSCO

The storied capital of the Inca Empire and gateway to the imperial city of Machu Picchu, Cusco (also spelled Cuzco) ★★★ is one of the highlights of South America. Stately and historic, with stone streets and building foundations laid by the Incas more than 5 centuries ago, the town is much more than a mere history lesson. It is also surprisingly dynamic, enlivened by throngs of travelers who have transformed the historic center around the Plaza de Armas into a mecca of sorts for South American adventurers. Yet for all its popularity, Cusco is one of those rare places able to preserve its unique character and enduring appeal despite its growing prominence on the tourism radar. Cusco's beautiful natural setting, colorful festivals, sheer number of sights—unparalleled in Peru—and facilities and services organized for travelers make it the top destination in Peru and one of the most exciting places in South America.

HISTORY   Cusco is a fascinating blend of pre-Columbian and colonial history and contemporary *mestizo* culture. It was the Inca Empire's holy city, the political, military, and cultural center of their continent-spanning empire.

SIGHTSEEING   Spaniards razed most of the city, but found some structures so well engineered that they built directly upon the foundations of Inca Cusco. Along with the cathedral, the city's top sights are the many perfectly constructed Inca stone walls, beginning with Quoricancha, the Incas' Temple of the Sun.

EATING & DRINKING   From Gastón Acurio's creative take on Cusqueña cooking at Chi Cha, to Limo's coastal fusion, and classic French gourmet dining at Le Soleil, Cusco is suddenly a dining capital. Don't miss a creative pisco cocktail at El Pisquerito or the bar at Limo.

ARTS & CULTURE   Where Cusco really thrives is in its vibrant expressions of Amerindian and *mestizo* culture: June's Inti Raymi, a deeply religious festival that's also a magical display of pre-Columbian music and dance, and raucous Paucartambo in mid-July are the highlights.

SHOPPING   The handicrafts center of Peru, Cusco's streets and markets teem with merchants and extraordinary textiles, many handwoven in rural mountain communities using the exact techniques of their ancestors. Pick up stylish alpaca fashions, folk art, and silver jewelry at boutiques in San Blas.

THE BEST TRAVEL EXPERIENCES IN CUSCO

- **Drinking in the Plaza de Armas at dusk.** In the early evening, lights cascading up the hills twinkle and street lanterns and the colored fountain glow against a blue-black sky and the silhouettes of the imposing Andes. Cusqueños of all ages parade across the square, window shop at the boutiques under the arcades, and dip into bars with coveted balconies for people-watching. See p. 169.

- **Catching a display of cultural pride.** You don't necessarily have to plan your trip to Cusco around Inti Raymi, one of Peru's greatest pageants of Andean culture, to see a spontaneous display, parade, or deeply felt homage to the city's Amerindian roots. See p. 181.

- **Marveling at Inca masonry.** Cusco's streets are a living history lesson, a mesmerizing mash-up of pre-Columbian and colonial cultures. The conquering Spaniards had the good sense to construct their mansions and churches right atop the Incas' brilliant stone foundations. The finest example is Qoricancha, the Temple of the Sun. See p. 175.

- **Strolling hilly San Blas.** Climbing the steep streets of atmospheric San Blas can feel like doing the StairMaster, but the city's most bohemian district is chock full of art galleries, bars and pubs, and squat, whitewashed colonial buildings with red-tile roofs. See p. 172.

- **Touring Cusco's Inca ruins.** The circuit of fine Inca ruins on the outskirts of Cusco is a terrific primer before heading on to famous ruins in the Sacred Valley. The star is Sacsayhuamán, a fortress of immense granite blocks magnificently perched on a hill overlooking the city. See p. 177.

The Air up Here

Cradled by the southeastern Andes Mountains that were so fundamental to the Inca belief system, Cusco sits at a daunting altitude of 3,400m (11,000 ft.). The air is noticeably thinner here than almost any city in South America, and the city, best explored on foot, demands arduous hiking up precipitous stone steps—leaving even the fittest of travelers gasping for breath and saddled with headaches and nausea. It usually takes a couple of days to get acclimatized. You'll need to take it easy for the first few hours or even couple of days in Cusco. Pounding headaches and shortness of breath are the most common ailments, though some travelers are afflicted with severe nausea (others may little feel effects of the altitude except when walking up Cusco's steep hills). Drink lots of water, avoid heavy meals, and do as the locals do: Drink *mate de coca*, or coca-leaf tea. (Don't worry, you won't get high or arrested, but you will adjust a little more smoothly to the thin air.) If that doesn't cure you, ask whether your hotel has an oxygen tank you can use for a few moments of assisted breathing. If you're really suffering, look for an over-the-counter medication in the pharmacy called "Soroche Pills." And if that doesn't do the trick, it may be time to seek medical assistance; see "Fast Facts" below. Increasingly, travelers are basing themselves in one of the lower-altitude villages of the Sacred Valley, but there is so much to see and do in Cusco that an overnight stay (at a minimum) is pretty much required of anyone who hasn't previously spent time in the area.

ESSENTIALS

Getting There

BY PLANE Flights arrive from Lima (1-hr.) as well as Arequipa, Juliaca, Puerto Maldonado, and La Paz, Bolivia, at **Aeropuerto Internacional Velasco Astete** (✆ 084/222-611), 5km (3 miles) southeast of the historic center of Cusco. All major Peruvian airlines fly into Cusco, including **LAN** (www.lan.com; ✆ 01/213-8200); **StarPeru** (www.starperu.com; ✆ 01/705-9000); **Taca** (www.taca.com; ✆ 01/511-8222); and **Peruvian Airlines** (www.peruvianairlines.pe; ✆ 01/716-6000), which recently began offering flights from Lima to Cusco. Flights to Cusco are very popular, so make reservations as far in advance as possible.

Transportation from the airport to downtown Cusco (20 min.) is by taxi or private hotel car. Most hotels, even less expensive *hostales,* prearrange airport pickup. Taxi fare is officially S/10 from the airport to the center.

BY BUS Buses to Cusco arrive from Lima, Arequipa, Puno/Juliaca, and Puerto Maldonado in the Amazon basin. The journey from Lima to Cusco takes 26 hours by land; from Puno, 9 to 10 hours; and from Arequipa, 12 hours. There is no single, central bus terminal in Cusco. Most buses arrive at the **Terminal Terrestre,** Av. Vellejos Santoni, Cdra. 2, Santiago (✆ 084/224-471), several kilometers from the city center on the way to the airport. Buses to and from the Sacred Valley (Urubamba buses, which go through either Pisac or Chinchero) use small, makeshift terminals on Calle Puputi s/n, Cdra. 2, and Av. Grau s/n, Cdra. 1. For service from Lima, contact the major companies, including **Ormeño** (www.grupo-ormeno.com.pe; ✆ 01/472-5000), **Cruz del Sur** (www.cruzdelsur.com.pe; ✆ 01/311-5050), **Oltursa** (www.oltursa.com.pe; ✆ 01/708-5000), and **Transportes Civa** (www.civa.com.pe; ✆ 01/418-1111). From Puno, the following offer daily service to Cusco: **Cruz del Sur** (see above), **Imexso Tours** (www.perucuzco.com/imexso tours; ✆ 084/240-801); and **Inka Express** (www.inkaexpress.com; ✆ 084/247-887). From Arequipa, your best bests are **Civa** and **Cruz del Sur.**

BY TRAIN Cusco has two main PeruRail train stations. Trains from Puno arrive at **Estación de Huanchaq** (also spelled Wanchaq), Av. Pachacútec s/n (www.perurail.com; ✆ 084/238-722), at the southeast end of Avenida El Sol. Trains from Ollantaytambo and Machu Picchu arrive at **Estación Poroy** (✆ 084/581-414), on the outskirts of Cusco. Visitors should be particularly cautious at train stations, where thieves have been known to prey on distracted passengers.

Visitor Information

As the top tourist destination in Peru, Cusco is well equipped with information outlets. There's a small, occasionally unoccupied branch of the **Oficina de Información Turística** (✆ 084/237-364) at the Velasco Astete Airport in the arrivals terminal; it's open daily from 6:30am to 12:30pm. The principal **Oficina de Información Turística** is located on Mantas 117-A, a block from the Plaza de Armas (✆ 084/222-032). It's open Monday through Saturday from 7am to 7pm and Sunday from 7am to noon. It sells the essential *boleto turístico* (tourist ticket; see "Cusco's *Boleto Turístico*" on p. 170). However, the **iPerú office,** Av. El Sol 103, Of. 102 (✆ 084/252-974), has been better stocked with information and much more helpful on recent visits; it's open daily from 8:30am to 7:30pm. Another information office is in the **Terminal Terrestre de Huanchaq** train station, Av. Pachacútec s/n (✆ 084/238-722); it's open Monday through Saturday from 8am to 6:30pm.

South American Explorers has an office and club in Cusco at Choquechaca 188, no. 4 (www.saexplorers.org; ✆ **084/245-484**). The office stores luggage, maintains lists of trail reports for members, and has a library of useful information for trekking and mountaineering. If you're traveling extensively, and independently, through Peru, it's worth becoming a member of this helpful group.

Tours

Pretty much every Cusco travel agency offers half-day city tours that take in the Cathedral and other major sights (as little as $15 per person). Agencies also promote tours of the Inca ruins circuit on the outskirts of town. The **Tranvía de Cusco** (www.tranviacusco.com; ✆ **084/223-840**) is a hop-on, hop-off tour of the city on a bus made up to look like an old cable car. It visits 40 historic and cultural sights (S/20 adults, S/10 students).

City Layout

The Incas designed their capital in the shape of a puma, with the head at the north end, at Sacsayhuamán (whose zigzagged walls are said to have represented the animal's teeth). This is pretty difficult to appreciate today; even though much of the original layout of the city remains, it has been engulfed by growth. Still, most of Cusco can be seen easily on foot, and walking is certainly the best way to take in this historic mountain city that is equal parts Inca capital, post-Conquest colonial city, and modern tourist magnet. For outlying attractions, such as the handful of Inca ruins that lie just beyond the center of town, taxis are the best option.

The old center of the city is organized around the stunning and busy Plaza de Armas, the focal point of life in Cusco. The streets that radiate out from the square—Plateros, Mantas, Loreto, Triunfo, Procuradores, and others—are loaded with travel agencies, shops, restaurants, bars, and hotels. The major avenue leading from the plaza southeast to the modern section of the city is Avenida El Sol, where most banks are located. The district of San Blas is perhaps Cusco's most picturesque barrio; the labyrinthine neighborhood spills on cobblestone streets off Cuesta San Blas, which leads to crooked alleys and streets and viewing points high above the city.

Much of what interests most visitors is within easy walking distance of the Plaza de Armas. The major Inca ruins are within walking distance for energetic sorts who enjoy a good uphill hike.

Neighborhoods in Brief

The only neighborhoods most visitors are likely to see are the **Centro Histórico** (radiating outward from the Plaza de Armas), home to most restaurants, hotels, bars, and tourist services, as well as the main historic sights; artsy **Barrio de San Blas,** which climbs into the hills just north from the Plaza de Armas, stretching to the Sacsayhuamán ruins overlooking the city and home to many boutique hotels, restaurants, art galleries, and shops; and **modern Cusco,** the extension of the city along Avenida de la Cultura and Av. El Sol on the way to the airport, which is the location of a few hotels, banks, and offices.

Getting Around Cusco

Getting around Cusco is straightforward and relatively simple, especially because so many of the city sights are within walking distance of the Plaza de Armas in the historic center. You will mostly depend on leg power and omnipresent, inexpensive taxis to make your way around town.

BY FOOT   Most of Cusco is best navigated by foot, although because of the city's 3,400-meter (11,000-ft.) elevation and steep climbs, walking is demanding. Allow extra time to get around, and carry a bottle of water. You can walk to the major ruins just beyond the city—Sacsayhuamán and Q'enko—but you should be rather fit to do so. It's also best to undertake those walks in a small group and not alone.

BY TAXI   Cusco is crawling with taxis. Unlike in Lima, taxis are regulated and charge standard rates (although they do not have meters). Taxis are inexpensive (S/3 for any trip within the historic core during the day, S/4–S/5 at night) and are a good way to get around, especially at night. Hailing a cab in Cusco is considerably less daunting than in Lima, but you still should call a registered taxi when traveling from your hotel to train or bus stations or the airport, and when returning to your hotel late at night (there have been reports of muggings and even rapes tied to rogue taxis). Licensed taxi companies include **Okarina** (© 084/247-080) and **AlóCusco** (© 084/222-222). Taxis can be hired for return trips to nearby ruins or for half- or full days. To the airport, taxis charge S/10 from the city center; to the distant Terminal Terrestre (bus station), they charge S/8.

BY BUS   Most buses—called variously *colectivos, micros,* and *combis*—cost S/1.50, slightly more after midnight, on Sunday, and on holidays. You aren't likely to need buses often, or ever, within the city, though the colectivos that run up and down Avenida El Sol are also a useful option for some hotels, travel agencies, and shopping markets (taxis are much easier and not much more expensive). A bus departs from Plaza San Francisco to the airport, but it isn't very convenient. Buses and combis are most frequently used to travel from Cusco to towns in the Sacred Valley, such as Pisac, Calca, and Urubamba. Those buses depart from small terminals on Calle Puputi s/n, Cdra. 2 (via Pisac) and Av. Grau s/n, Cdra. 1 (via Chinchero).

BY TRAIN   The most popular means to visit Machu Picchu and the Sacred Valley sights is by train. PeruRail trains from Cusco to Ollantaytambo and Machu Picchu Pueblo (also called Aguas Calientes) leave from **Estación Poroy,** a 15-minute cab ride from downtown. Reservations for these trains, especially in high season (May–Sept), should be made several days or weeks in advance. Make reservations online at www.perurail.com; also see p. 239 in chapter 9 for more information, including trains that travel between Machu Picchu and the Sacred Valley only.

BY CAR   Renting a car in the Cusco region—more than likely to visit the beautiful Sacred Valley mountain villages—is a more practical idea than in most parts of Peru. Rental agencies include **Avis,** Av. El Sol 808 (© 084/248-800) and **Localiza,** Av. Industrial J-3, Urbanización Huancaro (© 084/233-131). Rates range from $50 per day for a standard four-door to $75 or more per day for a Jeep Cherokee four-wheel-drive. Check also with **4x4 Cusco,** Urb. San Borja, Huanchaq (© 084/227-730) which has pickups and even Toyota Land Cruisers. For information on driving around the Cusco department, and in case of emergencies, contact the **Touring Automóvil Club del Perú,** Av. El Sol 349, 2nd Floor (© 084/224-561). The office is open Monday through Friday from 9am to 1pm and 3:30 to 7:30pm, and Saturday from 9am to 1pm.

FAST FACTS

ATMs/Banks Most banks with ATMs are located along Av. El Sol. Banks include **Banco Santander Central Hispano,** Av. El Sol 459; **Banco de Crédito,** Av. El Sol 189; and **Banco Continental,** Av. El Sol 366. The external ATMs nearest the Plaza de Armas are at **Banco de Crédito,** Av. El Sol 189; **Banco del Sur,** Av. El Sol 457; and **Banco Latino,** Av. El Sol 395. A few ATMs are also located at the entrances to stores and restaurants on the Plaza de Armas and at the Huanchaq train station.

Doctors & Hospitals In an emergency, contact **Tourist Medical Assistance** (TMA), Heladeros 157 (☎ **084/260-101**) for 24-hour emergency medical and dental services, as well as health information. English-speaking personnel are also available at: **Hospital EsSalud,** Av. Anselmo Álvarez s/n (☎ **084/237-341**); **Clínica Pardo,** Av. de la Cultura 710 (☎ **084/624-186**); **Hospital Antonio Loren,** Plazoleta Belén 1358 (☎ **084/226-511**); **Hospital Regional,** Av. de la Cultura s/n (☎ **084/223-691**); and **Clínica Paredes,** Lechugal 405 (☎ **084/225-265**). For **yellow-fever** vaccinations, go to Hospital Antonio Loren on Tuesday or Hospital Regional on Saturday from 9am to 1pm.

Embassies & Consulates The **U.S. consulate** is located at Av. Pardo 845 (CoresES@state.gov; ☎ **084/ 231-474**). The honorary U.K. consulate is at Manu Expeditions, Urbanización Magisterial, G-5 Segunda Etapa (bwalker@terra.com.pe; ☎ **084/239-974**).

Emergencies For general emergencies and **police,** call ☎ **105.** For **tourist police,** call ☎ **084/249-654.** For **fire,** call ☎ **103.** In a medical emergency, go to **Hospital EsSalud,** Av. Anselmo Álvarez s/n (☎ **084/223-030**), or contact **Tourist Medical Assistance** (☎ **084/ 260-101**).

Internet Access Internet *cabinas* are everywhere in the old section of Cusco, and many permit cheap overseas Internet-based calls for as little as S/1 per minute. Rates are generally S/2 per hour. Among the *cabinas*: **Explora,** Arequipa 251; **Speed X,** Procuradores 50 and Tecsecocha 400.

Language Schools For intensive Spanish courses, try **Escuela Amauta,** Suecia 480 (www.amautaspanish.com; ☎ **084/262-345**), **Academia Latinoamericana de Español,** Av. El Sol 580 (www.latinoschools.com; ☎ **084/243-364**), or **San Blas Spanish School,** Tandapata 688 (☎ **084/ 247-898**).

Mail & Postage Cusco's main post office, Serpost, is at Av. El Sol 800 (☎ **084/224-212**). A **DHL/Western Union** office is at Av. El Sol 627-A (☎ **084/ 244-167**).

Massage Most highly recommended is **Ying Yang Massage,** Av. El Sol 106 (Galerías La Merced) (yinyang_masajes@hotmail.com; ☎ **084/243-592** or cell **084/984-939717**), where the rooms are nice and a 1-hour full-body massage is S/75; hotel visits are also possible for a small supplement. The swankest massage center in town is **Inca Spa,** within the Hotel Eco Inn, Av. El Sol 1010 (www.incaspa.com.pe; ☎ **084/581-280**); it's excellent but prices are about double its competitors. Young women advertising "massage, massage" for as little as $7 (sometimes of dubious quality or intent) are found on virtually every street in the old town.

Pharmacies Find **Inka Farma** locations at Av. El Sol 210 and Ayacucho 175; **Botica Fasa** locations at Ayacucho 220 and Av. El Sol 130.

Police The **Policía Nacional de Turismo,** or National Tourism Police (Saphy 510; ☎ **084/249-654**) has an English-speaking staff trained to handle the needs of foreign visitors. Or contact **iPerú/INDECOPI** (Servicio de Protección al Turista, or Tourist Protection Bureau), Portal Carrizos 250, Plaza de Armas (☎ **084/ 252-974**).

Safety Cusco on the surface certainly seems to be an easygoing, if increasingly congested, Andean city, and I've never found it to

8

Fast Facts

CUSCO

be anything to the contrary. In Cusco, as in all of Peru, you're much more likely to find locals warm and welcoming than threatening. Yet over the years there have been isolated reports of violent muggings (some using the "chokehold" method) on empty streets, as well as reports of rapes, attempted rapes, and other sexual assaults. While I have never had a problem in the city in more than 20 years and never met anyone who has, it's advisable to take some precautions and remain vigilant at all times.

Incidents of drink-spiking at nightclubs have been reported; be aware of your drinking companions in bars and don't allow strangers to buy you drinks. Do not walk alone late at night (young women should travel in groups larger than two); have restaurants and bars call registered taxis to transfer you to your hotel. Young people staying in inexpensive hostels should be particularly cautious of hotel visitors and belongings. It's a good idea to be at your most vigilant, especially in

the neighborhoods of San Blas, in the side streets leading off the Plaza de Armas, near the Central Market, and at bus and train hubs; still, robberies and attacks have occurred at the ruins at Sacsayhuamán on the outskirts of the city and even along the Inca Trail.

Telephone Cusco's area code is **084**. The principal **Telefónica del Perú** office, where you can make long-distance and international calls, is at Av. El Sol 382–6 (📞 **084/241-114**). It's open Mon–Sat 8am–10pm.

EXPLORING CUSCO

The stately **Plaza de Armas ★★**, lined by arcades and carved wooden balconies, and framed by the Andes, is the focal point of Cusco and the heart of the *centro histórico*. Lively but still loaded with colonial character, it is one of the most familiar sights in Peru. You will cross it, relax on the benches in its center, and pass under the porticoes that line the square with shops, restaurants, travel agencies, and bars innumerable times during your stay in Cusco. It's the best people-watching spot in the city. The plaza—which was twice its present size in Inca days—is bordered by two of Cusco's most important churches and the remains of original Inca walls on the northwest side of the square, thought to be the foundation of the Inca Pachacútec's palace. Most of Cusco's main attractions are within easy walking distance of the Plaza.

Many principal sights both within the historic quarter of Cusco and beyond the city are included in the *boleto turístico* (see box p. 170), but a few very worthwhile places of interest, such as the Cathedral, Templo del Qoricancha (Temple of the Sun), Museo Machu Picchu, and Museo de Arte Precolombino (MAP), are not included.

Around the Plaza de Armas

La Catedral ★★★ CATHEDRAL Built on the site of the palace of the Inca Viracocha, Cusco's cathedral, which dominates the Plaza de Armas, is a beautiful religious and artistic monument. Completed in 1669 in the Renaissance style and now handsomely restored, the cathedral possesses some 400 canvasses of the distinguished Escuela Cusqueña that were painted from the 16th to 18th centuries. There are also amazing woodcarvings, including the spectacular cedar choir stalls. The main altar—which weighs more than 401 kilograms (884 lb.) and is fashioned from silver mined in Potosí, Bolivia—features the patron saint of Cusco. To the right of the altar is a particularly Peruvian painting of the Last Supper, with the apostles drinking *chicha* (fermented maize beer) and eating *cuy* (guinea pig). The **Capilla del Triunfo** (the first Christian church in Cusco) is next door, to the right of the main church. It holds a painting by Alonso Cortés de Monroy of the devastating earthquake of 1650.

CUSCO'S *BOLETO TURÍSTICO*

The city's *boleto turístico* includes admission to 16 places of interest in and around Cusco and the Sacred Valley. Though it is no longer much of a bargain, the *boleto* is the only way you can get into a number of churches, museums, and ruin sites (however, not all of these attractions are indispensable). In addition, arguably the city's top two sights, La Catedral and Qoricancha, are not included and charge separate admissions. The full ticket costs S/130 for adults and S/70 students with ID and children, and is valid for 10 days; it is available at the tourism office at Mantas 117-A (*C* **084/263-176**), open Monday to Friday 8am to 6:30pm and Saturday 8am to 2pm. In addition to the main Tourist Office, the *boleto* can be purchased at OFEC, Av. El Sol 103, office 101 (Galerías Turísticas; *C* **084/227-037**), Monday to Saturday 8am to 6pm, and Casa Garcilaso, at the corner of Garcilaso y Heladeros s/n (*C* **084/226-919**), Monday to Friday 8am to 5pm, and Saturday 8am to 4pm. You can also buy a partial ticket for S/70 that only covers either attractions in the city, or ruins and sights outside of Cusco. Make sure you carry the ticket with you when you're planning to make visits (especially on day trips outside the city), as guards will demand to see it so that they can punch a hole alongside the corresponding picture. Students must also carry their International Student Identification Card (ISIC), as guards often demand to see it. For additional information, visit www.boletoturisticocusco.com.

The full *boleto* allows admission to the following sights: in Cusco, Convento de Santa Catalina, Museo Municipal de Arte Contemporáneo, Museo Histórico Regional, Museo de Sitio Qoricancha, Museo de Arte Popular, Centro Qosqo de Arte Nativo, Monumento al Inka Pachacuteq; the nearby Inca ruins of Sacsayhuamán, Q'enko, Pukapukara, Tambomachay, Pikillacta, and Tipón; and the Valle Sagrado attractions of Pisac, Ollantaytambo, and Chinchero.

Plaza de Armas (north side). No phone. Admission not included in *boleto turístico;* S/25 adults, S/12.50 students. Mon–Sat 10am–6pm, Sun 2–6pm.

Museo Inka ★ MUSEUM Housed in the impressive Admirals Palace, this museum contains artifacts designed to trace Peruvian history from pre-Inca civilizations and Inca culture, including the impact of the Conquest and colonial times on the native cultures. On view are ceramics, textiles, jewelry, mummies, architectural models, and an interesting collection—reputed to be the world's largest—of Inca drinking vessels *(qeros)* carved out of wood, many meticulously painted. The museum is a good introduction to Inca culture, and there are explanations in English. The palace itself is one of Cusco's finest colonial mansions, with a superbly ornate portal indicating the importance of its owner; the house was built on top of yet another Inca palace at the beginning of the 17th century. In the courtyard is a studio of women weaving traditional textiles. Allow 1½ to 2 hours to see the entire collection.

Cuesta del Almirante 103 (corner of Ataúd and Tucumán). *C* **084/237-380.** Admission not included in *boleto turístico;* S/10 adults, S/5 students. Mon–Sat 9am–6pm.

Templo de la Compañía de Jesús ★★ CHURCH Cater-cornered to the cathedral is this Jesuit church, which rivals the former in grandeur and prominence on the square (an intentional move by the Jesuits, and one that had Church diplomats

Cusco Attractions

CUSCO | Exploring Cusco

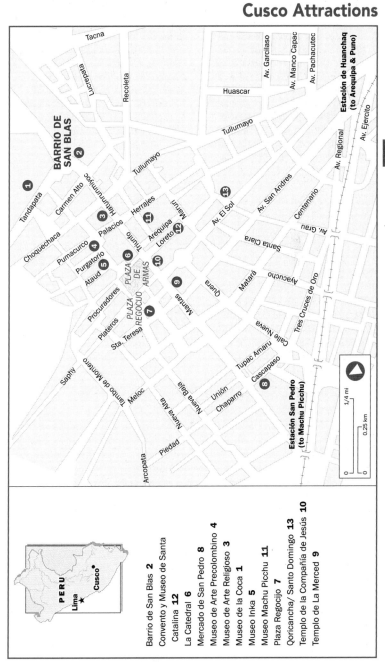

Barrio de San Blas **2**
Convento y Museo de Santa
Catalina **12**
La Catedral **6**
Mercado de San Pedro **8**
Museo de Arte Precolombino **4**
Museo de Arte Religioso **3**
Museo de la Coca **1**
Museo Inka **5**
Museo Machu Picchu **11**
Plaza Regocijo **7**
Qoricancha/ Santo Domingo **13**
Templo de la Compañía de Jesús **10**
Templo de La Merced **9**

El Negrito: Keeping Cusco Safe

A famous local figure is "El Negrito" (also known as "El Señor de los Temblores," or Lord of the Earthquakes), a brown-skinned figure of Christ on the cross known as the protector of Cusco. Found in La Catedral, at an altar to the right of the entrance to the Capilla (in the right nave, next to the choir stalls), the figure was originally paraded around the city by frightened residents during the 1650 earthquake. When the earthquake finally ceased, locals attributed it to a miracle and transformed El Negrito into an object of devotion (locals still deliver fresh flowers in his honor daily). The figure's crown was stolen a couple of years ago and not recovered; the one now adorning his head is gold, a gift of a parishioner.

running back and forth to the Vatican). Begun in the late 16th century, it was almost entirely demolished by the quake of 1650, rebuilt, and finally finished 18 years later. Like the cathedral, it was also built on the site of an important palace, that of the Inca Huayna Cápac (said to be the most beautiful of all the Inca rulers' palaces). Inside, it's rather gloomy, but the gilded altar is stunning, especially when illuminated. The church possesses several important works of art, including a picture of Saint Ignatius de Loyola, by the local painter Marcos Zapata, and the Cristo de Burgos crucifixion by the main altar. Also of note are the paintings to either side of the entrance, which depict the marriages of Saint Ignatius's nephews; one is the very symbol of Peru's *mestizo* character, as the granddaughter of Manco Inca weds the man who captured the last Inca, Tupac Amaru, the leader of an Indian uprising.

Plaza de Armas (southeast side). Admission not included in *boleto turístico*; S/10 adults, S/5 students. Mon–Sat 11am–noon and 3–4pm.

San Blas & East of the Plaza de Armas

Barrio de San Blas ★★ NEIGHBORHOOD   Cusco's most atmospheric and picturesque neighborhood, San Blas, a short but increasingly steep walk from the Plaza de Armas, is lined with artists' studios and artisans' workshops, and stuffed with tourist haunts—many of the best bars and restaurants and a surfeit of hostels. It's a great area to wander around—many streets are pedestrian-only—though you should exercise caution with your belongings, especially at night. The neighborhood also affords some of the most spectacular panoramic vistas in the city. In the square at the top and to the right of Cuesta San Blas is the small **Templo de San Blas ★**, said to be the oldest parish church in Cusco (no phone; admission not included in *boleto turístico*; S/15 adults, S/7.50 students; Mon–Sat 9am–5:30pm). Although it's a simple adobe structure, it contains a baroque gold-leaf main altar and marvelously carved Churrigueresque cedar pulpit. Some have gone as far as proclaiming it the finest example of woodcarving in the world; carved from a single tree trunk, it is certainly impressive. Most contend that the pulpit was created by a famous Quechua woodcarver, Juan Tomas Tuyrutupa, from Ayacucho, but one legend says that the artisan was a leper who created the pulpit to San Blaise after being miraculously cured, and it's his skull supposedly at the feet of San Pablo at the top.

Begins roughly at Calle Choquechaca, as the neighborhood climbs into the hills.

Museo de Arte Precolombino (MAP) ★★ 🛍 MUSEUM   This sophisticated and sumptuously designed archaeological museum features part of the vast collection of pre-Columbian works belonging to the Museo Larco in Lima. Housed in an erstwhile Inca ceremonial court, Santa Clara convent, and later colonial mansion (Casa Cabrera) of the Conquistador Alonso Díaz are 450 pieces—about 1% of the pieces in storage at the museum in Lima—dating from 1250 B.C. to A.D. 1532. Beautifully illuminated halls carefully exhibit gold and silver handicrafts, jewelry, ceramics, and other artifacts depicting the rich traditions from the Nasca, Moche, Huari, Chimú, Chancay, and Inca cultures. Although the number of pieces isn't overwhelming, they

THE MAGIC OF INCA STONES:
A walking TOUR ★★

Dominating the ancient streets of Cusco are dramatic **Inca walls,** constructed of mammoth granite blocks so exquisitely carved that they fit together without mortar, like jigsaw-puzzle pieces. The Spaniards razed many Inca constructions but built others right on top of the original foundations. (Even hell-bent on destruction, they recognized the value of good engineering.) In many cases, colonial architecture has not stood up nearly as well as the Incas' bold structures, which were designed to withstand the immensity of seismic shifts common in this part of Peru.

Apart from the main attractions detailed in this section, a brief walking tour will take you past some of the finest Inca constructions that remain in the city. East of the Plaza de Armas, **Calle Loreto,** originally called Intikkijllu, is the oldest surviving Inca wall in Cusco and one of the most distinguished. The massive wall on one side, composed of meticulously cut rectangular stones, once formed part of the Acllahuasi, or the "House of the Chosen Maidens," the Inca emperor's Virgins of the Sun. East of the Plaza de Armas, off Calle Palacio, is **Hatunrumiyoc,** a cobblestone street lined with impressive walls of polygonal stones. Past the Archbishop's Palace on the right side is the famed **12-angled stone** (now appropriated as the symbol of Cuzqueña beer), which is magnificently fitted into

the wall. Originally, this wall belonged to the palace of the Inca Roca. This large stone is impressively cut; the Incas almost routinely fitted many-cornered stones (with as many as 32, as seen at Machu Picchu, or even 44 angles) into structures. From Hatunrumiyoc, make your first right down another pedestrian alleyway, Inca Roca; about halfway down on the right side is a series of stones said to form the shape of a **puma,** including the head, large paws, and tail. It's not all that obvious, so if you see someone else studying the wall, ask him to point out the figure. **Siete Culebras (Seven Snakes),** the alleyway connecting Plaza Nazarenas to Choquechaca, contains Inca stones that form the foundation of the chapel within the Hotel Monasterio. Other streets with notable Inca foundations are **Herrajes, Pasaje Arequipa,** and **Santa Catalina Angosta.** Only a couple of genuine Inca **portals** remain. One is at Choquechaca 339 (the doorway to a recommended *hostal,* Rumi Punku), and another is at Romeritos 402, near Qoricancha.

Not every impressive stone wall in Cusco is Incan in origin, however. Many are transitional period (post-Conquest) constructions, built by local masons in the service of Spanish bosses. Peter Frost's *Exploring Cusco* (available in local bookstores) has a good explanation of what to look for to distinguish an original from what amounts to a copy.

THE CUSCO school OF ART

The colonial-era **Escuela Cusqueña,** or Cusco School of Art, that originated in the ancient Inca capital was a synthesis of traditional Spanish painting with local, *mestizo* elements—not surprising, perhaps, because its practitioners were themselves of mixed blood. Popular in the 17th and 18th centuries, the style spread from Cusco as far as Ecuador and Argentina. The most famous members of the school were Diego Quispe Tito, Juan Espinosa de los Monteros, and Antonio Sinchi Roca, even though the authors of a large majority of works associated with the school are anonymous. Most paintings were devotional in nature, with richly decorative surfaces. Artists incorporated recognizable Andean elements into their oil paintings, such as local flora and fauna, customs, and traditions—one depiction of the Last Supper has the apostles feasting on guinea pig and drinking maize beer—and representations of Jesus looking downward, like the Indians who were forbidden to look Spaniards in the eye. Original Escuela Cusqueña works are found in La Catedral, the Convent of Santa Catalina, the Museum of Religious Art, and a handful of other churches in Cusco. Reproductions of original paintings, ranging from excellent in quality to laughable, are available across Cusco, particularly in the galleries and shops of San Blas.

are all beautifully lit and displayed. Scattered about are comments about "primitive" art by major Western artists such as Paul Klee, and deviating from the museum's main thrust is a room of Cusqueña School religious painting. The museum is especially worthwhile for anyone unable to visit the major museums in Lima or any of the premier sites in northern Peru. Allow 1 or 2 hours for your visit. Within the courtyard, housed in a minimalist glass box, is MAP Café (p. 184), one of Cusco's most exclusive restaurants.

Casa Cabrera, Plaza de las Nazarenas s/n. map.perucultural.org.pe. ⓒ **084/237-380.** Admission not included in *boleto turístico;* S/22 adults, S/11 students and children. Daily 10am–10pm.

Museo de Arte Religioso (Palacio Arzobispal) MUSEUM   On the corner of one of Cusco's most extraordinary streets, Hatunrumiyoc, a pedestrian alleyway lined with magnificent Inca stonemasonry (see "The Magic of Inca Stones: A Walking Tour" on p. 173), the Museum of Religious Art is housed in a handsome colonial palace that previously belonged to the Archbishop of Cusco (before that, it was the site of the palace of Inca Roca and then the home of a Spanish marquis). Inside is a nice collection of colonial religious paintings, notable for the historical detail they convey, but the extravagant old house—with its impressive portal and Moorish-style doors, balcony, carved-cedar ceilings, stunning stained-glass windows, and small chapel—is pretty nearly the main draw. Plan to spend about 1 to 2 hours here.

Corner of Hatunrumiyoc and Palacio. ⓒ **084/225-211.** Admission not included in *boleto turístico;* S/10 adults, S/5 students. Mon–Fri 8am–12:30pm and 3–6pm.

Museo de la Coca   MUSEUM   If you're curious about the cultural role and science behind coca and coca leaves, this small museum tells the story of the "sacred leaf of the Incas" and how it's been used by locals throughout history in the Andes (including its more polemical present).

Calle Suyt'uqhatu, 705. ⓒ **084/974-772-505.** Admission S/10 adults, S/5 students, free for children. Daily 9am–8pm.

Qoricancha & South of the Plaza de Armas

Convento y Museo de Santa Catalina ★★ CONVENT/MUSEUM   A small convent a couple of blocks west of the Plaza de Armas, Santa Catalina was built between 1601 and 1610 on top of the Acllawasi, where the Inca emperor sequestered his chosen Virgins of the Sun. The convent contains a museum of colonial and religious art. The collection includes an excellent selection of Escuela Cusqueña paintings, featuring some of the greatest works of Amerindian art—a combination of indigenous and typically Spanish styles—in Cusco. The collection also includes four paintings of the Lord of the Earthquakes (El Señor de los Temblores) painted by Amerindians. The interior of the monastery is quite beautiful, with painted arches and an interesting chapel with baroque frescoes of Inca vegetation. Other items of interest include very macabre statues of Jesus and an extraordinary trunk that, when opened, displays the life of Christ in 3-D figurines. (It was employed by the Catholic Church's "traveling salesmen," who were used to convert the natives in far-flung regions of Peru.)

Santa Catalina Angosta s/n.© **084/226-032.** Admission included in *boleto turístico*. Daily 8am–5:30pm.

Museo Machu Picchu (Casa Concha) ★ MUSEUM   Inaugurated in 2011 to celebrate the centennial of Hiram Bingham's discovery for the world of Machu Picchu, and to display artifacts removed by Bingham for study at the Peabody Museum at Yale University—where they remained until recently, a matter of contentious dispute between Peru and the prestigious American university—this museum makes a good introduction before a visit to Machu Picchu. There are some interesting documents and items found at the ruins, including pages and sketches from Bingham's 1911 diary; a letter from Abercrombie & Fitch detailing provisions for the expedition; Inca ceramics and tools; the original map, which remained the best map of the ruins for nearly a century; and the first photograph taken at Machu Picchu. Although not yet the definitive or exhaustive exhibition of objects one might hope for, the museum, housed in a fine 1710 colonial mansion that was constructed on top of Tupac Inca Yupanqui's palace, it is expected to grow and become more complete in the coming years.

Santa Catalina Ancha, 320.© **084/255-535.** Admission not included in *boleto turístico*; S/20 adults, S/10 students. Mon–Fri 9am–5pm, Sat 9am–1pm.

Qoricancha (Templo del Sol)/Santo Domingo ★★★ CHURCH/MUSEUM   Qoricancha and Santo Domingo together form perhaps the most vivid illustration in Cusco of Andean culture's collision with Western Europe. Like the Great Mosque in Córdoba, Spain—where Christians dared to build a massive church within the perfect Muslim shrine—the temple of one culture sits atop and encloses the other. The extraordinarily crafted Temple of the Sun was the most sumptuous temple in the Inca Empire and the apogee of the Incas' naturalistic belief system. Some 4,000 of the highest-ranking priests and their attendants were housed here. Dedicated to worship of the sun, it was apparently a glittering palace straight out of El Dorado legend: *Qoricancha* means "golden courtyard" in Quechua, and in addition to hundreds of gold panels lining its walls, there were life-size gold figures, solid-gold altars, and a huge golden sun disc. The sun disc reflected the sun and bathed the temple in light. During the summer solstice, the sun still shines directly into a niche where only the Inca chieftain was permitted to sit. Other temples and shrines existed for the worship of lesser natural gods: the moon, Venus, thunder, lightning, and rainbows. Qoricancha was the main astronomical observatory for the Incas.

After the Spaniards ransacked the temple and emptied it of gold (which they melted down, of course), the exquisite polished stone walls were employed as the foundations of the Convent of Santo Domingo, constructed in the 17th century. The baroque church pales next to the fine stonemasonry of the Incas—and that's to say nothing about the original glory of the Sun Temple. Today all that remains is Inca stonework. Thankfully, a large section of the cloister has been removed, revealing four original chambers of the temple, all smoothly tapered examples of Inca trapezoidal architecture. Stand on the small platform in the first chamber and see the perfect symmetry of openings in the stone chambers. A series of Inca stones displayed reveals the fascinating concept of male and female blocks, and how they fit together. The 6m (20-ft.) curved wall beneath the west end of the church, visible from the street, remains undamaged by repeated earthquakes and is perhaps the greatest extant example of Inca stonework. The curvature and fit of the massive dark stones is astounding.

Once the Spaniards took Cusco, Francisco Pizarro's brother Juan was given the eviscerated Temple of the Sun. He died soon afterward, though, at the battle at Sacsayhuamán, and he left the temple to the Dominicans, in whose hands it remains.

Plazoleta Santo Domingo. ℂ **084/222-071.** Admission not included in *boleto turístico*; S/10 adults, S/5 students and children. Mon–Sat 8:30am–6:30pm; Sun 2–5pm.

West of the Plaza de Armas

Mercado de San Pedro ★★ PUBLIC MARKET The fascinating, frenzied Cusco central market is an amazing place to tap into the city at its most quotidian and traditional, a place where tourists are no more than an afterthought. The range of produce, meats, juice bars, household items, and oddities (such as medicinal plants from the rainforest) is daunting; for most, it's an experience not to be missed. However, exercise caution because the market is known to be frequented by pickpockets targeting tourists.

Calle Santa Clara, s/n. No tel. Admission free. Daily 7am–4pm.

Plaza Regocijo ★ PUBLIC SQUARE/MUSEUMS During Inca times, this pleasant, leafy square formed part of the main plaza, along with today's Plaza de Armas. Today it's full of shops and restaurants, as well as notable historic mansions, but is slightly less feverish than the main square. There is a pair of oft-overlooked

---

Hang a Right at Donkey Lips

Cusco is littered with difficult-to-pronounce, wildly spelled street names that date to Inca times. In the bohemian neighborhood of San Blas, though, they're particularly colorful. Here's a primer of atmospheric street names and their literal meanings:

Atoqsayk'uchi Where the fox got tired

Tandapata Place of taking turns

Asnoqchutun Donkey lips

Siete Diablitos Seven little devils

Siete Angelitos Seven little angels

Usphacalle Place of sterility/place of ashes

Saqracalle Where the demons dwell

Pumaphaqcha Puma's tail

Cajonpata Place shaped like a box

Rayanpata Place of myrtle flowers

One to seek out: **P'asñapakana** Where the young women are hidden

And, finally, one to avoid:

P'aqlachapata Place of bald men

Cusco = Cuzco = Q'osqo

Spanish and English spellings derived from the Quechua language are a little haphazard in Cusco, especially because there has been a linguistic movement to try to recover and value indigenous culture. Thus, you might see Inca written as Inka; Cusco as Cuzco, Qosqo, or Q'osqo; Qoricancha as Coricancha or Koricancha; Huanchaq as Huanchac or Wanchac; Sacsayhuamán as Sacsaywaman; and Q'enko as Qenko, Kenko, or Qenqo. You're likely to stumble across others, with similar alphabetical prestidigitation, all used interchangeably.

museums here, too: the **Museo Histórico Regional,** a regional history museum with archaeological and colonial artifacts, including furnishings and Escuela Cusqueña art, is housed in the mansion where Garcilaso de la Vega, an important Peruvian writer and chronicler of Inca history and culture, once lived (he was himself a descendent of Incas); and, within the Palacio Municipal, the small **Museo de Arte Contemporáneo,** which features the contemporary works of local artists.

Calles Garcilaso at Heladeros. Museo Histórico Regional and Museo de Arte Contemporáneo: daily 9am–5pm; admission by *boleto turístico.*

Templo de La Merced ★ CHURCH   Erected in 1536 and rebuilt after the great earthquake in the 17th century, La Merced ranks just below the cathedral and the La Compañía church in importance. It has a beautiful facade and lovely cloisters with a mural depicting the life of the Merced Order's founder. The sacristy contains a small museum of religious art, including a fantastic solid-gold monstrance swathed in precious stones. In the vaults of the church are the remains of two famous conquistadors, Diego de Almagro and Gonzalo Pizarro.

Calle Mantas s/n. ✆ **084/231-831.** Admission S/5, S/3 students. Mon–Sat 8:30am–noon and 2–5pm.

Inca Ruins near Cusco ★★★

The easiest way to see the following set of Inca ruins just outside Cusco is as part of a half-day tour. The hardy might want to approach it as an athletic archaeological expedition: If you've got 15km (9⅓ miles) of walking and climbing at high altitude in you, it's a beautiful trek. Otherwise, you can walk to Sacsayhuamán and nearby Q'enko (the climb from the Plaza de Armas is strenuous and takes 30–45 min.), and take a colectivo or taxi to the other sites. Alternatively, you can take a Pisac/Urubamba minibus (leaving from the bus station at Calle Intiqhawarina, off Avenida Tullumayo, or Huáscar 128) and tell the driver you want to get off at Tambomachay, the ruins farthest from Cusco, and work your way back on foot. Some even make the rounds by horseback. You can easily and cheaply contract a horse at Sacsayhuamán, but don't expect a chance to ride freely in the countryside—you'll walk rather slowly to all the sites alongside a guide.

Visitors with less time in Cusco or less interest in taxing themselves might want to join a guided tour, probably the most popular and easiest way to see the sites. Virtually any of the scads of travel agencies and tour operators in the old center of Cusco offer them. Some well-rated traditional agencies with a variety of programs include **Milla Turismo,** Av. Pardo 689 (www.millaturismo.com; ✆ **084/231-710**), and **SAS Travel,** Garcilaso 270, Plaza San Francisco (www.sastravelperu.com; ✆ **084/249-194**).

Inca Ruins near Cusco

To Machu Picchu

Ollantaytambo
Urubamba
Yucay
Calca
Moray
Maras
Chinchero
Rio Urubamba

To Abancay

Tambomachay
Puca Pucara
Q'enko
Anta
Sacsayhuamán
San Sebastián
Cusco

■ Ruins
- - - Unpaved Road

0 ———————— 5 mi
0 ———————— 5 km

Admission to the following sites is by *boleto turístico,* and they are all open daily from 7am to 6pm. Guides, official and unofficial, hover around the ruins; negotiate a price or decide upon a proper tip. There are a handful of other Inca ruins on the outskirts of Cusco, but the ones discussed below are the most interesting.

These sites are generally safe, but at certain times of day—usually dawn and dusk before and after tour groups' visits—several ruins are said to be favored by thieves. It's best to be alert and, if possible, go accompanied.

Note that new finds are continually being uncovered here, even as close to Cusco as the vicinity around Sacsayhuamán. Archaeologists recently announced the

  Those Fabulously "Sexy" Ruins

The pronunciation of Sacsayhuamán, like many Quechua words, proves difficult for most foreigners to wrap their tongues around, so locals and tour guides have several jokes that point to its similarity to the words "sexy woman" in English. You haven't really experienced Cusco until you've heard the joke with that punch line a dozen times—from old men, guides, and even little kids.

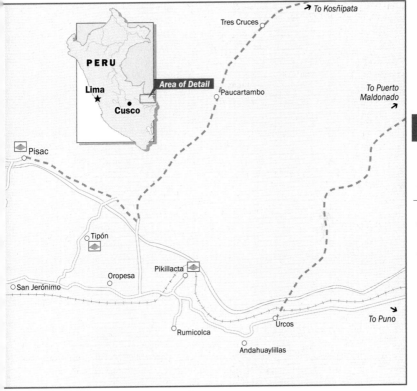

discovery of an ancient, pre-Inca temple, irrigation canals, and a series of rooms that held mummies and idols. The temple is believed to have been built by the Killke culture, which occupied the region around present-day Cusco from A.D. 900 to 1200.

Sacsayhuamán ★★★

The greatest and nearest to Cusco of the Inca ruins, Sacsayhuamán reveals some of the Incas' most extraordinary architecture and monumental stonework. Usually referred to as a garrison or fortress—because it was constructed with forbidding, castle-like walls—it was more likely a religious temple, although most experts believe it also had military significance. The Inca emperor Pachacútec began the site's construction in the mid-15th century, although it took nearly 100 years and many thousands of men to complete it. Massive blocks of limestone and other types of stone were brought from as far as 32km (20 miles) away.

The ruins, a steep 30-minute (or longer) walk from the center, cover a huge area, but they constitute perhaps one-quarter of the original complex, which could easily house more than 10,000 men. Today, what survive are the astounding outer walls, constructed in a zigzag formation of three tiers. (In the puma-shaped layout of the Inca capital, Sacsayhuamán was said to form the animal's head, and the zigzag of the defense walls forms the teeth.) Many of the base stones employed are almost unimaginably massive; some are 3.5m (11 ft.) tall, and one is said to weigh 300 tons. Like all Inca constructions, the stones fit together perfectly without the aid of mortar. It's easy to see how hard it would have been to attack these ramparts with 22 distinct zigzags; the design would automatically expose the flanks of an opponent.

Above the walls are the circular foundations of three towers that once stood here; they were used for storage of provisions and water. The complex suffered such extensive destruction that the primary function of Sacsayhuamán continues to be debated. What is known is that it was the site of one of the bloodiest battles between the Spaniards and native Cusqueños. More than 2 years after the Spaniards had initially marched on Cusco and installed a puppet government, the anointed Inca (Manco Inca) led a seditious campaign that took back Sacsayhuamán and nearly defeated the Spaniards in a siege of the Inca capital. Juan Pizarro and his vastly outnumbered but superior armed forces stormed Sacsayhuamán in a horrific battle in 1536 that left thousands dead. Legend speaks of their remains as carrion for giant condors in the open fields here. After the defeat of the Inca troops and the definitive Spanish occupation of Cusco, the Spaniards made off with the more manageably sized stone blocks from Sacsayhuamán to build houses and other structures in the city below.

The **Inti Raymi** festival is celebrated here annually, and it is truly a great spectacle—one of the finest in Peru (see "Cusco's Spectacular Celebrations" on p. 181). A flat, grassy esplanade (where the main ceremony of the festival is celebrated) separates the defense walls from a small hill where you'll find the "Inca's Throne" and large rocks with well-worn grooves, used by children and often adults as slides. Nearby is a series of claustrophobia-inducing tunnels—pass through them if you dare.

Night visits to the ruins are permitted from 8 to 10pm. Under a full moon in the huge starlit Andean sky, Sacsayhuamán is so breathtaking that you'll instantly grasp the Incas' worship of the natural world, in which both the sun and the moon were considered deities. If you go at night, take a flashlight and a few friends; security is a little lax, and assaults on foreigners have occurred.

Walking directions: A couple of paths lead to the ruins from downtown Cusco. You can take Almirante, Suecia, or Plateros. Head northwest from the Plaza de Armas. Take Palacio (behind the cathedral) until you reach stairs and signs to the ruins; or at the end of Suecia, climb either Huaynapata or Resbalosa (the name means "slippery") until you come to a curve and the old Inca road. Past the San Cristóbal church at the top, beyond a plaza with fruit-juice stands, is the main entrance to the ruins. Plan to spend about an hour here for a brief run-through, and up to 3 hours if you're a photography buff or if you have kids who want to play on the slides and in the tunnels.

Can't Leave Well Enough Alone

The Peruvian authorities are notorious for messing with ancient Inca ruins, trying to rebuild them rather than let them be what they are: Ruins. You'll notice at Sacsayhuamán and other Inca sites that unnecessary and misleading restoration has been undertaken. The grotesque result is that small gaps where original stones are missing have been filled in with obviously new and misplaced garden rocks—a disgrace to the perfection pursued and achieved by Inca stonemasons.

CUSCO'S spectacular CELEBRATIONS

Cusco explodes with joyous celebration of both its Amerindian roots and Christian influences during festivals, which are crowded but splendid times to be in the city if you can find accommodations. It's worth planning your trip around one of the following fiestas, if possible.

Inti Raymi ★★★, the fiesta of the winter solstice (June 24, but lasting for days before and afterward), is certainly the star attraction. It's an eruption of Inca folk dances, exuberant costumes, and grand pageants and parades, including a massive one that takes place at the stately Sacsayhuamán ruins overlooking the city. Inti Raymi is one of the finest expressions of local popular culture on the continent, a faithful reenactment of the traditional Inca Festival of the Sun. It culminates in high priests sacrificing two llamas, one black and one white, to predict the fortunes of the coming year. Cusco's **Carnaval week,** with lots of music, dance, and processions of its own, is part of the buildup for Inti Raymi.

Semana Santa, or Easter week (late Mar or Apr), is an exciting traditional expression of religious faith, with stately processions through the streets of Cusco, including a great procession led by El Señor de los Temblores (Lord of the Earthquakes) on Easter Monday. On Good Friday, booths selling traditional Easter dishes are set up on the streets.

In early May, the **Fiesta de las Cruces (Festival of the Crosses),** a celebration popular throughout the highlands, is marked by communities decorating large crosses that are then delivered to churches. Crucifix vigils are held on all hilltops that are crowned by crosses. Festivities, as always accompanied by lively dancing, give thanks for bountiful harvests. Early June's **Corpus Christi** festival is another momentous occasion, with colorful religious parades featuring 15 effigies of saints through the city and events at the Plaza de Armas and the cathedral (where the effigies are displayed for a week).

On December 24, Cusco celebrates the **Santuranticuy Festival,** one of the largest arts-and-crafts fairs in Peru. Hundreds of artisans lay out blankets in the Plaza de Armas and sell carved Nativity figures and saints' images, in addition to ceramics and *retablos* (altars). The tradition was begun by the Bethlehemite Order and Franciscan Friars.

A hugely popular Andean festival that attracts droves from Cusco and the entire region is the **Virgen del Carmen,** celebrated principally in Paucartambo (see "Side Trips from Cusco," later in this chapter) and with only a slightly lesser degree of exuberance in Pisac and smaller highland villages.

Q'enko ★

The road from Sacsayhuamán leads past fields where, on weekends, Cusqueños play soccer and have cookouts, to the temple and amphitheater of Q'enko (*Kehn*-koh), a distance of about a kilometer (½ mile). The ruins are due east of the giant white statue of Christ crowning the hill next to Sacsayhuamán; follow the main road, and you'll see signs for Q'enko, which appears on the right. A great limestone outcrop was hollowed out by the Incas, and, in the void, they constructed a cave-like altar. (Some have claimed that the smooth stone table inside was used for animal sacrifices.) Visitors can duck into the caves and tunnels beneath the rock. You can also climb on the rock and see the many channels cut into the rock, where it is thought that either *chicha* or, more salaciously, sacrificial blood coursed during ceremonies. (Q'enko might have been a site of ritual ceremonies performed in fertility rites and solstice and equinox celebrations.) Allow a half-hour to tour the site, not including travel time.

Puca Pucara

A small fortress (the name means "red fort") just off the main Cusco–Pisac road, this might have been some sort of storage facility or lodge, or perhaps a guard post on the road from Cusco to the villages of the Sacred Valley. It is probably the least impressive of the area sites, although it has nice views of the surrounding countryside. From Q'enko, Puca Pucara is a 90-minute to 2-hour walk along the main road; allow a half-hour for your visit.

Tambomachay

On the road to Pisac (and a short, signposted walk off the main road), this site is also known as Los Baños del Inca (Inca Baths). Located near a spring just a short walk beyond Puca Pucara, the ruins consist of three tiers of stone platforms. Water still flows across a sophisticated system of aqueducts and canals in the small complex of terraces and a pool, but these were not baths as we know them. Most likely this was instead a place of water ceremonies and worship. The exquisite stonework indicates that the *baños* were used by high priests and nobility only. Plan on spending an hour here.

ESPECIALLY FOR KIDS

Cusco is a blast to walk around, so entertaining the kids and finding suitable restaurants and things to do shouldn't be a problem for most families. Kids old enough to appreciate a bit of history might enjoy the exceptionally laid-out **Museo de Arte Precolombino (MAP),** as well as the **Museo Inka,** both of which will give them a good grounding in pre-Columbian civilizations and Inca culture. Beside ceramics and textiles, the Museo Inka displays cool mummies and tiny hand-painted Inca drinking vessels. You'll find Andean women weaving traditional textiles in the courtyard.

Cusco resonates with remnants of the ancient capital; a walking tour with the kids will take you past **Inca walls** with giant granite blocks that look like the pieces of a giant jigsaw puzzle. Have the kids count the hand-cut angles in the **12-angled stone** and find the outlines of the **puma figure** (see "The Magic of Inca Stones: A Walking Tour" on p. 173). Observing the walls will give you a chance to impress your family with your knowledge of Andean history. Explain that the Incas built these massive walls without mortar or cement of any kind and with no knowledge of the wheel or horses, and that they constructed one of the world's greatest empires, reaching from one end of South America to another, without a written language and with runners who relayed messages to rulers.

Another good activity for artistically inclined children is to pop into **artists' studios** in the funky neighborhood of San Blas. Then walk—if you have the energy—up to the ruins of **Sacsayhuamán.** There you'll find more massive stones and gorgeous views of the city and surrounding mountains, but kids will really dig the huge rocks with slick grooves that make fantastic slides. There are also some cool tunnels cut into stones nearby, which kids might enjoy much more than their parents.

And, of course, the biggest family attraction of all lies beyond Cusco: Few are the kids who aren't fascinated by the ruins of **Machu Picchu.** The easygoing towns of the **Sacred Valley** are also great spots for families; see chapter 9 for more information.

WHERE TO EAT

Visitors to Cusco have a huge array of restaurants and cafes at their disposal; eateries have sprouted up even faster than *hostales* and bars, and most are clustered around the main drags leading from Plaza de Armas. Many of the city's most popular restaurants are large tourist joints with Andean music shows, while many more are economical, informal places favored by backpackers and adventure travelers—some offer midday three-course meals *(menus del día)* for as little as S/10. However, Cusco is also blessed with a growing number of upscale dining options, and the dining scene has improved every year as it expands to accommodate new, and more sophisticated, visitors to the city. Prices, too, have crept steadily upward at the top end of the scale. Though you can still eat very inexpensively, Cusco is now also a place to reward yourself with a good meal if you've been in the jungle or been trekking in the mountains.

Cheap eateries line the narrow length of Calle Procuradores, which leads off the Plaza de Armas across from the Compañía de Jesús church and is sometimes referred to as "Gringo Alley." Many are pizzerias, as Cusco has become known for its wood-fired, crispy-crust pizzas. Lurking on Procuradores and Plaza de Armas are hawkers armed with menus, hoping to lure you inside restaurants. Most represent decent, upstanding restaurants (though some occasionally offer drugs and other services), but if you know where you want to dine, a polite "no, gracias" is usually all it takes to get them off your trail. Horror of horrors, McDonald's recently took over a coveted store-front right on the stately, ancient Plaza de Armas; fortunately, it's fairly discreet, with no giant glowing "M" to disrupt the harmonious appearance.

Several cool bars, such as The Muse, also double as (often quite good) restaurants, primarily for their young and hip clients who'd prefer to get their food the same place as their cocktails. Baco, owned by the folks that operate one of the best restaurants in Cusco, Cicciolina, is as much chic restaurant as wine bar, and serves great gourmet pizzas (closed on Sundays); see p. 184.

Not all restaurants in Cusco accept credit cards; many of those that do, especially the cheaper places, will levy a 10% surcharge to use plastic, so you're better off carrying cash (either *soles* or dollars). Top-flight restaurants often charge both a 10% service charge and 18% sales tax, neither of which is included in the prices listed below.

For restaurants in San Blas, see the "San Blas Hotels & Restaurants" map, on p. 207.

Very Expensive

Fallen Angel ★ ⚑ NOVO ANDINO/STEAK   It may be hard to conceive of this wildly eccentric, artistically designed funhouse as a restaurant rather than a nightclub. Though it takes a while to focus on the menu given the maximalist surroundings of flying pigs and floating cherubs, once you do, carnivores will be in heaven: It is dominated by beef tenderloin, with a choice of 15 different salsas, some with Asian and exotic combinations. Other than meat (including alpaca and guinea pig), the emphasis is on local produce from the Sacred Valley (where the creative owner spent much of his youth on a farm) for sides and salads. Non-meat eaters can also opt for pastas, such as sweet-potato tortellini, and ceviche, but the best bet by far are the steaks. From the baroque decor and creative cocktails to the menu, Fallen Angel is a place for adventurous diners.

Plazoleta Nazarenas 221. www.fallenangelincusco.com. ℂ **084/258-184.** Reservations recommended. Main courses S/40–S/58. MC, V. Mon–Fri 11am–11pm; Sat–Sun 2–11pm.

Le Soleil ★★★ CLASSIC FRENCH   A labor of love from a transplanted and polyglot French-Polish gentleman, Arthur Marcinkiewicz, this elegant and formal, minimalist-chic restaurant in a gorgeously converted *casona* is unique in Cusco (better said: Peru). It focuses solely on classical French dishes with impossible-to-get ingredients and prizes imported from France. The wine list is entirely French, and the dishes are *formidable*. Although you could order a la carte, this is the place to splurge with either the 5-course menu luxe de France, or the 8-course tasting menu. While neither is cheap, they represent good value given the quality of ingredients, careful preparation, and superb service. If you're less hungry but flexible, try the *menú sorpresa*, a 3-course chef's choice menu (carnivore and vegetarian versions available). On a recent visit I had snails followed by foie gras (and a glass of Sauterne) and duck neck stuffed with meats and foie, flambéed in Armgagnac. Le Soleil is a brilliant change of pace for Cusco, the kind of place to celebrate a trip to Peru in style.

San Agustín 275. www.restaurantelesoleilcusco.com. (*℃* **084/240-543.** Reservations recommended. Main courses S/42–S/65; Prix-fixe dinner menus (3–8 courses) S/69–S/159. AE, DC, MC, V. Daily noon–3pm and 6–11pm.

MAP Café ★★ INTERNATIONAL/NOVO ANDINO   Though the name might seem a bit misleading, causing one to conjure a globe-trotter's bohemian hangout, this is one of Cusco's most stylish restaurants. Housed in a stark, glass-and-steel box with few adornments other than views of the handsome colonial patio it sits in the middle of—Casa Cabrera, now the Museo de Arte Precolombino—it places its focus squarely on elegantly prepared and artistically presented food. At dinner, the chef presents a prix-fixe menu (including a pisco sour), a bit pricey for Cusco. Standouts include sampling of Lima-style *causas* (cold mashed-potato-and-vegetable casseroles), Andean-squash gnocchi, and quinua cannelloni. For diners in the mood for a taste of creative Andean cuisine, the guinea pig confit is a daring dish. As a bonus, the museum (see p. 173) is open late, making it possible to make a dinner-and-pre-Columbian date of the evening.

Casa Cabrera (in courtyard of Museo de Arte Precolombino), Plaza Nazarenas 231. www.cusco restaurants.com/en/mapcafe.html. (*℃* **084/242-476.** Reservations recommended. Main courses S/46–S/76; Prix-fixe 3-course dinner menu S/165. AE, DC, MC, V. Daily 11am–3pm and 6–10pm.

Expensive

Baco ★ WINE BAR/PIZZA/NOVO ANDINO   A spinoff from the wildly popular, Australian-owned Cicciolina (see below) and as much clubby wine bar as restaurant, this warmly lit spot with fresh flowers and modern art is perfect for a quiet or romantic evening. The focus is on wine—offering one of the city's most extensive cellars of Chilean, Argentine, and Spanish wines—and a menu of excellent gourmet pizzas and sophisticated *novo andino* and international fare.

Calle Ruinas 465. www.cicciolinacuzco.com/english/baco_home.html. (*℃* **084/242-808.** Main courses S/22–S/48. AE, DC, MC, V. Mon–Sat 3:30–10:30pm.

Chicha ★★ NOVO ANDINO/PERUVIAN   Gastón Acurio, Peru's celebrity chef who seemingly turns every kitchen he walks into to gold, has expanded beyond Lima and outposts in South and North America and put his spin on regional Peruvian cooking. The Cusco restaurant is his interpretation of Cuzqueña highland cuisine. In a warm and chic, nearly hidden second-story, long rectangular space with a high, white peaked ceiling and dark-stained wood floors, bookended by the open kitchen and the bar, Acurio works his magic again. Using local ingredients like quinoa for his tabbouleh and offering an upscale version of *pachamanca* (a traditional countryside barbecue

Central Cusco Restaurants

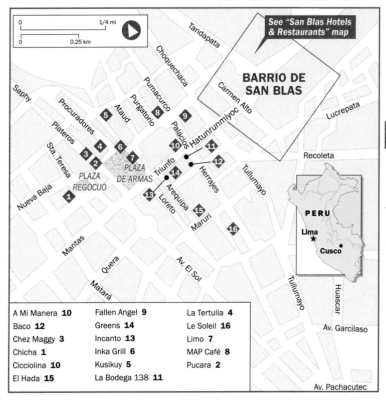

A Mi Manera **10**	Fallen Angel **9**	La Tertulia **4**
Baco **12**	Greens **14**	Le Soleil **16**
Chez Maggy **3**	Incanto **13**	Limo **7**
Chicha **1**	Inka Grill **6**	MAP Café **8**
Cicciolina **10**	Kusikuy **5**	Pucara **2**
El Hada **15**	La Bodega 138 **11**	

of meat and potatoes cooked underground), nearly everything works extremely well. I particularly loved the *codillo croquante,* slow-cooked pork shoulder wrapped in a thick slab of crunchy bacon. You can also get the ceviche and *causas* Acurio made famous in Lima.

Plaza Regocijo 261, 2nd floor. www.chicha.com.pe. ℂ **084/240-520.** Reservations recommended. Main courses S/26–S/49. AE, DC, MC, V. Mon–Sat noon–11pm; Sun noon–5pm.

Cicciolina ★★ MEDITERRANEAN/NOVO ANDINO   Upstairs in the court-yard of an old colonial house, this delightfully chic restaurant looks ripped from the Tuscan countryside. After several years, it remains one of the hottest spots in Cusco. The boisterous bar is decorated with bunches of garlic, peppers, and fresh-cut flowers and is great for an excellent cocktail (such as a maracuyá sour), or dinner itself, espe-cially the creative tapas (served only in the bar). The elegant, high-ceilinged dining room features deep-red walls and contemporary art. The dinner menu focuses on unusual spices and accents. You might start with spicy barbecued calamari, prawns, and scallops, served with a minty rice noodle salad. Main courses include large, delectable salads (a fave is rare roast beef and vegetables), excellent homemade pas-tas, and alpaca filet. There's a daily pasta lunch deal, and the bakery downstairs serves home-baked croissants, breads, and gourmet breakfasts.

Triunfo 393, 2nd floor. www.cicciolinacuzco.com/english/cicciolina_home.html. *C* **084/239-510.** Reservations recommended. Main courses S/23–S/48. AE, DC, MC, V. Daily 8–11am, noon–3pm and 6–10pm.

Greens ★ ORGANIC/NOVO ANDINO   It's been years since Greens was *the* destination restaurant in the bohemian heart of San Blas. It has grown comfortably into its home on the second floor of an old building just off the Plaza de Armas as a relaxed and intimate restaurant. It appeals to a wide audience, even as its organic menu caters to a healthy-eating crowd. The cool space, with overhead beams and warm woods, has just a handful of candelit tables and a soundtrack of laid-back dance beats. The creative and consistently good menu features a large number of vegetarian options, including delicious salads, as well as steaks, rack of lamb, and tropical chicken curry.

Santa Catalina Angosta 135, 2nd floor. www.cuscorestaurants.com/en/greensorganic.html. *C* **084/243-379.** Reservations recommended. Main courses S/28–S/45. No credit cards. Daily noon–9:30pm.

Inka Grill ★ PERUVIAN/NOVO ANDINO   A modern, large space right on the Plaza de Armas, popular with both young and old, the well-regarded Inka Grill serves dependable *novo andino* (modern Andean) dishes. There may not be much new here, but for most diners that's exactly what they want. Start with a bowl of *camote* (sweet potato) chips and green salsa. The best dishes are Peruvian standards such as sautéed alpaca tenderloin served over quinoa (a grain) and *ají de gallina* (shredded chicken with nuts, cheese, and chili peppers), and desserts such as a coca-leaf crème brûlée. The extensive menu also includes a wide range of international dishes such as pizza, pasta, and risotto.

Portal de Panes 115. www.cuscorestaurants.com. *C* **084/262-992.** Reservations recommended. S/23–S/55. AE, DC, MC, V. Mon–Sat 8am–midnight.

Limo ★★ PERUVIAN/SUSHI   This chic contemporary new restaurant has so much going for it that it's a place I—and I suspect many visitors—will return to multiple times, even on a short trip. The stupendous views of the Plaza de Armas and surrounding mountains from the enclosed terrace alone are enough to recommend it. The sleek transformation of a colonial structure preserves the high ceilings and beams (now painted a thick white) and is complemented by bold, large-format photographs. Start with an innovative cocktail and the complimentary starter of French-fried potatoes and three salsas. Then graduate to *causita* balls, ceviche, and imaginative sushi rolls (with a Peruvian bent) or *tiraditos* (Peruvian-style sashimi). Though seafood is the real attraction of Limo, meat-eaters can opt for more traditional highland entrees, such as pork shoulder and *adobo de cerdo*. Though it's not inexpensive for Cusco, for most international travelers it's a deal.

Portal de Carnes 236, 2nd floor. www.cuscorestaurants.com/en/limo.html. *C* **084/240-668.** Reservations recommended. Main courses S/21–S/46. AE, DC, MC, V. Daily 11am–11pm.

Moderate

A Mi Manera ★ 🏠 ANDEAN   A cozy and friendly little upstairs restaurant, entered through a colonial courtyard, this is one of the most relaxed spots in town. It serves excellent, creative Andean dishes with plenty of vegetarian options. For a taste of what Peruvian highlanders eat, this is the place. Traditionalists should check out the *rocoto relleno* (stuffed peppers with meat, peanuts, and raisins), *adobo de pollo* (chicken made with chichi and *yuca*), or the *orgía de papas* (an "orgy" of spicy and cheesy potatoes). The house specialty is the traditional oven-baked *cuy* (guinea pig) with stuffed pepper and potatoes. There are also homemade pastas, including several with twists, such as Andean quinoa gnocchi. Breakfast is served daily, and box lunches and cooking classes are available.

Triunfo 393, 2nd floor. www.amimaneraperu.com. © **084/222-219.** Reservations recommended. Main courses S/22–S/50. AE, DC, MC, V. Daily 8am–11pm.

Incanto ★ ☺ ITALIAN/PERUVIAN   From the outside, this restaurant—a large, airy space just off the Plaza de Armas, frequently filled with tourists—might not signal fine dining. But there's a reason it's often crowded. Focusing on homemade pastas and pizzas that emanate from a wood-burning oven in the center of the space, this laid-back restaurant, which sports a preserved interior Inca stone wall, is a definite crowd-pleaser. If you're looking for something uncomplicated, and especially if you've got kids in tow, this is a good choice. Vegetarians have plenty of options, including the tasty quinotto—risotto made from quinoa—and lasagna.

Santa Catalina Angosta 135. www.cuscorestaurants.com/en/incanto.html. © **084/254-753.** Reservations recommended. Main courses S/22–S/44. AE, DC, MC, V. Daily noon–11pm.

Kusikuy 🍴 ANDEAN/INTERNATIONAL   If you've resisted trying the Andean specialty that makes most foreigners recoil or at least raise an eyebrow, this could be the place to get adventurous. The restaurant's name in Quechua means "happy little guinea pig," so *cuy al horno* is, of course, the house dish. The rest of the menu focuses on other typical Peruvian dishes and adds stuff for gringos, such as pastas and basic chicken and meat dishes. It also serves a good-value lunch *menú* (which one day featured soup, chicken in red wine with rice, and pudding, plus juice). The cozy and good-looking loft-like space, on a hilly street above the Plaza de Armas, is warmly decorated with hardwood tables and couches and a mix of antiques and musical instruments from the Amazon. It's a cool, relaxed spot for a drink.

Suecia 339. © **084/262-870.** Reservations not accepted. Main courses S/16–S/42. MC, V. Mon–Sat 8am–midnight.

La Bodega 138 ★★ 🍴 PIZZA/ITALIAN   One of Cusco's newest and most attractive restaurants, this airy spot on a side street at the edge of San Blas does a modern take on rustic *casona* style, with whitewashed beams, pale blue textured walls, and brightly colored ceramic dinnerware. Ideal for a casual meal, it features a clay, wood-burning stove for excellent gourmet specialty pizzas (a big cut above most of the pizzas offered across Cusco), supplemented by a small menu of organic salads and delicious homemade pasta dishes. Everything is fresh, light, and nicely presented and prepared with excellent ingredients, and prices are very reasonable. Desserts (like the tiramisu) are great, and there's a nice little bar area with beers, wines, and fresh fruit juices. It's small and quickly becoming popular, so at peak hours you may have to wait a bit.

Herrajes 138. © **084/260-272.** Reservations not accepted. Main courses S/17–S/27. MC, V. Mon–Sat 1–11pm.

Pucara ★ 🍴 INTERNATIONAL/PERUVIAN   Just off the Plaza de Armas, this warm and dimly lit restaurant has small wood tables, exposed wood beams, and cloth lamps hanging low over the tables. As one of the first restaurants tourists stumble onto right off the main square, and as one of the better values in the historic center, it's generally packed. It has a few odd touches: On the walls are framed picture cut-outs of the dishes, and the waitstaff is a group of local women in yellow jackets and

CUSCO'S QUINTAS DINING AL FRESCO

When the day warms up under a huge blue sky in Cusco, you'll want to be outside. Cusco doesn't have many sidewalk cafes, but it does have a trio of *quintas*, traditional open-air restaurants that are most popular with locals on weekends. These are places to get large portions of good-quality Peruvian cooking at pretty reasonable prices. Among the dishes they all offer are *tamales*, *cuy chactado* (fried guinea pig with potatoes), *chicharrón* (deep-fried pork, usually served with mint, onions, and corn), alpaca steak, *lechón* (suckling pig), and *costillas* (ribs). You can also get classics such as *rocoto relleno* (stuffed hot peppers) and *papa rellena* (potatoes stuffed with meat or vegetables). Vegetarian options include *sopa de quinoa* (grain soup), fried *yuca*, and *torta de papa* (potato omelets). *Quintas* are open only for lunch (noon–5 or 6pm), and most people make a visit their main meal of the day. Main courses cost between S/15 and S/45.

Pachapapa ★ Across from the small church in San Blas, this popular *quinta* serves a full menu of authentic Andean dishes. Its delightful setting, in a relaxing and attractive courtyard with potted plants and whitewashed walls, also makes it an excellent place to take a breather while traipsing around hilly San Blas, to enjoy light items like soups and salads, as well as a full bar menu. From the wood-fired oven comes one of the house specialties, *cuy* (guinea pig served with Huacatay mint), as do the trout and even a spicy ham and cheese calzone. Plazoleta San Blas 120. ⓒ **084/241-318.**

Quinta Eulalia ★ ☺ Eulalia has been around since 1941, making it Cusco's oldest *quinta*. From a lovely colonial courtyard (only a 5-min. walk from the Plaza de Armas), there are views of the San Cristóbal district to the surrounding hills from the upper eating area. It's a great place to dine on a sunny day, and the Andean specialties are reasonably priced. Choquechaca 384. ⓒ **084/224-951.**

Quinta Zarate 🍴 Located at the eastern end of town, this relaxed place has a lovely, spacious garden area with great views of the Cusco Valley. Portions are very large, and the trout is a standout; try the ceviche de trucha (trout marinated in lime and spices). This *quinta* isn't difficult to find, though it's a decent hike from the square in San Blas. Totora Paccha 763, at the end of Calle Tandapata. ⓒ **084/245-114.**

hairnet caps. But don't let that turn you off; it has a nice selection of very reasonably priced traditional Peruvian and international dishes, including a tasty *lomo saltado* (strips of beef with fried potatoes, onions, and tomatoes), grilled trout, *palta rellena* (stuffed avocado), quinoa soup, and a variety of whitefish preparations.

Plateros 309. ⓒ **084/222-027.** Reservations not accepted. Main courses S/14–S/32. No credit cards. Mon–Sat 12:30–10pm.

Inexpensive

Chez Maggy ☺ PERUVIAN/PIZZERIA This bustling little joint, which has been around more than 3 decades and spawned several branches in other parts of Peru, has a bit of everything, from trout and alpaca to homemade pastas to Mexican food, but most people jam their way in for the pizzas made in a traditional brick oven. Chez Maggy is usually packed in the evenings, and there's often live Andean music. The restaurant is a long corridor with shared bench tables full of gringos. If you want a pizza on the terrace of your *hostal*, Chez Maggy will deliver for free.

Plateros 348. ☎ **084/234-861.** Reservations not accepted. Main courses S/14–S/34. MC, V. Daily 6–11pm.

Granja Heidi ★ 🍃 🏠 HEALTH FOOD/VEGETARIAN   Although easily overlooked, given its tucked-away, second-floor interior location, this clean and simple place with an emphasis on healthy, good-value meals (especially outstanding breakfasts) is worth tracking down. With a high ceiling and the look of an art studio, it's perfect for the San Blas neighborhood. Run by a German woman with a farm of the same name outside Cusco, it features farm-fresh ingredients, such as yogurt, cheese, and quiches. The menu also offers surprising meat dishes, including ostrich steak, and typical Peruvian dishes. The good-value daily *menú* (served until 9:30pm) offers vegetarian and nonvegetarian choices and might start with pumpkin soup, followed by lamb or a veggie stir-fry, fruit salad, and tea. Don't miss the rich, home-baked desserts.

Cuesta San Blas 525, San Blas. ☎ **084/238-383.** Reservations not accepted. Main courses S/14–S/32. No credit cards. Daily 8am–9:30pm.

Jack's Café Bar ★★ 🍃 CAFE/INTERNATIONAL   One of the most popular gringo hangouts in Cusco, owned by the guy who runs a thriving Irish pub in town, Jack's isn't just a spot to have a drink and check out some American and British magazines; it serves very fresh, very good, and frequently very large meals throughout the day, and features enough variety that you wouldn't be the first to eat here several times during your stay. For breakfast, try the big, fluffy pancakes. At lunch, order one of the towering salads or creative gourmet sandwiches (such as caramelized onions and salami). Finish with a dinner of "really hot green chicken curry" or a red wine, beef, and mushroom casserole. There are plenty of items for vegetarians, smoothies, wine and beer, as well as great coffee drinks and hot chocolate (for those cool Andean nights). And it's a friendly place to linger and meet fellow travelers, to boot.

Choquechaca 509 (corner of Cuesta San Blas). ☎ **084/806-960.** Reservations not accepted. Main courses S/12–S/26. No credit cards. Daily 7am–10pm.

La Tertulia ☺ BREAKFAST/CAFE FARE   A classic Cusco spot for breakfast or other light meals, this little place up a tight spiral staircase from a travel agency, is a gringo hangout par excellence. The name means "discussion," which is fitting because people gather here to read newspapers and foreign magazines, and to exchange books and advice on hiking the Inca Trail and other adventures. Many come to fuel up as early as 6:30am before setting out on one of those trips, and the superb breakfast buffet does the trick. You'll get all-you-can-eat eggs, fruit salads, yogurt, granola, amazing homemade wholemeal bread, French toast, *tamales,* fresh juices,

---

We Scream for *Helados Artesanales*

For the best artisanal ice creams and gelatos in Cusco, or maybe the best outside Italy, drop into **El Hada,** Arequipa 167 (☎ **084/253-744**), a sweet little joint scooping up coffee, cacao, passion-fruit, and other flavored organic ice creams made on a daily basis with the best local ingredients, as well as homemade cakes. Most unexpected is the Italian-made Rocket espresso machine, which cranks out excellent coffee drinks using the best small-batch Peruvian coffees from the Amazon, Puno, and other regions.

and coffee—truly the breakfast of champions and excellent value. The breakfast menu also features 16 types of crepes. There's a set-lunch deal and a nice salad bar, as well as pizzas, sandwiches, and fondues.

Procuradores 44, 2nd floor. *(C)* **084/241-422.** Reservations not accepted. Main courses S/8–S/24. MC, V. Daily 7am–3pm and 5–11pm.

SHOPPING

The Cusco region is Peru's center of handicraft production, especially handwoven textiles, and along with Lima is the country's premier shopping destination. Many Cusqueño artisans still employ ancient weaving techniques, and they produce some of the finest textiles in South America. Cusco overflows with tiny shops stuffed with colorful wares and large markets crammed with dozens of stalls.

Items to look for (you won't have to look too hard because shopping opportunities are pretty much everywhere you turn) include alpaca-wool sweaters, shawls, gloves, hats, scarves, blankets, ponchos, and *chullos,* the distinctive Andean knit caps with ear coverings; silver jewelry; antique blankets and textiles; woodcarvings, especially nicely carved picture frames; ceramics; and Escuela Cusqueña reproduction paintings.

The barrio of **San Blas,** the streets right around the **Plaza de Armas** (particularly calles Plateros and Triunfo), and **Plaza Regocijo** are the best and most convenient haunts for shopping outings. Many merchants sell similar merchandise, so some price comparison is always helpful. If sellers think you've just arrived in Peru and don't know the real value of items, your price is guaranteed to be higher. Although bargaining is acceptable and almost expected, merchants in the center of Cusco are confident of a steady stream of buyers, and, as a result, they are often less willing to negotiate than their counterparts in markets and more out-of-the-way places in Peru. Most visitors will find prices delightfully affordable, though, and haggling beyond what you know is a fair price, when the disparity of wealth is so great, is generally viewed as bad form. The best shops are the ones, like **Centro de Textiles Tradicionales del Cusco,** which guarantee that a high percentage of the sale price goes directly to the artisan.

Alpaca & Andean Fashions

It's difficult to walk 10 paces in Cusco without running into an alpaca goods shop. Almost everyone in Cusco will try to sell you what they claim to be 100% alpaca scarves and sweaters, but many sold on the street and in tourist stalls are of inferior quality (and might even be mixed with man-made materials such as fiberglass). What is described as "baby alpaca" might be anything but. (A trekking guide once joked to me that if you listen carefully, sellers claiming their wares are "baby alpaca" are, in fact, saying "may be alpaca.") To get better-quality, not to mention more stylish and original, examples, you need to visit a store that specializes in upscale alpaca fashions; they are more expensive but, compared to international alpaca prices, still a true bargain. Besides the following shops, see "Art & Handicrafts" and "Designer Apparel" below, for more and less traditional takes on alpaca goods.

My favorite alpaca-goods shops are: **Kuna ★★**, Plaza Recocijo 202 and Portal de Panes 127/Plaza de Armas (kuna.com.pe; *(C)* **084/243-233**), which features some of the finest, most modern alpaca and wool fashions for men and women, including great shawls, overcoats, and deconstructed and reversible, two-color jackets; and **Sol**

Alpaca ★★, San Juan de Dios 214 (www.solalpaca.com; ✆ 084/232-687), another of Cusco's most stylish and contemporary alpaca goods shops, with delicate sweaters, scarves, and shawls in great colors, nubby jackets, and the bonus of an excellent Indigo *artesanía* shop inside. Other boutiques, whose names let you know what you'll find inside, worth a look include: **Alpaca's Best ★**, Plaza Nazarenas 197–199 (✆ 084/245-331); **Alpaca 3,** Ruinas 472 (✆ 084/226-101); **Alpaca Treasures,** Heladeros 172 (✆ 084/438-557); and **World Alpaca,** Portal de Carnes 232/Plaza de Armas (✆ 084/244-098).

Many shops in Cusco feature sheep's wool or alpaca *chompas*, or jackets, with Andean designs (often lifted directly from old blankets and weavings). A different take on Peruvian fashions, sure to appeal to more stylish backpackers, is available at **Mundo Hemp,** Qanchipata 596, San Blas (✆ 084/258-411), where you'll find 100% natural hemp clothes and housewares, as well as a funky little cafe. For T-shirts with hip Andean motifs, check out **Mullu Arte Contemporáneo,** Triunfo 120 (✆ 084/229-831).

Antiques

Most of the best antiques dealers are found in the San Blas district. **Antigüedades Arcangel,** Cuesta de San Blas 591 (✆ 084/633-754), has a nice mix of religious and other antiques from the Cusco region and across Peru, including some accessibly priced gift items. **Antigüedades y Artesanías Sayre,** at Triunfo 352-B (✆ 084/236-981), and **Galería de Arte Cusqueño Antigüedades,** at Plazoleta San Blas 114 (✆ 084/237-857), stock a range of antiques, from textiles to art and furniture. Another shop worth a peek is **El Armario,** Carmen Alto 118 (✆ 084/229-809).

Art & Handicrafts (Artesanía)

Especially noteworthy is the **Centro de Textiles Tradicionales del Cusco ★★★**, Av. El Sol 603 (www.textilescusco.org; ✆ 084/228-117), an organization dedicated to "fair trade" practices. It ensures that 70% of the sale price of the very fine textiles on display goes directly to the six communities and individual artisans it works with. On-site is an ongoing demonstration of weaving and a very good, informative textiles museum. Prices are a bit higher than what you may find in generic shops around town, though the textiles are also higher quality, and much more of your money will go to the women who work for days on individual pieces. (There's also a small outlet of the Centro in the courtyard at the Museo de Arte Precolombino (MAP), Plaza Nazarenas 231.) For a massive selection of antique Andean textiles, visit the small shop that appears to have no name, but which the proud owner calls **Tienda-Museo de Josefina Olivera ★★**, Portal Comercio 173, Plaza de Armas (✆ 084/233-484). It stocks some fantastic vintage alpaca ponchos and blankets, though some age claims may be slightly exaggerated.

There are several large markets targeting the tourist trade in *artesanía*. For antique textiles, there's a good little stall at the end of the corridor (on the right side as you enter) within the **Feria Artesanal** at Plateros 334 (below). The stalls aren't numbered, and you might have to ask the owner to pull his older, more valuable pieces from a trunk he keeps them in, but he has some of the finest quality ceremonial textiles in Cusco. **Centro Artesanal Cusco,** at the end of Avenida El Sol, across from the large painted waterfall fountain, is the largest indoor market of handicrafts stalls in Cusco, and many goods are slightly cheaper here than they are closer to the plaza. Other centers with stalls and similar goods are **Feria Artesanal Tesoros del**

Inca, Plateros 334 (© **084/233-484**); **Centro Artesanal "Conde de Gabucha,"** Zetas 109 (© **084/248-250**); **Centro Artesanal El Inca,** San Andrés 218; **Centro Artesanal Sambleño,** Cuesta de San Blas 548; and **Feria Artesanal Yachay Wasi,** Triunfo 374.

More specialized shops congregate in the Centro Histórico. **Casa Ecológica Cusco,** Portal de Carnes 236 (interior)/Plaza de Armas (© **084/255-427**) has a good selection of high-quality, handmade textiles from highland communities (in addition to natural medicines and organic food products). Equal parts contemporary art gallery and shop dedicated to nicely selected, handmade *artesanía* (such as tablas de Sarhua) and jewelry, **Apacheta** ★, San Juan de Dios 250 (interior) (apachetaperu.com; © **084/238-210**) makes for good one-stop shopping. **Indigo Arte y Artesanía** ★, San Agustín 403–407 (© **084/240-145**) is similar, though more traditional and loaded with good gift ideas from across Peru. **La Casa de la Llama** ★, Palacio 121 (© **084/240-813**), features very nice quality and distinctive alpaca designs and leather goods, including embroidered reversible belts, baby alpaca stoles, and adorable and very colorful kids' sweaters. **Galería Latina,** Zetas 309 (© **084/236-703**), stocks a wide range of top-end antique blankets, rugs, alpaca-wool clothing, ceramics, jewelry, and handicrafts from the Amazon jungle in a large, cozy shop.

San Blas is swimming with art galleries, artisan workshops, and ceramics shops. You'll stumble upon many small shops dealing in reproduction Escuela Cusqueña religious paintings and many workshops where you can watch artisans in action. Several of the best ceramics outlets are also here, and a small handicrafts market usually takes over the plaza on Saturday afternoon. Several artists in the San Blas area open their studios as commercial ventures, although the opportunity to watch a painter work can be fairly expensive. Look for flyers in cafes and restaurants in San Blas advertising such workshops.

Arte Aller ★, Cuesta de San Blas 580 (© **084/241-171**), is a small and crowded shop crammed with great folk and religious art, including those uniquely Peruvian handmade Christmas ornaments. Marked by a sign that says ETHNIC PERUVIAN ART, **Aqlla** ★, Cuesta de San Blas 565 (© **084/249-018**), has great silver jewelry, folk and religious art, and fine alpaca items. For a general selection of *artesanía*, check out **Artesanías Mendivil** ★★, known internationally for its singular saint figures with elongated necks, but also featuring a nice selection of mirrors, carved wood frames, Cusco School reproductions, and other ceramics; it has locations at Plazoleta San Blas 619 (© **084/233-247**), Hatunrumíyoc 486 (© **084/233-234**), and Plazoleta San Blas 634 (© **084/240-527**). **Artesanías Olave** ★★, the outlets of a high-quality crafts shop that does big business with tourists, are located at Triunfo 342 (© **084/252-935**), Plazoleta San Blas 100 (© **084/246-300**), and Plazoleta San Blas 651 (© **084/231-835**). **Juan Garboza Taller** (workshop), Tandapata 676, Plazoleta San Blas (© **084/248-039**), specializes in pre-Inca-style ceramics. **Galería Sur,** Hatunrumiyoc 487-B (© **084/238-371**) sells fine, distinctive (and not inexpensive) tapestries from Ayacucho.

Designer Apparel

For women only, **Montse Aucells** ★★★, a Catalan designer resident in Cusco, has a small shop at Palacio 116 (© **084/226-330**) that features some of the most fashionable and original—but still largely traditional—alpaca designs and knitwear for women in town. The most unique designer that I've found in Cusco, or pretty much anywhere in Peru, for that matter, is a woman from Northern Ireland, Eibhlin

Cassidy, who sells her original clothing designs for women at her shop, **Hilo** ★★★, Carmen Alto 260, San Blas (www.hilocusco.com; ✆ 084/254-536). Eibhlin has a keen eye for patterns and sometimes startling combinations of fabrics and color and adornments like buttons; her whimsical but beautiful tops and jackets may not be for everyone, but to me it's wearable art. **Werner & Ana** ★, a Dutch–Peruvian design couple, sell stylish clothing in fine natural fabrics, including alpaca; they have a shop on Plaza San Francisco 295-A (at Garcilaso; ✆ 084/231-076).

Ollantay ★, Choquechaca 211 (✆ 984/616-844), makes handmade handbags and hats, but it's best known for the brightly colored suede boots, with swatches of antique Andean fabrics (and which can be custom-made). They've now proliferated across Cusco and can be found at several shops. Young and trendy sorts should check out the small shop **Pulga,** Carmen Alto 237, San Blas (www.pulgalatienda.com; ✆ 084/9844-93537), which focuses exclusively on the funky clothing, bags, and accessories (for both men and women) of young Peruvian designers from Lima and around the country. **Puquna,** Choquechaca 408 (✆ 084/255-257), is a small and stylish shop that features original design and popular art objects, including photography, textiles, and jewelry. **Puna** ★, Santa Teresa 375 (www.puna.com.pe; ✆ 084/225-590), is a contemporary gallery/shop with a pop and graphic sensibility, selling art prints, hip design notebooks, graphic T-shirts, CDs by Peruvian bands, and funky accessory items like colorful bags, pillows, gloves, and acrylic items.

Foodstuffs & Mercado Central

Cusco's famous, frenzied **Mercado Central** (Central Market, also referred to as Mercado San Pedro) ★★ near the San Pedro rail station is shopping of a much different kind—almost more of a top visitor's attraction than a shopping destination. Its array of products for sale—mostly produce, food, and household items—is dazzling; even if you don't come to shop, this rich tapestry of modern and yet highly traditional Cusco still shouldn't be missed. If you're an adventurous type who doesn't mind eating at street stalls (which are generally pretty clean), you can get a ridiculously cheap lunch for about $1. Don't take valuables (or even your camera), though, and be on guard because the market is frequented by pickpockets targeting tourists. The market is open daily from 8am to 4pm or so.

A great selection of homemade chocolates can be had at a small shop in San Blas, called, appropriately enough, **Chocolate** ★, Choquechaca 162 (✆ 084/229-001). **Mundo Hemp,** Qanchispata 596, San Blas (www.mundohemp.com; ✆ 084/258-411), has hemp-based sweets and soups in its cafe, in addition to the more expected hemp T-shirts and clothing and home-design accessories. **The Coca Shop,** Carmen Alto 115, San Blas (www.thecocashop.com; ✆ 084/260-774), features all things derived from coca leaves (save the obvious), including coca- and lúcuma-infused chocolates and teas. For Cusco's best artisanal ice cream and gelato, homemade cakes, as well as terrific Peruvian small-batch coffees from an Italian-made Rocket machine, drop into the adorable **El Hada** ★★, Arequipa 167 (no phone).

Jewelry & Silver

Ilaria ★★★, one of the finest jewelry stores in Peru, deals in fine silver and unique Andean-style pieces, and has several branches in Cusco: at Hotel Monasterio, Palacios 136 (www.ilariainternational.com; ✆ 084/221-192); at the Casa Andina Private Collection, Plazoleta de Limacpampa Chico 473 (p. 202); at Hotel Libertador, Plazoleta Santo Domingo 259 (✆ 084/223-192); and another at Portal Carrizos 258 on the Plaza de Armas (℗ **084/246-253**). Many items, although not inexpensive, are excellent value for handmade silver.

A collective of Lima jewelry designers share a small storefront at Choquechaca 162 (℗ **084/244-135**): **Claudia Lira ★★** (www.claudialira.com) works primarily in silver to create elegant contemporary pieces with clean lines and pure natural forms, while **Puro Diseño ★**(www.purodisenojoyas.com) features modern designs in wood and other materials in combination with silver. The contemporary jewelry designer **Carlos Chaquiras,** Triunfo 375 (℗ **084/227-470**), is an excellent craftsman; many of his pieces feature pre-Columbian designs. Another nice shop with silver items is **Platería El Tupo,** Portal de Harinas 181, Plaza de Armas (℗**084/229-809**). **Chimú Art & Gifts,** Carmen Alto 187-B, San Blas (℗**084/801-968**), is a funky shop featuring cool contemporary designs in silver, many based on interpretations of Chimú culture art. Rocío Pérez shows her original designs (packaged in handmade bags) at her little shop, **Jewelry Esma,** in the entryway to the Quinta Paccha Papa restaurant, at Plaza San Blas 120.

Outdoor Gear

As the gateway to outdoor highlands and Sacred Valley activities, including mountain climbing, trekking, and cycling, Cusco is well stocked with outdoor gear shops for those who aren't adequately equipped for their adventures. In the last few years, the selection of international, high-end name brands has increased while prices have come down to pretty standard international levels. **Tatoo Adventure Gear ★★**, Calle del Medio 130 leading just off Plaza de Armas (℗ **084/224-797**) has probably the best selection of camping, trekking, and mountain climbing shoes, backpacks, and equipment. Another good nearby shop with similar goods is **Cordillera ★**, Garcilaso 210 (℗ **084/244-133**).

Woodwork

Lots of shops have hand-carved woodwork and frames. However, the best spots for handmade baroque frames (perfect for your Cusco School reproduction or religious shrine) are **La Casa del Altar,** Mesa Redonda Lote A, near the Plaza de Armas (℗ **084/244-712**), which makes *retablos* (altarpieces) and altars in addition to frames; and **Taller Miguel Angel León,** Córdoba del Tucumán 372 (just off Plazoleta Nazarenas) (℗ **084/236-271**), a small studio where Señor León and his children and grandchildren make excellent handmade cedar frames to order (the kind one sees on most art from the Escuela Cusqueña originals and imitations).

ENTERTAINMENT & NIGHTLIFE

Most first-time visitors to Cusco are surprised to find that this Andean city with such a pervasive, gentle Amerindian influence and colonial atmosphere also has such a rollicking nightlife. It's not as diverse (or sophisticated) as Lima's, but the scene, tightly contained around the Plaza de Armas, is predominantly young and rowdy, a perfect diversion from the rigors of trekking and immersion in Inca and colonial history. Some older visitors might find the late-night, spring break party atmosphere a little jarring in such a historic, stately place. And no doubt that's what motivated the mayor's office to move to shut down several of the rowdiest, late-night clubs in the historic center in the last couple of years.

Even though the city is inundated with foreigners during many months of the year, bars and discos happily aren't just gringolandia outposts. Locals (as well as Peruvians from other cities, principally Lima, and other South Americans) usually make up a pretty healthy percentage of the clientele. Clubs are in such close range of each other—in the streets just off the Plaza de Armas and in San Blas (where the city's artsier bars and cafes proliferate)—that virtually everyone seems to adopt a pub-crawl attitude, bopping from one bar or disco to the next, often reconvening with friends in the plaza before picking up a free drink ticket and free admission card from one of the many girls on the square handing them out.

For those who are saving their energy for the Inca Trail and other treks, there are less rowdy options, such as Andean music shows in restaurants, more sedate bars, and English-language movies virtually every night of the week.

Bars & Pubs

In high season, bars are often filled to the rafters with gringos hoisting cheap drinks and trading information on the Inca Trail or their latest jungle or rafting adventure (or just trying to pick up Peruvians or each other). Most bars are open from 11am or noon until 1 or 2am. Many have elastic happy hours offering half-price drinks, making it absurdly cheap to tie one on. (Travelers still adjusting to Cusco's altitude, though, should take it easy on alcohol in their first days in the city.)

A handful of restaurants are excellent places to drop into for a cocktail or glass of wine. The mixologists at **Limo ★★★** (p. 186) can hold their own with any bartenders in the city, and the list of pisco cocktails, most with exotic fruit juices and other ingredients, is superb—a great place to begin or end the evening. **Baco ★**, (p. 184) is an oenophile's hangout, a good place to sample Chilean, Argentine, and Spanish wines in quiet, romantic environs. Its sister restaurant **Cicciolina ★★** (p. 185) also has a very appealing wine and cocktail bar right up front, with tons of ambience. Way too unique and inspired to be merely another restaurant, **Fallen Angel ★** (p. 183), has such a wild, over-the-top look—complete with glass tables topping porcelain bathtubs filled with brightly colored (live) fish—that it also makes a scene-stealing spot for a drink (note that it closes promptly at 11pm, however).

My favorite cocktail bar in Cusco, however, is **El Pisquerito ★★★**, San Juan de Dios 250 (interior) (✆ **084/235-223**), specializing in Peruvian piscos and a dizzying array of pisco sours and other cocktails. In its new, cozy location with a fireplace and open bar in the middle of a high, peaked-ceiling space, it's more a haunt of locals than gringos. **Los Perros ★**, Tecsecocha 436 (✆ **084/241-447**), is a laid-back but trendy lounge bar owned by an Australian–Peruvian couple. "The Dogs" has comfy sofas, good food and cocktails (including hot wine), and a hip soundtrack. The bar attracts an international crowd that takes advantage of the book exchange and magazines, and plenty of folks quickly become regulars, making it their spot for dining as well as just hanging out and drinking. **The Muse ★**, Triunfo 338, 2nd floor (✆ **984/762-602**), has a similar vibe, with boldly colored couches and neon-colored walls. The sedate and good-looking restaurant and cocktail lounge **Marcelo Batata,** Palacios 121 (✆ **084/224-424**) has a coveted rooftop terrace with amazing rooftop and star views.

One of the oldest pubs in town is the **Cross Keys ★**, Triunfo 350 (✆ **084/229-227**), owned by the English honorary consul and especially popular with Brits who come to play darts or catch up on European soccer on satellite, and knock back pints of ale; it's stuffed to the gills late at night. Pub grub is available, if you can manage to

Raw Fish: A Cure for What Ails You

If you hang out so much and so late in Cusco that you wind up with a wicked hangover—which is even more of a problem at an altitude of 3,300m (11,000 ft.)—adopt the tried-and-true Andean method of reviving yourself. For once, the solution is not coca-leaf tea—it's ceviche that seems to do the trick. Something about raw fish marinated in lime and chili makes for a nice slap in the face. When I lived in Ecuador (a country that fights with Peru not only over boundaries, but also over credit for having invented ceviche), late Sunday mornings at the *cevichería* were part of the weekly routine for pale-faced folks hiding behind sunglasses.

get an order in. American-owned **Norton Rat's Tavern,** Santa Catalina Angosta 116 (📞 **084/246-204**), next door to the La Compañía church, is a rough-and-tumble bar, the type of biker-friendly place that you might find in any American Midwestern city. Nice balconies overlook the action below on the plaza. **Paddy Flaherty's,** Triunfo 124, Plaza de Armas (📞 **084/247-719**), claiming to be the world's highest authentic Irish pub, is cozy, relaxed, and often crowded, with expats catching up on *fútbol* (soccer, of course) and rugby and downing Guinness on draft. **Rosie O'Grady's,** Santa Catalina Ancha 360 (📞 **084/247-935**), is the other Irish tavern of note, with fancier digs in which to down your (canned) Guinness. There's live music Thursday through Saturday, and several happy hours throughout the day. Rowdy late into the night in San Blas is **7 Angelitos, ★** Calle Siete Angelitos 638 (📞 **084/806-070**), with live music most nights; it's the place to go when all other bars have closed—its owners will still be buying folks drinks and encouraging hangovers until the sun comes up. **El Duende Lounge Bar,** Tecsecocha 429 (📞 **084/946 692-106**), is a good place for drinks and meeting Peruvian young people.

Live Music Clubs

Live music is a nearly constant feature of the Cusco nightlife scene, and it's less about itinerant bands of *altiplano* musicians in colorful vests and sandals playing woodwind instruments than live Latin rock, pop, and salsa. Live music tends to begin around 11pm in most clubs, and happy hours are generally from 8 to 9 or 10pm.

The coolest place in Cusco for nightly live music has long been **Ukuku's ★★,** Plateros 316, second floor (www.ukukusbar.com; 📞 **084/227-867**). It was recently closed down by the mayor for its loud, wee-hours antics, but locals hope to see it reopen. Check to see if it has, and if so expect again to see a range of acts that extends from bar rock to Afro-Peruvian, while the crowd comes to get a groove on, jamming the dance floor. **Inkabar,** Plateros 354, 2nd floor (📞 **084/237-000**) features occasional live bands in a handsome bar set in a restored colonial building (enter through Tayta Inta restaurant).

In San Blas, **Km. 0 ★,** Tandapata 100 (📞 **084/254-240**), is a Spanish-owned joint with a rocker's heart, a tiny ramshackle place with live rock, Latin, and blues music nightly, "happy hours all night," and a variety of tapas. A one-stop-shopping outlet for nightlife, **Garabato Video Pub,** Espaderos 135, 3rd Floor (📞 **084/620-336**), is a bar/restaurant that features nightly movies on a large screen, a variety of live shows, and a dance floor and lounge.

For a traditional folklore music-and-dance show with panpipes and costumes—well, ponchos, alpaca hats, and sandals, at a minimum—you'll need to check out one of the tourist-oriented restaurants featuring nightly entertainment. In addition to the long-time show restaurants **El Truco** (Plaza Regocijo 261; ✆ **084/232-441**) and **La Retama** (Portal de Panes 123, 2nd Floor; ✆ **084/226-372**), **Tunupa,** Portal Confiturías 233, 2nd Floor (✆ **084/252-936**), offers a good traditional music-and-dance show, as well as a panoramic view of the Plaza de Armas. They're not my cup of coca tea, but plenty of first-time visitors and groups get a kick out of them at least once.

Dance Clubs

Several late-night dance clubs have come and gone in the last few years, but a few of the old warhorses remain popular. A pretty young crowd, both backpackers and young Peruvians, is lured to the discos by all the free drink cards handed out on the Plaza de Armas. **Mama Africa ★★,** Portal de Panes 109, 2nd Floor (✆ **084/246-544**), boasts sweaty charm and features occasional live music and DJs who spin an international dance mix of Latin, reggae, rock, and techno music for a mix of locals and gringos (each often looking to hook up). The original club is now called **Mama Amerika,** Portal Belén 115, 2nd Floor (✆ **084/245-550**). It's just as crowded as ever, and besides serving free and cheap drinks, it also has good munchies and a large screen showing videos.

New on the scene are **Groove,** Teqsiqocha 282 (✆ **954/735-213**), a hopping place in a colonial building that's among the largest clubs in Cusco and, a few blocks from the Plaza de Armas in an area more populated with young local revelers, **Atika Disco Lounge Bar,** Av. El Sol 248/Pje. Chaski, s/n (www.atikadiversion.com; ✆ **984/777447**), the biggest dance club in Cusco and a full roster of events (like "Underwear Night").

CAFE society IN CUSCO

If you really just want to chill out and have a coffee, a beer, or some dessert, drop into one of the city's comfortable cafes. The following are all good places for a light meal during the day, but at night they tend to take on some of that smoky Euro-cafe sheen, and travelers get all metaphysical about their treks through the Andes.

Café Ayllu ★, Almagro 133 (✆ **084/232-357**), is a busy little place, a traditional Cusco cafe drawing as many locals as gringos. It's known for its *ponche de leche* (a milky beverage, often served with a shot of pisco) and *lenguas* (a flaky pastry with manjar blanco crème in the middle). It also offers good breakfasts, sandwiches, and the mainstay, coffee. **Trotamundos ★,** Portal de Comercio 177, second floor

(✆ **084/239-590**), has an excellent balcony on the main square, facing the cathedral. It also has an open fireplace, which is perfect for cold evenings, and a convenient Internet cafe. It's a good spot for coffee and cakes, and a lively nighttime bar atmosphere. **Café Varayoc,** Espaderos 142 (✆ **084/232-404**), is a sophisticated place to read and chill over coffee and excellent pastries and desserts, especially cheesecake. Removed from the center, but well located if you're making the rounds of Manu travel operators, **Manu Café** is a chic rainforest-style cafe, very swish for Cusco; it's attached to Manu Nature Tours at Av. Pardo 1046 (✆ **084/252-721**). It serves excellent coffee and light meals, and there are racks of foreign newspapers.

Cinema

There aren't many traditional cinemas in central Cusco, but there are a number of places showing movies, mostly to entertain international visitors in need of a break from trekking and sightseeing. Probably the best selection of international films, ranging from classic to art house to children's flicks, but mostly American, is found at **The Film Lounge & Danish Café,** Procuradores 389, 2nd floor (© **084/123-236**); it's got a cute little bar, serves food and drinks, and has three screenings daily (S/4). **Garabato Video Pub,** Espaderos 135, 3rd floor (© **084/620-336**) also screens movies on a daily basis.

Theater & Dance

For music and folkloric dance performances, **Teatro Municipal,** Mesón de la Estrella 149 (© **084/221-847**), and particularly the long-running **Centro Q'osqo de Arte Nativo ★**, Av. El Sol 684 (© **084/227-901**), feature good Peruvian music and folkloric dance performances. Check with the tourist information office for a schedule of events.

WHERE TO STAY

As the top tourist destination in Peru, where virtually every visitor seems to pass and stay at least a night or two, Cusco has developed a remarkable cornucopia of lodgings, with hundreds of hotels, inns, and *hostales* of all stripes and prices. More continue to sprout, and few seem to close. Although the sheer number of offerings, particularly at the midrange and budget levels, means that you can pretty confidently land in Cusco without a reservation (outside of popular festivals like Inti Raymi and Fiestas Patrias at the end of June and July) and find a decent place to stay, many of the better and more popular hotels at all levels fill up throughout high season and even in shoulder months. It's best to firm up a reservation as soon as you know your dates of stay in Cusco unless you're willing to wing it and aren't that picky.

Most of the city's most desirable accommodations are very central, in the Centro Histórico and within walking distance of the Plaza de Armas. The artsy San Blas neighborhood is also within walking distance, although many hotels and *hostales* in that district involve steep climbs up the hillside. (The upside is that guests are rewarded with some of the finest views in the city.) Some visitors may want to avoid hotels and inns too close to the Plaza de Armas; that zone's crowded bars and nightclubs, many of which are open until sunrise, tend to produce throngs of rambunctious and usually inebriated young people who stumble downstairs and howl at the moon or bellow at the people who just rejected them inside.

Hotels have really mushroomed in the last few years in Cusco, but the high-end boutique category in particular has exploded. In addition to those below, be on the lookout for the imminent arrival of two new properties that are certain to be among the most talked about in the city. After many years of restoration, Orient Express's new 55-room luxury property, **Palacio Nazarenas** (www.palacionazarenas.com; © **01/610-8300**), will open next door to the granddaddy of Peruvian luxury hotels, Hotel Monasterio (see p. 200), and offer personal butlers, a spa, and an infinity pool in a cloistered courtyard. Also on the horizon is the long-awaited debut of the 153-room **JW Marriott Hotel Cusco** (www.marriott.com/hotels/travel/cuzmc-jw-marriott-hotel-cusco; © **800-228-9290** in the U.S. and Canada or **01/217-7000**), Calle Ruinas 432 (at San Agustín), occupying an entire city block with spectacular

No Sleeping In

Most Cusco hotels have annoyingly early checkout times—often 9 or 9:30am—due to the deluge of early morning flight arrivals to the city. At least in high season, hotels are very serious about your need to rise and shine (and many travelers are up and out very early anyway, on their way to Machu Picchu or trekking excursions), but you can always store your bags until later.

installations that include an impressive spa and an oxygen-enriched system in all rooms. Though the style quotient has risen, along with the prices, Cusco remains a backpackers' delight, with a glut of inns of all stripes at the moderate and budget levels. Many *hostales* have more atmosphere and are likely to provide a better overall experience than more expensive—and more institutional—hotels. Prices listed below are rack rates for travel in high season and include taxes. During the low season (Nov–Apr), prices often drop precipitously, even at midrange inns and backpacker hostels—sometimes as much as 50%—as hotels fight for a much-reduced number of visitors.

At the lower end, hot water can be an issue at many hotels—even those that swear they offer 24-hour hot showers. Many hotels and inns will arrange free airport transfers if you communicate your arrival information to them in advance.

Near the Plaza de Armas
VERY EXPENSIVE

Aranwa Cusco Boutique Hotel ★★★ Aranwa's signature property is one of the new boutique hotels that has led the way at the upper echelon, by amping up luxury, personalized service, and modern technology within the confines of historic Cuzqueño architecture. This stately small hotel inhabits a brilliantly converted 16th-century colonial *casona*, filled with an impressive display of antiques, sculptures, and Cusqueña School art. The street it's on, just off Plaza Regocijo, has quickly become one of Cusco's most chic. Rooms, built around an enclosed courtyard, have incredibly high ceilings and are as large and elegant as any in Cusco, and bathrooms have heated floors. In fact, only the suites of La Casona and Hotel Monasterio come close. But the hotel's biggest competitive advantage may be its "intelligent oxygen system," which pumps purified air into the entire hotel—ideal for those affected by Cusco's high altitude. To keep up with the competition, a spa is on its way.

San Juan de Dios 255. www.aranwahotels.com. ☏ **084/604-444** or for reservations 01/434-1452. 43 units. $350–$390 double; $400–$450 suite. Rates include breakfast buffet. AE, DC, MC, V. **Amenities:** Restaurant; bar; concierge. *In room:* A/C, TV/DVD, fridge, Wi-Fi (free).

Fallen Angel: The Guest House ★★ 🎁 This idiosyncratic and fantasy-like guest house may not be for everyone, but it is certainly wildly unique. The brainchild of Andrés Zuniga, who created the surreal restaurant Fallen Angel, it takes that concept one step further—and literally upstairs. With just four rooms (with names like Passion, Liberty, and Tranquility), each decorated to the hilt as if part of some avant-garde art installation, this is a solar system removed from your expected Andean lodgings. A place for sybarites, rooms, filled with incredible original art and furnishings, are impossibly large and grand, adhering to an eclectic vision that's part Pedro Almodóvar, part Damien Hirst, and part Peter Greenaway. Staying here is something akin to sleeping on a trippy film set, so you need to have an open mind and sense of humor. If you do, Fallen Angel is a place you're unlikely to ever forget.

Plazoleta Nazarenas 221, Cusco. www.fallenangelincusco.com/TheGuestHouse/TheGuestHouse. html. © **084/258-184.** 4 units. $280–$330 suite. Rates include breakfast. MC, V. **Amenities:** Restaurant; bar. *In room:* A/C, TV/DVD, fridge, Wi-Fi (free).

Hotel Monasterio ★★★ Long Cusco's most extraordinary place to stay, though there's now plenty of competition from new luxury hotels, this Orient Express property is as much a museum as a hotel, with its own opulent gilded chapel and Escuela Cusqueña art collection. On quiet Las Nazarenas square, it occupies a 1592 monastery constructed on the foundations of an Inca palace. Rooms are impeccably decorated in both colonial and modern styles, with large Cusqueña School paintings; rooms off the first courtyard are more traditionally designed and feel more authentic. Enjoy the breakfast buffet as you're serenaded by Gregorian chants in the vaulted refectory of the monastery. As a special bonus, the hotel was the first in the world to offer oxygen piped directly into rooms through the ventilation. Orient Express is slated to open a similarly luxurious, more boutique-like sister property on the same square, and it's sure to be every bit as spectacular.

Palacios 136 (Plazoleta Nazarenas), Cusco. www.monasteriohotel.com. © **084/604-000** or 01/610-8300 for reservations. Fax 084/604-011. 126 units. $345–$475 double; $570–$2,100 suite. Rates include breakfast buffet. AE, DC, MC, V. **Amenities:** 2 restaurants; cafe; bar; concierge. *In room:* A/C, Cable TV/DVD, fridge, oxygen on demand ($45 surcharge).

La Casona ★★★ At the top of the ultraluxe boutique category is this eminently polished hotel, occupying a magnificent 16th-century colonial manor house on Plazoleta Las Nazarenas. A Relaís & Chateaux property, La Casona is meant not to feel like a hotel at all, but an elegant palace-home where guests are lucky (and affluent) enough to spend the night. There's no bell out front, no traditional lobby or check-in desk, and rooms have neither numbers nor names. The inn is about full-on luxury and attentive service (personal concierges take care of guests' every whim). The enormous suites, with heated floors and many stone fireplaces, are built around the elegant central courtyard, and the marble-and-stone bathrooms are the size of most NYC apartments. Rooms are outfitted with exquisite antiques, authentic Cusqueña School paintings, and feature radiant heat in the flooring. The elegant small dining room and sitting room are suitable for visiting dignitaries—which is how most guests will feel here.

Plazoleta Nazarenas 167, Cusco. www.inkaterra.com/en/cusco. © **800/442-5042** in U.S. and Canada, or 01/610-0400 for reservations. Fax 084/244-669. 11 units. $380–590 double; $720–$1,128 suite. Rates include breakfast buffet. AE, DC, MC, V. **Amenities:** Restaurant; concierge. *In room:* A/C, TV/DVD, fridge, Wi-Fi (free).

La Lune ★★★ ⚷ Above the stunning and resolutely French restaurant Le Soleil (see p. 184), and owned by the same gentleman, this privileged hideaway—for those that can afford it—is the most private and exclusive place in Cusco. Labeling itself a "one-suite hotel," on the second floor of an 18th-century *casona,* it is like staying in a friend's very privileged and elegantly appointed apartment in Old Cusco. The suites are incredibly spacious and exceedingly comfortable, perfect for the well-heeled family or couples traveling together. Perhaps the best bonus is that you'll eat all your meals (included) at Le Soleil. It's enough to think you've traveled to a swanky *arrondissement* of Paris rather than the old Andean capital.

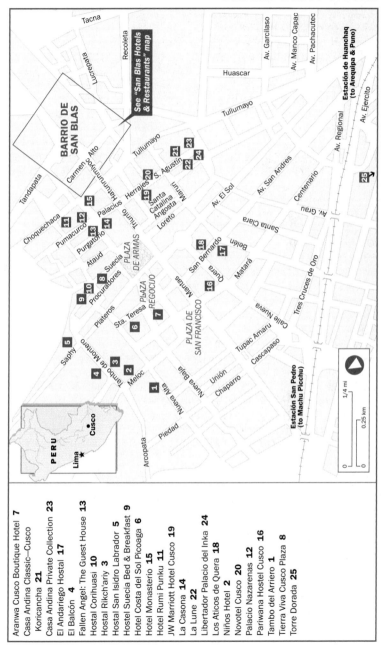

Central Cusco Hotels

- Aranwa Cusco Boutique Hotel **7**
- Casa Andina Classic—Cusco Koricancha **21**
- Casa Andina Private Collection **23**
- El Andariego Hostal **17**
- El Balcón **4**
- Fallen Angel: The Guest House **13**
- Hostal Corihuasi **10**
- Hostal Rikch'ariy **3**
- Hostal San Isidro Labrador **5**
- Hostel Suecia Bed & Breakfast **9**
- Hotel Costa del Sol Picoaga **6**
- Hotel Monasterio **15**
- Hotel Rumi Punku **11**
- JW Marriott Hotel Cusco **19**
- La Casona **14**
- La Lune **22**
- Libertador Palacio del Inka **24**
- Los Aticos de Quera **18**
- Niños Hotel **2**
- Novotel Cusco **20**
- Palacio Nazarenas **12**
- Pariwana Hostel Cusco **16**
- Tambo del Arriero **1**
- Tierra Viva Cusco Plaza **8**
- Torre Dorada **25**

San Agustín 275, Cusco. www.onesuitehotelcusco.com. ☏ **084/240-543.** 4 units. $550 suite–$1,000 2-bedroom apartment. Rates include 3 meals and massages. AE, DC, MC, V. **Amenities:** Restaurant. *In room:* A/C, TV/DVD, fridge, Wi-Fi (free).

Libertador Palacio del Inka ★   For years this hotel's only competition at the top was the Monasterio; the Libertador has now been overtaken by several newer and more intimate properties, but it remains a fine, large luxury hotel with attentive and professional service. Filled with art and antiques, and 4 blocks from the Plaza de Armas, directly across from the Inca Temple of the Sun and built on the foundations of the Aclla Huyasi (where the Inca chieftain kept maidens), this elegant traditional hotel occupies a historic house once inhabited by the conquistador Francisco Pizarro. It's built around a dramatic colonial courtyard marked by perfect arches, terracotta tiles, and a Spanish-style fountain. The swank lobby has a massive pyramidal skylight and exposed Inca walls. Guest rooms are spacious, soothing, and refined; furnishings have rustic colonial touches, and the marble bathrooms are large. Many rooms have small terraces.

San Agustín 400 (Plazoleta Santo Domingo 259), Cusco. www.summithotels.com. ☏**084/231-961.** Fax 01/233-152. 254 units. $305 deluxe double; $345 suite. AE, DC, MC, V. **Amenities:** Restaurant; coffee shop; concierge; fitness center; sauna. *In room:* A/C, Cable TV/DVD, fridge, hair dryer.

EXPENSIVE

Casa Andina Private Collection ★★ 🥗   In a handsome 18th-century mansion on a small square a bit removed from the heart of the old city, this sensitively restored hotel built around four interior patios is like a budget version of Hotel Monasterio. For travelers looking for a bit of that hotel's ambience but not its elevated price tag, Casa Andina is one of the best-value luxury options in town. Rooms are spacious and cleanly outfitted, with a minimalist take on Andean decor. While my favorites are the suites in the old section of the hotel, the newer rooms thankfully are not distractingly modern, and, tucked away as they are from the street, they're nice and quiet. The gorgeous, deep-red sitting room, with its massive, roaring fireplace, is the perfect place to warm up on a chilly Cusco night. The gourmet restaurant is one of those all too rare hotel restaurants that merits staying in for the night.

Plazoleta de Limacpampa Chico 473, Cusco. www.casa-andina.com. ☏ **866/220-4434** toll-free in the U.S., 08/082-343-805 in the U.K., or 01/213-9739. Fax 01/445-4775. 100 units. $219 double; $319–$389 suite. Rates include breakfast buffet. AE, DC, MC, V. **Amenities:** Restaurant; bar; babysitting; concierge. *In room:* TV, fridge, Wi-Fi (free).

Hotel Costa del Sol Picoaga ★   A nice, more reasonably priced alternative to Cusco's top luxury hotels, Picoaga also occupies a historic building—in this case a 17th-century mansion that once belonged to a Spanish nobleman, the marquis of Picoaga. Just minutes from the Plaza de Armas, part of the hotel is set around a lovely arcaded courtyard. A newer wing is in a much less appealing modern section at the rear of the hotel. Rooms are thus divided between Colonial and Modern. Ask for a room in the front section and on the back side of the courtyard; rooms there, about a third of the total, are larger, have high ceilings, and are decorated with colonial-style furniture and floral prints.

Santa Teresa 344, Cusco. www.costadelsolperu.com/peru/hotels/cusco. ☏ **01/711-3320000.** Fax 084/221-246. 77 units. $219–$247 double. Rates include breakfast buffet. AE, DC, MC, V. **Amenities:** 2 restaurants; fireplace cocktail bar; concierge. *In room:* A/C, TV, fridge, Wi-Fi (free).

MODERATE

Casa Andina Classic—Cusco Koricancha ★ 🍴   This professionally run, midprice hotel is one of five in Cusco belonging to this upstart Peruvian hotel chain. Casa Andina guests know what to expect: excellent service and clean, colorfully decorated rooms. Three blocks from the main square, this hotel is built around a restful colonial courtyard and is in a somewhat quieter neighborhood, while the other two, smaller locations, are virtually on top of the Plaza de Armas. All have similar prices and features (though the Cusco Catedral hotel has an Inca wall within the hotel and the smaller Cusco Plaza has views of the Plaza de Armas from its breakfast room).

San Agustín 371, Cusco. www.casa-andina.com. ✆ **866/220-4434** toll-free in the U.S., 08/082-343-805 in the U.K., or 01/213-9739. Fax 01/445-4775. 57 units. $129–$159 double. Rates include breakfast buffet. AE, DC, MC, V. **Amenities:** Concierge. *In room:* TV, fridge, Wi-Fi (free).

Hotel Rumi Punku ★ 🏨   This oddly charming, family-owned and ever-expanding small hotel, in a colonial house on the edge of San Blas, features a lovely rooftop terrace, flower-filled colonial courtyard with a cute little chapel, and gardens along a large Inca wall. As the owners have added more rooms, the style quotient and price ledger have also increased. The clean bedrooms are ample, with hardwood floors and Norwegian thermal blankets. The top-floor dining room, where breakfast is served, has excellent panoramic views of Cusco's rooftops. The massive portal to the street is a fascinating original Inca construction of cut stone, once part of a sacred Inca temple. (The door is one of three belonging to private houses in Cusco.) The hotel is on the way up to Sacsayhuamán, but only a short walk from the Plaza de Armas. Additional features include a spa with a "Finnish" sauna and Jacuzzi tub ($15 extra), perfect to take the edge off the altitude and area hikes.

Choquechaca 339, Cusco. www.rumipunku.com. ✆ **084/236-957.** Fax 084/242-741. 40 units. $100–$130 double; $200 suite. Rates include breakfast buffet and airport pickup. AE, DC, MC, V. **Amenities:** Restaurant; spa; gym; Jacuzzi; fireplace lounge. *In room:* Cable TV, Wi-Fi (free).

Novotel Cusco 🍴   This member of the French Novotel chain is built around the guts of a 16th-century colonial building with a lovely central courtyard. Most of the rooms, however, are in newly built additions. The hotel is modern and dependable, with good services and amenities, although, in most regards, it's a significant notch below the city's top-flight luxury hotels. The modern rooms are well equipped and brightly colored, but are otherwise standard accommodations. At this level, it's worth spending the extra money to get one of the superior rooms in the converted colonial section of the hotel; they are larger and much more atmospheric. The hotel, a short distance from the Plaza de Armas, features a nice garden-side restaurant serving French fare, and a warm bar with a fireplace. Deals are often available online.

San Agustín 239 (corner of Pasaje Santa Mónica), Cusco. www.novotel.com. ✆ **084/881-030.** Fax 084/228-855. 99 units. $127–$183 double. Rates include breakfast. AE, DC, MC, V. **Amenities:** Restaurant; bar; babysitting; concierge; sauna. *In room:* A/C, TV, fridge.

Tambo del Arriero ★ 🏨   On a quiet residential street, a bit off the beaten track—a good thing for travelers who quickly get enough of the Plaza de Armas hullabaloo 5 blocks away—this new family-owned boutique property is a loving restoration of a handsome 17th-century colonial house with two sunny, brightly colored courtyards and wooden balconies. Rooms are simply but warmly decorated and have plenty of character. I'm a fan of the rooms on the 2nd floor overlooking the first courtyard; No. 203, with a whitewashed, peaked ceiling and loft space; and, for a splurge, No. 108, an expansive suite with its own private patio. The inn, with its period details, bright colors, and Andean accents has a real sense of place and feels very Cusqueño, which is what most travelers to this alluring city are looking for.

Nueva Alta 484, Cusco. www.tambodelarriero.com. © **084/260-709.** Fax 084/263-378 18 units. $120–$150 double; $150–$300 suite. Rates include breakfast buffet and free airport pickup/drop-off. AE, DC, MC, V. **Amenities:** Coffee bar. *In room:* Cable TV, Wi-Fi (free).

Tierra Viva Cusco Plaza ★ ✦ Somewhere between boutique and midsize hotel, this relatively new addition to the Cusco hotel scene, carved out of an old *casona* and featuring a skylighted central patio and lovely stone fireplace, occupies a good niche: good service, fair prices, good location, and nicely equipped rooms. Decor is a notch above your typical small hotel, with Andean textiles, polished wood floors, and excellent-quality beds and linens. Most rooms have bathtubs. I particularly liked rooms 401 and 501, with their expansive views of the city; some interior rooms are rather dark, but they're very quiet. There are nice bonuses like free beers and soft drinks in the room fridges, and a bank of computers for guests' use. This small Peruvian group of hotels has another Cusco property on Calle Saphi, built around a pair of courtyards.

Suecia 345, Cusco. tierravivahoteles.com/hotels/cusco-plaza-hotel. ©/fax **084/245-848.** 20 units. $80–$140 double; $180 suite. Rates include breakfast buffet. AE, DC, MC, V. **Amenities:** Business center; fireplace lounge; *In room:* Cable TV, Wi-Fi (free).

INEXPENSIVE

El Andariego Hostal 🎒 ✦ ☺ This family-owned, cozy, and centrally located, though well hidden, *hostal* is a quiet, genial place that retains a great deal of the flavor of a 19th-century Cusco colonial house. Set back from a busy street across an interior patio, it has just eight rooms, a few of which are great value. Rooms nos. 101 (which fronts a small garden) and 103, which have functioning wood-burning fireplaces and exposed stone walls, are my favorites. They're large and comfortable, with hardwood floors and a smattering of antiques as well as clean tile bathrooms. Other rooms are also nice, if not quite as unique, and there's a family room that sleeps 5, perfect for the family on a budget. The owners offer cooking classes and will prepare dinners on request.

San Andrés 270, Cusco. www.andariegocusco.com. ©/fax **084/225-593.** 14 units. S/185 double. Rates include continental breakfast. MC, V. **Amenities:** Restaurant; bar. *In room:* TV, Wi-Fi (free).

Niños Hotel ★★★ ✦ ☺ The Dutch owner of the charming "Children's Hotel" says she has a story to tell, and it's certainly an inspirational one. Jolanda van den Berg has mounted a continually expanding empire of goodwill through the Niños Unidos Peruanos Foundation: Soon after arriving in Peru, she adopted 12 Peruvian street children, and constructed an extremely warm, stylish, and modern (not to mention great-value) hotel in the old section of Cusco that puts all its profits toward care for needy children. The project quickly grew to encompass a learning center, two restaurants feeding 500 kids a day, and athletic and day-care facilities with medical attention for other disadvantaged youths of Cusco. The foundation has added a second hotel, also in a historic building, and taken in two more adoptive families (totaling 20 girls and another two boys). On the same street as the second hotel are four terrific apartments (at Fierro 535) for longer stays, ideal for small families.

The good news for travelers is that, if you are lucky enough to get a room (reservations generally must be made about 6 months in advance for high season, though especially in the off season it's sometimes possible to score a reservation only days in advance), you won't have to suffer for your financial contribution to such an

Family-Friendly Hotels

Hostal Marani (p. 209) This relaxed and inviting, inexpensive boutique hotel has a mission similar to Niños Hotel. Families can learn about the programs of the HoPe Foundation, which funds schools and hospitals in the region.

Hotel Rumi Punku (p. 203) This family-owned *hostal* has a pretty, flower-filled colonial courtyard, gardens, and a historic Inca wall. There's plenty of room for the kids to run about behind the massive Inca portal.

Niños Hotel (p. 204) The very definition of a family-friendly hotel, this one was built to allow Cusco street kids to become part of a family. Profits go to care for another 500 needy children. The restored colonial house is one of the most charming and best-maintained small inns around. Reserve well in advance. Families should inquire about a second location and the excellent-value apartments for longer stays.

important cause. The main hotel, in a restored colonial house just 10 minutes from the Plaza de Armas, is one of the coolest, cleanest, and most comfortable inexpensive inns in Peru. The large rooms—named for the owner's adopted children—are minimalist chic, with white-painted hardwood floors and quality beds, and they ring a lovely sunny courtyard, where breakfast is served. Sister property Hotel Fierro, just 2 blocks away, is very similar in style and amenities, with lots of large contemporary art and 20 rooms. An excellent new option, for those also interested in visiting the countryside outside Cusco, is the **Niños Hotel Hacienda,** a beautiful, rustic inn in the town of Huasao, just 30 minutes from Cusco (rates $85–$125 double).

Meloq 442, Cusco (Hotel Fierro at Fierro 476). www.ninoshotel.com. © **084/231-424.** 20 units. $50 double with private bathroom; $46 double with shared bathroom; apartments $140 per person per week or $506 per month double. No credit cards. **Amenities:** Restaurant; cafe. *In room:* No phone.

Pariwana Hostel Cusco ★ ✒ This excellent youth hostel is a great option for students and young backpackers. Unusual for such a low-priced option, it occupies stately digs—an elegant 16th-century colonial manor house built around a beautiful courtyard just 2 blocks from the Plaza de Armas. Rooms are clean, safe, and very well thought out, with lockers and loads of options, from double rooms with bathrooms to standard dorm rooms of several sizes (overall capacity is for 220 people), including dorm rooms for women only. The hub of activity is the very cool bar/lounge (with video, Play Station, and ping-pong and pool tables), and all sorts of nightly group activities and excursions are offered. If you've come to Cusco to hang out, meet fellow travelers, and make new travel plans, this is the place. Knowing its audience well, breakfast is served until 1pm!

Mesón de la Estrella 136, Cusco. www.pariwana-hostel.com. © **084/233-751.** 60 units. S/110 double with private bathroom; S/95 double with shared bathroom; S/29–S/38 per person in dorm room with shared bathroom. Rates include breakfast. No credit cards. **Amenities:** Restaurant; bar; lockers. *In room:* Wi-Fi, no phone.

San Blas
MODERATE

Casa Andina Classic San Blas ★ Most inns in San Blas are small, simple *hostales*, but this is a definite step up in style, comfort, and service. It has the feel of an urbane country hotel. In a sprawling colonial structure built around a lovely interior stone courtyard, it has great views over the city. Rooms have a nice dose of colonial and Andean character. The most unique rooms are the seven in the tower, the highlight of which are open-air lounges overlooking the patio. The sunny courtyard and cozy fireplace bar are great places to relax after walking Cusco's hilly streets.

Chihuampata 278. www.casa-andina.com. © **866/220-4434** toll-free in the U.S., 08/082-343-805 in the U.K., or **01/213-9739.** Fax 01/445-4775. 38 units. $149–$189 double; $209 suite. Rates include breakfast buffet. AE, DC, MC, V. **Amenities:** Restaurant (lunch & dinner on request); concierge. *In room:* TV, fridge, Wi-Fi (free).

Casa San Blas Boutique Hotel
A modern boutique hotel tucked down a small, dead-end alleyway off pedestrian-only Cuesta San Blas, and approaching the artsy neighborhood of the same name, this place has a lot going for it. Excellent location and good services are principal among its advantages. I would opt for one of the two-level junior suites with kitchenettes and spectacular views of Cusco from upstairs; though the prices are up a bit from previous years, they're comparatively better value than the regular rooms, which are comfortable but plain and not nearly as inviting (all doubles are interior with no views). The hotel's panoramic-view terrace, though, is an excellent spot to relax and check out the city creeping up into the hills.

Tocuyeros 566, San Blas, Cusco. www.casasanblas.com. © **888/569-1769** in the U.S. and Canada or 084/251-563. Fax 084/237-900. 18 units. $110 double; $156–$192 suite. Rates include airport transfer and breakfast. AE, DC, MC, V. **Amenities:** Restaurant; piano bar; free Internet (in lobby); massage room; room service. *In room:* TV, Wi-Fi (free).

Quinua Villa Boutique ★★ 🎁 ✦
Tucked away, up a set of stairs in San Blas, this unique small hotel consists of just five apartments built around a lovely small courtyard, but they're so large and well-equipped enough that you might consider staying put for a while. All but one are two-story, and all have terrific kitchens and wood-burning fireplaces. It's one of the most laid-back and friendly spots you'll find, and the Italian owner, Cristiano, is on-site to make sure you've got everything you need. Each apartment is cozy and whimsically decorated, reflecting a period of Peruvian history; the one I stayed in recently took aim at the pop culture of the '60s and '70s, and it had a terrific balcony with views over Cusco. Breakfast is brought to your room. A good option for (close-knit) families is adding a couple of beds to an apartment and turning the apartment into a home for your stay in Cusco.

Pasaje Santa Rosa A-8 (Mirador T'oqokachi), San Blas, Cusco. www.quinua.com.pe. ©/fax **084/242-646.** 5 units. $97–$165 double. Rates include breakfast and airport pickup. AE, DC, MC, V. *In room:* Cable TV, Wi-Fi (free).

Second Home Cusco ★★ ✦ 🎁
In a meticulously reformed, colonial San Blas home with high ceilings, the inn is true to its name; it's like coming to stay at a friend's home. A sister property of my favorite place to stay in Lima (p. 123) and literally part of the family—the owner, Carlos, is the brother of Lillian who runs Second Home Peru, and both are the children of the famous Peruvian artist Victor Delfín—this tiny guesthouse has just three rooms, but it's a lovely and personable place to stay, and a very good value to boot. It has the comfort and exclusiveness of larger and more expensive hotels. Rooms have a modern sensibility, along with top-quality bedding and linens, and nicely appointed bathrooms. The house has several of Delfín's unique art pieces, including a stunning chimney, shaped like the massive head of a puma. Breakfast is a communal (but made-to-order) affair, and Carlos, the genial host, is generally around to share impressions of his Cusco.

San Blas Hotels & Restaurants

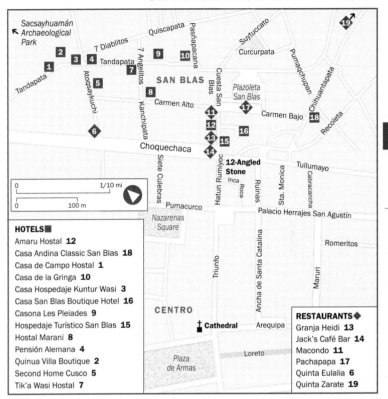

HOTELS ■
Amaru Hostal **12**
Casa Andina Classic San Blas **18**
Casa de Campo Hostal **1**
Casa de la Gringa **10**
Casa Hospedaje Kuntur Wasi **3**
Casa San Blas Boutique Hotel **16**
Casona Les Pleiades **9**
Hospedaje Turístico San Blas **15**
Hostal Marani **8**
Pensión Alemana **4**
Quinua Villa Boutique **2**
Second Home Cusco **5**
Tik'a Wasi Hostal **7**

RESTAURANTS ◆
Granja Heidi **13**
Jack's Café Bar **14**
Macondo **11**
Pachapapa **17**
Quinta Eulalia **6**
Quinta Zarate **19**

8

CUSCO | Where to Stay

Atocsaycuchi 616, San Blas, Cusco. www.secondhomecusco.com. ✆ **084/235-873.** Fax 084/242-200. 3 units. $120 double. Rates include breakfast. MC, V. *In room:* TV, Wi-Fi.

INEXPENSIVE

Amaru Hostal ★ 🐾   Popular with legions of backpackers, this hostel, in a pretty colonial-republican house in the midst of the San Blas artist studios and shops, has a lovely balconied patio, with a very nice garden area that tends to attract sunbathers and with good views of Cusco. Rooms are very comfortable, attractively decorated, and a good value (although some are quite small). Several have colonial-style furnishings and lots of natural light. (Ask to see several rooms, if you can.) It's a very friendly and relaxed place, as is its nearby sister property, **Amaru Hostal II,** on Chihmpata 642 (www.amaruhostal.com; ✆ **084/223-521**).

Cuesta San Blas 541, San Blas, Cusco. www.cusco.net/amaru. ✆/fax **084/225-933.** 16 units. $48–$59 double with bathroom; $29 double with shared bathroom. Rates include breakfast and airport/bus or train station pickup. No credit cards. **Amenities:** Coffee shop. *In room:* Wi-Fi (free), no phone.

Casa de Campo Hostal 🛏️   Lodged in the hills of San Blas, Casa de Campo indeed has the feel and freshness of country air. A growing, organic complex, its

207

MORE hotels & HOSTALES IN CUSCO

Despite the amazing number of accommodations strewn across the city, Cusco can get very crowded in high season; particularly if you're in town during the Inti Raymi festival (late June), July, and August, finding a place to rest your head can be headache inducing. Here are a few more recommended places to try (although a couple of them are often full).

Casa de la Gringa ★ 🏨 This tranquil and friendly South African-owned house is a real find and a favorite of those who come to Cusco on spiritual and mystical journeys. Its rooms are nicely decorated, with a touch of bohemian flair and lively, colorful art. It features a lounge and an annexed cottage, with a patio with glass-enclosed roof for star-gazing. Pasnapacana 148 (corner Tandapata), San Blas, Cusco. www.casadelagringa.com. ℂ/fax **084/241-168.** $30 double.

Casa Hospedaje Kuntur Wasi This tiny, family-run inn is popular with Europeans, tucked up in the San Blas district. The small terrace has amazing views of Cusco. Rooms are plain, but they have pretty good beds, and there's laundry service. Tandapata 352, San Blas, Cusco. ℂ/fax **084/227-570.** $20 double with shared bathroom; $35 double with private bathroom.

El Balcón ★ 🏨 This handsome and sprawling early-17th-century colonial building has beautiful long balconies and excellent views of the city. The rooms are comfortable, and there's an inviting atmosphere throughout. Tambo de Montero 222, Cusco. www.balconcusco.com. ℂ**084/236-738.** Fax 084/225-352. $65–$80 double (breakfast included).

Hostal Corihuasi 🏨 On a street leading up above Cusco, this small, cozy, and rustic hostal has a great living room/breakfast area with a fireplace and superlative panoramic views; those same views come with a handful of rooms (nos. 1, 6, 8, 10, and 20). Suecia 561, Cusco. www.corihuasi.com. ℂ/fax **084/232-233.** $49–$55 double (continental breakfast and airport pickup included).

rustic, chalet-style rooms appear to have sprouted one from the other. A friendly, charming and comfortable place, but not for everyone, especially not those affected by the altitude. The climb up to the hotel is taxing enough, but once inside guests have to amble up several more flights of stone steps. Of course, you're rewarded with gardens and terraces, and unparalleled sweeping views of the city, as well as a cozy lounge with a large fireplace. Rooms are smallish, but they have good, firm beds and are rustically decorated, with exposed wood beams and thick wool blankets. One special room has a fireplace; another is like a cottage towering above the city.

Tandapata 298, San Blas, Cusco. www.hotelcasadecampo.com. ℂ**084/244-404.** Fax 084/243-069. 49 units. $55–$60 double; $85 suite. Rates include breakfast buffet. AE, DC, MC, V. **Amenities:** Restaurant. *In room:* Phone in some units.

Casona Les Pleiades ★ 🖋 A small, French-owned boutique hotel tucked away on a pedestrian-only, hilly street in the San Blas neighborhood, this agreeable place is a relaxed refuge. A three-story house, it has a treasured sunny terrace, which is a great place to read and relax (and dry laundry), and to soak in great views of Cusco below. Rooms, accessed from an interior patio, are ample and colorfully decorated with bright down comforters. The friendly owners, Philippe and Melanie, are on hand to offer personal advice about activities in Cusco and the region, though Melanie spends a good part of each year working in California.

Hostal San Isidro Labrador The Labrador is a pleasant and safe but slightly overpriced choice, with 14 rooms set back from busy Calle Saphy in colonial digs set around a long courtyard. Rooms are rather small and dark but clean; several second-floor rooms have high ceilings, wood beams, and skylights. Saphy 440, Cusco. labrador@qnet.com.pe. (ℰ) **084/226-241.** $45 double.

Hostel Suecia Bed & Breakfast 🏷 This friendly and consistently popular backpackers' inn, housed in a 16th-century house 2 blocks from the main square, is a notch above most of Cusco's most economical *hostales*. It has comfortable rooms, an enclosed and covered courtyard, hot water, and nice beds. It's usually a great place to form Inca Trail groups. Suecia 332, Cusco. www.hostalsuecia1.com. (ℰ) **084/233-282.** S/90 double.

Los Aticos de Quera ☺ A great option for families, these cozy, clean rooms and apartments have a separate bedroom with a double bed, a living room with a sofa bed, a kitchenette, and a desk. It's excellent for long stays. Quera 253, Cusco. www.losaticos.com. (ℰ) **084/231-710.** Fax 084/231-388. $50 apartment (up to four people); $50 double.

Pensión Alemana This small, German-run San Blas hotel is like a large B&B. It is very clean, if a little spartan and functional-feeling, with a nice garden area and terrace with views of Cusco below. Room no. 1, which is large and light, has great views and is your best bet. Tandapata 260, San Blas, Cusco. www.cuzco.com.pe. (ℰ) **084/226-861.** S/165–S/180 double.

Tik'a Wasi Hostal A hostal with vehicular access—a rarity in this neighborhood—this clean and attractive inn has a cafeteria, comfortable carpeted rooms, a TV lounge, room service (another rarity among small *hostales*), and laundry service. Tandapata 491, San Blas, Cusco. www.tikawasi.com/hostel-cusco. (ℰ)/fax **084/231-609.** $50–$70 double.

Tandapata 116, San Blas, Cusco. www.casona-pleiades.com. (ℰ)/fax **084/506-430.** 7 units. S/165 double. Rates include breakfast. AE, MC, V. **Amenities:** Video lounge. *In room:* Cable TV, no phone, Wi-Fi (free).

Hospedaje Turístico San Blas About halfway up the principal artery that wends its way up (and up) the artsy San Blas district is one of its most attractive inexpensive inns. Rooms are decent-sized but pretty plain. The airy colonial house has a glassed-in courtyard and a sun terrace with good views (and 24-hr. hot water). This inn is a small step up from run-of-the-mill budget options in Cusco, and it's a good place to meet up with fellow travelers.

Cuesta San Blas 526, San Blas, Cusco. www.sanblashostal.com. (ℰ) **084/244-481.** Fax 084/225-781. 20 units. $43 double. Rates include continental breakfast and airport pickup. No credit cards. **Amenities:** Coffee shop. *In room:* No phone.

Hostal Marani ★ ☺ 🏷 Similar in commitment and heritage to the better-known and slightly more stylish Niños Hotel—both are Dutch-owned and very active in social programs to benefit disadvantaged Peruvian children—this handsome *hostal* is very well designed and maintained. It occupies an attractive colonial-era house in San Blas and features spacious, light, and impeccable rooms with spotless tiled bathrooms. The rooms are located around a traditional Spanish-style courtyard, where guests often take their breakfasts and read in the afternoon. Ask about off-season discounts. The *hostal* has a close affiliation with the HoPe Foundation, a Dutch non-profit that has funded dozens of schools, hospitals, and other development programs in Cusco and rural Andean villages.

Carmen Alto 194, San Blas, Cusco. www.hostalmarani.com. ℂ/fax **084/249-462.** 17 units. $51 double. Rates include buffet breakfast and airport/bus or train station pickup. No credit cards. **Amenities:** Cafe. *In room:* No phone.

Outskirts of Cusco

Torre Dorada ★ 🔥 I'm generally hesitant to recommend hotels outside city centers, because convenience is of the utmost importance. However, this personalized boutique hotel in a quiet residential neighborhood (5 min. from downtown, and staff generously ferry guests back and forth for free) is so exceptional that I can't overlook it. While not luxurious, the four-story, modern construction offers attention to detail nearly the equal of 5-star hotels (but it's much friendlier doing it). It's a particularly good place to stay if you are concerned about safety, undisturbed about not being able to walk to and from the city, and perhaps uncertain about a trip to Cusco or lacking in Spanish skills. The staff goes out of its way to look out for guests and make their trips enjoyable and easygoing. Rooms are very well outfitted and impeccable. The breakfast buffet, served in a top-floor dining room with great views, outclasses most luxury hotels.

Calle los Cipreses, Residencial Huancaro, Cusco. www.torredorada.com.pe. ℂ**084/241-698.** Fax 084/224-255. 21 units. $110 double. Rates include airport pickup and buffet breakfast. AE, DC, MC, V. **Amenities:** TV lounge; free taxi service to downtown; Wi-Fi (free).

SIDE TRIPS FROM CUSCO

Many visitors "do" Machu Picchu in a single day, taking a morning train out and a late-afternoon train back to Cusco. In my book, Machu Picchu is much too important and impressive a sight to relegate it to a day trip, but that's all many people have time for. The Sacred Valley villages and famed markets (especially Pisac and Chinchero) also constitute day trips for loads of travelers. Again, though, the area is so rich and offers so much for travelers with time to do more than whiz through it that the area—including Pisac, Urubamba, Ollantaytambo, Calca, Chinchero, and Moray—is treated separately in chapter 9, along with the great Inca ruins of Machu Picchu.

 Jungle Adventure

Cusco is the gateway to the southern Amazon region. If you're interested in a jungle expedition to the Manu Biosphere Reserve or the Tambopata National Reserve, don't miss chapter 11.

A Cusco-area **ruins hike,** either on foot or on horseback, of the Inca sites within walking distance of the capital—Sacsayhuamán, Q'enko, Puca Pucara, and Tambomachay—makes for a splendid day-long (or half-day, if you make at least some use of public transportation or a taxi) excursion. For more information on the individual sites, see the earlier "Inca Ruins Near Cusco" section and the map in "What to See & Do in Cusco," earlier in this chapter.

Adventure travelers might want to concentrate on other **outdoor sports,** including treks, biking excursions, and white-water rafting that can be done around Cusco. See "Extreme Sacred Valley: Outdoor Adventure Sports" in chapter 9.

Paucartambo ★★

110km (68 miles) NE of Cusco

Most visitors who venture to very remote Paucartambo (and there aren't many of them) do so for the annual mid-July **Fiesta de la Virgen del Carmen ★★★**, one of Peru's most outrageously celebrated festivals (it lasts several days, and most attendees, be they villagers or foreigners, camp out because there is nowhere else to stay); see the "Cusco's Spectacular Celebrations" box on p. 181 for more details. Yet the beautiful, small, and otherwise quiet mountain village might certainly be visited during the dry season (May–Oct), if you've got the patience to venture way off the beaten track. A few travelers stop en route to Puerto Maldonado and the Manu Biosphere Reserve.

The peaceful colonial town, once a mining colony, has cobblestone streets and a lovely Plaza de Armas with white structures and blue balconies, but not a whole lot else—that is, until it is inundated by revelers donning wildly elaborate and frequently frightening masks, and drinking as if Paucartambo were the last surviving town on the planet. The colorful processions and traditional dances are spectacular, and a general sense of abandonment of inhibitions (senses?) reigns. Mamacha Carmen, as she's known locally, is the patron saint of the *mestizo* population. During the festival, there's a small office of tourist information on the south side of the plaza. More information on the celebrations is available from the main tourist office in Cusco (p. 165).

Depending on when you visit, you might be able to get a simple bed at one of two small and very basic inexpensive inns in town: the **Hostal Quinta Rosa Marina** and the **Albergue Municipal** (neither has a phone).

Another 45km (28 miles) beyond Paucartambo is **Tres Cruces (Three Crosses) ★**, sacred to the nature-worshiping Incas and still legendary for its mystical sunrises in the winter months (May–July are the best). Tres Cruces occupies a mountain ridge at the edge of the Andes, before the drop-off to the jungle. From a rocky outcropping at nearly 4,000m (13,100 ft.) above sea level, hardy travelers congratulate themselves (for having gotten there, as much as for the sight they've come to witness) as they gaze into the distance out over the dense, green Amazon cloud forest. The sunrise is full of intense colors and trippy optical effects (including multiple suns). Even for those lucky enough to have experienced the sunrise at another sacred Inca spot, Machu Picchu, it is truly a hypnotic sight.

GETTING THERE   Gallinas de Rocas minibuses leave daily for Paucartambo from Cusco's Avenida Huáscar, near Garcilaso (departure times vary; the journey takes 4–6 hr.). For the Virgen del Carmen festival (July 15–17), some small agencies organize 2- and 3-day visits, with transportation, food, and camping gear (or arrangements for use of a villager's bed or floor) included. Look for posters in the days preceding the festival. To get to Tres Cruces, see whether any Cusco travel agencies are arranging trips; otherwise, you'll either have to hire a taxi from Cusco or hitchhike from Paucartambo. (Ask around; some villagers will be able to hook you up with a ride.) Make sure you leave in the middle of the night to arrive in time for the sunrise.

Tipón ★

23km (14 miles) SE of Cusco

Rarely visited by tourists, who are in more of a hurry to see the villages and Inca ruins of the Sacred Valley north of Cusco, the extensive complex of Tipón is nearly the equal of the more celebrated ruins found in Pisac, Ollantaytambo, and Chinchero.

AND THEN THERE WERE 12:
THE inca EMPERORS

The Inca Empire, one of the greatest the Americas have ever known, had 12 rulers over its lifetime from the late 12th century to the mid-16th century. The emperors, or chieftains, were called Incas; the legendary founder of the dynasty was Manco Cápac. The foundations of the palaces of the sixth and eighth leaders, Inca Roca and Viracocha Roca, respectively, are still visible in Cusco.

Pachacútec was a huge military figure, the Inca responsible for creating a great, expansive empire. He was also an unparalleled urban planner. He made Cusco the capital of his kingdom, and, under his reign, the Incas built Qoricancha, the fortresses at Pisac and Ollantaytambo in the Sacred Valley, and mighty Machu Picchu. Huayna Cápac, who ruled in the early 16th century, was the last Inca to oversee a united empire. He divided the Inca territory, which, by that time,

stretched north to Ecuador and south to Bolivia and Chile, between his sons, Huáscar and Atahualpa, which resulted in a disastrous civil war. Atahualpa eventually defeated his brother but was captured by Francisco Pizarro in Cajamarca and killed by the Spaniards in 1533, which led to the ultimate downfall of the Incas. The 12 Incas, in order, are as follows:

1. Manco Cápac
2. Sinchi Roca
3. Lloque Yupanqui
4. Mayta Cápac
5. Cápac Yupanqui
6. Inca Roca
7. Yahuar Huácac
8. Viracocha Inca
9. Pachacútec
10. Tupac Inca
11. Huayna Cápac
12. Atahualpa

For fans of Inca stonemasonry and building technique, Tipón's well-preserved agricultural terracing is among the best created by the Incas and makes for a rewarding, if not easily accessible, visit. Peter Frost writes in *Exploring Cusco* (Nuevas Imágenes, 1999) that the terracing is so elaborately constructed that it might have been instrumental in testing complex crops rather than used for routine farming. There are also baths, a temple complex, and irrigation canals and aqueducts that further reveal the engineering prowess of the Incas. The ruins are a healthy hour's climb (or more, depending on your physical condition) up a steep, beautiful path, or by car up a dirt road. The uncluttered distant views are tremendous. The truly adventurous and fit can continue above the first set of ruins to others perched even higher (probably another 2 hr. of climbing). During the rainy season (Nov–Mar), it's virtually impossible to visit Tipón.

GETTING THERE   Combis for "Urcos" leave from Avenida Huáscar in Cusco; request that the driver drop you off near Tipón, which is between the villages of Saylla and Oropesa. The site is 4km (2½ miles) from the highway; it's open daily from 7am to 5:30pm. Admission is by Cusco's *boleto turístico*.

Pikillacta & Rumicolca

38km (24 miles) SE of Cusco

These pre-Inca and Inca ruins might go unnoticed by most, were it not for their inclusion on the Cusco tourist ticket. Although the Cusco region is synonymous with the

Incas, the Huari and other cultures preceded them. **Pikillacta** is the only pre-Inca site of importance near Cusco. The Huari culture built the complex, a huge ceremonial center, between A.D. 700 and 900. The two-story adobe buildings, of rather rudimentary masonry, aren't in particularly good shape, although they are surrounded by a defensive wall. Many small turquoise idols, today exhibited in the Museo Inka in Cusco, were discovered at Pikillacta.

Less than a kilometer from Pikillacta, across the main road, is **Rumicolca,** an Inca portal—a gateway to the Valle Sagrado—constructed atop the foundations of an ancient aqueduct that dates to the Huari. The difference in construction techniques is readily apparent. The site was a travel checkpoint controlling entry to the Cusco Valley under the Incas.

GETTING THERE   Combis for "Urcos" leave from Avenida Huáscar in Cusco and drop passengers for Pikillacta near the entrance. Both sites are open daily from 7am to 5:30pm. Admission is by Cusco's *boleto turístico.*

MACHU PICCHU & THE SACRED VALLEY

9

The Urubamba Valley was sacred to the Incas, and it's not hard to understand why. Better known as The Sacred Valley, it's a serene and incomparably lovely stretch of small villages and ancient ruins spread across a broad plain, split by the Urubamba River and framed by magnificent Andes peaks and a massive sky. The Incas built several of the empire's greatest estates, temples, and royal palaces between the sacred centers of Cusco and Machu Picchu, positioned like great bookends at the south and north ends of the valley. Whether you get to Machu Picchu by train or trekking four days along the Inca Trail, nearly everyone who comes to Peru makes it to one of the most spectacular sites on Earth. Many visitors are using the valley as a base for visiting the region, as it's about 300m (1,000 ft.) lower than Cusco, making it a better introduction for visitors prone to altitude-related health problems.

HISTORY   The entire valley is suffused by the great, if brief, presence of the Incas. From extraordinary temples to fortresses, topped by the imperial retreat of Machu Picchu, no region in Peru is more marked by the continent-spanning civilization. Today, Quechua-speaking residents work fields with primitive tools and harvest salt with methods unchanged since the days of the Incas.

SIGHTSEEING   The Valle Sagrado has taken off as a destination on its own, rather than just a blitzkrieg-style coach trip. There are superb ruins, traditional markets and villages, and of course the granddaddy of them all: Machu Picchu. Several highlights, such as the ruins of Pisac and Ollantaytambo, and the market town Chinchero, are visited as part of Cusco's *boleto turístico.*

NATURE   Through the verdant valley rolls the revered Río Urubamba, a pivotal religious element of the Incas' cosmology (counterpart to the Milky Way). The fertile valley was a major center of agricultural production for native crops such as white corn, coca, and potatoes along terraced mountain slopes. And of course the valley is surrounded on all sides by the stunningly beautiful Andes.

WHERE TO STAY & EAT   Home to some of Peru's finest country lodges, the valley is perfect for either a relaxing pace or nonstop activity.

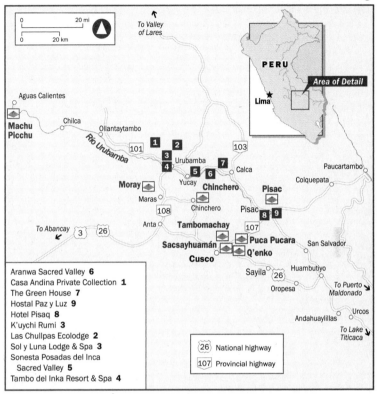

Aranwa Sacred Valley **6**
Casa Andina Private Collection **1**
The Green House **7**
Hostal Paz y Luz **9**
Hotel Pisaq **8**
K'uychi Rumi **3**
Las Chullpas Ecolodge **2**
Sol y Luna Lodge & Spa **3**
Sonesta Posadas del Inca
  Sacred Valley **5**
Tambo del Inka Resort & Spa **4**

26 National highway
107 Provincial highway

The kings of swank and serenity are Tambo del Inka and Inkaterra Machu Picchu, but there are affordable alternatives like The Green House. Dining focuses on the produce and grains that made the region the Incas' breadbasket.

ACTIVE PURSUITS The Sacred Valley region is one of the best in Peru for trekking, white-water rafting, mountain biking, hang-gliding and hot-air ballooning. It's best known for classic treks, including the Inca Trail, and alternative ruins treks for adventurers seeking solitude and authenticity.

THE BEST TRAVEL EXPERIENCES IN THE SACRED VALLEY

- **Climbing to Pisac's ruins.** Leave the busy artisans' market behind and hike the trail up the mountainside to the Inca fortress ruins. At the top are spectacular views of the valley's agricultural terracing, mountain vistas, and Pisac laid out beneath your feet. See p. 218.
- **Appreciating Ollanta's genius.** In the shadow of imposing ruins is a superb example of Inca engineering: Ollantaytambo's 15th-century grid of *canchas*, a

masterful urban plan of cobblestone streets, courtyards, and canals that still carry water rushing down from the mountains. See p. 233.

o **Taking the train to Machu Picchu.** Wending your way through the valley's lush green fields, on the banks of the rushing Urubamba River and far below the towering Andes is reward enough, but the sense of anticipation makes most people positively giddy. See p. 239.

o **Kicking back at a luxe hotel.** Revel in the lower altitude and greater serenity of the Urubamba Valley by relaxing at a country hotel, complete with spa, stunning views, and all the activities you could want—or not. See p. 228.

o **Strolling in the valley.** The pretty and rural Urubamba Valley is perfect for gentle walks. My favorite is the gorgeous 3-hour route from the enigmatic and, some say, mystical Inca site Moray to the ancient Salineras salt mines. See p. 223.

PISAC ★★

32km (20 miles) NE of Cusco

The pretty Andean village of Pisac lies at the eastern end of the valley. Although prized principally for its hugely popular Sunday artisan market, an obligatory stop on most Sacred Valley tours, Pisac deserves to be more widely recognized for its splendid Inca ruins, which rival Ollantaytambo. Perched high on a cliff is the largest fortress complex built by the Incas, with commanding, distant views from atop the mountain, over a luxuriously long valley of green patchwork fields.

Essentials

GETTING THERE   A *combi* or *colectivo* (S/5) from Cusco (Calle Puputi s/n, Cdra. 2; no phone) to Pisac takes 45 minutes to an hour, dropping passengers just across the river at the edge of town, a 3-block walk uphill from the main square (and market). From Pisac, buses return to Cusco and depart for other parts of the valley—Yucay, Urubamba (both a half-hour journey), and Ollantaytambo (1 hr.)—from the same spot. Although a taxi to Pisac on your own costs about S/35, it is often possible to go by hastily arranged private car for as little as S/10 per person. Private cars congregate near the bus terminal and leave when they have three or four passengers; just get in and ask the price (everyone pays the same fare).

 Getting Around the Sacred Valley

Local buses (usually small *combis* or *colectivos*) are the easiest and cheapest way to get to and around the Sacred Valley. They are often full of local color, if not much comfort. (Tall people forced to stand will not find them much fun.) Buses to towns and villages in the Sacred Valley—primarily to Pisac, Urubamba, and Chinchero—use small, makeshift terminals on Calle Puputi s/n, Cdra. 2 and Av. Grau s/n, Cdra. 1, in Cusco. They leave regularly throughout the day, departing when full; no advance reservations are required. Fares are S/3.

You can also hire a taxi from Cusco to get to any of the valley towns or for a day-long tour of the Sacred Valley—expect to pay about S/90. Shared private cars (*autos*) to Urubamba leave from Calle Pavitos 567, with four passengers per car (they're generally station wagons with room for luggage in back and take just 50 min.).

The Cusco *boleto turístico* (tourist pass) is essential for visiting the Sacred Valley, in particular the ruins of Pisac and Ollantaytambo, as well as the market and town of Chinchero. You can purchase it at any of those places if you haven't already bought it in Cusco before traveling to the valley. You can also purchase the partial ticket that just covers the Sacred Valley sites if you aren't planning to make use of the full ticket in Cusco. See p. 170 in chapter 8 for more information.

VISITOR INFORMATION You're best off getting information on Pisac and the entire Sacred Valley before leaving Cusco at the **Tourist Information Office,** Mantas 117-A, a block from the Plaza de Armas (℃ **084/263-176**) or the **iPéru office,** Av. El Sol 103, Of. 102 (℃ **084/252-974**). Cusco's **South American Explorers Club** (℃ **084/245-484**) is also an excellent source of information, particularly on the Inca Trail and alternative treks, mountaineering, and white-water rafting in the valley. Inquire there about current conditions and updated transportation alternatives. Beyond that, the best sources of information are hotels.

TOURS Pretty much every Cusco travel agency offers a good-value, 1-day Sacred Valley tour (as little as $25 per person for a full-day guided tour), and most provide English-speaking guides. The tours tend to coincide with market days (Tues, Thurs, and Sun) and generally include Pisac, Ollantaytambo, and Chinchero. It's not enough time to explore the ruins, though a quickie tour gives at least a taste of the valley's charms. The first Sacred Valley visit on most itineraries is Pisac. Although you will travel comfortably by chartered, air-conditioned bus and will not have to worry about connections, you won't be able to manage your time at each place (indeed, you'll have precious little time in each place—only enough for a quick look around and a visit to ruins or the local market).

FAST FACTS There's an **ATM** on the main square, but it's probably wise to exchange much of the money you'll need before leaving Cusco (especially if coming on Sun to the crowded market). There's a **post office** on the corner of Comercio and Intihuatana.

Exploring Pisac

Pisac (also spelled Pisaq) has just two items of interest to most visitors, but they're biggies: The famed market and the hilltop ruins. You could manage a superficial visit to both in just a couple of hours, but an in-depth visit, especially if hiking to the ruins, requires a very full morning or afternoon.

PISAC MARKET ★

Pisac's extremely popular *mercado de artesanía,* or artisans' market, draws many hundreds of shoppers on Sunday morning in high season, when it is without a doubt one of the liveliest in Peru. (There are slightly less popular markets on Tues and Thurs as well.) Hundreds of stalls crowd the central square—marked by a small church, San Pedro el Apóstolo, and massive *pisonay* trees—and spill down side streets. Sellers come from many different villages, many of them remote populations high in the Andes, and wear the dress typical of their village. Dignitaries from the local villages

The Virgen del Carmen Festival

Pisac celebrates the Virgen del Carmen festival (July 16–18) with nearly as much enthusiasm as the more remote and more famous festival in Paucartambo (p. 211). It's well worth visiting Pisac during the festival if you are in the area.

usually lead processions after Mass (said in Quechua), dressed in their versions of Sunday finery. The market is much like Cusco: rather touristy, though endearing and an essential experience in Peru. Even if you're not a committed shopper, it's an event. If you've never been to a Peruvian market, this is the place to start, though the market at Chinchero (p. 225) strikes me as considerably more authentic.

The goods for sale at the market—largely sweaters and ponchos, tapestries and rugs, musical instruments, and carved gourds—are familiar to anyone who's spent a day in Cusco, but prices are occasionally lower on selected goods such as ceramics. While tourists shop for colorful weavings and other souvenirs, locals are busy buying and selling produce on small streets leading off the plaza. The market begins at around 9am and lasts until mid-afternoon. It is so well-worn on the Cusco tourist circuit that choruses of, "¿Foto? Propinita," (photograph for a tip) ring out among the mothers and would-be mothers who come here to show off their children, dressed up in adorable local outfits. On nonmarket days, bustling Pisac becomes a very quiet, little-visited village with few activities to engage travelers.

PISAC RUINS ★★

The Pisac ruins are some of the finest and largest in the entire valley. Despite the excellent condition of many of the structures, little is conclusively known about the site's actual purpose. It appears to have been part city, part ceremonial center, and part military complex. It might have been a royal estate of the Inca emperor (Pachacútec). It was certainly a religious temple, and although it was reinforced with the ramparts of a massive citadel, the Incas never retreated here to defend their empire against the Spaniards (and Pisac was, unlike Machu Picchu, known to Spanish forces).

The best but most time-consuming way to see the ruins is to climb the hillside, following an extraordinary path that is itself a slice of local life. Trudging along steep mountain paths is still the way most Quechua descendants from remote villages get around these parts; many people you see at the Pisac market will have walked a couple of hours or more through the mountains to get there. To get to the ruins on foot (about 5km/3 miles, or 60 min.), you'll need to be pretty fit and/or willing to take it very slowly. Begin the ascent at the back of Pisac's main square, to the left of the church. (If you haven't already purchased a *boleto turístico,* required for entrance, you can do so at the small guard's office at the beginning of the path as you climb out of town.) The path bends to the right through agricultural terraces. There appear to be several competing paths; all of them lead up the mountain to the ruins. When you come to a section that rises straight up, choose the extremely steep stairs to the right. (The path to the left is overgrown and poorly defined.) If an arduous trek is more than you've bargained for, you can hire a taxi in Pisac (easier done on market days) to take you around the back way. (The paved road is some 9.5km/6 miles long.) If you arrive by car or colectivo rather than by your own power, the ruins will be laid out the opposite way to that described below.

9

Pisac

MACHU PICCHU & THE SACRED VALLEY

From a semicircular terrace and fortified section at the top, called the **Qori-huayrachina,** the views south and west of the gorge and valley below and agricultural terraces creeping up the mountain slopes are stunning. Deeper into the nucleus, the delicately cut stones are some of the best found at any Inca site. The most important component of the complex, on a plateau on the upper section of the ruins, is the **Templo del Sol (Temple of the Sun),** one of the Incas' most impressive examples of masonry. The temple was an astronomical observatory. The **Intihuatana,** the so-called "hitching post of the sun," resembles a sundial but actually was an instrument that helped the Incas to determine the arrival of important growing seasons rather than to tell the time of day. Sadly, this section is now closed to the public, due to vandals who destroyed part of it a few years ago. Nearby (just paces to the west) is another temple, thought to be the **Templo de la Luna (Temple of the Moon),** and beyond that is a ritual bathing complex, fed by water canals. Continuing north from this section, you can either ascend a staircase path uphill, which forks, or pass along the eastern (right) edge of the cliff. If you do the latter, you'll arrive at a tunnel that leads to a summit lookout at 3,400m (11,200 ft.). A series of paths leads from here to defensive ramparts **(K'alla Q'asa),** a ruins sector called **Qanchisracay,** and the area where taxis wait to take passengers back to Pisac.

In the hillside across the Quitamayo gorge, at the back side (north end) of the ruins, are hundreds of dug-out holes where *huaqueros* (grave robbers) have ransacked a cemetery that was among the largest known Inca burial sites.

The ruins are open daily from 7am to 5:30pm; admission is by Cusco's *boleto turístico* (p. 217). Note that to explore the ruins thoroughly by foot, including the climb from Pisac, you'll need 3 to 4 hours. Most people visit Pisac as part of a whirlwind day tour through the valley, which doesn't allow enough time either at the market or to visit the ruins. Taxis leave from the road near the bridge and charge around S/15 to take you up to the ruins.

Where to Eat

For eats in Pisac, check out **Ulrike's Café ★**, Plaza de Armas 828 (✆ **084/203-195**), a relaxed spot on the main square. Run by a German expat, Ulrike's is a genial and inexpensive place for any meal, from breakfast to hearty lunches and vegetarian options, such as homemade lasagna, omelets, salads, and great desserts (like Ulrike's famous strudel or any number of cheesecakes). It serves a great-value lunch menu (S/21, for a three-course meal). For a snack or lunch on the run, check out the excellent *hornos coloniales* (colonial bakeries), which use traditional, wood-fired ovens; one, called **Horno Colonial Santa Lucía,** is on the southwest corner of the main square next to Hotel Pisaq, while the other (unnamed) is on Mariscal Castilla 372, a short walk from the plaza. Both serve excellent empanadas and breads, and are especially popular on market days (often selling out of empanadas by 2pm). Another good lunch or dinner option is **Ayahuasca,** Bolognesi s/n (✆ **084/797-625**), a cute little cafe a couple of blocks from the plaza, on the way to the bus stops. You can get a simply prepared but very good-value menu (*lomo saltado* and other classic Peruvian highlander dishes) for just S/10.

Where to Stay
MODERATE
Hostal Paz y Luz ★ About a 20-minute walk from the village along a road up to the Inca ruins is this convivial B&B and healing center run by a woman from New

EXTREME sacred VALLEY: OUTDOOR ADVENTURE SPORTS

Peru has become a star on South America's burgeoning adventure and extreme sports travel circuit, a far cry from the days when just traveling to Peru was adventure enough. These days, many gringos in Peru have Gore-Tex boots on their feet and adrenaline rushes on their minds.

The Cusco–Sacred Valley region is one of the best in Peru—and the whole of South America—for white-water rafting, mountain biking, trekking, hang-gliding, and paragliding.

Many tour operators in Cusco organize adventure trips, some lasting a single day and some lasting multiple days, with a focus on one or more extreme sports. Participants range from novices to hardcore veteran adventure junkies; no experience is required for many trips, but make sure you sign up for a program appropriate for your level of interest and ability. Extreme sports being what they are, I suggest that you thoroughly check out potential agencies and speak directly to the guides, if possible. Booking a tour in Cusco rather than your home country may lead to a large discount. Trips booked in advance may be changed if there are not enough participants or farmed out to another, subcontracting, agency.

Bungee Jumping & Zipline New to the Sacred Valley (and as far as I know, Peru) is this favorite activity of thrill-seekers the world over. **Action Valley Cusco Adventure Park,** Calle Santa Teresa 325 (Plazoleta Regocijo), Cusco (www.action valley.com; ☎ 084/240-835) is an adventure park 11km (7 miles) from Cusco,

with not just bungee jumping but paintball and other suspended line activities, such as "swing" and "slingshot." **Cola de Mono Canopy** (www.canopyperu. com; ☎ 084/792-413), claims to operate the highest zipline in South America; zip among the lush treetops of Santa Teresa, 15 km (9 miles) from Machu Picchu, at speeds of up to 30 mph.

Horseback Riding Perol Chico, Carretera Urubamba-Ollantaytambo Km 77, Urubamba (www.perolchico.com; ☎ 01/994-147-267 or 084/984-624-475), is a ranch in the Sacred Valley and one of the top horseback-riding agencies in Peru. It offers full riding vacations, with Peruvian Paso horses and stays at the ranch (in rustic cottages), as well as 1- and 2-day rides.

Hot-Air Ballooning & Paragliding Now that you can no longer hop on a helicopter to Machu Picchu, there are other, less intrusive ways to get aerial views of the Sacred Valley. **Aero Sports Club of the Sacred Valley (Globos de los Andes),** Av. de la Cultura 220, Ste. 36 (www.globosperu.com; ☎ 084/232-352), run by an American, Jeff Hall, is the only outfit organizing such trips. If you've got the money (ballooning isn't cheap, no matter where you do it) and you want aerial panoramas of the Sacred Valley, Inca ruins, and the majestic Andes, contact Aero Sports Club to verify current flight programs. You might also check around Cusco for posters advertising tandem paraglide flights over the Sacred Valley.

York, Diane Dunn, author of the book *Cusco: Gateway to Inner Wisdom.* It spells out its mission in the name: Peace and Light (also the names of the two dogs that make their home at the inn). Andean healing workshops, meditation, and sacred-plant ceremonies (administered by Javier, a Swiss national of Spanish descent) are a good part of the attraction for guests interested in the Sacred Valley's spiritual offerings and

Mountain Biking Mountain biking has started to catch on in Peru, and tour operators are rapidly expanding their services and equipment. Cusco's nearby ruins and the towns, villages, and gorgeous scenery of the Sacred Valley (and the Manu jungle, for more adventurous excursions) are the best areas. **Peru Discovery** (www.perudiscovery.com; ✆ 054/274-541) is one of the top specialists, with a half-dozen bike trips that include hard-core excursions. **Amazonas Explorer, Apumayo Expediciones, Eric Adventures, Instinct Travel** (for contact information, see "White-Water Rafting," below), and **Manu Adventures** (www.manuadventures.com; ✆ 084/261-640; or 213/283-6987 in the U.S. or Canada), all offer 1- to 5-day organized mountain-biking excursions ranging from easy to rigorous. For a locally based group, including mountain bike rentals and extended as well as shorter cyclotourism rides around Urubamba, contact Omar Zarzar at **Eco Montana** (www.ecomontana.com). A popular day's ride is from Moray to Salineras de Maras.

Trekking Too many highland-trekking adventures are offered to fully describe here. In addition to the groups listed in "Inca Trail Agencies" (p. 253) and "Some Alternatives to the Inca Trail," on p. 256, which organize Inca Trail and other regional treks, the following companies handle a wide variety of trekking excursions: **Andina Travel** (www.andina travel.com; ✆ 084/251-892); **Apuandino**

Expediciones (www.apuandino-expeditions.com; ✆ 084/274-789); **Aventours** (www.ecoinka.com; ✆ 084/224-050); **Enigma** (www.enigmaperu.com; ✆ 084/221-155); **Manu Expeditions** (www.manuexpeditions.com; ✆ 084/225-990); U.S.-based **Andean Treks ★★** (www.andeantreks.com; ✆ 800/683-8148 or 617/924-1974); and **Peru for Less ★★** (www.peruforless.com; ✆ 877/2609-0309). **Peru Discovery** (see "Mountain Biking," above) also organizes excellent trekking expeditions, and Chalo, the Chilean-born owner of the cool ecostyled lodge **Las Chullpas** in Urubamba (p. 230), leads small-group treks into nearby ranges.

White-Water Rafting There are some terrific Andean river runs near Cusco, ranging from mild Class II to moderate and world-class IV and V, including 1-day Urubamba River trips (Huambutío–Pisac and Ollantaytambo–Chillca), multi-day trips to the more difficult Apurímac River, and, for hard-core rafters, the Tambopata (10 days or more) in the Amazon jungle. Recommended agencies include **Amazonas Explorer ★★** (www.amazonas-explorer.com; ✆ 084/252-846); **Apumayo Expediciones** (www.apumayo.com; ✆ 084/246-018); **Eric Adventures** (www.ericadventures.com; ✆ 084/234-764); **Instinct Tour Operator** (www.instinct-travel.com; ✆ 084/233-451); **Loreto Tours** (www.loretotours.com; ✆ 084/228-264); **Mayuc** (www.mayuc.com; ✆ 084/242-824); and **Swissraft Peru ★** (www.swissraft-peru.com; ✆ 084/264-124).

self-exploration, though plenty of guests come simply for the restful spirit and perhaps a massage—treating it as a relaxed country inn. Rooms are in comfortable and colorful adobe bungalows with thick blankets, high ceilings, and splendid views of the Pisac ruins and surrounding valley.

Carretera Pisac Ruinas s/n. www.pazyluzperu.com. © **084/203-204.** 86 units. S/170 double; S/220 suite (weekly and monthly rates also available). Rates include continental breakfast. AE, DC, MC, V. **Amenities:** Massage; healing workshops and sacred plant ceremonies. *In room:* No phone.

Hotel Pisaq ★★ 🌿 Owned by a friendly Peruvian–American couple, this small, pleasant, and central inn is a superb option in town. If you've come to Pisac to get a full taste of the market and ruins, it's the best spot to be. Located right on the main square in Pisac (the sign outdoors says "Pisac Inn"), it features nicely decorated color-ful rooms full of Andean textiles, murals hand-painted by the owners, a sauna, and an attractive courtyard with flowers. The hotel also operates a small bar/restaurant with good pizza from a wood-burning oven and home-cooked meals.

Plaza Constitución 333, Pisac. www.hotelpisaq.com. ©/fax **084/203-062.** 11 units. $50–$65 dou-ble with private bathroom; $40–$45 with shared bathroom. Rates include breakfast. AE, MC, V. **Amenities:** Restaurant; bar; sauna; computer room. *In room:* No phone.

URUBAMBA & ENVIRONS ★★

78km (48 miles) NW of Cusco

Centrally located Urubamba, the transportation hub of the valley, is also its busiest town and the best equipped to handle visitors. The town itself doesn't have a whole lot more than a handsome main plaza and a few restaurants to offer, but the surround-ing region is lovely, and several of the best hotels in the region are located within a radius of a few miles, either just south near Yucay, an attractive colonial village, or north on the road toward Ollantaytambo. The area as a whole makes a fine base from which to explore the Sacred Valley.

Essentials

GETTING THERE

BY BUS   To Urubamba (1½–2 hr. from Cusco), you can go either via Pisac or via Chinchero (a slightly more direct route). Buses, or combis (S/5), depart from Av. Grau s/n, Cdra. 1, in Cusco and arrive at **Terminal Terrestre** (no phone), the main bus terminal, about a kilometer (½ mile) from town on the main road to Ollantaytambo. Buses from the Urubamba terminal depart for Cusco and Chinchero (1 hr.), as well as Ollantaytambo (30 min.). Combis for other points in the Sacred Valley depart from the intersection of the main road at Avenida Castilla. To continue on to Yucay, just a couple of kilometers down the road, catch a mototaxi or a regular taxi in Urubamba or a colectivo along the highway (headed east, the opposite direction of the bus ter-minal from town).

BY TAXI   From Cusco, you can catch a cab to Urubamba for about S/70. Shared cars in Cusco leave from Calle Pavitos 567 for Urubamba; they charge just S/10 per person and take about an hour. If you're headed directly to the valley upon arrival in Cusco, have your hotel arrange for pickup at the airport. If it's a market day, you can easily arrange for the driver to take you to Pisac or Chinchero for a brief stopover along the way. For taxi or minivan trips around the valley, try **Roberto Angles Ochoa** (© **084/984-752-565**) or **Jorge Flores** (© **984/629-821**).

VISITOR INFORMATION

You should pick up information on the Sacred Valley before leaving Cusco, at the main **Tourist Information Office,** Mantas 117-A, a block from the Plaza de Armas (© **084/263-176**); **iPerú** Av. El Sol 103, Of. 102 (© **084/252-974**), or from

Cusco's **South American Explorers Club** (✆ 084/245-484). In Urubamba, you might be able to scare up some limited assistance at Av. Cabo Conchatupa s/n; in Yucay, try the office of **Turismo Participativo,** Plaza Manco II 103 (✆ 084/201-099).

FAST FACTS

If you need cash, you'll find ATMs on either side of the main road to Yucay from Urubamba. For medical assistance, go to **Centro de Salud,** Av. Cabo Conchatupa s/n (✆ 084/201-334), or **Hospital del Instituto Peruano de Seguridad Social,** Av. 9 de Noviembre s/n (✆ 084/201-032).

Urubamba is the best spot for Internet *cabinas* in the Sacred Valley region, with a good supply of machines and fast connections all around town. **Academia Internet Urubamba** (no phone), established with the help of an American exchange student, is 2 blocks northeast of the Plaza de Armas, on the corner of Jirón Belén and Jirón Grau. There are also a couple of Internet *cabinas* on the main square. If you need a post office in Urubamba, you'll also find one on the Plaza de Armas.

Exploring Urubamba

The main square of Urubamba, the **Plaza de Armas,** is attractively framed by a twin-towered colonial church and *pisonay* trees. Dozens of mototaxis, a funky form of local transportation not seen in other places in the valley (and widely seen in only a few other places in Peru), buzz around the plaza in search of passengers. Worth visiting in town is the beautiful home workshop of **Pablo Seminario ★**, a ceramicist whose whimsical work features pre-Columbian motifs and is sold throughout Peru. Visitors either love or hate the style, which was once sold by Pier 1 Imports in the U.S. The grounds of the house, located at Berriozábal 111 (www.ceramicaseminario.com; ✆ 084/201-002), feature a minizoo, with llamas, parrots, nocturnal monkeys, falcons, rabbits, and more. The workshop is open Monday through Saturday from 10am to 6pm. Seminario now has shops in the Sonesta Posadas del Inca hotel in Yucay as well as Cusco.

Yucay, just south of Urubamba, is a pleasant and quiet little village with extraordinary views of the surrounding countryside. The Spaniards "bequeathed" the land to their puppet Inca chieftain, Sayri Tupac, who built a palace here. Inca foundations are found around the attractive **main plaza,** and some of the best agricultural terracing in the valley occupies the slopes of mountains around the village. However, the most interesting sights are all beyond Urubamba: the ancient salt pans of Maras, the Inca site at Moray, and Chinchero, a historic market town.

SALINERAS DE MARAS ★★

10km (6 miles) NW of Urubamba

Near Urubamba (about 6km/3½ miles down the main road toward Ollantaytambo but from there only accessible by foot) is the amazing sight of the **Salineras de Maras** (also called Salinas), thousands of individual ancient salt mines that form unique terraces in a hillside. The mines, small pools thickly coated with crystallized salt like dirty snow, have existed in the same spot since Inca days and are still operable. Families pass them down like deeds and continue the backbreaking and poorly remunerated tradition of salt extraction (crystallizing salt from subterranean spring water). Although the site as a whole is extraordinary and photogenic—from afar it looks like a patchwork quilt spread over a ravine, or some sort of sprawling, multilevel cake with white and caramel-colored icing—and I found it almost surreal to watch

Chicha Here, Get Your Warm Chicha

Throughout the valley, you'll see modest homes marked by long poles topped by red flags (or red balloons). These *chicha* flags indicate that home-brewed fermented maize beer, or *chicha*, is for sale inside. What you'll usually find is a small, barren room with a handful of locals quietly drinking huge tumblers of pale yellow liquid. Tepid *chicha*, which costs next to nothing, is definitely an acquired taste.

workers standing ankle-deep and mining salt from one of nearly 6,000 pools cascading down the hillside, I suppose there are some travelers who might be somewhat less captivated by the sight of salt pans. If you have a good sense of balance, you can walk among salt-encrusted paths to get good close-up photographs. A small fee (S/5) is collected at the entrance; opening hours are from dawn to dusk.

GETTING THERE   To get to Salineras, take a taxi (S/10) from Urubamba to a point near the village of Tarabamba (next to the restaurant Tunupa); you can either have the taxi wait for you or hail a combi on the main road for your return. From there, it's a lovely 4km (2½-mile), or 1-hour, walk under a huge sky and along a footpath next to the river. There are no signs; cross the footbridge and bend right along the far side of the river and up through the mountains toward the salt pans. As you begin the gentle climb up the mountain, stick to the right path to avoid the cliff-hugging and only inches-wide trail that forks to the left. Even better is the walk (5km/3 miles) along a path (a little over an hour) from the village of Maras, a route taken by some of the salt-mine workers (as if their work weren't grueling enough). Still more extreme and rewarding is the trek to the salt mines from the Inca ruins at Moray. It is one of the most stunningly beautiful walks in the region, a feast of blue-green cacti, deep red-brown earth, snowcapped mountains, plantings of corn and purple flowering potatoes, and small children tending to sheep. It's only for those who are in good shape, however; allow about 4 hours to cover the entire 14km (7½ miles), all the way out to the main Urubamba–Ollantaytambo road.

MORAY ★★

9km (5½ miles) NW of Maras

Among the wilder and more enigmatic Inca sites in Peru are the concentric ring terraces found in Moray. Unique in the Inca oeuvre, the site is not the ruins of a palace or fortress or typical temple, but what almost appears to be a large-scale environmental art installation. Three main sets of rings, like bowls, are set deep into the earth, forming strange sculpted terraces. The largest of the three has 15 levels. From above, they're intriguing, but it's even cooler to go down into them and contemplate their ancient functions. Many spiritually inclined travelers who come to the Sacred Valley for its special energy find that Moray possesses a very strong, and unique, vibe. The site may have had ritualistic purposes, but most likely it was an agricultural development station where masterful and relentlessly curious farmers among the Incas tested experimental crops and conditions. The depressions in the earth (caused by erosion) produced intense microclimates, with remarkable differences in temperature from top to bottom, that the Incas were evidently studying. Moray is at its most spectacular after the end of the rainy season, when the terraces are a magnificent emerald green.

Entrance to Moray is by Cusco *boleto turístico*, but you can also pay S/10 at the entrance if you don't have one.

GETTING THERE   Unfortunately, Moray is not easy to get to because it's removed from the main road that travels from Urubamba to Chinchero, with no public transportation of any kind, so it tends to draw only independent travelers and Inca completists, although increasingly Sacred Valley tours are beginning to include the site on their itineraries. The most convenient option is to take a taxi from either Urubamba or Chinchero; the driver will have to wait for you because there's nothing nearby, so the trip is sure to set you back at least S/120. Another option is to take a colectivo or bus that climbs up to Chinchero from Urubamba (or vice versa), getting off on the road to the village of Maras. (Make sure you ask the driver for the *desvío a Maras.*) From that point, there are usually taxis waiting to take visitors to Moray (negotiate a round-trip price). If you do go to Moray, it's possible to add on to your hike by walking another 9km (5½ miles) along a trail down to the Salineras de Maras (meaning you could take a one-way taxi for S/60 or so). (See the trek described above, under "Salineras de Maras.") Along the path you'll likely encounter workers from the salt mines, who walk the distance back and forth to work.

CHINCHERO ★★
28km (17 miles) NW of Cusco

Popular among tour groups for its bustling Sunday market that begins promptly at 8am, Chinchero is spectacularly sited and much higher than the rest of the valley and even Cusco; at 3,800m (12,500 ft.) and far removed from the river, technically Chinchero doesn't belong to the Urubamba Valley. The sleepy village has gorgeous views of the snowy peak of Salcantay and the Vilcabamba and Urubamba mountain ranges in the distance. Sunset turns the fields next to the church—where child shepherds herd their flocks and grown men play soccer without goal posts—gold against the deepening blue sky.

It might once have been a great Inca city, but except on the main market day, Chinchero remains a graceful, traditional Andean Indian village. Its 15,000 inhabitants represent as many as 12 different indigenous communities. The town's main points of interest, in addition to the fine market, are the expansive main square, with a handsome colonial church made of adobe and built on Inca foundations, and some Inca ruins, mostly terraces that aren't quite as awe-inspiring today as their counterparts in Ollantaytambo and Pisac.

In the main plaza is a formidable and famous Inca wall composed of huge stones and 10 trapezoidal niches. The foundations once formed the palace of the late-15th-century Inca Tupac Yupanqui. The early-17th-century *iglesia* (church) ★ has some very interesting, if faded, frescoes outside under the porticoes and mural paintings that cover the entire ceiling. The church is open Monday through Saturday from 9am to 5pm and Sunday from 9am to 6pm. Across the plaza is a **Museo de Sitio** (no phone), the rather spare municipal museum that holds a few Inca ceramics and instruments; it's open Tuesday through Sunday from 8am to 5pm, and admission is free.

The market comprises two marketplaces: one focusing on handicrafts and the other consisting mainly of produce. The **Chinchero market ★★** is one of the best places in the entire valley for Andean textiles and common goods such as hats, gloves, and shawls. Even on Sunday, it is more authentic than the one at Pisac (although some visitors might find Pisac more lively and fun). Chinchero's sellers of *artesanía*—who are more often than not also the craftspeople, unlike the mere agents you'll find in Pisac and other places—dress in traditional garb, and even the kids seem less manipulative in pleading for your attention and *soles*. Midweek (especially Tues and Thurs), there are usually fewer sellers who set their wares on blankets around the main square, and you'll have a better chance of bargaining then.

Through the terraces to the left of the church is a path leading toward a stream and to some finely sculpted Inca masonry, including stone steps, water canals, and huge stones with animal figures.

GETTING THERE Colectivos leave every half-hour or so from Tullumayo in Cusco for Chinchero (a 90-min. journey). Buses also leave every 20 minutes or so from the Terminal Terrestre in Urubamba (a 50-min. trip). Entrance to Chinchero—officially to just the market and church, but, in practice, to the whole town, it seems—is by *boleto turístico* (see p. 217). If you try to visit the church and main square without a *boleto,* you will be asked to purchase one (you can purchase the partial version that covers only Sacred Valley sites if you wish, rather than the entire Cusco ticket). Nearly everyone visits Chinchero on a half-day visit from either Cusco or Urubamba; there's not much else in the way of infrastructure to detain you, although there are a handful of inexpensive restaurants on the main road where the bus drops you off for lunch. One serving pretty good Andean specialties is **Abarrotes Bar Restaurant,** Av. Mateo Pumacahua 143 (✆ **084/306-052**). There are a just a couple of spots in town to spend the night (the better of the two is the small and inexpensive Hostal Los Incas), unless you want to camp in the fields just beyond the plaza where the market is held. You're much better off visiting during the day and staying elsewhere in the Sacred Valley, where there are considerably more services.

Where to Eat

Because so many hotels are scattered about the Urubamba region, and somewhat isolated, many guests, especially at the upscale accommodations in the region, dine at their hotels; the major ones listed above (Tambo del Inka, Casa Andina, Rio Sagrado, and Sonesta) all have good—but pricey for the area—restaurants. Perhaps best for drop-ins is the fine **restaurant** of Sol y Luna Lodge & Spa (p. 228). Its restaurant, **Killa Wasi,** is a two-story space with an open fireplace and pub on the second floor, and it serves very nicely prepared *criollo* and Nouveau Andean specialties, including *ají de gallina* (spicy, creamy chicken) and stuffed river trout, as well as fresh pastas. The restaurant's new incarnation has gone very upscale and gourmet, with wine-pairing dinners and the like. Call for reservations because the restaurant is often full with hotel guests.

However, easily the best and coolest restaurant in the Urubamba area is right in town: **El Huacatay ★★★**, Jr. Arica 620 (www.elhuacatay.com; ✆ **084/201-790**), popular with both wealthier Peruvians and visiting gringos. A few blocks from the main square, this surprising gourmet restaurant, in an old home built around a garden set back from a nondescript Urubamba street, is the perfect place for a long, relaxing lunch on the patio under bamboo shade or a more elegant dinner in the warm, intimate dining room (which has only five tables) or brightly colored lounge area. Run by a Peruvian chef, Pío, and his German wife Iris, the restaurant's chef-driven menu is a bit of a rarity in these parts, and it focuses on Andean specialties, such as quinoa soup, alpaca lasagna, and coca-infused (but street-legal!) gnocchi. Portions are large and attractively presented, and although fairly priced for the setting, service, and quality, the restaurant is more upscale than most in the area. Open Monday to

Saturday from 2 to 10pm, the restaurant accepts only cash and Visa cards; reservations on weekends and evenings are recommended. Another very good restaurant, also right in town, is **Tres Keros** ★, Av. Sr. de Torrechayoc (main road Urubamba–Ollantaytambo), second floor [tel] **084/201-701**), the work of a very hands-on chef and owner, Ricardo Behar (either unfailingly charming or a blowhard, depending on your disposition). He prepares surprisingly creative Peruvian cuisine, with great local ingredients and fish that comes in from the capital, at this cozy upstairs spot with a high, pitched bamboo ceiling and corner fireplace. The restaurant has become a favorite of diners fleeing the fancier, pricier digs at Tambo del Inka and other nearby hotels. The fresh salads, *lomo saltado* (made with beef tenderloin), and alpaca steak are particularly good, as is the small selection of wines. Lunch and dinner are served Monday through Saturday. A good spot for a simple breakfast or lunch of sandwiches, soups, and salads (you can also get lunch to go if you're off on a hike), is **Café Restaurant Plaza,** Bolivar 440 (no phone). The wildly colorful little cafe also serves more sophisticated dishes, such as river trout and alpaca steak in pepper sauce, as well as sandwiches that sound a bit odd to my ears: peach chicken and pineapple chicken.

A unique valley restaurant for fine dining is **Huayoccari Hacienda Restaurant** ★★, Carretera Cusco–Urubamba, Km 64 (① **084/962-2224** or **084/226-241** in Cusco), several miles southeast of Urubamba. The restaurant, in an exceedingly elegant farmhouse high in the hills above the Sacred Valley, is tough to make reservations at and hard to find. (It works almost exclusively with tour agencies such as **Lima Tours,** ① **01/424-5110,** to arrange lunches and dinners; if you're not with a group, it's worth having your hotel call to see if it's possible to get in and get directions.) The $35 (cash only) prix-fixe menu starts with a pisco sour in the antique-filled common room or out among the gardens. Then diners, who feel as though they belong to an exclusive club, are admitted to the wood-paneled dining room—which has large picture windows framing views of the Andes—for a simple but well-prepared meal of local vegetables, soups (such as *crema de maiz*), and fresh river trout. The place is rather emphatically designed to feel like one is a guest in the home of a local agricultural patron (and in fact, the home and restaurant belong to the Orihuela family, one of the valley's most distinguished, and oldest, families).

Alhambra ★, Ctra. Urubamba–Ollantaytambo s/n (near Hotel Sol y Luna; ① **084/201-200**), is a relaxed hacienda-style restaurant targeting groups. There are tables outdoors under a thatched roof, with lovely garden and mountain views. Its buffets are only on market days (Tues, Thurs, and Sat). At other times, the three-course *menú turístico* ($15) is excellent; choose main courses such as stuffed lake trout with quinoa in a nut sauce.

Shopping

In addition to the famous valley handcrafts markets in **Pisac** and **Chinchero** and renowned ceramicist **Pablo Seminario** (see p. 223), **Wasi Alpaca,** Av. Berriozabal (① **084/201-394**) is a little shop across from Pablo Seminario with a nice selection of alpaca capes, scarves, sweaters, and handcrafted boiled-wool items. **Lanandina** ★, Los Girasoles s/n (past Torrechayoc church) (① **084/201-390;** call for directions, as it's very complicated to find), is operated by an Austrian artist and resident of Urubamba, Christa Quiroz. She makes fantastic, funky handmade wool slippers, handbags, and hats using a centuries-old Mongolian formula.

Entertainment & Nightlife

Urubamba is a pretty sleepy town at night, and most guests stick close to their hotels, especially if they have early-morning plans. Best bets for a drink are the top-echelon hotel bars: **Chichi Wasi** (Sol y Luna Lodge & Spa); **El Bar del Huerto** (Hotel Rio Sagrado), a lounge with views of the Urubamba River and a well-heeled rustic look; and **Kiri Bar ★★** (Tambo del Inka), which has a super chic cocktail bar just off the swank lobby, with high ceilings and a cool backlit onyx photography mural over the bar, as well as superb cocktails. See the section that follows for addresses of each.

Where to Stay

This section of the Sacred Valley continues to attract hoteliers and developers, who all seem intent on adding new country luxury resort hotels—a sure sign of the region's growing importance and affluence, at least in terms of foreign travelers. A simpler, in-town alternative to the more upscale hotels reviewed below is the pleasant and good-value **Posada Las Tres Marías,** Jr. Zavala 307, Urubamba (www.posadatres marias.com; ✆ 084/201-006 or 984-650-225), a modern house in the center of town with gardens and seven large rooms (doubles $50).

VERY EXPENSIVE

Aranwa Sacred Valley ★★ ☺   Part of a small Peruvian hotel group begun by a Lima doctor, this well-conceived and picturesque country hotel has so much to offer that it may preclude some guests from exploring the valley. The sprawling complex, part of which was originally a 17th-century hacienda, contains a lake, riverside trails, a movie theater, colonial chapel, art gallery, beautifully landscaped grounds, and luxe spa. The spacious, elegant accommodations feature lovely antique pieces and are divided by small "villages": colonial manor house rooms and modern rooms and suites on the bank of the river and lake (suites have kitchenettes and Jacuzzis). And while it may seem a bit over the top for some in the rustic, peaceful Sacred Valley, it is leagues removed from your typical, faceless all-inclusive resort; in fact, it blends nicely with its rustic surroundings.

Antigua Hacienda Yaravilca, Huayllabamba. www.aranwahotels.com. ✆ 01/434-1452 for reservations, or **084/205-080.** Fax 01/434-6199. 115 units. $225–$300 double; $400 and up suite. Rates include breakfast buffet. AE, DC, MC, V. **Amenities:** 3 restaurants; bar; concierge; exercise room; outdoor pool; spa; theater. *In room:* TV, fridge, Wi-Fi.

Sol y Luna Lodge & Spa ★★ ☺   The continually expanding Sol y Luna is one of the more attractive properties in the valley. Though the hotel has many fans, including Bono, travelers may find that they can do as well or better at one of its newer competitors (unless ensconced in one of the new premium *casitas* with chimneys and private terrace Jacuzzis). Set back from the main road on the way to Ollantaytambo, amid spectacularly landscaped gardens, the French- and Swiss-owned cluster of invitingly decorated, circular bungalow-style rooms (including four family bungalows) comes with rustic decor, private terraces, and gorgeous mountain views. The hotel has a nice but rather small outdoor pool, a super-sleek restaurant and pub, appealing spa, and horse stables. The newest additions are five superluxe suites—no doubt where the U2 singer stayed when he passed through the Sacred Valley.

Ctra. Urubamba–Ollantaytambo s/n, Huicho (2km/1¼ miles west of Urubamba). www.hotelsoly luna.com. ✆ **084/201-620.** Fax 084/201-184. 33 units. $256 double; $416 family bungalow; casitas premium $576–$960. Rates include breakfast buffet. AE, DC, MC, V. **Amenities:** Restaurant; pub; small pool; room service; tennis court. *In room:* TV.

Tambo del Inka Resort & Spa ★★★ ☺ Sacred Valley hotels have been trending upscale for the last few years, but this magnificent hotel, urbane and stylish, is without doubt my favorite in the valley. Ingeniously designed by the celebrated Lima architect, Bernardo Fort-Brescia, with exquisite nods to Inca design motifs, this Starwood Luxury Collection property blends in beautifully in a site that backs up to the Urubamba River, just across from town (making it considerably less isolated than most upscale valley hotels). Rooms are top notch in every way, with sumptuous bathrooms; I especially like the ones that back up to the gardens and river, which also have mountain views. What really distinguishes this property, though, are the soaring two-story public rooms, gorgeous indoor/outdoor lap pool, and luxurious spa with one of the most impressive water circuits I've seen. The hotel even has its own PeruRail train station for service direct to Machu Picchu. Of course, all this comes at a price, but if you're splurging or just have deep pockets, this is the place to be.

Avenida Ferrocarril s/n, Urubamba. www.starwoodhotels.com/luxury/property/overview/index. html?propertyID=3285. ☏**800/325-3589** in the U.S. and Canada or **01/581-777.** Fax 01/581-778. 128 units. $515 and up double. Rates include breakfast buffet. AE, DC, MC, V. **Amenities:** Restaurant; bar; concierge; exercise room; indoor/outdoor pool; spa and water circuit. *In room:* TV, fridge, Wi-Fi.

EXPENSIVE

Casa Andina Private Collection ★★ ☺ One of the upstart Casa Andina group's select upscale offerings, this large, mountain-chalet type hotel is very professionally run and has a beautiful setting, with abundant gardens and excellent views of the countryside. Rooms are large and handsomely decorated, with high ceilings and spacious bathrooms; the two-story suites with balconies are especially enticing. The hotel features a very good, though occasionally boisterous, restaurant, a spectacular full-service Andean-styled spa—one of the finest I've seen in Peru—and even a planetarium and observatory for stargazing in the huge, clear sky, making this an excellent retreat for sybarites, families, and groups of diverse size. A full range of activities, such as river rafting, trekking, mountain biking, and horseback riding, is offered. New additions include four apartment-like Andean Suite cottages—ideal if you're looking for some added privacy and luxury.

Quinto paradero, Yanahuara. www.casa-andina.com. ☏ **866/220-4434** toll-free in the U.S., **08/082-343-805** in the U.K., or **01/213-9739.** Fax 01/445-4775. 85 units. $179 double; $279 suite. Rates include breakfast buffet. AE, DC, MC, V. **Amenities:** Restaurant; concierge; exercise room; room service; spa. *In room:* TV, fridge, Wi-Fi (free).

MODERATE

K'uychi Rumi ★ ☺ 🎒 One of the more interesting and relaxing, if least pronounceable, lodging options in the Sacred Valley, this property isn't a hotel, per se. It's a complex of a half-dozen condos: rustic two-story, two-bedroom adobe houses. The houses are connected by walkways and gardens, and all have excellent mountain views. For a couple that wants a bit of space, privacy, a kitchen, and a great fireplace, it's perfect, and it's also a bargain for families or two couples who occupy the whole house. The architect who built the houses lives on-site and administers the property. A buffet breakfast is extra (S/25), and there's no restaurant on the premises. Still, if you're looking for a serene retreat, this might be it.

Carretera Urubamba–Ollantaytambo s/n, Urubamba. www.urubamba.com. ☏/fax **084/201-169.** 6 units. S/440 double; S/690 family bungalow (four people). AE, DC, MC, V. *In room:* Kitchen, fridge.

Sonesta Posadas del Inca Sacred Valley ★ ☺ This handsome, ranch-style hotel remains one of the better options in the valley, even as its high-end competition has passed it by. Originally a monastery in the late 1600s and then a hacienda, it was converted into an atmospheric colonial-village-like complex with mountain views and relaxed comfort in 1982. The grounds feature a chapel brought in whole from a provincial town, nice gardens, a good restaurant, and a cool little museum with ancient ceramics and textiles. Room no. 115 in the old section is a nice loft space, and room no. 312 has fantastic windows and superior views. There are mountain bikes for guests' use; and lots of excursion and soft-adventure programs, including rafting, mountain biking, and horseback riding.

Plaza Manco II de Yucay 123, Yucay. www.sonesta.com. ✆ **084/201-107,** or **01/222-4777** for reservations (**800/SONESTA [766-3782]**) in the U.S. and Canada). Fax 084/201-345. 84 units. $119–$189 double; $170–$250 suite. Rates includes breakfast buffet. AE, DC, MC, V. **Amenities:** Restaurant; bar; lounge; spa. *In room:* TV, fridge.

INEXPENSIVE

Las Chullpas Ecolodge ★ 🎒 This self-described "ecological guesthouse" is the sort of place you might expect to find in the Amazon. It has a bohemian feel but enough creature comforts (including hot showers) for all but the most demanding guests. Run by a young Chilean and his German ex-wife (a midwife who works with *campesina* women from the countryside), the rooms are connected huts that have the feel of tree forts, with comfortable beds, stovepipe heaters, and hand-painted tiles in the bathrooms. Profits from the huge suite go toward Leonie's midwifery practice, and Chalo prepares excellent organic and vegetarian meals in the fireplace-warmed dining room. He's also a great mountain guide, who runs multi-day treks (visit www.peru.uhupi.com for info).

Querocancha s/n, Urubamba (up a long dirt road 3km/2 miles from Urubamba). www.chullpas.pe. ✆ **084/201-568.** 9 units. $50 double; $70 suite. Rates include breakfast buffet. No credit cards. **Amenities:** Restaurant; bar/lounge. *In room:* No phone, Wi-Fi (free).

The Green House ★★ 🎒 A unique, secluded B&B at the edge of the Sacred Valley, this terrifically relaxing inn, run by an Englishman and his Argentine partner (who live on the grounds), features gardens with great mountain views, a soaring, wall-of-glass living space with a fireplace, and simple, cozy rooms with attractive tiled bathrooms. In the less-traveled section of the valley, Huarán, it's the kind of place folks decamp at for several days. Gabriel prepares delicious home-cooked meals in the evenings, the three dogs keep visitors company in the gardens and on walking trails leading from the property, and hiking, rafting, horseback riding, and biking tours can be arranged.

Carretera, Km 60, Pisac–Ollantaytambo, Calca (11km/7 miles from Urubamba). www.thegreen houseperu.com. ✆ **084/984-770-130.** 4 units. S/210 double. Rates include breakfast. No credit cards. **Amenities:** Restaurant, video lounge. *In room:* No phone, Wi-Fi.

OLLANTAYTAMBO ★★★

97km (60 miles) NW of Cusco; 21km (13 miles) W of Urubamba

A tongue twister of a town—the last settlement before Aguas Calientes and Machu Picchu—this historic and lovely little place at the northwestern end of the Sacred Valley is affectionately called Ollanta (Oh-*yahn*-tah) by locals. Plenty of outsiders who can't pronounce it fall in love with the town, too, and the town, which was

Ollantaytambo

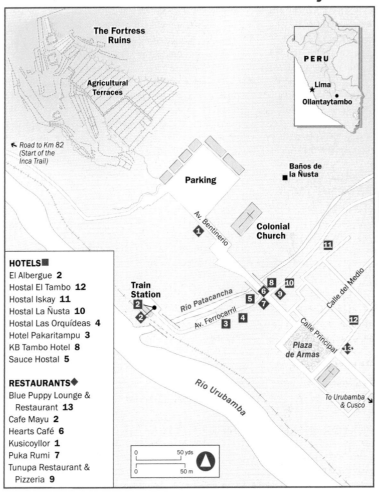

The Fortress
Ruins

Agricultural
Terraces

↖ Road to Km 82
(Start of the
Inca Trail)

PERU

★ Lima
● Ollantaytambo

Parking

Baños de
■ la Ñusta

Av. Bentinerio

Colonial
Church

11

HOTELS ■
El Albergue **2**
Hostal El Tambo **12**
Hostal Iskay **11**
Hostal La Ñusta **10**
Hostal Las Orquídeas **4**
Hotel Pakaritampu **3**
KB Tambo Hotel **8**
Sauce Hostal **5**

RESTAURANTS ◆
Blue Puppy Lounge &
  Restaurant **13**
Cafe Mayu **2**
Hearts Café **6**
Kusicoyllor **1**
Puka Rumi **7**
Tunupa Restaurant &
  Pizzeria **9**

Train
Station

2

2

Río Patacancha

Av. Ferrocarril

5

3 **4**

8 **10**
6
9
7

Calle del Medio

Calle Principal

12

Plaza
de Armas

To Urubamba ↘
& Cusco

Río Urubamba

0   50 yds
0   50 m

9

MACHU PICCHU & THE SACRED VALLEY

Ollantaytambo

oh-so-quiet just a few years ago, is now firmly on the tourist trail, fast on its way to becoming a tiny version of Cusco. New cafes, restaurants, and *hostales* now ring the main square and line the street that connects the old town to the ruins, but Ollanta is trying to negotiate its newfound popularity and doing its best to avoid being overrun with shoddy tourist establishments like Aguas Calientes. Despite its quick transformation, though, Ollantaytambo remains one of the most enjoyable places in the Sacred Valley, the one place (other than Machu Picchu, of course) not to be missed. The scenery surrounding Ollantaytambo is stunning: The snowcapped mountains that embrace the town frame a much narrower valley here than at Urubamba or Pisac, and both sides of the gorge are lined with Inca stone *andenes*, or agricultural terraces. Most extraordinary are the precipitous terraced ruins of a massive temple-fortress built by the Inca Pachacútec. Below the ruins, Ollantaytambo's old town is a splendid grid of streets dating to Inca times and lined with adobe brick walls, blooming bougainvillea, and perfect canals, still carrying rushing water down from the mountains. Though during much of the day tour buses deposit large groups at the foot of the fortress (where a handicrafts market habitually breaks out to welcome them) and tourists overrun the main square, the old town remains pretty quiet, a traditional and thoroughly charming Valle Sagrado village.

Ollantaytambo is one of the best spots to spend the night in the Sacred Valley—although accommodations are limited to small inns and simple hotels—especially if you want to be able to wander around the ruins alone in the early morning or late afternoon, before or after the groups overtake them. With the town's expanding roster of traveler services, it's now a good place to hang out for several days, not just an overnight on the way to or back from Machu Picchu.

Essentials

GETTING THERE

BY TRAIN Ollantaytambo lies midway on the Cusco–Machu Picchu train route. Trains traveling to Aguas Calientes (Machu Picchu) from Cusco stop first at Ollantaytambo; two new competitors of PeruRail originate in Ollanta for travel to Machu Picchu. Peru Rail trains depart Cusco from **Estación Poroy** (© 084/221-352), a 15-minute taxi ride from Cusco, and arrive in Ollantaytambo 90 minutes later. The train station in Ollantaytambo is a long 10-minute walk from the main square. For additional details, see "Getting There" in "Machu Picchu & the Inca Trail," later in this chapter.

BY BUS The cheapest way to Ollantaytambo is to catch a combi or colectivo from Cusco to Urubamba (S/5) and transfer at the terminal there to a frequent combi (S/3) for Ollanta (30 min.). Buses drop passengers at the Plaza de Armas in the old town, about a kilometer (½-mile) from the ruins.

BY TAXI Taxis between Ollantaytambo and Cusco generally charge about S/90–S/100 each way. Shared taxis (for about S/10 per person) to Urubamba are frequently available; a private taxi from the bus station in Urubamba to Ollanta will run to another S/10 to S/15.

VISITOR INFORMATION

You're better off getting information on the Sacred Valley before leaving Cusco, either at the main **Tourist Information Office** (© 084/263-176), Av. El Sol 103, or at Cusco's branch of the **South American Explorers Club** (© 084/245-484). Your best bet for exchanging cash in Ollantaytambo is in small shops. If you need medical assistance, go to **Centro de Salud,** Calle Principal (© 084/204-090). The **post office** is on the Plaza de Armas.

FAST FACTS

If you need cash, you'll find ATMs on either side of the main road to Yucay from Urubamba. For medical assistance, go to **Centro de Salud,** Av. Cabo Conchatupa s/n (© 084/201-334), or **Hospital del Instituto Peruano de Seguridad Social,** Av. 9 de Noviembre s/n (© 084/201-032).

Exploring Ollantaytambo

FORTRESS RUINS ★★★

The Inca elite adopted Ollantaytambo, building irrigation systems and a crowning temple designed for worship and astronomical observation. Rising above the valley and an ancient square (Plaza Mañaraki) are dozens of rows of stunningly steep stone terraces carved into the hillside. The temple ruins, which appear both forbidding and admirably perfect, represent one of the Inca Empire's most formidable feats of architecture. The Incas were able to successfully defend the site against the Spanish in 1537, protecting the rebel Manco Inca after his retreat here from defeat at Sacsayhuamán. In all probability, the complex was more a temple than a citadel to the Incas.

The upper section—reached after you've climbed 200 steps—contains typically masterful masonry of the kind that adorned great Inca temples. A massive and supremely elegant door jamb—site of many a photo—indicates the principal entry to the temple; next to it is the **Temple of Ten Niches.** On the next level are six huge pink granite blocks, amazingly cut, polished, and fitted together; they appear to be part of rooms never completed. This **Temple of the Sun** is one of the great stone-masonry achievements of the Incas. On the stones, you can still make out faint, ancient symbolic markings in relief. Across the valley is the quarry that provided the stones for the structure; a great ramp descending from the hilltop ruins was the means by which the Incas transported the massive stones—thousands of workers essentially dragged them around the river—from several kilometers away.

A footpath wends up the hill behind an outer wall of the ruins to a clearing and a wall with niches that have led some to believe prisoners were tied up here—a theory that is unfounded. Regardless of the purpose, the views south over the Urubamba Valley and of the snowcapped peak of Verónica are outstanding.

The ruins are open daily from 7am to 5:30pm; admission is by *boleto turístico* only (see p. 217). To experience the ruins in peace before the tour buses arrive, plan on getting to them before 11am. Early morning is best of all, when the sun rises over mountains to the east and then quickly bathes the entire valley in light.

At the bottom of the terraces, next to the Patacancha River, are the **Baños de la Ñusta (Princess Baths),** a place of ceremonial bathing. Wedged into the mountains facing the baths are granaries built by the Incas (not prisons, as some have supposed). Locals like to point out the face of the Inca carved into the cliff high above the valley. (If you can't make it out, ask the guard at the entrance to the ruins for a little help.)

OLD TOWN ★★★

Below (or south of) the ruins and across the Río Patacancha is the finest extant example of the Incas' masterful urban planning. Many original residential *canchas,* or blocks, each inhabited by several families during the 15th century, are still present; each *cancha* had a single entrance opening onto a main courtyard. The finest streets of this stone village are directly behind the main square. On my last visit to Ollanta, stonemasons were busy redoing every last old cobblestone street, so the Old Town should be in pristine shape again. Get a good glimpse of community life within a *cancha* by peeking in at **Calle del Medio** (Chautik'ikllu St.), where a couple of neighboring houses have a small shop in the courtyard and their ancestors' skulls are displayed as shrines on the walls of their living quarters. The entire village retains a solid Amerindian air to it, unperturbed by the crowds of gringos who wander through it, snapping photos of children and old women. It's a starkly traditional place, largely populated by locals in colorful native dress and women who pace up and down the streets or through fields absent-mindedly spinning the ancient spools used in making handwoven textiles.

Ollantaytambo is an excellent spot in the valley for gentle or more energetic walks around the valley and into the mountains. One of the more accessible walks is the climb up to **Pinkuylluna ★★** and the hills overlooking the old town; take the stairs

WE CALL IT CHOCLO: foods OF THE INCAS

Wondering what the Incas cultivated on all those amazing, steeply terraced fields that so elegantly grace the hillsides? Sure, they grew *papas* (potatoes) and *coca* (coca leaves), but corn was perhaps the Incas' most revered crop. Although corn was important throughout the Americas in pre-Columbian times, the Inca Empire raised it to the level of a sacred state crop. Corn was a symbol of power, and the Incas saved their very best lands for its cultivation. The *choclo* of Cusco and the Sacred Valley was considered the finest of the empire. It is still an uncommon delight: Huge, puffy, white kernels with a milky, sweet taste, it's best enjoyed in classic corn-on-the-cob style, boiled and served with a hunk of mountain cheese.

Pachamanca is a classic *sierra* dish, an indigenous barbecue of sorts, perfected by the Incas. The word is derived from *Pachamama*, or "Mother Earth," in Quechua. A *pachamanca* is distinguished by its underground preparation. Several types of meat, along with potatoes, chopped *ají* (hot pepper), herbs, and cheese, are baked in a hole in the earth over hot stones. Banana leaves are placed between the layers of food. The act of cooking underground was symbolic for the Incas; they worshiped the earth, and to eat directly from it was a way of honoring Pachamama and giving thanks for her fertility. Peruvians still love to cook *pachamancas* in the countryside.

Quinoa, which comes from the word that means "moon" in Quechua (another central element in the Inca cosmology), was the favored grain of the Incas. The grain, which expands to four times its original volume when cooked and contains a greater quantity of protein than any other grain, remains central to the Andean diet. Most often seen in *sopa a la criolla*, it is often substituted for rice and incorporated into soups, salads, and puddings.

off Calle Lares K'ikllu, northeast of the Plaza de Armas and with the widest rushing canals in town. A simple sign reads "To Pinkuylluna." Though the climb is initially very steep, you can clamber over the entire hilltop and explore old Inca granaries. The views of Ollantaytambo, across town to the ruins and of the surrounding valley are stupendous.

Where to Eat

Every year more and more small, tourist-oriented cafes and restaurants pop up in Ollantaytambo to cater to the crowds that hang out in the day and increasingly spend the night here. If you're staying in Ollanta and don't mind a drive, you might also consider catching a taxi to one of the fine restaurants along the main road from Urubamba to Ollantaytambo; see "Where to Eat" in "Urubamba & Environs," earlier in this chapter.

My favorite spot in Ollantaytambo is **Cafe Mayu** ★★, Estación de Tren Ollantaytambo (www.elalbergue.com; ✆ **084/204-014**), part of El Albergue *hostal* (see below) and right on the train tracks. The attractive cafe, which looks like it's been around much longer than it has, features homemade pastas (such as fettuccine with three Andean cheeses), quinoa and other salads, and tasty sandwiches. It also serves excellent breakfasts and great coffee and a locally famous brownie with vanilla ice cream. If you're headed out on a hike or to Machu Picchu, you can also pick up a boxed lunch for S/30.

The next best choice, although simple and unadorned, may be **Hearts Café ★**, in a new location on Av. Ventiderio, s/n (✆ **084/436-726**) begun by a British woman, Sonia Newhouse, who operates an NGO (www.heartscafe.org) that works with highland community women and children—to which all profits of this restaurant are donated. Besides feeling good about spending your *soles* here, it's a cozy little spot for breakfast (served all day), sandwiches, empanadas, fruit juices, and full, good-value dinners. **Blue Puppy Lounge & Restaurant ★**, Calle Horno s/n (Plaza de Armas) (✆ **084/630-464**) is an upstairs joint just off the main square and as much bar as it is restaurant, but if you're in need of some uncomplicated comfort food, it does the trick, with quesadillas, burritos, pizzas, salads, and chicken and steaks with a wide variety of sauces. There's a full menu of veggie items, too.

Puka Rumi, Av. Beniterio s/n (✆ **084/204-091**), is a little bar/cafe that serves everything from eggs to *churrasco* (barbecue) and chicken; it's especially good for a cold beer on the tiny terrace. Across the street, **Tunupa Restaurant & Pizzeria**, Av. Beniterio s/n (✆ **084/204-077**), the main drag between the ruins and Old Town, is an inexpensive family-run terrace joint with a very agreeable open-air atmosphere. It serves breakfast, lunch, and dinner, from pancakes to pizza and *chifa* (Peruvian–Chinese dishes). Other cheap restaurants in the Old Town, mostly serving cheap, serviceable pizzas, such as **Bar Ollantay** and **La Fortaleza,** ring the main square. Right next to the entrance to the ruins, **Kusicoyllor,** Plaza Araccama s/n (✆ **084/204-114**), is a cozy cafe/bar that is expectedly a tad touristy and overpriced. It serves standard Peruvian and predominantly Italian dishes and offers a fixed-price *menú*. Breakfast is especially good, making it a fine stop after an early morning tour of the ruins.

Shopping

While most shoppers make a beeline for the market directly in front of the entrance to the ruins, those in search of higher-quality, handwoven textiles (with all-natural dyes and fibers), produced by artisans from Quechua mountain communities, should visit **Awamaki ★**, Calle Chaupi (✆ **084/792-529**), the retail outlet of an NGO that runs a weaving project and ensures that profits make it back to the women of the Patacancha Valley. The organization also organizes trips to the Patacancha communities for weaving demonstrations and visits with local families and artisans.

 Sacred Valley Festivals

The traditional Andean villages of the Sacred Valley are some of the finest spots in Peru to witness vibrant local festivals celebrated with music, dance, and processions. Among the highlights are Christmas, **Día de los Reyes Magos (Three Kings Day,** Jan 6), **Ollanta-Raymi** (celebrated in Ollantaytambo the week after its big brother, Cusco's Inti Raymi, during the last week of June), and Chinchero's **Virgen Natividad** (Sept 8), the most important annual fiesta in that village. The **Fiesta de las Cruces (Festival of the Crosses,** May 2–3) is celebrated across the highlands with enthusiastic dancing and the decoration of large crosses. Pisac celebrates a particularly lively version of the **Virgen del Carmen** festival held in Paucartambo (July 16).

Entertainment & Nightlife

Blues Bar Café ★, Calle Chaupi (between the ruins and main square) (☏ **984/322-911**) is a rock-n-roll joint with the slightest hint of attitude (for laid-back Ollanta) and a good spot if you're staying in town and need a fix of tunes, munchies, and beer and cocktails. There are nightly 2-for-1 happy hours. Another spot for decent cocktails, as well as fruit juices and milkshakes, is **Blue Puppy Lounge & Restaurant,** Calle Horno s/n (☏ **084/630-464**), a combination restaurant and upstairs lounge-bar. Tables at one end have views of the main square.

Where to Stay

In addition to the hotels below, budget travelers gravitate toward the first inexpensive options (which, for the most part, don't offer hot water) they come across: **KB Tambo Hotel** (www.kbtambo.com; ☏ **084/204-091**), owned by a mountain-biking American and with nice new rooms constructed a couple of years ago ($15–$20 per person); **Hostal Las Orquídeas,** Av. Ferrocarril s/n (☏ **084/204-032**), which has clean and simple rooms with a shared bathroom around a courtyard for $20; and **Hostal La Ñusta,** Ctra. Ocobamba s/n (☏ **084/204-035**), a clean and friendly place with good views from the balcony but small and plain rooms ($20 for a double). Tucked into the Old Town on a quiet street, simple and comfortable **Hostal El Tambo,** Calle Horno s/n (☏ **084/204-003**), is built around an attractive, verdant patio. Rates are $15 for doubles.

EXPENSIVE

Hotel Pakaritampu ★   On the road from the train station to town, this hotel is surprisingly upscale for unassuming Ollantaytambo. With beautiful gardens, great views, and cozy touches such as a fireplace lounge and a library, it has a reasonably authentic, lived-in country feel. Rooms are tasteful, with sturdy, comfortable furnishings, and there's a nice restaurant/bar. It's owned by one of Peru's best-known athletes, a former Olympic volleyballer.

Av. Ferrocarril s/n, Ollantaytambo. www.pakaritampu.com. ☏ **084/204-020.** Fax 084/205-105. 39 units. $151 double; $317 suite. Rates include breakfast. AE, DC, MC, V. **Amenities:** Restaurant; bar; TV lounge.

MODERATE

El Albergue ★★ ✎   This rustic and homey boutique inn, owned by a long-time American resident of Ollantaytambo and with hotel roots dating to 1925, is my favorite place to stay, having steadily gotten more stylish over the years. It has large and very nicely furnished rooms—the aesthetic is a kind of clean, modern rusticity—with excellent beds, luxuriant gardens, a wood-fired sauna, Labrador retrievers roaming the grounds, and a spot right next to the train to Machu Picchu. It's frequently full, even though it's more expensive than other budget accommodations in town (and prices have climbed steadily over the years). The inn now sports an excellent cafe/restaurant, **Café Mayu,** with its entrance through the hotel or from the train tracks—also my favorite spot in town for a meal or even just dessert and coffee.

Av. Estación s/n (next to the railway station platform), Ollantaytambo. www.elalbergue.com. ☏/fax **084/204-014.** 16 units. $74–$99 double with shared bathroom. Rates include continental breakfast. No credit cards. **Amenities:** Restaurant; cafe; sauna. *In room:* Wi-Fi (free); no phone.

Sauce Hostal   Sandwiched between the main square of the village and the road to the ruins, this modern and comfortable free-standing building has a smattering of

HIKING TRAILS IN THE sacred VALLEY

Energetic travelers with a fierce desire to get outdoors and exercise their legs in the Sacred Valley can do much more than the standard ruins treks and even the Inca Trail, although the latter is certainly the best-known trek in Peru. Other trails are considerably less populated, so if you're looking for isolation in the Andes, give some of the following treks a try.

The entire valley is virtually tailor-made for treks, but Ollantaytambo and Yucay are particularly excellent bases for treks into the lovely, gentle hillsides framing the Urubamba Valley. The Cusco office of **South American Explorers** (☏ **084/245-484**) is very helpful with trip and trail reports for members.

○ **Km 82 of the Inca Trail:** Whether or not you're planning to do the Inca Trail, hiking the section from Km 82 to Km 88 is a nice addition to the classic or mini route. By staying to the north (or railroad) side of the Río Urubamba, you'll pass several good ruin sites, including Salapunku and Pinchanuyoq, finally reaching the Inca bridge at Km 88.

○ **Pumamarca ruins:** You can reach the small but well-preserved Inca ruins of Pumamarca by a pretty trek along the banks of the Río Patacancha, which takes you through tiny villages. The walk from Ollantaytambo takes about 5 hours round-trip. To get there, take the road that leads north out of Ollanta along the Patacancha. After it crosses the river, it turns into a footpath and passes the village of Munaypata. Veer left toward the valley and terracing, and then turn sharply to the right (northeast), toward the agricultural terraces straight ahead.

○ **Pinkulluna:** The mountain looming above Ollantaytambo makes for an enjoyable (though initially very steep) couple-hour trek up, past Inca terracing and old granaries. However, the trail isn't very clearly marked in sections, so it might be worthwhile to ask around town for a guide.

○ **Huayoccari:** Adventurous trekkers in search of solitude should enjoy the 2-day hike (one-way) from Yucay to the small village of Huayoccari, which passes some of the valley's loveliest scenery, from the Inca terraces along the San Juan River ravine to Sakrachayoc and ancient rock paintings overlooking caves. After camping overnight, trekkers continue to the Tuqsana pass (4,000m/13,100 ft.) and descend to Yanacocha Lake before arriving at Huayoccari.

very clean, nicely equipped rooms and a small restaurant. Some rooms have superb views of the ruins. The inn's name might strike some English speakers as a little odd, but it refers to the *sauce* tree out front.

Ventiderio 248, Ollantaytambo. www.hostalsauce.com.pe. ☏ **084/204-044.** Fax 084/204-048. 8 units. S/280 double ($10 discount if paying cash). Rates include breakfast. V. **Amenities:** Restaurant; bar; Wi-Fi.

INEXPENSIVE

Hostal Iskay ★ 🖉   This new, comfortable *hostal* down a quiet street in Old Town has something no one else can claim: killer views of the Ollantaytambo ruins. That's enough to recommend it, but this friendly and cool place, run by a Catalan guy with dreadlocks, also has very clean and sparsely decorated but comfortable rooms that are a bargain. Ask for a room that opens onto the terrace with the incredible views.

Patacalle s/n, Ollantaytambo. www.hostaliskay.com. © **084/204-004.** 5 units. $30–$49 double; $57–$67 mini-suite/family room. Rates include breakfast. MC, V.

MACHU PICCHU & THE INCA TRAIL ★★★

120km (75 miles) NW of Cusco

The stunning and immaculately sited Machu Picchu, the fabled "lost city of the Incas," is South America's greatest attraction, one that draws ever-increasing numbers of visitors from across the globe to Peru. The Incas hid Machu Picchu so high in the clouds that it escaped destruction by the empire-raiding Spaniards, who never found it. It is no longer lost, of course—you can zip there by high-speed train or trek there along a 2- or arduous 4-day trail—but Machu Picchu retains its perhaps unequaled aura of mystery and magic. From below it remains totally hidden from view, although no longer overgrown with brush, as it was when it was rediscovered in 1911 by the Yale archaeologist and historian Hiram Bingham with the aid of a local farmer who knew of its existence. The majestic setting the Incas chose for it, nestled in almost brooding Andes mountains and frequently swathed in mist, also remains unchanged. When the early morning sun rises over the peaks and methodically illuminates the ruins' row by row of granite stones, Machu Picchu leaves visitors as awe-struck as ever.

Machu Picchu's popularity continues to grow by leaps and bounds, straining both its infrastructure and the fragile surrounding ecosystem, forcing state officials to limit the number of visitors in high season. The great majority of visitors to Machu Picchu still visit it as a day trip from Cusco, but many people feel that a few hurried hours at the ruins during peak hours, amid throngs of people following guided tours, simply do not suffice. That certainly is my opinion. By staying at least 1 night, either at the one upscale hotel just outside the grounds of Machu Picchu or down below in the town of Aguas Calientes (also officially called Machu Picchu Pueblo, though most Peruvians and visitors still call it by the original name), you can remain at the ruins later in the afternoon after most of the tour groups have gone home, or get there for sunrise—a dramatic, unforgettable sight. Many visitors find that even a full single day at the ruins does not do it justice.

The base for most visitors, Aguas Calientes is a small and humid, ramshackle tourist-trade village with the feel of a frontier town, dominated by sellers of cheap *artesanía* and souvenirs and weary backpackers resting up and celebrating their treks along the Inca Trail over cheap eats and cheaper beers. The Peruvian government has been doing its level best to spruce up the town, lest its ramshackle look turn off visitors to Peru's greatest spectacle. It has fixed up the Plaza de Armas, built a nicely paved *malecón* riverfront area, and added new bridges over and new streets along the river. Attempts to give it a makeover have long been complicated by flooding and mudslides, the most recent in 2010 (when five people died and some 2,000 tourists were stranded at Machu Picchu, eventually evacuated by helicopter). Although Aguas Calientes does look considerably better than at any time I can remember, and despite its spectacular setting—surrounded by cloud forest vegetation and Andes peaks on all sides—it's still probably not a place you want to hang out for long. There are some additional good hikes in the area, but most people head back to Cusco after a day or so in town.

Essentials

GETTING THERE

BY TRAIN   Most people travel to Machu Picchu by train (indeed, the only other way to get there is by foot). You can go to Aguas Calientes, at the base of the ruins, from either Cusco or two points in the Sacred Valley (Ollantaytambo and now Urubamba). The 112km (70-mile) trip from Cusco is a truly spectacular train journey. It zigzags through lush valleys hugging the Río Urubamba, with views of snowcapped Andes peaks in the distance. From Cusco, **PeruRail** (www.perurail.com; © **01/612-6700** in Lima, **084/581-414** in Cusco) operates three tourist trains from **Estación Poroy,** a 15-minute taxi ride from Cusco, all arriving in under 3½ hours: the **Expedition,** the slowest and least expensive ($72–$76 one-way); the **Vistadome,** the faster first-class service ($79–$81); and the top-of-the-line and very pricey luxury line **Hiram Bingham,** named after the discoverer of Machu Picchu ($329–$389 one-way, including meals, cocktails, and a guided tour at the ruins). Among other regularly scheduled times, the Expedition departs Cusco daily at 7:42am and arrives in Aguas Calientes at 10:51am (returning at 4:43pm and arriving in Cusco at 8:13pm); the Vistadome leaves at 6:40am and arrives at 9:53am (returning at 3:20pm and arriving at 6:50pm); and the Hiram Bingham leaves Cusco at 9:05am and arrives in Aguas Calientes at 12:24pm (returning at 5:50pm and arriving in Cusco at 9:16pm). Make your train reservations as early as possible; tickets can be purchased online or at **Estación Huanchaq** on Avenida Pachacútec (in cash, either dollars or *soles*) for tickets reserved in advance. It's open Monday through Friday from 8:30am to 5:30pm, Saturday and Sunday from 8:30am to 12:30pm.

Travelers already based in the Urubamba Valley have additional options to travel by train to Machu Picchu. **PeruRail** now travels to Machu Picchu from its new, private train station on the grounds of **Tambo del Inka Resort & Spa** (see p. 229) in Urubamba. Autovagón trains make the 2½-hour journey, with brunch included.

From the station in Ollantaytambo to Machu Picchu, the journey takes under 2 hours. **Inca Rail,** Portal de Panes 105/Plaza de Armas, in Cusco (www.incarail.com; © **084/233-030** in Cusco or **01/613-5272** in Lima), operates Tourist, Executive, and First Class trains, with fares ranging from $60 to $65 for adults, $50 for children. Trains (five per day) begin running at 6:40am, with the last return at 7pm. On **Machu Picchu Train,** Av. El Sol 576, in Cusco (www.machupicchutrain.com; © **084/221-199**), fares from Ollantaytambo to Machu Picchu range from $50 to $63 one-way for adults, $35 for children, with the first train leaving at 7:20am and the last return at 7:15pm. PeruRail's Expedition and Vistadome services also originate in Ollantaytambo, leaving several times a day, from 5:10am to 9pm. Fares range from $43 to $80 each way.

Tip: For the best views on the way to Machu Picchu, sit on the left side of the train. All three train companies permit online booking and ticketing, with major credit cards accepted, and Machu Picchu Train accepts PayPal.

Estación Machu Picchu Pueblo, the train station in Aguas Calientes, is along the river side of the tracks, just beyond the market stalls of Avenida Imperio de los Incas. Porters from several hotels greet the trains upon arrival each morning.

BY BUS You can't travel from Cusco to Machu Picchu by bus until the final leg of the journey, when buses wend their way up the mountain, performing exaggerated switchbacks for 15 minutes before suddenly depositing passengers at the entrance to the ruins. The cost is $17 round-trip. There's no need to reserve in advance; just purchase your ticket at the little booth in front of the lineup of buses, at the bottom of the market stalls. Buses begin running at 6:30am and come down all day, with the last one descending at dusk. Some people choose to purchase a one-way ticket ($9) up and walk down (30–45 min.) to Aguas Calientes.

BY FOOT The celebrated **Inca Trail (Camino del Inca)** is almost as famous as the ruins themselves, and the trek is rightly viewed as an attraction in itself rather than merely a means of getting to Machu Picchu under your own power. There are two principal treks: one that takes 4 days (43km/27 miles) and another shorter and less demanding route that lasts just 2 days. The trails begin outside Ollantaytambo (at Km 82 of the Cusco–Machu Picchu railroad track); you can return to Cusco or Ollantaytambo by train. See "Hiking the Inca Trail," later in this section, for more details; many new regulations have been introduced in the past few years.

For those who take the train to Aguas Calientes but still want a small dose of what it's like to walk to Machu Picchu, it's straightforward (if a little difficult) to walk up to the ruins from town up a steep path that cuts across the switchback road. It takes a little over an hour to make it up and about 45 minutes to descend. Because you'll probably want to save your energy for exploring Machu Picchu, if you are fit and want to walk at least one-way, I recommend walking down from the ruins (which is still pretty strenuous on one's knees).

VISITOR INFORMATION

Aguas Calientes has an **iPerú** office, Av. Pachacútec, Cdra. 1 s/n (📞 **084/211-104**), about one-third of the way up the main drag in town. It has photocopies of town maps and some basic hotel and Machu Picchu information.

FAST FACTS

The lone bank in Aguas Calientes is **Banco de Crédito,** Av. Imperio de los Incas s/n. To exchange money (cash or traveler's checks), try **Gringo Bill's Hostal** at Colla Raymi 104, just off the main square. Shops and restaurants along the two main

---

 Train Schedules to Machu Picchu

Train schedules have changed with alarming frequency in the past few years, according to season and, it seems, the whims of some scheduler—and that's likely to be especially true now that there are three companies handling service (rather than just one), all employing the same tracks. It's wise to make your reservation at least several days (or more) in advance, especially in high season. For PeruRail's high-end Hiram Bingham service, reservations several weeks or more in advance are recommended. It's also smart to verify hours and fares at your hotel (if you're staying in one of the better ones with good service and informed personnel), the Tourist Information Office in Cusco (p. 165), or via PeruRail (www.perurail.com; 📞 **084/ 238-722**); Inca Rail (www.incarail.com; 📞 **084/233-030**); or Machu Picchu Train (www.machupicchutrain.com; 📞 **084/ 221-199**).

ENDANGERED machu PICCHU

Machu Picchu survived the Spanish onslaught against the Inca Empire, but in the last few decades it has suffered more threats to its architectural integrity and pristine Andean environment than it did in nearly 500 previous years of existence. In the past, UNESCO has threatened to add Machu Picchu to its roster of endangered World Heritage Sites and not to withdraw that status unless stringent measures were taken by the Peruvian government to protect the landmark ruins.

Clearly, the preservation of Machu Picchu continues to face significant challenges. In the past few years, the ruins have again been named on another notorious list, the 2010 World Monuments Watch, which details the 100 Most Endangered Sites in the World. (In 2002, in recognition of the Peruvian government's adoption of tougher regulations on the Inca Trail and the suspension of a proposed cable-car plan, Machu Picchu was removed from the list.) Today, World Monuments Fund maintains that "little has been done to address the impacts of tourism on the site or the resulting environmental degradation of the area." Planned projects, which include building a bridge across the Vilcanota River, are representative of "uncontrolled development and environmental mismanagement in Aguas Calientes." Add to that the reality that tourism at Machu Picchu has increased from 9,000 visitors in all of 1992 to close to 5,000 on a single busy day (the site receives more than 1 million visitors annually), and Peru has significant environmental and conservation issues to face.

In 2001, a film company shooting a TV ad for a Peruvian beer sneaked equipment into the site and irreparably damaged the stone Intihuatana atop the ruins (the camera crane operator was sentenced to 6 years in prison in 2005). Developers' plans for a tram to the site have not been entirely dropped, as once reported, though they have been altered to minimize its impact should it ever be built. The Peruvian government has only slowly responded to pressure from UNESCO, foreign governments, and watchdog groups, introducing measures to clean up and restrict access to the historic Inca Trail. One unique measure adopted was a debt-swap initiative, in which the government of Finland traded 25% of Peru's then-outstanding debt (more than $6 million) for conservation programs targeting Machu Picchu. Yet clearly much more needs to be done to protect these singular ruins, Peru's most acclaimed treasure.

streets, Avenida Imperio de los Incas and Avenida Pachacútec, also buy dollars from travelers in need at standard exchange rates.

You'll find the **police** on Avenida Imperio de los Incas, down from the railway station (© **084/211-178**).

There are Internet *cabinas* at the **Café Internet** (no phone) on Avenida Imperio de los Incas, a block away from the main square on the railroad tracks, and at a couple of places on the Plaza de Armas. There's a **post office** on the corner of Avenida Collasuyo s/n. A **posta de salud** (health clinic) is located at Av. Imperio de los Incas, s/n. The **Telefónica del Perú** office is at Av. Imperio de los Incas 132.

Exploring Machu Picchu ★★★

Since its rediscovery in 1911 and initial exploration by an American team of archaeologists from Yale during the next 4 years, the ruins of Machu Picchu have resonated far beyond the status of mere archaeological site. Reputed to be the legendary "lost city of the Incas," it is steeped in mystery and folklore. The unearthed complex, the only significant Inca site to escape the ravenous appetites of the Spanish conquistadors in the 16th century, ranks as the top attraction in Peru, arguably the greatest in South America and, for my money, one of the world's most stunning sights. Countless glossy photographs of the stone ruins, bridging the gap between two massive Andean peaks and swathed in cottony clouds, just can't do it justice. I distinctly remember seeing pictures of Machu Picchu in a textbook when I was 5 years old and dreaming that someday I would go there. When I did, for the first time in 1983, the glorious city of the Incas more than lived up to all those years of expectation. It is dreamlike and remains so, even though it's a mandatory visit for virtually everyone who travels to Peru.

Invisible from the Urubamba Valley below, Machu Picchu lay dormant for more than 4 centuries, nestled nearly 2,400m (8,000 ft.) above sea level under thick jungle and known only to a handful of Amerindian peasants. Never mentioned in the Spanish chronicles, it was seemingly lost in the collective memory of the Incas and their descendants. The ruins' unearthing, though, raised more questions than it answered, and experts still argue about the place Machu Picchu occupied in the Inca Empire. Was it a citadel? An agricultural site? An astronomical observatory? A ceremonial city or sacred retreat for the Inca emperor? Or some combination of all of these? Adding to the mystery, this complex city of exceedingly fine architecture and masonry was constructed, inhabited, and deliberately abandoned all in less than a century—a mere flash in the 4,000-year-history of Andean Peru. Machu Picchu was very probably abandoned even before the arrival of the Spanish, perhaps as a result of the Incas' civil war. Or perhaps it was drought that drove the Incas elsewhere.

Bingham mistook Machu Picchu for the lost city of Vilcabamba, the last refuge of the rebellious Inca Manco Cápac (see "Bingham, the 'Discoverer' of Machu Picchu" on p. 248). Machu Picchu, though, is not that lost city (which was discovered deeper in the jungle at Espíritu Pampa). Most historians believe that the 9th Inca emperor, Pachacútec (also called Pachacuti Inca Yupanqui)—who founded the Inca Empire, established many of the hallmarks of its society, and built most of the greatest and most recognizable of Inca monuments—had the complex constructed sometime in the mid-1400s, probably after the defeat of the Chancas, a rival group, in 1438. Machu Picchu appears to have been both a ceremonial and agricultural center. Half its buildings were sacred in nature, but the latest research findings indicate that it was a royal retreat for Inca leaders rather than a sacred city, per se. Never looted by the Spaniards, many of its architectural features remain in excellent condition—even if they ultimately do little to advance our understanding of the exact nature of Machu Picchu.

One thing is certain: Machu Picchu is one of the world's great examples of landscape art. The Incas revered nature, worshiping celestial bodies and more earthly streams and stones. The spectacular setting of Machu Picchu reveals just how much they reveled in their environment. Steep terraces, gardens, and granite and limestone temples, staircases, and aqueducts seem to be carved directly out of the hillside. Forms echo the very shape of the surrounding mountains, and windows and instruments appear to have been constructed to track the sun during the June and December solstices. Machu Picchu lies 300m (1,000 ft.) lower than Cusco, but you'd imagine the exact opposite, so nestled are the ruins among mountaintops and clouds.

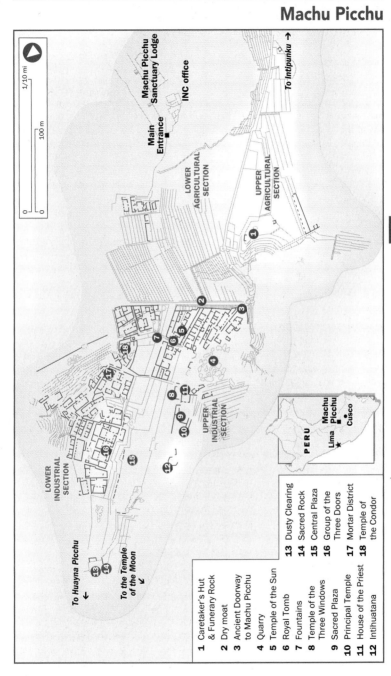

1 Caretaker's Hut & Funerary Rock
2 Dry moat
3 Ancient Doorway to Machu Picchu
4 Quarry
5 Temple of the Sun
6 Royal Tomb
7 Fountains
8 Temple of the Three Windows
9 Sacred Plaza
10 Principal Temple
11 House of the Priest
12 Intihuatana
13 Dusty Clearing
14 Sacred Rock
15 Central Plaza
16 Group of the Three Doors
17 Mortar District
18 Temple of the Condor

Not a Woman's World

For years, the world thought Machu Picchu had been almost entirely populated by the Inca's chosen "Virgins of the Sun." Bingham and his associates originally reported that more than three-quarters of the human remains found at the site were female. Those findings have been disproved, however; the gender makeup of the inhabitants of Machu Picchu was no different than anywhere else in society: pretty much 50/50.

The ruins are cradled at the center of a radius of Andean peaks, like the pistil at the center of a flower.

Appreciating Machu Picchu for its aesthetic qualities is no slight to its significance. The Incas obviously chose the site for the immense power of its natural beauty. They, like we, must have been in awe of the snowcapped peaks to the east; the rugged panorama of towering, forested mountains and the sacred cliff of Putukusi to the west; and the city sitting gracefully like a proud saddle between two huge *cerros*, or peaks. It remains one of the most thrilling sights in the world. At daybreak, when the sun's rays creep silently over the jagged silhouette, sometimes turning the distant snowy peaks fiery orange, and then slowly, with great drama, cast brilliant light on the ruins building by building and row by row, it's enough to move some observers to tears and others to squeals of delight.

VISITING THE RUINS

Named a UNESCO World Heritage Site in 1983 and declared one of the "New Seven Wonders of the World," Machu Picchu's image around the world continues to grow, as does the number of people who want to visit the ruins. Until recently, as many as 5,000 visitors a day visited Machu Picchu during high season, but the number of visitors permitted on a daily basis has now been capped at 2,500—making reservations in advance of your visit pivotal. I'd recommend purchasing online at least 1 week in advance (but if you're traveling in high season, from May to October, make them as early as possible to avoid a crushing disappointment). Even with the new regulations, you've got to arrive very early in the morning or stay past 3pm for a bit of splendid Inca isolation. Still, the place is large enough to escape most tour-group bottlenecks. Perhaps the worst times to visit are from July 28 to August 10, when Peruvian national holidays land untold groups of schoolchildren and families at Machu Picchu, or solstice days (June 21 and Dec 21), when everyone descends on the ruins for a glimpse of the dazzling effects of the sun's rays. During the rainy season (Nov–Mar), you are very likely to get rain for (often) brief periods during the day, and Machu Picchu is usually obscured by clouds in the morning.

For information on the shuttle buses to the ruins, see "Getting There," earlier.

The ruins are open daily from dawn to dusk. The first visitors, usually those staying at the hotel or arriving from the Inca Trail, enter at 6am. Everyone is ushered out by 6pm. Tickets no longer can be purchased at the entrance: They may be reserved, purchased **online** (Visa only) and printed (www.machupicchu.gob.pe; ℂ 084/582-030). Tickets can also be purchased in Aguas Calientes at the **Centro Cultural Machu Picchu,** Av. Pachacútec s/n (ℂ 084/211-196), near the main plaza (cash only, *soles*). In Cusco, tickets may be purchased (cash or Visa only) at the **Dirección Regional de Cultura,** Av. de la Cultura 238 (ℂ 084/236-061), **Dircetur** offices,

Portal de Mantas 117-A (**℡** **084/246-074**), **PeruRail,** Av. Pachacútec s/n; **IncaRail,** Portal de Panes, 105/Plaza de Armas; or **Hotel Monasterio,** Calle Palacios, 136/Plazoleta Nazarenas. The entrance fee is S/128 adults (S/65 students with an ISIC card; free for children under 8). Tickets are valid for 3 days from date of purchase, but are good for a single day's entrance only. Note that another new regulation is that advance tickets are required for additional access to **Huayna Picchu,** the steep trail to the mountaintop overlooking Machu Picchu, and **Templo de la Luna** (see p. 247). Access for these components frequently sells out weeks in advance. Capacity is limited to two groups of 200 people each, with the first entry from 7–8am and the second from 10–11am. The combination ticket (Machu Picchu–Huayna Picchu–Templo de la Luna) is S/150 adults, S/75 students.

Along with your entrance ticket, you will be given an official Institute of National Culture map of the ruins, which gives the names of the individual sections, but no detailed explanations. The numbers indicated in brackets below follow our own map, "Machu Picchu," on p. 243. English-speaking guides can be independently arranged on-site; most charge around $30 for a private 2-hour tour. Individuals can sometimes hook up with an established group for little more than $5 per person.

For more information on the confusing (and potentially still evolving) ticketing process at Machu Picchu, see a helpful independent website, www.machupicchu tickets.com.

EXPLORING MACHU PICCHU

After passing through the entrance, you can either head left and straight up the hill, or go down to the right. The path up to the left takes you to the spot above the ruins, near the **Caretaker's Hut** and **Funerary Rock** [1] that affords the classic postcard overview of Machu Picchu. If you are here early enough for sunrise (6:30–7:30am), by all means do this first. The hut overlooks rows and rows of steep agricultural terraces (generally with a few llamas grazing nearby). In the morning, you might see exhausted groups of trekkers arriving from several days and nights on the Inca Trail. (Most arrive at the crack of dawn for their reward, a celebratory sunrise.)

From this vantage point, you can see clearly the full layout of Machu Picchu, which had defined agricultural and urban zones; a long **dry moat** [2] separates the two sectors. Perhaps a population of 1,000 lived here at the high point of Machu Picchu.

Head down into the main section of the ruins, past a series of burial grounds and dwellings and the **main entrance to the city** [3]. A section of stones, likely a **quarry** [4], sits atop a clearing with occasionally great views of the snowcapped peaks (Cordillera Vilcabamba) in the distance (looking southwest).

 Beware: Bogus Machu Picchu Entrance Tickets

With the increased interest in Machu Picchu (and higher prices associated with a visit), perhaps it's inevitable that counterfeit entrance tickets have become a reality. The Peruvian Ministry of Culture warns tourists not to purchase tickets to Machu Picchu or any other archaeological site in the Cusco region from anyone other than official outlets (see above). The falsified tickets are frequently offered in the Plaza de Armas in Cusco.

Down a steep series of stairs is one of the most famous Inca constructions, the **Temple of the Sun ★★★** [5] (also called the Torreón). The rounded, tapering tower has extraordinary stonework, the finest in Machu Picchu: its large stones fit together seamlessly. From the ledge above the temple, you can appreciate the window perfectly aligned for the June winter solstice, when the sun's rays come streaming through at dawn and illuminate the stone at the center of the temple. The temple is cordoned off, and entry is not permitted. Below the temple, in a cave carved from the rock, is a section traditionally called the **Royal Tomb** [6], even though no human remains have been found there. Inside is a meticulously carved altar and series of niches that produce intricate morning shadows. To the north, just down the stairs that divide this section from a series of dwellings called the **Royal Sector,** is a still-functioning water canal and series of interconnected **fountains** [7]. The main fountain is distinguished by both its size and excellent stonework.

Back up the stairs to the high section of the ruins (north of the quarry) is the main ceremonial area. The **Temple of the Three Windows ★★** [8], each trapezoid extraordinarily cut with views of the bold Andes in the distance across the Urubamba gorge, is likely to be one of your lasting images of Machu Picchu. It fronts one side of the **Sacred Plaza** [9]. To the left, if you're facing the Temple of the Three Windows, is the **Principal Temple** [10], which has masterful stonework in its three high walls. Directly opposite is the **House of the Priest** [11]. Just behind the Principal Temple is a small cell, termed the **Sacristy,** renowned for its exquisite masonry. It's a good place to examine how amazingly these many-angled stones (one to the left of the door jamb has 32 distinct angles) were fitted together by Inca stonemasons.

Up a short flight of stairs is the **Intihuatana ★** [12], popularly called the "hitching post of the sun." It looks to be a ritualistic carved rock or a sort of sundial, and its shape echoes that of the sacred peak Huayna Picchu beyond the ruins. The stone almost certainly functioned as an astronomical and agricultural calendar (useful in judging the alignment of constellations and solar events and, thus, the seasons). It does appear to be powerfully connected to mountains in all directions. The Incas built similar monuments elsewhere across the empire, but most were destroyed by the Spaniards (who surely thought them to be instruments of pagan worship). The one at Machu Picchu survived in perfect form for nearly 5 centuries until 2001, when a camera crew sneaked in a 1,000-pound crane, which fell over and chipped off the top section of the Intihuatana.

Follow a trail down through terraces and past a small plaza to a **dusty clearing** [13] with covered stone benches on either side. Fronting the square is a massive, sculpted **Sacred Rock** [14], whose shape mimics that of Putukusi, the sacred peak

 Huayna Picchu: Advance Reservations Required

Advance tickets are now required for additional access to **Huayna Picchu,** the steep climb to the mountaintop overlooking Machu Picchu, and **Templo de la Luna** (see p. 247). Access frequently sells out weeks in advance, as capacity is limited to two groups of 200 people each, with the first entry from 7–8am and the second from 10–11am. The combination ticket (Machu Picchu–Huayna Picchu–Templo de la Luna) is S/150 adults, S/75 students. Climbing to the top of Huayna Picchu for those physically able is one of the highlights of visiting Machu Picchu, making advance planning more necessary than ever.

that looms due east across the valley. This area likely served as a communal area for meetings and perhaps performances. Many locals (as well as visitors) believe that the Sacred Rock transmits a palpable force of energy; place your palms on it to see if you can tap into it.

To the left of the Sacred Rock, down a path, is the gateway to **Huayna Picchu ★★**, the huge outcrop that serves as a dramatic backdrop to Machu Picchu. Although it looks forbidding and is very steep, anyone in reasonable physical shape can climb it. The steep path up takes most visitors about an hour or more, although some athletic sorts ascend the peak in less than 25 minutes. Note that only 400 people per day (admitted in two groups: 7–8am and 10–11am) are permitted to make the climb, and there is now an additional cost associated with it. If you are keen on ascending Huayna Picchu for the views and exercise, make your reservations as far in advance as possible (for more information, see the sidebar on p. 246). At the top, you'll reach a platform of sorts, which is as far as many get, directly overlooking the ruins. Most who've come this far and are committed to reaching the apex continue on for a few more minutes, up through a tight tunnel carved out of the stone, to a rocky perch with 360-degree views. There's room for only a handful of hikers up there, and the views are so astounding that many are tempted to hang out as long as they can—so new arrivals might need to be patient to win their place on the rock. The views of Machu Picchu below and the panorama of forested mountains are quite literally breathtaking.

Ascending Huayna Picchu is highly recommended for energetic sorts of any age (I've seen octogenarians climb the path at an enviable clip), but young children are not allowed. In wet weather, you might want to reconsider, though, because the stone steps can get slippery and become very dangerous.

Returning back down the same path (frighteningly steep at a couple of points) is a turnoff to the **Temple of the Moon,** usually visited only by Machu Picchu completists. The trail dips down into the cloud forest and then climbs again, and is usually deserted. Cleaved into the rock at a point midway down the peak and perched above the Río Urubamba, it almost surely was not a lunar observatory, however. It is a strangely forlorn and mysterious place of caverns, niches, and enigmatic portals, with some terrific stonework, including carved thrones and an altar. Despite its modern name, the temple was likely used for worship of the Huayna Picchu mountain spirit. The path takes about 1 to 1½ hours round-trip from the detour.

Passing the guard post (where you'll need to sign out), continue back into the main Machu Picchu complex and enter the lower section of the ruins, separated from the spiritually oriented upper section by a **Central Plaza** [15]. The lower section was more prosaic in function, mostly residential and industrial. Eventually, you'll come to a series of cells and quarters, called the **Group of the Three Doors** [16] and the **Mortar District** or Industrial Sector [17]. By far the most interesting part of this lower section is the **Temple of the Condor** [18]. Said to be a carving of a giant condor, the dark rock above symbolizes the great bird's wings and the pale rock below quite clearly represents its head. You can actually crawl through the cave at the base of the rock and emerge on the other side.

Apart from the main complex, west of Machu Picchu, is **the Inca Bridge,** built upon stacked stones and overlooking a sheer, 600 meter (nearly 2,000 ft.) drop. Critical to the citadel's defense, the bridge can be reached in an easy half-hour from a clearly marked narrow trail.

BINGHAM, THE "DISCOVERER" OF
machu PICCHU

Hiram Bingham is credited with the "scientific discovery" of Machu Picchu, but, in fact, when he stumbled upon the ruins with the aid of a local *campesino,* he didn't know what he'd found. Bingham, an archaeologist and historian at Yale University (and later governor of Connecticut), had come to Peru to satisfy his curiosity about a fabled lost Inca city. He led an archaeological expedition to Peru in 1911, sponsored by Yale University and the National Geographical Society. Bingham was in search of Vilcabamba the Old, the final refuge of seditious Inca Manco Cápac and his sons, who retreated there after the siege of Cusco in 1537.

From Cusco, Bingham and his team set out for the jungle through the Urubamba Valley. The group came upon a major Inca site, which they named Patallacta (Llaqtapata), ruins near the start of the Inca Trail. A week into the expedition, at Mandorpampa, near today's Aguas Calientes, Bingham met Melchor Arteaga, a local farmer, who told Bingham of mysterious ruins high in the mountains on the other side of the river and offered to guide the expedition to them. In the rain, the two climbed the steep mountain. Despite his grandiose claims, the ruins were not totally overgrown; a small number of *campesinos* were farming among them.

In *The Lost City of the Incas,* Bingham writes: "I soon found myself before the ruined walls of buildings built with some of the finest stonework of the Incas. It was difficult to see them as they were partially covered over by trees and moss, the growth of centuries; but in the dense shadow, hiding in bamboo thickets and toggled vines, could be seen here and there walls of white granite ashlars most carefully cut and exquisitely fitted together . . . I was left truly breathless."

Bingham was convinced that he'd uncovered the rebel Inca's stronghold, Vilcabamba. Yet Vilcabamba was known to have been hastily built—and Machu Picchu clearly was anything but—and most accounts had it lying much deeper in the jungle. Moreover, the Spaniards were known to have ransacked

For those who haven't yet had their fill of Machu Picchu, the climb up to **Intipunku (Sun Gate)** is well worth it. The path just below the **Caretaker's Hut** leads to the final pass of the route Inca Trail hikers use to enter the ruins. The views from the gateway, with Huayna Picchu looming in the background, are spectacular. Two stone gates here correspond to the all-important winter and summer solstices; on those dates, the sun's rays illuminate the gates like a laser.

For a more detailed guide of the ruins and Machu Picchu's history, Peter Frost's *Exploring Cusco* (Nuevas Imágenes, 1999), available in Cusco bookstores, is quite excellent.

Hiking the Inca Trail

At its most basic, the Inca Trail (Camino del Inca) was a footpath through the Andes leading directly to the gates of Machu Picchu. Contrary to its image as a lone, lost, remote city, Machu Picchu was not isolated in the clouds. It was the crown of an entire Inca province, as ruins all along the Inca Trail attest. Machu Picchu was an administrative center in addition to its other putative purposes. That larger purpose

Vilcabamba, and there is no evidence whatsoever of Machu Picchu having suffered an attack. Despite these contradictions, Bingham's pronouncement was accepted for more than 50 years. The very name should have been a dead giveaway: Vilcabamba means "Sacred Plain" in Quechua, hardly a description one would attach to Machu Picchu, nestled high in the mountains.

In 1964, the U.S. explorer Gene Savoy discovered what are now accepted as the true ruins of Vilcabamba, at Espíritu Pampa, a several-day trek into the jungle. Strangely enough, it seems certain that Hiram Bingham had once come across a small section of Vilcabamba, but he dismissed the ruins as minor.

The Machu Picchu ruins were excavated by a Bingham team in 1915. A railway from Cusco to Aguas Calientes, begun 2 years earlier, was finally completed in 1928. The road up the hillside to the ruins, inaugurated by Bingham himself, was completed in 1948. Bingham died still believing Machu Picchu was Vilcabamba, even though he'd actually uncovered something much greater—and more mysterious.

Bingham took some 11,000 pictures of Machu Picchu on his second visit in 1912 and eventually removed more than 45,000 artifacts for study in the U.S. (with the permission of the Peruvian government under the agreement that they would be returned to Peru when there was a suitable place for their storage and continued study). Peru claims the agreement was for 18 months, but the objects remained at Yale University's Peabody Museum in New Haven, Connecticut for nearly a century. After years of negotiations and threats of lawsuits, Yale and the Peruvian government finally came to an agreement that recognizes that Peru holds title to the artifacts. Some 40,000 museum-quality Bingham artifacts have, at long last, been returned to Peru, a selection of which are on display at the new **Museo Machu Picchu** (Casa Concha) in Cusco; see p. 175), which was inaugurated to celebrate the centennial of Bingham's 1911 discovery of Machu Picchu.

is comprehensible only to those who hike the ancient royal route and visit the other ruins scattered along the way to the sacred city.

More than that, though, the Incas conceived of Machu Picchu and the great trail leading to it in grand artistic and spiritual terms. Hiking the Inca Trail—the ancient royal highway—is, hands down, the most authentic and scenic way to visit Machu Picchu and get a clear grasp of the Incas' overarching architectural concept and supreme regard for nature. As impressive as Machu Picchu itself, the trail traverses a 325-sq.-km (125-sq.-mile) national park designated as the Machu Picchu Historical Sanctuary. The entire zone is replete with extraordinary natural and man-made sights: Inca ruins, exotic vegetation and animals, and dazzling mountain and cloud-forest vistas.

Today the Inca Trail—which, as part of the Machu Picchu Historical Sanctuary, has been designated a World Heritage natural and cultural site—is the most important and most popular hiking trail in South America, followed by many thousands of ecotourists and modern-day pilgrims in the past 3 decades. Its extreme popularity in recent years—more than 75,000 people a year hike the famous trail—has led to concerns among environmentalists and historians that the trail is suffering potentially irreparable degradation. The National Institute of Culture (INC) and the Ministry of Industry, Tourism, Integration, and International Trade (MITINCI), reacting to pressure from groups such as UNESCO (which threatened to rescind Machu Picchu's World Heritage Site status), instituted far-reaching changes in practices designed to limit the number of visitors and damage to Machu Picchu and the Inca Trail, though these alone may not be enough to forestall the trail's damage; see the "Inca Trail Regulations" box on p. 255.

There are two principal ways to walk to Machu Picchu: either along the traditional, fairly arduous 4-day/3-night path with three serious mountain passes, or as part of a more accessible 2-day/1-night trail (there's also an even shorter 1-day trek that covers just the last part of the trail, which is suitable for inexperienced walkers). You can hire porters to haul your packs or suck it up and do it the hard way. Independent trekking on the Inca Trail without an official guide has been prohibited since 2001. **You must go as part of an organized group arranged by an officially sanctioned tour agency** (at the end of 2011, 177 agencies, both in Cusco and beyond, were allowed to sell Inca Trail packages). A couple or a small number of people can organize their own group if they are willing to pay higher prices for the luxury of not having to join an ad hoc group.

Sadly, even with the new regulations, hiking the Inca Trail, beautiful and mystical as it remains for most, is not a silent, solitary walk in the clouds. At least in high season, you will contend with groups walking the trail both in front of and behind you, and some will invariably be noisy student groups.

PREPARING FOR THE INCA TRAIL

The classic **4-day route** is along hand-hewn stone stairs and trails through sumptuous mountain scenery and amazing cloud forest, past rushing rivers and dozens of Inca ruins. The zone is inhabited by rare orchids, 419 species of birds, and even the indigenous spectacled bear. The trek begins at Qorihuayrachina near Ollantaytambo—more easily described as Km 88 of the railway from Cusco to Aguas Calientes. The 43km (26-mile) route passes three formidable mountain passes, including the punishing "Dead Woman's Pass," to a maximum altitude of 4,200m (13,800 ft.). Most groups enter the ruins of Machu Picchu at sunrise on the fourth day, although others, whose members are less keen on rising at 3:30am to do it, trickle in throughout the morning.

The **2-day version** of the trail is being promoted by authorities as the Camino Sagrado del Inca, or "Sacred Trail," although it might also be called the Camino "Lite." It is a reasonable alternative to the classic trail if time or fitness is lacking. The path rises only to an elevation of about 2,750m (9,020 ft.) and is a relatively easy climb to Huiñay Huayna and then down to Machu Picchu. The minitrail begins only 14km (8¾ miles) away from Machu Picchu, at Km 104, and it circumvents much of the finest mountain scenery and ruins. Groups spend the night near the ruins of Huiñay Huayna before arriving at Machu Picchu for sunrise on the second day. More and more people of all ages and athletic abilities are tackling the Inca Trail; the Peruvian government, in addition to adopting more stringent regulations governing its use, also placed flush toilets in campsites several years ago in an attempt to make the trail cleaner and more user-friendly.

Either way you go, it is advisable to give yourself a couple of days in Cusco or a spot in the Sacred Valley to acclimatize to the high elevation. Cold- and wet-weather technical gear, a solid backpack, and comfortable, sturdy, broken-in (and waterproof)

The Inca Trail

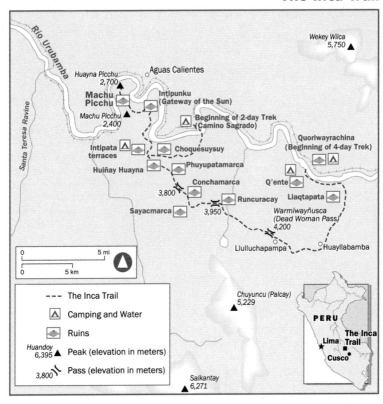

hiking boots are musts (also needed: sleeping bag, flashlight/headlamp, and sun block). Above all, respect the ancient trail and its environment. Whatever you pack in, you must also pack out. You should also choose your dates carefully. The dry season (June–Oct) is the most crowded time on the trail, but it's excellent in terms of weather. Shoulder seasons can be best of all, even with the threat of a bit of rain; May is perhaps best, with good weather and low numbers of trekkers. Other months—especially December through March—are simply too wet for all but the hardest-core trail vets. The entire trail is closed for maintenance and conservation during the month of February—which is one of the rainiest and least appealing months for trekking to Machu Picchu anyway. For the most popular months (May–Sept), early booking (at least 3 months in advance) is essential.

The Peruvian government has sought to limit the number of trekkers on the Inca Trail (now capped at 200 trekkers and 300 trek staff, or 500 total per day), but also to maximize revenue from one of its foremost attractions. Thus, the cost of hiking the trail has steadily climbed—it now costs at least three times what it did just a few years ago. Standard-class 4-day treks, the most common and economical service, start at around $500 per person, including entrance fees ($93 adults, $47 students) and return by tourist rail. Independent trekkers generally join a mixed group of travelers;

ON THE TRAIL OF "NEW" INCA CITIES: THE discovery CONTINUES

Ever since the demise of the Inca Empire, rumors, clues, and fabulous tales of a fabled lost Inca city stuffed with gold and silver have rippled across Peru. The tales prompted searches, discoveries, and, often, reevaluations. Machu Picchu wasn't the lost and last city Hiram Bingham thought it was—Vilcabamba the Old was the last refuge of the Incas. The search continues, though, and incredibly, new discoveries continue to occur in the Andes. First, it was Choquequirao in the early 1990s. More recently, other teams have announced the discoveries of other lost Inca cities.

The discovery of **Qorihuayrachina** (also called **Cerro Victoria,** the name of the peak it rests on), 35km (22 miles) southwest of Machu Picchu in the Andes, was announced by the National Geographic Society in March 2002. Led by Peter Frost, a group of explorers uncovered the ruins of a large settlement that might have been occupied by the Incas long before they'd built a continent-spanning empire. Among the ruins are tombs and platforms, suggestive of an important burial site and sacred rites, although there are also indications that the site was an entire city. The ruins cover 6 sq. km (2⅓ sq. miles) and occupy a spectacular mountaintop location with panoramic views of the Vilcabamba range's snowcapped peaks, which were considered sacred by the Incas. Archaeologists, claiming that Qorihuayrachina is one of the most important sites found in the Vilcabamba region since it was abandoned by the Incas nearly 500 years ago, have high hopes that the ruins will help them piece together the Inca Empire from beginning to end.

Frost claimed the site was the largest of its kind found since 1964. Comprising 100 structures, including circular homes, storehouses, cemeteries, funeral towers, roadways, waterworks, farming terraces, a dam, and a pyramid, the city might have been occupied by the Incas who fled Cusco after the Spanish conquest. The ruins are secluded in cloud forest in the remote Vilcabamba region.

Just months after the discovery of Qorihuayrachina in 2002, the British Royal Geographic Society, led by Hugh Thompson and Gary Ziegler, announced the finding of a major new Inca site, **Cota Coca,** only a few kilometers away but across a deep canyon from Choquequirao (a road might have connected the two). Wholly unknown to the outside world until its discovery, Cota Coca—97km (60 miles) west of Cusco—appears to have been an administrative and storage center.

Llaqtapata, rediscovered by a U.S. and British team using remote (aerial) infrared technology and reported in November 2003, is the most recent Inca city to (re)surface. Just 3km (1¾ miles) from Machu Picchu, it, too, had been visited by Bingham and several explorers in the 1980s, so it's open to interpretation how new its "discovery" in fact is.

How long these discoveries might go on is anyone's guess. According to Hugh Thomson, "The physical geography of southeast Peru is so wild, with its deep canyons and dense vegetation, that it is possible that there are even more ruins waiting to be discovered. The fact that we have found two in 2 years means there could be many more out there."

groups tend to be between 12 and 16 people, with guaranteed daily departures. The cost includes a bus to Km 88 to begin the trek, an English-speaking guide, tents, mattresses, three daily meals, and porters who carry all common equipment. Tips for porters or guides are extra (and considered mandatory). Personal porters, to carry your personal items, can be hired for about $150 for the 4 days. Premium-class services generally operate smaller group sizes (a maximum of 10 trekkers), and you generally get an upgrade on the return train. Prices for premium group treks, organized for small private groups, range from $750 to as high as $1,500 per person. Note that entrance fees to the Inca Trail and Machu Picchu should always be included in your package price.

Prices vary for trail packages based on services and the quality and experience of the agency. For the most part, you get what you pay for. Rock-bottom prices (anything below $500, generally) will probably get you an inexperienced guide who speaks little English, food that is barely edible, camping equipment on its last legs, and a large, rowdy group (usually 16 young trekkers). Especially important is the ability of an agency to guarantee departure even if its desired target number of travelers is not filled. Students with ISIC identification can expect about a $40 discount.

Be wary of hidden costs; never purchase Inca Trail (or, for that matter, any tour) packages from anyone other than officially licensed agencies; and be careful to make payments (and get official receipts) at the physical offices of the agencies. If you have questions about whether an agency is legitimate or is authorized to sell Inca Trail packages, ask for assistance at the main tourism information office in Cusco.

To guarantee a spot with an agency (which must request a trek permit for each trekker) it is imperative that you make a reservation and pay for your entrance fee a minimum of 15 days in advance (though in practice you'd be wise to do this at least 4–6 months or more in advance if you plan to go during peak months of May–Oct). Reservations can be made as much as a year in advance. Gone are the days when trekkers could simply show up in Cusco and organize a trek on the fly. Changing dates once you have a reservation is difficult, if not impossible. If spots remain on agency rosters, they are offered on a first-come, first-served basis.

The entrance ticket for the 2-day Camino Sagrado, purchased in Cusco, is $51 for adults and $44 for students. Basic pooled service (maximum 16 trekkers) costs about $200 to $250 per person (including the entrance fee). There are no premium-class services for the 2-day trek.

A good independent website with current information on the Inca Trail (and alternative trails arriving at Machu Picchu) is: www.andeantravelweb.com/peru/treks/incatrail4.html.

Inca Trail Agencies

Only officially sanctioned travel agencies are permitted to organize group treks along the Inca Trail; an overwhelming number, nearly 180 tour operators (!)—both Peruvian and international—have been granted government licenses to sell and operate Inca Trail treks. With the higher-end agencies, it is usually possible to assemble your own

Howling at the Moon

For a truly spectacular experience on the Inca Trail, plan your trip to coincide with a full moon (ideally, departing 2 or 3 days beforehand). Locals say the weather's best then, and having your nights illuminated by a full or near-full moon, especially for the early rise and push into Machu Picchu on the last day, is unforgettable.

private group, with as few as two hikers. Budget trekkers will join an established group. In addition to cost, hikers should ask about group size (12 or fewer is best; 16 is the most allowed), the quality of the guides and their English-speaking abilities, the quality of food preparation, and porters and equipment. You should also make certain that the agency guarantees daily departures so that you're not stuck waiting in Cusco for a group to be assembled.

Recommended agencies that score high on those criteria follow. (Note that the phone numbers below change frequently; the websites are more reliable sources of info.) Some of the larger international adventure-tour operators, including several listed in chapter 4, "The Best Special Interest Trips," also handle the Inca Trail and alternative treks in Cusco and the Sacred Valley.

- **Andean Life** (www.andeanlifeperu.com; ℂ **084/221-491**): A reputable mid-range company offering both pooled basic and premium private treks with good guides.

- **Andean Treks ★★** (www.andeantreks.com; ℂ **800/683-8148** in the U.S. and Canada, or **617/924-1974**): A long-time (since 1980), well-thought-of outdoors operator based in Watertown, Massachusetts, running 5-day treks along the Inca Trail as well as numerous other programs in Latin America.

- **Andina Travel ★** (www.andinatravel.com; ℂ **910/805-7139** in the U.S. or **084/251-892** in Cusco): A progressive company interested in sustainable development, owned by a Cusco native and his North American business partner, offering classic Inca Trail and alternative treks.

- **Big Foot Cusco** (www.bigfootcusco.com; ℂ **084/233-836**): A popular and dependable budget agency.

- **Chaska Tours ★** (www.chaskatours.com; ℂ **084/240-424**): A very capable midrange company, run by a Dutch and Peruvian team, praised for its private and group treks to Machu Picchu as well as Choquequirao.

- **Enigma Adventure Tours ★** (www.enigmaperu.com; ℂ **084/222-155**): A relatively new adventure travel operator with a good reputation and specialized and alternative hiking and trekking options, good for small-group and private treks.

- **Explorandes ★★** (www.explorandes.com; ℂ **01/715-2323** or **084/238-380** in Cusco): One of the top high-end agencies and among the most experienced in treks and mountaineering across Peru. Especially good for forming very small private groups.

- **Inca Explorers ★★** (www.incaexplorers.com; ℂ **084/241-070**): One of the best midrange agencies offering well-planned and comfortable Inca Trail treks. Porters carry hikers' packs, and groups are small (including private group treks).

- **Mayuc ★** (www.mayuc.com; ℂ **855/819-5899** in the U.S. and Canada or **084/242-824** in Cusco): Especially good for pampered Inca Trail expeditions (porters carry all packs). It aims to be low impact, and hosts smaller groups.

- **Q'Ente ★★** (www.qente.com; ℂ **084/222-535**): Receives high marks from budget travelers. It's very competitively priced, with responsible, good guides, and also offers a premium trek with a maximum of eight trekkers.

- **SAS Travel ★** (www.sastravelperu.com; ℂ **084/249-194**): Large, long-established agency serving budget-oriented trekkers. Very popular, responsible, and well organized.

- **United Mice ★** (www.unitedmice.com; ℂ **084/221-139**): Started by one of the trail's most respected guides, this is another of the top trekking specialists organizing affordable midrange treks.

INCA trail REGULATIONS

For decades, individuals trekked the Inca Trail on their own, but hundreds of thousands of visitors—more than 75,000 a year—left behind so much detritus that not only was the experience compromised for most future trekkers, but the very environment was also placed at risk. The entire zone has suffered grave deforestation and erosion. The Peruvian government, under pressure from international organizations, has finally instituted changes and restrictions designed to lessen the human impact on the trail and on Machu Picchu itself: In the first couple of years, regulations were poorly enforced, but in 2003, the government announced its intentions to fully and strictly enforce them.

All trekkers are now required to go accompanied by a guide and a group. In addition, the overall number of trekkers permitted on the trail was significantly reduced, to 200 per day (with an additional 300 trek staff, for a total daily number admitted of 500); the maximum number of trekkers per group outing is capped at 16; only professionally qualified and licensed guides are allowed to lead groups on the Inca Trail; the maximum loads porters can carry has been limited to 20 kilograms (44 lb.); and all companies must pay porters the minimum wage (about $15 per day).

These changes have cut the number of trekkers on the trail in half and have made reservations essential. Guarantee your space on the trail by making a reservation at least 15 days in advance of your trip (but 4–6 months or more in advance for high season May–Oct; reservations can be made as much as a year in advance). Travelers willing to wing it stand an outside chance of still finding available spots a week or a few days before embarking on the trail, perhaps even at discounted rates, but waiting until you arrive in Cusco is a ridiculous risk if you're really counting on doing the Inca Trail.

The key changes for travelers are that it is no longer possible to go on the trail independently and no longer dirt-cheap to walk 4 days to Machu Picchu. The good news is that the trail is more organized and that hope for its preservation is greater. But if you're looking for solitude and a more spiritual experience, you might consider one of the "alternative ruins treks"; see the sidebar on p. 256 for more details.

9

MACHU PICCHU & THE SACRED VALLEY

Machu Picchu & the Inca Trail

Day-by-Day: The Classic Inca Trail Trek

The following is typical of the group-organized 4-day/3-night schedule along the Inca Trail.

DAY 1 Trekkers arrive from Cusco, either by train, getting off at the midway stop, Ollantaytambo, or Km 88; or by bus, at Km 82, the preferred method of transport for many groups. (Starting at Km 82 doesn't add an appreciable distance to the trail.) After crossing the Río Urubamba (Vilcanota), the first gentle ascent of the trail looms to Inca ruins at **Llaqtapata** (also called **Patallacta,** where Bingham and his team first camped on the way to Machu Picchu). The path then crosses the Río Cusicacha, tracing the line of the river until it begins to climb and reaches the small village (the only one still inhabited along the trail) of **Huayllabamba**—a 2- to 3-hour climb. Most groups spend their first night at campsites here. Total distance: 10 to 11km (6¼–6¾ miles).

DAY 2 Day 2 is the hardest of the trek. The next ruins are at **Llullucharoc** (3,800m/12,460 ft.), about an hour's steep climb from Huayllabamba. **Llulluchapampa,** an isolated village that lies in a flat meadow, is a strenuous 90-minute to 2-hour climb through cloud forest. There are extraordinary valley views from here. Next up is the dreaded Abra de Huarmihuañusqa, or **Dead Woman's Pass,** the highest point on the trail and infamous among veterans of the Inca Trail. (The origin of the name—or who the poor victim was—is anybody's guess.) The air is thin, and the 4,200m (13,780-ft.) pass is a killer for most: a punishing 2½-hour climb in the hot sun, which is replaced by cold winds at the top. It's not uncommon for freezing rain or even snow to meet trekkers atop the pass. After a deserved rest at the summit, the path descends sharply on complicated stone steps to **Pacamayo** (3,600m/11,810 ft.), where groups camp for the night. Total distance: 11km (6¾ miles).

 # SOME alternatives TO THE INCA TRAIL

The legendary Inca Trail was once very much off the beaten path and at the cutting edge of adventure travel—for hardcore trekkers only. Although the Peruvian government adopted new measures to restrict the numbers of trekkers along the trail, it has become so popular and well-worn that in high season it's tough to find the solitude and quiet contemplation such a sacred path deserves. Trekkers and travelers looking for more privacy, greater authenticity, or bragging rights are seeking out alternatives, and many adventure-travel companies are catering to them by offering less accessible trails to keep one step ahead of the masses. Several international operators now offer custom-designed alternatives to the traditional Inca Trail, and many Peru cognoscenti believe this is the future of trekking in Cusco and the Sacred Valley. Some of the challenging treks terminate in visits to Machu Picchu, while others explore stunning but much less-visited Inca ruins like Choquequirao. **Adventure Life** ★ (www.adventurelife. com; ✆ 800/344-6118) promotes a 10-day Cachiccata trek and 11-day Ausangate trip Alternative; **Andean Treks** ★★ (www.andeantreks.com;

✆ 800/683-8148) offers a 4-day "Moonstone to Sun Temple" trek, as well as others to Choquequirao and Ausangate; **Mountain Travel Sobek** ★★ (www. mtsobek.com; ✆ 888/831-7526) offers a 12-day (7 days hiking) "Other Inca Trail"; **Peru for Less** ★★ (www.peruforless. com; ✆ 877/2609-0309), originally based in the U.S., recently launched a series of small-group, alternative treks in the Vilcabamba region, with trips to Choquequirao, Ausangate, and Espíritu Pampa; and **Wilderness Travel** ★★ (www.wildernesstravel.com; ✆ 800/368-2794) has a 17-day (13 days hiking) "Choquequirao to Machu Picchu Hidden Inca Trail" tour. Most treks range from about $600 to $4,000 per person.

The trend toward luxury, or soft, adventure has gained traction in the Peruvian Andes, and companies offering treks to Machu Picchu and other highland destinations are targeting more affluent and creature comfort-oriented travelers who want the adventure experience without roughing it too much. **Mountain Lodges of Peru** ★★★ (www.mountainlodgesofperu.com; ✆ 01/421-6952 or 877/491-5261 in the U.S. and Canada), a Peruvian adventure

DAY 3   By the third day, most of the remaining footpath is the original work of the Incas. (In previous sections, the government "restored" the stonework with a heavy hand.) En route to the next mountain pass (1 hr.), trekkers encounter the ruins of **Runcuracay.** The circular structure (the name means "basket shaped") is unique among those found along the trail. From here, a steep 45-minute to 1-hour climb leads to the second pass, **Abra de Runcuracay** (3,900m/12,790 ft.), and the location of an official campsite just over the summit. There are great views of the Vilcabamba mountain range. After passing through a naturally formed tunnel, the path leads past a lake and a stunning staircase to **Sayacmarca** (3,500m/11,480 ft.), named for its nearly inaccessible setting surrounded by dizzying cliffs. Among the ruins are ritual baths and a terrace viewpoint overlooking the Aobamba Valley, suggesting that the site was not inhabited but instead served as a resting point for travelers and as a control station.

travel company, has constructed four lodges on private lands in the Vilcabamba mountain range west of the Sacred Valley. The inns are stunning, not only for their high-altitude locations but also their sophisticated architecture and amenities—which include whirlpools, hot showers, fireplaces, and sleek dining rooms. Mountain Lodges offers its own 7-day treks (beginning at $2,390 per person), culminating in a visit to Machu Picchu, but the company has also contracted with international trekking and adventure companies, including **Backroads** (www.backroads.com; ☏ 800/462-2848), **Wilderness Travel,** and **Mountain Travel Sobek** (see p. 51), which have booked the lodges for their own 9-day (5 days trekking) "Machu Picchu Lodge to Lodge" or "Inn to Inn" packages. Prices for full trips, including stays in Cusco, run to $4,995 per person. **Andean Lodges ★** (www.andeanlodges. com; ☏ 305/434-7167 in the U.S. and Canada, or 084/224-613), a rare joint initiative between the Cusco tour group Auqui Mountain Spirit and local Quechua shepherding communities, operates four simple and ecofriendly mountain lodges, which it claims are the highest altitude

lodges in the world (at 4,000–4,500m/13,000–15,000 ft.), along the Camino del Apu Ausangate (in the Vilcanota range). Trek prices start at $845 per person.

If the notion of soft or luxury adventure travel doesn't excite your inner hard-core adventurer, consider one of the spectacularly scenic (and arduous 4- to 11-day) treks that have gained wider traction in the last few years: **Salcantay, Vilcabamba, Espíritu Pampa,** and **Choquequirao,** the last two "lost" Inca cities only truly unearthed in the past decade. All are increasingly offered by local trek tour agencies in Cusco and some of the most established international trekking and Peruvian travel companies (see above). Much as I hate to disparage the legendary Camino Inca, it has become too popular and laden with restrictions and hassles for many adventure travelers to enjoy it the way it was intended. By going off the standard trekking grid, not only can you be sure that when you get back to Cusco not everyone in the coffeehouse will have the same bragging rights, you are likely to have a more authentic, peaceful, and exhilarating outdoors and cultural experience.

The trail backtracks a bit on the way to **Conchamarca,** another rest stop. Here, the well-preserved Inca footpath drops into jungle thick with exotic vegetation, such as lichens, hanging moss, bromeliads, and orchids, and some of the zone's unique bird species. After passing through another Inca tunnel, the path climbs gently for 2 hours along a stone road, toward the trail's third major pass, **Phuyupatamarca** (3,800m/12,460 ft.); the final climb is considerably easier than the two that came before it. This is a spectacular section of the trail, with great views of the Urubamba Valley. Some of the region's highest snowcapped peaks (all over 5,500m/18,040 ft.), including Salcantay, are clearly visible, and the end of the trail is in sight. The tourist town of Aguas Calientes lies below, and trekkers can see the backside of Machu Picchu (the peak, not the ruins).

From the peak, trekkers reach the beautiful, restored Inca **ruins of Phuyupatamarca.** The ancient village is another one aptly named: It translates as "Town above the clouds." The remains of six ceremonial baths are clearly visible, as are retaining-wall terraces. A stone staircase of 2,250 steps plummets into the cloud forest, taking about 90 minutes to descend. The path forks, with the footpath on the left leading to the fan-shaped **Intipata terraces.** On the right, the trail pushes on to the extraordinary ruins of **Huiñay Huayna ★★,** which are actually about a 10-minute walk from the trail. Back at the main footpath, there's a campsite and ramshackle trekkers' hostel offering hot showers, food, and drink. The grounds are a major gathering place for trekkers before the final push to Machu Picchu, and for some, they're a bit too boisterous and unkempt, an unpleasant intrusion after all the pristine beauty up to this point on the trail. Although closest to Machu Picchu, the Huiñay Huayna ruins, nearly the equal of Machu Picchu, were only discovered in 1941. Their name, which means "Forever Young," refers not to their relatively recent discovery, but to the perpetually flowering orchid of the same name that is found in abundance nearby. The stop was evidently an important one along the trail; on the slopes around the site are dozens of stone agricultural terraces, and 10 ritual baths, which still have running water, awaited travelers. Total distance: 15km (9⅓ miles).

DAY 4 From Huiñay Huayna, trekkers have but one goal remaining: reaching Intipunku (the Sun Gate) and descending to Machu Picchu, preferably in time to witness the dramatic sunrise over the ruins. Most groups depart camp at 4am or earlier to reach the pass at Machu Picchu and arrive in time for daybreak, around 6:30am. Awaiting them first, though, is a good 60- to 90-minute trek along narrow Inca stone paths, and then a final killer: a 50-step, nearly vertical climb. The descent from Intipunku to Machu Picchu takes about 45 minutes.

Having reached the ruins, trekkers have to exit the site and deposit their backpacks at the entrance gate near the hotel. There, they also get their entrance passes to Machu Picchu stamped; the pass is good for 1 day only. Total distance: 7km (4⅓ miles).

About Tipping

At the end of the Inca Trail, guides, cooks, and especially porters expect—and fully deserve—to be tipped for their services. They get comparatively little of the sum hikers pay to form part of the group, and they depend on tips for most of their salary, much like wait staff in American restaurants. Tip to the extent that you are able (for guides and porters that should probably be about $5–$10 per day, in *soles*). Tipping a relatively huge amount relative to what they earn—I've heard stories of trekkers tipping a couple of hundred dollars—is going way overboard.

AGUAS CALIENTES (MACHU PICCHU PUEBLO)

Renamed Machu Picchu Pueblo by the Peruvian government—a name adopted by few—Aguas Calientes is quite literally the end of the line. It's a gringo outpost of *mochileros* (backpackers) outfitted in the latest alpaca and indigenous weave fashions: Hats, gloves, sweaters—they are walking (if unshaved) advertisements for Peruvian artisanship. Making it Peru's own little Katmandu, the trekkers hang out for a few days after their great journey to Machu Picchu, sharing beers and tales, and scoring a final woven hat or scarf, or at least celebratory T-shirt, to wear as a trophy back home.

To be honest, there's not much else to do in Aguas Calientes, which might as well be called Aires Calientes, given its sweltering heat and humidity. A purpose-built jumble of cheap construction and a blurry of pizza joints, souvenir stalls, and *hostales,* it's a place I'm sure tourism officials would like a do-over on. But if you squint hard enough, and your legs are tired enough, you might just find a little ramshackle charm in it. The town has a river rushing through its middle and *baños termales,* or outdoor **hot springs**—the source of the town's name—at the far end of Avenida Pachacútec. Many visitors find springs to be hygienically challenged, but they're popular with folks who've completed the Inca Trail and are in desperate need of muscular relaxation (not to mention a bath). The one pool with freezing mountain water can be tremendously restorative if you've just finished a long day at the ruins, but the smell of iron is overpowering. The springs are open from 5am to 9pm; admission is S/10. Just be sure to leave your valuables locked up at the hotel.

Adventurous sorts not yet exhausted from climbing might want to climb the sacred mountain **Putukusi ★★**, which commands extraordinary distant views across the river to the ruins of Machu Picchu. Note: Check with the local tourism office or your hotel to determine if the trail is open and "doable"; massive flooding and mudslides in 2010 wiped out a bunch of the wood steps and ladders to the top, making it all but impossible for anyone but the most adventurous, experienced, and athletic trekkers (rope pulls have replaced the ladders). If the trail is repaired, look for the trailhead on the right side of the railroad just out of town. (A signpost reads KM 111.) Veer to the right up stone steps until you reach a clearing and series of stone-carved switchbacks. At the summit, the view of Machu Picchu, nestled like an architectural model between its two famous peaks, is incredible. In good condition, the trek up takes about 75 minutes; the descent takes 45 minutes.

Another good trail, particularly for bird-watchers, is the short trail to **Mandor Ravine** and a waterfall found there. From the railroad tracks, walk downstream (beyond the old train station) until you come to the ravine (about 3km/1¾ miles). A short climb takes you to the waterfall.

Where to Eat

Scores of small and friendly restaurants line the two main drags (okay, the only two real streets) in Aguas Calientes, Avenida Imperio de los Incas and Avenida Pachacútec. There's a proliferation of cheap pizzeria pit stops hugging the railroad tracks; if you're looking for an easy meal of wood-fired pizza, almost any spot in town can accommodate you. Menu hawkers, often the children of the cook or owner, will try to lure you in with very cheap menu deals.

For lunch during visits to the ruins, you have two choices: the expensive buffet lunch at Machu Picchu Sanctuary Lodge or a sack lunch. I recommend the latter,

Mudslides at Machu Picchu

The most recent mudslide at Machu Picchu occurred in January 2010, when five people (including two on the Inca trail) were killed and 2,000 tourists stranded, requiring airlift evacuations by helicopter. Officials said the rains that swelled the Urubamba River were the heaviest in 15 years, and floods affected 80,000 people living in or near Aguas Calientes, leaving many homeless. Train service to Machu Picchu was not restored for more than a month. It was the latest in a series of catastrophic rain-related events near the ancient ruins. In October 2005, an avalanche destroyed part of the train track leading from Cusco to Machu Picchu, stranding 1,400 travelers, and before that, in April 2004, two massive mudslides at the tail end of the rainy season hit Aguas Calientes, killing six local people and stranding as many as 1,500 tourists for the duration of Easter weekend.

Such destructive rains may not be the norm, but they highlight both the dangers of traveling in the highlands during the wet season as well as the precarious infrastructure of Aguas Calientes and its ill-preparedness to handle the explosive growth of tourism in recent years.

especially because lunchtime is when lots of tourists vacate the ruins (pick one up at Rupa Wasi, Gringo Bill's, or assemble one from the breakfast buffet of your hotel). Note that you cannot enter Machu Picchu with disposable plastic water bottles.

Chez Maggy 🔴 PERUVIAN/PIZZA   On the right side of restaurant row, as you walk toward the hot springs, this long-time favorite and branch of the legendary Chez Maggy in Cusco is a good, relaxed place for wood-fired pizzas, pisco sours, and cold beers. You can also get a whole range of Peruvian *comida típica* and Mexican dishes, but everyone I've seen here is always gorging on pizza or pasta.

Av. Pachacútec 156. 🕾 **084/211-006.** Reservations not accepted. Main courses S/18–S/36. MC, V. Daily 10am–10pm.

Indio Feliz ★★ 🔴 PERUVIAN/FRENCH   A restaurant named "The Happy Indian" might not sound too PC, especially for a place that sits at the foot of a city abandoned by the Incas sometime before the Spanish invaded, but this is one of Aguas Calientes's best restaurants. A folksy two-level place chock full of carvings, antiques, and paintings, it's usually jampacked with gringos. Starters include quiche Lorraine and *sopa a la criolla* (Peruvian milk-based soup); the standout among main courses is the lemon or garlic trout. The ginger chicken is also quite nice, as are the desserts.

Lloque Yupanqui 103 (down an alley to the left off Av. Pachacútec). www.indiofeliz.com. 🕾 **084/211-090.** Reservations recommended in high season. Main courses S/26–S/44. MC, V. Daily noon–midnight.

La Cafeteria (El MaPi) ★ PERUVIAN/BUFFET   The hip and mod restaurant of the equally cool hotel of the same name, this is a good spot with a decent-value buffet lunch and tasty a la carte items like empanadas, organic salads, pastas, panini, and Peruvian standards (*lomo saltado,* grilled trout). It has a lot of style—cement floors, contemporary white plastic chairs, a menu that takes the form of a local newspaper—for this ramshackle, one-horse town.

Av. Pachacútec 109. www.elmapihotel.com/la_cafeteria.php. 🕾 **084/211-011.** Reservations not accepted. Main courses S/18–S/38. MC, V. Daily 7am–11pm.

Aguas Calientes (Machu Picchu Pueblo)

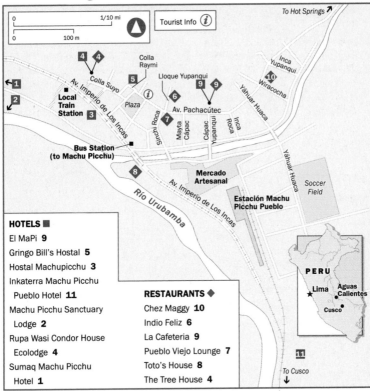

HOTELS ■
El MaPi **9**
Gringo Bill's Hostal **5**
Hostal Machupicchu **3**
Inkaterra Machu Picchu
  Pueblo Hotel **11**
Machu Picchu Sanctuary
  Lodge **2**
Rupa Wasi Condor House
  Ecolodge **4**
Sumaq Machu Picchu
  Hotel **1**

RESTAURANTS ◆
Chez Maggy **10**
Indio Feliz **6**
La Cafeteria **9**
Pueblo Viejo Lounge **7**
Toto's House **8**
The Tree House **4**

Pueblo Viejo Lounge ★ PERUVIAN   One of the more animated spots on restaurant row (right at the beginning, off the plaza), the airy Pueblo Viejo has a pretty hip vibe, with a pitched ceiling, terrace seating, DJs, and a roaring fire. It specializes in *parrilladas*, or grilled lamb, pork, and alpaca, and grilled trout. Choose from vegetarian, *menú de la casa*, and *menú turístico* menus. You can also get good wood-fired pizza.

Av. Pachacútec 108. *✆* **084/211-193.** Reservations not accepted. Main courses S/24–S/39. MC, V. Daily noon–midnight.

The Tree House ★★ 🍴 NOVO ANDINO   The in-house restaurant of the Rupa Wasi ecolodge (see below) is a cut above other restaurants in Aguas Calientes. Indeed reminiscent of a tree house, up an imposing flight of stairs, it has a cozy, rustic charm, with a fireplace and indigenous wood paneling on the ceilings and walls. The chef prepares creative Novo Andino dishes, using local ingredients from the inn's garden. For a treat, opt for one of the tasting menus (6, 8, or 10 courses), or try the quinotto (red-quinoa risotto), alpaca filet mignon, or spinach, ricotta, and quinoa raviolis. If you're a passion-fruit freak like me, save room for the maracuyá pie. While it's easily one of the best options in town, it's also a bit pricey for Aguas Calientes (although the

$35, three-course meal with a glass of wine is a decent deal). The chef does well-regarded cooking lessons ($35).

Jr. Huanacaure Mz. 6, Lt. 26. www.rupawasi.treehouse.net. ℂ **084/211-101.** Reservations recommended. Main courses S/35–S/49. AE, MC, V. Daily noon–midnight.

Toto's House PERUVIAN/PIZZA This large, touristy restaurant, perched between the railroad tracks and the banks of the Río Vilcanota, is one of the nicer spots in town. It features an open area overlooking the river with refreshing mountain views. The dining room is dominated by a barbecue pit and, most days, it features live Andean music. The menu is extensive and varied, ranging from a mixed grill and trout to the standby of all restaurants in town, pizza. The lunch buffet is a good deal and popular with folks waiting for the train back to Cusco.

Av. Imperio de los Incas s/n. ℂ **084/211-020.** Reservations not accepted. Main courses S/25–S/40. MC, V. Daily noon–midnight.

Shopping

Shopping may not be very exciting in Aguas Calientes—it's pretty much limited to Machu Picchu souvenirs and touristy alpaca (or would-be alpaca) goods—but it's everywhere. The main **Mercado Artesanal** (*artesanía* and souvenir market) is a jumble of stalls clustered between the Río Aguas Calientes and the train station. You can't miss it. If you're going to pick up a T-shirt, cap, or other memento of your journey to Machu Picchu, this is the place.

Entertainment & Nightlife

Most gringos congregate at innumerable and largely indistinguishable bars along the train tracks. My vote for the best bar in town is **El Bar ★,** Av. Pachacútec 109 (ℂ **084/211-011**), the house watering hole at **El MaPi,** the hipster hotel that took over a former government-run inn. It's a cool lounge with a funky library aesthetic, great mixologists, and a daily happy hour. A good spot for music and drinks is **Blues Bar Café,** Av. Pachacútec s/n (ℂ **084/211-125**), an airy, cabin-like two-level place next to the park on restaurant row. In the late afternoon and early evening, the terrace is a fine place to chill and gaze out at Putukusi, the mountain across from Machu Picchu.

Where to Stay

At the upper end, hotels in and around Machu Picchu Pueblo have suddenly gotten very expensive—more costly than anything comparable in all of Peru. And it's usually only the very fortunate—those who not only plan far ahead, but who also have very healthy bank accounts—who have the option of staying at the one upscale hotel next to the ruins. For the rest of us, below the ruins in Aguas Calientes, there are scores of *hostales* (inns) aimed at the grungy backpacker crowd, a couple of midrange options, and a couple of self-styled ecolodges (one quite upscale, the other more adventurous).

Although a few new hotels have popped up to take advantage of Machu Picchu's ever-expanding popularity, there are growing concerns about the environmental impact of new construction. Indeed, UNESCO, which named the whole Machu Picchu Historical Sanctuary a World Heritage Site, has threatened to withdraw the honor if Peru doesn't address growth and environmental concerns.

VERY EXPENSIVE

Inkaterra Machu Picchu Pueblo Hotel ★★★ ☺ This unique and appealingly rustic, exceedingly private and overall splendid hotel is one of my favorites in

Peru. It's a world removed from the town's unappealing commercial chaos, a place to disconnect and engage with nature. The compound of Spanish colonial, tile-roofed *casitas* (bungalows) and candle- and lantern-lit pathways is surrounded by 5 hectares (12 acres) of cloud forest beside the Vilcanota River, with a tea plantation and more than 100 species of birds, 250 species of butterflies, and 372 species of orchids. Regular rooms are large and comfortable, and junior suites have crackling fireplaces and small terraces. A pretty spring-water pool makes this great place to relax after taking in the grandeur of Machu Picchu. Environmentally conscious and carbon neutral, it's the best retreat for naturalists within the Machu Picchu Historical Sanctuary: The hotel offers orchid tours, bird-watching, and guided ecological hikes (including a visit to rescued, rare spectacled bears).

Av. Imperio de los Incas (Km 10 Línea Férrea Cusco, Quillabamba), Aguas Calientes. www.inkaterra. com/en/machu-picchu. (*C*) **800/442-5042** in the U.S. and Canada or 084/211-122; 01/610-0400 for reservations. Fax 084/211-124. 85 units. $498–$547 double; $598–$1,063 suite. Rates include breakfast buffet, one dinner, and guided excursions within the property. AE, DC, MC, V. **Amenities:** Restaurant; cafe; bar; outdoor pool; room service; spa. *In room:* Wi-Fi (free), fireplaces (some rooms).

Machu Picchu Sanctuary Lodge ★ Once a government-built, temporary hotel in the 1970s, this property, now owned by Orient Express, won a begrudged permanence and today stands as the only major alteration to the ruins' isolated setting. As hotels go, it is pretty sensitively inserted into the hill and is not visible from the ruins themselves. It has been transformed into a very pricey luxury lodge, now with a full meal plan program for guests. As the only hotel perched right next to the ruins, it can pretty much charge what it wants (and does). Rooms are not especially large, but they now have a good deal of Peruvian character, with some lovely modern furnishings, and most have small terraces that open to lovely gardens with impressive views of the ruins and the surrounding Andes. If you can afford it as a special treat, you'd be wise to reserve 3 to 6 months in advance during high season (May–Oct). The buffet lunch ($35) is open to all ruins visitors.

Machu Picchu (next to the ruins). www.machupicchu.orient-express.com. (*C*) **084/984-816-956** or 01/610-8300 for reservations. Fax 084/246-983. 31 units. $979 to $1,400 double; $1,600 and up suite. Rates include three meals daily. AE, DC, MC, V. **Amenities:** Restaurant; cafeteria; snack bar; room service. *In room:* TV, fridge.

Sumaq Machu Picchu Hotel ★ This large, upscale hotel in Aguas Calientes is a sprawling, cantilevered structure—with stonework designed to echo Inca masonry—near the river and a 10-minute walk from the train station. It offers spacious and handsomely appointed, tiled-floor rooms with excellent bedding, soft linens, and Andean motifs in bathrooms and on the headboards. Many rooms have small balconies. Guests who are beat from scaling Machu Picchu will revel in the full-service on-premises spa, where they can pick up a relaxing massage or indulge in the steam sauna. The restaurant terrace, with views of the surrounding mountains, is a good spot to celebrate making it to Machu Picchu.

Av. Hermanos Ayar Mz 1 Lote 3, Aguas Calientes. www.sumaqhotelperu.com. (*C*) **084/211-059** or 01/445-7828 for reservations. Fax 01/211-081. 60 units. $479–$603 double; $587–$932 suite. Rates include breakfast buffet. AE, DC, MC, V. **Amenities:** Restaurant; cafe; bar; room service; spa. *In room:* Fridge.

EXPENSIVE

El MaPi ★★ Filling a couple of niches is this modern and hip midsize hotel (a former government-run *hostal*, now owned and transformed by Inkaterra, a groundbreaking group that operates the Inkaterra Machu Picchu Hotel, the top upscale property in town). The hotel has an ecofriendly, surprisingly urban, and young vibe, though its rates might eliminate many backpackers from staying here. The contemporary, Ikea-like rooms are a bit tight and more functional than the cool public spaces, but the beds are excellent, and there's a small hot springs pond, computer room, sleek restaurant, and happening bar. The hotel is awash in typographics and messages, some of which advertise its commitment to being carbon neutral and exhort guests to live green. Look for the addition of another 20 or so rooms soon.

Av. Pachacútec 109, Aguas Calientes. www.elmapihotel.com. ✆ **084/211-011** or 084/244-598. 48 units. $200–$250 double w/ breakfast. AE, DC, MC, V. **Amenities:** Restaurant; bar; room service. *In room:* TV, fridge.

MODERATE

Gringo Bill's Hostal   A long-time backpackers' institution, Gringo Bill's, established by an American expat, has been around since 1979, steadily making improvements. Tucked into the hillside behind the Plaza de Armas, the plant-filled *hostal* has gone upscale. But it still has a funky vibe, with a lounge bar with a fireplace where travelers hang out watching videos and trippy cosmic murals painted by the Cusco artist Gonzalo Medina. Many of the comfortable rooms have views of cloud forest. Visitors headed to Machu Picchu or out on treks can pick up bagged lunches to go. Although a stay of 2 or 3 nights will earn you a 10% discount, some backpackers still find it comparatively expensive for budget travel.

Colla Raymi 104, Plaza de Armas, Aguas Calientes. www.gringobills.com. ✆/fax **084/211-046,** or 084/241-545 for reservations. Fax 084/211-046. 86 units. $75 double; $105–$135 suite. Rates include continental breakfast. AE, MC, V. **Amenities:** Restaurant; bar; TV room. *In room:* TV in newer rooms, no phone (in older rooms).

Rupa Wasi Condor House Ecolodge ★ 🏠   This cool, tree-house-like lodge isn't for everybody. While it's one of the only good midrange options in Aguas Calientes and uses sustainable materials, alternative energy, and biodegradable products, it's out of the way and up a long flight of about 80 stairs—which, after a visit to Machu Picchu or the Inca Trail, may not be welcome. Built from recycled woods, it's surrounded by dozens of species of orchids and native trees but can be damp. The three cheery upstairs suites with private balconies and great views of the surrounding Andean peaks are vastly superior to the plain downstairs standard rooms. The inn's calling card is its excellent restaurant (The Tree House), which offers terrific cooking classes and boxed lunches.

Jr. Huanacaure 180, Mz. 6, Lt. 26, Aguas Calientes. www.rupawasi.net. ✆ **084/211-101.** 5 units. $41–$83 double; $76–$142 suite. Rates include breakfast. AE, DC, MC, V. **Amenities:** Restaurant.

INEXPENSIVE

Hostal Machupicchu   Across from the police station and, in true frontier fashion, right on the train tracks (a better location than it sounds—a balcony on the other side overlooks the Vilcanota River, and the hostel is perfectly positioned for barhopping), this midsize hotel is one of the better less-expensive options in Aguas Calientes, though that's not saying a whole lot. It has very clean, well-furnished, and airy rooms, some painted in funky colors. Its sister hotel next door, the Presidente, has 28 rooms and is pretty similar but slightly costlier.

Av. Imperio de los Incas s/n, Aguas Calientes. www.hostalmachupicchu.com. ✆ **888/790-5264** in the U.S., 800/7297-2900 in the U.K., or 084/211-065. Fax 084/212-034. 24 units. $55 double. Rates include continental breakfast. MC, V. **Amenities:** Cafe; bar.

SOUTHERN PERU

Southern Peru ranks just behind Cusco and the Sacred Valley in terms of show-stopping travel highlights. The region's natural beauty, from the world's highest navigable body of water to a canyon twice as deep as the Grand Canyon, as well as colonial cities and villages, are major draws. The deep sapphire expanse of Lake Titicaca is one of the world's unique sights, as are the astounding folkloric festivals—eruptions of Amerindian folklore and wildly creative, modern-day partying—Puno has become famous for. And while Puno's not a terribly appealing town, curiously underrated Arequipa, ringed by volcanoes and with a historic quarter carved out of *sillar*, or white volcanic stone, is Peru's most elegant city. Nearby, Colca Valley is home to colonial villages, colorful peoples, and a patchwork of ancient agricultural terraces lining the Río Colca.

HISTORY The region is rich in indigenous cultures that predate not only the Spaniards but Incas. Lake Titicaca is equal parts Aymara and Quechua, expressed most vibrantly in local religious festivals. Manco Cápac, the original Inca chieftain believed to be a direct descendant of the sun, is said to have risen from Titicaca's waters to found the Inca Empire. Arequipa is one of Peru's most complete ensembles of colonial architecture. The Collaguas and Cabanas peoples of the Colca Valley trace their history back 2,000 years, while the agricultural terraces along the Colca River have been farmed for a millennium.

THINGS TO DO The way to experience Lake Titicaca is **by boat,** traveling to the lake's inhabited islands and taking in its serene beauty. Visit **pre-Inca ruins** on the windswept *altiplano*. Stroll **Arequipa's historic quarter,** full of resplendent colonial churches and manor houses, many carved out of local volcanic stone, and get lost behind the thick walls of the **Santa Catalina monastery,** a world unto itself. Arequipa's **Museo Santuarios Andinos** holds an astounding local discovery: a perfectly preserved Inca teenage maiden sacrificed more than 500 years ago.

EATING & DRINKING The biggest culinary draw is **Arequipeña** cooking, one of Peru's greatest and most distinctive regional cuisines, famous for its spicy *ají* peppers. There's plenty of drinking in the region, but it's less an exalted pastime and more a party time; you'll find variety ranging from Puno's **inebriated festivals** to Arequipa's 3-for-1 happy hours at bars across the historic quarter.

NATURE   Southern Peru is dominated by fabled **Lake Titicaca,** South America's largest lake and the world's highest navigable body of water (3,830m/12,566 ft. above sea level); and the volcanoes and canyons near Arequipa. The city is surrounded by towering volcanic peaks, all about 6,000m (20,000 ft.) or higher. Elusive Andean condors, one of the world's great birds, soar directly over the heads of spectators every morning at a spot above **Colca Canyon.**

ACTIVE PURSUITS   The high-altitude altiplano and mountainous desert landscapes are a beacon to outdoors enthusiasts. From **canoeing** and **kayaking** on placid Lake Titicaca and **white-water rafting** on world-class rapids near Arequipa and Colca, to high-altitude **mountain biking** and **climbing** to the summits of volcanoes, the region—Colca especially—has emerged as one of Peru's top outdoors destinations.

THE BEST TRAVEL EXPERIENCES IN SOUTHERN PERU

- **Partying like mad:** Puno is known as the folklore capital of Peru, and its festivals, including Candlemas (La Candelaria) and Puno Week, are spectacular expressions of local culture, with wild masks and fervent dancing, as well as wild orgies of intoxication. See p. 272.

- **Trekking to the top of Suasi:** As the sun begins to lower over the lake, take an easy hike up to this tiny private island's hilltop, where the sunset is a thing of beauty. At 4,000 meters (13,000 ft.) above sea level, the colors are incredible—and there's little doubt why ancient peoples used to stone offerings (*apachetas*) to the gods in places like this. See p. 278.

- **Staying overnight with an Amantaní family:** The floating Uros Islands are touristy, but at the other extreme on Titicaca is the height of authenticity: sleeping at a family's home on rustic Isla Amantaní, where locals craft some of the finest textiles in the Americas. See p. 277.

- **Relishing nightfall at Santa Catalina:** Peru's finest religious monument, this 16th-century convent of cloistered nuns is a mesmerizing ensemble of architecture, and it feels like a small Andalusian village. But at night, with candles and fires burning in the nuns' former cells and an eerie quiet in the complex, a visit is true time travel. See p. 290.

- **Soaking on the banks of the Río Colca:** Chic Colca Lodge has something no other hotel in Colca does: thermal hot springs pools carved out of stone and perched right on the banks of the river running through the canyon. It's the height of rustic luxury. See p. 317.

PUNO & LAKE TITICACA ★★★

388km (241 miles) S of Cusco; 297km (185 miles) NE of Arequipa; 1,011km (628 miles) SE of Lima

Puno is a ramshackle town that draws numbers of visitors wholly disproportionate to its innate attractions. A mostly unlovely city on the altiplano (a high, wind-swept plateau), Puno has one thing going for it that no other place on Earth can claim: It hugs the shores of fabled Lake Titicaca, the world's highest navigable body of water, a sterling expanse of deep blue at 3,830m (12,566 ft.) above sea level. Titicaca is South America's largest lake (8,500 sq. km/3,282 sq mi.) as well as the largest lake in

the world above 2,000m (6,560 ft.). The magnificent lake straddles the border of Peru and Bolivia, and many Andean travelers move on from Puno to La Paz—going around or, in some cases, over Lake Titicaca.

Before leaving Puno, almost everyone hops aboard a boat to visit at least one of several ancient island-dwelling peoples that seem to have materialized straight out of the pages of *National Geographic*. A 2-day tour takes travelers to the Uros Floating Islands—where Indian communities consisting of just a few families construct tiny islands out of totora reeds—and two inhabited natural islands, Amantaní and Taquile. A special bonus, for travelers who have the time and the funds, is a visit to the lake's only private island, Suasi, home to a luxury ecolodge.

Puno has one other thing in its favor. Though dry and often brutally cold, the city is renowned for its spectacular festivals, veritable explosions of *cultura popular*. The unassuming town, where locals are mostly descendants of the Aymara from the south and the Quechua from the north, reigns as the capital of Peruvian folklore. Its traditional fiestas, dances, and music—and consequent street partying—are without argument among the most vibrant and uninhibited in Peru. Among those worth planning a trip around are February's **Festival de la Virgen de la Candelaria**

In Juliaca, Hit the Ground Running

Juliaca, site of the regional airport, is perhaps the most disgraced city in all of Peru. If you are flying into Juliaca on your way to Puno, don't linger. The town is a chaotic and ugly mess of half-finished houses, potholed dirt roads, and trash-strewn streets clogged with sales carts and *ciclotaxis*. If that weren't enough, Juliaca is also reputed to be downright dangerous. The only reason it was awarded an airport is that Puno is boxed in by mountains and local politicians had a stranglehold on Lima's purse strings.

(Candlemas) ★★★ and **Puno Week ★★**, celebrating the birth of the city and the Inca Empire, in early November.

Essentials
GETTING THERE

BY PLANE   Puno proper does not have an airport; the nearest is **Aeropuerto Manco Capac** (✆ 051/322-905) in Juliaca, 45km (28 miles) north of Puno. **LAN** (www.lan.com; ✆ 01/213-8300) flies daily from Lima, Arequipa, and (finally) Cusco to Juliaca; flights start at about $139 one-way from Lima. Tourist buses run from the Juliaca airport to Puno (a 1-hr. trip), depositing travelers on Jirón Tacna for S/15. **Rossy Tours** (✆ 051/366-709) runs inexpensive *combi* taxis to the airport in Juliaca (picking passengers up at their hotels) for S/20 per person.

BY TRAIN   The Titicaca Route journey from Cusco to Puno, along tracks at an altitude of 3,500m (11,500 ft.), is one of the most scenic in Peru. Though it is slower (10 hr. and prone to late arrivals) and has experienced its share of onboard thievery, it is a favorite of travelers in Peru and preferable to the bus if you've got the time and money. Keep a careful eye on your bags and, if possible, lock backpacks to the luggage rack; keep valuables close to your person. PeruRail's **Andean Explorer** trains (www.perurail.com) from Cusco to Puno depart from **Estación Huanchaq** (✆ 084/238-722), at the end of Avenida El Sol. Service to Puno is Monday, Wednesday, and Saturday year-round, departing at 8am and arriving at 5:50pm. The fare is $210 one-way in swank coaches and includes lunch in luxurious dining cars. Tickets can be pre-reserved. The Puno train station (✆ 051/351-041) is at Av. La Torre 224, only a few blocks north of downtown. Inexpensive taxis are widely available; hotels along the banks of Lake Titicaca definitely require a taxi, unless you're staying at Casa Andina Private Collection, which has its own train stop.

Train service from Arequipa to Puno is available by group charter only; see www.perurail.com for details.

BY BUS   Puno has a modern, safe bus station, **Terminal Terrestre** (✆ 051/364-733), Av. Primero de Mayo 703, Barrio Magistral. Road service to Puno from Cusco has been greatly improved in recent years, and many more tourists now travel by bus, which is faster and cheaper than the train. The terrific views during the day are pretty much the same. Most buses drop passengers at Melgar, a few short blocks from downtown.

From Cusco, executive-, imperial-, or royal-class buses make the trip in less than 7 hours (though some services, such as Inka Express, make stop-offs at Inca ruins en route, extending the trip by a couple of hours, highly recommended if you have the extra

Puno

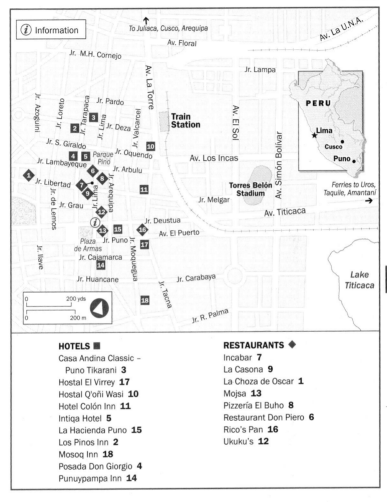

HOTELS ■

Casa Andina Classic –
  Puno Tikarani **3**
Hostal El Virrey **17**
Hostal Q'oñi Wasi **10**
Hotel Colón Inn **11**
Intiqa Hotel **5**
La Hacienda Puno **15**
Los Pinos Inn **2**
Mosoq Inn **18**
Posada Don Giorgio **4**
Punuypampa Inn **14**

RESTAURANTS ◆

Incabar **7**
La Casona **9**
La Choza de Oscar **1**
Mojsa **13**
Pizzería El Buho **8**
Restaurant Don Piero **6**
Rico's Pan **16**
Ukuku's **12**

10

SOUTHERN PERU | Puno & Lake Titicaca

time) and cost about $50. **Cruz del Sur** (www.cruzdelsur.com.pe; ☎ **01/311-5050**); **Imexso** (www.perucuzco.com/imexsotours; ☎ **084/240-801**), and **Inka Express** (www.inkaexpress.com; ☎ **084/247-887**) operate buses with videos and English-speaking tour guides. **Ormeño** (www.grupo-ormeno.com.pe; ☎ **01/472-5000**) has daily direct departures between Cusco and Puno (6 hr.). Regular buses are as cheap as S/30, but they are uncomfortable, have no restrooms or videos, and are potentially dangerous—and not recommended.

The trip between Puno and Arequipa by bus is no longer tortuous; the long-awaited highway between the cities has dramatically shortened travel time from 12 hours to just

5. **Cruz del Sur** (www.cruzdelsur.com.pe; ✆ 01/311-5050) and **Ormeño** (www.grupo-ormeno.com.pe; ✆ 01/472-5000) make the trip for around S/45.

GETTING AROUND

Few visitors spend more than a day or two in Puno (unless lingering at a festival), and the little getting around that needs to be done in town is either on foot or by taxi to your hotel. The small downtown area is pretty easily managed on foot, although several of Puno's nicest hotels lie several kilometers away, on the banks of Lake Titicaca. The port is only about 10 blocks east from the Plaza de Armas in the center of town. The main pedestrian thoroughfare, Jirón Lima, connects the Plaza de Armas to Parque Pino.

Visits to Lake Titicaca and its islands, as well as the ruins on the outskirts of town, are most conveniently done by organized tour.

BY TAXI   Taxis are inexpensive and plentiful, easily hailed on the street, and best used at night and to get back and forth from the hotels on the banks of Lake Titicaca. Most trips in town cost no more than S/3. Taxis can also be hired for round-trips to nearby ruins or for half- or full days. Call **Taxi Milenium** (✆ 051/363-134) or **Taxi Tour Puno** (✆ 051/369-900).

BY FOOT   Puno is small enough to get around almost entirely on foot, unless you're staying at one of the upscale hotels on the shores of Lake Titicaca several kilometers from the center of town.

BY BOAT   You can independently hire boats at Puno harbor to take you out on Lake Titicaca, but it's simpler to sign up for economical organized tours to the islands (see "Organized Tours," later in this section).

VISITOR INFORMATION

An **iPerú tourist information office** is located at the pedestrian-only main drag of Puno, Jr. Lima 549 (✆ 051/365-088; at Jirón Deustua, just off the Plaza de Armas). There you can pick up a map and get a couple of hints on sights in town. However, you're better off going to one of the travel agencies that organizes Lake Titicaca-area trips, such as **All Ways Travel** or **Edgar Adventures** (see "Organized Tours," below), for information on Puno's most important attractions, all of which lie beyond the city.

ORGANIZED TOURS

Most travel agencies in Puno handle the conventional tours of Lake Titicaca and Sillustani, along with a handful of other ruins programs. Two of the best agencies are **All Ways Travel** ★★, Jr. Deustua 576 (in the courtyard of La Casa del Corregidor; www.titicacaperu.com; ✆ 051/353-979), which is run by the friendly and very helpful Victor Pauca and his daughter Eliana, with good guides and progressive cultural trips in addition to the standard tours (including a library bus that takes tourists to rural communities to donate books and toys to children); and **Edgar Adventures,** Jr. Lima 328 (www.edgaradventures.com; ✆ 051/353-444), which is run by a Peruvian husband/wife team. Both agencies can arrange bus and air travel as well, including travel to Bolivia.

Uros Islands half-day trips cost about $12 per person. Uros Islands and Taquile Island full-day trips cost $25 per person. Uros, Taquile, and Amantaní trips, lasting 2 days and 1 night, cost $30 to $35 per person. Sillustani and Chucuito tours, usually 3 hours long, cost $12 per person.

Puno & Lake Titicaca

SOUTHERN PERU

Take It Easy: You're on Top of the World

Puno's extreme elevation of 3,830m (12,566 ft.) is even higher than Cusco, so unless you've already spent time in the Andes, you'll almost certainly need to rest for at least a day to acclimatize. See "Health," in "Fast Facts" in chapter 13, for more information on how to address altitude sickness.

FAST FACTS

You'll find banks and ATMs along Jirón Lima (aka Pasaje Lima), as well as at Hotel Casa Andina, Jr. Independencia 185. Banks include **Banco Continental,** at Jr. Lima 400, and **Banco de Crédito,** on the corner of Jirón Lima and Jirón Grau. Money-changers can generally be found along Jirón Tacna, where most bus stations are located, and at the market near the railway and Avenida de los Incas.

For those crossing into Bolivia, the **Bolivian Consulate** is located at Jr. Arequipa 120 (② **051/351-251**). North Americans, Europeans, New Zealanders, and Australians do not need a visa to enter Bolivia, but the border is a historically problematic one (it was closed in 2005 during the widespread strikes that paralyzed parts of Bolivia), so you might need to check on the status of the crossing before traveling to Bolivia.

In a medical emergency, go to **Clínica Puno,** Jr. Ramón Castilla 178–180 (② **051/368-835**), or **Hospital Nacional,** Av. El Sol 1022 (② **051/369-696**). The **tourist police** are located at Jr. Deustua 538 (② **051/352-720**).

Pretty fast Internet connections are available at **Qoll@internet,** Jr. Oquendo 340 (Parque Pino), where you can make inexpensive international calls; rates are S/2 per hour. A nice, quiet spot for surfing the Internet is behind the cafe at **La Casa del Corregidor,** Jr. Deustua 576 (② **051/351-921**). Other Internet *cabinas* are located along Pasaje Lima. Puno's main **Serpost post office** (② **051/351-141**) is at Moquegua 269. The **Telefónica del Perú** office is on the corner of Moquegua and Arequipa.

Exploring the Area

Most of the year, Puno itself is a rather bleak and unimpressive place if you don't count its enviable geography. The main attractions in Puno are outside the city: the communities of Lake Titicaca and the ancient Sillustani ruins. What there is to see in Puno doesn't delay most visitors for more than a half-day or so. However, if you stumble upon one of Puno's famously colorful festivals, you might want to linger.

Titicaca's Antique British Steamship

Nowadays, fleets of tourist boats set out daily for the floating and natural islands of Lake Titicaca. The oldest ship to ply the world's highest navigable waterway, the **Yavarí,** built in 1862 in Birmingham, England, today sits inactive on the shore of the lake (outside the Sonesta Posada del Inca hotel). The restored steamship, which was originally shipped as a kit to Arica, Chile (and then carried by mule over the course of 6 years to Lake Titicaca), sailed Titicaca for 100 years. It has now been converted into a small museum and bar. The ship is owned by a foundation, Asociación Yavarí. To arrange a free visit with Capt. Carlos Saavedra and his crew, call ② **051/369-329,** visit www.yavari.org, or stop by the ship on most afternoons.

PUNO HIGHLIGHTS

The large **Catedral** (cathedral), on the west side of the Plaza de Armas at the end of Jirón Lima, is the focal point of downtown Puno. The 18th-century baroque church is large, but no great shakes; the elaborate exterior is much more impressive than the spartan, spacious, chilly interior. Also on the main square is the 17th-century **La**

PUNO & lake TITICACA FESTIVALS

Official travel literature rarely tires of labeling Puno the folkloric capital of Peru. Its festivals, celebrated with spectacularly vibrant pre-Columbian dances and costumes, certainly rank among the most spectacular in the country. Festivals in Puno are not just colorful; they're usually wild affairs. (Excessive imbibing seems to be as important a ritual as singing or dancing.) Locals zealously guard their ancestral traditions and cultural expressions, which are known for their unusual variety, singular choreography, and lilting *altiplano* music. The local cultures are responsible for registering more than 360 dances in the National Institute of Culture.

Foremost among local festivals is the **Festival de la Virgen de la Candelaria (Candlemas) ★★★**, held during the first 2 weeks of February. The celebration of Puno's patron saint brings bands and more than 200 groups of dancers from villages and towns all over the region. The festival owes its origins to ancient rituals linked to agricultural cycles and harvests. Festivities blend traits associated with the dominant native local groups: the sobriety of the Quechua people and the *joie de vivre* of the Aymara. The principal Candlemas dance is the *diablada*, or devil dance. Dancers wearing spectacular costumes and grotesque masks play panpipes and make offerings to Pachamama, or "Mother Earth." You'll see terrifying devil masks with twisted horns and angelic, sequined "suits of lights." Official functions are held in the stadium, while more popular exercises are on the streets of Puno. The

more informal events are a real highlight for most observers. Festival dances are divided clearly between two historical epochs: pre-Columbian dances, celebrated on Saturday, and the post-Columbian dances, which take place on Sunday. On Monday is a grand 12-hour Folkloric Parade throughout Puno. Street dancing is observed every day of the week, so even if you miss the first couple of days, you're sure to get a healthy dose of the Virgen de la Candelaria.

Puno Week ★★, celebrated during the first week of November, remembers Manco Cápac, who, according to legend, rose from the waters of Lake Titicaca to found the Inca Empire. A major procession leads from the shores of the lake to the town stadium. Dances and music pervade the city, and things sometimes get pretty wild, with plenty of people staggering and falling down drunk by the end of the evening.

Puno is also well known for its pre-Lenten **Carnaval** celebrations (late Feb to early Mar). Not quite the same as Brazil's hedonistic party, Carnaval here is celebrated with native dances, lots of drinking, and water bombs.

Other lively festivals in and around Puno and Lake Titicaca, worthy of planning your trip around, include **San Juan de Dios** (St. John; Mar 7–8); **Fiesta de las Cruces Alasitas** (May 8); **San Juan, San Pedro, and San Pablo** (St. John, St. Peter, and St. Paul; June 24–29); and **Apóstol Santiago** (St. James; July 25), which is the most enthusiastically celebrated day on Isla Taquile.

To many Peruvians, Lake Titicaca is a mystical and sacred place. Manco Cápac, the original Inca chieftain believed to be a direct descendant of the sun, is said to have risen from the lake's waters along with his sister to found the Inca Empire. The Uros Indians might remain on their floating islands because they believe themselves to be lake people by birth—the very descendants of the royal siblings.

Casa del Corregidor, Jr. Deustua 576 (© **051/351-921**), purportedly Puno's oldest house, with an impressive Spanish balcony; it now houses a very nice "cultural cafe" and is the best spot in town to take a breather. Nearby, the **Museo Municipal Carlos Dryer,** Conde de Lemos 289, is the town's principal (but small) museum. It has a decent selection of pre-Inca ceramics and textiles, as well as mummies with cranial deformations, but the collection is not very well illuminated. The museum is open Monday through Friday from 7:30am to 3:30pm; admission is S/5.

For a superb view of Lake Titicaca and a vantage point that makes Puno look more attractive than it really is, climb the steep hill to **Mirador Kuntur Wasi** and **Huajsapata Park,** about 10 minutes southwest of the main square. On top is a blazing white statue of Manco Cápac, the legendary first Inca and founder of the empire. Back down below, Jirón (Pasaje) Lima is a pedestrianized mall, chock-full of shops, restaurants, and bars, that runs from the Plaza de Armas to pretty **Parque Pino,** a relaxed square populated by locals just hanging out. Puno's seedy **central market** is 2 blocks east of here, and it spills across several streets. While unattractive, it's a realistic look at the underbelly of the Peruvian economy. Beyond the railroad tracks is a *mercado de artesanía* (artisans' market) targeting tourists with all kinds of alpaca and woven woolen goods, often much cheaper those than found in Cusco and other cities. (Try on the sweaters, though; they rarely seem to fit as well as you'd expect.)

LAKE TITICACA ★★

South America's largest lake and the world's highest navigable body of water, Lake Titicaca has long been considered a sacred place among indigenous Andean peoples. The people who live in and around the lake consider themselves descendants of Mama Qota, or Sacred Mother, and they believe that powerful spirits live in the lake's depths. According to Andean legend, Lake Titicaca—which straddles the modern border between Peru and Bolivia—was the birthplace of civilization. Viracocha, the creator deity, lightened a dark world by having the sun, moon, and stars rise from the lake to occupy their places in the sky.

Worthy of such mystical associations, Lake Titicaca is a dazzling sight. Its deep azure waters seemingly extend forever across the altiplano, under the monstrously wide sky. Daybreak and sunset are particularly stunning to witness.

Massive Titicaca has been inhabited for thousands of years. Totora-reed boats roamed the lake as early as 2500 B.C. Titicaca's islands—both man-made and natural—are home to several communities of Quechua and Aymara Indians, groups with remarkably different traditions and ways of life. Visiting them and staying overnight on one of the islands if you can is certainly one of Peru's highlights and one of the most unique experiences in South America.

10

SOUTHERN PERU | Puno & Lake Titicaca

The most convenient way to visit is by an inexpensive and well-run guided tour, arranged by one of several travel agencies in Puno (see "Organized Tours," above). Although it is possible to arrange independent travel, the low cost and easy organization of group travel don't encourage it. Even if you were to go on your own, you'd inevitably fall in with groups, and your experience wouldn't differ radically. You can go on a half-day tour of the Uros Floating Islands or a full-day tour that includes Taquile Island, but the best way to experience Lake Titicaca's unique indigenous life is to stay at least 1 night on either Taquile or Amantaní, preferably in the home of a local family. Those with more time and money to burn may want to explore the singular experience of staying on private **Isla Suasi,** home to little more than a solar-powered hotel and a dozen llamas and vicuñas.

Uros Floating Islands (Las Islas Flotantes) ★
5km (3 miles) N of Puno

As improbable as it sounds, the Uros Indians of Lake Titicaca live on floating "islands" made by hand from totora reeds that grow in abundance in the shallow waters of the lake. This unique practice has endured since the time of the Incas, and today there are some 45 floating islands in the Bay of Puno. The islands first came into contact with the modern world in the mid-1960s, and their inhabitants now live mostly off tourism. To some visitors, this obvious dependency is a little unseemly.

Many visitors faced with this strange sight conclude that the impoverished islanders can't possibly still live on the 40-odd islands, that it must be a show created for their benefit. True, the islands can seem to be little more than floating souvenir stands; the communities idly await the arrival of tourist boats and then seek to sell handmade textiles and reed-crafted items while gringos walk gingerly about the spongy islands—truly an odd sensation—photographing houses and children. Yet the islands and their people are not just a tourist show. Several hundred Titicaca natives continue to live year-round on the islands, even if they venture to Puno for commercial transactions. The largest island, Huacavacani, has not only homes, but also a floating Seventh-day Adventist church, a candidate for one of the most bizarre juxtapositions you're likely to find in Peru—or anywhere. Others have schools, a post office, public telephone, small hotel, and souvenir shops. Only a few islands are actually set up to receive tourists. The vast majority of the Uros people live in continual isolation and peace, away from curious onlookers and camera lenses.

The Uros Indians might remain on their floating islands because they believe themselves to be lake people by birth—the very descendants of the royal siblings. The Uros, who fled to the middle of the lake to escape conflicts with the Collas and Incas, long ago began intermarrying with the Aymara Indians, and many have now converted to Catholicism. Fishers and birders, they live grouped by family sectors, and entire

Lake Titicaca

HOTELS ■
Casa Andina Private
  Collection – Isla Suasi **1**
Casa Andina Private Collection –
  Puno **5**
Kantuta Lodge **2**
Las Cabañas **6**
Puno Hotel Libertador
  Lake Titicaca **3**
Sonesta Posadas del Inca
  Lake Titicaca **4**
Titilaka Lodge **7**

families live in one-room tent-like thatched huts constructed on the shifting reed island that floats beneath. They build modest houses and splendid gondolas with fanciful animal-head bows out of the reeds and must continually replenish the fast-rotting mats that form their fragile islands. Visitors might be surprised, to say the least, to find some huts outfitted with televisions powered by solar panels (which were donated by the Fujimori administration after a presidential visit to the islands). Incredibly, the Fujimori government also built some solar-powered aluminum houses

  Organized Lake Tours

Most travel agencies in Puno handle conventional tours of Lake Titicaca and Sillustani, along with a handful of other ruins programs. The two best are **All Ways Travel** (Jr. Deustua 576, in the courtyard of La Casa del Corregidor; www.titicacaperu.com; ☎ **051/353-979**), with good guides and several well-thought-out, progressive cultural trips; and **Edgar Adventures** (Jr. Lima 328, www.edgaradventures.com; ☎ **051/353-444**).

on several islands, but few, if any, locals actually dwell in them, because they are very hot during the day and brutally cold at night. For a fee, locals will take visitors on short rides from one island to another in the reed boats, but you should consider it a contribution to the community: At S/10 or so a head for a 5-minute jaunt, it's hardly the best deal in Peru, but may be worth it if you're looking for a photo op.

GETTING THERE   Inexpensive tours (normally $12 per person) that go only to the Uros Islands last about 3 hours and include hotel pickup, an English-speaking guide, and motorboat transportation to the islands. Unless you're unusually pressed for time, it's much more enjoyable and informative to visit the Uros as part of a brief stop en route to the natural islands of Amantaní or Taquile. You can go on your own by catching a *lancha* (small boat) at the port. Depending on how many people you or the skipper are able to assemble, the cost will usually be about S/25.

Taquile Island (Isla Taquile) ★★★
35km (22 miles) E of Puno

Life on the natural islands of Lake Titicaca is more authentic feeling and less overtly dependent on tourism than on the man-made Uros islands. Taquile is a fascinating and stunningly beautiful island about 4 hours from Puno. The island is narrow, only a kilometer (½-mile) wide, but about 6km (3¾ miles) long, and it rises to a high point of 264m (866 ft.). The island is a rugged ruddy color, which contrasts spectacularly with the blue lake and sky, and its hillsides are laced with formidable Inca stone agricultural terraces and other Inca and pre-Inca stone ruins.

The island is as serene as the distant lake views. Taquile has been inhabited for 10,000 years, and life remains starkly traditional; there isn't electricity, you won't run into vehicles, and islanders quietly go about their business. Taquile natives, of whom there are still about 3,000 or so, allow tourists to stay at private houses (in primitive but not uncomfortable conditions), and there are a number of simple restaurants serving visitors near the central plaza. Although they're friendly to outsiders, the

⊙ CELEBRATION & quiet ON TAQUILE

If you are lucky enough to catch a festival on the island, you will be treated to a festive and stubbornly traditional pageant of color, marked by picturesque dances and women twirling in circles, revealing as many as 16 layered, multi-colored skirts. (Easter, Fiesta de Santiago on July 25 and Aug 1–2, and New Year's are the best celebrations.) Any time on the island, though, offers unique experiences—especially once the day-trippers have departed and you have the island and incomparable views of the blue waters framed by stone archways virtually to yourself. Taquile then seems about as far away from modernity and "civilization" as one can travel on this planet. At the top of the island on a clear night, under a carpet of blazing stars, Taquile is more magical still.

Access to the island from the boat dock is either by a long path that wends around the island or by an amazing 533-step stone staircase that climbs to the top, passing through two stone arches with astonishing views of the lake. Independent travelers sign in and pay a nominal fee. Those who want to stay the night can arrange to be put up in a family house. If you stay, expect to rough it a bit without proper showers. Many islanders do not speak Spanish, and English is likely to be met with blank stares.

Quechua-speaking islanders remain a famously reserved and insular community. Their dress is equally famous: Taquile textiles are some of the finest in Peru. Men wear embroidered, woven red waistbands (*fajas*) and embroidered wool stocking caps (*chullos*)—so tightly knitted that they can hold water—that indicate marital status: red for married men, red and white for bachelors. Women wear layered skirts and black shawls over their heads. Taquile textiles are much sought after for their hand-woven quality, though they are considerably more expensive than mass-produced handicrafts in other parts of Peru. Along with agriculture, textiles are the island's main source of income. A cooperative shop operates on the main plaza, and laid-back stalls are set up during festivals and the high season of tourist travel (June–Sept). Sadly, a hideously modern municipal building now dominates the main square, looking woe-fully out of place.

Locals are much more resistant to haggling than are artisans in other parts of Peru. (Usually they simply refuse to bargain.) There's very little of the noise and activity that's present at most Peruvian markets. If you go with a group, you're also likely to visit one of the individual communities on the island, and perhaps have a home-cooked meal after a low-key demonstration of their quotidian customs. Buying lunch is one way to contribute money to a community, although many guests also like to tip the head of the community for opening their doors to outsiders.

GETTING THERE   The only feasible way to visit Taquile is as part of an inexpensive and convenient organized tour, which also takes in the Uros Islands ($25 per person). Most single-day tours of the Uros and Taquile islands depart early in the morning and stop at the islands of Uros for a half-hour en route. For most visitors, a day trip, which allows only an hour or two on the island and 8 hours of boat time, is too grueling and insufficient to appreciate the beauty and culture of Taquile Island. A 2- or 3-day visit ($30–$35), with time to spend the night on either Taquile or Amantaní, is preferable.

Amantaní Island (Isla Amantaní) ★★
36km (22 miles) NE of Puno

Amantaní, a circular island located about 4½ hours from Puno (and about 2 hr. from Taquile), is home to a very different, although equally fascinating, Titicaca community. Also handsomely terraced and home to farmers, fishers, and weavers, in many ways Amantaní is even more rustic and unspoiled than Taquile. It is a beautiful but barren and rocky place, with a handful of villages composed of about 800 families and ruins clinging to the island's two peaks, Pachatata (Father Earth) and Pachamama (Mother Earth). The island presents some excellent opportunities for hikes up to these spots, with terrific views of the lake and the sparsely populated island land-scape. The agricultural character of the island is perhaps even more apparent than on Taquile. Long, ancient-looking stone walls mark the fields and terraces of different communities, and cows, sheep, and alpacas graze the hillsides.

The islanders, who, for the most part, understand Spanish, are more open and approachable than natives of Taquile. The highlight of a visit to Amantaní is an overnight stay with a local family. Not only will the family prepare your simple meals, but you will also be invited to a friendly dance in the village meeting place. For the event, most families dress their guests up in local outfits—the women in layered, multicolored, embroidered skirts and blouses, and the men in wool ponchos. Although the evening is obviously staged for tourists' benefit, it is low-key and charming rather than cheesy.

Amantaní islanders also make lovely handwoven textiles, particularly the show-stopping black shawls embroidered with seven colors. The main festival on Amantaní, Fiesta de la Santa Tierra, is on the third Thursday in January, when the population splits in two—half at the Temple of Pachamama and the other half at the Temple of Pachatata (a perfect illustration of their dualistic male/female belief system). Other good festivals are the anniversary of Amantaní (Apr 9, lasting 3 days) and Carnaval (Feb or Mar).

Amantaní is best visited on a tour that allows you to spend the night (visiting the Uros Islands en route) and travel the next day to Taquile. Tour groups place groups of four or five with local families for overnight stays. The tour price normally includes accommodations, lunch, and dinner on the first day and breakfast the following morning.

It's a good idea to bring small gifts for your family on Amantaní because they make little from stays and must alternate with other families on the island. Pens, pencils, and batteries all make good gifts.

If you want to appreciate the utter quiet and remoteness of the island after the day-trippers depart, a nice place to spend the night is **Kantuta Lodge** (www.punored.com/titicaca/amantani/img/lodge.html; ☎ **051/812-664**), an inn run by the family of Segundino Cari near the port of Comunidad Pueblo. Clean and brightly decorated rooms, featuring local textiles, are $20 per person. Meals only are $5.

GETTING THERE   The only feasible way to visit Amantaní is by organized tour. Almost all tours that go to Amantaní also visit the Uros and Taquile islands, stopping en route at Uros and spending the night on Amantaní before visiting Taquile the following day.

Suasi Island (Isla Suasi) ★★★
80km (50 miles) NE of Puno

The only island in private hands on Lake Titicaca, S-shaped Isla Suasi is tiny (just 48 hectares, or 117 acres), isolated, serene, and beautiful. And it makes for a wholly unique getaway, even if it is a long way to go for isolation and relaxation. Though reachable by fast *lancha* (motorized boat) in under 3 hours, most boats take upwards of 5 or 6 to get there (and either way, you'll have to shell out a couple of hundred dollars for the privilege of round-trip transportation). However, once you arrive, you really have traveled far. There are no inhabitants other than the island's owner and part-time resident, the sociologist Martha Giraldo, the few employees of the solar-powered refuge she started (which has since become an upscale ecolodge, administered since 2005 by the Casa Andina hotel chain), and a dozen alpacas and eight free-ranging vicuñas. There are no cars, no TV, and no electricity. If you're lucky, you'll be one of just a handful of guests to enjoy the stunning high-altitude sunsets, gorgeous panoramic views of Titicaca—which extends in all directions like a sterling, placid cobalt sea—and total peace and quiet. The ecofriendly lodge, **Casa Andina Private Collection – Isla Suasi ★★★**, is luxurious but sensitively designed (rooms have great lake views), its restaurant is outstanding, and the personnel friendly. Activities are pretty much limited to reading in hammocks, canoeing around the island (which is small enough that it takes just about an hour to circle), hiking and trying to spot the vicuñas, trekking up to the *cerro* (hilltop) for sunset, and stargazing at night. I can't think of a more peaceful place in all of Peru. Many guests find their sunset visits to the hilltop to be a mystical experience; the sky at 4,000 meters (13,000 ft.) above sea level blazes with unimaginable streaks of violet, red, and gold. At the top of the hill is an *apacheta*, a small tower of stacked, balanced stones,

Fun with Language & Geography

Lake Titicaca, which covers some 8,288 square kilometers (3,200 sq. mi) and is South America's largest lake, is more or less evenly shared by Peru and Bolivia. Yet Peruvians are fond of claiming it is, in fact, more like a 60/40 breakdown, and there are maps that label the lake with "Titi" covering the Peruvian half and "caca" designating the Bolivian half.

echoing an ancient native practice of leaving stones at high elevations (where one is presumably closer to the *apus*, or gods). You can return to Puno either by boat again or by a very scenic but extremely rough ride in a car or van (the first 38km/24 miles are murder, but then it gets worse; asphalt only arrives after 2 hr.). For additional information, including arranging transportation, see www.casa-andina.com, or call *C* **866/220-4434** toll-free in the U.S., **08/082-343-805** in the U.K., or **01/213-9739.** Rates are $199 to $319 per person.

OTHER ATTRACTIONS NEAR PUNO
Sillustani Ruins ★
32km (20 miles) NE of Puno

Just beyond Puno are mysterious pre-Inca ruins called *chullpas* (funeral towers). The finest sit on the windswept altiplano on a peninsula in Lake Umayo at Sillustani. The Colla people—a warrior tribe that spoke Aymara—buried their elite in giant cylindrical tombs, some as tall as 12m (39 ft.). The stonemasonry is exquisite (many archaeologists and historians find them more complex and superior even to Inca engineering), and the structures form quite an impression on such a harsh landscape.

The Collas dominated the Titicaca region before the arrival of the Incas. After burying their dead along with foodstuffs, jewels, and other possessions, they sealed the towers. The high-altitude altiplano has a reputation as one of the windiest and coldest places in Peru, so dress warmly for your visit here.

GETTING THERE By far the best way to visit Sillustani is by guided tour, usually in the afternoon around 2 or 2:30pm (see "Organized Tours," below). Tours are inexpensive ($12–$15) and very convenient. Going on your own generally isn't worth it because the site is a pain to reach and, once there, you've no guide to explain the significance of the ruins. If you insist, though, catch a "Juliaca" *colectivo* from downtown Puno and request to be let off after about 20 minutes, at the fork in the road that leads to Sillustani (DESVIO PARA SILLUSTANI). From that point, it's 15km (9⅓ miles) and a half-hour farther away, but colectivos aren't frequent. To return, you're best off trying to hitch a ride back to Puno.

Chucuito: Fertility Temple
18km (11 miles) S of Puno

On a small promontory on the southern shore of Lake Titicaca, Chucuito, a small Aymara town, is one of the oldest in the altiplano region. The town, capital of the province during colonial times, has a lovely main square and a colonial church, **Nuestra Señora de La Asunción** (built in 1601). Chucuito was also the primary Inca settlement in the region. Another colonial church, **Santo Domino,** is a most curious—though many would say dubious—construction, and the town's main attraction.

Landing on Lampa

The windswept altiplano beyond Puno and Lake Titicaca can be forbidding, but the sweet little, largely unknown colonial town of Lampa ★ is an unexpected gem. With its peaceful town squares, faded pastel-colored houses, and unique 17th-century stone cathedral, it has been bypassed by time and progress. The spectacular **Imaculada Concepción cathedral** is the centerpiece of town; beyond its honey-colored stone exterior and unique roof of green-glazed ceramic tiles, are a labyrinth of catacombs (including tunnels, now sealed, said to stretch all the way to Puno, Arequipa, and even Cusco!) and,

peculiarly, an exact copy of the Vatican's *La Pietá*. Near best-overlooked Juliaca (site of the regional airport but little else; in fact, the seedy place is big into contraband and corruption), Lampa isn't on most tours but is worth a visit for anyone with an extra day or so in the region to see a once-important town seemingly preserved in aspic. Few of the Puno agencies tend to offer organized tours to Juli and Lampa, so taxis or your own private transportation are your best bet. Colectivos travel to Lampa from Av. 2 de Mayo in Juliaca (S/3), but it's a bit of a slog.

Said to date to pre-Columbian times, Inca Uyo is composed of dozens of large, mushroom-shaped phallic stones, most a few feet high, which locals claim were erected as part of fertility rituals. The anatomically correct stones, which until a few years ago were kept in a sterile museum, leave little doubt as to what their creators were getting at. Some point up at the sun god, Inti, while others are inserted into the ground, directed at Pachamama, or Mother Earth. At the center of the ring, lording over the temple, is the king phallus. Local guides tell tales of the exact rituals during which virgins purportedly sat for hours atop the phalluses to increase fertility. The stones might predate the Incas, but some contend that they, or at least the manner in which they are displayed, are fake, a hoax perpetrated by locals to rustle up tourist business. Spanish missionaries did everything in their power to destroy all symbols and structures they considered pagan, and it is highly unlikely that they would have constructed two churches nearby but left this temple intact.

If you find yourself drawn to the stones at Inka Uyo and want to spend the night, the best option in town is **Las Cabañas ★**, a very smart, comfortable and well-priced inn with pretty gardens, an attractive setting by the lake, and a cute restaurant, at Jr. Tarapacá 538 (www.chucuito.com; ℂ/fax **051/368-494**). Rooms (some of which have chimneys) have private bathrooms and run to S/96 for a double, while cool duplex bungalows, which sleep six and have chimneys and balconies, are S/168.

GETTING THERE Acora-bound colectivos leave from Puno's Avenida El Sol. The ride to Chucuito costs S/3 and takes 15 to 20 minutes; tell the driver you want to get off at Chucuito, which lies about halfway between Chimú and Acora.

Where to Eat

Chilly, drab Puno is hardly a place for particularly sophisticated dining. It's better suited for pizzas from wood-fired ovens and simple, straightforward Peruvian cooking. On those scores, it succeeds. Besides, at this altitude, it's not a great idea to overindulge in eating or drinking. Most of Puno's more attractive restaurants, popular with gringos, are located just off the pedestrian-only main drag, Jirón Lima. In addition to those listed below, check out the two restaurants at **Hotel Colón Inn** (p. 286) and, especially for a light and inexpensive lunch, the attractive cafe **Casa del Corregidor,** Jr. Deustua 576 (☏ **051/351-921**), which serves good salads and sandwiches and has a nice, quiet courtyard.

MODERATE

Incabar INTERNATIONAL/PERUVIAN   Stylish and downright funky (as well as relatively expensive) for rough-around-the-edges Puno, this lounge bar/restaurant aims high. The menu is much more creative and flavorful than other places in town (even if dishes don't always succeed), with interesting sauces for lake fish and alpaca steak, curries, and stir fries, and artful presentations. Try the *pescadito crocante*—lake kingfish *(pejerrey)* in quinoa grain. Interesting pastas and big salads, as well as sandwiches and snacks, are served until 5pm, and breakfast is served daily. Incabar is also a good place to hang out, have a beer or coffee, and write postcards—the colorful back room has comfortable sofas.

Jr. Lima 348. ☏ **051/368-031.** Reservations recommended. Main courses S/22–S/35. AE, DC, MC, V. Daily 9am–10pm.

La Casona 🍴 INTERNATIONAL/PERUVIAN   With its traditional, rather old-school Spanish decor, with lace tablecloths, La Casona seems a little stale. Its specialty is Titicaca lake fish, such as trout and kingfish *(pejerrey)*, served La Casona style, which means with a kitchen-sink preparation of rice, avocado, ham, cheese, hot dog, apple salad, french fries, and mushrooms. Chicken and beef are prepared the same way. If that's a little overwhelming for you, go with the simple trout served with mashed potatoes. Service can be awfully slow.

Jr. Lima 517. ☏ **051/351-108.** Reservations recommended. Main courses S/15–S/35. DC, MC, V. Daily 9am–10pm.

La Choza de Oscar PERUVIAN/SHOW   Specializing in nightly Andean folklore shows, this restaurant may seem touristy, but that doesn't mean you can't get a quality meal along with colorful song and dance numbers. The menu runs the gamut from the ubiquitous pastas and pizzas to the house specialty, *pollos a la brasa* (rotisserie chicken) and more exotic fare like alpaca. It's pricier than most restaurants in Puno, but then it's pretty obvious you're paying for the *espectáculo.*

Jr. Libertad 354. www.lachozadeoscar.com. ☏ **051/351-199.** Reservations recommended. Main courses S/24–S/40. MC, V. Daily 11am–10pm.

Mojsa ★★ PERUVIAN/PIZZA   Easily the best option in Puno is this attractive and surprisingly sophisticated second-floor restaurant just off the Plaza de Armas. Using fresh local ingredients, it serves good thin-crust pizza (dinner only), Peruvian specialties like ceviche, trout *causa* (a *Creole* casserole), quinoa tabbouleh, and *rocoto relleno* (spicy stuffed peppers), steaks, and desserts (including lemon pie). Service can be a little haphazard, but that's pretty much true for anywhere in Puno. If you're here during festival time, jockey for a table out on the balcony for great views of the action.

Jr. Lima 635 (2nd floor). www.mojsarestaurant.com. ☏ **051/363-182.** Reservations recommended. Main courses S/15–S/30. AE, DC, MC, V. Daily 11am–11pm.

Restaurant Don Piero INTERNATIONAL/PERUVIAN   A long-time standard of Pasaje Lima, the pedestrian boulevard at the heart of Puno, Don Piero seems pretty stale. It still cranks out the same standard Peruvian and international fare in large portions as it always has, but the nondescript, midrange place doesn't appeal much to backpackers, and more interesting competition has cropped up on the street for more discriminating palates. Outside on slow days, bow-tied waiters looking bored halfheartedly appeal to tourists to enter. The menu has barbecued chicken and a long list of Peruvian favorites such as *palta rellena* (avocado stuffed with chicken salad) and *lomo saltado* (beef strips with french fries, onions, and peppers).

Jr. Lima 348–364. ℭ **051/351-766.** Reservations not accepted. Main courses S/14–S/34. DC, V. Daily 11am–10pm.

Ukuku's PERUVIAN/PIZZA In a second-story space overlooking Jirón Lima, the main drag, this large pizzeria is a relaxed spot that's good looking enough for Puno, with hardwood floors and wood tables and chairs. It focuses on pizzas from a wood-burning oven, but also offers a full menu of Peruvian specialties, such as alpaca steak cooked in red wine, ceviche, and even *chifa* (Peruvian-Chinese cooking). If that's not enough, you can also get a passable plate of pasta. There's a second location at Libertad 216.

Jr. Grau 172 (at Jirón Lima). ℭ **051/367-373.** Reservations not accepted. Main courses S/12–S/27. MC, V. Daily 11am–midnight.

INEXPENSIVE
Pizzería El Buho 🔥 ITALIAN/PIZZA El Buho's wood-burning oven/chimney kicks out some of Puno's best pizzas. It's extremely popular with both gringos and locals. The menu also lists a good number of pastas and a handful of soups, but I swear I've never seen anyone have anything other than pizza.

Jr. Lima 347. ℭ **051/363-955.** Reservations not accepted. Main courses S/10–S/25. DC, V. Daily 4:30–11pm.

Rico's Pan BAKERY/CAFE You know what to expect at a small cafe and bakery with a name like "Tasty Bread," and Rico's Pan doesn't disappoint. Drop by for inexpensive sandwiches, pastries, and cakes. It also serves very good coffees, including espresso and cappuccino, and is a good spot for breakfast or for stockpiling goodies for boat trips on Titicaca. There's now a second, convenient location right on the main drag, Jirón Lima.

Lima 420, Puno. ℭ **051/354-179.** Reservations not accepted. Main courses S/6–S/12. No credit cards. Daily 7am–11pm.

Shopping
Although it has few nice shops on the order of Lima, Cusco, or Arequipa, Puno is one of the better places to load up on inexpensive woolen and alpaca goods, including hats, gloves, scarves, shawls, and blankets. They are cheaper here than in those cities, although you might not encounter the quality found at some upscale shops. The **open-air market** just beyond the railroad tracks (btw. Jirón Melgar and Avenida Titicaca) has a couple of dozen stalls specializing in alpaca and woolen goods. There is a cluster of souvenir and clothing shops along **Jirón Lima,** the pedestrian-only main drag, as well as on Jirón Grau (just off Lima). A place worth seeking out is the nonprofit **Fair Trade Store (La Tienda de Comercio Justo)** ★ in the patio of La Casa del Corregidor, Jr. Deustua 576 (ℭ **051/365-603**). Fifty percent of the purchase price of alpaca and wool scarves, ponchos, and the like here goes directly to the artisans (identified by name on the garments) in rural communities (decidedly

not the case in most transactions). It's open 10am to 6pm daily but does not accept credit cards.

Entertainment & Nightlife

Though the city is the country's capital of folklore, there's not a whole lot happening in Puno after dark. Outside of festivals, nightlife is pretty much confined to a single street, consisting of a handful of bars and discos strung along (or just off) the pedestrian mall, Jirón Lima. My favorite watering hole, just off Jirón Lima, is **Kamizaraky Rock Pub ★**, Pasaje Grau 148 (no phone). A cozy and cool hangout with a loft space, it looks like a graffiti-filled mountain cabin and serves excellent cocktails to a young, gregarious clientele (with occasional live rock music). Along Jirón Lima itself, the jungle lodge and reggae-themed **Positive Vibrations** (no. 378; no phone) is one of the better bets for some decent music and hot drinks. **La Hostería** (no. 501) and **Ekeko's** (no. 355, 2nd Floor; ℰ 051/365-986) often have live bands, and the latter has a large-screen TV showing soccer or videos, and a small dance floor. **Kusillo's Pub,** Libertad 259 (ℰ 051/351-301), has a nightly happy hour and reggae, jazz, and blues, as well as occasional folklore shows. **Shaman,** Jr. Puno 505 (on the Plaza de Armas; no phone), is a second-floor bar that has free Internet access, pizzas, and drinks.

Where to Stay

VERY EXPENSIVE

Titilaka Lodge ★★★ 🛏   Far removed from the unseemly chaos of Puno, on a private peninsula jutting out onto Lake Titicaca, this chic boutique hotel is about as much of a private retreat as you'll find (short of remote Isla Suasi). Easily the most stylish place in the area, it has just 18 starkly modern rooms, all with large windows facing the immense lake ,and is ideal for a tranquil aesthetic experience (which doesn't come cheap). Rooms have heated wooden floors, high-quality bed linens, and deep bathtubs. The hotel is enlivened by folk art and superb lake views at every turn, including 270-degree views of Titicaca in the dining room. Though you'll be tempted just to gaze at the lake, Titilaka caters to active travelers, with guided hiking, mountain biking, and kayak and sailing excursions, and coming soon are a full spa and indoor pool. The hotel is 45 minutes by road from Puno: either out of the way or perfectly out of the way, depending on your perspective.

Chucuito Peninsula, Lake Titicaca (36 km/21 miles from Puno). www.titilaka.com. ℰ **866/628-1777** toll-free in the U.S. or **01/700-5100.** 18 units. $301–$1,070 suite "full board"; $589–$1,450 suite "comprehensive experience" (including pressurized oxygen). Rates include all meals, cocktails, and hotel activities (full board); plus excursions and transfers (comprehensive). AE, DC, MC, V. **Amenities:** Restaurant; bar; concierge. *In room:* A/C, fridge, hair dryer, Wi-Fi (free).

EXPENSIVE

Casa Andina Private Collection–Puno ★★ 🍴   One of the best options on the banks of Lake Titicaca is this low-slung and attractively rustic hotel, which has marvelous lake views from its deck, dining room, and, especially, the single enormous suite. Regular rooms are spacious but not pretentious; they are decorated in a warm, Andean style. About half the rooms have lake views; be sure to ask for one, as it's well worth the small difference in price. While Casa Andina is similar to the nearby Posadas del Inca, it is considerably newer and has a couple of singular amenities, including a pier, with its own floating island a la Uros, extending over the lake, and a private train station—so that if you're coming from Cusco, you can get off right at the hotel without having to go into Puno.

Av. Sesquicentenario 1970–72, Sector Huaje, Lake Titicaca (Puno). www.casa-andina.com. ✆ **866/220-4434** toll-free in the U.S., 08/082-343-805 in the U.K., or 01/213-9739. Fax 051/364-082. 46 units. $159–$199 double; $289 suite (including pressurized oxygen). Rates include breakfast buffet. AE, DC, MC, V. **Amenities:** Restaurant; bar; concierge. *In room:* A/C, TV, fridge, hair dryer, Wi-Fi (free).

Puno Hotel Libertador Lake Titicaca ★

Ensconced in serenity and splendid isolation on the shore of a small island 5km (3 miles) from Puno, overlooking the expanse of Titicaca, this large, stark-white hotel, built in the late 1970s, may stick out on the banks of the lake, but it takes full advantage of its privileged or inconvenient location, depending on your perspective. Part of the luxury Libertador chain, the hotel has rooms that are spacious if a little bland, and about half have panoramic views of the lake. Those views, though, are spectacular. Service is excellent and the large, white-block hotel has soaring ceilings, but it doesn't have as much character as the better-value Sonesta Posadas del Inca (below), which has views that are almost as good. The hotel is linked to the mainland by a causeway, and the only way back and forth to Puno is by taxi (about S/10 each way).

Isla Esteves s/n, Lake Titicaca. www.libertador.com.pe. ✆ **877/778-2281** toll-free in the U.S. and Canada, or 051/367-780. Fax 051/367-879. 123 units. $155–$260 deluxe double; $235–$350 suite. Rates include breakfast buffet. AE, DC, MC, V. **Amenities:** Restaurant; bar; concierge; fitness center; sauna. *In room:* A/C, TV, fridge, hair dryer.

Sonesta Posadas del Inca Lake Titicaca ★ ☺

Like the Libertador, Posada del Inca hugs the shores of Titicaca and boasts splendid views, but it fits more sensitively into its enviable surroundings. The hotel is imaginatively designed, with warm colors and Peruvian touches, including bright modern art and folk artifacts. Rooms are large and comfortable, and bathrooms are also large and nicely equipped. The restaurant and many rooms look over the lake; other rooms have views of the mountains. The relaxed lobby has a cozy fireplace. Service is friendly, and the staff can arrange visits to Titicaca's islands. Children will enjoy the mini version of a floating lake community in the grounds by the lake.

Av. Sesquicentenario 610, Sector Huaje, Lake Titicaca. www.sonesta.com/LakeTiticaca. ✆ **800/SONESTA [766-3782]** in the U.S. and Canada, or 051/364-111. Fax 051/363-672. 62 units. $276 double. Rates include breakfast buffet. Children 8 and under stay free in parents' room. AE, DC, MC, V. **Amenities:** Restaurant; cocktail lounge; concierge. *In room:* A/C, TV, fridge, hair dryer.

MODERATE

Casa Andina Classic – Puno Tikarani ★ ✦

This professional Peruvian chain of popular and comfortable midsize hotels offers dependably good service and impeccable, if predictably decorated, rooms across the board. The group now operates just one location in downtown Puno (one of their signature upscale hotels, Private Collection Puno, is just outside town, on the banks of Lake Titicaca). Ideal both for small groups and individual travelers, this branch is 5 blocks from the Plaza de Armas, and its rooms are a good size, extremely clean, and well-equipped. Those on the second floor in the interior are quietest.

Jr. Independencia 185, Puno. www.casa-andina.com. ✆ **866/220-4434** toll-free in the U.S., 08/082-343-805 in the U.K., or 01/213-9739. Fax 051/365-333. 53 units. $84 double. Rates include breakfast buffet. AE, DC, MC, V. **Amenities:** Concierge. *In room:* A/C, TV, fridge, hair dryer, Wi-Fi (free).

festival TIME? ADDITIONAL HOSTALES

If you arrive in Puno during festival time and there's a crunch on affordable accommodations, try these modest hotels and budget-backpacker places. None of these is my first choice, but they'll do when you need a place to crash.

Hostal El Virrey El Virrey has pretty clean rooms with private bathrooms, TVs, and hot water. Some rooms even have views of Titicaca. Tacna 510. ℂ 051/354-495. $25 double.

Hostal Q'oñi Wasi Located across from the train station, this *hostal* has very simple rooms with twin beds, private bathrooms, and electric showers. It also has a decent little breakfast room. Av. La Torre 119. ℂ 051/365-784. $12 double.

Los Pinos Inn 🔥 One of the best values at the budget range, this agreeable and clean place in a modern building has clean bathrooms, ample but cold rooms, and good natural light, as well as 24-hour hot showers. Jr. Taracapá 182. ℂ 051/367-398. $20 double.

Posada Don Giorgio A step up from the others listed here, this *hostal* is quite a good midrange choice, though perhaps not as good value as Los Pinos. Its carpeted rooms (all with private bathrooms) are comfortable and nicely decorated for the price. Jr. Tarapacá 238. www. posadadongiorgio.com. ℂ/fax **051/363-648.** $40 double.

Intiqa Hotel ★ 🔥 Exceptionally clean and a particularly good midrange value, this small hotel, just 1 block from Pino Park and Jirón Lima, is a dependable alternative to the more upscale hotels along the banks of Titicaca. Although not quite luxurious, the large rooms are well appointed, stylishly contemporary, and very comfortable for the price, with high-quality bedding and linens, double-paned windows, and thermal floors (and hot water bottles warm beds in cold months). Service is friendly and uniformly excellent, with a very accommodating staff eager to help guests with travel, tours, and dining suggestions (going as far as ordering pizza and soup for guests who aren't feeling well).

Jr. Tarapacá 272, Puno. intiqahotel.com. ℂ **051/366-900.** Fax 051/355-933. 24 units. $70 double; $80 suite. Rates include buffet breakfast and free pickup from bus or train station. MC, V. **Amenities:** Coffee shop. *In room:* TV, fridge, hair dryer upon request, Wi-Fi (free).

La Hacienda Puno Built around a pair of sunny courtyards on a busy downtown street, this midsize hotel is cozy, impersonating a hacienda-style inn. The lobby has a nice fireplace, and a large, impressive spiral staircase leads to the large rooms, which are carpeted, and, on the whole, pretty nice. Half the hotel's rooms were newly constructed a few years ago; it's certainly brighter and more welcoming than it was in the past. Request one of the newer accommodations because they have much-improved bathrooms (with tubs) and double beds.

Jr. Deustua 297, Puno. www.lahaciendapuno.com. ℂ **051/367-340.** Fax 051/365-134. 40 units. $90 double; $160 suite. Rates include continental breakfast. MC. **Amenities:** Restaurant; cafe; bar; concierge. *In room:* TV, Wi-Fi.

Punuypampa Inn ★ 🔥 With a very central location, just a block from the Plaza de Armas, this small hotel may have a mouthful of a name, but it excels in every respect, especially at this moderate price point. Rooms are modern and spotless, with

TRAVELING TO bolivia

Plenty of travelers make their way across the Andes to Puno not only to visit Lake Titicaca, but also to continue on to Bolivia, which shares a border with Peru. Several travel agencies (see "Organized Tours," below) in Puno sell packages and bus tickets to Bolivia.

The most common and scenic route is from Puno to La Paz via **Yunguyo** and **Copacabana.** You get dropped off at the border and then pick up a colectivo or taxi shuttle across, where you go through Customs and passport control. If you're going on your own, you'll need to catch another colectivo to Copacabana, just

over a half-hour away. The trip to La Paz takes 7 or 8 hours by bus. Buses also go to La Paz via **Desaguadero.** Or, you can go by a combination of overland travel and hydrofoil or catamaran, a unique but very time-consuming journey (13 hr.).

At the border, visitors get an exit stamp from Peru and a tourist visa (30 days) from Bolivia. Foreigners are commonly tapped for phony departure and entry fees; resist the officials' blatant attempts at corruption.

For more information about Bolivia, pick up a copy of *Frommer's South America.*

---

nicely outfitted bathrooms. There are communal sitting areas on each floor offering complimentary coffee and tea, and the breakfast buffet is surprisingly ample for a budget-level inn. It's safe and offers friendly service, too. The only knock against it might be something that's hard to avoid in Puno, especially for a hotel on the corner of two busy streets: there's street noise, so see if you can get a room on the top floor and away from the street.

Jr. Lima 787, Puno. punuypampa.com. © **051/352-881.** Fax 051/352-744. 20 units. $70 double; $85 suite. Rates include buffet breakfast. AE, DC, MC, V. **Amenities:** Restaurant; room service. *In room:* Wi-Fi (free).

INEXPENSIVE

Hotel Colón Inn   A small and rather charming, Belgian-owned hotel in the heart of Puno, the Colón inhabits a 19th-century republican-era building on a corner. Built around an airy, sky-lit, colonial-style lobby, it has three floors of good-size and comfortably appointed carpeted rooms with desks and marble bathrooms. The cozy top-floor pub is advertised for its panoramic views, but in reality, all you can see are the tops of concrete buildings. The two restaurants, Sol Naciente and Pizzeria Europa, are a couple of the better places in Puno for lunch or dinner.

Calle Tacna 290, Puno. www.coloninn.com. © **051/351-432.** Fax 051/357-090. 21 units. $60 double. Rates include taxes and breakfast buffet. AE, DC, MC, V. **Amenities:** 2 restaurants; bar; room service. *In room:* TV, fridge.

Mosoq Inn ★ 🛅   As budget hotels go (at least those a step up from backpacker hostels), this unassuming but charming little place a couple of blocks off busy Jr. Lima is your best bet. The ample rooms are brightly colored, clean, and well equipped for the price, with wall-to-wall carpeting—looking a tad outdated but otherwise perfectly presentable—cable TV, good breakfasts, plus hot showers all day long. Best of all is the very friendly and responsive service from a dedicated staff, something not often seen at the budget level.

Jr. Moqueque 673, Puno. www.mosoqinn.com. ©/fax **051/367-518.** 15 units. $50 double. Rates include taxes and breakfast buffet. MC, V. **Amenities:** Bar; room service. *In room:* TV, Wi-Fi (free).

AREQUIPA: LA CIUDAD BLANCA ★★★

1,020km (634 miles) S of Lima; 521km (324 miles) S of Cusco; 297km (185 miles) SW of Puno

The southern city of Arequipa, Peru's second largest, might be the most handsome in the country. Founded in 1540, it retains an elegant historic center constructed almost entirely of *sillar* (a porous, white volcanic stone), which gives the city its distinctive look and the nickname *la ciudad blanca*, or "the white city." Colonial churches, mansions, a splendid Plaza de Armas, and the sumptuous 16th-century Santa Catalina convent gleam beneath palm trees and a brilliant sun. Ringing the city, in full view, are three delightfully named volcanic peaks: El Misti, Chachani, and Pichu Pichu, all of which hover around 6,000m (20,000 ft.). And the city's small Museo Santuarios Andinos holds an astounding local discovery: a perfectly preserved Inca teenage maiden sacrificed more than 500 years ago.

Arequipa has also emerged as a favorite base of outdoors enthusiasts who come to climb volcanoes, raft on rivers, trek through the valleys, and, above all, head out to Colca Canyon—twice as deep as the Grand Canyon and the best place in South America to see giant Andean condors soar overhead. Suiting its reputation as an outdoor paradise, Arequipa also enjoys perfect weather: more than 300 days a year of sunshine, huge blue skies, and low humidity.

The commercial capital of the south, Arequipa not only looks different; it feels dissimilar from the rest of Peru. Arequipeños have earned a reputation as aloof and distrusting of centralized power in Lima. Relatively wealthy and home to prominent intellectuals (including Mario Vargas Llosa, the winner of Peru's first Nobel Prize for Literature), politicians, and industrialists, Arequipa has a self-satisfied air about it— at least in the view of many Peruvians who hail from less distinguished places—but you'd hardly know it in the evenings, when the historic quarter is alive with rowdy bar and restaurant patrons.

Essentials
GETTING THERE
BY PLANE   There are daily flights to Arequipa from Lima and Juliaca on **LAN** (www.lan.com; ✆ 01/213-8200) and from Lima on the cheaper **Peruvian Airlines** (www.peruvianairlines.pe; ✆ 01/716-6000). Flights from Lima start at about $100 one-way on LAN.

Aeropuerto Rodríguez Ballón (✆ 054/443-464 or 054/443-458), Av. Aviación s/n, Zamácola, Cerro Colorado, is about 7km (4⅓ miles) northwest of the city.

 The Withering Snows of Arequipa's Volcanoes

The three volcanoes that encircle Arequipa have, as long as most people can remember, been snowcapped year-round. In recent years, however, that has sadly changed. In 2009, the peaks of Chachani, El Misti, and Pichu Pichu were white with snow for just 3 months (June–Aug). Locals are mystified and heartbroken. The effects of global warming and, presumably, ozone deterioration, have not only altered the look of their city; they also bode ill for future discoveries of Inca sacrifices preserved in icy mountaintops.

From the airport to downtown hotels, transportation is by taxi (S/15) or shared colectivo service (about S/5 per person). See "Getting Around" below for more taxi info.

BY BUS The main **Terminal Terrestre** (© 054/427-798), Avenida Andrés Avelino Cáceres, at Av. Arturo Ibáñez s/n, is about 4km (2½ miles) south of downtown Arequipa. Nearby is a newer station, **Nuevo Terrapuerto** (© 054/348-810), Av. Arturo Ibáñez s/n. A huge number of bus companies travel in and out of Peru's second city from across the country, and you'll need to ask if your bus departs from Terminal or Terrapuerto. Taxis are usually present at both stations, though if you had trouble at Terrestre, you'd certainly find one at Terrapuerto; to town it's a 5-minute drive.

From Lima (a 16-hr. ride), recommended companies include **Ormeño** (www.grupo-ormeno.com.pe; © 01/472-5000), **Cruz del Sur** (www.cruzdelsur.com.pe; © 01/311-5050), **Civa Transportes** (www.civa.com.pe; © 01/418-1111), and **Oltursa** (www.oltursa.com.pe; © 01/708-5000). For service from Puno (5 hr.) and Juliaca, contact **Cruz del Sur** or **Civa.** **Ormeño** travels to Arequipa from Puno (as well as Cusco). Other options from Cusco (10–12 hr.) are **Civa Transportes** and **Cruz del Sur.** From Chivay/Colca Canyon (3–4 hr.), call **Reyna** (© 054/426-549) or **Cristo Rey** (© 054/213-094).

Note: Arequipa's bus stations—and especially the buses themselves—are notorious for attracting thieves. Travelers are advised to pay very close attention to their belongings, even going so far as to lock them to luggage racks. The route between Arequipa and Puno especially has earned a bad reputation. It's best to opt for the more exclusive and safer bus companies recommended above.

BY TRAIN Puno-to-Arequipa trains are now available only by private charter for groups of 40 or more, and there are no trains to or from Lima. However, there's always the possibility that the former trajectory might be reinstated at some point in the future (for updates or charters, visit www.perurail.com). The Arequipa rail station is 8 blocks south of the city center, at Av. Tacna y Arica 201 (© 054/215-640).

GETTING AROUND

Arequipa is compact, and most of its top attractions can easily be seen on foot and with an occasional taxi. The historic center is built around the stately Plaza de Armas, marked by the cathedral on the north flank and porticoed buildings on the other three sides. Most sites of visitor interest, including most hotels and restaurants, are found in the blocks immediately north of the plaza. A few blocks west of the main square is the Río Chili and, beyond it, the residential neighborhood Yanahuara and La Recoleta monastery. Two bridges, Puente Grau and Puente Bolognesi, lead from the center to these areas. A double-decker bus offering tours of the city and countryside is the imaginatively named **Bustour,** Portal de San Agustín 111, Plaza de Armas (www.bustour.com.pe; © 054/203-434); with daily departures ranging from 2½ to 4 hours in length (S/25–S/40).

BY TAXI Taxis are inexpensive and plentiful, easily hailed on the street, and best used at night. Most trips in town cost no more than S/4. To call a taxi at night, try **Taxi Seguro** (© 054/450-250), **Taxi Sur** (© 054/465-656), **Master Taxi** (© 054/220-505), or **Ideal Taxi** (© 054/288-888). An excellent private driver for trips to Colca and elsewhere is Manuel Pino Torres of **Privatour** (© 054/952-6495).

BY CAR A car isn't necessary in Arequipa unless you want to explore the countryside, especially Colca and/or Cotahuasi canyons, independently. Try **Lucava Rent-a-Car,** Aeropuerto Rodríquez Ballón (© 054/650-565) and Centro Comercial Cayma no. 10

(☎ **054/663-378**); and **Avis,** Aeropuerto Rodríquez Ballón (☎ **054/443-576**) and Palacio Viejo 214 (☎ **054/282-519**).

VISITOR INFORMATION

There's a **tourist information booth** at the Aeropuerto Rodríquez Ballón (☎ **054/444-564**), open Monday through Friday from 9am to 4pm. The best information office in town is in **Casona de Santa Catalina,** Santa Catalina 210 (across from the convent; ☎ **054/221-227**); it's open daily from 9am to 9pm. There's also an office on the Plaza de Armas across from the cathedral at Portal de la Municipalidad 112 (☎ **054/223-265**); it's open daily from 8am to 6pm. You can also get information and free maps from the **tourist police,** Jerusalén 315, at the corner of Ugarte (☎ **054/201-258**).

ORGANIZED TOURS

Most travel agencies in Puno handle the conventional tours of Lake Titicaca and Sillustani, along with a handful of other ruins programs. Two of the best agencies are **All Ways Travel ★★**, Jr. Deustua 576 (in the courtyard of La Casa del Corregidor; www.titicacaperu.com; ☎ **051/353-979**), which is run by the friendly and very helpful Victor Pauca and his daughter Eliana, with good guides and progressive cultural trips in addition to the standard tours (including a library bus that takes tourists to rural communities to donate books and toys to children); and **Edgar Adventures,** Jr. Lima 328 (www.edgaradventures.com; ☎ **051/353-444**), which is run by a Peruvian husband/wife team. Both agencies can arrange bus and air travel as well, including travel to Bolivia.

Uros Islands half-day trips cost about $12 per person. Uros Islands and Taquile Island full-day trips cost $25 per person. Uros, Taquile, and Amantaní trips, lasting 2 days and 1 night, cost $30 to $35 per person. Sillustani and Chucuito tours, usually 3 hours long, cost $12 per person.

FAST FACTS

You'll find ATMs in the courtyards of the historic Casa Ricketts at San Francisco 108, now the offices of **Banco Continental.** Other banks in the historic center include

A Note about Safety

Arequipa—which on the surface seems to be one of Peru's most placid, easy-going cities—has earned a reputation for rife pickpocketing, although some locals talk about staged tourist robberies and even "strangle muggings." Based on my experience, I've found some citizens to be quite alarmist. Several people have been outspoken about what you should carry on your person (nothing of value, including a camera) and how to conduct yourself (be on guard at all times), even in the daytime, when plenty of police patrol the streets in the old quarter. I've never had a problem in Arequipa, but I do think that late at night you should be especially cautious when exiting bars and restaurants in the historic center; as always, leave your daypack and other unnecessary belongings in your hotel. Some taxi drivers in Arequipa also warn about their colleagues who set tourists up for ambushes. They suggest either calling for a cab or getting into taxis with older drivers because most of the crimes have been perpetrated by younger drivers.

Banco Latino, at San Juan de Dios 112, and **Banco de Crédito,** at General Morán 101. Money-changers can generally be found waving calculators and stacks of dollars on the Plaza de Armas and major streets leading off the main square. There are several *casas de cambio* near the Plaza de Armas and Global Net ATMs in several shops around the plaza; one is **Arequipa Inversiones,** Jerusalén 109.

The general emergency number in Arequipa is ℂ **105.** If you need the police, call the **Policía Nacional** (national police) at ℂ **054/254-020,** or **Policía de Turismo** (tourist police), Jerusalén 315, at the corner of Ugarte, at ℂ **054/201-258.** For fire emergencies, call ℂ **116.** If you need medical attention, go to **Clínica Arequipa,** Avenida Bolognesi at Puente Grau (ℂ **054/253-416**), which has good service and English-speaking doctors. You can also try **Hospital General,** Peral s/n (ℂ **054/231-818**) or **Hospital Regional,** Av. Daniel Alcides Carrión s/n (ℂ **054/231-818**).

Arequipa has plenty of Internet *cabinas.* Most are open daily from 8am to 10pm, charge S/2 per hour, and have Net2Phone or other programs that allow very cheap Web-based international phone calls. Two of the cheapest and fastest *cabinas* are **La Red,** Jerusalén 306B (ℂ **054/286-700**), and **TravelNet,** Jerusalén 218 (ℂ **054/205-548**). An only slightly more expensive option that's open a bit later is **Catedral Internet,** Pasaje Catedral 101 (ℂ **054/282-074**), on the pedestrian mall just behind the cathedral.

The main **Serpost** (post office) is located at Moral 118 (ℂ **054/215-247**). A **DHL** office is located at Santa Catalina 115 (ℂ **054/220-045**). **Telefónica del Perú** offices are located at Alvarez Thomas 209 (ℂ **054/281-112**) and Av. Los Arces 200B, in the Cayma district (ℂ **054/252-020**).

Exploring the City

AREQUIPA HIGHLIGHTS

Monasterio de Santa Catalina ★★★ ☺ HISTORICAL MONUMENT

Arequipa's serene Convent of Santa Catalina, founded in 1579 under the Dominican order, is the most important and impressive religious monument in Peru. The 16th-century convent remained a mysterious world unto itself until 1972, when local authorities forced the sisters to install modern infrastructure, a requirement that led to opening the convent for tourism. Today only 19 cloistered nuns, ages 20 to 90, remain, mostly out of sight of the hundreds of tourists who arrive daily to explore the huge and curious complex. Although the nuns, all from wealthy Spanish families, entered the convent having taken vows of poverty, in the early days they lived in relative luxury, having paid a dowry to live the monastic life amid servants (who outnumbered the nuns), well-equipped kitchens, and art collections.

Behind tall, thick *sillar* fortifications are walls painted sunburned orange, cobalt blue, and brick red, hiding dozens of small cells where more than 200 sequestered nuns once lived. Santa Catalina is a small, labyrinthine village, with narrow cobblestone streets, plant-lined passageways, and pretty plazas, fountains, chapels, and secret niches and quiet corners. Not by accident does it look and feel like a small village in southern Spain, with its predominantly *mudéjar* (Moorish–Christian) architecture and streets named for Spanish cities. In all, it contains 3 cloisters, 6 streets, 80 housing units, an art gallery, and a cemetery. The interplay of intense sunlight and shadows, tiny white-stone windows suddenly framing brilliant bursts of color, and sense of splendid isolation from the city beyond make for an incredible aesthetic experience. No less an expert than the great Portuguese architect Alvaro Siza called

Arequipa Attractions

Casa Arango **11**	Iglesia de San Agustín **6**
Casa Arróspide **5**	Iglesia de San Francisco **16**
Casa del Moral **4**	Iglesia de Santo Domingo **18**
Casa Goyeneche **10**	Iglesia de Yanahuara **1**
Casa Ricketts **15**	La Compañía **13**
Casona Flores del Campo **14**	Monasterio de la Recoleta **2**
Catedral **8**	Monasterio de Santa Catalina **3**
Convento de Santa Teresa **17**	Museo Santuarios Andinos **9**
Iglesia de La Merced **12**	Plaza de Armas **7**

Santa Catalina a "magnificent lesson in architecture." Yet, alarmingly, it is on World Monuments Watch list of Most Endangered Monuments; experts say the great convent is threatened by structural damage caused by pollution and earthquakes.

Among the convent's highlights are the Orange Tree Cloister, with mural paintings over the arches; Calle Toledo, a long boulevard with a communal *lavandería* at its end, where the sisters washed their clothes in halved earthenware jugs; the 17th-century kitchen with charred walls; and the rooms belonging to Sor Ana, a 17th-century nun at the convent who was beatified by Pope John Paul II and is on her way to becoming a saint. Visitors can enter the choir room of the church, but it's difficult to get a good look at the main chapel and its marvelous painted cupola. To see the church, slip in

10 SOUTHERN PERU | Arequipa: La Ciudad Blanca

THE discovery OF JUANITA, THE AMPATO MAIDEN

The mummy of the teenage Inca maiden, now christened Juanita, is one of the most important archaeological finds of the last few decades in the Americas. The first frozen female found from the pre-Columbian era in the Andes, her body, packed in ice and thus not desiccated like most mummies, preserved a wealth of information about her culture and life.

Juanita was discovered at the summit of the Ampato volcano in September 1995 by the American anthropologist Dr. Johan Reinhard, the *National Geographic* explorer-in-residence. She immediately became news around the world. Reinhard, who had spent 2 decades looking for clues in the volcanoes of the western Andes near Arequipa, was working on a project co-sponsored by Arequipa's Catholic University of Santa María and was accompanied by Carlos Zárate, a locally famous mountaineer who for years has run one of the best mountain-climbing-expedition tour companies in Peru. Juanita had been remarkably preserved in ice for more than 500 years, but hot ashes from the eruption of the

nearby Mount Sabancaya volcano melted the snowcap on Ampato and collapsed the summit ridge, exposing what had been hidden for centuries. Reinhard and Zárate at first saw only the feathers of a ceremonial Inca headdress. It took the two men 2 days to descend the peak with the 80-pound mummy, fighting against time to conserve her frozen body and get her back to Arequipa and the Catholic University labs.

Juanita was selected by Inca priests to be sacrificed as an appeasement to Ampato, whose dominion was water supply and harvests. The offering was almost certainly a desperate plea to stave off drought and starvation. Reinhard and his team later discovered two additional mummies, a girl and a boy, several thousand feet below the summit—probably companion sacrifices leading to the more important sacrifice of the princess on Ampato's summit.

The mummy's incredibly well-preserved corpse allows scientists to examine her skin, hair, blood, and internal organs, and even the contents of her stomach. Her

during early morning Mass (daily at 7:30am); the cloistered nuns remain at the back, in view behind a wooden grille. Visitors are advised to take an informative guided tour (in English and other languages, available for a tip of about S/20), though it's also fun just to wander idly around discovering its myriad spaces, especially before or after the crowds arrive. For an especially transfixing experience, visit at night, when cells and the huge kitchen are illuminated by wood fires and flickering candles (come in the early evening as the sun sets). Allow at least a couple of hours to see the convent in all its glory.

Santa Catalina 301. www.santacatalina.org.pe. (C) **054/608-282.** Admission S/35. Fri–Mon 9am–5pm (summer high season, 8am–5pm); Tues–Thurs 8am–8pm.

Museo Santuarios Andinos ★★ ☺ MUSEUM The small Museum of Andean Sanctuaries features a collection of fascinating exhibits, including mummies and artifacts from the Inca Empire, but it is dominated by one tiny girl: Juanita, the Ice Maiden of Ampato. The victim of a ritualistic sacrifice by Inca priests high on the volcano Mount Ampato and buried in ice at 6,380m (20,932 ft.), "Juanita"—named after the leader of the expedition, Johan Rhinehard—was discovered in almost

DNA makeup is being studied. Juanita was dressed in superior textiles from Cusco, clues to her probable nobility. Incredibly important was the fact that the ceremonial site was undisturbed, with all ritual elements in place, allowing anthropologists to essentially re-create the ceremony.

The peak of Apu Ampato was sacred to the Incas, and only priests were allowed to ascend to it. It is most extraordinary that the Incas were able to climb 6,000m (20,000-ft.) peaks without the assistance of oxygen or other modern climbing equipment. Juanita's transfer and sacrifice there, at the age of 13, was part of an elaborate ritual. Having first met with the Inca emperor in Cusco, she must have known her fate: an imminent journey to meet the mountain gods so revered by the Incas. Sacrifice was the greatest honor bestowed upon an individual. Led up the frozen summit by priests, in sandals and surely exhausted, she was probably made to fast and might have been given drugs or an intoxicating beverage before she was killed by a swift blow to her right temple. Scientists at Johns Hopkins University in Baltimore examined the mummy with a CT scan that revealed a crack in the skull, just above the right eye, and internal bleeding.

More than 100 sacred Inca ceremonial sites have been found on dozens of Andes peaks, although no mummies have been uncovered in the frozen condition of Juanita. Anthropologists believe that hundreds of Inca children might be entombed in ice graves on the highest peaks in South America from central Chile to southern Peru. The Incas believed that they could approach Inti, the sun god, by ascending the highest summits of the Andes. The mountain deities they believed to live there were considered protectors of the Inca people. Sacrifices were frequently responses to cataclysmic events: earthquakes, eclipses, and droughts.

Juanita and many of the ritualistic elements found at the ceremonial site are now exhibited at the Museo Santuarios Andinos (below). More information about the Mount Ampato expedition can be found at www.nationalgeographic.com.

perfect condition in September 1995 after the eruption of the nearby Sabancaya Volcano melted ice on the peak. Juanita had lain buried in the snow for more than 550 years. Only Inca priests were allowed to ascend to such a high point, where the gods were believed to have lived. Juanita, who became famous worldwide through a *National Geographic* report on the find, died from a violent blow to the head; she was 13 at the time of her death. Her remarkable preservation has allowed researchers to gain great insights into Inca culture by analyzing her DNA. Today, she is kept in a glass-walled freezer chamber here, less a mummy than a frozen body, in astoundingly good condition, nearly 600 years old—visitors should leave feeling truly privileged at the chance to observe such a monumental discovery and window onto the legacy of the Inca people. Displayed nearby and in adjacent rooms are some of the superb doll offerings and burial items found alongside Juanita's corpse and those of three other sacrificial victims also found on the mountain. Guided visits, which begin with a good *National Geographic* film, are mandatory. Allow about an hour for your visit.

La Merced 110. www.ucsm.edu.pe/santury. (© **054/200-345.** Admission S/15 adults, S/5 children, free for seniors. Mon–Sat 9am–6pm; Sun 9am–3pm.

Plaza de Armas ★★ PUBLIC SQUARE Arequipa's grand Plaza de Armas, an elegant and symmetrical square of gardens and a central fountain lined by arcaded buildings on three sides, is the focus of urban life. Dominated by the massive, 17th-century neoclassical Catedral ★, it is perhaps the loveliest main square in Peru, even though its profile suffered considerable damage when the great earthquake of 2001 felled one of the cathedral's two towers and whittled the other to a delicate pedestal. The cathedral, previously devastated by fire and other earthquakes, has now been fully restored to its original grandeur and you'd never know an earthquake struck. The interior is peach and white, with carved arches and a massive pipe organ. The cathedral is open Monday to Saturday from 7 to 11:30am and 5 to 7:30pm, Sunday from 7am to 1pm and 5 to 7pm.

La Compañía ★, just off the plaza at the corner of Alvarez Thomas and General Morán, opposite the cathedral, is a splendid 17th-century Jesuit church with an elaborate (Plateresque) facade carved of *sillar* stone. The magnificent portal, one of the finest in Peru, shows the end date of the church's construction, 1698—more than a century after work began on it. The interior holds a handsome carved-cedar main altar, bathed in gold leaf, and two impressive chapels: the Capilla de San Ignacio, which has a remarkable painted cupola, and the Capilla Real, or Royal Chapel. Painted murals in the sacristy feature a jungle motif in brilliant colors. Next door to the church are the stately Jesuit cloisters, of stark *sillar* construction, now housing upscale boutiques (enter on Calle Morán). Climb to the top for good views of the city's rooftops and distant volcanoes. The church is open Monday through Saturday from 9 to 11am and 3 to 6pm; admission is free.

On the east side of the plaza at Portal de Flores 136 is the **Casona Flores del Campo** (𝄐 054/244-150), the oldest house in Arequipa. Begun in the late 1500s but not finished until 1779, today it is in deplorable condition, having suffered through earthquakes and a lack of funds that have left it barely standing, and is now closed to the public for safety considerations.

MORE ATTRACTIONS

Casa del Moral ★★ HISTORIC HOME An extraordinary *mestizo* baroque mansion, built in 1733 by a Spanish knight and nicely restored with period detail in 1994, Casa del Moral offers one of the best windows onto colonial times in Arequipa.

Photo Op: Yanahuara

One of the best views in Arequipa is from the elevated *mirador* (lookout point) in the tranquil suburb of Yana-huara ★★ just across Puente Grau. Next to the delightful Plaza de Yana-huara, with its tall palm trees and lovely gardens, a series of *sillar* stone arches beautifully frames the volcanic peaks of El Misti and Chachani. Across from the mirador is the Iglesia de Yanahuara, also built of *sillar* in the mid-18th century and featuring a splendid baroque carved facade and bell tower. The Plaza de Yanahuara, about a 25-minute walk up to Avenida del Ejército from down-town Arequipa, makes a very pleasant place to duck out of Arequipa's intense sun. A bar-restaurant on one side of the square, **Tinto & Asado,** Calle Cuesta del Olivo 318 (𝄐 054/272-380), has a relax-ing terrace with superlative views of El Misti and happy-hour drinks. Or visit the mirador after lunch at **Sol de Mayo** (p. 298), just a few blocks south.

HOUSE TOUR: AREQUIPA'S colonial MANSIONS ★★

Arequipa possesses one of the most attractive and harmonious colonial nuclei in Peru. Several extraordinary seigniorial houses were constructed in white *sillar* stone. They are predominantly flat-roofed, single-story structures, a construction style that has helped them withstand the effects of frequent earthquakes that would have toppled less solid buildings. Most of these houses have attractive, though small, interior patios and elaborately carved facades. Best equipped for visitors is the restored **Casa del Moral** (p. 294), but several others are worth a look, especially if you have an interest in colonial architecture.

Just off the main square at San Francisco 108, **Casa Ricketts** (also called **Casa Tristán del Pozo**), a former seminary and today the offices of Banco Continental, is one of the finest colonial homes in Arequipa. Built in the 1730s, it has a beautiful portal, perhaps Arequipa's finest expression of colonial civil architecture, with delicate representations of the life of Jesus. Inside are two large, beautiful courtyards with gargoyle drainage pipes.

On the other side of the cathedral at the corner of Santa Catalina 101 at San Agustín, **Casa Arróspide** (also called **Casa Iriberry**), from the late 18th century, is one of the most distinguished *sillar* mansions in the city. Now the Cultural Center of San Agustín University ((© **054/204-482**), its several *salas* host temporary exhibits of contemporary art and photography; you'll also find an art shop and nice little cafe with a terrace and great views over the top of the cathedral.

Other colonial houses of interest include **Casa Arango,** a squat and eclectic 17th-century home located on Consuelo at La Merced; **Casa Goyeneche,** La Merced 201, today the offices of Banco de Reserva; and **Casa de la Moneda,** Ugarte at Villaba.

About a 15-minute cab ride outside of town, in Huasacache, is the **Mansión del Fundador** ((© **054/442-460**), one of the most important *sillar* mansions in Arequipa. It is said to have been constructed by the founder of Arequipa, Manuel de Carbajal, for his son. It features terrific vaulted ceilings and a large interior patio. The house is open daily from 9am to 5pm; admission is S/10.

Parroquia de Yanahuara, a stunningly carved church with a long, single nave and vaulted ceiling, dates to 1730 and is the centerpiece of the Yanahuara main square overlooking Arequipa.

10

SOUTHERN PERU

Arequipa: La Ciudad Blanca

Named for an ancient mulberry tree—the *moral* found in the courtyard—the home is also distinguished by a magnificent stone portal with heraldic emblems carved in *sillar*. Handsome furnishings, carved wooden doors, and Cusco School oil paintings decorate large salons, built around a beautiful courtyard, the largest of the colonial residences in the city. Look for 17th-century maps that depict the borders and shapes of countries quite differently from their usual representations today. A second courtyard, painted cobalt blue, was used as the summer patio. Climb to the rooftop for a great view of Arequipa and the surrounding volcanoes. Visits are by guided tour (at no extra cost).

Moral 318 (at Bolívar). (© **054/210-084.** Admission S/5 adults, S/3 students. Mon–Sat 9am–5pm; Sun 9am–1pm.

Arequipa has a wealth of colonial churches that are well worth a visit if you have the time. They include **Iglesia de San Francisco** (Zela 103), built of *sillar* and brick in the 16th century with an impressive all-silver altar and a beautiful vaulted ceiling; **Iglesia de San Agustín** (at the corner of San Agustín and Sucre), with a superbly stylized baroque facade, an excellent example of 16th- and 17th-century *mestizo* architecture (it was rebuilt in 1898 after earthquake damage and was restored, with an unfortunate new bell tower, again in October 2005); **Iglesia de Santo Domingo** (at Santo Domingo and Piérola), with handsome 1734 cloisters; **Iglesia de La Merced** (La Merced 303), built in 1607 and possessing a lovely carved *sillar* facade and an impressive colonial library; **Convento de Santa Teresa** (Melgar at Peral), of brilliant *sillar* and newly restored, with a museum and lovely outdoor terrace; and **Iglesia de Yanahuara** (see p. 294).

Monasterio de la Recoleta ★ MONASTERY/MUSEUM A 10-minute walk from the Plaza de Armas across the Río Chili, distinguished by its tall brick-red-and-white steeple, is the Recoleta convent museum. Founded in 1648 and rebuilt after earthquakes, the peaceful Franciscan convent contains impressive cloisters with *sillar* columns and lovely gardens; today just four of the original seven remain. The convent museum includes several collections. In one room is a collection of pre-Inca culture artifacts, including funereal masks, textiles, and totems; in another are mummies and a series of paintings of the 12 Inca emperors. At the rear of the convent is a small Amazonian museum, stocked with curious items collected by Franciscan missionaries in the Amazon basin. The missionaries were understandably fascinated by prehistoric-looking fish, crocodiles, piranhas, and the clothing of indigenous communities. These souvenirs pose an interesting contrast to the Dominicans' fine library containing some 20,000 volumes, including rare published texts from the 15th century. Guides (tip basis) are available for 1-hour tours in English, Spanish, and French.

Recoleta 117. www.aqplink.com/recoleta. Ⓒ **054/270-966.** Admission S/5 adults, S/3 students, free for seniors. Mon–Sat 9am–noon and 3–5pm.

Where to Eat

Arequipa ranks just behind Lima for gastronomic adventures, and at very reasonable prices. Arequipeño cooking is famous throughout Peru, and several restaurants specialize in traditional regional specialties, a couple of them with fabulous outdoor seating and excellent views of the volcanoes. Several restaurants in the historic quarter—the two streets leading north from the Plaza de Armas, Santa Catalina, and San Francisco are the main hub of nighttime activity—specialize in traditional Arequipeño cooking, though two of the best are a short taxi ride beyond downtown.

EXPENSIVE

Chi Cha ★★★ 🔖 AREQUIPEÑO The full name of this stylish new restaurant is "Chi Cha por Gastón Acurio," which, for anyone who's been following Peruvian cuisine, is pretty much all you need to know. Acurio hit it big in Lima with Astrid & Gastón and La Mar and then expanded to other parts of South and North America. His latest venture is Chi Cha in both Cusco and Arequipa, taking on regional

Arequipa Hotels & Restaurants

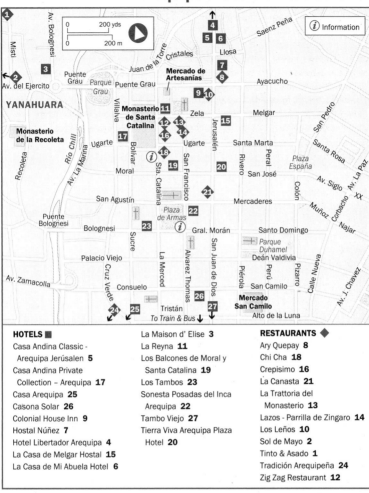

HOTELS ■

Casa Andina Classic -
 Arequipa Jerúsalen **5**
Casa Andina Private
 Collection – Arequipa **17**
Casa Arequipa **25**
Casona Solar **26**
Colonial House Inn **9**
Hostal Núñez **7**
Hotel Libertador Arequipa **4**
La Casa de Melgar Hostal **15**
La Casa de Mi Abuela Hotel **6**

La Maison d' Elise **3**
La Reyna **11**
Los Balcones de Moral y
 Santa Catalina **19**
Los Tambos **23**
Sonesta Posadas del Inca
 Arequipa **22**
Tambo Viejo **27**
Tierra Viva Arequipa Plaza
 Hotel **20**

RESTAURANTS ◆

Ary Quepay **8**
Chi Cha **18**
Crepisimo **16**
La Canasta **21**
La Trattoria del
 Monasterio **13**
Lazos - Parrilla de Zingaro **14**
Los Leños **10**
Sol de Mayo **2**
Tinto & Asado **1**
Tradición Arequipeña **24**
Zig Zag Restaurant **12**

Peruvian cuisines. The inviting space, a colonial *sillar* mansion with vaulted ceilings, features a variety of dining rooms ranging from an intimate bar room to an open patio with a communal table at the center (and views of the open kitchen). While several of Acurio's signature dishes from his *cevichería* and other restaurants are on the menu, go for his local-accented fare labeled "la tradición." Those plates include *escribano,* a tangy, spicy potato salad; and *rocoto relleno,* a spicy pepper stuffed with minced meat. The excellent pisco cocktails, with local fruit juices and named for Arequipa landmarks, such as the Chachani, are superb. Though not inexpensive, by international comparisons, it's a downright bargain for top-flight, creative cooking using indigenous ingredients and advancing local cuisine.

Santa Catalina 210 (interior). www.chicha.com.pe. ☎ **054/287-360.** Reservations recommended. Main courses S/18–S/49. AE, DC, MC, V. Mon–Sat 1pm–midnight; Sun noon–5pm.

Lazos – Parrilla de Zingaro ★★ ARGENTINE GRILL   I'd venture to say this Argentine steakhouse would satisfy the purist carnivore instincts of my friends from Buenos Aires. It does what it must: a great job with its charcoal-and-wood *parrilladas* (mixed grills to share), chorizo sausages with chimichurri sauce, and excellent cuts of beef. You can also try alpaca ribs, or if you're not a meat eater, a nice selection of fresh seafood and shellfish. The long space carved out of *sillar* is handsome, with a modern, minimalist aesthetic and burnished, dark-wood floors. The wine list is focused on big, juicy Argentine malbecs, which go perfectly with the superbly grilled meats.

San Francisco 313–315. www.lazos-parrilla.blogspot.com. ☎ **054/215-729.** Reservations recommended. Main courses S/21–S/45. MC, V. Daily noon–midnight.

Sol de Mayo ★ 🦐 AREQUIPEÑO/PERUVIAN   A 5-minute taxi ride from the *centro* in Yanahuara, the city's nicest residential neighborhood, this long-time stalwart (it's been around for more than a century) is the standard-bearer for Arequipeño cooking. A favorite of upscale locals and tourists alike—and yes, it can seem a little touristy—it has the most delightful setting of the city's restaurants. The colonial tables are set around the edges of a breezy, picture-perfect courtyard with thick grass, geraniums, a small pool and cascading waterfall, and strolling altiplano musicians. There are also indoor dining rooms inside the brick-red and yellow *sillar* stone building, but nothing beats eating outdoors here. Peruvian specialties are Sol de Mayo's calling card: *chicharrón de chancho* (fried pork), ostrich, fresh shellfish, and a tantalizing lineup of ceviche. Starters include a yummy mixed salad of *choclo* (white corn), tomato, and avocado.

Jerusalén 207, Yanahuara. www.restaurantsoldemayo.com. ☎ **054/254-148.** Reservations recommended. Main courses S/15–S/48. AE, DC, MC, V. Daily 11am–10pm.

Zig Zag Restaurant ★★ GRILL/SWISS   Calling its cuisine "Alpandino," Zig Zag has an awful lot going for it. Occupying a cool two-level, *sillar*-walled space with a fantastic, twisting iron staircase, it's chic enough to appeal to young people on dates and comfortable enough for families and small tourist groups. If you're in need of a meat fix, this is the place. The house specialty is stone-grilled meats, including ostrich and alpaca, ordered by quantity (10–250 grams) and served either unadorned on a sizzling stone or with a variety of sauces. The owners like to educate their customers about these lean meats as a healthy alternative to other meats. Try the ostrich carpaccio in lemon or ostrich stone-grilled with Swiss-style hash browns. If you're not a carnivore, other favorites are trout and shrimp, or fondues and pastas (such as the interesting Peruvian–Italian quinoa gnocchi). The two-level restaurant plays hip music and has attentive service, and a couple of tables upstairs are perched on a ledge overlooking the attractive Plazuela San Francisco.

Zela 210. www.zigzagrestaurant.com. ☎ **054/206-020.** Reservations recommended. Main courses S/28–S/48. AE, DC, MC, V. Daily 6pm–midnight.

MODERATE

Ary Quepay AREQUIPEÑO/PERUVIAN   A relaxed and friendly, family-owned restaurant with a gardenlike dining room under a bamboo roof and skylights, Ary Quepay specializes in traditional Peruvian cooking. It's less fancy than a couple of the better-known restaurants specializing in Arequipeño cooking, but the others are on the outskirts of the city, and more expensive. That said, this place has the feel of a restaurant resting on past laurels, and service is lacking. Main courses are classic: *Rocoto relleno* (stuffed spicy red peppers), *adobo* (pork stew with *ají*), and *escabeche de pescado* (spicy fish stew). The menu also features a number of dishes for vegetarians, and good breakfasts, juices, and milkshakes. In the evenings, there's often live folkloric music, but to some diners, that will feel unappetizingly touristy.

Jerusalén 502. ✆ **054/672-922.** Main courses S/16–S/30. DC, MC, V. Daily 10am–11pm.

La Trattoria del Monasterio ★★ 🍴 ITALIAN   Cleaved into the outer *sillar* wall of the Santa Catalina monastery, this chic but cozy and unassuming Italian eatery is a personal favorite for lingering over an intimate dinner. It's considerably quieter than the hopping restaurant row just 1 block over on San Francisco. Spilling into three elegant, small, and whitewashed dining rooms, it specializes in Italian favorites like risottos, lasagnas, ravioli, and *osso buco*. For cognoscenti, it features both long and short pastas. The menu was prepared by the hot chef of the moment in Peru, Gastón Acurio of Astrid & Gastón, La Mar, and others in Lima and up and down South America. You'll also find a good selection of wines, great desserts, and fine, attentive service.

Santa Catalina 309 www.latrattoriadelmonasterio.com. ✆054/204-062. Reservations recommended. Main courses S/22–S/36. AE, DC, MC, V. Mon–Sat noon–2:30pm and 7–11pm; Sun noon–2:30pm.

Tradición Arequipeña ★★ 🍴 AREQUIPEÑO/PERUVIAN   It's a few kilometers outside town on a busy avenue in the district called Paucarpata, so you'll need to grab a taxi to get to this classic open-air restaurant. Elegantly set amid beautiful gardens and stunning views of snowcapped El Misti from the upper deck, it's open only for lunch (although you could also squeeze in an early dinner at 5 or 6pm). Most encouraging is how popular it is not only among tourists, but also among locals. In fact, it's the restaurant that seems most highly recommended to foreigners by Arequipeños. It serves large portions of classic Peruvian and Arequipeño dishes, such as *cuy, adobo,* and ceviche, but they're more carefully prepared here than in many other *comida típica* restaurants. A good starter is combination fried cheese and fried *yuca* with picante sauce and salsa verde. The prices are quite affordable for such an elegant place.

Av. Dolores 111, Paucarpata. ✆054/426-467. Reservations recommended Fri–Sat. Main courses S/15–S/39. AE, DC, MC, V. Daily noon–7pm.

INEXPENSIVE

Crepisimo ★ 🍴 ☺ CREPES   Owned by the folks who operate the excellent Zig Zag, this laid-back little restaurant looks more like a bar or cafe. It's a great spot for lunch, especially if you nab one of the tables on the interior courtyard and opt for the superb-value *menú*, which, for about $7, gets you a great salad, choice of savory crepe, dessert, and a drink. Or go a la carte and pick any of a long roster (more than 100 varieties) of sweet and savory crepes.

Santa Catalina 208 www.crepisimo.com. ✆ 054/206-620. Reservations recommended. Main courses S/12–S/25. AE, DC, MC, V. Daily noon–11pm; Sun noon–5pm.

La Canasta BREAKFAST/BAKERY   A charming bakery and lunch and breakfast nook, hidden away inside the courtyard of a massive colonial mansion on a heavily trafficked street, La Canasta only has a couple of tables on the patio. You can get pizzas, *empanadas* (stuffed pastries), sandwiches, and hamburgers, as well as some of the best breakfasts you're likely to come across in Peru.

Jerusalén 115. ☎ **054/287-138.** Reservations not accepted. Main courses S/5–S/9. No credit cards. Mon–Sat 7am–8:30pm.

Los Leños 😊 PIZZERIA   At this fun cave of a pizza place, diners share long wooden tables, and the footprints of many hundreds of travelers carry on in the graffiti that covers every square inch of stone walls up to a vaulted ceiling. It looks and feels like a college tavern. The house specialty is pizza from the wood-fired oven; among the many varieties, the Leños house pizza is a standout: cheese, sausage, bacon, ham, chicken, and mushrooms. Those who've had their fill of pizza can opt for other standards, such as lasagna and a slew of other pastas. Los Leños opens early, and you can choose from among 20 different "American breakfasts" offered here.

Jerusalén 407. ☎ **054/289-179.** Reservations not accepted. S/12–S/21. No credit cards. Daily 7am–11pm.

Shopping

Arequipa is perhaps the number one spot in Peru—better even than Cusco and Lima—to shop for top-quality baby alpaca, vicuña, and woolen goods. Although many items are more expensive than the lesser-quality goods sold in other parts of Peru, in Arequipa you'll find nicer designs and export-quality knit sweaters, shawls, blankets, and scarves. In many parts of Peru, what is sold as alpaca or baby alpaca is often a mix of alpaca and synthetics. Many of the finest pure alpaca woven items in Peru come from Arequipa. Vicuña wool, which is softer, rarer, and more expensive than alpaca, is also now found at a couple of shops, but keep in mind that a simple shawl runs to about $1,600. The city also produces very nice leather goods, and several excellent antiques shops feature colonial pieces and even older items (remember, though, that these antiques cannot legally be exported from Peru; see "Fast Facts," in chapter 13, for regulations). **Casona de Santa Catalina,** Santa Catalina 210 (☎ **054/281-334**) and **Patio del Ekeko,** Mercaderes 141 (☎ **054/215-861**), are two small shopping malls near the Plaza de Armas with several good, upscale shops, including alpaca goods, handicrafts, jewelry, and food shops. Calle Mercaderes is newly pedestrian-only and more than ever the city's top shopping avenue.

ALPACA GOODS   Three general areas are particularly good for alpaca items. One is the **cloisters** next to La Compañía church, where you'll find several alpaca boutiques and outlets. Another good place is **Pasaje Catedral,** the pedestrian mall just behind the cathedral, and a third is **Calle Santa Catalina.** Shops with fine alpaca items include **Kuna** ★★, Santa Catalina 210 and Calle Mercaderes 141 (☎ **054/282-485** and **054/225-550**); **Millma's Baby Alpaca,** Pasaje Catedral 177 (☎ **054/205-134**); **Baby Alpaca Boutique,** Santa Catalina 208 (☎ **054/206-716**); **Anselmo's Souvenirs,** Pasaje Catedral 119 (no phone); **Wari,** San Francisco 311 (☎ **054/223-301**); **Alpaca Azul,** Moral 223–225 (☎ **054/228-331**); and **Alpaca 111** ★, Zela 212 (☎ **054/223-238**). Two **Incalpaca** (Grupo Inca) ★ factory outlets are good spots to get last season's items at discounted prices: One is in town, within the courtyard of La Compañía, on General Moran and Álvarez Thomas (☎ **054/205-931**); the other is about 10 minutes outside of town, Av. Juan Bustamante s/n, in the Tahuaycani district (☎ **054/251-025**). The latter also has a small zoo of camelids to entertain the kids while parents shop for alpaca and hard-to-find and expensive vicuña items.

ANTIQUES   Calle Santa Catalina and nearby streets have several antiques shops. I found lots of items I wished I could have taken home at the following three stores: **Curiosidades,** Zela 207 (☎ **054/952-986**); **Álvaro Valdivia Montoya**'s two well-stocked shops at Santa Catalina 204 and Santa Catalina 406 (☎ **054/229-103**); and **Arte Colonial,** Santa Catalina 312 (☎ **054/214-887**).

BOOKS   A very good and friendly bookstore with art books and English-language paperbacks is **Libería El Lector,** San Francisco 221 (☎ **054/288-677**).

HANDICRAFTS   A general handicrafts market *(mercado de artesanía)* with dozens of stalls in the old town jail, is next door to the Plazuela de San Francisco (btw. Zela and Puente Grau). For handmade leather goods, stroll along Puente Bolognesi, which leads west from the Plaza de Armas, and you'll find numerous small stores with handbags, shoes, and other items.

Entertainment & Nightlife

Arequipa has a pretty hopping nightlife in the old quarter, with plenty of bars, restaurants, and discos catering to both gringos and locals. On a busy night, Arequipa does its best impression of the Cusco bar scene, and the alleyway just behind the Cathedral (Pasaje de la Catedral) is Arequipa's version of Cusco's "gringo alley," though more respectable. Just as in Cusco many bars are housed in impressive colonial digs, in Arequipa you're likely to do your drinking in a bar with vaulted *sillar* ceilings. Sunday through Wednesday is usually pretty quiet, with things heating up beginning on Thursday night. Virtually every bar in town advertises elastic happy hours, with basic cocktails going for as little as three for S/12. Calles San Francisco and Zela are the main hot spots, while there are also a number of bars along Santa Catalina.

   Las Quenas ★, Santa Catalina 302 (☎ **054/281-115**), is a peña bar and restaurant featuring live Andean music Monday through Saturday from 9pm to midnight, and special dance performances on Friday and Saturday nights. It's a cozy little place that serves pretty good Peruvian dishes. You can also catch peña music most evenings at **El Tuturutu,** Portal San Agustín 105 (☎ **054/201-842**), a restaurant on the main square, and Afro-Peruvian and folkloric music at **La Troica,** Jerusalén 522 (☎ **054/ 225-690**), a tourist-oriented restaurant in an old house.

   As for pubs and bars, **Brujas ★,** San Francisco 300 (no phone) is a cozy little watering hole, popular with local young people and serving up good happy-hour drink specials. **Istambul,** San Francisco 231 (no phone) also draws young people to its happy hours. **Siwara ★,** Santa Catalina 210 (☎ **054/626-218**) is a good-looking beer tavern that spills into two patios in the building of the Santuarios Andinos museum, across from the Santa Catalina monastery. **Farrens Irish Pub,** Pasaje Catedral 107 (☎ **054/238-465**), very popular with visiting gringos, is a cool two-level joint with good drink specials, a pool table, and a rock and pop soundtrack. Another good spot for a drink is **Montreál Le Café Art ★,** Ugarte 210 (☎ **054/ 931-2796**), which features an eclectic variety of live music Wednesday through Saturday and has happy hours between 5 and 11pm. **La Casa de Klaus,** Zela 207 (☎ **054/203-711**), is a simple and brightly lit tavern popular with German, British, and local beer drinkers.

   For a little more action, check out **Forum Rock Café ★★,** San Francisco 317 (☎ **054/202-697**), a huge place that is equal parts restaurant, bar, disco, and concert hall. It sports a rainforest theme, with jungle vegetation and "canopy walkways"

SOUTHERN PERU

Arequipa: La Ciudad Blanca

everywhere. Live bands (usually rock) take the stage Thursday through Saturday. The upstairs grill has great panoramic views of the city. Just down the street, **Déjà Vu ★**, San Francisco 319 (© **054/221-904**), has a good bar with a mix of locals and gringos, a lively dance floor, and English-language movies on a big screen every night at 8pm. It also has a spectacular rooftop terrace, which is a good spot for dinner or even breakfast after a long night partying. **Frog's ★**, Zela 216 (www.frogslive.com; no phone) is a happening local club and *cevichería* frequented by locals and featuring live Peruvian rock bands. **Kibosh,** Zela 205 (© **054/626-218**), is an upscale pub with four bars, wood-oven pizza, a dance floor, and live music Wednesday through Saturday (ranging from Latin to hard rock).

Where to Stay

Arequipa has an ample roster of very good hotels and *hostales* at all levels. A number of them occupy historic houses in the old quarter, within very easy walking distance of major sights, restaurants, and bars. Even budget travelers can do very well in Arequipa—it's a good place for a significant step up in comfort and style (but not price) from the usual backpacker dregs. Indeed, even travelers not accustomed to looking at hotels in the inexpensive or moderate range may well find a very welcome surprise in here in terms of comfort and value. The area north of the Plaza de Armas is nicer and less chaotic (though full of restaurants and bars) than the streets south of the square.

Note: If you hop in a taxi from the airport or bus station, insist on going to the hotel of your choice; local taxi drivers often claim that a particular hotel is closed in order to take you to one that will pay them a commission.

EXPENSIVE

Casa Andina Private Collection – Arequipa ★★★   This upscale midsize hotel, in one of Arequipa's emblematic colonial buildings, the storied Mint House—a national historic monument—is one of the city's few true luxury options, and a splendid place to stay. Just 3 blocks from the Plaza de Armas, around the corner from the Santa Catalina convent, it's ideally located. It features beautiful *sillar* walls, two lovely interior courtyards, an elegant gourmet restaurant, and even a small on-site museum depicting the minting of old coins. Accommodations in the modern wing are elegantly understated and spacious, with nice bathrooms, while the sprawling suites in the historic main house are downright sumptuous. Intimate, with a boutique feel but all the services of a larger luxury hotel, and prices that, while not inexpensive, seem merited, it has immediately become Arequipa's top place to stay, and one of the top hotels in Peru.

Ugarte 403, Arequipa. www.casa-andina.com. © **866/220-4434** toll-free in the U.S., 08/082-343-805 in the U.K., or 01/213-9739. Fax 054/226-908. 41 units. $239 double; $289–$449 suite. Rates include breakfast buffet. AE, DC, MC, V. **Amenities:** Restaurant; bar; concierge. *In room:* A/C, TV, fridge, hair dryer, Wi-Fi (free).

Hotel Libertador Arequipa ★ ☺   Arequipa's swankest large hotel within reach of the historic center is in this handsome, sprawling 1940s colonial-style building. In the midst of quiet Selva Alegre, the largest park in Arequipa, the midsize hotel, recently renovated and part of a small upmarket Peruvian chain, is about a 15-minute walk from the main square. It maintains a colonial theme throughout, with soaring ceilings, historical murals, and older-style dark-wood period furnishings in expansive, elegantly appointed rooms. Accommodations, equipped with marble bathrooms, are about as large as you're likely to find. The hotel has a lovely, large outdoor pool among nice gardens and tall palm trees. Families will appreciate the outdoor recreation and game area for children.

Plaza Bolívar, Selva Alegre, Arequipa. www.libertador.com.pe/en/2/2/1/arequipa-hotel-general-information. ℂ **01/518-6500** for reservations or 054/215-110. Fax 054/241–933. 88 units. $125–$160 deluxe double; $185 suite. Rates include buffet breakfast. AE, DC, MC, V. **Amenities:** 2 restaurants; bar; concierge; fitness center; Jacuzzi; large outdoor pool; sauna. *In room:* A/C, TV, fridge.

Sonesta Posadas del Inca Arequipa   This hotel has perhaps the most coveted location in Arequipa: right on the stately Plaza de Armas. Even if that's the best thing about this large hotel, it's still plenty. It's perfectly located to allow you to see and do everything in Arequipa with ease. The hotel has gotten a partial but not yet full make-over, so the dated casino lobby decor, an awkward step back into the 1970s, is thank-fully gone. Rooms are spacious and comfortable, if not luxurious, with a retro feel to them; the desirable executive rooms on upper floors have attractive terraces under the porticoes with plaza views. There's also a nice little rooftop pool framed by flower beds and sweeping views of the cathedral and volcanoes in the distance, and the restaurant bar has seats overlooking the plaza.

Portal de Flores 116, Plaza de Armas, Arequipa. www.sonesta.com/Arequipa. ℂ **054/215-530.** Fax 054/234–374. 58 units. $276 double; $350 suite. Rates include buffet breakfast. AE, DC, MC, V. **Amenities:** Restaurant; bar; concierge; outdoor rooftop pool. *In room:* A/C, TV, fridge.

MODERATE

Casa Andina Classic–Arequipa Jerúsalen   With a curved and colorful, con-temporary facade, this downtown hotel is the largest in the Casa Andina group. It's at the edge of the historic quarter, about a 10-minute (6-block) walk from the Plaza de Armas—good for some travelers, who prefer to be removed from the bar noise, but less good for those who'd prefer to be right in the thick of things. Rooms are pretty spacious and modern, with splashes of color and bold fabrics, as well as rustic touches like *sillar* volcanic stone. There's a nice terrace on the fourth floor with views of the El Misti volcano. Other than that, the hotel doesn't have a whole lot of flavor, but the services and facilities are particularly good for small groups.

Santa Catalina 300, Arequipa. www.casa-andina.com. ℂ **866/220-4434** toll-free in the U.S., 08/082-343-805 in the U.K., or 01/213-9739. Fax 054/226-908. 94 units. $89–$119 double; $139 suite. Rates include breakfast buffet. AE, DC, MC, V. **Amenities:** Cafe; concierge. *In room:* A/C, TV, hair dryer upon request, Wi-Fi (free).

Casa Arequipa ★ ✦   This intimate inn, akin to a European boutique hotel—something very unusual for Peru—is one of the most surprisingly luxurious places to stay in the country and boasts bargain prices. It occupies a beautifully restored, pink 1950s mansion in the quiet Vallecito residential district, a short walk or cab ride from the Plaza de Armas (which some may find a bit inconvenient; others will appreciate being removed from the hubbub). The inn features elegantly designed guest rooms, with nicely chosen furnishings (including many antiques), very comfortable beds, and the finest towels and bed linens you'll find in Peru. Photographs of the Andes, taken by the owner (who splits his time between Arequipa and Washington, D.C.), decorate the rooms, and fresh flowers are placed in every room and throughout the house. The excellent bathrooms, several of which have tubs, are of gleaming marble. The breakfast buffet and personal attention are worthy of a five-star hotel.

Av. Lima, Vallecito, Arequipa. www.arequipacasa.com. ✆ **054/284-219** or 202/518-9672 for reservations in the U.S. Fax 054/253-343. 10 units. $65–$99 double. Rates include buffet breakfast. AE, DC, MC, V. **Amenities:** Concierge; CD library. *In room:* A/C, TV, CD player, fridge.

Casona Solar ★ 🏠 In a gem of a *sillar* noble house from 1702, this homey place, built around two lovely, sun-drenched courtyards and just 2 blocks from the Plaza de Armas, is run by a Peruvian–Dutch couple and has the feel of a B&B. Rooms have high, vaulted brick ceilings and attractive wood floors, and many have exposed volcanic stone walls. Those that don't are much less appealing. All are simply, even sparsely, decorated. By far the best room—and a worthwhile splurge, as it's not much more than a standard double—is the elegant Colonial Suite, which has a fireplace and sitting area. On cold evenings, the fireplace lounge is a nice spot for a warming cocktail.

Consuelo 116, Cercado, Arequipa. www.casonasolar.com. ✆ **054/228-991.** 12 units. S/175 double; S/199 suite. Rates include breakfast. V. **Amenities:** Restaurant; bar; Wi-Fi (free). *In room:* Cable TV, Wi-Fi (free).

La Maison d' Elise This small gem of a hotel is hidden behind a nondescript, rather unappealing facade. Across from the park on the other side of Puente Grau, just beyond the historic center, this 14-year-old hotel is like a small Mediterranean village. Ocher-and-white villas are clustered around courtyards ripe with cactus and colorful flowering plants. Double rooms are very large and comfortably furnished; matrimonial suites have a lower-level sitting room. There are also apartments with private terraces. The hotel has a small pool with a rock waterfall, and a notable and nicely decorated restaurant. Deals are sometimes available. The hotel is less luxurious overall than the Libertador (above), but it's got a quirkier charm and is much more affordable.

Av. Bolognesi 104, Yanahuara, Arequipa. www.hotel-lamaisondelise-arequipa.com. ✆ **054/256-185.** Fax 054/253-343. 88 units. $70 double; $80–$110 suite. AE, DC, MC, V. **Amenities:** 2 restaurants; bar; pool. *In room:* A/C, TV. Wi-Fi (free).

Los Tambos ★★ 🗝 A homey boutique inn just around the corner from the Plaza de Armas, with warm and colorful rooms with plenty of natural light and wood floors, this is a delightful surprise. Rooms are spotless and the staff exceedingly friendly and responsive, going out of their way to make guests feel at home (and the inn more like a B&B). Although the hotel is on a busy road, it has good soundproof windows and rooms are quiet. There's a cozy fireplace lounge, two terraces with volcano views, fresh flowers in the lobby and rooms, and breakfast is abundant and tasty.

Puente Bolognesi 129, Arequipa. www.lostambos.com.pe. ✆ **054/600-900.** 26 units. $89 double. Rates include buffet breakfast and airport transfers (2-night minimum stay). AE, DC, MC, V. **Amenities:** Lounge. *In room:* A/C, TV, Wi-Fi (free).

Tierra Viva Arequipa Plaza Hotel ★★ 🗝 A brand-new hotel in the historic quarter—just 2 blocks from the Plaza de Armas—this terrific addition is racking up the accolades right out of the gates. A boutique hotel with the exemplary services and amenities of a larger place, and bargain prices more in line with much lesser hotels, this is the perfect hotel for most types of travelers (except perhaps for those in need of a pool). The spacious rooms are quiet and immaculate, minimalist but with a sense of warmth. They feature excellent orthopedic mattresses, sleek modern bathrooms, and large LCD TVs. The lobby sets a chic tone with chandeliers and *sillar* volcanic stone walls. Tierra Viva is a small Peruvian hotel group, with just two other hotels in Cusco.

Jerusalén 202, Arequipa. tierravivahoteles.com/hotels/arequipa-plaza. © **054/234-161.** 26 units. $60–$80 double; $100 suite. Rates include buffet breakfast. AE, DC, MC, V. **Amenities:** Restaurant; bar; business center. *In room:* A/C, TV, Wi-Fi (free).

INEXPENSIVE

Colonial House Inn 🎁 A rambling 200-year-old house—continually owned by the same family—in the old quarter, this friendly, eclectic inn is perfect for backpackers or budget travelers in search of some local flavor. It has a great rooftop terrace, nice large rooms (all with a private bathroom), a comfortable covered patio, a library and book exchange, and good breakfasts in a little cafe area. Book in advance, as it is frequently full.

Puente Grau 114, Arequipa. www.colonialhouseinn-arequipa.com. ©/fax **054/223-533.** 7 units. $20 double. Rates include continental breakfast. No credit cards. **Amenities:** Restaurant.

Hostal Núñez 🗡 This colonial inn is attractive and affordable—and thus popular. Friendly and family-owned, it's on a street in the old quarter loaded with travel agencies. Rooms aren't anything special, but they are ample and have hardwood floors and cable TV, and they're decorated with actual color schemes, a rarity at these prices. Public rooms are congenial and loaded with plants. A huge rooftop terrace has excellent views of the city, and there are other unusual amenities at this level, including an on-site salon. Breakfast on the terrace is a great perk. Couples or friends sharing a room are best off: single rooms are tiny.

Jerusalén 528, Arequipa. www.hotel-nunez.de. ©/fax **054/218-648.** 7 units. $30 double. Rates include continental breakfast. No credit cards. **Amenities:** Restaurant; bar. *In room:* TV.

La Casa de Melgar Hostal ★ 🎁 A handsome colonial house made of white *sillar* (volcanic stone), this charming small hotel is one of the nicest and most relaxed in Peru, as well as one of the best value. Just 3 blocks from the Plaza de Armas, the restored 18th-century mansion—the former residence of the bishop of Arequipa—has thick walls and three interior courtyards. It echoes the rich, brick-red and royal-blue tones of the Santa Catalina Monastery and is the perfect place to stay if you're a fan of colonial architecture. Some rooms—especially those on the ground floor that have high vaulted brick ceilings—exude colonial character; if the hotel isn't full, ask to see a couple. A newer wing of rooms, also in a colonial building with *sillar* walls at the rear, behind a nice garden and terrace, are also lovely; some have incredibly high ceilings. Breakfast is served in the neat little cafe next door in one of the courtyards. Advance reservations are a must in high season.

Melgar 108, Cercado, Arequipa. www.lacasademelgar.com. ©/fax **054/222-459** or 01/446-8343 for reservations. 30 units. $50 double. Rates include breakfast. V. **Amenities:** Bar.

La Casa de Mi Abuela Hotel One of the best-run small hotels in Arequipa, "my grandmother's house" is tucked behind a security gate but welcomes everyone with an easygoing atmosphere. An organic, quirky place that has grown from a tiny B&B operation into a very popular 50-room hotel, it is still family run. Today it's a self-contained tourism complex and miniresort, with a live-music peña bar, book exchange, travel agency, and beautiful, relaxing gardens with views of El Misti. Some rooms have roof terraces; others have balconies. Many rooms are plainly decorated and cramped, but the *hostal* compensates with services, facilities, and security. The inn is about a 10-minute walk (6 blocks) north of the main square; it's often filled, so make advance reservations. Nice breakfasts are served in the garden (extra charge).

Jerusalén 606, Cercado, Arequipa. www.lacasademiabuela.com. (C) **054/241-206.** Fax 054/242-761. 50 units. $59 double; $74 suite. DC, MC, V. **Amenities:** Restaurant; bar; outdoor pool. *In room:* TV, fridge.

La Reyna   A backpacker inn in town, La Reyna is smack in the middle of the historic center, just a block from the famed Santa Catalina monastery and paces away from plenty of bars and restaurants. The *hostal*'s many rooms feed off a labyrinth of narrow staircases that climb up three floors to a roof terrace, a popular spot to hang out and write postcards and plan hiking expeditions, or to veg out and stargaze late at night. There are simple, rock-bottom dormitory rooms for zero-budget travelers and a couple of rooftop casitas that, although basic in their decoration, have private bathrooms and their own terraces with awesome views of the mountains and the monastery below—something akin to backpacker penthouse suites. (Number 20 is worth reserving, if you can.) The *hostal,* though a little haphazardly run, organizes lots of canyon treks and volcano-climbing tours, and even offers Spanish classes.

Zela 209, Arequipa. (C)/fax **054/286-578.** 20 units. $12 double without bathroom; $15 double with bathroom. No credit cards.

Los Balcones de Moral y Santa Catalina ⚑   This inviting small hotel is very comfortable and decently furnished, a nice step up from budget hostels for not too much more money. In the heart of the old quarter, it's only a couple of blocks from the Plaza de Armas. Half of the house is colonial (first floor); the other is republican, dating from the 1800s. The house is built around a colonial patio with a sunny terrace. Furnishings are modern, with wallpaper and firm beds. Eleven of the good-size rooms have hardwood floors and large balconies with nice views looking toward the back of the cathedral; the other rooms are carpeted and less desirable (though quieter). All have good, tiled bathrooms.

Moral 217, Arequipa. www.balconeshotel.com. (C)/fax **054/201-291.** 17 units. S/135 double. MC, V. **Amenities:** Restaurant. *In room:* TV.

Tambo Viejo 👪   This quirky and charming budget *hostal,* occupying an old colonial family home, is a 15-minute walk south of the Plaza de Armas, but it's popular and usually full of backpackers drawn by good word of mouth about the tranquil and genial atmosphere. There are rooms with shared and private bathrooms, a big garden with sun terraces and volcano views, a cafe serving veggie breakfasts and other meals, a book exchange, a TV lounge, and hot water all day.

Av. Malecón Socabaya 107, Arequipa. www.tamboviejo.com. (C) **054/288-195.** Fax 054/284-747. 20 units. S/75–S/99 double; S/25 per person in dorm room. Rates include American breakfast and bus station pickup. DC, MC, V. **Amenities:** Cafe; bike rental; Internet (in lobby).

Side Trips from Arequipa

Easy day trips from Arequipa include jaunts to the relaxed small towns of **Paucarpata** and **Sabandía,** in the beautiful countryside surrounding the city. But the excursions of primary interest to visitors—for many, the main reason for a visit to Arequipa—is **Colca Canyon,** where the highlight is **Cruz del Cóndor,** a lookout point where giant Andean condors soar overhead; see "Colca Valley & Canyon," below, for more information. The region around Arequipa is unimaginably blessed by nature. It has soaring, active volcanoes, perfect for experienced mountaineers and trekkers; the two deepest canyons in the world, Colca and Cotahuasi; and chilly rivers that lace the canyons. The opportunities for trekking, rafting, and mountaineering expeditions through the valley are some of the finest in Peru. Out in the desert are ancient petroglyphs at **Toro Muerto.**

Tour agencies have mushroomed in Arequipa, and most offer very similar city and countryside (*campiña*) highlight trips (about $30 per person). Going with a tour operator is economical and by far the most convenient option for visitors with limited time and patience—public transportation is poor and very time-consuming in these parts. Of the many agencies that crowd the principal streets in the old quarter, only a handful of tour operators in Arequipa are well run, and visitors need to be careful when signing up for guided tours to the valley. Avoid independent guides who don't have official accreditation; see p. 289 for recommendations.

THE OUTSKIRTS (CAMPIÑA TOURS)

Paucarpata, 7km (4⅓ miles) southeast of Arequipa, is a pretty little town surrounded by Inca-terraced farmlands and El Misti volcano in the distance. About a kilometer down the road, the peaceful village of **Sabandía** is where many Arequipeños visit on weekends to dine at country-style restaurants. For out-of-town visitors, the highlight of the village is a large, early 17th-century stone *molino,* or water-powered mill. There are several nice colonial estates in the surrounding countryside. One of the nicest is **La Mansión del Fundador ★** (www.lamansion delfundador.com; ✆ **054/213-423**), a handsome colonial mansion in the suburb of **Huasacache,** 10km (6¼ miles) from Arequipa. The house, once the property of the founder of Arequipa, Don García Manuel de Carbajal, is nicely outfitted with original antique paintings and furnishings. It's open daily from 9am to 5pm; admission is S/10.

GETTING THERE If you are one of the few who decides not to go with an organized tour, you can catch a Sabandía colectivo from San Juan de Dios or Independencia, a few blocks from the Plaza de Armas, but it's much simpler to take a taxi for S/10. The *molino* is on the same road as the **El Lago Resort** at Camino al Molino s/n, Sabandía (✆ **054/448-383**), a good spot for lunch.

TORO MUERTO

About 3 hours from Arequipa, near the town of Corire, is **Toro Muerto,** touted as the world's largest field of petroglyphs. Whether it is actually the world's largest number of petroglyphs in one place is hard to say; many contend that other places have more. But the site is certainly exceptionally big, unique, and fascinating: Carved on hundreds of volcanic boulders, the glyphs lie scattered in an area at least a couple of kilometers long. Most historians believe that they were created by the Huari culture more than 1,000 years ago (and perhaps added to by subsequent peoples such as the Incas).

The enormous scale and the beautiful desert setting, more so than the individual drawings, are what most impress visitors to the site. The carvings comprise somewhat crude animal, human, and geometric representations. Although some estimates claim that there are 6,000 engraved stones at Toro Muerto, many more stones are not carved, so walking among the boulders in the sand and under a hot desert sun in search of the engraved stones requires considerable effort. The site draws very few tourists. Its distance from Arequipa and the difficulty getting there (and, no doubt, the competing popularity of Colca Canyon) preclude many groups from going to Toro Muerto.

GETTING THERE General-service tour agencies in Arequipa arrange group trips to Toro Muerto; see "Organized Tours" under "Essentials" in the "Colca Valley & Canyon" section, below. You can also hire a taxi from Arequipa at a cost of $35 to $40.

COLCA VALLEY & CANYON ★★

165km (103 miles) N of Arequipa

Mario Vargas Llosa, the Peruvian novelist, Nobel Prize winner, and most famous Arequipeño, described Colca as "The Valley of Wonders." That is no literary overstatement. Colca is one of the most scenic regions in Peru, a land of imposing snow-capped volcanoes, narrow gorges, artistically terraced agricultural slopes that predate the Incas, arid desert landscapes and vegetation, and remote traditional villages, many visibly scarred by seismic tremors common in southern Peru. Some of Peru's most recognizable wildlife, including llamas, alpacas, vicuñas, and the celebrated giant Andean condors, roam the region.

The Colca River, one of the sources of the mighty Amazon, slices through the massive canyon, which remained largely unexplored until the late 1970s, when rafting expeditions descended to the bottom of the gorge. Reaching depths of 3,400m (11,150 ft.)—twice as deep as the Grand Canyon—*el Cañón del Colca* forms part of a tremendous volcanic mountain range more than 100km (62 miles) long. Colca, though, is no longer considered the world's, or even southern Peru's, deepest canyon; Cotahuasi, at the extreme northwest of the Arequipa department, has wrested away that honor. Among the region's great volcanoes, several of which are still active, are Mount Coropuna (6,425m/21,079 ft.), Peru's second-highest peak, and Mount Ampato (6,310m/20,702 ft.), where a sacrificed Inca maiden, known to the world as Juanita, was discovered frozen in 1995 (see "The Discovery of Juanita, the Ampato Maiden" on p. 292). The valley and its summits are a rapidly growing extreme-sports destination for hiking, mountain climbing, river rafting, and mountain biking.

Dispersed across the Colca Valley are 14 colonial-era villages, which date to the 16th century and are distinguished primarily by their small, but often richly decorated, churches. Local populations in the valley, descendants of the Collaguas and Cabanas, pre-Inca ethnic communities that have lived in the region for some 2,000 years, preserve ancient customs and distinctive traditional dress. They speak different

---

 The Air up There

The road from Arequipa to the Colca Valley climbs impressively, reaching 4,910m (16,100 ft.) at the Patapampa lookout point. The air is very thin at this altitude, and breathing is not at all easy. The main town in the valley, Chivay, sits at an altitude of nearly 3,600m (11,800 ft.), and nights can be brutally cold.

Travelers who haven't yet spent time in either Cusco or Puno/Lake Titicaca should take it easy for a couple of days in Arequipa before heading out to Colca. *Soroche,* or acute altitude sickness, is common. See "Health," in "Fast Facts" in chapter 13, for additional information on how to combat it.

Colca Valley & Canyon

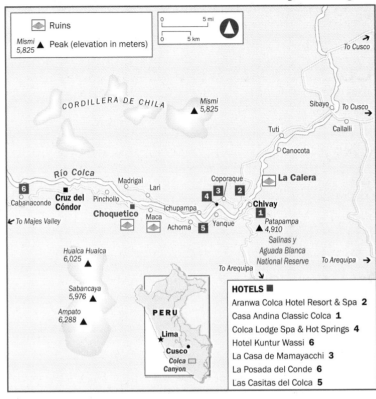

HOTELS ■

Aranwa Colca Hotel Resort & Spa **2**
Casa Andina Classic Colca **1**
Colca Lodge Spa & Hot Springs **4**
Hotel Kuntur Wassi **6**
La Casa de Mamayacchi **3**
La Posada del Conde **6**
Las Casitas del Colca **5**

languages and can be distinguished by their hats; Collagua women wear straw hats with colored ribbons, while the Cabanas sport elaborately embroidered and sequined felt headgear. (The men once wore distinctive dress as well but today are decidedly less colorful.) Colca villages are also celebrated for their vibrant festivals, which remain as authentic as any in Peru, throughout the year. The valley's meticulous agricultural terracing, even more extraordinary and extensive than the Inca terraces seen in the Sacred Valley near Cusco, were first cultivated more than 1,000 years ago.

Travelers are now spending more time in the Colca Valley, lapping up its extraordinary beauty, quiet traditional life, and opportunities for outdoor adventure sports, but the number-one draw remains the almost ineffable wonder of seeing majestic condors with massive wingspans soar overhead at Cruz del Cóndor lookout point over Colca Canyon and head out along the river.

The Colca Valley is lush and emerald green just after the heavy rains from January to March, but most of the rest of the year it is arid and dusty. Apart from that, the best time to visit Colca is during the dry season—May through November. The condors put on their best show from June to September, although recent reports of dwindling numbers of Andean condors in the canyon, perhaps due to continuing development in the region, are certainly cause for concern. Though sunny during the day, it can also get quite cold (below freezing) at night—which is not unexpected, since Chivay is higher than Cusco.

Essentials
GETTING THERE
Colca Valley is a long half-day (3–4 hr.) trip from Arequipa along dusty roads that climb steadily, passing through the **Reserva Nacional Salinas y Aguada Blanca,** populated only by a collection of grazing alpacas and vicuñas, en route. The road imposes less suffering than it did just a few years ago; the section of unpaved and bumpy travel is down to just 23km (14 miles), from 120km (75 miles). The **Mirador de los Andes** (also called Patapampa), 27km (17 miles) outside Chivay, is the highest point in the valley, ringed by eight snowcapped volcanoes, and a small army of *apachetas,* tiny towers of piled stones, marks the spot locals considered closest to mountain *apus* (gods). (Originally *apachetas* were offerings to the gods, but most, if not all, of these have been left behind by tourists.)

The great majority of visitors to the Colca Valley and the canyon do so on guided tours, arranged in Arequipa. Entry to Colca is $7 per person; you'll get a *boleto turístico* that serves for admission to a half-dozen sights in the region, including churches and the Cruz del Cóndor.

ORGANIZED TOURS
Conventional travel agencies offer day trips to Cruz del Cóndor, usually leaving at 3 or 4am, with brief stops at Chivay before returning to Arequipa—it's an awful lot to pack into a single day, especially at a high altitude, and it leaves no time to enjoy what makes the region unique (though you do arrive in time to see the condors at 8 or 9am). Expect to pay $30 to $40 per person. Two-day "pool" (grouped) tours are much more enjoyably paced and cost $50 to $130, depending on hotel arrangements (they include transportation, a guide, hotel accommodations, and breakfast; other meals are extra). Other campiña tours offered by many agencies include the Toro Muerto petroglyphs; Mejía lagoons, a bird sanctuary; Laguna Salinas, a saltwater lagoon populated by flamingos; Aguada Blanca Nature Reserve; and the remote Valley of the Volcanoes, a lunar landscape located more than 13 hours from Arequipa. The best all-purpose agencies in Arequipa, which offer everything from city tours to general and private tours of Colca, as well as hard-core adventure, are **Giardino Tours ★**, Jerusalén 604-A (www.giardinotours.com; ✆ **054/241-206**); **Colonial Tours,** Santa Catalina 106 (www.helloarequipa.com/colonial_tours; ✆ **054/286-868**); **Illary Tours,** Santa Catalina 205 (✆ **054/220-844**); **Ideal Tours,** Urbanización San Isidro F-2, Vallecito (idealperu@terra.com.pe; ✆ **01/9883-5617**); and **Santa Catalina Tours,** Santa Catalina 219 (santacatalina@star.com.pe; ✆ **054/216-994**). All of these agencies are also equipped to organize private transportation and hotel packages, which range from $95 per person for 1-day trips to $400 per person with accommodations at one of the top lodges in the region, such as Colca Lodge or the Las Casitas del Colca.

BY BUS   Local buses travel from Arequipa to Cabanaconde (6 hr.), near Cruz del Cóndor, with stops in Chivay (4 hr.). Two companies that make these runs are **La Reyna,** Terminal Terrestre, Arequipa (✆ **054/426-549**), and **Cristo Rey,** San Juan de Dios 510, Arequipa (✆ **054/213-094**). The ride costs S/15. Unless you have plenty of time and patience, or a real need to be on your own, your best bet for getting to Colca is to go with an organized group.

VISITOR INFORMATION

A **Centro de Visitantes (Visitors' Center),** open daily 8am to 5pm, with maps and a small exhibit on the region, is located within Aguada Blanca National Reserve, 45km (28 miles) outside of Arequipa. The office of the local **Tourist Police (℡ 054/ 488-623**) can be found on the Plaza de Armas in Chivay. It's open daily in the afternoon and should be able to provide hiking information. You can also pick up information in Arequipa from the tourist information office or one of the travel agencies that organize Colca trips.

Exploring the Area
MAIN COLCA VILLAGES: CHIVAY & CABANACONDE

The Valle del Colca is generally thought of in terms of left (south) and right (north) banks of the canyon, with villages and hotels of interest on both. Villages aren't separated by many kilometers, but the roads on both sides are rocky, dusty, and meandering, making for arduous and time-consuming driving. The left bank, which leads to Cruz del Cóndor, sees most of the tourists.

Although **Chivay,** on the left bank, is the valley's main town, it is still a largely sleepy little place that not long ago got on just fine without electricity. For many travelers on their way to Cruz del Cóndor and other spots in the valley, Chivay, which has the lion's share of restaurants and affordable hotels in the region, amounts to little more than a stopover. For those adhering to a leisurely pace, though, Chivay can be an enjoyable place to hang out; it benefits from an extraordinarily scenic natural setting. The attractive, low-key Plaza de Armas is the focus of attention in town and the site of several restaurants and *hostales.*

Most visitors hit the soothing and clean **La Calera hot springs ★** while in town. Though they can't compare with the thermal baths of Colca Lodge (see later in this chapter), they're enjoyable and easy to get to, just a 4km (2½-mile) walk or a colectivo ride from town, and inexpensive (S/10); they're open daily from 8am to 8pm.

The first village past Chivay (10km/6¼ miles) is **Yanque,** a modest town with a baroque 18th-century church. In **Maca ★,** a village on the way to Cruz del Cóndor that was destroyed by a 1979 earthquake, you'll find Santa Ana, a restored, brilliant white church with a surprising gilded interior. Nearby, perched overlooking the river, is the **Choquetico stone,** a pre-Inca carved-stone scale model of the mountains across the canyon, as well as a handful of Inca tombs carved out of the cliff face.

The remote, reserved village of **Cabanaconde,** the last town in the Colca Valley, is a couple of hours from Chivay. Some independent travelers prefer to stay here because it is within (hearty) walking distance, 15km (9⅓ miles), or a 15-minute drive, from the Cruz del Cóndor lookout point, and it's well positioned for other hikes in the canyon and throughout the valley. The views of the canyon are tremendous, and short walks take you to excellent vantage points overlooking some of the most brilliant agricultural terracing in the area. The locals are descendants of the Cabanas people, and they maintain traditional dress and customs; women wear hats embroidered with flowers and wide skirts. There is a good small hotel and a couple of inexpensive *hostales* in the village (see "Where to Stay & Eat," below).

The right (north) side of Colca Canyon is less visited. **Coporaque ★**, just across the river from Chivay, is a sleepy village with the oldest church in the valley, the charming **Templo de Coporaque,** built in 1569 with twin bell towers. Just outside the village, and on the way to Colca Lodge, is the stunning **Mirador de Ocolle ★★**, an amphitheater formed by agricultural terraces of varying shades of green. A new bridge from **Pinchollo** to **Lari** leads across a gorgeously terraced valley of pink rock and abundant cacti. Lary's primary attraction is its splendidly simple 1886 church, **Templo de la Purísima Concepción de Lari ★**. White with red trim, an orange and green portal, and double bell towers, it looks like a rural Mexican church or something that would decorate the top of a cake. It has recently been restored, and the interior is full of colorful murals and paintings, while the entire altar is adorned with brilliant baroque murals and painted columns. If you're not on a tour, you may have to ask at the shop next door for the key.

CRUZ DEL CÓNDOR ★★★

Cruz del Cóndor, or Condor Cross, about 50km (31 miles) west of Chivay, is just a lookout point on one side of Colca Canyon. However, it has become famous throughout Peru for its spectacular inhabitants: graceful Andean condors (*Vultur gryphus*). At a spot 1,200m (3,937 ft.) above the canyon river, large crowds gather every morning, zoom lenses poised, to witness a stunning wildlife spectacle. Beginning around 9am, the condors—the largest birds in the world, with awesome wingspans of 3.5m (12 ft.)—suddenly begin to appear, theatrically circling far below in the gorge and gradually gaining altitude with each pass, until they literally soar silently above the heads of awe-struck admirers before heading out along the river in search of prey. Condors are such immense and heavy creatures that they cannot simply lift off from the ground; instead, they take flight from cliff perches. The condors return late in the afternoon, but only a small group of people attends the show then. Witnessing the condors' majestic flight up close is a memorable and mesmerizing sight, capable of producing goose bumps on even the most jaded travelers (though photographing the

A TYPICAL guided TOUR OF COLCA VALLEY

Most organized tours of the region are very similar, if not identical. The road that leads out of Arequipa and into the valley, bending around the El Misti and Chachani volcanoes, is poor and unbearably dusty. It passes through the **Laguna Salinas** and **Aguada Blanca Nature Reserve,** where you'll usually have a chance to see rare vicuñas, llamas, and alpacas from the road. The altiplano landscape is barren and bleak. Most tours stop at volcano and valley lookout points along the way before heading to Chivay.

From **Chivay,** the valley's main town and the gateway to the region, many organized tours embark on short hikes above the canyon and visit the wonderfully

relaxing hot springs of **La Calera** (p. 311). Evening visits to the hot springs allow visitors to bathe in open-air pools beneath a huge, starry sky; artificial light in the valley is almost nonexistent. Charming colonial villages in the valley that are often visited by tours include Yanque, Coporaque, Maca, and Lari. Most 2-day tours head out early the following morning for **Cruz del Cóndor** to see the Andean condors begin to circle around 9am.

Organized tours generally include transportation, an English-speaking guide, hotel accommodations in Chivay or a nearby village (with breakfast), and park entrance fees to Colca and Cruz del Cóndor. Additional meals are extra.

ON those CAMELIDS

You'll likely have a chance to see three types of South American camelids common to the Andes: the domesticated llama and alpaca, and the considerably rarer wild vicuña. Llamas have been domesticated in the Andes for more than 5,000 years, used for meat, clothing, shelter, and fertilizer. Pre-Columbian civilizations also sacrificed llamas and alpacas as offerings to gods. Vicuñas are the smallest members of the camelid family, as well as the most prized and endangered. These camelids are native to the high plains of the Andes Mountains in Bolivia, Chile, and, primarily, Peru.

Alpacas and llamas differ in size and fiber quality. Adult alpacas are usually about a foot shorter than llamas, and the former produces 10 pounds a year or more of high-quality fiber in a single fleece. Alpaca hair is extremely fine, soft, smooth, and lightweight. It is stronger, warmer, and longer lasting than wool. "Baby alpaca" is the first clipping of the shearling, and, extraordinarily soft, it is universally prized and expensive. Llamas, on the other hand, have a less fine dual-fiber fleece, and the animals are better equipped to serve as excellent beasts of burden, perfect for mountain-trekking expeditions. Both llamas and alpacas graze at elevations of 3,000m (9,800 ft.) and higher. Llamas and alpacas are intelligent and gentle animals, but they have a reputation for a nasty habit: spitting. They usually spit at each other over food, but female llamas also spit at male llamas to ward off advances.

The vicuña is a national symbol in Peru, which is home to more than half the world's vicuña population. The Incas dressed their nobility in its ultrasoft fibers, considered the finest and warmest in the world, considerably lighter even than cashmere. Vicuña fleece sells for as much as $1,600 a pound; a man's sport coat made of vicuña costs at least $5,000. Poaching nearly rendered the vicuña extinct; it was declared endangered, and trade in vicuña products was banned internationally in 1975. With the vicuña community back up to approximately 200,000 animals throughout the Andean highlands, the animal is now considered threatened rather than endangered, and control over the harvesting of vicuña coats was placed under the ownership and management of Peru's Indian communities in the 1990s. Limited vicuña trade is now allowed; only garments stamped with the "Vicuñandes" trademark or "Vicuña" and the country of origin are deemed legal.

condors in flight demands skill, patience, and a substantial zoom lens). It's little wonder that the Incas believed them to be sacred creatures.

The dry months of June through September are when you're likely to see the largest group of condors in flight, and that's when they tend to circle and circle just over spectators' heads as they gain altitude, catch hold of a current, and set off down the river. The smallest number of condors is visible during the wet months of January through April and even October to December. On one trip to Colca in the last decade, I saw at least two dozen condors take off over the canyon, and a guide I spoke with claimed he once saw 54 in a single morning. On my most recent visit, however, I saw just three. There is great concern that the number of resident Andean condors has decreased dramatically, likely in response to the rapid hotel development and increased traffic near the canyon.

INDEPENDENT HIKING IN COLCA ★

Those looking to spend some quality hiking time in the valley and canyon can get to the region by public transportation or rental car from Arequipa and go out on their own. The largest number of inexpensive hotel accommodations is in Chivay. You can also camp throughout the canyon and valley, with the exception of Cruz del Cóndor.

The region is loaded with excellent hikes that can be done independently if you have suitable gear and camping equipment. Unless you're an experienced hiker, however, it's best to go with a guide (see "Tour Agencies for Rafting, Trekking & Mountaineering Expeditions," below).

Among the best hikes is a 2- to 3-hour, 1,300m (4,265-ft.) **descent into Colca Canyon** from the Cruz del Cóndor lookout. Because of the arduous, lengthy 5- or 6-hour climb back out, most travelers who do this hike end up camping down below near the **Sangalle oasis** with palm trees and water suitable for swimming. Hikes down to the canyon floor require good physical conditioning and preparedness (plenty of water, food, sunscreen, and so on). The trails are quite difficult in sections, and the altitude complicates the trek—the drop is more than 1,000m (3,281 ft.). An even longer and more demanding hike is to the village of **Tapay,** beginning at Cabanaconde and following a good trail from the oasis via the Río Colca (about 6 hr. each way). The path is very steep.

Less taxing hikes are possible by simply walking from one village to another in the region. From **Chivay** to **Yanque** along the main road is about 7km (4⅓ miles). You can continue from Yanque to the villages of **Achoma** (another 7km/4⅓ miles), **Maca** (12km/7½ miles), and **Pinchollo** (10km/6¼ miles). From there, on the way to Cabanaconde, it's about an hour to the **Colca Geyser (Hatun Infiernillo).**

EXTREME COLCA VALLEY: RAFTING, TREKKING & VOLCANO CLIMBING ★★

The countryside around Arequipa, laced with canyons and volcanoes, is one of the best in Peru for outdoor adventure travel. Trails crisscross the Colca Valley, leading across mountain ridges, agricultural terraces, and curious rock formations, and past colonial towns and fields where llamas and vicuñas graze. The most common pursuits are river running, treks through the canyon valleys, and mountain climbing on the volcanoes just beyond the city. Many tour agencies in Arequipa offer conventional 2- and 3-day visits to Colca Canyon, as well as longer, more strenuous treks through the valley and to Cotahuasi Canyon. Some of the most interesting (but most time-consuming and difficult) expeditions combine rafting and trekking. Your best bet for organizing any of these activities is with one of the tour operators mentioned below; several in Arequipa focus solely on eco- and adventure tourism.

RIVER RAFTING

The rivers and canyons around Arequipa pose some excellent river-running opportunities for both novices and experts. The best months for rafting are May through September, when water levels are low. (In the rainy season, when water levels are high, the canyon rivers can be extremely dangerous.) The most accessible rafting, suitable for first-timers, is on the **Río Chili,** just 15 minutes from downtown. It offers Class III and IV runs, and is a great way to get your feet wet during a half-day trip. Year-round runs of similarly moderate difficulty and scenic beauty can be arranged on day trips to the **Río Majes** (the Río Colca beyond the gorge). Rafting in Cotahuasi and Colca canyons is serious stuff for confident rafters; there are 3-day

Cotahuasi Canyon

Reputedly the deepest canyon in the world, Cotahuasi (3,354m/11,000 ft. at its deepest point) was only explored by rafting teams a few years ago. As enticing as trekking or rafting in the world's deepest canyon no doubt is to many, the effort required to get to Cotahuasi is substantial. It's a full 12 to 15 hours from Arequipa by bus, more than 400km (250 miles) on pretty difficult roads. Although some adventurers do go independently, trekking or rafting in the Cotahuasi is much better and more safely organized by a professional outfit such as Zárate Aventuras (see "Tour Agencies for Rafting, Trekking & Mountaineering Expeditions," below).

rafting trips to Colca (about $175) for those with moderate experience, and longer, 10- to 12-day trips to either canyon for serious white-water runners. The **Río Colca** (Class IV–V) is extremely technical, although some upriver sections are less dangerous and difficult. **Río Cotahuasi** was first explored only in 1994; it has 120km (75 miles) of Class IV and V rapids (and some Class VI). A few agencies offer annual trips that combine trekking with hard-core white-water rafting in Cotahuasi. These organized trips are expensive ($2,000 and up) and lengthy, usually 12 to 14 days total.

MOUNTAIN & VOLCANO CLIMBING

At the foot of the western Andes, Arequipa is ideally positioned for a variety of ascents—many of them not technically challenging—to volcano summits and mighty Andes peaks. Climbers in good physical condition can bag 5,000m (16,400-ft.) summits on ascents of 2 days or less. The best months for climbing are July through September, although some peaks can be climbed year-round. Climbers should be sufficiently acclimatized before making any ascents; if you've spent several days in Cusco or Puno before arriving in Arequipa (and are in good physical shape), you should be fine. Adventure travel operators in Arequipa provide logistical support, porters, and guides, but you must provide your own sleeping bag and boots. Be sure to ask plenty of questions about weather conditions, equipment, and experience before setting out with any guide.

El Misti, a nearly 6,000m (19,680-ft.) volcano, dominates the Arequipa landscape from a distance of about 20km (12 miles). The most popular climb among both locals and visitors, Misti is a demanding 2- or 3-day trek with few technical challenges. It is suitable for inexperienced climbers accompanied by professional guides. Most climbers stay the first night at the base camp Nido de Aguilas (Eagle's Nest) and reach the summit after about 7 hours of climbing on the second day. Arequipa's other major volcano, **Chachani** (6,075m/19,931 ft.), also presents an excellent and technically straightforward climb, a good opportunity for inexperienced climbers to brag about reaching a 6,000m (19,680-ft.) summit.

The Colca Valley has a number of peaks that draw serious climbers, including the **Ampato** volcano (6,288m/20,630 ft.), a 3- or 4-day climb, and the **Hualca Hualca** glacier (6,025m/19,767 ft.). **Coropuna** (6,425m/21,079 ft.), perhaps the most stunning mountain in the Cotahuasi Valley, requires a couple of days of travel from Arequipa to begin the difficult climb.

TOUR AGENCIES FOR RAFTING, TREKKING & MOUNTAINEERING EXPEDITIONS

The best general agencies in Arequipa (see "Getting There," earlier) arrange entry-level rafting and trekking itineraries. Almost all are located on just two streets in Arequipa—Jerusalén and Santa Catalina—so it's pretty simple to browse up and down and get a feel for an agency.

Apumayo Expediciones ★★, Jirón Ricardo Palma, N-5 Santa Monica, Wanchaq, Cusco (www.apumayo.com; ☎ **084/246-018**), is excellent for adventure trips in the region, including long trekking/rafting expeditions to Cotahuasi and Colca, as is **Amazonas Explorer ★★**, Zela 212, Cusco (www.amazonas-explorer.com; ☎ **054/252-846**), an international company that organizes hardy multisport trips to Cotahuasi and Colca (which can be combined with tours to Cusco, the Inca Trail, and Machu Picchu). **Cusipata Viajes y Turismo ★**, Jerusalén 408-A (www.cusipata.com; ☎ **054/203-966**), is the local specialist for Chili and Colca rafting and kayaking (including courses), and its guides, led by Gianmarco Vellutino, frequently subcontract out to other agencies in Arequipa. **Ideal Tours,** Urbanización San Isidro F-2, Vallecito (☎ **054/244-439**), handles Chili and Majes rafting, as well as Colca and other standard tours.

Colca Trek ★, Santa Catalina 204 (www.colcatrek.com; ☎ **054/202-461**), offers canyon treks of 3 to 5 days or more and a number of other adventure activities, such as horseback riding, mountain biking, rafting, and climbing.

For hard-core mountain climbing and trekking, one agency stands out: **Carlos Zárate Aventuras ★★**, Santa Catalina 204, no. 3 (www.zarateadventures.com; ☎ **054/202-461**), is run by Carlos Zárate, the top climbing guide in Arequipa (a title his dad held before him). He can arrange any area climb and has equipment rental and a 24-hour mountain-rescue service. Climbing expeditions (per person) start at: El Misti, $50; Chachani, $70; and Colca Canyon, $75. Mountain biking and rafting trips are also arranged.

For specialized birding programs (as well as other nature tours), **Tanager Tours,** La Estrella F-9, in the J. L. Bustamante y Rivero district (www.tanagertours.com; ☎ **054/426-210**), is the top choice in Arequipa.

Where to Stay & Eat

Most agencies offering 2- and 3-day trips to Colca Canyon put passengers up at modest hotels in the village of Chivay. If you can afford to step up a notch from budget accommodations, the following rustic inns in and around the canyon—primarily between Chivay and Cabanaconde—are the most comfortable and atmospheric places to stay in Colca. Comparatively luxurious, they are by far the best choices if offered by tour operators (often at bargain rates) or if you're traveling to Colca independently.

In the center of Chivay, **Casa Andina Classic Colca ★**, Huayna Cápac s/n, Chivay (www.casa-andina.com; ☎ **866/220-4434** toll-free in the U.S., or **054/531-020;** fax 054/531-098), is the latest entry into the Colca rustic hotel category and an indication that many people in the industry are betting on Colca's further development. It's easily the nicest place in the hub of Chivay. It recently expanded to 52 accommodations in the style that has become so popular in the region: Stone walls, thatched roofs, and cozy furnishings with thick wool blankets. The new bungalow-style rooms are slightly larger and have higher ceilings. A double room costs $89. The restaurant features folk music and dance shows as well as a cool planetarium and telescope.

Las Casitas del Colca ★★★, Parque Curiña s/n, on the outskirts of Yanque (www.lascasitasdelcolca.com; ✆ **800/237-1236** in the U.S. and Canada or **01/610-8300** or **054/959-672-480**), part of the upscale Orient Express chain that owns the Hotel Monasterio in Cusco and Machu Picchu Sanctuary Lodge, is easily the most exclusive inn in the valley. All-inclusive and the height of country luxury, it has undergone a stunning transformation in recent years. Its extraordinary casitas (individual thatched-roof bungalows) were inaugurated in 2008. Elegantly decorated and nestled about the property, the 20 casitas have private terraces and plunge pools. They're joined by a spectacular spa and free-form swimming pool. Perched on the lip of the canyon, the ecolodge features solar energy and electricity, a breakfast terrace with gorgeous valley views of extensive gardens, terraced fields, and the river. The kitchen turns out wonderfully fresh dinners and excellent breakfasts using ingredients from the garden, and the lodge also offers horseback riding. Although the place was once an incredible bargain, those days are gone, as is much of the old charming rustic simplicity. As handsome and studiously perfect as the place is, I miss what it once was, not to mention the old tariffs! A night in a private casita, with all meals and activities (such as horseback riding, cooking lessons, and fly-fishing) included, runs to $1,000 for a double (though much-cheaper deals are usually available online). But it is an unmatched, luxurious retreat in a beautiful place.

Colca Lodge Spa & Hot Springs ★★★, about 10km (6¼ miles) from Chivay (www.colca-lodge.com; ✆ **054/202-587; fax 054/220-407**), is beautifully situated across the river from Yanque and has one feature no other lodge can match: Its own private thermal baths, carved in stone and secluded along the banks of the river. The continually expanding lodge is a very comfortable, ecostyle hotel with adobe, stone, and thatched-roof architecture, solar power, and a swank new spa. Its level of luxury is just a small step down from the Las Casitas del Colca (above), the fanciest lodge in the region (although those hot springs make it a close call). The views of the valley are excellent from nearly everywhere. The hotel also has a sophisticated lodge-style restaurant serving fairly expensive lunches and dinners. The lodge's 45 rooms cost $165 per double (suites from $262). If you're not a guest, you can experience the thermal pools for $10.

The Aranwa hotel group is planning its own high-end addition to the Colca lodge scene, **Aranwa Colca Hotel Resort & Spa** (www.aranwahotels.com/colca_canyon_hotel.php); when completed in mid-2013, its 32 rooms and 8 bungalows should rival Las Casitas del Colca and Colca Lodge.

Giardino Tours books its Colca tour guests at **La Casa de Mamayacchi ★**, Coporaque (www.lacasademamayacchi.com; ✆ **054/241-206;** fax 054/242-761). Located just outside the village of Coporaque, it has 50 very comfortable rooms with exposed beams, great views, a fireplace lounge, and an attractive rustic restaurant featuring good local preparations. It's owned by the same folks who run La Casa de Mi Abuela Hotel in Arequipa. Rooms cost a very reasonable $70 per double.

There are just a few *hostales* and one hotel in quiet Cabanaconde, which will appeal to those who spend a couple of days hiking in the canyon. The top spot is **Hotel Kuntur Wassi ★**, La Ladera 360 (www.kunturwassi.com; ✆ **054/233-120** or **958/797-217**). On a hill above the village, this rambling small hotel, built of adobe and stone, has nicely decorated rooms with high ceilings, faux stone bathrooms, and lots of plants lining the walkways along the property. With a good restaurant and bar overlooking town, it's a nice place to relax after a long hike. The 25 rooms

10

SOUTHERN PERU | Colca Valley & Canyon

are $55 for doubles, $70 to $100 for suites. Ask about special multi-night package deals. **La Posada del Conde,** San Pedro at Bolognesi (© **054/440-197**), is the next best choice in the village: a decent, clean place, with private bathrooms; doubles are good value at $30.

Although most visitors eat all meals at their hotels, especially when staying at one of the lodges in the valley, a hodgepodge of restaurants (mostly in Chivay) host the lunchtime tourist groups that come through town. **Mama Tierra ★**, Calle Arequipa 504 (© **054/531-133**), a new restaurant a couple of blocks from the Casa Andina hotel, is a winner—a warm and cozy place with a stone oven and meats grilled on volcanic stone. **Witite,** Calle Siglo XX 328 (© **054/531-036**), named for a locally famous dance competition, serves a general Andean menu. **Solar Rosario,** Calle Arequipa 504 (© **054/531-133**), is a good-looking spot that offers a pretty good buffet lunch, and **Casablanca,** Plaza de Armas 705 (© **054/521-019**), serves a good-value *menú* and boasts a handful of vegetarian dishes. In Cabanaconde, the **Hotel Kuntur Wassi** (see above) has a nice little, good-value restaurant, serving alpaca and other local specialties as well as pizzas from a wood-fired oven. If you stay the night in Chivay, you may want to check out a little peña action (served up with dinner) at **El Encanto del Colca,** Calle Mariscal Castilla 500 (no phone), down a little side street. Good folkloric peña music can also be found at **El Nido,** Zarumilla 216 (© **054/531-010**), around the corner from El Encanto.

AMAZONIA

I ncredibly, nearly two-thirds of Peru is Amazon rainforest, which thrives with some of the richest biodiversity on the planet. Covering 6,475,000 sq. km (2,500,000 sq. miles), the Amazon basin represents 54% of all remaining rainforest on the planet. This vast, largely impenetrable region, with the smallest human population in the country and few towns of any significant size, stands in stunning contrast to the country's rugged Andean peaks and arid desert coasts. Jungle ecotourism has exploded in Peru, and the country's jungle regions are now much more accessible than they once were—a two-edged sword, of course—and there are more lodges and eco-options, including river cruises on Amazon tributaries, than ever. The southern Amazon region includes the immense protected zones Tambopata National Reserve and Manu National Park, while the northern Amazon, primarily accessible from Iquitos, reaches all the way to Peru's borders with Colombia and Brazil.

FLORA & FAUNA   The Peruvian Amazon is home to more than 400 species of mammals (of which about 70 are endemic and about 100 are threatened or endangered), 2,000 species of fish, 1,800 birds, and more than 50,000 plants (including 3,000 species of orchids). Incredibly, Peru boasts 84 of the world's existing 103 ecosystems and 28 of 32 total climates.

NATURE   The tropical rainforest east of the Andes, which occupies more than 60% of Peru, is one of the world's richest habitats, with tremendous plant and animal life. Peru has 72 million hectares (178 million acres) of natural-growth forests—70% in the Amazon jungle region—and Manu Biosphere Reserve, Tambopata National Reserve, and Pacaya-Samiria National Reserve constitute three of the largest protected rainforest areas in the world. Rivers define life in the jungle even more than do the forests; for both locals and visitors, almost all transport along the vast river system that stretches across the whole of eastern Peru is by dugout canoe, motorboat, or large riverboats (*lanchas*).

EATING & DRINKING   Fishing is a way of life in Amazon jungle regions, and most diets consist almost entirely of fish such as river trout and *paiche* (a huge river fish now endangered). Common accompaniments are *yuca* (a root), *palmitos* (palm hearts) and *chonta* (palm-heart salad), bananas and plantains, and rice *tamales* known as *juanes*. It's not uncommon to see wild boar, piranha, river and land turtles, caiman, and even monkey on menus—the last three of these animals are officially endangered, illegally hunted, and ought not to be consumed by travelers, no matter how exotic sounding. Fruit juices made from indigenous jungle fruits and beer are the most common beverages.

TOURS   The most common and convenient way to visit the Amazon jungle is by contracting a stay at a lodge (or lodges), either directly with it or with a travel outfitter that handles jungle tours. Packages generally include all local travel, accommodations, food and activities, including boating and nightlife viewing excursions, nature walks, and more. Jungle tours range from light and easily accessible 2-day, 1-night trips only a half-hour or so from the main city of entry (Puerto Maldonado or Iquitos) to deep immersion tours of 10 days or more. The more remote a lodge or camping trek is, and the more pristine and unspoiled the environment is, the more it's going to cost you to get there in terms of both time and money.

ACTIVE PURSUITS   Most of the active travel in the jungle is the travel itself: getting to a lodge aboard a riverboat. But once there, activities include ziplines, canopy walks, nature trail trekking, boating, and wildlife spotting excursions (including nighttime).

THE BEST TRAVEL EXPERIENCES IN AMAZONIA

o **Dangling above the treetops:** Get a thrill, as well as perspective on the density of the Amazon rainforest, by teetering above the trees on a canopy walkway or darting between them on a zipline. Reserva Amazónica Lodge and ExplorNapo have excellent canopy walks, and there's a great zipline at Tahuayo Lodge. See p. 352.

o **Marveling at a macaw clay lick:** Bring your binoculars for an unforgettable nature show: hundreds of brilliantly colored and squawking *guacamayos* (macaws) gathering for their daily feed at a clay lick. See p. 333.

o **Luxuriating at an ecolodge:** Although staying at a jungle ecolodge is generally equated with roughing it, there are several surprisingly luxo ecolodges, and you don't have to go all that deep into the jungle for pampering and a taste of the rainforest. One of the best is Reserva Amazónica, with a thatched-roof cocktail lounge and full-service spa overlooking the river. See p. 330.

o **Spotting giant river otters and pink dolphins:** You're unlikely to spot a jaguar or tapir, but don't despair: your chances of seeing endangered giant river otters and fabled pink river dolphins are actually pretty good if you get out on an oxbow lake or the river tributaries of the Northern Amazon. See p. 343.

o **Rolling on an Amazon river boat:** You could jump in a dugout canoe, but cruising the mighty Amazon on a rubber boom-era riverboat or the sleek, stunningly modern M/V *Aqua* of Aqua Expeditions will give you a real appreciation for the jungle's dramatic waterways. See p. 353.

THE SOUTHERN AMAZON JUNGLE ★★★

Easily accessible from Cusco, the southern jungle boasts some of Peru's finest and least spoiled Amazon rainforest. The area has been less penetrated by man than has the northern Amazon; indeed, the southern jungle remained largely unexplored until expeditions into the remote rainforest were undertaken in the 1950s. Two of Peru's top three jungle zones—and two of the finest in South America—dominate the southeastern department of Madre de Dios. The region's two principal protected areas, the **Manu Biosphere Reserve** (which encompasses the Parque Nacional del

Manu, or Manu National Park) and the **Tambopata National Reserve (Reserva Nacional de Tambopata),** are both excellent for jungle expeditions, although they differ in terms of remoteness and facilities.

Manu, one of the largest protected natural areas in the Americas and considered to be one of the most pristine jungle regions in the world, remains complicated and time-consuming to visit. Flights in and out of Boca Manu are now handled by the National Air Force rather than commercial carriers, and travel is possible only with one of eight officially sanctioned agencies. Expeditions last a minimum of 5 or 6 days (and most are a week or more), involve both significant overland and air (not to mention extensive river) travel, are expensive, and are very rustic, with the focus much more on contact with nature than creature comforts. Access is easiest from Cusco, although it involves a (spectacular) day's travel overland (or a half-hour flight), followed by a couple of days by boat.

Travelers without the time or budget to reach Manu often find Tambopata a most worthy alternative: Its wildlife and jungle vegetation are nearly the equal of Manu in some parts. Most lodges in Tambopata are considerably easier to get to and cheaper than those in Manu, although a couple require up to 8 or even 12 hours of travel by boat from Puerto Maldonado. The jungle frontier city of Puerto Maldonado, which is the capital of Madre de Dios department and just a half-hour flight from Cusco, is the jumping-off point to explore Tambopata. Travelers interested in the least time-consuming and least expensive way to see a part of the Peruvian jungle can visit one of the lodges on Madre de Dios River or Lago Sandoval, the latter an oxbow lake within a couple of hours of Puerto Maldonado.

In travel packages to both destinations, round-trip airfare from Cusco to Puerto Maldonado or Boca Manu (the gateway to the Manu Biosphere Reserve) is usually extra. Cheaper tours travel overland, stay at lesser-quality lodges (or primarily at campsites), and might travel on riverboats without canopies. Independent travel to Tambopata and two-way overland travel to either are options only for those with a lot of time and patience on their hands. Independent travelers not only find it complicated to enter many parts of the jungle, but they are also not permitted to enter the most desirable section of Manu, the Reserve Zone. Organizing a trip with one of the lodges or specialized tour operators listed below is highly recommended, in terms of both access and convenience. Most have fixed departure dates throughout the year. Do not purchase any jungle packages from salesmen on the streets of Cusco; their agencies might not even be authorized to enter restricted zones, and last-minute "itinerary changes" are likely.

Searing heat and humidity are year-round constants in the jungle (though in the southern jungle, occasional cold fronts called *friajes* are common). Appropriate gear for steamy tropical conditions is a must. Dry season (May–Oct) is the best time for southern jungle expeditions—during the rainy season, rivers overflow and mosquitoes gobble up everything in sight. Be careful to note when a tour operator's fixed departures leave (some are every Wed, others every Sun, and so on). Most lodge visits include boat transportation and three meals daily, as well as guided visits and activities (some, such as canopy walks and distant clay-lick outings, entail additional fees).

 Preventive Medicine for the Jungle

Yellow fever vaccinations are a wise idea before visiting the jungles of southeastern Peru. Even though the only reported outbreaks of yellow fever in the last couple of years have been in the northern Amazon around Iquitos, local authorities in Puerto Maldonado make sure that visitors who want to be protected are. At the airport arrival terminal, yellow fever shots are administered by Health Ministry nurses.

Other vaccinations worth considering are those for Hepatitis A and typhoid. Malaria pills are also a good idea, especially if you're planning to venture deep into the jungle. You should carry your vaccination records with you while traveling in Peru. For more information on health issues, see p. 439; also speak to your doctor or consult the World Health Organization or Centers for Disease Control and Prevention websites.

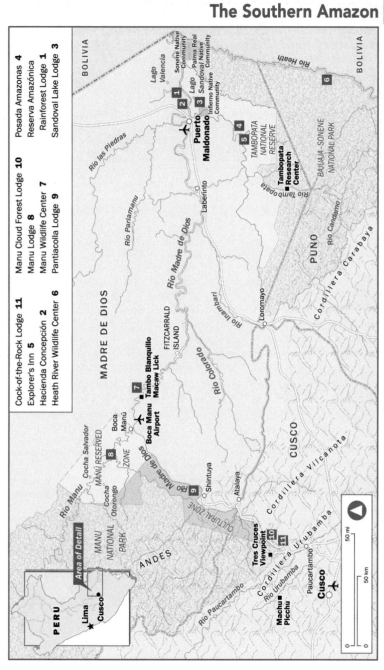

Posada Amazonas **4**
Reserva Amazónica
Rainforest Lodge **1**
Sandoval Lake Lodge **3**

Manu Cloud Forest Lodge **10**
Manu Lodge **8**
Manu Wildlife Center **7**
Pantiacolla Lodge **9**

Cock-of-the-Rock Lodge **11**
Explorer's Inn **5**
Hacienda Concepción **2**
Heath River Wildlife Center **6**

The southern Amazon region, which extends to the Bolivian and Brazilian borders, is concentrated in the Madre de Dios department, the least populated area in Peru. Although accessible by land from Cusco, it is an exceedingly difficult route. Most travelers fly to Puerto Maldonado (the gateway to the Tambopata National Reserve) and travel overland to the Manu Biosphere Reserve, returning by small aircraft.

Essentials

GETTING THERE

BY PLANE The **Aeropuerto Internacional Padre Aldamiz Puerto Maldonado** (𝄢 082/571-531) is 8km (5 miles) outside of the city. Flights arrive daily from Cusco and Lima on **LAN** (www.lan.com; 𝄢 01/213-8200) and **Star Perú** (www.starperu.com; 𝄢 01/705-9000) starting from $105 one-way from Cusco, $135 one-way from Lima. Health Ministry nurses are on hand to vaccinate visitors against yellow fever (*fiebra amarilla*). To get from the airport to town, the best bet is a *motocarro* (a motorcycle rickshaw), which costs about S/7.

Adventurous budget travelers with bountiful patience and perseverance, particularly those looking for a new warrior experience and the bragging rights that go with it, can travel by truck to Puerto Maldonado from Cusco. The journey takes at least 3 days in the dry season and up to 10 days in wetter conditions, and the route traverses more than 500km (310 miles) with zero comfort to speak of; it's certainly one of the worst (if not *the* worst) roads in Peru connecting two points of obvious interest. It costs about $15 and will provide you with stories for months, but you will definitely suffer for the dubious privilege. Trucks leave from Plaza Tupac Amaru in Cusco and arrive in Puerto Maldonado at the Mercado Modelo on Calle Ernesto Rivero. Take the challenge at your own risk; though the scenery is said to be astounding, the trip is not something I can recommend.

GETTING AROUND

In Puerto Maldonado, quick, easy, and cheap *motocarros* are everywhere; most rides in town cost S/2. Ferries cross the Ríos Madre de Dios and Tambopata daily. If you just want to cruise across the river you'll have to negotiate the price, but expect to spend about S/20 per person.

VISITOR INFORMATION

In Puerto Maldonado, there's a small booth at the airport that can give very limited information on the city and jungle lodges. Most visitors leave for the southern jungle from Cusco, so if you spend a few days there first, it's worthwhile to pick up more complete information on Puerto Maldonado and the rest of the jungle at the main **Tourist Information Office** at Mantas 117-A, a block from the Plaza de Armas (𝄢 082/263-176). Anyone traveling to Manu or Tambopata with an organized expedition should be able to get all the necessary information from the tour organizer.

ORGANIZED TOURS

See p. 329 for information on travel outfitters and lodges.

FAST FACTS

Banks on the Plaza de Armas include **Banco de la Nación,** Jr. Carrión 233 (𝄢 082/571-064), and **Banco de Crédito,** Arequipa 334 (𝄢 082/571-001). Only Banco de Crédito changes traveler's checks. There are also *casas de cambio* along Jirón Puno. Credit cards are not widely accepted in Puerto Maldonado, so you should plan on bringing cash for incidentals if you've already booked a lodge or tour program.

The best time to visit the Amazon is during the dry season—May through the end of October. During the rainy season in the southern Amazon, parts of the jungle are flooded and impassable. The northern jungle does not have a rainy season, per se, and travel there is less restricted during the winter. However, water levels can rise from 7.5m (25 ft.) to more than 15m (50 ft.) from December to May, and some jungle villages become flooded. Many naturalists find high-water months best for wildlife observation.

For required exit stamps to travel to Bolivia via Puerto Heath (a trip of 3–4 days by boat), visit the **Peruvian Immigration Office** at 26 de Diciembre 356, a block from the Plaza de Armas. It's open Monday through Friday from 9am to 1pm.

For medical attention, go to **Hospital Santa Rosa,** Jr. Cajamarca 171, at Velarde (✆ **082/571-019**). The **police station** can be found at Jr. Carrión 410 (✆ **105** or **082/571-022**). The **post office** is on Av. León Velarde 675 (✆ **082/571-088**). There's a **Telefónica del Perú** office at Jr. Puno 670 (✆ **082/571-600**). Several pharmacies are located along Jr. León de Velarde.

Internet cafes are located on the Plaza de Armas and along León de Velarde.

Puerto Maldonado
EXPLORING PUERTO MALDONADO & VICINITY

Founded in 1902 and once a prosperous rubber town, Puerto Maldonado is a humid, scruffy, and fast-growing place, a frontier market town that has gone through several phases of boom and bust, as have most jungle outposts. After the rubber boom came the game hunters and loggers. Today the town's primary industries continue to be based on exploiting the rainforest that surrounds Puerto Maldonado: gold prospecting, Brazil-nut harvesting, and ecotourism. It's the kind of place where streets just off the main square are still unpaved and full of muddy potholes, and colorful tin-roofed houses speak to the town's frontier ethos. For most travelers, Puerto Maldonado is merely a gateway to the jungle, and groups booked on Tambopata package tours often blow through town with little notice, ferried directly from the airport to waiting riverboats. Though it's a stiflingly hot one-horse (and motor-scooter) town, the frontier atmosphere, which continues to draw dreamers from across Peru, proves interesting to some visitors, at least for a day or two before they push on into the jungle.

The **Plaza de Armas,** or main square, is distinguished by tall palm trees and a peculiar, blue-and-yellow clock tower-cum-gazebo at its center. **Mercado Modelo** (Av. Fitzcarrald at Ernesto Rivero), the main market, throbs with noisy *chiringuitos* (storefronts serving food and fruit juices), Brazil nuts and other jungle produce, and natural rainforest remedies. Just out of town, on the road to the airport, is **La Casa de Mariposas** (www.inkaterra.com/en/reserva-amazonica/butterfly-house; ✆ **01/610-0400**), a conservation and learning center that has several hundred species of butterflies (of the 3,800 that exist in Peru).

Good jungle experiences, with possibilities of some fauna sightings and attractive walks in primary and secondary forest, are within easy reach of Puerto Maldonado. However, your experience will be vastly improved if you go farther from the city, particularly for stays of 2 nights or more at one of the lodges discussed below. Still, a couple of easy and inexpensive day trips from the regional capital—vastly better than comparable close-in trips from Iquitos—can be arranged.

LAGO SANDOVAL ★★   Sandoval Lake is about 5km (3 miles), or an hour by boat, from Puerto Maldonado. Even if you don't stay at the lodge on the lake or one of those nearby along the Río Madre de Dios (see "Tambopata Lodges," below), this pretty and serene oxbow lake, ringed by palm trees, makes an excellent day trip downriver from Puerto Maldonado. It boasts a surprising diversity of wildlife, including macaws, parrots, herons, kingfishers, caimans, turtles, and even a family of giant river otters that can frequently be spied in the lake. The best way to get here is to catch a canoe or motorboat at the port. You'll then have to walk a couple of kilometers along a path through the jungle, but it's a beautiful (if very hot) hour-long trek. Most jungle lodges along the Madre de Dios offer excursions to Lago Sandoval among their activities, though they usually arrive in the heat of the day, when wildlife activity is least observable (birds, monkeys, and the lake's caimans and resident river otters are much more active in the early morning and early evening hours).

WHERE TO STAY & EAT

Most people who stay overnight in Puerto Maldonado are either resting up from a trip to the jungle or trying to arrange one. In town, there are only a couple of decent and comfortable hotels, in addition to about a dozen very basic hostels.

The best place to stay in Puerto Maldonado is **Wasaí Maldonado Lodge ★**, Jr. Guillermo Billinghurst (www.wasai.com; ✆ **01/436-8792**). Although it's only a block from the main square in town, this inn is built much more like a mini-jungle lodge, with 6 of the 18 bungalows perched on stilts. The location is quite stunning, overlooking the Madre de Dios River. The spacious and comfortable bungalows are cabin-like paneled rooms with refrigerators, private bathrooms with hot water, air-conditioning (or fan), and TV. The small swimming pool, which looked abandoned on my last visit, overlooks the river. The lodge restaurant, the best and most upscale in town, is in a gazebo that sits above the riverbank; on the second floor is a new bar with good river views. Doubles in bungalows with river views cost $52. Ecotours and jungle expeditions with stays at the **Wasaí Tambopata Lodge,** 120km (75 miles)—about 6 hours—upriver on the Río Tambopata, and visits to Sandoval Lake (4 days/3 nights, $504 per person; day rate, $80 per person), as well as other jungle junkets, can be arranged.

Hotel Don Carlos Maldonado, Velarde 1271 (www.hotelesdoncarlos.com; ✆ **082/571-029**), sits above the banks of Tambopata River about 5 blocks south of the center of town and is surrounded by native flora. Smaller, more rustic, and more low-key than the chain's other hotels, this inn nonetheless has a host of services and

---

 Native Foods

Local jungle dishes worth a try include *patarashca,* a steamed river fish wrapped in banana leaves; *timbuche,* a thick soup made with local fish; and *tacacho,* or bananas cooked over coals and served with fried pork and chopped onions. Locals also eat *motelo* (turtle soup served in its shell) and *muchangue* (turtle eggs with steamed bananas), but, given that river and sea turtles are endangered species protected by Peruvian law, it seems especially criminal for gringos to indulge this custom. *Mazato* is a local beverage of fermented *yuca,* bananas, and milk.

Río Madre de Dios

Port

Jr. Billinghurst

Jr. Loreto

PLAZA DE ARMAS

Jr. Carrión

Jr. 26 de Diciembre

Jr. Ernesto River

Jr. Cusco

Jr. Puno

Jr. Arequipa

Av. 2 de Mayo

← To Airport

Jr. Moquegua

Jr. González Prada

Av. Léon Velarde

PERU

Lima

Cusco

Puerto Maldonado

Jr. J. Troncoso

Jr. Tacna

ATTRACTIONS ●
La Casa de Mariposas 2
Mercado Modelo 9

HOTELS ■
Hotel Cabañaquinta 3
Hotel Don Carlos Maldonado 10
Wasaí Maldonado Lodge 4

RESTAURANTS ◆
Bulevard Video-Pub 5
El Califa 1
Hotel Cabañaquinta Restaurant 3
La Casa Nostra 8
Pizzería Trattoria El Hornito 6
Pollos a la Brasa La Estrella 7
Wasaí Maldonado Lodge Restaurant 4

amenities, including a restaurant, laundry, 24-hour room service, an outdoor swimming pool, and air-conditioning. The 15 rooms are nice enough, but hardly a steal, at $60 for a double. **Hotel Cabañaquinta,** Cusco 535 (www.hotelcabanaquinta.com. pe; ✆ **082/571-045**), is a comfortable inn with 50 pretty decent but simple rooms with private bathrooms, a nice garden, small pool and sauna, and one of the better restaurants in town. Double rooms cost S/130–S/170.

The top restaurant in town is the one at **Wasaí Maldonado Lodge** ★ (see above). The hotel restaurants at **Don Carlos** and **Cabañaquinta** are also frequented by visitors to town, but there are a slew of basic eateries, *chifas,* and cafes clustered near the Plaza de Armas and lining León de Velarde, the main street. **La Casa Nostra,** Jr. León de Velarde 515 (✆ **082/573-833**), is a good little cafe stop for hamburgers, *tamales,* typical Peruvian dishes like *papas rellenas* (stuffed potatoes) and a host of desserts and cakes, as well as tropical fruit juices. **Pizzería Trattoria El Hornito,** Jr. Carrión 271, Plaza de Armas (✆ **082/572-082**), is a good and cozy pizza joint and pub serving wood-fired pies. It's open daily until midnight and accepts credit cards. **El Califa,** Piura 266 (✆ **082/571-119**), on a small side street, is a local, open-air joint that, with bright green paneling, ceiling fans, a tin roof, and verdant garden, very much looks the part of small-town tropical eatery. It serves local jungle cuisine and good Peruvian meals, including ceviche, at lunch. Grilled and rotisserie chicken, always a good bet in Peru, can be had at **Pollos a la Brasa La Estrella,** Velarde 474 (✆ **082/573-107**).

A great stop for dessert on the Plaza de Armas is **Heladería Gustitos del Cura,** Loreto 258 (no phone), a sweet little ice cream parlor. It serves *sorbetes* (sorbets) and ice creams made from Amazonian fruits and donates profits to a local charity organization.

Tambopata National Reserve ★★★

650km (404 miles) NE of Cusco; 37km (23 miles) SW of Puerto Maldonado

Upstream from Puerto Maldonado, jungle lodges in and around the **Tambopata National Reserve (Reserva Nacional de Tambopata)**—a massive tract of humid subtropical rainforest in the department of Madre de Dios—are located either along the Tambopata or Madre de Dios rivers. The National Reserve covers 275,000 hectares (nearly 680,000 acres), while the entire area, including the Bahuaja-Sonene National Park, encompasses some 1.5 million hectares (3.7 million acres) of Amazonian jungle. The Peruvian government prohibited hunting and logging in the area in 1977 and created the reserve, then called the Tambopata-Candamo Reserve Zone, in 1990. Nearly one-third the size of Costa Rica, Tambopata has more species of birds (595) and butterflies (more than 1,200) than any place of similar size on Earth.

Visits to lodges here are considerably more accessible than those in Manu. Most trips involve flying a half-hour from Cusco and then boarding a boat and traveling by river for 45 minutes to up to 5 hours to reach a jungle lodge. Primary lodges are those that travelers can get to the same day they arrive by plane in Puerto Maldonado. Although mankind's imprints are slightly more noticeable in the Tambopata region, the area remains one of superb environmental diversity, with a dozen different types of forest and several gorgeous oxbow lakes. Environmentalists claim that Tambopata's great diversity of wildlife is due to its location at the confluence of lowland Amazon forest with three other ecosystems. At least 13 endangered species are found here, including the jaguar, ocelot, giant armadillo, harpy eagle, and giant river otter. The farther one travels from Puerto Maldonado, the greater the chances of significant wildlife viewing.

The Tambopata Macaw Clay Lick (*collpa de guacamayos*) within the reserve is one of the largest natural clay licks in the country and one of the wildlife highlights of Peru. Thousands of brilliantly colored macaws and parrots arrive daily at the cliffs to feed on mineral salts.

Most visitors prearrange tours to Tambopata in Cusco or in their country of origin, although one could also book a lodge visit by stopping in the local offices of travel agents and tour operators in the center of Puerto Maldonado or at the airport (though you will have less information and opportunity to compare offerings). Access to Tambopata is by boat from Puerto Maldonado. Packages begin with 2-day/1-night arrangements, but 3-day/2-night packages are preferable. Lodge stays generally allow visitors to see a large variety of trees, plants, and birds, but sightings of wild mammals, apart from monkeys and otters, are rare. Large and rare species such as jaguars and tapirs are infrequently seen, though visitors to Lago Sandoval, an oxbow lake, have the exciting opportunity to see an extended family of resident giant river otters (known in Spanish as *lobos de río*).

The weather in the Madre de Dios region is usually extremely hot and sticky, as you would expect. But the southern jungle's proximity to the Andes produces periodic cold spells called *friajes,* which originate in the South Pole, from June through September. When they hit, *friajes* drop the temperature to 48°F (9°C) for a period of 2 or 3 days. It's a good idea to pack a jacket and even some gloves on the off chance that the jungle turns cold on you.

Lodges are located predominantly either along the Río Tambopata, which extends south of Puerto Maldonado, or the Río Madre de Dios, east of the city. The area around the Río Tambopata, with greater primary forest, is generally considered better for wildlife viewing.

EAST OF PUERTO MALDONADO: ALONG THE RIO MADRE DE DIOS

Lodges within a couple of hours by boat from Puerto Maldonado are generally cheaper (and, of course, less time-consuming to get to) than those deeper in the Tambopata National Reserve. Because they are located in secondary jungle and are not nearly as remote, they best serve as introductory visits to the Amazon. The forest along the Madre de Dios is generally not as pristine as that found along the Tambopata River. The following lodges are several of the best that are easily accessible from Puerto Maldonado (as little as a half-hour by boat).

○ **Sandoval Lake Lodge ★★** (www.inkanatura.com; ℭ **888/870-7378** in the U.S. and Canada or **01/440-2022**). This pioneering lodge, on high bluffs overlooking lovely Sandoval Lake (p. 326) and surrounded by palm trees and thick forest, is the best option close to Puerto Maldonado if you're more into wildlife than plush accommodations. It is one of just three in the Amazon in a nationally protected zone, and by far its greatest advantage is its unique location on one of the jungle's prettiest oxbow lakes. The journey to the lodge is part of the experience; after a 45-minute boat ride, you walk a couple of kilometers (another 45 min.) through secondary forest, then you hop in a wooden canoe and paddle along a canal and then across the lake. The rustic, spacious facility consists of a large main dining room and lounge, and two wings of rooms with private bathrooms (but open ceilings). Visitors have their choice of wildlife-viewing centers and leisurely paddled catamaran and canoe trips on the lake at prime viewing hours; most visitors not only see a wealth of aquatic and jungle birds, including macaws, but several species of monkeys, caimans, and the elusive, highly prized community of giant river otters (on my last trip here I witnessed the complete group of 10 playing and lounging on a log in the lake). Prices range from $325 to $475 for 3- to 4-day stays. InkaNatura's newest lodge is the remote **Heath River Wildlife Center,** situated another 3 hours downriver near the Bolivian border, within easy reach of a large macaw clay lick and owned and staffed by the indigenous Ese'Eja Sonene people; it is possible to combine a couple of nights at both lodges. Heath River prices range from $575 for 4 days to $645 for 5 days. InkaNatura, which administers the lodge, is the Peruvian partner of the American environmental organization Tropical Nature (which handles international marketing). Outside Peru, trips can be organized through **Tropical Nature Travel,** P.O.

What's an Oxbow Lake?

An oxbow lake is a natural lake formed by the normal shifting of river waters, which have fashioned a new streambed in the riverbanks. The old riverbed fills with water and forms a lake. Oxbow lakes are essentially designed to become extinct. After forming, they have life expectancies of perhaps 400 years; they expand but then become shallower as river flooding and runoff deposits sediment, sand, and leaves, and then begin to dry up as grasses and trees take root. Oxbow lakes, which can be very large and superb spots for wildlife viewing, are so named because they are shaped like an old-fashioned U-shaped yoke.

Box 5276 Gainesville, FL 32627-5276 (www.tropicalnaturetravel.com; ☎ **877/827-8350** toll-free in the U.S. and Canada).

○ **Reserva Amazónica Rainforest Lodge ★★** (www.inkaterra.com/en/reserva-amazonica; ☎ **800/442-5042** in the U.S., **808/101-2224** in the U.K., or **01/610-0400** in Lima). Although one of the oldest lodges in the Peruvian Amazon, this completely upgraded place—operated by the folks behind the swanky Machu Picchu Pueblo Hotel—just 15km (9⅓ miles), or 1 hour down the Madre de Dios from Puerto Maldonado, is also one of the plushest. In other words, it is *the* place for an upscale jungle experience and creature comforts. Its large main house, stylishly designed like an Indian roundhouse, features a dining room and upstairs lounge, perfect for swilling drinks after a day in the jungle. The 43 thatched-roof, African-style bungalows, attractively strewn about the riverside property, are a model of rustic chic, a fancy step up from most accommodations in the jungle. Rooms have private bathrooms and terraces with hammocks. Though there's no electricity in the rooms, the kerosene lamps left at the door add to the romance of the place. The superior cabanas and suites are particularly luxurious. Food is excellent, and the guides are very professional (they even wear matching Disney-like eco-outfits). Although the surrounding forest doesn't teem with wildlife (except for sonorous russet-backed Oropendola birds that make waking up a treat), there's a good system of trails nearby, as well as an island that is home to a dozen or so rescued monkeys and a terrific canopy walk (which leads to a canopy tree house). An unusual bonus in the Amazon, the lodge's expanded ENA spa, overlooking the river, offers Reiki, cold stone massage, reflexology, and other types of massage services. Rates range from $865 to $1,399 (the latter in a suite and including spa treatments) for 4 days.

○ **Hacienda Concepción ★** (www.byinkaterra.com/hacienda-concepcion; ☎ **800/442-5042** in the U.S., **808/101-2224** in the U.K., or **01/610-0400** in Lima). Near Lago Sandoval, just 20 minutes (or 8 km) downriver from Puerto Maldonado, this newly refurbished lodge is a secondary property of the Inkaterra group (which owns Reserva Amazónica). The small and intimate lodge has just 15 rooms (8 doubles and 7 cabañas or bungalows, including several with views over a small, private *cocha*, or lake) that are smart and jungle sleek. It's walking distance to the Sandoval oxbow lake and its giant river otters, and guests can also venture over to Reserva Amazónica (another 20 min. downriver) to take advantage of its canopy walkway. Rates range from $280 per person for 3 days in a double to $806 per person for 5 days in a cabaña.

SOUTH OF PUERTO MALDONADO: ALONG RÍO TAMBOPATA

○ **Explorer's Inn ★★★** (www.explorersinn.com; *(©)* **01/447-8888**). The only lodge located within the Tambopata National Reserve, this comfortable 30-year-old lodge hosts both ecotourists and scientists. It's a little over 3 hours upriver from Puerto Maldonado along the Tambopata River, and is excellent for viewing fauna, including otters, monkeys, and particularly jungle birds. (It's probably the top spot in Tambopata for birding.) Established in 1976, the complex has seven rustic, thatched-roof bungalows and 30 rooms with private bathrooms. The lodge has a good network of nearly 32km (20 miles) of trails, including several to nearby oxbow lakes. Guides are Peruvian and international biologists (or biologists in training). The organization **Amazonia Tours** (www.peruviansafaris.com) arranges travel in Peru; prices range from $230 for 2 nights to $557 for a 7-day Bird Watching program.

○ **Posada Amazonas ★★**. About 45 minutes up the Tambopata River from Puerto Maldonado, this lodge is owned jointly with the Infierno indigenous community and is quite good for inexpensive, introductory nature tours. It has an eagle nest site and a canopy observation tower, and two parrot clay licks are located within a kilometer of the lodge. The lodge, inaugurated in 1998, featuring 30 rustic rooms and a wall open to the forest, is operated by the award-winning **Rainforest Expeditions ★★★** (www.perunature.com; *(©)* **01/719-6422** or **51/997-511-024**). This veteran ecotourism company promotes tourism with environmental education, research, and conservation, and operates two Tambopata lodges. Prices are $375 to $695 for 3- to 5-day trips. The 13-room **Tambopata Research Center ★★★** is more remote (8 hr. upriver from Puerto Maldonado), just 500m (1,640 ft.) from the jungle's largest and most famous macaw clay lick. Just one of three Peruvian lodges in a protected national nature reserve, it is the best lodge in Tambopata for in-depth tours and viewing wildlife, including several species of monkeys. It's certainly *the* place to see flocks of colorful macaws and parrots. Trips usually entail an overnight at Posada Amazonas before continuing on to the Research Center. A 5-day trip runs to $795. The newest

---

Birds, Plants? Check. Monkeys & Macaws? Check. Caimans? Check. Jaguars? Not So Fast!

Peru's Amazon jungle regions have some of the greatest recorded biodiversity and species of plants and animals on Earth. However, you may be disappointed if you go expecting a daily episode of *Wild Kingdom*. An expedition to the Amazon is not like a safari to the African savanna. Many mammals are extremely difficult to see in the thick jungle vegetation, and though the best tour operators employ guides skilled in ferreting them out, there are no guarantees. Even in the most virgin sections, after devoting several patient days to the exercise, you are unlikely to see a huge number of mammals, especially the rare large species such as tapirs, jaguars, and giant river otters. If you spot a single one of these prized mammals, your jungle expedition can be considered a roaring success. (Your best shot at seeing jaguars is in Manu during the months of May and June.) However, in both Manu and Tambopata you are very likely to see a wealth of jungle birds (including the region's famous and fabulous macaws), several species of monkeys, black caimans, butterflies, and insects.

lodge run by the group is the 32-room **Refugio Amazonas ★**, adjacent to the Tambopata National Reserve and about 4 hours by boat upriver from Puerto Maldonado. Prices are $375 for a 3-day trip to $2,300 for a 7-day Biology and Ecology seminar.

Manu Biosphere Reserve ★★★

242km (150 miles) NE of Cusco

Manu, a UNESCO World Biosphere Reserve and World Heritage Site, certainly doesn't lack for distinctions and accolades. The Biosphere Reserve encompasses the least accessible and explored jungle of primary and secondary forest in Peru, and it is about as close as you're likely to come to virgin rainforest anywhere in the world. In fact, it's so remote that not only did the Spaniards, who found their way to virtually every corner of Peru except Machu Picchu, never enter the jungle, but the Incas, who created an empire that stretched from Ecuador to Chile, never conquered the region either. The forest wasn't really penetrated until the late 1800s, when rubber barons and loggers set their sights on it. Peru declared it a national park in 1973.

Only slightly smaller than the Pacaya-Samiria National Reserve (see "Into the Wild: Farther Afield from Iquitos" on p. 354), Manu—about half the size of Switzerland—is one of the largest protected areas in South America, with just less than 2 million hectares (nearly 5 million acres). Its surface area of varied habitats includes Andes highlands, cloud forests, and lowland tropical rainforests. The park encompasses an area of almost unimaginable diversity, climbing as it does from an altitude near sea level to elevations of 3,500m (11,480 ft.).

A single hectare of forest in Manu might have 10 times the number of species of trees that a hectare of temperate forest in Europe or North America has. Manu, which contains the highest bird, mammal, and plant diversity of any park on the planet, offers visitors perhaps their best opportunity for viewing wildlife that has been pushed deep into the rainforest by man's presence. It boasts nearly 1,000 species of birds, 1,200 species of butterflies, 20,000 plants, 200 species of mammals, and 13 species of primates. Species in danger of extinction include the spectacled bear, giant armadillo, and Andean cock-of-the-rock.

Birders thrill at the prospect of glimpsing bird populations that account for 10% of the world's total, more than what's found in all of Costa Rica. Hugely prized among wildlife observers are giant river otters, parrots, and macaws at a riverbank clay lick; preening and bright red cocks-of-the-rock; and lumbering lowland tapirs gathering at a forest clay lick. Scientists estimate that perhaps 12,000 to 15,000 animal species remain to be identified. Manu is also home to dozens of native Amerindian tribes, some of which have contact with the modern world and others that remain secluded.

 All Alone in the Forest . . . with a Few Good Friends

As remote and huge as the Manu Reserve Zone is, don't expect to find yourself enveloped and alone in the quiet of the jungle during high season. The few lodges and tour operators with a presence in the zone are very busy during the months of June, July, and August, and travelers' contact with each other might greatly outdistance their contact with species native to the rainforest. This is the case despite the official limits of 30 travelers per agency per week. (If all 10 agencies have full loads, that's still 300 people traveling many of the same waterways and racing to arrive first at primary observation points.)

While Tambopata is superb for bird-watching, with nearly 600 species, Manu enjoys a nearly mythic reputation among birders. And it should: It has the highest concentration of birdlife on the planet. In addition to its many thousands of species of plants, more than a dozen species of monkeys, and hundreds of mammals, the Manu Biosphere Reserve contains some 1,000 species of birds, including seven species of colorful macaws. That's more than half the bird species in all of Peru—one of the top countries in the world (along with Colombia and Indonesia) for recorded bird species within its borders. That's more species than are found in all of Costa Rica, and it's one of every nine birds in the world! The forests of the western Amazon enjoy the highest density of birds per square mile of any on Earth.

The immense variety of birds is due to the diversity of altitudinal zones, habitats, and ecosystems spread across Manu, which encompasses cloud forest and upper and lowland tropical forest. In addition, Manu shimmers with vastly different types of forests, lakes, and microclimates. From the Andes Mountains surrounding Cusco, the road to Manu plummets an amazing 4,000m (13,120 ft.) down to the dense tropical forests of the Amazon basin. For every 1,000m (3,280 ft.) of change in elevation, the indigenous bird life changes just as dramatically. The twisting road near the Cock-of-the-Rock Lodge has been called "the best road in the world" by leading bird-tour companies.

In visits of just 2 to 3 weeks in Manu, dedicated birders have recorded a staggering 500 species. Birders can expect to come into contact with quetzals, toucanets, tanagers, and the famed, blazing-red Andean cocks-of-the-rock at their numerous leks. Also of interest to birders, among many dozens more, are the blue-headed macaw, white-cheeked tody-tyrant, bamboo antshrike, and Manu antbird.

For most visitors, the spectacle of viewing hundreds of *guacamayos*, or macaws, and other birds feeding at a *collpa* (clay lick) in Tambopata or Manu remains the holy grail of Amazon bird-watching. Many birds and mammals (such as tapirs) supplement their diets with minerals found in clay, which is loaded with minerals and salts. Early in the morning, parrots gather in trees above the river. They then descend in large numbers and feed at the clay. Gorgeously colored and noisy macaws arrive next. Visitors often view the scene from a small catamaran. **Blanquillo Macaw and Parrot Lick,** the subject of a 1994 *National Geographic* report and subsequent TV special on macaws, is the most famous *collpa* in Manu. *Collpa* viewings are during the dry season only and are best from July to September; macaws do not feed at the clay licks during the month of June, for reasons unknown.

All the Manu tour operators focus to some extent on birding, of course, but for specialists, the **Manu Wildlife Center ★★★** (www.manu-wildlife-center.com), jointly owned by Manu Expeditions, itself run by a well-known ornithologist, is perhaps best suited for enthusiastic birding in Manu. Also recommended by birders is **Pantiacolla Lodge ★** (p. 337) where birders have recorded 500 birds in a month's worth of observation. **Tanager Tours ★**, La Estrella F-9, J. L. Bustamante y Rivero, Arequipa (www.tanagertours.com; ✆ **054/426-210**), organizes birding trips to Manu, Puerto Maldonado, and many other spots in Peru; the Dutch-owned group also has a branch in Cusco.

Birders and would-be birders should check out **Birding Peru** (www.birding peru.org) and **Ornifolks** (www.ornifolks. org) for additional bird-watching trips to Peru. **WorldTwitch** (www.worldtwitch. com) has helpful links to birding lodges, tour operators, and organizations throughout Peru, as well as the Americas and the Caribbean.

THE amazon IN DANGER

Could the vast Amazon rainforest disappear from the face of the Earth during our lifetimes? Some scientists now maintain that the forest itself—not to mention the many thousands of plant, animal, bird, and insect species that call it home—is in imminent danger of extinction. A mathematical model by an American researcher, presented at a 2001 Geology Society conference in Scotland, suggests that the destruction of Amazonian rainforests could be irreversible in a few years, and forecasts the wholesale destruction of Brazil's rainforest in about 40 years.

Peru, the origin of the great Amazon River, boasts some of the largest and most biologically diverse rainforests in the world. The country counts 84 of 103 existing ecosystems and 28 of the 32 climates on the planet among its remarkable statistics. Peru has 72 million hectares (178 million acres) of natural-growth forests—70% in the Amazon jungle region—that comprise nearly 60% of the national territory. But it's losing nearly 300,000 hectares (740,000 acres) of rainforest annually. In other Amazon basin countries, the picture is even bleaker. Half the world's known plant and animal species live in rainforests, but according to the World Resources Institute, more than 100 species become extinct in the world every day due to tropical deforestation. The destruction of their habitats is estimated at 81,000 hectares (200,150 acres) each day—an area larger than New York City. Less than 50 years ago, 15% of the Earth's land

surface was rainforest. Today that total has been reduced to a mere 6%.

The primary threats to Peru's tropical forests are deforestation caused by agricultural expansion, cattle ranching, logging, oil extraction and spills, mining, illegal coca farming, and colonization initiatives. Deforestation has shrunk territories belonging to indigenous peoples and wiped out more than 90% of the population. In the southern Amazon's Madre de Dios department, 3 decades of gold prospecting have pushed isolated tribes to the edge of extinction. Along with the threats to communities comes cultural extinction: Knowledge of plants and natural medicines, traditional ways of life, and even languages are lost. In Peru's Amazon jungle, new languages are being discovered even as others become extinct. Once-isolated communities in the jungle spoke up to 150 languages; today, only 53 survive and 25 of them are in danger of extinction, according to the Summer Institute of Linguistics.

Governments in developing countries have traditionally been reluctant to adopt tough measures to halt deforestation, bowing to the need for "economic development" and offering inducements to industry and extraction practices that have ranged from rubber extraction to logging and oil drilling. Slash-and-burn clearing of land, unproductive farming, and overhunting by marginalized people living in and around the jungle have further denuded the landscape of vegetation and animals. Five hundred years ago, an estimated 10 million indigenous

Going with a group tour to Manu is the only realistic way to visit the park, and only a handful of travel agencies in Cusco are authorized to organize excursions to the Manu Biosphere Reserve. The Reserve comprises three zones: **Manu National Park,** an area of dedicated conservation reserved for scientific study (the largest zone, it occupies 3.7 million hectares/9.1 million acres, or about three-fourths of the entire reserve); the **Reserve Zone,** up the River Manu northwest of Boca Manu,

people inhabited the Amazon rainforest; by the 21st century, that population had dropped to less than 200,000.

Can anything be done to save the Amazon and its people, plants, and animals? Leaving the rainforests intact, with their wealth of nuts, fruits, oil-producing plants, and medicinal plants, has greater economic value than destroying them for unsustainable short-term interests. More than six times as much can be earned from sustainable harvests of fruit, cocoa, timber, and rubber from the rainforest tract than commercial logging produces. Slash-and-burn practices, which involve no preparation of the land and no safeguards to make its yield sustainable, destroy the land's capacity to produce: A plot can be burned just twice before a farmer must abandon it and search for another, uncultivated piece of land.

For most of the 20th century, Peru gave carte blanche to oil and gas exploration by multinationals in the Amazon basin, and the government looked the other way with regard to invasive gold mining in Indian communities. However, Peru has done a slightly better job of setting aside tracts of rainforest as national park reserves and regulating industry than have some other Latin American and Asian countries. The Manu Biosphere Reserve, the Tambopata National Reserve, and the Pacaya-Samiria National Reserve are three of the largest protected rainforest areas in the world, and the government regulates entry of tour groups. Peru augmented the Bahuaja-Sonene National Park, which

was created in 1996, by 809,000 hectares (nearly 2 million acres) in 2001. INRENA, Peru's Institute for Natural Resource Management, enforces logging regulations and reseeds Peru's Amazon forests. A handful of international and Peruvian environmental and conservation groups, such as ProNaturaleza and Conservation International, are active in Peru, working on reforestation and sustainable forestry projects.

Many conservationists have mixed feelings about promoting ecotourism in endangered habitats. Responsible tourism has the potential to educate people about the rainforest and its threats and could spur much-needed activism. The income produced by ecotourism is vital to local communities—many of whom are increasingly dependent upon tourists to buy their handicrafts or to lead on treks into the jungle—and to countries, as an incentive to protect the very things tourists come to see. A small handful of lodges in the rainforest have successfully integrated local tribes into the running of the lodges. The lodges and tour operators I've recommended for travel in the Amazon all profess to practice responsible, low-impact tourism. Please do your utmost to follow suit. If you witness a tour group or lodge practicing unsafe ecotourism, by all means report it to either **INRENA** (© **01/224-3298**) or **PromPerú** (© **01/ 224-3279**), or to the tourist information offices in Cusco (© **084/263-176**) or Iquitos (© **065/235-621**).

accessible by permit and accompanied by an authorized guide only for ecotourist activities; and the Multiuse or **Cultural Zone,** home to traditional nomadic groups and open to all visitors. Traveling independently to the Cultural Zone is possible but extremely demanding and time-consuming—too much so for all but the hardiest ecoadventurers with plenty of time.

Most trips to Manu visit jungle trails and lakes Cocha Salvador and Cocha Otorongo. Both are uniquely endowed with wildlife, including several types of caimans and wild monkeys. Cocha Otorongo is home to a prized, endangered group of giant otters. Virtually all tours make stops at key observation piers, platforms, and towers for wildlife viewing. Many longer Manu trips include visits to a macaw clay lick.

Getting to Manu is itself an ecoadventure. Overland access to the Manu Reserve Zone from Cusco (from Puerto Maldonado is much more difficult) is a stunning (and stunningly beautiful) 2-day journey through 4,000m (13,120-ft.) mountains and cloud forest before descending into lowland rainforest. The scenery along the narrow road, full of switchbacks and great panoramic views of glaciers and the eastern Andes, is so extraordinary that many lodges and tour operators travel overland and return to Cusco by small aircraft (a 25-min. flight from Boca Manu). The trip passes through Paucartambo (see chapter 8) and travels along roads whose steep descents are thrilling—though unsettling to some travelers—on the way to high jungle. Bus or plane travel to Boca Manu is followed by up to a couple of days of river travel to lodges, campsites, and principal points of interest in the reserve. Because Manu is so isolated and access is so restricted, reserve visits are expensive and plainly beyond the scope of most budget travelers ($700 to more than $2,500 or more per person for a 5- to 8-day trip). Most visits to Manu require about a week.

MANU TOUR OPERATORS

Only eight tour companies are permitted to run organized expeditions to Manu, and the number of travelers they can take there each week is strictly limited. The best firms listed below are closely involved with conservation efforts and local development programs. The least expensive expeditions bus travelers in and out or return by small plane. Land (and river) travel is very time-consuming, but it makes for an excellent opportunity to experience the diverse terrain and types of forest that comprise Manu. Note that most companies operate with fixed departure dates only in the dry season, from May to November. The prices below do not include air transportation from Cusco.

Most of the tour operators below post detailed itineraries and information about their Manu trips on their websites.

o **InkaNatura ★★★** (www.inkanatura.com; © **888/870-7378** in the U.S. and Canada or **01/440-2022**): Perhaps the most serious and sophisticated outfit operating ecotourism trips in the Peruvian Amazon, InkaNatura, associated with the Peruvian conservation group PerúVerde and the American organization Tropical Nature, organizes stays at the famed **Manu Wildlife Center** (of which Inka-Natura is a joint owner). The lodge, opened in 1996, is located near the world's largest tapir clay lick, as well as the Blanquillo macaw clay lick, and it features 48km (30 miles) of nature trails and two canopy-viewing platforms. Accommodations are in 22 spacious, private bungalows with tiled bathrooms. Packages at the Manu Wildlife Center range from 4 days/3 nights for $1,095 to 5 days/4 nights for $1,315. InkaNatura also operates shorter trips to the **Cock-of-the-Rock Lodge** ($635, 3 days/2 nights) in the Selva Sur Nature Reserve at an elevation of 1,600m (5,250 ft.), excellent for birders; several lodges in Tambopata (see above); and multi-lodge sojourns that include trips to Cusco and Machu Picchu. Outside Peru, trips can be organized through the excellent organization **Tropical Nature Travel,** P.O. Box 5276, Gainesville, FL 32627-5276 (www.tropicalnaturetravel. com; © **877/827-8350** toll-free in the U.S.).

○ **Manu Expeditions ★★★** (www.manuexpeditions.com; ℂ **084/225-990**): One of the pioneering ecotourism operators in southern Peruvian Amazon, Manu Expeditions—run by a well-known ornithologist who is also the British Consul in Cusco—has been organizing rainforest tours for more than 2 decades. Tours include stays at the **Manu Wildlife Center,** of which the group is part owner (above), near the famed macaw clay lick, and a safari camp facility deep at Cocha Salvador within the Manu Biosphere Reserve. The Wildlife Center is considered the best lodge in Peru for birding. The longer tours include initial stays at the **Cock-of-the-Rock Lodge** in cloud forest. Four-, six-, and nine-day fixed-departure tours range from $990 to $2,445 per person.

○ **Manu Nature Tours ★★★** (www.manuperu.com; ℂ **084/252-721**): A highly professional, prizewinning outfit with 20 years' experience in Manu—it was one of the first to send expeditions to the reserve—Manu Nature Tours operates the well-known and comfortable **Manu Lodge,** situated next to a pristine oxbow lake and the only full-service lodge within Manu National Park itself (5-day/4-night trips cost $1,029–$1,500 per person), and the excellent **Manu Cloud Forest Lodge,** the first of its kind in Peru, overlooking a waterfall (3-day/2-night trips for $849 per person). The agency claims that the oxbow lake is one of the best spots anywhere in the jungle to view giant river otters. Add-on options include mountain biking, rafting, and tree canopy climbs. The office in Cusco is attached to a Patagonia outdoor gear shop and a rainforest cafe, in case you needed any reassurance of their commitment. The agency has expanded its activities to include trekking programs in the southern and central highlands, as well as more traditional tourist trips throughout Peru.

○ **Pantiacolla ★** (www.pantiacolla.com; ℂ **084/238-323**): An initiative of a Dutch biologist and Boca Manu-born conservationist, this agency operates the small **Pantiacolla Lodge,** with double rooms in bungalows, on bluffs overlooking the Madre de Dios River at the edge of Manu National Park. The organization also operates **Yine Lodge,** a community-based ecotourism project with the Yine Indians of the Manu rainforest. Pantiacolla is favored by ecotravelers on a budget, offering camping and lodge trips ranging from $990 for 5 days to $1,064 for 7 days.

IQUITOS & THE NORTHERN AMAZON ★★★

1,860km (1,156 miles) NE of Lima

Iquitos, the gateway to the northern Amazon, is Peru's largest jungle town and the capital of its largest department, Loreto, which occupies nearly a third of the national territory and is nearly the size of Germany. You must fly to get here—unless you have a week to kill for hot and uncomfortable river travel—but the pockets of jungle down- and upriver from Iquitos are among the most accessible of the Peruvian Amazon basin. Some of the best jungle lodges in the country, some of which are well into their fifth decade of ecotourism, are located just a few hours by boat from Iquitos. Because the region is the most trafficked and developed of the Peruvian Amazon, costs are lower for most jungle excursions than they are in the more exclusive Manu Biosphere Reserve in southeastern Peru.

The most important port city of the Amazon lies at the confluence of the Nanay and Itaya rivers. The city was founded in 1754 by Jesuit missionaries, although some

According to the Centers for Disease Control and Prevention, epidemic malaria rapidly emerged in the northern Amazon most recently in the 1990s. Peru has the second-highest number of malaria cases in South America (after Brazil), with the majority of cases from the Loreto department. From 1992 to 1997, malaria increased 50 times in Loreto, a rate more than 10 times greater than in the rest of the country. Malaria around the city of Iquitos accounts for the greatest number of cases in Loreto.

In 2001, the Peruvian Ministry of Health also reported an outbreak of yellow fever in the Loreto department in three districts, including Iquitos. Eight cases of yellow fever were confirmed, with two deaths. In 2003, the Pan American Health Organization recorded 22 cases and 13 deaths in Peru, just one of five Latin American nations grappling with an outbreak that claimed 99 lives by the end of the year.

These outbreaks should not deter most travelers from visiting the Amazon of northern Peru, but they should emphasize the need for proper vaccinations and medication before (and during) traveling to the region. See "Health" in "Fast Facts" in chapter 13, for more information.

continue to claim that it actually was not founded until nearly a century later. The city's proximity to South America's greatest rainforest and its isolation from the rest of Peru have created a unique tropical atmosphere. In the late 1860s and 1870s, pioneering merchants got rich off the booming rubber trade and built ostentatious mansions lined with glazed tiles along the river. Iquitos rivaled Manaus in Brazil for leadership of the rubber trade. The city went from boom to bust, although oil exploration, shipping, logging, and other export trade later revived and sustained the city's fortunes. Today tourism is quite evidently among Iquitos's most important industries.

Iquitos is far from the grand port of old. The modern city of nearly a half-million is composed of descendants of original ethnic groups such as the Yaguas, Boras, Kukama, and Iquitos, as well as significant populations of immigrant groups from Europe and Asia. Those great homes along the *malecón* are now faded monuments to the city's glory days, and just blocks from the main square lies the fascinating Belén district, where families live in a squalid pile of ramshackle wooden houses on the banks of the river. Some are propped up by spindly stilts, while others float, tethered to poles, when the river rises 6m (20 ft.) or more.

The Belén district looks distinctly Far Eastern, and Iquitos has more in common with steamy tropical Asian cities than the highlands of Peru. Like a South American Saigon, the air is waterlogged and the streets buzz with unrelenting waves of motorcycles and mototaxis. Locals speak a languid, mellifluous Spanish unmatched in other parts of the country, and pretty prostitutes loll about the Plaza de Armas. Locals dress not in alpaca sweaters and shawls, but in flesh-baring tank tops and short skirts.

Essentials

GETTING THERE

Water-locked Iquitos can be reached only by airplane or boat. For most travelers, air is the only practical option.

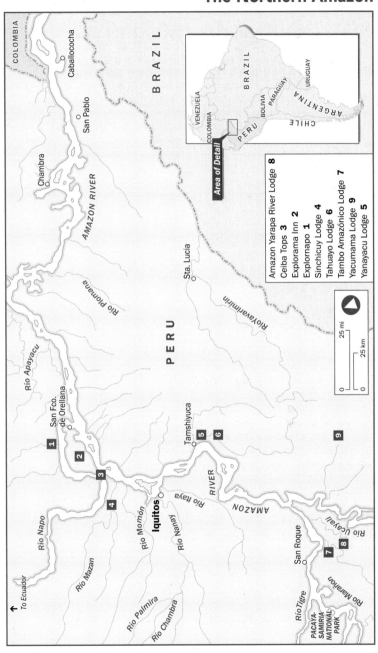

Area of Detail

Amazon Yarapa River Lodge **8**
Ceiba Tops **3**
Explorama Inn **2**
Explornapo **1**
Sinchicuy Lodge **4**
Tahuayo Lodge **6**
Tambo Amazónico Lodge **7**
Yacumama Lodge **9**
Yanayacu Lodge **5**

25 mi
25 km

BY PLANE   Iquitos's **Aeropuerto Francisco Secada Vigneta,** Avenida Abelardo Quiñones, Km 6 (☏ **065/260-251**), was once an international airport, receiving flights from Miami, but those were suspended several years ago. **LAN** (www.lan.com; ☏ **01/213-8200**), **Peruvian Airlines** (www.peruvianairlines.pe; ☏ **01/716-6000**), and **Star Perú** (www.starperu.com; ☏ **01/705-9000**) fly daily to Iquitos from Lima and from Pucallpa and Tarapoto, other cities in the Loreto department (where flights from Lima often make stopovers). Flights from Lima start at $72 one-way.

To downtown Iquitos, an automobile taxi costs about S/15; a *motocarro* costs S/10. If a taxi driver offers to take you for less, he will certainly take you directly to a hotel where he can earn commission, not where you necessarily want to go. (The difference could be a lot more than the few *soles* you save on the taxi fare.) City buses (S/1) are available outside the gates of the airport on the main road (they travel along Ocampo/Tacna/Grau), but unless you have a very manageable backpack as your only luggage, it's not worth the hassle.

BY BOAT   Arriving by boat is an option only for those with the luxury of ample time and patience. It takes about a week when the river is high (and 3–4 days in the dry season) to reach the capital city of Loretos upriver along the Amazon from Pucallpa or Yurimaguas.

To travel to Colombia or Brazil (Manaus, Santarém, and Belém) by boat, your best bet is by river cruise. The Iquitos port, Puerto Masusa, is about 3km (1¾ miles) north of the Plaza de Armas. See "River Cruises," below, for more details.

GETTING AROUND

For all practical purposes, Iquitos is an island city, defined by water—not just the mighty Amazon and its tributaries, which border it to the west, but also a complex network of smaller rivers and streams, and a series of lakes just outside the city. The riverfront along the Itaya River is a long boulevard with a pedestrian walkway; Malecón Maldonado morphs into Malecón Tarapacá as it moves away from the focal point of downtown to the shabby but picturesque Belén district. Próspero is the main avenue of communication from the main square to residential zones south.

BY MOTOTAXI & TAXI   Mototaxis are everywhere in Iquitos; if you don't mind the noise and wind in your face (and aren't worried about accidents), it's a great way to get around. In-town fares are S/2. Regular car taxis are only slightly less ubiquitous; most trips in town cost less than S/5. To order a taxi, call ☏ **065/232-014.**

BY BUS   *Combis* and *omnibuses* (buses) travel principal routes but are much less comfortable and not much less expensive than more convenient *motocarros*. The fare is S/1.50.

BY MOTORCYCLE   If you want to travel around town as Iquiteños do, rent a small *moto,* or motorcycle. Try **Visión Motos,** Nauta 309 (☏ **065/234-759**). Rates are about $45 per day or $5 per hour.

BY FOOT   Although the city is spread over several square miles, the core of downtown Iquitos is compact and easy to get around on foot, and even the waterfront Belén district is easy to walk to. Some hostels and hotels are a distance from the main square, though, requiring at least the occasional use of inexpensive mototaxis.

VISITOR INFORMATION

A municipal **tourism information booth** (☏ **065/260-251**) is at the arrivals terminal baggage claim at the airport. It maintains a chart of hotels and costs, and the staff is happy to dispense information (and frequently opinions) about the various jungle-tour

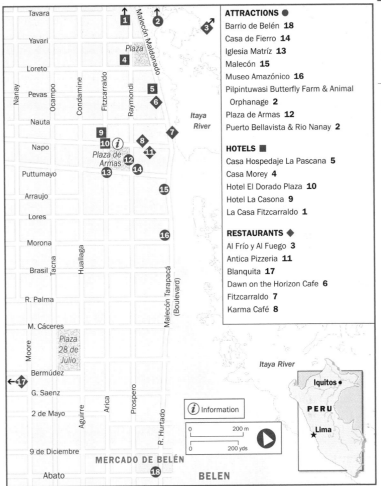

ATTRACTIONS ●
Barrio de Belén **18**
Casa de Fierro **14**
Iglesia Matríz **13**
Malecón **15**
Museo Amazónico **16**
Pilpintuwasi Butterfly Farm & Animal
  Orphanage **2**
Plaza de Armas **12**
Puerto Bellavista & Rio Nanay **2**

HOTELS ■
Casa Hospedaje La Pascana **5**
Casa Morey **4**
Hotel El Dorado Plaza **10**
Hotel La Casona **9**
La Casa Fitzcarraldo **1**

RESTAURANTS ◆
Al Frío y Al Fuego **3**
Antica Pizzeria **11**
Blanquita **17**
Dawn on the Horizon Cafe **6**
Fitzcarraldo **7**
Karma Café **8**

and lodge operators. One of Peru's more helpful tourism information offices is just off the Plaza de Armas at Jr. Napo 161 (℗ **065/236-144**). The English-speaking staff has free maps and lists of recommended hotels and tour operators, and will try to sort through the (often intentionally) confusing sales pitches of jungle-tour companies. The office is open Monday through Saturday from 9am to 6pm, Sunday from 9am to 1pm. A free monthly English-language newspaper, *Iquitos Times,* is given out at restaurants on the Malecón and area around the Plaza de Armas, often by the publisher himself.

FAST FACTS
ATMs and banks are located along Putumayo and Próspero, on the south side of the Plaza de Armas. Two banks that exchange traveler's checks and cash are **Banco de**

Crédito, Putumayo 201, at Próspero, and **Banco Continental,** Sargento Lores 171. Money-changers can usually be found hanging around the Plaza de Armas and along Putumayo and Próspero, but calculate the exchange beforehand and count your money carefully.

If you're looking to cross into Brazil or Colombia, the **Brazilian Consulate** is located at Sargento Lores 363 (☎ 965/956-060), and the **Colombian Consulate** is at Calvo de Araujo 431 (☎ 065/231-461). You should make contact with the embassies in Lima or even at home before traveling to Peru. For questions about border-crossing formalities for jungle travel to and from Brazil and Colombia, visit or call the **Migraciones** office at Malecón Tarapacá 382 (☎ 065/235-371). The **United States Embassy** in Lima has named the owner of Dawn on the Amazon, Bill Grimes, as a warden for Iquitos, but the office at Malecón Maldonado 185 (☎ 065/223-730) is not trained in visa regulations and cannot answer visa-related questions. The **British Consular Agent,** with consular service for Irish and New Zealand nationals, is located at Calle San José 113, 2nd floor (☎ 065/253-364).

In an **emergency,** call ☎ 105. You can also call **Cruz Roja (Red Cross)** at ☎ 065/241-072 for medical emergencies, and ☎ 065/267-555 for **fire emergencies.** For medical attention, go to one of the following hospitals or clinics: **Clínica Ana Stahl,** Av. la Marina 285 (☎ 065/252-535); **EsSalud,** Av. la Marina 2054 (☎ 065/250-333); or **Hospital Regional de Loreto,** Av. 28 de Julio s/n, Punchana (☎ 065/252-004). The **tourist police** office is located at Sargento Lores 834 (☎ 065/242-081). There's also a **Tourist Protection Service** office at Huallaga 311 (☎ 065/243-490).

Most Internet cafes or *cabinas* in Iquitos stay open late, and rates are about S/2 per hour. One to try is **Estación Internet,** Fitzcarrald 120 (☎ 065/223-608). Several other *cabinas* are located near the Plaza de Armas, particularly on Próspero and Putumayo. Iquitos's **post office** is at Arica 403, on the corner of Morona (☎ 065/223-812). The **Telefónica del Perú** office is at Arica 276.

Exploring the City
IQUITOS HIGHLIGHTS

Although the **Plaza de Armas** is perhaps not Peru's most distinguished, it is, as always, one of the focal points in town. It is marked by the early-20th-century neo-Gothic **Iglesia Matríz** (parish church), built in 1919. Many of the church's most attractive elements, such as the tower, were later additions. Across the square stands the now-abandoned **Casa de Fierro,** or Iron House, designed by none other than Gustave Eiffel for the 1889 Paris Exhibition. The walls, ceiling, and balcony are plastered in rectangular sheets of iron. Said to be the first prefabricated house in the Americas, it was shipped unassembled from Europe and built on-site where it currently stands.

One block back from the plaza, facing the Itaya River, (a tributary of the Amazon) the riverfront promenade **Malecón (Maldonado/Tarapacá)** was enlarged and improved a few years back with fountains, benches, and street lamps, making it the focus of Iquitos urban life. The *malecón* is lined with several exquisite 19th-century mansions, relics from the rubber heyday, lined with Portuguese glazed tiles, or *azulejos.* The most spectacular is probably **Casa Hernández,** nos. 302–308. Other houses worth checking out along the boulevard are **Casa Fitzcarrald,** Napo 200–212, an adobe house belonging to a famed rubber baron; **Casa Cohen,** Próspero

401–437; **Casa Morey** (now a handsome boutique hotel), Av. Raimondi (at Av. Loreto/Plaza Ramón Castilla), on the first block off the *malecón;* and the **Logia Unión Amazónica,** Nauta 262.

The **Museo Amazónico,** Malecón Tarapacá 386 (🕿 **065/231-072**), occasionally has interesting exhibits of Amazon folklore and tribal art, and has a curious collection of 76 Indian statues made of fiberglass but fashioned as if they were bronze. Reportedly, some of the mothers whose children served as models for the works freaked out when they were covered in plaster for the moulds, thinking the children would be buried alive. The museum building, which dates to the mid-19th century, is a nicely restored example of the *malecón's* period mansions. The museum is open Monday through Friday from 8am to 1pm and 3 to 7pm, and Saturday from 9am to 1pm. Admission is S/3.

The curious and spectacular waterfront **Barrio de Belén ★★**, about a 15-minute walk south along the *malecón,* is Iquitos's most unusual quarter. Known for its floating houses (locals call it, somewhat generously, the "second Venice") and **Mercado de Belén**—its sprawling, colorful, claustrophobic, and odiferous open-air market, where you'll find a bounty of strange and wonderful Amazon fish, fauna, and fruits—Belén's residential district is a rather squalid and extremely poor but endlessly fascinating shantytown. Houses are constructed above the waters of the Itaya River, and when the river is high, transportation is by canoe or motorboat. Visitors are free to walk about in dry season (or, for much of the year, to take a locally arranged canoe trip) and see the houses—some on stilts, others floating during the rainy season. For safety's sake, though, go in a group and during the day only. Belén is an atmospheric and photogenic place, akin to Calcutta—you'll see scrappy kids tumbling out of clapboard houses and playing with pet monkeys, and a few houses proudly outfitted with cable TV and other modern conveniences (the "streets" are illuminated by electric street lights). There are even a couple of discos where, during high-water season, the floor heaves under the weight of revelers, who often end up "dancing" in water up to their hips. If you're squeamish and/or severely affected by extreme heat and humidity or crowds or pungent smells, you may want to visit for a very short time only, as it can quickly add up to sensory overload; carry water and plan your egress. Exercise some caution and restraint if walking around the area with expensive camera equipment. Most residents of the neighborhood, while more nonplussed than puzzled at

Out on the River(s)

Iquitos sits not quite on the banks of the mighty Amazon River; rather it's on the Río Itaya, an Amazon tributary, which flows into the Amazon at the point where it also meets with the Río Nanay. A great idea is to hire a covered motorboat to get out to the confluence of the three rivers, where you may spot pink dolphins, and also take you around the floating Barrio de Belén. Near the Boulevard, you can hire a manned motorboat with guide (who likely speaks little English) for as little as S/40 for a few hours. If you'd rather a somewhat more formally organized boating excursion and a native English speaker, inquire at Dawn on the Amazon, Malecón Maldonado 185 (🕿 **065/223-730**). To wend your way by water among the small canals of Barrio de Belén, you can hire a canoe at the Puerto de Belén for about S/30 for a couple of hours.

foreigners' interest in the aesthetics of their dilapidated streets, are more than approachable for photos, if you ask respectfully. The animated market, which extends over several blocks, is itself a wild place to visit, with all sorts of extraordinary exotic items for sale, including yummy Amazonian fruits such as *maracuyá* (passion fruit), *aguaje, cocona,* and others. Look for the stands set up with blenders, cranking out fruit juices and smoothies (*refrigerios* and *jugos*). Less appetizing items include endangered animals such as butchered land and sea turtles, alligators, and even monkeys—all officially illegal for capture and sale (see chapter 2, "Peru In Depth," p. 12). An entire block, **Pasaje Paquito,** is full of traditional Amazonian folk remedies and quirky and bizarre potions used by faith healers, many of which claim aphrodisiac qualities.

ATTRACTIONS NEAR IQUITOS

Pilpintuwasi Butterfly Farm and Animal Orphanage ★★★ ☺ WILDLIFE REFUGE   This very special nonprofit and non-exploitative garden refuge and learning center, started by an Austrian woman, Gudrun Sperrer, is home to some 25 species of colorful butterflies bred in captivity, as well as orphaned, rescued exotic animals, including red uakari and Capuchin monkeys, macaws, and turtles, as well as a jaguar, capybara, tapir, and an ocelot. It's a superb Amazon biodiversity learning experience and adventure for individuals of all ages and families.

Padre Cocha, Iquitos. www.amazonanimalorphanage.org. ⓒ **063/232-665.** Admission S/20 adults, S/10 students. Guided 1-hour visits, Tues–Sun 9am–4pm. To get there, take a mototaxi (S/3) or colectivo marked BELLAVISTA/NANAY, which leaves from points along Próspero, and then arrange for a boat (S/30) that will deliver you to banks of the river (a 5-minute walk from Pilpintuwasi) and wait to take you back to the port.

Puerto Bellavista & Rio Nanay   BEACH/PORT   This small Río Mañon port and village, a couple of kilometers from downtown at the northern edge of Iquitos, has a pretty white-sand beach (Playa Nanay) that locals enjoy and that is safe for swimming during summer months. It's also a good spot to hire a boat and cruise down to the confluence of the Amazon and Nanay rivers, where you can appreciate the difference in water colors (muddy brown and black), passing beaches, and a handful of local communities—among them the Boras and Yaguas—along the way. To get there, take a mototaxi (S/3) or colectivo marked BELLAVISTA/NANAY, which leaves from points along Próspero.

Quistococha   PARK/ZOO   A resort complex about 13km (8 miles) south of Iquitos, the Quistococha Lagoon and Tourist Park has a pretty nice beach and swimming area. It's mostly a spot for local families to hang out on weekends. Attractions include picnic grounds, paddleboats, an aquarium, botanical garden, a walking path around the lagoon, a zoo with exotic jungle animals and fish, including macaws, giant river otters, monkeys, serpents, jaguars, and pumas, and a fish

---

  Amazonian Fruit Delicacies

Throughout South America, the Amazon region is famed for its exotic fruits. In Iquitos, check out stands around the Plaza de Armas for natural fruit juices and ice creams made from stuff hard to get at home, such as *aguaje, maracuyá, camu camu, carambola, guayaba, mamey, cocona,* and *tumbo,* among many others.

hatchery that's populated by giant *paiche* fish (some of the large animals, such as the jungle cats, are not in suitable spaces, so if you're not a fan of zoos in general and in particular those with sub-optimal conditions, you might be wise to avoid this one). There's a restaurant on the grounds, as well as informal food stalls set up near the entrance to the park. Nearby is the **Centro de Rescate Amazónico** (Amazon Rescue Center), where you'll find a handful of manatees that have been rescued from poachers. To get there, you can take a 20-minute ride in a *motocarro* (about S/15) or catch a colectivo marked QUISTOCOCHA (S/2) on the corner of Moore and Bermúdez.

Where to Eat

Restaurants in Iquitos feature dishes straight out of the Amazon, *patarashca* (steamed river fish wrapped in banana leaves) and *juanes* (rice *tamales* made with minced chicken, pork, or fish, prepared with black olives and egg and wrapped in *bijao* leaves). Although protected species appear illegally on menus, they still do. *Paiche* (Amazon river fish) is now endangered, and many are worried about the sustainability of hearts of palm (*chonta* or *palmitos*), which goes into a good many salads locally. Think twice before encouraging shifty restaurateurs by ordering turtle-meat soup or alligator. If you venture into the Belén market, be prepared to see even more exotic foodstuffs, such as monkey and alligator meat.

EXPENSIVE

Al Frío y Al Fuego ★★ INTERNATIONAL/PERUVIAN   For a unique experience and splurge in Iquitos, check out this cool restaurant, floating in the middle of the Itaya River, with a huge swimming pool to boot (yes, you can bring a bathing suit during the day if you come for lunch). A private boat ferries you out across the river; climb to the second floor open-air, thatched-roof dining room for great views of the river and Iquitos on the river bank. Start with ceviche or very good salads. Main courses include well-prepared, if comparatively expensive, fresh catch of the day (usually *doncella* or trout), as well as a variety of beef tenderloin dishes and grilled meats (the mixed grill is an awful lot of food, but surely it's the most expensive main course in Iquitos). The restaurant is touristy, but out on the river you're unlikely to care.

Embarcadero El Hequito (Av. de La Marina at Angel Blanco). www.alfrioyalfuego.com. © **065/262-713.** Reservations recommended on weekends. Main courses S/24–S/70. AE, DC, MC, V. Mon–Sat noon–4pm and 7–11pm; Sun noon–5pm.

MODERATE

Antica Pizzeria ★ ITALIAN/PIZZA   A sister to several popular branches in Lima's coolest neighborhoods, this good-looking, rustic Italian restaurant with wooden tables and massive wood-burning ovens, a half-block from the Plaza de Armas, is a welcome addition to Iquitos's more local dining scene. Though you can feast on very good thin-crust pizzas or straightforward pastas, the menu also includes more sophisticated fare, such as octopus salad and porcini mushroom risotto, as well as *maracuyá* (passion fruit) cheesecake for dessert. The place has a cool, relaxed atmosphere, with a reggae and pop soundtrack and young clientele.

Jr. Napo 159. © **065/241-988.** Reservations recommended for groups. Main courses S/16–S/32. AE, MC, V. Daily 7am–midnight.

Dawn on the Horizon Cafe ★ 🍴 INTERNATIONAL   Featuring a truly massive menu, with everything from breakfast served all day to Peruvian, Italian,

Mexican, American, Chinese, and vegetarian—as well as a special Ayahuasca diet menu for those about to trip and a roster of Cuban cigars—this American-owned restaurant is a good spot along the *malecón* when you're not sure exactly what to have, or want some comfort food. It's like the owner accepted a bet to be as global as possible! Items are well prepared and a good value. Breakfast is my go-to meal here.

Malecón Maldonado 185 (at Nauta). ☎ **065/234-921.** No reservations. Main courses S/18–S/36. MC, V. Daily 7:30am–midnight.

Fitzcarraldo ★ INTERNATIONAL   This popular joint right on the *malecón* has a diverse menu to appeal to travelers of all stripes and appetites, from salads or excellent pizzas, sandwiches, and hamburgers (as well as some ill-advised "bush meats"). The convivial restaurant is an open-air house (which once belonged to a British rubber company) featuring updated colonial touches and views of the Amazon, along with good music and sidewalk tables but underpowered ceiling fans.

Napo 100. ☎ **065/600-536.** Reservations recommended for groups. Main courses S/13–S/40. MC, V. Daily noon–midnight.

Karma Café ★ INTERNATIONAL/VEGETARIAN   A cozy, dimly lit, and vaguely hippieish new spot with sofas, bean-bag chairs, trippy art on the walls, and free Wi-Fi (everyone seems to be surfing the net), this makes for a good spot to duck out of the traffic and noise for a beer and salad, huge burgers and toasted sandwiches, and curry and stir-fry dishes. There are good rock and pop tunes on the soundtrack and a good nightly happy hour.

Napo 138, Plaza de Armas (2nd Floor). ☎ **065/222-732.** Reservations not accepted. Main courses S/12–S/24. MC, V. Daily noon–10pm.

INEXPENSIVE

Blanquita INTERNATIONAL/PERUVIAN   A truly local experience and a hike from the Plaza de Armas—take a mototaxi, for sure—this is a place where you're almost certain to be the only gringo. With a woman out front preparing *tamales* and banana-leaf *juanes,* and resolutely local menu featuring massive portions of *chifa* (Peruvian-Chinese) and Amazon specialties such as *cecina* (flat, tough grilled pork with plantains). It's brightly lit, clean and friendly, and full of families. If you're curious about the local diet but don't dare eat in the Belén market, this is your place.

Av. Bolognesi 1181. ☎ **065/266-015.** Reservations not accepted. Main courses S/10–S/18. No credit cards. Mon–Sat 5:30pm–midnight.

📎 *Chifas* in Iquitos

To some observers, there's something distinctly Asian-feeling about hot, humid, and motorcycle-crazed Iquitos. Waves of Chinese immigrants came as laborers to Iquitos throughout the 20th century, which is the biggest reason there are so many *chifas* (Peruvian-Chinese restaurants) in town. Eating Chinese food at the edge of the Amazon instead of exotic jungle fruits and fish might not be your first impulse in Iquitos, but *chifas* are plentiful and reasonably priced—perfect fallback dining options. Try **Chifa Long Fung,** San Martín 454 (☎ **065/233-649**); **Chifa Can Chau,** Huallaga 165 (☎ **065/241-384**); and **Chifa Pekin,** Putumayo 900 (☎ **065/242-892**). Other dirt-cheap *chifas* line Avenida Grau near Plaza 28 de Julio.

Shopping

The most intriguing shopping option is **Mercado de Belén,** the redolent open-air market (see above), although you'll likely find more to photograph and smell than to actually buy (unless you're in the market for faith-healers' potions). For local artisans' goods, there aren't many options; try **Centro Artesanal Anaconda,** Malecón Tarapacá (Boulevard), the sparsely populated market of stalls downstairs from the *malecón,* the **mercadillo** of souvenir stalls on Jr. Nauta (between Raimondi and Malecón Maldonado), or **Mercado Artesanal de San Juan,** the larger market with wooden outdoor stalls selling hammocks, woodcarvings, and paintings, on Avenida Quiñones, Km 4.5, on the way out to the airport (about 3km/1¼ miles from downtown). Unlike most markets in Peru, here many of the sellers are also the craftspeople behind the work. Some of the best crafts, including textiles and pottery, come from the Shipibo Indian tribe of the Amazon.

Camu-Camu Gallery, Trujillo 498 (© **065/253-120**), showcases the work of a local artist, Francisco Grippa, whose colorful paintings evoke Amazonian themes, including jungle flora and fauna. Grippa's exuberant and expressive style, known in the United States and Europe, has been labeled "grippismo." He uses local materials, including a canvas made from tree bark. The gallery is open daily from 10am to 1pm and 4 to 7pm. Tour groups often visit the Grippa's home/gallery in Pevas, the oldest town in the Peruvian Amazon, about 150km (93 miles) downriver from Iquitos.

Entertainment & Nightlife

Along the *malecón* (frequently called the Boulevard) are a couple of lively bars with good views of the river; it's the place to mill about on Friday and Saturday evenings. **Arandú Bar,** Malecón Maldonado 113 (© **065/243-434**), is particularly hopping, a good place for sharing a pitcher of sangria and loud rock 'n' roll. A unique option is to have a cold beer or cocktail on the floating deck on the river of the ramshackle, and rowdy, **Camiri Lounge,** Pevas Cdra.1 Parte Baja, a "floating" *hostal.* The views of the river are great, and the music goes late (I don't think the backpackers staying in the thatched-roof bunks are expecting much sleep anyway). You can grab a more sophisticated drink or, shockingly, a Belgian beer, at the **Amazon Bistro,** Malecón Tarapacá 286 (© **065/600-785**), an attractive two-level spot with a French feel that also serves meals and is a nice break from the Boulevard. The biggest nightspot for locals is **Noa-Noa,** Pevas 298 at Fitzcarraldo (© **065/232-902**), a disco and rock bar near the Plaza de Armas. When the two-level dance floor is happening, the smoke machines crank and the sound system pumps out salsa and Latin rock.

Where to Stay

For many visitors, Iquitos is essentially a way station on their journey to the Amazon. As a result, the city has fewer good hotels than its environs have attractive jungle lodges. Things are improving, though, and Iquitos finally got its first high-end, full-service hotel a few years back. All but the cheapest *hostales* (inns) will usually arrange for a free airport transfer if you pass on your arrival information ahead of time. Even so, be careful whom you tell at the airport that you're expecting a certain hotel to pick you up and always make sure that the driver already knows your name before going anywhere with him.

EXPENSIVE

Hotel El Dorado Plaza ★   In a privileged location on the Plaza de Armas, the El Dorado Plaza fills a gaping hole in the Iquitos hotel scene—the city's only bona fide, large high-end hotel. A modern high-rise building, with a soaring lobby, a good restaurant, and an excellent outdoor pool, this is clearly the fanciest and best-equipped hotel in town. Rooms are large and nicely outfitted, if not quite at the upper-echelon levels found in Lima or Cusco. Guests have a view of either the main square or the pool. The hotel has quickly become popular with foreigners who come to Iquitos for top-of-the-line jungle tours. See the website for frequent deals—occasionally as much as half the rack rate.

Napo 258 (Plaza de Armas), Iquitos. www.grupo-dorado.com/doradoplaza. ☏ **065/222-555.** Fax 065/224-304. 65 units. $240–$300 double; $385–$600 suite. Rates include breakfast buffet. AE, DC, MC, V. **Amenities:** Restaurant; 2 bars; coffee shop; concierge; fitness center; Jacuzzi; outdoor pool; sauna. *In room:* A/C, TV, fridge, Wi-Fi (free).

MODERATE

Casa Morey ★★   A recently restored and English-owned, 1910 rubber-baron's mansion near the riverfront, this spectacular, large white corner house is the city's newest boutique hotel. It has the feel of an inherited palace or sparsely furnished museum, with rooms that are unfathomably immense. They're so large, with such high ceilings, that they appear to be missing some pieces among the collection of antiques. A few details, such as run-of-the-mill bathroom fixtures, keep it from being a top-of-the-line luxury hotel, but if you're looking for character and a great place to spread out before or after an Amazon cruise or jungle lodge experience—but not a roster of business-hotel amenities—it's a better choice than the El Dorado Plaza, and the small outdoor pool in a sparkling white courtyard is a great place to relax.

Loreto 200 (at Av. Raimondi/Plaza Ramón Castillo), Iquitos. www.lacasamorey.com. ☏/fax **065/ 231-913.** 14 units. $85–$100 double. Rates include breakfast buffet. AE, DC, MC, V. **Amenities:** Outdoor pool. *In room:* A/C, TV, fridge, Wi-Fi (free).

La Casa Fitzcarraldo ★★ 🎒   Occupying the house where the German film-maker Werner Herzog lived when making the legendary and troubled *Fitzcarraldo*—and still owned by the Swiss producer of that film and many others by Herzog—this one-of-a-kind boutique inn exudes tropical flavor. It's a lovely retreat from Iquitos's bustle, with a gorgeous pool, lush gardens, nice outdoor restaurant, and even a crazy, soaring four-story tree house. Rooms are brightly colored, spacious (except for the "Small Room," which is definitely that) and well outfitted. Film and pop-culture buffs will be enthralled; Herzog loved the bungalow out back, and among the guests were the star of the film, Klaus Kinski, and (in the blue room) Mick Jagger, who was to be featured in the film but ended up getting cut out when he went on tour with the Stones and couldn't complete his role. The one thing I can fault this place for is its lack of political correctness: the presence of certain "bush meats" and endangered species on the menu, as well as an ocelot that's in a tiny cage.

Av. La Marina 2153, Iquitos (on the way to Nanay/Puerto Bellavista). casafitzcarraldo.com. ☏ **065/601-138.** 8 units. $40–$90 double. Rates include breakfast buffet. MC, V. **Amenities:** Restaurant; bar; outdoor pool. *In room:* TV, fridge, Wi-Fi (free).

INEXPENSIVE

Casa Hospedaje La Pascana 🌿   One of the better basic budget inns in Iquitos, the Pascana is a friendly, small place with rooms built around a long, plant-lined, and open-air courtyard. Rooms are very simple, even plain, but not uncomfortable, and they have fans rather than air-conditioning. The place is quiet and peaceful, and just a 2-minute walk from the *malecón* and the Plaza de Armas—reasons why it's often full and popular with small budget-level groups. Don't expect much hot water at this price, although you probably won't care in the sweltering heat.

Pevas 133, Iquitos. www.pascana.com. ⓒ **065/231-418.** Fax 065/233-466. 18 units. S/50 double. Rates include continental breakfast buffet. MC, V. **Amenities:** Cafeteria.

Hotel La Casona ★ 🍴 A cut above other budget inns in Iquitos, this family-owned small hotel just off the Plaza de Armas is amiable, safe, well-equipped, and a good value. Though it doesn't look like much from the street, it's a better bet than several hotels double its price. Rooms are very simply decorated but spacious and clean, equipped with either fans or air-conditioning. And they count with several amenities hard to find at this price: wireless (albeit very slow) Internet, cable TV, and guaranteed hot water. You'll also find a communal kitchen and leafy little patio. Add to that excellent, friendly service, and you've got a winner. For even cheaper rooms, the hotel owns a *hostal* and backpacker-oriented *hospedaje* across the street.

Calle Fitzcarraldo 147, Iquitos. www.hotellacasonaiquitos.com. ⓒ**065/234-394.** 23 units. S/75–S/80 double with fan; S/90–S/100 double with A/C. MC, V. *In room:* A/C (some rooms), TV, Wi-Fi (free).

Jungle Tours, Lodges & River Cruises

The mighty Amazon reaches widths of about 4km (2½ miles) beyond Iquitos, and the river basin contains 2,000 species of fish (among them, everyone's favorite, piranhas); 4,000 species of birds (including 120 hummingbirds); native mammals such as ant-eaters, tapirs, marmosets, and pink dolphins; and 60 species of reptiles, including caimans and anacondas.

Although the town itself holds a kind of sultry fascination, ecotourism is the primary draw for visitors to Iquitos, and the giant Amazon river system just beyond the city holds a wealth of natural wonders: rustic jungle lodges, canopy walks, and opportunities for bird-watching, piranha fishing, visits to Indian villages, and wildlife spotting (as well as less-standard activities, such as shaman consultations and *ayahuasca* drug ceremonies). Your options for exploring the jungle are **lodge stays,** which include jungle activities such as treks and canoe excursions; **river cruises;** or more adventurous **camping treks** with private guides. Most people head for lodges of varying degrees of rusticity and distance from Iquitos. The jungle is immense, and most parts of it are inaccessible. Immersing yourself in anything resembling pristine jungle is both costly and time-consuming. The northern Amazon basin within reach of Iquitos has been explored and popularly exploited far longer than the more remote southern jungle areas of Manu and Tambopata.

Don't expect to spend your time in the jungle checking off a lengthy wildlife list of sightings; no matter where you go, your opportunities for viewing more than a couple of species of birds, fish, and mammals will be severely limited. You'll see lots of birds and, if you're lucky, perhaps a few monkeys, caimans, and pink dolphins. (For deeper and more adventurous treks into the jungle, see "Into the Wild: Farther Afield from Iquitos," on p. 354, and "Independent Guides," later in this section.)

For a quick and simple experience, you can stay at a lodge only an hour or two (within a 50km/31-mile radius) by boat from Iquitos, in secondary jungle. You're likely to see more fauna and have a more authentic experience in primary rainforest, but

📎 **Eco-nomizing in Iquitos**

Although the prices of some lodges might seem steep to backpackers accustomed to dropping $10 for a place to sleep in other parts of Peru, getting by on $60 a day or so is really a pretty decent bargain, considering that food, river transportation, English-speaking guides, fishing and wildlife trips and treks, and shelter are all included. That said, you can almost certainly get a better deal when signing up with a lodge or tour on the ground in Iquitos by going door-to-door to the sales offices and comparing programs and prices than you would contracting one in Lima or from your home country before stepping foot in Peru. Especially during the off season, lodges are willing to negotiate. However, you risk not getting the tour you want when you want it. For many travelers, the extra hassle and uncertainty might not be worth the dollars saved. Prices quoted on websites and through travel agents might be quite negotiable if you contact operators directly, depending on season and occupancy levels.

you'll have to travel much farther (beyond a radius of 80km/50 miles; up to 4 hr. by boat) and pay quite a bit more for the privilege. Generally, you must trade comforts for authenticity. Very short trips (2–3 days) are unlikely to produce much in the way of wildlife, although you can still expect enjoyable contact with the Amazonian habitat. A true foray into virgin jungle, far from the heavy footsteps of thousands of guides and visitors before you, requires at least a week of demanding camping and trekking. Hard-core ecotypes might want to contract private guides to go deep into the *selva* and camp. (Ask at the tourism information office for a list of licensed, official guides; the office also has a list of blacklisted guides.)

Prices for lodges and tours vary tremendously. For conventional, easy-to-reach lodges contracted in Iquitos, lodge tours average around $75 per person per day, and $175 or more per person per day for lodges located farthest from the city. Some budget lodges offer bargain rates, as little as $40 a day (although, in most cases, you get what you pay for), and independent guides might charge as little as $20 a day. Costs are directly related to distance from Iquitos; the farther they are, the more expensive they are. Costs include transportation, lodging, buffet-style meals, and guided activities (beverages cost extra).

Be careful: There are lots of lookalike lodges and tours. Lodges and ecotourism companies come and go, and everyone's competing for your dollars. Hustlers, con artists, and all manner of disreputable touts abound in Iquitos, and you need to exercise a certain amount of caution before handing over money for a promised itinerary. The local tourism office (✆ **065/260-251**) can be of help ferreting out guides, tours, and lodges with bad reputations. If you're making a tour decision on the ground in Iquitos, it's a good idea to visit the office first for the most up-to-date information.

Most jungle lodges feature either individual rustic thatched-roof bungalows or main buildings with individual rooms, beds with mosquito netting, communal dining areas, hammock lounges, covered plank walkways, toilets, and either hot- or cold-water sinks and showers. A few lodges have extras such as swimming pools, lookout towers, canopy walkways, and electricity. Guests are taken on guided day- and nighttime excursions, including jungle walks, piranha fishing, and canoe and motorboat trips to spot birds, caimans, and dolphins. Many lodges offer artificial, even cheesy, visits with local Indian tribes, staged for your pleasure, and some host *ayahuasca* rituals (see "Trippin' Amazon Style" on p. 352).

JUNGLE LODGES

The following are tour operators and lodges with good reputations in the area. The list is not by any means exhaustive; there are dozens more agencies and lodges, but reports on many of them are less than stellar.

- **Amazon Explorama Lodge ★★** (www.explorama.com; ℂ **065/252-530,** or **800/707-5275** in the U.S. and Canada). The longest-established jungle-tour company in Iquitos (now into its 5th decade) and owned by an American, Explorama operates three lodges and a campsite, ranging from 160km (100 miles) to 40km (25 miles) downriver from Iquitos. The company has one of the best reputations of the Northern Amazon lodge operators, bolstered by good guides, very good facilities and food, and a range of flexible activities. The company's first lodge, **Explorama Inn** (80km/50 miles from Iquitos), is large and attractive, with two long wings and a lovely restaurant/bar and communal area. Explorama owns the jungle's most luxurious lodge, **Ceiba Tops** (40km/25 miles from Iquitos), a jungle resort hotel with air-conditioning, a spectacular pool with a slide, and a Jacuzzi. There are trails nearby, and boats can take you out onto the river for dolphin-spotting and fishing, but Ceiba Tops is much more about relaxing in style surrounded by jungle. Near **Explornapo** (the Explorama lodge deepest in the jungle), there's a splendid **canopy walkway ★**, one of the longest in the world. At a height of 36m (118 ft.) and a rambling length of 500m (1,640 ft.), it alone is one of the highlights of a visit to this part of the Peruvian Amazon. It's possible to mix and match lodges; a popular plan for many travelers is several days at Explornapo (or, more adventurous still, the rustic Explortambos campsite) followed by a couple of days of relative luxury at Ceiba Tops. Prices range from $280 for a 2-day/1-night trip to Ceiba Tops to $950 for a 5-day/4-night trip to Explornapo. Web specials as well as special programs are frequently available.

- **Amazon Yarapa River Lodge ★★★** (www.yarapa.com; ℂ **065/993-1172,** or **315/952-6771** in the U.S. and Canada). Associated with Cornell University (which built a tropical biology field lab for students and faculty here), this terrific conservation-minded lodge—two-time winner of a World Travel Award as the top resort in Peru—is 177km (110 miles) upriver on the Yarapa River, an Amazon tributary, near the Reserva Nacional Pacaya-Samiria. Surrounded by pristine jungle and oxbow lakes that teem with wildlife, the beautiful lodge features full solar power, composting, and flush toilets with a waste-management system. Both lodge facilities and guides are first-rate and among the finest in the Peruvian Amazon; spacious private bungalows are almost luxurious. A 4-day/3-night trip (with private bathroom) runs to $840–$920 per person; a 7-day/6-night trip is $1,260–$1,470 per person. Travelers can opt for an overnight in the remote Pacaya-Samiria National Park Reserve, 4 hours away by boat.

- **Paseos Amazónicos** (www.paseosamazonicos.com; ℂ **065/231-618** or **01/417-576** in Lima). This company operates three well-run lodges, **Tambo Amazónico, Sinchicuy,** and **Yanayacu.** The farthest, Tambo Amazónico, is 180km (112 miles) upriver from Iquitos on the Yarapa River; the other two are much closer and focus on quick in-and-out tours. The Sinchicuy (30km/19 miles from Iquitos) is one of the oldest established lodges in the zone. Yanayacu lodge is 60km (37 miles) from

Iquitos & the Northern Amazon

AMAZONIA

Several Amazon lodges offer *ayahuasca* ceremonies, which involve the privilege of taking a natural hallucinogenic potion prepared by an "authentic" Indian shaman, at $15 a shot. It's the local version of taking peyote with Don Juan, but at some joints, it teeters on the edge of spring break at the ecolodge. *Ayahuasca* is an authentic ritual and herbal drug with deep roots in local communities. A shaman boils diverse Amazonian plants and roots for up to 6 hours, and the resulting potion can indeed be very hallucinogenic. It is taken as part of a cleansing ritual, to purify the body and mind. The ceremony is not to be taken lightly, although some lodges seem to do just that, for the sake of selling a cool Amazon experience. Reports circulate about some travelers losing their minds, but it's hard to say if they should be taken seriously. At a minimum, *ayahuasca* is a cultural practice that should be respected and not abused by gringos.

the city. The company is honest and professionally run, and offers good and clean budget- to midrange standard tours in rustic shared lodges. The lodges are offered by several Peruvian and international travel agents and tour operators. Adventurers might be interested in the company's camping trips to the Pacaya-Samiria National Reserve, one of the best opportunities to rough it and catch glimpses of Amazonian wildlife (see "Into the Wild: Farther Afield from Iquitos" on p. 354). A 4-day/3-night trip to the Sinchicuy and Yanayacu lodges starts at $296 per person, while 2-night trips to the nearer lodges start at $259; camping trips to the Pacaya-Samiria National Reserve start at $759 per person.

○ **Tahuayo Lodge ★★★** (www.perujungle.com; ℰ **800/262-9669**). One of the most outstanding Amazon ecolodges in Peru, this low-impact ecoproperty, associated with the Rainforest Conservation Fund, lies on the shores of the River Tahuayo, about 4 hours from Iquitos. *Outside* magazine has touted it as one of the top-10 travel finds in the world. It is the only lodge with access to the Tamshiyacu-Tahuayo Reserve, a splendid area for primate and other wildlife viewing (it counts 500 species of birds). Because of its remoteness, it recommends visits of at least a week; programs are individually tailored. The 15 cabins are open year-round, and the lodge offers an excellent schedule of excursions ranging from rugged (jungle survival training) to relaxed; most enticing are zipline canopy ropes for treetop viewing. An 8-day/7-night trip is $1,295 per person (additional days $100), although trips as short as 3-days/2-nights are possible.

○ **Yacumama Lodge ★★** (www.yacumamalodge.com; ℰ **065/235-510,** or **800/854-0023** in the U.S. and Canada). Yacumama is an American-owned, first-class lodge with a handsome main house, private bungalows, solar power, and ecosensitive flush toilets deep in the Amazon—186km (116 miles) upriver on Río Yarapa (a tributary of the Río Ucayali). It's on an excellent 7,000-hectare (17,290-acre) forest reserve with a cool 10-story canopy tower; the treetop perspective is nearly as spectacular as the Explorama canopy walkway, although you miss the possibility of walking above the trees. In operation since 1993, Yacumama has built a solid reputation with its environmentally sound engineering, good jungle treks, and possibilities for dolphin sightings, and the company dedicates a percentage of its profits to conservation efforts. The company offers Machu Picchu/Cusco program extensions. A 4-day/3-night stay starts at $750.

RIVER CRUISES

Riverboat cruises down the Amazon and along its tributaries generally don't allow you to see much in the way of fauna or pristine jungle, although you will likely spot lots of birds and dolphins and get out on the waterways that are such a fundamental part of life and ecosystems in the northern Amazon. Cruises are best for people who don't want to rough it too much and who like the romance of traveling the Amazon by boat, although varying degrees of rusticity and luxury are available. Many cruises stop off at reserves for jungle walks and visits to local villages. Some of the best cruises are those to the Pacaya-Samiria National Reserve; see "Into the Wild: Farther Afield from Iquitos," below, for details. Most cruises have fixed departures, so arranging in advance of your visit is critical.

- **Aqua Expeditions ★★★** (www.aquaexpeditions.com; ☎ **866/603-3687** in the U.S. and Canada, or **065/601-053** in Peru) has blown the old concept of creaky, uncomfortable Amazon cruises out of the water. Its luxury river cruises are aboard the gorgeous, modern 130-foot M/V *Aqua,* designed by the well-known Peruvian architect Jordi Puig. The company's newest ship is the equally stunning, 147-foot M/V *Aria.* The menu is overseen by a celebrated Lima chef, Miguel Schiaffino. Sleeping quarters are sleekly contemporary, with swank indoor and outdoor lounge spaces, air-conditioned rooms with high-quality bedding, and large, panoramic windows that make it look like you're watching a big-screen movie of the Amazon. Cruises depart from Iquitos and go through the Pacaya-Samiria National Reserve. Prices range from $2,685 to $6,965 per person for 3-, 4-, and 7-day cruises, with weekly departures.

- **Dawn on the Amazon** 🛶 (www.dawnontheamazon.com; ☎ **065/223-730**). Run by Captain Bill Grimes, an enthusiastic one-time Indiana farmer who relocated to Iquitos and built a couple of handsome hardwood riverboats, this custom-oriented cruise company gets high marks for its service, honesty, and flexibility. There are both day trips and multi-day excursions (but not set departures) (ranging from $159 per person, per day to $2,450 per person for a 6-day cruise into Pacaya-Samiria). If you've come to Iquitos hoping to arrange a trip, pop into the office at Malecón Maldonado 185 to have a chat with Bill and see what can be worked out (even if it's only a day trip out on the rivers).

- **Delfin Amazon Cruises ★★** (www.delfinamazoncruises.com; ☎ **01/719-0998**). This Peruvian-owned luxury cruise company operates ships that are about as stylish as Aqua Expeditions, just less starkly contemporary. Its high-end cruises are aboard the Delfin I and Delfin II, gorgeously new and refurbished river vessels, luxurious but with warm and spacious suites. Four- to five-night riverboat cruises range from $3,150 to $4,400 per person.

- **Jungle Expeditions ★** (www.junglex.com; ☎ **065/261-583**). This company offers luxury river cruises on a fleet of six very elegant, 19th-century style boats, and cruises upriver along the Río Ucayali. Prices start at $3,898 per person for 10-day expeditions. The company accepts passengers through its Lima booking office (☎ **01/241-3232**) or **International Expeditions** (www.international expeditions.com; ☎ **800/234-9620**) in the United States, which offers air-inclusive packages and programs with Cusco and Machu Picchu extensions.

INDEPENDENT GUIDES

For travelers who want to get away from the lodges and groups and riverboats, more flexible independent treks into the jungle could be the way to go. You'll see more

INTO THE WILD: FARTHER afield FROM IQUITOS

The opportunities for enjoying spectacular wildlife sightings and experiencing how locals truly live in the Amazon are severely diminished in most areas where the jungle lodges are located. For primary rainforest and more authentic native villages, you have to be willing to rough it more than traditional lodges force you to. However, as jungle tourism in Peru continues to grow, several mid-range and luxury cruise operators are now organizing river cruises to one of Peru's greatest jungle zones.

About 300km (190 miles) south of Iquitos, a couple of days removed by boat and sandwiched between the Marañón and Ucayali rivers, is the **Pacaya-Samiria National Reserve ★★★**, the largest protected area in Peru and one of the most pristine in the world. Established in 1982, it contains 2,080,000 hectares (5,139,800 acres) of thick, untouched rainforest and wetlands. Incredibly, that accounts for 1.5% of Peru's total surface area. Riddled with rivers and 85 lakes, it's huge and daunting, and should be explored only with an experienced guide. Some of the Amazon's finest and most abundant wildlife resides in the reserve, such as pink dolphins, macaws, black caimans, spider monkeys, and giant river turtles. The reserve's numbers are staggering: It is home to 539 species of birds, 101 species of mammals, 256 kinds of fish, and 22 species of orchids. Guides typically take visitors by dugout canoe from **Lagunas** (upstream from Iquitos) through the reserve. Villages on the outskirts of the reserve worth visiting are **San Martín de Timpishia** and **Puerto Miguel.** To enter the reserve, officially you need permission from **INRENA,** the Peruvian parks authority. Contact its office in Iquitos (Pevas 350; ℰ **065/231-230**) or in Lima

(Los Petirrojos 355, Urbanización El Palomar; ℰ **01/224-3298**) for additional information. You'll need a minimum of 4 or 5 days to do the trip from Iquitos. Aqua Expeditions, Delfin Amazon Cruises, and Jungle Expeditions all organize Pacaya-Samiria National Reserve river cruises, while Paseos Amazónicos operates camping trips to the Reserve (for contact information, see "River Cruises" and "Jungle Lodges," above).

Another option for down-and-dirty exploration of Amazon culture and sights is to cruise the rivers not on (relatively) pampered boats that take tourists out to lodges, but aboard the **three-decked riverboats** that form the transportation backbone of the region, ferrying people back and forth from villages on Amazon tributaries to Iquitos and other towns. The boats are rough going, stuffed with animals and densely packed families and their household goods, and are almost entirely absent of comforts. You should take along plenty of bottled water, a hammock, and foodstuffs such as fruit and canned items. Journeys can last several days, but slinging yourself into a hammock on the top deck and floating slowly down the Huallaga or Ucayali will certainly win points among your friends when it comes to regaling them with vacation heroics. For budget travelers, it's a perfect antidote to high-priced lodges and river cruises: It's virtually impossible to spend more than $15 a day, including transportation.

For more details about how to organize trips to Pacaya-Samiria or simple river transport along the rivers, contact the helpful folks at the tourist information office in Iquitos for up-to-the-minute suggestions. See also "Independent Guides," below, for information on treks with independent guides.

fauna, and especially flora, than will other travelers, and you'll get to visit native communities that aren't merely putting on a show for your benefit. You'll rough it in varying degrees (everything from eating cans of tuna and rice and beans cooked over an open fire, to enjoying fresh-caught fish straight from the river, to camping in makeshift sites along the way). To immerse yourself in the dense Amazonian jungle, you need an experienced, reliable wilderness guide. Scores of independent guides operate in the jungle around Iquitos and scout for tourists in the city. Their quality and professionalism vary tremendously, however, and many plainly are not to be trusted. Several guides in Iquitos have criminal records for robbing the very tourists who trusted them. The local tourism office maintains a book of disreputable, blacklisted guides.

Because you're going to be spending all your time in the jungle with the guide, depending on him to lead you, communicate with you, cook for you, and build good campsites, selecting a competent guide is of the utmost importance. Most guides are "extralegal"; only a couple of guides in Iquitos are officially licensed to operate as full-fledged independent jungle guides (possessing a license, an expensive bureaucratic requirement out of reach of most guides, isn't the only determination, however). No matter what you hear from other travelers, if you're considering hiring a guide for a solo or small-group trek into the jungle, visit the tourism information office in Iquitos before exchanging money; ask for the office personnel's recommendations—which they're usually happy to dispense—and take a look at the review books of comments about guides. Rates depend on the number of travelers and length of trips; they can range from $40 to $50 a day per person to more than $100 per day.

If you manage to locate a guide for an independent trip, never pay upfront before your arrival in Iquitos; some travelers have been scammed.

NORTHERN PERU

12

Northern Peru is curiously underappreciated, at least as compared to the vastly more popular south, despite a fascinating blend of coastal desert and mountain landscapes, ancient archaeological treasures, fine colonial cities, the country's best beaches, and the legendary peaks of the north-central Andes. For travelers willing to venture off Peru's proverbial beaten track, there's much to discover, even if it doesn't have the tourist-friendly immediacy and famed attractions of Cusco, the Sacred Valley, and Titicaca. For archaeology buffs, there's Chan Chan, the great adobe city of the Chimú civilization and the great royal tomb of Lord of Sipán, Peru's very own King Tut. Urban explorers can explore the colonial gems Trujillo and Cajamarca. Surfers and beach lovers can hit the Pacific's great waves and fast-developing resorts around Máncora, while outdoors adventurers can challenge themselves in the Cordillera Blanca, one of the world's premier destinations for mountain climbing and trekking. If there's less tourist infrastructure in the north, well, there are also many fewer tourists.

HISTORY Several of Peru's greatest pre-Inca civilizations inhabited the north, including the Chavín (1200 to 300 B.C.), Moche (A.D. 100 to 700), Chimú (A.D. 1000 to the 15th century), and Sicán (A.D. 100 to 1100). Evidence of these great cultures ranges from inscrutable adobe pyramids to a pre-Inca aqueduct at Cumbe Mayo, which dates to 1000 B.C.

SIGHTSEEING Archaeology buffs have their hands full with Chan Chan, the great adobe city of the Chimú civilization; 1,500-year-old Moche temples; the royal tomb of the Lord of Sipán; and the Sicán's so-called "Valley of Pyramids." Cajamarca's colonial core is one of Peru's loveliest, and it too is surrounded by evocative archaeological sites, such as Cumbe Mayo.

NATURE Northern Peru's natural diversity is astounding: a vast Pacific coastline, where two currents, the cold Humboldt from the south and Ecuatorial from the north, meet; coastal deserts; and the snowcapped 5,000m (16,400-ft.) peaks of the Cordillera Blanca (part of the protected Huascarán National Park, a UNESCO Biosphere Reserve and World Heritage Trust site).

RELAXATION The long coastline offers leisurely beach strolling and fresh seafood from the small fishing village of Huanchaco, just outside Trujillo, up to the burgeoning resorts near Máncora, home to Peru's best beaches and new stylish boutique hotels perched right on the beach.

ACTIVE PURSUITS Northern Peru beckons outdoors adventurers, from surfing some of the greatest waves in South America, along the north coast, to the all-around playground of the Cordillera Blanca and Callejón de Huaylas Valley, where the smorgasbord includes world-class mountain climbing and trekking, ice and rock climbing, mountain biking, and river rafting.

THE BEST TRAVEL EXPERIENCES IN NORTHERN PERU

○ **Marveling at Peru's King Tut.** The Lord of Sipán's royal tomb is one of the great archaeological discoveries in the Americas. The Moche royal figure was buried more than 1,700 years ago in many levels of treasures, now on display at the cool Museo Tumbas Reales de Sipán. See p. 378.

- **Singing along at Usha Usha.** Late at night in Cajamarca, the place to be is this tiny, graffiti-filled peña bar, where regulars join the owner and musicians in singing Andean protest songs until the wee hours. See p. 395.
- **Finding your way to Kuélap.** Nearly as spectacular as Machu Picchu, but comparatively undiscovered, these 800-year-old Chachapoyas ruins atop a mountain ridge comprise a massive fortress complex of round buildings and monumental defensive wall. Tough to get to, but with quite the payoff. See p. 384.
- **Gazing at Lagunas de Llanganuco.** High in the Andes—3,850m (12,631 ft.) above sea level and surrounded by Peru's most stunning peaks—this duo of brilliant turquoise lakes is a gorgeous sight. Get to them on a day trip or at the end of a multi-day trek. See p. 421.
- **Strolling deserted beaches.** Once the province of hippies, surfers, and budget backpackers, Máncora and its surrounding beaches—the best in Peru—are now welcoming chic boutique hotels. Midweek you may have the sands all to yourself. See p. 398.

TRUJILLO ★

561km (349 miles) N of Lima; 200km (124 miles) S of Chiclayo; 298km (185 miles) SW of Cajamarca

Trujillo, the capital of La Libertad department, is the third-largest city in Peru and one of only two of commercial importance on the entire north coast. Yet the town, founded in 1534 by Diego Almagro on the orders of Francisco Pizarro, retains the Spanish colonial feel of a much smaller town. Locals saunter along the grandly laid-out Plaza Mayor, and the downtown area is a handsome grid of streets lined with elegant, pastel-colored colonial mansions embellished by wrought-iron window grilles.

The importance of the region greatly predates the arrival of the Spaniards, however, and Trujillo is celebrated mostly for a stunning collection of pre-Columbian sites that abound on the outskirts of the city. Looming in the desert are five major archaeological sites, including two of the richest ensembles of Moche temples and ruins of the Chimú culture in Peru. Chan Chan, a monumental adobe complex of royal palaces covering more than 52 sq. km (20 sq. miles), is the primary draw for visitors, but archaeological tours also visit the fascinating Temples of the Moon and Sun (Huacas del Sol y de la Luna), built by the Moche culture around A.D. 500. Several of these sites have been partially restored, but they still require some imagination to conjure a sense of their immensity, the busy daily activity, and the grandeur of the ceremonies once held there.

Just northwest of Trujillo is Huanchaco, a laid-back beach resort that serves as a virtual bedroom community for many visitors, particularly younger travelers with an interest in surfing. Ideally positioned for ruins visits, Huanchaco is less hectic than Trujillo and has a better roster of cheaper small hotels, budget *hostales* (inns), and seaside seafood restaurants.

Essentials

GETTING THERE

BY PLANE **LAN** (www.lan.com; © **01/213-8200**) and **Star Peru** (www.star peru.com; © **01/705-9000**) fly daily to Trujillo from Lima (1 hr.); flights arrive at the **Aeropuerto Carlos Martínez de Pinillos** in the Huanchaco district

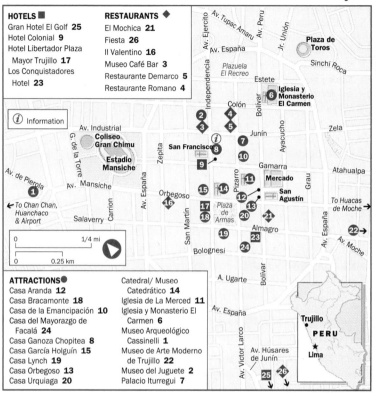

HOTELS ■
Gran Hotel El Golf **25**
Hotel Colonial **9**
Hotel Libertador Plaza
  Mayor Trujillo **17**
Los Conquistadores
  Hotel **23**

RESTAURANTS ◆
El Mochica **21**
Fiesta **26**
Il Valentino **16**
Museo Café Bar **3**
Restaurante Demarco **5**
Restaurante Romano **4**

ⓘ Information

ATTRACTIONS ●
Casa Aranda **12**
Casa Bracamonte **18**
Casa de la Emancipación **10**
Casa del Mayorazgo de
  Facalá **24**
Casa Ganoza Chopitea **8**
Casa García Holguín **15**
Casa Lynch **19**
Casa Orbegoso **13**
Casa Urquiaga **20**

Catedral/ Museo
  Catedrático **14**
Iglesia de La Merced **11**
Iglesia y Monasterio El
  Carmen **6**
Museo Arqueológico
  Cassinelli **1**
Museo de Arte Moderno
  de Trujillo **22**
Museo del Juguete **2**
Palacio Iturregui **7**

(𝄞 **044/464-013**), about 20 minutes northwest of downtown (a taxi to downtown Trujillo costs about S/20).

BY BUS   The major companies making the 9-hour trip from Lima are **Ormeño** (www.grupo-ormeno.com.pe; 𝄞 **01/472-5000**), **Cruz del Sur** (www.cruzdelsur.com.pe; 𝄞 **01/311-5050**), and **Oltursa** (www.oltursa.com.pe; 𝄞 **01/708-5000**). **Transportes Línea** (www.transporteslinea.com.pe; 𝄞 **044/286-538** in Trujillo, **076/823-956** in Cajamarca, or **074/233-497** in Chiclayo) makes the 6-hour trip from Cajamarca, 3-hour journey from Chiclayo and the 8-hour journey from Huaraz. **ITTSA** (www.ittsabus.com; 𝄞 **044/222-541**) goes to Trujillo from Lima, Chiclayo, and Piura.

GETTING AROUND

Downtown Trujillo is a grid of relatively short blocks ringed by Avenida España. At the heart of the *centro* is the Plaza de Armas, and the main sights are all nearby on the major streets leading off the square. Getting around the small *centro* is thus best managed on foot. However, you'll need to take either a taxi or a public bus to visit the major archaeological sites outside Trujillo, or the beachside suburb, Huanchaco.

Confusing as can be are Trujillo's street names: Nearly every street and avenue has two names and two corresponding signs, one a smaller printed version and the other a fancier painted sign. Most maps go by the smaller, printed name, which is what I give in this chapter.

Several *urbanizaciones,* or residential districts, lie just beyond Avenida España. Urbanización El Recreo, where several resort-style hotels are located, is just west of Av. 28 de Julio. Chan Chan is just 5km (3 miles) northwest of the city, on the way to the airport and Huanchaco. The Huacas de Moche are 8km (5 miles) south of town beyond the Carretera Industrial.

BY TAXI   Taxis are plentiful in Trujillo. Most in-town fares, inside the Avenida España ring, are about S/4. A taxi ride to Chan Chan or Huanchaco costs about S/20. You can hire taxis by the hour (S/20) or by the day (S/100–S/125) to tour archaeological sites in the environs. Be sure to negotiate or ask first in the tourist office to determine the fare.

BY BUS   *Combis* cost S/1; buses travel from just outside the *centro histórico* in Trujillo to Huanchaco (S/3).

BY CAR   If you want to rent a vehicle to make trips to Chan Chan and other sites, or even to travel around the northern region, try **Global Car Rental,** Ecuador 122, Of. 201, Urbanización El Recreo (© **044/295-548**).

ORGANIZED TOURS

Agencies offering standard city and archaeological tours include **Guía Tours,** Jr. Independencia 580 (© **044/245-170**); **Chacón Tours,** Av. España 106 (© **044/255-212**); **Consorcio Turístico del Norte,** Jr. Pizarro 478 (© **044/205-645**); and **Trujillo Tours,** Diego de Almagro 301 (© **044/233-091**). Most standard tours cost S/45 to S/60 per person. Tours to El Brujo are generally S/90 to S/120.

VISITOR INFORMATION

The **iPerú** offices are located at the airport (© **044/464-226**) and downtown at Jr. Diego de Almagro 420, on the Plaza Mayor (also called the Plaza de Armas; © **044/294-561**); the downtown office is open Monday through Friday from 9am to 1pm and 2 to 5pm. It has free maps, and the staff can advise you on the easiest way to visit Chan Chan and the other major archaeological sites beyond the city. The city's tourism website is www.trujillodelperu.com.

FAST FACTS

Banks that exchange traveler's checks and cash and that have ATMs are **Banco de Crédito,** Jr. Gamarra 562 (© **044/242-360**); **Banco Latino,** Jr. Gamarra 572 (© **044/243-461**); and **Banco Continental,** Pizarro 620, in the colonial Casa de la Emancipación. **Interbanc,** located at Pizarro and Gamarra, has a Cirrus/PLUS ATM. Money-changers can usually be found hanging about the Plaza de Armas or along Gamarra.

In case of emergency, call © **105.** The helpful **tourist police** are located at Independencia 630, in the Casa Ganoza Chopitea (© **044/291-705**). For complaints, you can also call the **Tourist Protection Service** at © **044/204-146.**

If you need medical attention, you're likely to find English-speaking doctors at **Clínica Peruana-Americana,** Av. Mansiche 702 (© **044/231-261**). Other hospitals are **Hospital Regional Docente de Trujillo,** Av. Mansiche 795 (© **044/231-581**), and **Hospital Belén,** Bolívar 350 (© **044/245-281**). In Huanchaco, a clinic (*posta médica*) is located at Atahualpa 437 (📞 **044/461-547**). In Trujillo, there are InkaPharma locations at Jr. Pizarro 525 and Jr. Bolívar 623; Botica Fasa at Jr. Pizarro 525 and Jr. Bolívar 393.

For Internet access, two *cabinas* to try are **Cibercafé Internet,** Manuel María Izaga 716 (📞 **044/228-729**), and **Deltanet/Telecom,** Orbegoso 641 (📞 **044/294-327**). Both charge about S/2 per hour.

Trujillo's **post office** is at Independencia 286 (📞 **044/245-941**). A **DHL/Western Union** branch is at Almagro 579 (📞 **044/203-686**). The **Telefónica del Perú** office is at Pizarro 561. A *locutorio* (public calling place) is located at Gamarra 454.

Exploring the Area
COLONIAL TRUJILLO

Trujillo has an impressive collection of elegant colonial- and republican-era houses (*casas antiguas*) and baroque churches, as well as one of Peru's odder museums of ancient ceramics. A tour of Trujillo rightly begins with the graceful **Plaza de Armas,** where vendors hang out and families in their Sunday finery pose for pictures in front of the Libertad monument. On the square is the **Catedral,** built in the mid-17th century but rather sober and uninteresting, although it has a **Museo Catedrático** (📞 **044/235-083**) with silver and gold chalices and bishops' vestments. The museum is open 9am to 1pm and 4 to 7pm Monday to Friday, 9am to 1pm Saturday; admission is S/5. The plaza is ringed by colorful examples of fine colonial-era mansions, including the one that is now home to the Hotel Libertador. Trujillo's pastel colonial buildings are distinguished by their ornamental wrought-iron window grilles, unusual in Peru.

Casa Ganoza Chopitea ★   HISTORIC HOUSE   Better known in Trujillo as La Casa de los Leones (House of the Lions) because of the lions crowning the main door, this 17th-century house is one of the most splendid of the colonial era. Opposite the San Francisco church, the entrance is loaded with baroque and rococo details, including river stones (*canto rodado*) on the ground. A *concha venera,* or welcoming shell, is placed above the door. Inside the house, you'll pass through the Salón de Varones (Men's Hall), with a high wooden ceiling, followed by the Salón de Damas (Women's Hall). Look for the curious air holes in the latter—they go all the way to the roof to allow fresh air to circulate.

Jr. Independencia 630. No phone. Free admission. Mon–Fri 9am–1pm and 3–5pm.

Casa Orbegoso ★   HISTORIC HOUSE   This huge yellow-and-brown mid-18th-century house, once the property of former president Luis José de Orbegoso, stretches around the block and has its own plaza facing the San Agustín church. In the entrance are Moorish–Christian mural paintings that were buried beneath successive baroque, rococo, and finally neoclassical murals. Inside are some original furnishings and mural paintings that can still be seen around the lower sections of some rooms. The front part of the house still belongs to descendants of the original owners. Orbegoso, who fought alongside Bolívar in the War of Independence, is buried in a mausoleum in the house.

Orbegoso 553. 📞 **044/234-950.** Free admission. Tues–Sun 9:30am–7pm.

Casa Urquiaga (Casa Calonge) ★★   HISTORIC HOUSE   This grand colonial mansion, royal blue with white window grilles, conserves the 18th-century desk of Simón Bolívar, who lived here for 2 years after proclaiming Peru's independence in

1824. The home, with three lovely interior courtyards, is one of Trujillo's most magnificently restored and most historic. It hosted the first viceroy of Peru in 1604 and was the headquarters of the first bank in Trujillo. The dining room features spectacular French porcelain, and throughout there are beautiful chandeliers and mirrors. In a second patio is an exhibit of Moche and Nasca ceramics. Look for the gold Chavín necklaces and several Chimú ornamental pieces, also in gold. Today the mansion is owned by the Banco Central.

Jr. Pizarro 446 (Plaza Mayor). No phone. Free admission; passport or other identification required. Mon–Fri 9am–3pm; Sat–Sun 10am–1pm.

Iglesia de La Merced CHURCH On a small square set back from the street and next to the Corte Superior de Justicia (itself worth a peek), La Merced, one of Trujillo's most impressive churches, dates to 1636. It's especially notable for the colorful carved figures in relief around the cupola, including alternating series of small angels and cherubs supporting the top section—perhaps 100 in all. Inside, the church is salmon and white, with white stone arches. At the rear, apparently jammed into the organ loft, is a massive rococo pipe organ.

Jr. Pizarro 550. No phone. Free admission. Daily 8am–noon and 4–6pm.

Iglesia y Monasterio El Carmen ★ CHURCH/MONASTERY This lovely church and monastery, founded in 1724 and occupying an entire city block, has the most important collection of colonial art in Trujillo. Its Carmelite museum (Pinacoteca Carmelita) possesses 150 baroque and rococo paintings, the majority of them from the 17th and 18th centuries, as well as paintings of the Quito Art School. The final room shows the process of restoration of paintings, although explanations are in Spanish only. The church's central gilded altar is marvelous. The main *retablo* (altar) was created by Master Fernando Collado de la Cruz, a free black Peruvian. Floral murals in soft pastels line each side of the church. The monastery has two cloisters (and 10 cloistered nuns) and contains a fair portion of the convent's art collection, but it cannot be visited.

Jirón Bolívar (at Colón). ℂ **044/233-091.** Admission to church and museum S/3 adults, S/1 children. Mon–Sat 9am–1pm.

Museo Arqueológico Cassinelli ★ 📷 MUSEUM One of the most curious places you'll ever see fine ceramics exhibits is this private museum, about a 10-minute walk from the Plaza de Armas, housed in a dumpy space beneath a Mobil gas station. What are the odds of a gas-station and car-wash owner devoting all his money, time, and attention to assembling and displaying one of the largest private collections of ancient ceramics? Going on over 40 years of existence, with dreams of greater recognition and expansion, Señor Casinelli's superb collection of the Moche, Nasca, Chavín, Huari, and Chimú cultures (among others) holds about 4,000 pieces (although Casinelli says only 2,000 can be displayed "for lack of space and lack of support from the Peruvian government") and spans more than 2,500 years. There are some excellent examples of all those cultures displayed on pressboard shelves, including, behind a wall meant to protect innocent eyes, the famed erotic ceramics of the Moche. (You might have to ask the old guy to open the case, a feeling akin to asking the pharmacist for condoms.) Casinelli owns the gas station upstairs and has an architect's model of the much larger museum, along with a hotel, he'd like someday to build (but he's now in his 80s, so that dream is growing dim). Guided tours are in Spanish only.

Av. Nicolás de Piérola 607 (at intersection of Huanchaco and Ctra. Panamericana). © **044/246-110.** Admission S/7. Mon–Sat 9am–1pm and 3–7pm.

Museo de Arte Moderno de Trujillo ★ 💼 MUSEUM Unusual for this city that celebrates its colonial past is its relatively new Museum of Modern Art. The private collection of the *Trujillano* painter and sculptor Gerardo Chávez includes, in addition to his own pieces, the contemporary works of renowned international artists such as Alberto Giacometti, Paul Klee, and the celebrated Latin American painters Roberto Sebastián Matta, Wilfredo Lam, Joaquín Torres-García, Oswaldo Guayasamin, and Rufino Tamayo. The small, handsome museum (with fewer than 100 works) is located about 4 km (2 miles) outside Trujillo.

Ctra. Industrial s/n. mamtrujillo.blogspot.com. © **044/215-668.** Admission S/10. Mon–Sat 9:30am–5:30pm.

Museo del Juguete ☺ TOY MUSEUM Upstairs from my favorite watering hole in Trujillo (Museo Café Bar; see p. 370), this small and sweet museum of antique toys—assembled by the artist Gerardo Chávez, whose collection of modern art forms the Museu de Arte Moderno de Trujillo—includes examples dating from the pre-Columbian era all the way to the 1950s.

Jr. Independencia 705 (at Junín). © **044/208-181.** Admission S/6 adults, S/3 children. Mon–Sat 10am–6pm; Sun 10am–2pm.

Palacio Iturregui ★ HISTORIC HOUSE This bright yellow mansion, an excellent example of neoclassical civil architecture that dates to the 19th century, is home to the Club Central, Trujillo's traditional social club. Although the club continues to be members-only, visitors can tool around for a view of an only slightly dilapidated exclusivity. The two-story mansion, with a large central courtyard, is outfitted with window grilles, thin columns, and Italian marble statues. Upstairs is a small museum containing Moche ceramics. Members in semiformal dress still drop by for lunch or dinner at the club, followed by a game of cards.

Jr. Pizarro 688. © **044/234-212.** Admission (guided tour) S/5. Mon–Sat 11am–6pm.

ARCHAEOLOGICAL SITES NEAR TRUJILLO ★★

Chan Chan ★★ ARCHAEOLOGICAL SITE One of the most important archaeological sites in Peru (although, in its present state it might not seem as "complete" to the layman observer as some of the Inca stone ruins in the highlands), Chan

Chan is an enormous adobe city in the Moche Valley, just 5km (3 miles) from Trujillo. The great capital of the Chimú Empire, which stretched some 966km (600 miles) along the northern coast of Peru from Lima to the Ecuadorian border, is the largest complex of its kind from pre-Columbian America. The urban Chimú was the chief state in Peru before the continental conquest of the Inca Empire. Begun around 1300, it reaches all the way from Huanchaco port to Campana Mountain, an area covering more than 25 sq. km (9¾ sq. miles) of desert floor.

First excavated in the mid-1960s, the crumbling mud city was once home to perhaps as many as 60,000 inhabitants. In all, the UNESCO Cultural Mankind Heritage Monument comprises more than a dozen citadels and a maze of living quarters, thick defensive walls, ramps, plazas, gardens, workshops, warehouses, narrow streets, a huge reservoir, a royal cemetery, and pyramidal temples. Nine palaces were the personal domains of Chimú chieftains; when one died, he was buried in an elaborate ritual in the palace and a new royal compound was built for his successor. These were almost certainly overflowing with gold and silver riches, and were later ransacked not by the Incas, but by the Spaniards and subsequent *huaqueros* (grave robbers, or treasure hunters). The fragile buildings themselves have fallen victim to erosion caused by recurring El Niño floods; in 1986, Chan Chan was listed on World Heritage Sites in Danger due to both physical erosion and acts of continued pillaging.

The Chimú kingdom began around A.D. 1000 and reached its apex in the 15th century before succumbing to the Incas in 1470 and 1471, after more than a decade of resistance. Today one can only imagine what this massive complex looked like and the sophisticated society that once inhabited it. Unfortunately, no written records or documents aid our understanding of the establishment of the city or reconstruct the daily activities that took place there. Long walls are embellished with friezes of geometric figures, stylized birds and fish, ocean motifs, and mythological creatures—although some might be considered a bit too impeccably restored. There are no doors or arches in the entire complex, and there are no stairs—only ramps.

There are four main sites at Chan Chan, all spread over a large area that requires either a lot of walking or a couple of taxi rides. (The Palacio Nik-An is the site of greatest interest; the others, including Huaca Arco Iris, Huaca Esmeralda, and a site museum, are less impressive, so if you're pressed for time, you could make do with a visit only to Nik-An.) The principal complex, the **Palacio Nik-An,** or royal palace, was home to a noble population of 500 to 1,000. It has been partially restored, and a walking tour is indicated by painted arrows. The first area of interest is a ceremonial

 Chan Chan Crime Report

Chan Chan is spread out over several kilometers, and some visitors walking alone among the component parts have reported robberies and attacks. To be safe, stick to the main paths between major sites and avoid wandering along smaller paths in the open fields around Tschudi Palace. Chan Chan is just a couple of kilometers from the beach, but the route to the water has a very bad reputation and should be avoided; too many reports of muggings and worse have been registered over the years to risk it. There have also been crime reports in the neighborhoods around Huaca Arco Iris and Huaca Esmeralda; it's best to take a taxi there from the Museo de Sitio de Chan Chan.

The Hairless Peruvian Dog

Near the Chan Chan site museum and elsewhere in northern Peru, you might spot a peculiar smooth, black-skinned creature, often with blotches. This less than blessed creature is the *biringo,* or Peruvian hairless dog. Ancient and—to my Labrador-loving tastes—ugly as all get out, these dogs were kept by several of the pre-Inca cultures of the region, and they're still around and kept as pets. These dogs are hot to the touch, and it is said that ancient nobles kept them as portable heaters. The Lambayeque and Chimú not only domesticated the animal, though; they also made it part of their diets. *Eeww.*

courtyard decorated with meticulously restored, aquatic-themed friezes. The original walls were 18m (59 ft.) high. Just beyond the courtyard are walls with interesting friezes of fish and seabirds. The most fascinating component of the palace is the large area known as the Sanctuary, whose walls are textured like fishing nets.

The **Museo de Sitio de Chan Chan,** along the road back toward Trujillo, has a small collection of ceramics from Chan Chan and some exhibits about the nature of the city and its history. The museum is equipped with an auditorium and models of Chan Chan; an audio and light presentation is given in English as well as Spanish. The museum is at least a 20-minute walk from Tschudi Palace.

Huaca Esmeralda and Huaca Arco Iris are two smaller pyramidal temples that are rather removed from the main palace. They are included in the Chan Chan ticket, but one must go to either the museum or Nik-An first. **Huaca Esmeralda** is in the Mansiche district, midway between Chan Chan and Trujillo (several blocks behind the church, to the right). The *huaca* consists of a couple of platforms and some friezes that have not yet been restored; although they are less impressive than others, at least visitors get a clear chance to see original reliefs.

Huaca Arco Iris (**Rainbow Temple,** also called **Huaca El Dragón**), lies in the La Esperanza suburb a couple of kilometers from Trujillo, west of the Pan-American Highway. It is in much better condition than Huaca Esmeralda, having been excavated only in the 1960s, and its well-conserved rainbow-shaped friezes are fascinating. Some have interpreted the central motif to be that of a dragon. Outer walls have reliefs of snakes and peculiar lizards. The fairly large structure has several ramps, and visitors can climb to platforms at the top of the temple.

To visit all the sites, you'll need the better part of a day. Many people choose to break up the visit over 2 days. A visit can begin at either Palacio Nik-An or at the Museo de Sitio, transferring between them by bus or taxi, and then going to the adjunct temple sites by taxi.

Valle de Moche. (Huaca Arco Iris: Jr. Pedro Murillo 1681, La Esperanza, Trujillo, Panamericana Norte). Admission S/11; ticket is good for 48 hr. and all four sites of the complex. Guides are available at the entrance to Nik-An for S/35 per group. Daily 9am–4pm. Catch the Huanchaco bus (S/4) on Av. España (at the corner of Independencia/Ejército) and ask to be let off at the turnoff to Chan Chan. Occasionally, there are taxis waiting here; otherwise, walk nearly a mile down a dirt road to the left, to the Tschudi Palace. For the Museo de Sitio, catch a bus returning to Trujillo. Taxis from Trujillo cost about S/20. Because transportation among the four sites is not always available, it might be worthwhile to contract a taxi to take you to the sites and wait for you (round-trip, S/75).

El Brujo 🎁   ARCHAEOLOGICAL SITE   Difficult to get to and explore without a private guide, the remote Moche complex of El Brujo nonetheless makes a very worthwhile visit for those intrigued by what they've seen at Chan Chan and the huacas near Trujillo. Because it is so little explored—until recently, it was closed to the public—many visitors enjoy El Brujo even more than those other sites. (Because of ongoing excavations, some groups are reportedly still occasionally turned away.)

El Brujo lies in the Chicama Valley, about 60km (37 miles) north of Trujillo along the coast, or 1½ hours by car. A number of cultures developed in the Chicama Valley region since the pre-ceramic period, and at least one of the three temples here, **Huaca Prieta,** is about 5,000 years old. Oddly enough, it's essentially a giant, prehistoric garbage dump—not much to see for nonspecialists, but containing a wealth of nonbiodegradable information for archaeologists researching the ancient people of the same name. (The Huaca Prieta civilization inhabited the area from around 3500–2200 B.C.) The main temple of interest at El Brujo is **Huaca Cao,** a leveled-off pyramid with terrific and huge multicolored friezes—some of the finest in northern Peru. They depict figures of warriors, priests, and sacrificial victims. Nearby, **Huaca Cortada** has some cool and menacing figures in high relief brandishing a knife in one hand and a recently decapitated head in the other.

Near Magdalena de Cao, Valle de Chicama. Admission S/20. Daily 9am–4pm. Several tour agencies in Trujillo organize excursions to El Brujo; be sure to ask about the status of the current admissions policy at the site. Private guides who frequently take individuals and small groups are Michael White and Clara Luz Bravo (📞 **044/243-347**). Ask at the Tourism Information Office (📞 **044/938-922**) about other guides.

Huacas de Moche ★   ARCHAEOLOGICAL SITE   About 8km (5 miles) south of Trujillo in the desert Valle de Moche, this complex of Moche ruins is enigmatic from a distance. Two imposing rounded-off and weathered adobe pyramids, partially eroded, sit in a dusty open field at the foot of Cerro Blanco. Built by the Moche people around A.D. 500, they are about 7 centuries older than the ruined city of Chan Chan. The two masses constituted a religious center and an urban settlement.

The first pyramid, the **Huaca del Sol (Temple of the Sun),** is nearly 20m (66 ft.) high, although it was once bigger by perhaps two-thirds, and it was very likely the largest man-made structure in the Americas in its day. Heavy rains of the El Niño phenomenon, and the Spaniards' diversion of the nearby Moche River, precipitated the erosion. It is said to have been built by 250,000 men and 140 million adobe bricks. The pyramid once surely was composed of multiple staircases and platforms. The huaca remains unexcavated, and it looks very fragile, as though a major rainstorm could easily take it out. Signs warn visitors against climbing on the ruins (NO ESCALAR), but plenty do climb up to the top along steep trails. Additional foot traffic only furthers the erosion, though, and the views are equally good from the Huaca de la Luna across the way. Some visitors inevitably find this lumped mass a bit of a disappointment, just a massive mound of muddy earth; if you find yourself in that camp, hurry over to the neighboring huaca.

Across the open field, where burial sites have been found and living quarters were once erected, is the smaller but more interesting **Huaca de la Luna (Temple of the Moon).** It is better preserved than the Temple of the Sun and has been excavated; many of the most important finds took place in the 1990s, and excavations are ongoing. The structure consists of five independent levels, with no communication among them—perhaps a result of the fact that the huaca (pyramid) was constructed in major phases over 600 years. Inside the adobe walls (at the top of an entrance

MOCHE culture

Anyone who has spent time in a small museum room crammed with the famed erotic ceramics of the Moche culture might feel that we know almost too much about this ancient civilization, certainly more than plenty of people are comfortable seeing depicted on vases and other vessels. But our knowledge isn't limited to the Moche's sexual mores. The Moche, who inhabited the northern coastal desert of Peru from A.D. 100 to 700, left detailed information about their entire civilization in their finely detailed ceramics, which are some of the finest produced in pre-Columbian Peru. The Moche are, along with the contemporary Nasca people from the desert coast south of Lima, the best-documented culture of the Classical period.

The apogee of Moche society was A.D. 500 to 600. Although they possessed no written language, their superior painted pottery presents evidence of nearly all elements of their society, from disease and dance to architecture, transportation, agriculture, music, and religion. The Moche (also referred to as "Mochica," although the latter term is losing some currency) were a strictly hierarchical, elite-dominated society that developed into a theocracy. They also constituted one of the first true urban cultures in Peru. Religious temples or pyramids, called huacas, were restricted to nobles, warriors, and priests; common citizens—farmers, artisans, fishers, and slaves—lived in areas removed from the temples.

The finest selection of Moche ceramics in the country is found at the Museo Arqueológico Rafael Larco Herrera (p. 89) in Lima, the largest private collection of pre-Columbian art in the world. The founder of the museum is the author of the classic study *Los Mochicas*. The Museo de Arte Precolombino (p. 173) in Cusco also has a fine, although small, collection of Moche artifacts.

ramp) are polychromatic friezes of large rhomboids, featuring a repeated motif of the fearsome anthropomorphic figure Ai-Apaek, known as *El Degollador* (the decapitator), and several secondary figures. The yellow, red, white, and black designs are quite remarkable; the god is said to have the hair of the sea and eyes of an owl. From the top of the Huaca de la Luna, there are excellent views of Huaca del Sol and the surrounding countryside. Near the ticket booth, where you can arrange for a guide, is a small refreshment stand and souvenir shop.

Valle de Moche. ☎ **044/291-894.** Admission S/10; cost includes a Spanish- or English-speaking guide (tip expected). Daily 9am–4pm. Catch the yellow "Campiña de Moche" *colectivo* (S/2) on Suárez (at Av. Los Incas), several blocks northeast of the Plaza de Armas. Otherwise, you can take a taxi there for about S/20. In high season, you won't need to have the driver wait because there are frequent buses and taxis returning to Trujillo. If there are few people around, however, you can usually get the driver to wait an hour or so to take you back to Trujillo for around S/35.

HUANCHACO ★

Huanchaco, 13km (7½ miles) northwest of Trujillo, is a tranquil and traditional fishing village now doubling as a pretty low-key resort. On summer weekends, though, it gets jumping with folks from Trujillo and vacationing Peruvians. Huanchaco is a very good alternative to Trujillo as a base for exploring the archaeological sites of the Chimú and Moche (and a day's visit to the capital city is easily accomplished from Huanchaco).

The town's fishing character is apparent in the long jetty that juts out over the water and the pointy handcrafted boats called *caballitos del mar* (or *caballitos de totora*), for which Huanchaco has become famous and which remain the photogenic vessel of choice for fishers. These small boats, made of bound totora reeds, have been used by fishermen for more than 1,000 years, since the reign of the Moche. The area around Huanchaco is one of the few places in Peru where this ancient sea-vessel tradition has not disappeared from use. When not out on the water, they're parked on the beach in groups like slender tepees.

Besides a stroll on the beach or out onto the long piers, and a visit to Huanchaco's pleasant *artesanía* market, there's not too much to see or do. A 16th-century colonial church clings to a cliff, but it's a long walk uphill from town. More than anything else, Huanchaco's easy pace and proximity to the sea are its main attractions. It has several agreeable resort hotels, seafood restaurants, and nice stretches of beach. The big waves here attract local surfers and a few board-carrying tourists, although the biggest and best waves are at **Puerto Chicama** (also known as **Malabrigo**), about 80km (50 miles) farther up the coast. Waves there can be ridden up to a half-mile, and it's the site of the largest left wave in the world. (Another good spot in the far north is **Cabo Blanco,** about 110km/68 miles south of Tumbes.) La Casa Suiza *hostal* (p. 374) rents out body boards.

GETTING THERE   Pick up a Huanchaco bus (S/3) along Independencia in Trujillo; the buses go along the first part of the beach before turning on Los Ficus. You can get to Puerto Chicama by colectivos, which depart hourly from the Terminal Interurbano on Calle Santa Cruz in Trujillo; the journey takes about 90 minutes. A taxi from Trujillo is about S/25.

Where to Eat

Dining out is a mostly low-key affair in Trujillo. Though it's Peru's third-largest city, it doesn't have many sophisticated restaurants—though a branch of Fiesta, which specializes in the renowned cuisine of Chiclayo, opened a couple of years ago and is by far the finest restaurant in Trujillo. One hotel restaurant that's worth a visit even if you're not staying there—especially for brunch on the weekend—is the **Las Bóvedas** restaurant at the Hotel Libertador (p. 372). Most visitors also enjoy eating out in Huanchaco, which has one chic beachside restaurant, **Club Colonial,** and a number of seafood places with ocean views.

TRUJILLO
Expensive
Fiesta ★★★ NORTHERN PERUVIAN   Although Chiclayana cuisine (from the region around Chiclayo, just north of Trujillo) is a well-kept secret that few foreigners are privy to, Peruvians know it's one of the country's most sophisticated regional cuisines. Outside of Chiclayo, this is the best place to indulge in hearty northern cooking, including roasted baby goat and the restaurant's legendary "grilled ceviche." Portions are large and filling, and the cocktails—mixed right at your table—are superb. And though Trujillo's best and most elegant restaurant is inconveniently

located outside of the centro, in the Vista Alegre residential district, it's very much worth the cab fare for a very good, and filling, lunch or dinner.

Av. Larco 854 (Vista Alegre district). www.restaurantfiestagourmet.com. ℃ **044/421-572.** Main courses S/21–S/48. AE, DC, MC, V. Tues–Sun noon–4pm and 7–11pm.

Moderate

El Mochica ★ PERUVIAN   The one restaurant that it seems everyone in Trujillo recommends is a bit of a surprise. From the outside, it looks to be a pretty sophisticated joint: It's housed within a beautiful colonial building with an impressive carved-wood balcony. Inside, though, the dining room is a little jarring, with white plastic chairs and a large TV blaring videos in the front room. A second room has a bar and a stage for live music on weekends. Despite the inauspicious surroundings, service is good—waiters are even dressed in black tie. El Mochica also produces well-prepared and good-value *criollo* cooking and classic dishes such as roasted guinea pig and *parrilladas* (mixed grilled meats), in addition to fresh fish such as *corvina* (sea bass).

Bolívar 462. ℃ **044/293-441.** Reservations recommended for live music Fri–Sat. Main courses S/14–S/36. AE, DC, MC, V. Daily 8pm–1am.

Il Valentino ITALIAN   Across from Trujillo's jampacked Cine Primavera is the city's classiest-looking restaurant. An attractive, vaguely Mediterranean-style place, it has yellow walls and arched doorways, subdued lighting, and tables on two levels with tablecloths and fake flowers. The menu is dominated by pizzas and pastas of the upscale variety, plus a few steaks. It's perfectly located for dinner before or after a movie (Cine Primavera shows films in their original language), although service here can be a bit slow, so I recommend going to the movie first and having dinner afterward.

Orbegoso 224. ℃ **044/221-328.** Reservations recommended on Fri–Sat. Main courses S/15–S/35. AE, DC, MC, V. Tues–Sun noon–11pm.

Restaurante Demarco INTERNATIONAL/ITALIAN   A pleasant-enough, cafe-style restaurant, which resembles an ice-cream parlor crammed with small tables and ceiling fans, Demarco has something for just about everyone and every time of day. It draws a consistent crowd of locals for its good breakfast selection, its sandwiches, pizza, pastas, and other Italian fare, as well as its excellent cakes and ice creams. The extensive menu also has *criollo* specialties such as *asado de res con puré y arroz* (roast beef with mashed potatoes and rice), *churrasco con tacu tacu* (grilled meats served with rice and beans), and the classic *lomo saltado* (strips of beef with onions, tomatoes, and french fries over rice). Though it boasts a daily lunch *menú* (inexpensive set-price meal), it's just as good for a midafternoon snack or late dessert.

Pizarro 725. ℃ **044/234-251.** Reservations not accepted. Main courses S/14–S/32. AE, DC, MC, V. Daily 8am–midnight.

Restaurante Romano 🌶 INTERNATIONAL/ITALIAN   Located on one of the city's main thoroughfares, this uncomplicated and cheery restaurant is a good, easygoing place for pizzas, rice dishes, salads, and omelets, as well as more substantial items such as steak, pork loin, and filet mignon with mushrooms. There are also homemade pastas, including ravioli, lasagna, and cannelloni. The weekday set-price menu is a good value; it might be a tuna and vegetable salad to start, followed by baked chicken with rice and mashed potatoes, plus juice and bread. Romano is open for breakfast and has a nice selection of desserts and coffees, including cappuccino and espresso. It's very popular with local regulars, especially at lunch. Waiters bring the food

Trujillo

through the front door, which looks odd, as if they are going out to the street to fetch your meal. (The kitchen is around the other side of the restaurant.)

Pizarro 747. ☏ **044/252-251.** Reservations not accepted. Main courses S/12–S/29. AE, DC, MC, V. Daily 8am–midnight.

Inexpensive

Museo Café Bar ★ SANDWICHES/SNACKS   I guess this doesn't qualify as a proper restaurant, since it's really a sumptuous old cafe/bar. But it's a great place to pop in for a snack, light lunch, or a cocktail. The bar looks like a turn-of-the-20th-century Buenos Aires cafe, with a stunning wood and marble-topped bar, cozy booths, and a nice little menu of sandwiches and *piqueos* (snacks), as well as a whole roster of breakfasts. It's the kind of place you may want to camp out in, or return to several times. I do both.

Jr. Independencia 713 (at Junín). ☏ **044/297-200.** Entrees S/8–S/15. AE, DC, MC, V. Daily 7pm–midnight.

HUANCHACO

Moderate

Big Ben ★ SEAFOOD   It's hard to miss this white, three-level restaurant on a curve in the beach. For fresh seafood and commanding views from the open-air, top-floor dining room, this is a favorite upscale destination of vacationing Peruvians. The ceviche and fresh fish dishes are excellent.

Av. Larco 1182 (Urb. El Boquerón). www.bigbenhuanchaco.com. ☏ **044/461-378.** Entrees S/18–S/42. AE, DC, MC, V. Lunch and dinner daily.

Club Colonial ★★★ BELGIAN/FRENCH   This romantic Belgian-owned restaurant, now in a new incarnation right on the Huanchaco beachfront, is more inviting than ever. Decorated with antiques and colorful contemporary art, it has an elegant outdoor, candelit terrace that looks out to the promenade and sea. The menu is an interesting mix of Peruvian and Franco–Belgian items, including *cordon bleu* and nicely prepared fish dishes, such as sole *en papillote* with herbs and artichoke sauce. Desserts, such as *crêpes suchards* (crepes with ice cream and chocolate), are also outstanding. If you plan on eating here a couple of days, you could add to the convenience by staying in one of the comfortable rooms upstairs (p. 373).

Av. La Rivera 541. ☏ **044/461-639.** Entrees S/20–S/34. AE, DC, MC, V. Daily 8am–10pm.

📎 Old World Cafe

Casona Deza Café, Jr. Independencia 630 (☏ **044/474-756**), is both cafe stop and tourist sight, and a great place to stop in for a coffee and snack. The 17th-century *casona*, Casa Ganoza Chopitea—better known as La Casa de los Leones (House of the Lions) because of the carved stone lions crowning the main door—is one of Trujillo's most magnificent colonial buildings. The mansion originally belonged to the first tax collector in Trujillo, and the entrance is loaded with baroque details, including river stone walkways and a *concha venera,* or welcoming shell, above the door. The front room of the house and courtyard have been converted into a cool, old-Europe-style cafe (soon to be joined by a lounge-bar and, according to the owner, a boutique hotel in the near future).

Inexpensive

El Peñón 🐟 SEAFOOD   Huanchaco, a fishing village, is rightly famous for its fresh fish. And there are few better places to plunge into the local catch than this casual and comfy place, one of the first tourist-oriented restaurants in Huanchaco. It couldn't be simpler: white plastic chairs, tables with green tablecloths, and the roar of the sea. (Indoor seating is also available, but the best spot is on the small terrace.) Located right across the street from the surf, this family-run restaurant is a favorite of locals, and the amiable owner seems to know everyone. Try one of the excellent ceviches, seafood omelets, or main courses such as *arroz con mariscos* (shellfish rice), *calamares* (squid), or *pulpo* (octopus).

Av. Víctor Larco 549 (at Raymondi). ℂ **044/461-549.** Reservations recommended in high season. Main courses S/10–S/30. DC, MC, V. Daily noon–10pm.

Shopping

Trujillo doesn't have a whole lot to interest potential shoppers (unless you need eyeglasses; Calle Bolívar is loaded with opticians). For a taste of what shopping means to most Trujillo natives, check out the sprawling **street mercado** that operates daily along Avenida Los Incas. It's one of the more unruly (and headache-inducing) markets in Peru, with vendors struggling to be heard over the incessant sounds of car horns. The market stretches across several blocks and spreads out into the street, selling an unending variety of vegetables, fish, and household items; there are even carts full of charcoal. Most visitors will be better off shopping in Huanchaco. **Artesanía del Norte,** Los Olivos 504 (ℂ **044/461-220**), has some of the coolest exclusive ceramics designs in Peru. They'll ship pieces to your home if you can't limit yourself to just one. The *mercado de artesanía* fronting the beach in Huanchaco has a number of stalls and is also a good place for jewelry, including pieces made with the sought-after blue stone lapis lazuli.

Entertainment & Nightlife

Trujillo is pretty quiet except on weekends, when it springs to life. A few nightclubs and peñas are clustered in the *centro,* but most of the hopping discos that go all night are very local and young affairs, on the outskirts of the city. Trujillo has a surprising roster of casinos and movie houses (including two multiplexes showing recently arrived English-language films). My favorite place for a quiet cocktail is **Museo Café Bar,** Jr. Independencia 713 (ℂ **044/297-200**), a beautiful old-world cafe, with a gorgeous antique bar. If you're not a drinker, it also has great fresh fruit juices and a nice menu of snacks.

More lively options include **Las Tinajas,** Pizarro 383 (ℂ **044/296-272**), with a balcony overlooking the Plaza de Armas, a popular bar with a downstairs disco. On weekends, it features live rock and pop; the cover is usually S/10. **El Estribo,** San Martín 810, is a lively and large open music hall with peña music and Mariah Carey wannabes occasionally performing. **La Canana,** San Martín 791 (ℂ **044/232-503**), is another nearby peña with a good restaurant and live music and dancing on weekends. **Luna Rota,** at América Sur 2119 in the Santa María district at the end of Huayna Cápac (ℂ **044/228-877**), is an all-in-one complex with a thumping disco for teenagers, a pub, and a casino for slightly more mature folks. The cover in the disco and pub is usually S/10.

Cine Primavera, Orbegoso 239, near the Plaza de Armas (☏ **044/241-277**), has first-run American and European films in their original languages and draws long lines of moviegoers.

Among the collection of casinos along Orbegoso and Pizarro is **Casino Solid Gold,** Orbegoso 554 (☏ **044/207-662**). Open daily 24 hours, the club features cocktail waitresses in flashy short skirts and has a low-rent Vegas feel to it.

In Huanchaco, **El Kero,** Av. La Ribera 612 (☏ **044/461-184**), is a beachfront restaurant with a stylish bar upstairs and terrace lounge on the third floor, with a bamboo ceiling and white leather sofas and chairs. The terrace is a great spot for an early-evening cocktail to see the sun set over the ocean.

Where to Stay

Visitors have the option of staying in downtown Trujillo, which despite its nice colonial feel can be rather noisy and harried—and truth be told, not exactly possessing of a stellar roster of hotels—or staying in the less expensive and more relaxed beachside town of Huanchaco, just 12km (7½ miles) away, where there are several laid-back resort hotels and some good budget *hostales*. Because the focus of many travelers' attentions is Chan Chan, which is located northwest of the city toward Huanchaco, staying beachside is a very practical option.

TRUJILLO
Expensive

Gran Hotel El Golf ★ ☺   This massive, modern resort hotel, the largest in the north of Peru, is built around a large circular swimming pool and is close to a golf country club in one of the most upscale residential districts of Trujillo (5 min. driving from the Plaza de Armas). While the hotel certainly doesn't have the character of the Hotel Libertador on the main square, which wins with its location and historic building, this beats it for quiet and space. Rooms are ample, as are bathrooms, but they fall short of being luxurious. The Golf's two-story units overlook the pool and nice gardens. For those (particularly families) looking for some relaxation and space for the kids to run around in, it's not a bad bet. Additional distractions include tennis courts, a spa, children's games, and nearby beaches.

Los Cocoteros 505, Urbanización El Golf, Trujillo. www.granhotelgolftrujillo.com. ☏ **044/484-150.** Fax 044/282-231. 120 units. $110–$135 double; $200–$275 suite. Rates include breakfast buffet. AE, V. **Amenities:** Restaurant; bar; cafe; concierge; *frontón* court; nearby golf course w/guest privileges; outdoor pool; gym; spa; 2 tennis courts. *In room:* A/C, TV, fridge, Wi-Fi (free).

Hotel Libertador Plaza Mayor Trujillo ★ ☺   The top place to stay in Trujillo, and not a bad value given its superb location right on the Plaza de Armas, in a beautiful salmon-colored colonial mansion with a courtyard patio and spectacular pool overlooked by palm trees. The place has a fair amount of colonial elegance and flavor. Rooms aren't spectacularly luxurious, but they are certainly comfortable and well outfitted, although with somewhat dated furnishings. Rooms on the interior are quieter and have views of the pool. Other rooms look out onto the busy but pretty plaza, and some have small balconies that are perfect for people-watching (but be prepared for the trade-off: street noise until late). The hotel has a handsome bar, a good restaurant, and both dry and steam saunas. On Sunday, there's a big-time brunch starting at noon, with both Peruvian and international foods.

Jr. Independencia 48, Plaza de Armas, Trujillo. www.libertador.com.pe. ☏ **044/232-741,** or 01/518-6500 for reservations. Fax 044/235-641. 78 units. $145 double; $175–$1,950 suite. Rates include breakfast buffet. AE, DC, MC, V. **Amenities:** Restaurant; bar; concierge; gym; excellent outdoor pool; sauna. *In room:* A/C, TV, fridge.

Moderate
Los Conquistadores Hotel 🗡
On a busy street just a couple of blocks from the Plaza de Armas, this clean midsize independent hotel is your best bet in this price range, even if it's hardly an exciting option. With nice-looking public rooms set way back from the street and its hubbub, it counts with a welcoming atmosphere and good service. Accommodations are quiet, large, and carpeted, with outmoded, almost retro, hotel decor; beds are decked out in flowery bedspreads. Suites are especially large, with separate sitting areas. Walk-in discounts are frequently available.

Jr. Diego de Almagro 586, Trujillo. www.losconquistadoreshotel.com. ✆ **044/481-650.** Fax 044/235-917. 50 units. S/343 double; S/473–S/563 suite. Rates include continental breakfast. AE, DC, MC, V. **Amenities:** Restaurant; bar. *In room:* A/C, TV, Wi-Fi (free).

Inexpensive
Hotel Colonial 🗡
Having upgraded over the years from cheap *hostal* to respectable midsize hotel, this is a good option if you want colonial flavor in the center of town but aren't prepared to spend more at the Libertador. Inhabiting a handsome colonial house just a block from the Plaza de Armas, its best feature may be the interior patio. Rooms that overlook the courtyard are pretty cozy, with deep brick-red walls, but a little plain. For the low price, though, they're plenty comfortable. However, by far the best rooms are those that open up to a great rooftop balcony with views of the Plaza.

Jr. Independencia 618. www.hostalcolonial.com.pe. ✆ **044/258-261.** 40 units. S/90 double. No credit cards. **Amenities:** Restaurant/bar. *In room:* TV, Wi-Fi (free).

HUANCHACO
Moderate
Club Colonial ★ 🏠
Being tucked away above a restaurant might not sound that appealing, but in this case, since the restaurant in question is the terrific, Belgian-owned restaurant of the same name, it's an asset. Like a boutique hideaway, it has just five pretty chic rooms, nicely decorated with artwork and antiques. Several rooms have fantastic sea views and a couple even have balconies overlooking the promenade. With the best restaurant in town right downstairs, this is a smart choice.

Av. La Rivera 541. ccolonial@hotmail.com. ✆ **044/461-015.** 5 units. S/90–S/230 double. Rates include breakfast. AE, MC, V. **Amenities:** Restaurant; bar. *In room:* A/C, TV.

Hostal Bracamonte 🗡 ☺
A miniresort tucked behind a high gate and a couple of blocks from the beach, this relaxed *hostal* has a bit of a motel atmosphere. Rooms and bungalows are positioned around a large pool, and the hotel has a playground and gardens for kids to run around, as well as several terraces, a barbecue grill area, and a game room. Bungalows have room for three or four guests each. Rooms have a beachy, unadorned feel, with tile floors but comfortable beds. Overall, it's a pretty good, if not outstanding, value, and it's an especially welcome retreat for those traveling with children.

Jr. Los Olivos 503, Huanchaco. www.hotelbracamonte.com.pe. ✆044/461-162. Fax 044/461-266. 28 units. S/132–S/209 double; S/283–S/322 family suite. AE, DC, MC, V. **Amenities:** Restaurant; cafeteria; bar; outdoor pool. *In room:* A/C, TV.

Hotel Caballito de Totora ★★ 🗡
Only a few years ago, this was a very simple *hostal* whose best asset was its location facing the beach. Having undergone a

dramatic transformation, into a chic and contemporary boutique-style hotel, it is now Huanchaco's top place to stay. Rooms are smart, contemporary, and spacious, and many have excellent sea views. Some suites have elevated Jacuzzi tubs in the middle of the bedroom, which I guess guests might find either really odd or very romantic (maybe it depends on whom you're with!). In the back is a great, quiet garden area and terrifically inviting pool, and there's a rooftop terrace with lounge chairs and great ocean views.

Jr. Los Olivos 503. www.hotelcaballitodetotora.com.pe. ✆ **044/462-636.** 21 units. $68–$79 double; $129–$161 suite. AE, DC, MC, V. **Amenities:** Restaurant; bar; outdoor pool. *In room:* A/C, TV, Wi-Fi (free).

Huanchaco International Hotel ★ ☺   This Belgian-owned modern beach resort hotel, positioned right on the beach but a bit out of town, on the road to Huanchaco, is a welcoming place, particularly for families. Popular with vacationing Peruvians, it has a huge pool, yellow and white bungalow accommodations dotting the property, and gardens with sea views. Breakfast is served on a terrace overlooking the beach. Rooms are large and clean; many of the little, houselike bungalows— which can house four adults—are attractively positioned up stone steps. If you're staying for a few days, ask about package deals that include area visits.

Autopista a Huanchaco, Km 13.5, Playa Azul, Huanchaco. www.huanchacointernational.com. ✆/fax **044/461-754.** 40 units. S/147–S/207 double/bungalow; S/267 two-room bungalow. Rates include breakfast. AE, DC, MC, V. **Amenities:** Restaurant; bar; cafe; large outdoor pool; solarium. *In room:* TV, Wi-Fi (free).

Inexpensive
La Casa Suiza ★ 🏄   A favorite of backpackers for more than a quarter of a century, this inn run by a Swiss–Peruvian family—still referred to as "Heidi's house" by long-time vets—is an extremely friendly place to hang out and meet up with other travelers. It's a warren of somewhat plain rooms of all shapes and sizes scattered across three floors, but the star at this *hostal* is the great rooftop terrace, where guests line-dry their laundry and write in their journals. There's a cable TV room, a book exchange, and Wi-Fi (and even a laser printer). Would-be surfers are well cared for here; the *hostal* has gear (including wet suits and boards) for rent. And the prices are tough to beat.

Los Pinos 451, Huanchaco. www.lacasasuiza.com. ✆ **044/461-285.** 16 units. S/50–S/75 double with private bathroom; S/20–S/25 per person in shared room with shared bathroom. No credit cards. **Amenities:** Breakfast room. *In room:* No phone, Wi-Fi (free).

CHICLAYO

770km (478 miles) N of Lima; 200km (124 miles) N of Trujillo; 235km (146 miles) NW of Cajamarca

Although it's Peru's fourth-largest city, with a population of just under a half-million, Chiclayo would be just another busy commercial town, generating little notice among travelers, were it not for the city's strong associations with Peru's ancient cultures. The primary draw is Chiclayo's proximity to the archaeological sites Sipán and Túcume, two of the most important related to the Moche and Lambayeque cultures, and the spectacular Museo Tumbas Reales de Sipán, which houses one of the country's most remarkable finds of the past several decades: the tomb of the Lord of Sipán.

Chiclayo is a modern and relatively new city. Although it was founded in the mid-16th century, most of its real development dates to the late 1800s and early 1900s. (The Parque Principal, or main square, didn't come into existence until 1916.) Today

HOTELS ■
Gran Hotel Chiclayo **2**
Hostería San Roque **3**
Hotel Costa del Sol Chiclayo **10**
Hotel Embajador **6**
Los Horcones de Túcume **3**

RESTAURANTS ◆
Chez Maggy **4**
Fiesta Chiclayo Gourmet **1**
La Parra **9**

ATTRACTIONS ●
Catedral **8**
Mercado Modelo **5**
Parque Principal **7**
Paseo de las Musas **11**

Chiclayo is a sprawling, bustling place; the city itself holds little interest for most visitors. Frankly, most people come here to get out of town. The capital of the Lambayeque department, Chiclayo calls itself "La Ciudad de la Amistad"—the City of Friendship. There's no real reason for such a distinction as far as I can see, but why not? It's not Peru's prettiest, biggest, or most fascinating city, but it is an agreeable, down-to-earth place.

About 12km (7½ miles) northwest of Chiclayo, Lambayeque, site of the distinguished archaeological museums, Museo Tumbas Reales de Sipán and Museo Brüning, was once the more important of the two towns. Today that is true only from the traveler's perspective. It is a slow-moving, rather dilapidated town with a smattering of interesting colonial buildings, none of which is particularly well restored or open to visitors. Except for the draw of the Lord of Sipán, the town lives in the shadow of Chiclayo's ever-growing commercial importance.

Essentials

GETTING THERE
BY PLANE   **Star Peru** and **LAN** also fly daily from Lima to Chiclayo (90 min. if direct; 2 hrs with stopover in Trujillo), with flights starting at around $95 one-way.

There are also flights north to and from Piura. Flights arrive at **Aeropuerto José Quiñones González,** Av. Bolognesi s/n (✆ **074/233-192**), 2km (1¼ miles) east of downtown (a taxi costs S/7).

BY BUS   Chiclayo is serviced by several domestic bus companies from Lima and most major points along the north coast and northern highlands. Many long-distance buses travel at night only. There is no central bus station in Chiclayo; most companies have their own terminals at offices on Avenida Bolognesi, 5 blocks south of the Parque Principal. The major carriers making the 8-hour trip from Lima are **Ormeño** (www.grupo-ormeno.com.pe; ✆ **01/472-5000**), **CIVA Transportes** (www.civa.com.pe; ✆ **01/418-1111**), **Cruz del Sur** (www.cruzdelsur. com.pe; ✆ **01/311-5050**), and **Oltursa** (www.oltursa.com; ✆ **01/708-5000**). **Transportes Línea** (www.transporteslinea.com.pe; ✆ **044/286-538** or **074/ 233-497**) and **ITTSA** (✆ **044/222-541**) make the 3-hour trip from Trujillo to Chiclayo, as do a number of colectivos and *combis*. **Transportes Línea** is also the major carrier from Cajamarca.

GETTING AROUND

Chiclayo is a busy and fairly congested city. The center of town is, as always, the Plaza de Armas—although, in Chiclayo, it more often goes by the name Parque Principal. About 4 blocks north of the main square is the other focal point in the city: the Mercado Modelo, a sprawling, spirited open street market with stalls spread across several blocks. The main axis in town is Avenida José Balta, which runs north to south and extends on either side of the Parque Principal (with designations Sur [south] and Norte [north]). Lambayeque is 12km (7½ miles) due west of Chiclayo; the airport and Sipán are to the east of Chiclayo.

Walking around the *centro* is easy enough, but you'll need public or private transportation to get to Lambayeque or the major archaeological sites.

BY TAXI   Inexpensive mototaxis buzz about downtown, as do regular taxis. You can hire the latter by the hour (S/25) or by the day (S/120–S/150) to tour archaeological sites or to visit Lambayeque. A round-trip taxi ride to Túcume from Chiclayo costs about S/70.

BY BUS   Combis and *omnibuses* are most useful for getting to Lambayeque and several archaeological sites outside Chiclayo. There are several terminals around the city serving different destinations. The fare is S/2.

ORGANIZED TOURS

Sipán Tours, 7 de Enero 772 (✆ **074/229-053**), is willing to dispense information without giving you the hard sell for package tours (but if you're interested, it's one of the most reputable agencies in town offering city and archaeological tours). Another excellent agency, which has specialized in archaeology tours and independent travel in northern Peru and offers bilingual guides in several languages, is **Indiana Tours,** Colón 556 (www.indianatoursperu.com; ✆ **074/222-991** or **01/9883-5617**).

VISITOR INFORMATION

Chiclayo has two accessible tourist information kiosks, run not by the municipal government, but by two related restaurants. One is on the Parque Principal, or the main plaza. Another is on Avenida José Balta Sur (at Manuel María Izaga), in front of the Hebrón restaurant. Both kiosks give out maps of the city and the area, and they'll give you some basic information about how to get around (and they'll put in a plug for barbecue chicken, to boot). The **iPerú** tourism information office is located on Av. Sáenz Peña 838 (✆ **074/205-703**).

FAST FACTS

Most banks are clustered around the Parque Principal, including **Banco de Crédito,** José Balta 630, and **Interbanc,** Elías Aguirre 680. Money-changers usually hang around in front of banks.

In an **emergency,** call ✆ **105.** The helpful **tourist police** are located at Sáenz Peña 830 (✆ **074/236-700**). For medical attention, go to **Hospital Las Mercedes,** González 635 (✆ **074/237-021**); **Clínica Lambayeque,** Vicente de la Vega 415 (✆ **074/237-961**); or **Clínica Santa Cecilia,** González 668 (✆ **074/237-154**). In Lambayeque, head to **Hospital Belén de Lambayeque,** Ramón Castilla 597 (✆ **074/281-190**). If you need a pharmacy, in Chiclayo, there are **InkaPharma** outlets at Av. Balta 1095, and **Botica Fasa** at Av. Balta 390 and 999.

For Internet access, try **Sic@n Internet,** Vicente de la Vega 204 (✆ **074/227-668**), or **Efenet,** Elías Aguirre 181 (no phone). There are also Internet *cabinas* clustered around the Parque Principal and on Manuel María Izaga near Avenida Balta.

Chiclayo's **post office** is at Elías Aguirre 140 (✆ **074/237-031**), about 6 blocks from the Parque Principal. The **Telefónica del Perú** office is behind the cathedral at Elías Aguirre 631 (✆ **074/232-225**).

Exploring the Area

CHICLAYO

A brief look around Chiclayo should be sufficient. Start at the **Parque Principal,** the attractive and overwhelming focal point of life in the city. People camp out on park benches and slurp on ice-cream cones, shoeshine boys scurry from one pair of scuffed-up loafers to the next, and pigeons flutter from treetops to sidewalks to roof-tops. The white, twin-domed neoclassical **Catedral** that dominates the square dates to 1869. About 10 long blocks south of the plaza, the **Paseo de las Musas** is an attractive park area rather inexplicably outfitted with neoclassical statuary of mytho-logical figures.

The fascinating **Mercado Modelo ★,** 5 blocks north of the Parque Principal, is one of Peru's most raucous open street markets. Open daily from dawn to dusk, it carries virtually everything under the sun, but it's famed for the section of small stalls crammed with the elixirs and potions of shamans and faith healers. The so-called *mercadillo de brujas* (witches' little market), near Calle Arica, is redolent with exotic spices and drying herbs, wild with visual overload: hanging shells, small altarpieces, and bottles filled with hooves and claws, snake skins, miniature desiccated crocs, claws, skunks, and fish eggs. Echoing throughout are the distinctive come-ons of vendors. This city of stalls is about as close as you'll get to India or Morocco in Peru, but it's nonetheless a primer on the country's extensive informal economy. You'll find luggage, natural Viagra substitutes, baskets, guitars, hats, calf brains, children's clothes, vats of peanut butter, stuffed ani-mals, shops of canned goods, machetes, and butcher knives, plus dozens of beauty salons and shoe and electronics repair headquarters.

LAMBAYEQUE

The **Museo Tumbas Reales de Sipán** (below) is the undisputed highlight of this small, quiet, and dusty town that was once considerably more important than its bigger neighbor but which has long since been overtaken, at least in terms of commercial importance, by it. The new museum has stolen much of the thunder of the **Museo Arqueológico Brüning** (below), where the Lord of Sipán used to reside. A few clues to Lambayeque's former status are evident in a number of colonial houses and the baroque **Iglesia de San Pedro** (daily 8am–4pm), a large and impressive yellow-and-white church built in 1700 and located on the main square. It's worth a look inside to see the impressive mural paintings on the ceiling of the central nave and the cupola. Columns are painted to look like real marble, which I suppose they do if you squint hard enough. The rest of the church is done up in pastel hues of green, blue, and yellow.

On the corner of Dos de Mayo and San Martín is Lambayeque's other building of import, **Casa de la Logia ★** (also known as **Casa Montjoy**). Erected in the 16th century, it claims the longest colonial balcony in Peru, a splendidly carved wooden wraparound structure 67m (220 ft.) long. It can be viewed only from outside.

Lambayeque really springs to life on market day, Sunday. Otherwise, there's little to detain visitors. If you're looking for a bite to eat after visiting the Brüning Museum, check out Dos de Mayo, where there are several *cevicherías* and other restaurants.

Museo Arqueológico Brüning ARCHAEOLOGY MUSEUM Until its Sipán treasures were removed and transferred to the new Tumbas Reales Museum 2 blocks away (below), this was the preeminent museum in northern Peru. Without its star attraction, the museum, founded in 1966, no longer draws crowds, but it still retains some important archaeological finds, such as Sicán masks from Batán Grande, excellent Moche ceramics, and an assortment of artifacts found at Túcume. The collection includes some 1,500 items from the Lambayeque, Moche, Chavín, Vicus, and Inca civilizations. Some pieces date back 10,000 years.

Av. Huamachuco (Block 7), Lambayeque. www.perucultural.org.pe/sipan/excava3.htm. ℭ **074/282-110.** Admission S/8 adults, S/3 students. Guides available for S/10. Daily 9am–5:30pm. Colectivos to Lambayeque depart Chiclayo from the corner of Avenida Angamos and Vicente de la Vega, and pass right in front of the Brüning Museum about a half-hour later. The main plaza is a couple of blocks from the museum (across the street).

Museo Tumbas Reales de Sipán ★★★ ARCHAEOLOGY MUSEUM This stunningly modern museum certainly stands out in northern Peru, land of dusty archaeological pyramids and colonial towns. Its daring architecture of bold angles, glass, and orange concrete makes a statement by echoing the ancient Moche pyramids of the region, but the principal attraction is within. It holds one of Peru's most spectacular exhibits, the tomb of the **Lord of Sipán,** discovered in 1987, which ranks as one of the most important archaeological discoveries in Peru of the past 50 years. Unearthed at the Huaca Rajada at Sipán, the multilevel royal funeral tomb of El Señor de Sipán, a Moche royal figure buried more than 1,700 years ago, was remarkable for its undisturbed, methodical layers and wealth of ceremonial ornaments and treasures that provided key clues to Moche culture. Buried along with the king, who was presumed to be a sort of living deity, were companions joining him on his journey to the afterlife: a Moche warrior, a priest, three female concubines, a dog, two llamas, a child, 212 food and beverage vessels, and a guard with a copper shield, gold helmet, and amputated feet—symbolic of his everlasting protection over the king's tomb.

The space dedicated to the Lord of Sipán is one of the most impressive and unforgettable sights under a roof in Peru—a revelation for visitors who've visited several of the archaeological sites in northern Peru and been disappointed to find little more than difficult-to-decipher colossal piles of clay. In this marvelously designed three-level museum, the spectacular Sipán finds articulate the grandeur and achievements of pre-Inca cultures and help us comprehend their religious beliefs, social structure, and sophistication. On display from the main funerary chamber—amazingly, never looted—are headdresses, garments, and breastplates of gold, silver, and precious stones that tell an intricate story of power and rank. Several pieces, such as the royal necklace of 20 peanuts, half gold and half silver, are stunning. Other tombs uncovered and re-created here are those of the priest, the mythical "Bird-Man" and top-ranking religious official, and the Viejo Señor de Sipán (or Old Lord of Sipán), a Moche spiritual dignitary whose death preceded that of the newer lord's and whose remains were found buried farther below.

The Tumbas Reales Museum is one of the best organized and best designed in Peru, an eminently worthy resting place for this monumental discovery. You'll need at least a couple of hours to explore it fully.

Juan Pablo Vizcardo y Guzman s/n, Lambayeque. www.museotumbasrealessipan.pe. © **074/283-977.** Admission S/10 adults, S/4 seniors, S/1.50 students. Guides available for S/15. Tues–Sun 9am–5pm. Colectivos to Lambayeque depart Chiclayo from the corner of Av. Angamos and Vicente de la Vega, and pass right in front of the Tumbas Reales Museum about a half-hour later.

FERREÑAFE

Museo Nacional Sicán ★★ ARCHAEOLOGY MUSEUM Although not quite as celebrated as the Museo Tumbas Reales, this handsome, modern, and excellent museum, inaugurated in 2001, is very much worth a visit to round out an understanding of the region's ancient civilizations. Like its better-known sibling, it too is pyramid-shaped and a study in cement and glass, but it focuses on the Sicán culture (also called Lambayeque) that succeeded the Moche and thrived until the 14th century. The Sicán (which means "Temple of the Moon"), who were the first to discover bronze in northern Peru, buried their dead in unique vertical rooms and surrounded them with large collections of valuable metals. Those graves provided looters throughout Peru with a wealth of sought-after gold objects. Sicán masks with *ojos alados,* or "winged eyes," are very prized among institutions and collectors, and some excellent examples are on view here. The museum is located in Ferreñafe, 20km (12 miles) north of Chiclayo, along the road that leads to Batán Grande (below).

Av. Batán Grande (Block 9), Carretera a Pítipo, Ferreñafe. © **074/286-469.** Admission S/10 adults, S/4 seniors, S/1.50 students. Guides available for S/15. Tues–Sun 9am–5pm. Colectivos to Ferreñafe depart Chiclayo from the Terminal de Epsel, Av. Oriente at Nicolás de Piérola.

ARCHAEOLOGICAL SITES NEAR CHICLAYO

Colectivos (buses) to the archaeological sites Batán Grande, Templo de Sipán, and Zaña leave from the Terminal de Epsel at the corner of Avenida Oriente and Nicolás de Piérola in Chiclayo, a somewhat unsavory area. It's more convenient to visit these sites by organized tour; contact **Sipán Tours** at © 074/229-053.

Batán Grande ARCHAEOLOGY SITE The Batán Grande archaeological complex is a set of ruins from the Sicán culture that comprises some 50 adobe pyramids and a network of tombs from the middle Sicán period (A.D. 900–1000). Some of the finest pre-Columbian artifacts in Peruvian museums were found by archaeologists here, including a nearly 7-pound gold Tumi (ceremonial knife) figure and an estimated 90% of all gold pieces from the Lambayeque civilization. Set amid a large nature reserve of mesquite forest (El Bosque Seco de Pómac), there's an on-site interpretation center for visitors, but the pyramids are not as established on the tourist circuit as are those at Túcume.

Located 57km (35 miles) SE of Chiclayo, and 5km (3 miles) NE of Túcume. © **074/201-470.** Admission S/10 adults, S/4 students. Guides available for S/10. Daily 7am–4pm. Colectivos leave from the Terminal de Epsel at the corner of Av. Oriente and Nicolás de Piérola in Chiclayo. It's more convenient to visit Batán Grande by organized tour; contact Sipán Tours at © **074/229-053.**

Templo de Sipán   ARCHAEOLOGY SITE   The site where the Lord of Sipán was discovered in 1987, this Moche burial ground 35km (22 miles) from Chiclayo was overlooked by archaeologists for decades. Grave robbers, who'd beaten scientists to countless other valuable sites in Peru, had just begun to loot the ones here, tipping off Peruvian archaeologist Dr. Walter Alva to the presence of the tomb in time to save it. The Sipán sarcophagus held greater riches than any other found to date in Peru and, today, is recognized as one of the most outstanding of the Americas. The twin adobe pyramids, connected by a platform, held five royal tombs. The most elaborate was that of El Señor de Sipán; deeper still was the tomb of an older spiritual leader, now referred to as El Viejo Señor. The remains of both are exhibited at the Museo Tumbas Reales in Lambayeque. Near the original site, Huaca Rajada ("Cracked Pyramid") is a small site museum with photos of the excavations and some replicas of tombs. Although it's interesting to see where the tombs were found, and the views from the top of the large pyramid across from the Sipán excavation site are excellent, Templo de Sipán is no substitute for the splendor of jewels and ornaments now housed at the Museo Tumbas Reales.

Complejo Arqueológico de Huaca Rajada, Sipán. © **074/800-048.** Admission S/5. Guides available for S/10. Daily 8am–6pm. Colectivos leave from the Terminal de Epsel at the corner of Av. Oriente and Nicolás de Piérola in Chiclayo, and take about 45 min.

Túcume ★★   ARCHAEOLOGY SITE   Located 33km (20 miles) north of Chiclayo, this magnificent, massive complex of 26 adobe pyramids (not for nothing do locals call it "El Valle de las Pirámides") was constructed by the Sicán civilization around A.D. 1000 and developed over a period of nearly 500 years. The site was settled and enlarged by the Chimú culture in the 14th century and, finally, occupied by the Incas. Túcume was the most important elite urban center of the region and is considered the last great capital of the Lambayeque culture.

You can wander freely around the maze of courtyards and pyramids, and even scale several of them, which are still being excavated and together present an enigmatic desert ensemble. Walking around sites such as these is almost more evocative of what a contemporary archaeologist's life is like than of the lives of those ancient cultures that lived there. The Túcume complex's stunning size, more than a mile long in each direction (a total of 32 hectares/79 acres), is more impressive than any individual structure. The pyramid toward the back of the complex, known as **Huaca Larga,** is reputed to be the largest adobe brick structure in South America. It measures (even after erosion) 700m (2,297 ft.) long, 280m (919 ft.) wide, and 30m (98 ft.) high. A massive platform with several patios and courtyards connected by ramps and corridors, the huaca has walls covered in red, white, and black murals. Archaeologists have uncovered evidence of the three major stages of construction in Huaca Larga, from the original Lambayeque to Chimú, whose "Temple of the Mythical Bird" dates to 1375, and finally an Inca structure built on top of the Chimú building at the end of the 15th century. Inside the Inca room was a burial tomb, where 22 bodies were discovered, including a local ruler and warrior, interred along with two other males and 19 females.

THE SICÁN civilization

The Sicán culture (often designated the Lambayeque civilization, referring to the region where it grew to prominence) developed on the north coast of Peru in the 7th century following the collapse of the Moche civilization. A sophisticated culture whose economic mainstay was agriculture, the Sicán specialized in irrigation engineering. The society reached its apogee between A.D. 900 and 1100, and established religious and administrative headquarters at Batán Grande in the Pómac forest, near the Leche River. The site there is known as the "Temple of the Moon" in the ancient local dialect, Muchik. Around 1100, the Sicán abandoned Batán Grande, which they appear to have set fire to, and moved their capital across the valley to El Purgatorio, a hill in the midst of what are now the Túcume ruins. There they built a splendid urban center, the most important in the region, but the civilization was eventually conquered by the Chimú in 1375.

An interestingly conceived site museum exhibits photographs of the excavations and discusses the involvement of a Norwegian explorer, the late Dr. Thor Heyerdahl, who sought to connect ancient Peruvian culture to that of Polynesia. (He sailed a balsawood craft called the *Kon Tiki* from Peru to the Polynesian islands.) Heyerdahl was the director of the 1989 to 1994 Túcume Project, which carried out excavations at the site. Also on-site are a handicrafts-and-ceramics workshop and a snack shop. You'll often find women cooking out in the open on the grounds.

Complejo Arqueológico, Caserío La Raya, Campo. www.museodesitiotucume.com. © 074/422-027, or 074/800-052 site museum. Admission S/12 adults, S/4 students. Guides available for S/10. Daily 8am–4:30pm. Colectivos leave from Av. Angamos, btw. Naturaleza and Pardo in Chiclayo (a 45-min. ride), although they leave travelers a good mile or so from the site. Look for a taxi or mototaxi, or walk along the road. A good idea is to visit the Museo Arqueológico Brüning in the morning and head out to Túcume in the afternoon. Buses leave for Túcume from very near the museum in Lambayeque; the ticket office can indicate exactly where. Tell the driver you'll be getting off at Túcume.

Zaña HISTORIC SITE   Ruins of an entirely different sort, this 16th-century ghost town was once an important and wealthy colonial outpost, loaded with churches and monasteries. On the fast track toward becoming the Peruvian capital, it underwent a turbulent period of slave rebellion and pirate attacks. Wealthy families fled to Lambayeque city, and Zaña was soon afterward wiped out by a massive flood in 1720. The overflowing Río Zaña caused such structural damage that the population abandoned the city. Today it's a curious sight of ornate columns, church arches, and the remains of the once-grand Gothic Convento de San Agustín (as well as three other convents). A small, inhabited village (also called Zaña) is nearby.

46km (29 miles) SE of Chiclayo. Admission by organized tour only. Colectivos leave from the Terminal de Epsel on the corner of Av. Oriente and Nicolás de Piérola in Chiclayo. Numerous tour agencies also include Zaña in organized outings, probably the most efficient way of visiting the town; try Sipán Tours at © 074/229-053.

NEARBY BEACHES

Pimentel is a beach resort 14km (8¾ miles) west of Chiclayo, with a nice enough beach that's very popular in summer and a small fishing community that still employs the *caballitos de mar* (totora-reed boats) seen in Huanchaco, near Trujillo. Just 6km

(3¾ miles) south of Pimentel is **Santa Rosa,** a more attractive beach and fishing village with totora-reed and gaily painted wooden fishing boats. It has a handful of good seafood restaurants. Both beaches are low-key and a good antidote to touring archaeological sites.

Buses and colectivos run from Vicente Vega and Angamos in Chiclayo to Pimentel. In summer, they continue along a "circuito de playas" to Santa Rosa, Puerto Etén, and Monsefú, none of which is spectacular.

Where to Eat

The hearty cuisine of the Lambayeque region is recognized by Peruvians as one of the country's outstanding regional cuisines. Yet for visitors, it's not a city that's loaded with fine-dining establishments. By far the best place to sample Chiclayo's signature dishes is Fiesta (see below).

CHICLAYO
Expensive

Chez Maggy ☺ PIZZA/ITALIAN   Long-time locations in Cusco and Aguas Calientes have become well known to travelers to Peru for the kind of good, low-risk meal one is often looking for on foreign territory. The pizzas that come out of the wood-fired oven are always dependable, and frequently delicious. Other items of note include a nice roster of salads and calzone. This new and larger locale retains much of the coziness of Maggy's previous chez.

José Balta 413. ✆ **074/209-253.** Reservations not accepted. Main courses S/14–S/30. AE, DC, MC, V. Daily 10am–11pm.

Fiesta Chiclayo Gourmet ★★★ NORTHERN PERUVIAN   This terrific restaurant, where all the clients seem to be regulars and even friends, specializes in a very underrated cuisine. Chiclayo is definitely the best place to indulge in its distinctive, hearty fare (although there are Fiesta branches in Lima and Trujillo). Behind an unassuming facade with a mural representation of the region's rich ancient cultures and archaeology is one of the north's best restaurants. Have an excellent cocktail in the cozy Bar Sipán before moving on to the straightforward dining room, with parquet wood floors, straw window treatments, and simply framed photographs on the walls. Start with the pork or corn *humitas* (*tamales*) or grouper *causa* (with mashed potatoes), a dish that in Chiclayo is typically eaten only on Sundays (but here is served daily), followed perhaps by succulent barbecued goat ribs. Service is impeccable and friendly. Just be sure to bring your appetite, as this is rich and filling food.

Salaverry 1820. www.restaurantfiestagourmet.com. ✆ **074/201-970.** Reservations recommended. Main courses S/24–S/48. AE, DC, MC, V. Daily noon–11pm.

La Parra ★ ☺ GRILL   At the entrance of this restaurant is a busy, open grill—an indication of the meat-dominated menu inside. This comfortable, relaxed restaurant is nice, if a tad nondescript, with a vaulted wood ceiling, wood paneling, stucco walls, and hardwood floors—and odd incongruous touches such as a framed portrait of Jesus and a deer head. Everyone chows down on grilled meats, served with fries and a salad, not just because it's the house specialty, but also because it's the only thing La Parra serves. *Lomo fino* (sirloin), shish kabob, sausage, and chicken are among the excellent choices from the grill. Shareable menu options like the *parrillada* for four make this place popular with families. Next door is a good *chifa* (Peruvian-Chinese restaurant) by the same owner.

Manuel María Izaga 752. 𝄞 **074/227-471.** Reservations recommended Fri–Sat. Main courses S/11–S/32. AE, DC, MC, V. Daily noon–11pm.

Where to Stay

CHICLAYO

Chiclayo isn't brimming with good hotel options, and especially not at the upper end. Anyone looking for luxury in Chiclayo will be disappointed. With the exception of the city's largest hotel, Gran Hotel Chiclayo, currently being managed by Casa Andina, and a new boutique-style hotel (Hotel Embajador), most are merely functional. The most interesting options are actually outside the city, especially for archaeology buffs who intend to see several of the sites beyond Chiclayo.

Expensive

Gran Hotel Chiclayo ★ Several blocks removed from the heart of downtown, Chiclayo's largest hotel is a modern, massive concrete block with mainstream corporate style. It is currently being managed by the very professional Peruvian group of hotels, Casa Andina, in transition to becoming one of its "Select" hotels, and when the makeover is finished, it should have some of the style this iconic building always deserved, with the stamp of clean, contemporary rooms and local touches that Casa Andina stands for. This hotel has all the amenities and services that business travelers demand, as well as a nice round pool for leisure visitors.

Av. Federico Villarreal 115, Chiclayo. www.casa-andina.com. 𝄞 **866/220-4434** toll-free in the U.S., 08/082-343-805 in the U.K., or 01/213-9739. Fax 01/445-4775. 129 units. $179–$209 double; $229 suite. Rates include breakfast buffet. AE, DC, MC, V. **Amenities:** Restaurant; bar; concierge; outdoor pool. *In room:* A/C, TV, fridge, Wi-Fi (free).

Moderate

Hotel Costa del Sol Chiclayo A miniature high-rise building on Chiclayo's most important and busiest street, this midsize hotel, part of a Peruvuan chain, offers a good mix of amenities and easygoing charm. The remodeled, newly sedate rooms are spacious and comfortable, and bathrooms are also of a good size. Unexpected features are the cute rooftop pool and the Jacuzzi with a dry sauna. All in all, it's a good value with enough personality to set it apart from the more expensive and more standard Gran Hotel Chiclayo.

Av. José Balta 399, Chiclayo. www.costadelsolperu.com. 𝄞 **074/227-272.** Fax 074/209-342. 82 units. $76 double; $120 suite. Rates include continental breakfast buffet. AE, DC, MC, V. **Amenities:** Restaurant; bar; concierge; Jacuzzi; outdoor pool; sauna. *In room:* A/C, TV, fridge.

Inexpensive

Hotel Embajador ★ 🛍🔑 One of the city's best (and best-value) options is this smart little family-run hotel, close to the main square in Chiclayo. Behind a gleaming mirrored exterior are brightly colored, cheerful, and spotless rooms. Bedding and bathrooms are both exceptional for a budget hotel, and service is extremely friendly and attentive (although you can't depend on a lot of English being spoken). Bonuses at this price include free Wi-Fi and a nice little coffee shop and cafeteria.

Calle 7 de Enero 1368. hotelembajadorchiclayo.com. 𝄞 **074/204-729.** 20 units. S/100–S/120 double; S/150 suite. Rates include pickup from bus station. MC, V. **Amenities:** Cafeteria. *In room:* A/C, TV, Wi-Fi (free).

BEYOND CHICLAYO

Hostería San Roque ★ One of the best options for anyone primarily interested in the great museums in and near Lambayeque is this boutique hotel with plenty of

ruins OF KUÉLAP ★★

Everyone—at least everyone on his or her way to Peru—has heard of Machu Picchu. Very few have heard of Kuélap, though. Yet it's one of the archaeological wonders of Peru, a formerly lost city that stands as the true adventurer's alternative to Machu Picchu, which today is easily accessible and exceedingly popular. Tucked in highland cloud forest on top of an Andean mountain ridge at an altitude of 3,000m (9,840 ft.), Kuélap is a stupendous and titanic set of ruins that in fact predates the Incas—it's more than 800 years old. Though ripe for discovery by a wider swath of visitors to Peru, Kuélap is still primarily a destination for independent travelers with plenty of time and a keen sense of adventure.

Located northeast of Cajamarca, near the small town of Chachapoyas (itself something of a poor man's Cusco, given the assortment of ruins littered about it), and discovered in the mid-19th century, the site is said to have employed more stone during its 200-year construction than even the Great Pyramids of Egypt. A fortress complex of nearly 400 buildings, most of them round, and surrounded by a 30m-high (98-ft.) defensive wall, Kuélap was home to 2,000 people from A.D. 1100 to 1300. Very little is known about its builders and inhabitants, though. They were most likely the Chachapoyans or Sachupoyans, both groups that were later brought into the Inca fold that unified the highlands.

Unlike other ruins in Peru, most of what exists at Kuélap is original, although some reconstruction has been initiated.

The ruins are open daily from 8:30am to 5pm; admission is S/12. Getting to Kuélap remains time-consuming and difficult, involving long buses to Chachapoyas, capital of the Amazonas department, or Tingo, plus a 3-hour combi ride to the site. (From Cajamarca to Chachapoyas, it's a scenic but wearying 16- to 20-hour bus ride, or a less exciting 10-hour journey from Chiclayo.) Organized visits might not suit modern-day explorers, but they are the most convenient way to get to what remains a remote outpost. Group trips from Cajamarca begin at $250 per person. Agencies handling Kuélap trips include **Cumbe Mayo Tours** and **Inca Baths Tours** (p. 386), both in Cajamarca. But much better is **Chachapoyas Tours** (Jr. Grau 534, Chachapoyas; www.chachapoyastours. com; ☏ **041/478-078** or **866/396-9582** in the U.S.), an American–Peruvian-owned agency that specializes in tours of Kuélap and the region departing from Chachapoyas. Smaller tour groups in Chachapoyas run day trips to Kuélap for as little as $10 per person. There is a small Institute of National Culture albergue (lodge) at the site, which sleeps eight in dorm rooms, and Chachapoyas Tours runs two comfortable lodges in Choctamel and Levanto (www.kuelap.org; ☏ **866/396-9582** in the U.S or **041/478-838**).

personality and colonial flavor. In a handsomely renovated, 19th-century manor house, it features colorful and simply furnished rooms that are built around three interior patios and a large, inviting outdoor pool. Rates are a tad elevated given how simple the rooms are.

Dos de Mayo 437, Lambayeque. www.hosteriasanroque.com. ☏ **074/282-860.** 12 units. S/190 double. Rate includes continental breakfast. MC, V. **Amenities:** Cafeteria; bar; outdoor pool. *In room:* A/C, TV, Wi-Fi (free).

Los Horcones de Túcume ★★ 📖 The best place to stay in the Chiclayo/ Lambayeque area—especially for anyone interested in visiting the region's archaeological sites—is this stylish rural lodge in the shadow of the Túcume pyramids, about 30km (19 miles) outside of town. This relaxing inn, constructed of adobe and local *algarrobo* beams and designed by the owner, a Lima architect, sits in an open area of corn fields, and it has peaceful private and common terraces swathed in trees and flowers. Rooms are airy and colorfully decorated, and there's a nice little, affordable restaurant on-site. The inn offers horseback riding in the valley, making it the perfect place to enjoy the sunny valley of the pyramids, but little else in terms of service. It's a place for guests who enjoy peace and quiet and being on their own.

Antigua Panamericana Norte Lambayeque–Túcume. loshorconesdetucume.com. © **01/242-1866** or 951/831-705 for reservations. Fax 01/445-5186. 12 units. $40 double. Rates include breakfast. MC, V. **Amenities:** Restaurant. *In room:* A/C, no phone.

CAJAMARCA ★★

855km (531 miles) NE of Lima; 298km (185 miles) NE of Trujillo; 235km (146 miles) SE of Chiclayo

Delightful and historic Cajamarca, the jewel of Peru's northern highlands, deserves to be more widely appreciated. Those who know the city often call it "the Cusco of the north," and comparisons to that tourist magnet farther south are not illegitimate. This graceful and traditional mountain town possesses some of the same attributes as Cusco, but it is refreshingly free of many of the hassles associated with the gringo capital of South America. Although it's surrounded by the Andes at an altitude of nearly 2,700m (8,900 ft.) above sea level, Cajamarca is a down-to-earth and unassuming place that doesn't get caught up in its colonial beauty and Andean grace. Townspeople, nearly all of them decked out in marvelously distinctive *sombreros de paja* (straw hats), merely go about their business.

Cajamarca is the largest city in a fertile agricultural region (though see the box on p. 391 for info on the growing mining industry here) that is virtually unsurpassed in Peru for its luxurious, verdant countryside. (The climate is pleasantly springlike, with clear blue skies most of the year.) It's also known for its splendid dairy products, so any visit here should involve stops at some of the many ice-cream and cheese shops. And Cajamarca is ringed by archaeological sites and handsome hacienda estates, which make getting out to the country a must.

Essentials

GETTING THERE

BY PLANE There are daily 2-hour flights from Lima on LAN (www.lan.com; © 01/213-8200) and **LC Busre** (www.lcbusre.com.pe; © 01/619-1313). Flights start at $115 one-way.

The **Armando Revoredo Aeropuerto de Cajamarca** (© 076/362-523) is just 3km (1¾ miles) east of the Plaza de Armas. To downtown Cajamarca, a taxi costs S/5.

BY BUS **Cruz del Sur** (www.cruzdelsur.com.pe; © 01/311-5050) and **Expreso Cia** (© 01/428-5218) make the 12-hour trip from Lima to Cajamarca. **Transportes Línea** (www.transporteslinea.com.pe; © 076/222-221 or 044/297-000) travels from Lima, Trujillo (6 hr.), and Chiclayo (5–6 hr.). The bus terminals are located on Avenida Atahualpa and Avenida Zavala, about 3km (1¾ miles) from the center of town.

GETTING AROUND

The major sights of interest in Cajamarca are all around the Plaza de Armas or within easy walking distance of it. Except for the Inca Baths, you're unlikely to require

CAXAMARCA: A brief HISTORY

The Cajamarca Valley was the epicenter of a pre-Inca culture called Caxamarca (as it was spelled pre-conquest) which reached its apex between A.D. 500 and 1000. Cajamarca was part of a small northern highlands kingdom called Cuismango, which was influenced by two great cultures, Chavín and Huari. The Incas, led by Cápac Yupanqui, conquered Caxamarca around 1465, annexing the territory and solidifying the empire's hold on the northern Andes. Cajamarca soon became an important administrative, political, and religious center and a major link in the transcontinental Andes highway; the Incas constructed great palaces and temples in the city.

Francisco Pizarro and a small band of troops, numbering around 160, reached the Cajamarca Valley in November 1532. November 16 shook the very

foundations of the Inca Empire and changed Spanish-American and Peruvian history. Pizarro's men ambushed Atahualpa, the last Inca emperor, and held him prisoner. Inca troops, numbering more than 50,000 but already in the midst of civil war, offered no resistance. Atahualpa proposed a huge ransom to win his release, but the Spaniards killed him anyway, 7 months after a staged trial condemning him for attempting to arrange his rescue. The end of the Inca Empire was near, as the Spanish moved south toward Cusco. Cajamarca became a colonial city in 1802. Besides a few stone foundations, only Atahualpa's Cuarto de Rescate (Ransom Room) remains of the grand Inca masonry that once distinguished Cajamarca. But the city's post-Inca colonial roots are very much evident in Spanish-style architecture throughout Cajamarca.

transportation unless you're staying at one of the country hotels on the outskirts of town, which are serviced by taxi and, to a lesser extent, colectivo. The most convenient way to get to the major sights beyond Cajamarca are inexpensive organized tours (the only way to get to most of them on your own would be by contracting a taxi that would wait for you).

BY TAXI   Taxis are easy to come by in the center of Cajamarca. They circulate around the Plaza de Armas and the streets leading off it. Most in-town fares are about S/3. To call a cab, try **Taxi Seguro** (✆ **076/365-103**) or **Taxis Unidos** (✆ **076/368-888**).

ORGANIZED TOURS

Reliable tour agencies include **Inca Baths Tours,** Jr. Amalia Puga 653 (✆ **076/362-938**); **Cumbe Mayo Tours,** Jr. Amalia Puga 635 (✆ **076/822-938**); and **Cajamarca Travel,** Jr. Dos de Mayo 570 (✆ **076/365-651**). These companies offer city tours and inexpensive, pooled half- and full-day tours to sights in the countryside around Cajamarca (including Cumbe Mayo, Otuzco, Colpa, and Inca Baths). Most standard tours cost S/30 to S/35. Several agencies also offer long-distance tours to the famed but remote Kuélap ruins for around $600 per person. All agencies advertise English-speaking guides, but fluency is a relative term. The best bets are Inca Baths Tours and Cumbe Mayo Tours.

VISITOR INFORMATION

There's a branch of the **Regional Tourism Office** within the massive Conjunto Monumental de Belén complex at Jr. Belén 600 (✆ **076/362-997**). It's open Monday through Friday from 8:30am to 1pm and 2:30 to 6:30pm. The office has a handful

Cajamarca

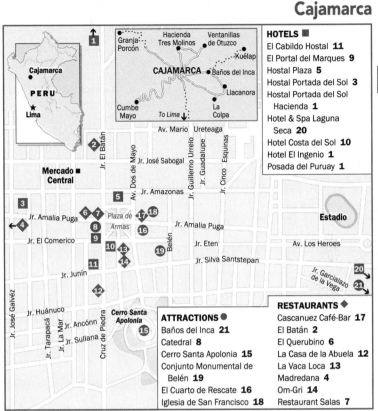

HOTELS ■
El Cabildo Hostal **11**
El Portal del Marques **9**
Hostal Plaza **5**
Hostal Portada del Sol **3**
Hostal Portada del Sol
 Hacienda **1**
Hotel & Spa Laguna
 Seca **20**
Hotel Costa del Sol **10**
Hotel El Ingenio **1**
Posada del Puruay **1**

ATTRACTIONS ●
Baños del Inca **21**
Catedral **8**
Cerro Santa Apolonia **15**
Conjunto Monumental de
 Belén **19**
El Cuarto de Rescate **16**
Iglesia de San Francisco **18**

RESTAURANTS ◆
Cascanuez Café-Bar **17**
El Batán **2**
El Querubino **6**
La Casa de la Abuela **12**
La Vaca Loca **13**
Madredana **4**
Om-Gri **14**
Restaurant Salas **7**

of photocopied materials and some brochures for sale, including a self-published tourist information guide. There's another small **Oficina de Información Turística,** associated with the university, at Batán 289 (☏ 076/361-546), which is very helpful and gives out free city maps. It's open Monday through Friday from 8:30am to 1pm. The city's tourism website is www.cajamarcaperu.com/turismo.

FAST FACTS

Two banks are **Interbank,** Dos de Mayo on the Plaza de Armas (☏ **076/362-4600**), and **Banco de Crédito,** Jr. del Comercio 679 (☏ **076/362-742**). Neither of these banks exchanges traveler's checks. There are generally money-changers on the Plaza de Armas and Jirón del Batán; there are also several small *casas de cambio* in the same area.

   In an **emergency,** call ☏ **105.** The **police** are located at Amalia Puga 807 (☏ **076/362-832**). For medical attention, go to **Hospital Regional,** Mario Urteaga 500 (☏ **076/362-156**); **Clínica San Francisco,** Avenida Grau (☏ **076/362-050**); or **Clínica Limatambo,** Puno s/n (☏ **076/364-241**).

   There are **InkaPharma** outlets at Amazonas 580 and Av. Sor Manuela Gil 151, and **Botica Fasa** at Jr. del Batán 137.

Carnaval in Cajamarca

Cajamarca is a very traditional Andean highland city, but it lets loose once a year during Carnaval. Its pre-Lenten festivities are said to be the wildest in Peru. Full of music and dance, it also takes on aspects of a high-school locker room. Paint, water, and even bodily fluids (!) are flung around with abandon, so wear a raincoat. If you want to experience (or subject yourself to?) Cajamarca's Carnaval, plan ahead. It's very popular with Peruvians, and hotels sell out. Another festive time in Cajamarca, formerly Peru's grandest Inca celebration, is Corpus Christi (May or June), which includes lots of processions, music, bullfights, and horse shows.

For Internet access, try **Efenet,** Jirón Dos de Mayo, **CyberNet,** Comercio 924, or **Atajo,** Jr. del Comercio 716 (© **076/362-245**). Atajo is open until 1am and offers cheap international Internet calls.

Cajamarca's **Serpost** (post office) is at Amalia Puga 778 (© **076/364-065**). There's a **DHL/Western Union** office at Dos de Mayo 323 (© **076/364-674**), within the Cajamarca Tours office. The **Telefónica del Perú** office is at Dos de Mayo 460 on the Plaza de Armas (© **076/364-008**).

Exploring the Area
CAJAMARCA

Colonial Cajamarca has several sights of interest, although the town's principal appeal might lie in its relaxed and proudly traditional air, as yet undisturbed by a tourist onslaught. Many of Cajamarca's premier tourist attractions are just outside the city in the beautiful pastoral countryside, within easy reach for day trips. Most are best visited by convenient organized tour (see "Getting Around," above).

Plaza de Armas ★★ PUBLIC SQUARE The heart of city life, Cajamarca's peaceful Plaza de Armas is one of the loveliest in Peru. In the days of the Incas, it was also the focal point of town, but it was a triangular courtyard rather than a square, per se. The plaza was taken in dramatic fashion by Pizarro's small band of invading troops in 1532, and the Inca Emperor Atahualpa was killed there after a mock trial. The fountain at the center of the square dates back more than 300 years, and the plaza is marked by handsome topiaries and low trees. Two grand churches front the square, and it can be difficult to determine which one is the cathedral. On one side is the **Catedral** (cathedral), built in the 17th and 18th centuries. Its baroque facade is ornately carved from volcanic stone. The gloomy interior features a bold, amazingly carved main altar and a pulpit of carved wood and gold leaf. If the cathedral looks a bit squat and unfinished, it's because its belfry was never completed, a drastic measure to avoid payment of a Spanish tax on finished ecclesiastical buildings. As seen in colonial churches in Cusco, the cathedral is built upon original Inca stonework.

Get Out of Town on Tuesday

Most of Cajamarca's top sights are closed on Tuesday. If you're in town that day, it would be wise to schedule a visit to the Inca Baths or another out-of-town excursion, such as Cumbe Mayo or Otuzco.

The grander of the two churches, though, is directly across the plaza. The **Iglesia de San Francisco ★**, which once formed part of the San Francisco Convent, is entirely wrought from volcanic rock. Built in the first half of the 18th century, the parish church did not add the two bell towers until 1951. Covering every inch of the facade is terrific stone sculpting. Inside is a **Museo de Arte Religioso Colonial,** Jr. Dos de Mayo 435 (✆ **076/322-994**); it's open Monday through Saturday from 3 to 6pm and admission is S/3. The collection of colonial art includes interesting icons and paintings. Beneath the museum are the church's catacombs, good for an eerie visit. Next door to the church is the small and beautiful Santuario de la Virgen de Dolores, or the chapel of **La Dolorosa,** named for the patron saint of Cajamarca. The 18th-century facade is one of the greatest examples of stone carving in the city.

Conjunto Monumental de Belén ★★★ HISTORIC LANDMARK On block 6 of Belén is the city's most important and historic architectural complex, almost entirely constructed of volcanic stone. Dating to the 18th century, it includes a church and colonial women's and men's hospitals, now housing ancient medical and archaeological exhibits. The entire complex is run by the National Institute of Culture. On a small and pretty square, the **Iglesia Belén** might be the most extraordinary work of colonial architecture in Cajamarca. The church, which replaced a primitive adobe-and-wood church on the spot, was begun in 1699 and completed a half-century later. Its decorative baroque stone facade is one of the finest in Peru. The interior is replete with delightful and large, carved polychromatic figures of angels and warriors; the carved pulpit is particularly impressive. The richly decorative cupola, supported by eight almost cartoon-like cherubs, was painted by highland natives.

The **Hospital de Hombres (Men's Hospital)** is located on a lovely courtyard marked by a fountain. The austere hospital, run by Franciscans, began receiving patients in 1630. So that they could focus on prayer, the patients' beds faced the altar and the Virgen de la Piedad. To the right of the entrance is a gallery of vibrant paintings, several of them portraits of highlands *campesinos,* by Andrés Zevallos. Across the street is the **Hospital de Mujeres (Women's Hospital);** on the facade, note the woman with child above the portal and, on either side of it, female figures with four breasts, symbols of the valley's super-potent fertility. Today the building houses perhaps the most interesting component of the Belén complex, a **Museo de Arqueología y Etnografía,** well laid out and exhibiting textiles and ceramics dating from as far back as 1500 b.c., replicas of Moche vessels, and local artisanship, dress (including Carnaval costumes), and silver *milagros* (prayer fetishes).

Jr. Belén s/n (at Junín). ✆ **076/322-601.** Admission is by *boleto* (S/7.50 adults; S/4 students), a combination ticket that also admits visitors to El Cuarto de Rescate (below). Mon and Wed–Fri 9am–1pm and 3–6pm; Sat–Sun 9am–1pm.

El Cuarto de Rescate ★ Across the street from La Dolorosa Chapel is the most famous building in Cajamarca. When Atahualpa was taken prisoner by Pizarro and his band of men in 1532, the Inca emperor was held in a cell, which he promised to fill with gold and silver many times over if the Spaniards would spare his life. The so-called "Ransom Room" is a small, rectangular stone room, set in the back of a colonial courtyard, once part of Atahualpa's palace. It is made of unadorned Inca masonry—the last intact example of Inca architecture in the city—and is barren except for a red line drawn across one wall, supposedly the very line Atahualpa drew to demonstrate to the Spanish how high his men would fill the cell with treasures. No one knows for sure whether this was simply Atahualpa's prison cell or if it was

CAJAMARCA'S colonial MANSIONS & CHURCHES

In the center of Cajamarca are several notable large houses that feature carved stone porticoes, slanted roofs, long wooden balconies, and the type of pretty garden courtyards favored by Spanish colonialists. Visitors with an interest in 17th- and 18th-century colonial and republican architecture should check out the following *casonas* and churches, in addition to those discussed elsewhere in greater detail.

- **Casa Santiesteban,** Junín 1123.
- **Casa Toribio Casanova,** Jr. José Gálvez 938.
- The **house** at Cruz de Piedra 613. Now the property of the municipal government, the house has another excellent carved portico. Also on Cruz de Piedra is a

stone cross, which supposedly marks the spot where Simón Bolívar, the Great Libertador, swore to avenge the death of Atahualpa.

- **La Recoleta,** a church about 6 blocks south of the Plaza de Armas, at the end of Amalia Puga.
- **Palacio del Obispo,** next to the cathedral.
- **Palacio de los Condes de Uceda** (now the Banco de Crédito), Apurímac 717. A splendid yellowish-orange, well-restored noble house with a carved stone portico.
- **San Pedro,** a church at the corner of Gálvez and Junín.

indeed a ransom room. What we do know is that the Inca chief was later executed by Pizarro's men, presumably on a stone right here, even before the Incas had surrendered all of the promised riches. The Cuarto de Rescate represents a crucial moment in Peruvian history, a clash in cultures with ramifications for the entire continent, but it might take some imagination to conjure the drama of the moment. The large painting at the entrance near the ticket booth, of Atahualpa being burned at the stake by the Spanish, is not entirely accurate; after accepting baptism, Atahualpa was merely strangled to death.

Amalia Puga 750 (½-block from Plaza de Armas). © **076/322-601.** Admission by *boleto* (S/7.50 adults; S/4 students), which admits visitors to the component parts of the Conjunto Monumental de Belén (above). Mon and Wed–Fri 9am–1pm and 3–6pm; Sat–Sun 9am–1pm.

OUTSKIRTS OF CAJAMARCA

Baños del Inca ☺   Just beyond Cajamarca lies the Inca Baths complex of gardens and pools with Cajamarca's famed thermal waters. In use since the time of the Incas (supposedly, Atahualpa had to be roused from his beloved bath when Pizarro and his troops entered the city), the baths are a wonderful respite of clean air and hot waters, ideal for relaxing after days of travel in the highlands. Set in a serene valley, at an elevation of nearly 2,650m (8,700 ft.) with wonderful mountain views, the park's thermal waters are said to be medicinal and effective for treating bronchial and rheumatic conditions. The waters, which reach temperatures of 165°F (74°C, but you can control the temperature with spigots in private pools), come from two different sources, Los Perolitos and El Tragadero. The open pools with rising steam make clear the scalding nature of the waters. The modern complex is extremely popular with locals and visitors alike. You can either opt for a private, indoor bath, in which you wait for a room to be vacated and cleaned and the deep pool filled with fresh sulfurous spring waters, or the sauna or outdoor pool. Take a bathing suit and towel with you. Bath products are for sale at the entrance.

6km (3¾ miles) from Cajamarca. ℂ **076/821-563.** Admission to the tourist complex (individual bathing cabins) S/5; to the communal baths S/3. Outdoor pool has assigned entrance times. Daily 5am–7pm. Colectivos labeled BAÑOS DEL INCA leave from Calle Amazonas and take about 15 min.; virtually everyone gets off at the same stop, across the street from the complex. A taxi costs about S/8.

Cerro Santa Apolonia   A steep but lovely climb up the stairs at the southeast end of the Dos de Mayo leads to Santa Apolonia hill. On the way to the top is a small white chapel, the Virgen de Fátima, built in 1854. Often locked, the interior can still be glimpsed through the doorway. Up more paths, through terraced gardens where there are also a handful of caged animals, is a mirador with splendid panoramic views of Cajamarca laid out at your feet. Rocks at the top, carved with petroglyphs, are believed to date to the Chavín civilization (1000–500 B.C.). Nearby, to the right of the white cross (if you're looking down at Cajamarca), sits a stone altar that has earned the popular name "the Inca's Throne." At this altar, carved like a chair, the Inca chief reportedly sat and gazed down on his city and troops. There's also a small tunnel that, according to legend, went all the way from Cajamarca to Cusco.

Reached by stairs at the end of Dos de Mayo. Park admission S/1. Daily 8am–6pm.

BEYOND CAJAMARCA

The countryside (*campiña*) around Cajamarca is extraordinary: a luxuriant expanse of rolling hills, eucalyptus trees, and meadows. If you're not staying at one of the country-style hacienda hotels outside of Cajamarca, a visit to the country is highly recommended to see this gorgeous, fertile region.

Among the standard organized campiña visits are excursions to several rural haciendas, including the worthwhile **Granja Porcón** (ℂ **076/365-631**), a huge cooperative farm and agrotourism experiment supported by the Peruvian government and the European Union. It's about 30km (19 miles) north of Cajamarca. The community runs entirely on hydroelectric power, and hilltop forests have been planted at an altitude of 3,700m (12,139 ft.) to provide paper and wood products without harming the area's natural forests. There is a small *albergue* (lodging) and a restaurant on the premises. In **Lower Porcón,** the Festival of the Crosses (on Palm Sunday at the beginning of Easter week) is a famous expression of local folklore. Huge wood and

Mining Gold—& Digging Up Controversy

Cajamarca's rural roots and agriculture-based economy have been given a jolt with the discovery in the late 1980s of one of the world's largest and most productive gold mines, Yanacocha. The mine, about 48km (30 miles) north of Cajamarca, has quickly become the region's largest employer and brought an influx of foreign executives and their families, as well as controversy and conflict. Newmont Mining Corporation, with headquarters in Denver, Colorado, gained majority control of the Peruvian mine in 2000 through reported dealings with some of the Fujimori government's more unsavory officials. Since then, the firm has been engulfed in charges of contaminating local water supplies and protests over its proposed expansion to a nearby mountain, Cerro Quilish.

cane crosses, adorned with images of Jesus and saints, flowers, and palm fronds, are carried in devout processions.

Other area cooperatives have not been well maintained and are less worthy of a visit. They include **La Colpa** (no phone), a cattle ranch and manor house in a beautiful setting; **Llacanora** (no phone), a small mountain village with ancient cave paintings and hikes to a pretty waterfall; and **Tres Molinos** (no phone), an agricultural center and gardens, where dairy products are sold.

The best way to visit one or more of the archaeological sites beyond Cajamarca is to sign on with one of the tour operators in town. Several of the sites are not accessible by public transportation; going with a guide in a small private colectivo is economical and convenient. Most agencies charge S/20 for standard day trips. Many combine visits (for example, to the Inca Baths, Colpa, and Llacanora; or to Otuzco and Tres Molinos).

Cumbe Mayo ★★ ☺ A stunning natural spot of huge and fascinating rock formations set amid rolling green hills at an elevation of 3,400m (11,150 ft.), Cumbe Mayo has been called a stone forest. Equally remarkable, if not more so, is the evidence of human intervention here, first discovered in 1937: caves etched with petroglyphs and a **pre-Inca aqueduct** that is a marvel of hydraulic engineering. The remarkable open canal, carved out of volcanic stone in perfect, polished lines, served to collect and redirect water from various sources on its way to the Pacific Ocean. At points, the canal narrows and introduces right angles to slow the flow of water and lessen the effects of erosion. In all, the aqueduct stretches more than 9km (5½ miles). Created, incredibly, around 1000 B.C., it is perhaps the oldest known manmade structure in South America.

Elsewhere in the park is a cliff referred to as the **sanctuary,** which looks like a human head from the outside; a grotto inside is adorned with enigmatic petroglyphs and is said to have been a place of ritual. Stairs carved in stone lead to sacrificial altars (llamas, not humans) and platforms, signs of the ceremonial importance of the zone. As guides lead groups through the "stone forest," they point out figures that can be seen in the stones, such as a group of monks as well as phalluses, breasts, a dog climbing a hill, a tortoise, a pirate's head, and mushrooms—the latter and perhaps former shapes all fun for kids to pick out. Some are clear, amusing likenesses; others are like trying to identify someone else's images in cloud formations.

20km (12 miles) SW of Cajamarca. Daily 8am–5pm. To get there, take an organized tour (S/30). It is also possible to take a colectivo that leaves from behind Cerro de Santo Apolonia; it leaves passengers a short walking distance from the entrance to Cumbe Mayo.

Kunturwasi Three to four hours away from Cajamarca, in the province of San Pablo, these ceremonial stone ruins date to 1100 B.C. Besides a series of courtyards, plazas, and platforms, many marked with large petroglyphs, burial sites were discovered here. The gold treasures from the tombs are now exhibited in a small museum in the nearby town of San Pablo.

110km (68 miles) from Cajamarca. Tours to Kunturwasi cost about S/50 per person and last a full day. Daily 8am–5pm.

Ventanillas de Otuzco ★ A large necropolis whose gravesites are small square window niches carved out of a hillside, Otuzco was created by the Caxamarca culture, probably around 500 B.C. The niches were funereal tombs for elites. Many held just one body; others housed several corpses. Another 20km (12 miles) beyond Otuzco are the even more impressive (and better preserved) burial niches of

Ventanillas de Comboyo. More extensive than Otuzco, they are holed out of a sheer volcanic cliff.

7km (4½ miles) NW of Cajamarca. Admission S/3. Daily 8am–5pm. To get there, take an organized tour (S/35), which combines visits with stops at a hacienda. You can also hop on a colectivo along Batán, a few blocks from the Plaza de Armas.

Where to Eat

Cajamarca has a laid-back selection of good-value restaurants, all within easy walking distance of the Plaza de Armas. The city is famous for its desserts and ice cream— and bakeries and cafes stuffed with cakes line the streets. In addition to the restaurants below, **Cascanuez Café-Bar,** Amalia Puga 554 (✆ **076/366-089**) is good for either dessert or a quick meal. For ice cream (as well as light snacks), the two best spots are **La Cremería,** Comercio 964 and Amazonas 741 (✆ **076/362-235**), and **Heladería Holanda,** Amalia Puga 657 (✆ **076/340-113**).

MODERATE

El Batán PERUVIAN   A fairly sophisticated restaurant, with perhaps the most elevated reputation in town, El Batán uses the tag line "buffet de arte." In fact, the place is part art gallery upstairs. In a handsome 18th-century colonial house entered through the courtyard, it offers a series of relatively expensive fixed-price menus, but there's also a bargain hunter's *menú ejecutivo.* You can mix and match appetizers with main courses. You might have a stuffed avocado to start, followed by chicken in mushroom sauce. The menu is meat-heavy, as seems typical in Cajamarca. Meat eaters will appreciate dishes such as stuffed tenderloin with peppercorns or filet mignon in whiskey sauce. On weekends, there's peña music. You can dine in either the covered courtyard or the relaxed, art-filled interior.

Jr. del Batán 369. ✆ **076/366-025.** Reservations recommended. Main courses S/14–S/30. AE, DC, MC, V. Daily noon–midnight.

El Querubino PERUVIAN   An elegant place a half-block off the Plaza de Armas, El Querubino has been a Cajamarca trendsetter for a few years. With mustard-yellow walls, decorative tiles, and a live music duo playing *altiplano* tunes, it's bright, cheery, friendly, and intimate, and just a few paces from the cathedral. The restaurant qualifies as upscale for low-key Cajamarca, but it's quite popular with locals. House specialties include *mollejas al ajillo* (sweetbreads in garlic) and mustard chicken. Other options among meat dishes are also nice: beef stroganoff, filet mignon, and pork chops. There's a daily list of bargain specials such as lemon chicken written on a board at the entrance. Finally, a Cajamarca restaurant with fish on the menu! (Okay, it's only sole, but it's a start.) The wine list is a bit more extensive than at most local restaurants.

Jr. Amalia Puga 589. ✆ **076/340-900.** Reservations recommended. Main courses S/15–S/32. AE, DC, MC, V. Daily 9am–midnight.

La Casa de la Abuela DESSERT/INTERNATIONAL   This cute, country-kitchen-style place has wood beams, a preponderance of baskets with dried flowers, and little tables with blue-and-white-checked tablecloths and blue candles. In short, it's very unusual for Peru—one of the few small restaurants with a conscious and consistent design or look. The first thing to draw your attention will be the wide selection of desserts, including ice cream, cheesecakes, and several other colorful and delectable cakes, in the case at the entrance. But "Grandma's House" also serves a variety of items for breakfast, lunch, and dinner, such as sandwiches and hamburgers, pizzas, pastas, and a gourmet selection of meats. Plenty of people pop in just for dessert and coffee.

Jr. Cruz de Piedra 671. © **076/362-027.** Reservations recommended Fri–Sat. Main courses S/10–S/27. MC. Daily 8am–midnight.

Magredana ★★ ITALIAN/INTERNATIONAL   Locals seem to concur that this deceptively simple-looking spot is the best new restaurant in Cajamarca. It serves delectable versions of home-cooked Italian favorites, such as lasagna, spaghetti a la Bolognesi, and prawns in garlic and herb sauce with tagliatelle, as well as a handful of Peruvian dishes, including ceviche (kind of a rarity in landlocked Cajamarca) and even some Asian dishes—even though the chef is Irish. Everything is made to order and with fresh local ingredients, and desserts are exceptional. There are also very good-value *menús ejecutivos* at lunctime. Unusually for a restaurant, Thursday nights are "Ladies Night," with 20% discounts offered to women.

Jr. Sara MacDougall, 140–144. © **076/506-786.** Reservations recommended. Main courses S/22–S/34. MC, V. Mon–Sat 1–11pm; Sun 6:30–11pm.

Om-Gri ★ 📖 ITALIAN   Eating at this tiny place is pretty much like eating in a friend's kitchen. The amiable Tito Carrera Montes prepares only pastas, topped by a dozen or so sauces—which he spends 8 hours preparing—from a tiny stove tucked behind a bar and a ton of well-used pans. There are just five tables set up in a haphazardly decorated room with salon doors that advertise "Pastas! Lo Mejor!" (Pastas! The Best!) Tito fetches sauces from the freezer and proceeds to whip up dishes from what appears to be little more than a hot plate. Choose the pasta—fettuccine, spaghetti, lasagna—and the sauce, and watch Tito go to work. Wondering about the restaurant's odd name? It's a play on words and nod to Tito's years spent in French-speaking Europe and his full head of gray hair: a made-up, multilingual name meaning *hombre gris*—gray man.

Jr. San Martín 360. © **076/367-619.** Reservations not accepted. Main courses S/12–S/28. No credit cards. Mon–Sat 1–11pm; Sun 6:30–11pm.

INEXPENSIVE

La Vaca Loca 🍴 ☺ ITALIAN/PIZZA   If you're in need of a pizza fix, this is your place. "The Crazy Cow" is cute, and fun, and though it's inexpensive, it pays more attention to decor than any other restaurant in Cajamarca. It's brightly colored and stuffed with cows in all sorts of incarnations, from paintings, to figurines, to cartoons. Seats and booths are black-and-white faux cowhide, the walls are deep red and orange, and the ceilings are lined with rustic beams. It serves 19 different types of pizzas, from standard options to more adventurous combinations, as well as fresh salads, pastas, and lasagnas. Few people seem to order anything but the pizza, however, which is available in both personal and family size.

Jr. San Martín 320. © **076/828-230.** Reservations not accepted. Main courses S/8–S/18. No credit cards. Daily noon–10pm.

Restaurant Salas 🍴 PERUVIAN   From the lines at the entrance, you might expect this traditional restaurant to be good—it's packed with locals daily (even though some veterans carp that it's not as good as it used to be). Occupying the same spot on the Plaza de Armas since 1947, Salas is a huge eating hall with high ceilings and white-coated waiters scurrying about. Perhaps it's so popular because of the monstrous portions. There's a daily typed list of *platos especiales* (specials), *platos del* *día* (daily specials), and a set menu for about $2. The *humitas* (sweet corn *tamales*) are excellent. Most of the menu focuses on typical Peruvian dishes and things such as *churrasco* and *asado* (roasted and barbecued meats).

Amalia Puga 637. © **076/362-867.** Reservations not accepted. Main courses S/8–S/26. V. Daily 9am–10pm.

Shopping

Relaxed and untouristy Cajamarca isn't brimming with chic shops and merchants hawking *artesanía* to visitors. Yet its colorful central market is an enjoyable place to absorb the flavor of an authentic Andean town market and pick up a regional specialty: Cajamarca has excellent handicrafts, including ceramics and Cajarmarquiña mirrors with decorative glass frames. The **Mercado Central ★★** on Amazonas (between Batán and Apurímac), which sprawls among several streets daily 7am to 5pm, is a great place to score one of those amazing, finely woven tall straw hats that virtually all natives wear. Those *sombreros de paja* are famous throughout Peru, but some are so finely made that you might be shocked at the prices. I'm told that some campesinos spend up to $400 for their hat, which is their most prideful article of clothing. As you'll see, the hats beg all sorts of individual style; forming and wearing the hat according to one's taste is part of the fashion. They're perfect for gardening—though finding ones to fit large, non-Andean heads can be trying. Ask the seller to show you how to roll up the hat for easy packing. Other items of interest include saddlebags *(alforjas)*, decorative glass-and-silkscreen mirrors, and dairy products.

Cajamarca's modern shopping mall east of downtown, **El Quinde Shopping Plaza,** Av. Hoyos Rubio (at Jr. Sor Manuela Gil) (© **076/344-099**) has everything from shoe and clothing stores, a supermarket and a book shop, to ice cream shops and a movie theater. On a much more intimate scale, **Colors & Creations,** Belén 628 (© **076/343-875**) is an artisans' cooperative, selling good-quality crafts, including ceramics, jewelry, and textiles.

Cajamarca is famous for its dairy products and ice cream. **Heladería Holanda ★★★** Amalia Puga 657 (© **076/340-113**) is a Dutch-owned ice cream shop and local favorite right on the Plaza de Armas. Nearly its equal is **La Cremería ★★** Comercio 964 (second branch at Amazonas 741) (© **076/362-235**), a small ice cream shop with great fruit flavors.

Entertainment & Nightlife

For the most part—or at least outside of carnaval—Cajamarca is a pretty quiet town. Most bars and nightclubs downtown are clustered along José Galvez between Amalia Puga and Amazonas; among those popular with locals are **Orni, Bambolé,** and **Indio Bar.**

Considerably more interesting is **Peña Usha Usha ★★**, at Amalia Puga 142 (© **076/997-4514**), about 4 blocks from the Plaza de Armas, a funky little peña bar with kerosene lamps, a smattering of tables and benches, a small altar, and graffiti everywhere. It's atmospheric and intimate, and Jamie Valera Bazán has been singing politically motivated songs here, either alone or with a couple of friends, for years. The bar, which serves simple mixed drinks only, opens at 9pm and doesn't close its doors sometimes until 6am. Very popular with local young folks is **Gruta 100 ★★**, Av. Silva Sant Estéban 100 (next to stairs to Santa Apolonia hill, on Jr. Junín), a lively two-level bar near the Plazuela de Belén. It has good, unique cocktails (such as "El Frailón") and live music and dance (including peña on weekends). The most upscale disco in town is **Los Frailones,** Av. Perú 701 (℅ **076/364-113;** at Cruz de la Piedra, at the base of Santa Apolonia hill). The cover charge is generally S/15 for men and S/10 for women.

Where to Stay

Like the mini-Cusco it appears to be, Cajamarca has a very nice selection of affordable small hotels, many of them in converted colonial mansions, all quite close to the main square. The finest and most relaxing hotel, however—one of the nicest in Peru—is in the countryside on the outskirts of town.

EXPENSIVE

Hotel & Spa Laguna Seca ☺ A country-style hotel renowned for its proximity to the Baños del Inca, this spa resort hotel is where to stay if you're looking for things you don't typically find in Peru: aerobics, massages, and in-room thermal baths. It also features thermal pools (two for adults, one for children), Turkish baths, and a host of outdoor activities (including horseback riding). Rooms are large and pretty nicely equipped, but they're not nearly as luxurious as those at the Hotel Posada del Puruay (below), and are quite a bit more expensive even than the better-located Costa del Sol (below).

Av. Manco Cápac 1098, Baños del Inca, Cajamarca. www.lagunaseca.com.pe. ℅ **076/584-300.** Fax 044/584-311. 40 units. $146–$164 double; $175–$206 suite. Rates include breakfast buffet and thermal and Turkish baths. AE, DC, MC, V. **Amenities:** Restaurant; cafeteria; bar; concierge; Jacuzzi; 3 thermal-water pools; aerobics, massage room; spa. *In room:* A/C, TV, fridge.

Hotel Costa del Sol ★★ ⚑ An excellent hotel in a handsome colonial building next to the cathedral on the Plaza de Armas—hands-down the most enviable location in town—and part of a small Peruvian chain with several properties in northern Peru, this is the best, and really only, upscale place to stay if you want to be right in town. For visiting business travelers, including those who come to oversee operations in the mines outside town, it's the top choice. It has very comfortable, good-size, and nicely decorated rooms, as well as the most complete menu of amenities and services in Cajamarca, including a pool, spa, casino, and a very nice glass-enclosed restaurant. Given all it offers, it's a good value.

Jr. Cruz de Piedra 707, Cajamarca. www.costadelsolperu.com. ℅ **076/362-472.** 71 units. $95 double; $135–$200 suite. Rates include continental breakfast. V. **Amenities:** Restaurant; bar; exercise room; outdoor pool; sauna; spa. *In room:* A/C, TV, fridge, Wi-Fi (free).

MODERATE

Hotel El Ingenio ★ 🛍 This engaging hotel, a bit inconveniently located on the outskirts of town and about a 15-minute walk to the Plaza de Armas, nonetheless has real flavor and feels like a small village within the city. The colonial hacienda style-buildings are built around pretty courtyards and gardens; rooms are quite large, if a tad dark.

Vía de Evitamiento 1611–1709. www.elingenio.com. ℅ **076/368-733.** 15 units. $60–$75 double. Rates include breakfast buffet. MC, V. **Amenities:** Restaurant; bar. *In room:* A/C, TV, fridge, Wi-Fi (free).

Posada del Puruay ★★★ ⚑ ☺ An extraordinary country hotel housed in an impeccably restored, elegant 1830 salmon-colored hacienda about 20 minutes from downtown Cajamarca, this is one of the most refined and relaxing hotels in Peru. And it's also a flat-out bargain. Set amid more than 202,350 hectares (500,000 acres) of land, with eucalyptus forest, beautifully landscaped gardens, and views of the verdant, mountainous countryside, the hotel feels light-years removed from any city, yet it's only 7km (4½ miles) away. The lovely house, built around a pretty courtyard, has rooms with names such as La Mansión and La Prisión. The first couldn't be truer: Rooms are gigantic and extremely well equipped, with large, luxurious bathrooms. The second room name, though, is misleading: If this is prison, I want to be thrown in the slammer. The restaurant and public rooms are decorated with well-chosen antiques. Outdoors, horses beckon, as does the trail up the hill to a small structure with stupendous panoramic views. The charming and loquacious owner, Nora, and her husband and daughter live on the premises and couldn't be more gracious. The terrific restaurant and serene grounds make this a perfect spot to kick back for several days in the northern highlands.

Ctra. Porcón-Hualgayoc, Km 4.5, Cajamarca. www.posadapuruay.com.pe. ℂ 076/367-028. 14 units. $90 double; $100–$130 suite. Rates include breakfast buffet and airport pickup. AE, DC, MC, V. **Amenities:** Restaurant; bar; concierge; Wi-Fi. *In room:* A/C, TV, fridge.

INEXPENSIVE

El Cabildo Hostal ☺   One block from the Plaza de Armas, this charming small hotel has the swankest colonial courtyard in town: It's sunny, with a central fountain, arches, and balconies on all four sides—a perfect spot to relax. Rooms have a cozy vibe, though they're a bit run down; the beds have carved-wood headboards. Furnishings aren't plush, and the brown-carpet-and-orange-bedspread look could probably do with an update, but given the friendly services and pedigree of the building, if you're not looking for perfection it's not a bad deal. Four of the rooms are loft-style, which is perfect for families.

Jr. Junín 1062, Cajamarca. cabildoh@latinmail.com. ℂ/fax **076/367-025.** 22 units. S/105 double. Rates include taxes and continental breakfast. DC, MC, V. **Amenities:** Restaurant; bar; small gym; spa. *In room:* TV, fridge.

El Portal del Marques ✦   An attractively furnished colonial *casona* located a block and a half from the main square, this comfortable and friendly hotel is a pretty decent midrange option. The carpeted rooms, placed around the brightly painted central courtyard and interior garden, are a good size and feature very clean bathrooms. Public rooms are inviting and warm, with wood-beam ceilings, stone portals, original paintings, local ceramics, and cozy armchairs and sofas. The good-looking bar and renovated restaurant on the premises isn't a bad spot for dinner in town, and it features a happy hour every afternoon from 6 to 8pm.

Jr. del Comercio 644, Cajamarca. www.portaldelmarques.com. ℂ/fax **076/368-464,** or 01/9880-5440 for reservations. 20 units. $30 double; $75 family suite. Rates include continental breakfast. V. **Amenities:** Restaurant; bar. *In room:* TV/DVD, Wi-Fi (free).

Hostal Plaza   This large and rambling old colonial wooden house, a favorite of backpackers, is loaded with character, even if the rooms are dorm-like and completely unadorned. For the adventurous traveler, it's not uncomfortable, though, and it certainly has a great location—right on the Plaza de Armas—for the cheap price. The hotel is spread across two interconnected wings that are built around a pair of courtyards. Hot water comes and goes. The rickety wooden floors and varied levels have their own kind of charm for travelers looking for a bargain but who need little in the way of creature comforts.

Plaza de Armas, Cajamarca. ✆ **076/362-058.** 22 units. S/60 double with private bathroom; S/35 double with shared bathroom. No credit cards. *In room:* No phone.

Hostal Portada del Sol ★ 🌊 A cozy family inn occupying a beautiful colonial house about 5 minutes from the Plaza de Armas, this is one of the best affordable hotels in town. Rooms have wood-beam ceilings, older-style furnishings, and small bathrooms. Some rooms have upstairs loft areas. The small, covered central courtyard has a marble fountain and is set up with tables beneath the wooden balcony on three sides. El Sol Grill, a charming restaurant with a wood-burning stove, is on the premises, and service is personal and accommodating. The inn owns the handsome hacienda hostel of the same name in the countryside outside Cajamarca (below).

Jr. Pisagua 731, Cajamarca. www.hostalportadadelsol.com. ✆/fax **076/365-395** or 01/225-4306 for reservations. 20 units. S/115 double. AE, DC, MC, V. **Amenities:** Restaurant; bar. *In room:* TV.

Hostal Portada del Sol Hacienda ★ 🌊 ☺ A great-value country hacienda, only 6km (3¾ miles) from the Plaza de Armas in Cajamarca, this pretty house with beautiful gardens and comfortable, nicely decorated but simple rooms is an excellent option for a relaxed stay. Owned by the same people who run a similarly named inn in town (above), this cozy Spanish-style hacienda doesn't have the luxury of Puruay, but it's a good middle-of-the-road choice. Almost unheard of at this price, the hotel has tennis courts, football fields, games for children, horseback riding, and trails for walking.

Camino al Cumbe Mayo Km 6, Cajamarca. www.hostalportadadelsol.com. ✆ **076/365-395** or 01/225-4306 for reservations. 15 units. S/115 double. AE, DC, MC, V. **Amenities:** Restaurant; bar; tennis courts. *In room:* TV.

MANCORA & THE NORTHERN BEACHES ★★

1,172km (727 miles) N of Lima; 599km (371 miles) N of Trujillo; 396km (246 miles) N of Chiclayo

Despite its nearly 2,500 km (1,500 miles) of coastline, Peru has never been widely celebrated for its beaches. The northern desert coast, inaccessible and poorly developed for decades, possesses the finest long, sandy beaches in the country. They have been prized mostly by pioneering locals, travelers on their way down the coast by land from Ecuador, and especially surfers drawn to the Pacific Ocean's extraordinary swells and breaks. Only recently has the region really begun to take off with a more diverse crowd; moneyed Limeños are building chic beachside homes, and small hotel groups and entrepreneurs are descending on the region to put a stake in the market before it's too late. Accommodations had previously been largely limited to thatched-roof bungalows that had the benefit of being, like the area, authentic, cool, and cheap, but they weren't ideal for a wider population of national and international travelers. That has quickly changed in just the past few years, and the area is experiencing a boom.

Piura and Tumbes are the two northern departments that share the finest of Peru's beaches. **Máncora** (in Piura), 120km (75 miles) south of the Ecuadoran border and 1,165km (722 miles) north of Lima, is the epicenter of the surfer and beach craze, popular with young travelers and hippies, even if to some newcomers it may still seem rough around the edges and not your classic beach resort. Away from the beach, Máncora is essentially a main drag, lined end-to-end with open-air casual bars and

Máncora & the Northern Beaches

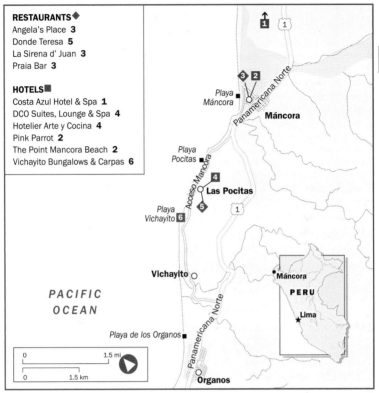

RESTAURANTS◆
Angela's Place **3**
Donde Teresa **5**
La Sirena d' Juan **3**
Praia Bar **3**

HOTELS■
Costa Azul Hotel & Spa **1**
DCO Suites, Lounge & Spa **4**
Hotelier Arte y Cocina **4**
Pink Parrot **2**
The Point Mancora Beach **2**
Vichayito Bungalows & Carpas **6**

restaurants, with the craggy desert to one side and the open sea the other. The long, sandy beaches in Máncora and extending about 25km (15 miles) north and south are excellent—even if they can't quite compete with the sparkling white sands of Brazil or the Caribbean. But the water is warm, the sun shines virtually all year (as opposed to farther south, in and around Lima, where it seems rarely to peek through the gray haze), the seafood and ceviche are supreme, and the waves are, well, killer. The area gets a bit crazed during the Peruvian summer and during other holiday periods, but the rest of the year is charmingly low-key.

Essentials

GETTING THERE

BY AIR LAN (www.lan.com; ✆ 01/213-8200) flies daily to Piura or Tumbes from Lima. The drive to Máncora from Piura is longer (2½ hours), but flights arrive throughout the day, giving you daylight hours to make it to your destination. Flights to Tumbes, about an hour north of Máncora, depart daily only at 7:15pm, arriving at 9pm. Flights start at about $115 one-way. From the airports, private taxis to Máncora run to about $80 from Piura and $40 from Tumbes; buses make the trip for $6. **Máncora Travel** (www.mancoratravel.com.pe; ✆ **073/258-571**) arranges shared

Surf's Up, Fish are Jumping

Two Pacific Ocean currents, the cold Humboldt from the south and Ecuatorial from the north, meet just south of Cabo Blanco, creating vastly different water temperatures (the north being considerably warmer year-round). For surfing fanatics, this section of the Pacific is renowned for its excellent swells, long waves, perfect barrels, superb point breaks, and awesome lefts. The tourist zone stretches from Órganos in the south to Punta Sal and Zorritos (part of Tumbes) north of Máncora. The top beaches for swimming and sunning are Vichayito, Pocitas, Punta Sal, and Zorritos. To the south, Cabo Blanco, a fisherman's village (off which the largest black marlin on record was caught) is said by many locals to have been the inspiration for Ernest Hemingway's *The Old Man and the Sea* (Hemingway did spend time in the area in 1956 deep-sea fishing and carousing, but I'm sure a good many Cubans would argue the point). Top spots for surfing, some of which are for advanced boarders only, include Cabo Blanco, Punta Ballenas, Órganos, Panic Point, Lobitos, and El Golf.

and private minivans from Piura and Tumbes ($50–$150). Piura is 185km (115 miles) south of Máncora; Tumbes is 102km (63 miles) north.

BY BUS   The bus from Lima is about 16 hours (overnight is recommended); fares range from about S/60 to S/100. **Cruz del Sur** (www.cruzdelsur.com.pe; ℂ 01/311-5050), **Oltursa** (www.oltursa.com.pe; ℂ 01/708-5000) and **CIVA Transportes** (www.civa.com.pe; ℂ 01/418-1111) are the best options.

CAR RENTAL   Most car rental agencies are located in Piura. **Rent-a-Car San José** (ℂ 073/303-240) has good cars ($40–$50 per day) in Piura and meets travelers at the airport.

GETTING AROUND

Unless you have a rental car, getting around the region is almost entirely by mototaxis (S/2), which are as ubiquitous as the tiny crabs on the beaches. For a couple of *soles,* you can go about anywhere the dirt roads will take you.

VISITOR INFORMATION

A very good site with information on the entire area, including distances, details on the best surf spots, breaks and equipment and lessons, and fishing and diving, is **www.vivamancora.com**.

FAST FACTS

There are ATMs on Av. Piura in Máncora. In an **emergency,** call ℂ **105.** The **national police** are located on Av. Piura s/n. There's a Botica San José **pharmacy** at Av. Piura 525.

Exploring the Area

The best beaches for swimming, strolling, and relaxing are just south and north of Máncora. To the south, **Vichayito ★★** is blessed with wide sands and calm waters, a beautiful stretch that's one of the top beaches along the north coast for swimming, sunning, and kitesurfing. It's perfect for a relaxing vacation, but still close enough to the restaurants and bars of Máncora for easy access. There are two entrances to Vichayito: either at Km 1150 of the Panamericana Norte highway, just past

Los Órganos, or along the dusty, unpaved road back from Las Pocitas. **Orígenes, Panamericana Norte Km. 1155** (www.spaorigenes.com; ☎ **073/694-460**), is an excellent spa right on the beach, with a full menu of services and open-air massages, as well as a hot tub and gorgeous pool overlooking the ocean. (The very nice little spa at **DCO Hotel** (see below) is also open to nonguests.) **Las Pocitas ★★**, an upscale zone just south of (and virtually contiguous to) Máncora, is pretty similar to Vichayito, albeit with a bit more in the way of development. It also has a narrower, palm tree-lined beach and is home to a growing number of chic hotels and weekend and summer houses. The waters are calm and excellent for swimming.

North of Máncora, **Punta Sal ★** is perhaps the best pure beach in the region, a beautiful, long stretch of white sand and calm waters. It's a relaxed resort with a couple of large hotels frequented mostly by Peruvian (largely Limeña) families. **Zorritos ★** marks the northern end of the region's stretch of beaches. A mellow, often empty beach destination south of Tumbes, the capital of the department just 30 km (19 miles) from the Ecuadoran border, it has a pretty beach with a tropical feel, good waves, and a smattering of rustic, thatched-roof *cabaña* accommodations. Zorritos is quickly morphing into a young people's alternative to Máncora (an alternative to the alternative, as it were). Access to it is faster and simpler from Tumbes than Piura.

Although the beaches are the logical focus of a visit to Máncora, some seeking diversion head to the thermal and mineral-rich mud baths of **Poza del Barro,** 30 km (19 miles) northeast of Máncora (admission S/3; open daily 8am–6pm). The rustic baths (where the temperature reaches about 40°C/ 104°F) are said to have healing properties and are surrounded by *algarrobo* trees. Some people choose to hike, bike, or ride horses to get here, but the easiest way is to hop on a mototaxi (since there's no real address, but most people and mototaxi drivers know where they are).

Where to Eat in Máncora

In addition to the restaurants listed below, for a chic date night, the restaurant at **DCO Suites, Lounge & Spa** (see below) is the most upscale in the area. Things in town on the main drag in Máncora are generally a bit scrappier and cheaper than the hotel restaurants on the beaches.

Angela's Place ★ A little vegetarian spot, owned by an Austrian woman who passed through Máncora and never left, this is the perfect place for budget travelers who've grown "tired of chicken and rice," as Angela herself puts it. She offers instead great hummus, salads, whole-grain bread, veggie main-course options (quinoa with sautéed vegetables and vegetarian burritos), carnivore-friendly goulash, apple strudel, and a great meal deal. For S/15, you get a starter, main course, and a beverage.

Av. Piura 396, Máncora. www.praiabar.com. pe. ☎ **073/258-603.** Main courses S/18–S/34. No credit cards. Daily noon–10pm.

Donde Teresa ★★ PERUVIAN/ SEAFOOD Named for the mother of one of the owners of this boutique hotel (Teresa Ocampo, a celebrity chef in Peru who had the country's first TV

High Season Crush

Limeños and other Peruvians descend on the beaches in the north during high season. The Peruvian summer (January through March) is when the region is busiest, but specific dates you might want to avoid are Christmas, New Year's, and Easter week, as well as Peru's Fiestas Patrias (National Celebration), the week of July 28. Off-season is from mid-March to late December.

cooking show), the open-air restaurant "Donde Teresa" serves excellent local seafood and specialties like *chancho al barril* (wood-fired, slow-cooked pork).

Las Pocitas s/n (1 km/½ mile south of Máncora). www.hotelier.pe. ☎ **073/258-702.** Main courses S/24–S/60. MC, V. Daily noon–10pm.

La Sirena d'Juan ★ A cute little sliver of a place, with hip music and terrace seating, this is an excellent spot for an intimate night out in Máncora. It serves terrific seafood, including tuna sashimi and seared tuna with ginger and passion-fruit salsa (tuna is big in Máncora), and creative Novo Andino dishes. The passion-fruit cheese-cake is also a winner.

Av. Piura 316, Máncora. ☎**073/258-173.** Main courses S/30–S/35. MC, V. Mon–Sat 7pm–midnight.

Praia Bar ★★ The most stylish bar in Máncora, this cool all-white cocktail lounge behind a sliding metal shop door is not only a great place for a drink, such as a tremendous maracuyá sour, it is a place to stick around for dinner. Portions are obscenely large, and the fresh tuna sashimi my wife and I had there recently—caught just hours earlier, and enough for a family of four, all for $6—was so amazing we took photographs of it and emailed them to jealous friends. Less exalted, but just as likely to hit the spot, are the generous *lomo saltado* and yummy, messy cheeseburger. There are killer nightly drink specials; Monday night's three-for-one pisco drinks (superb sours of several stripes) take the prize.

Av. Piura 336, Máncora. www.praiabar.com.pe. ☎ **073/258-571.** Main courses S/24–S/38. MC, V. Mon–Sat 7pm–midnight.

Shopping

Check out the artisans' market on the main drag, Avenida Piura, or the chic little shop **Sirena** (Av. Piura 336), featuring very stylish bikinis, sundresses, *pareos* (beach wraps), sandals, and other beach apparel and accessories designed by an Argentine woman and made in Máncora. **Soledad Surf Shop** (Av. Piura 316; ☎ **01/9983-0425**) is the go-to place for hard-core *surfistas* and beachy types who just want to look the part.

Board rentals and surfing lessons are easily arranged in Máncora (ask at **Soledad Surf Shop;** see above). For those interested in a full-scale surfing tour of northern Peru, contact **Octopus Surf Tours** (www.wavehunters.com/peru-surfing/nperu.asp; ☎ **19/9400-5518**). Kitesurfing is also taking off—pardon the pun—and several outfits, including **Máncora Kite Club** (www.mancorakiteclub.com) and **Máncora Kite Surf** (www.mancorakitesurf.com), arrange lessons, gear, and trips.

Entertainment & Nightlife

Máncora has a rowdy bar scene in season, with lots of young Peruvians, international travelers, and surfing fans hitting the rustic bars along the main drag, Avenida Piura, and the clubs in hotels and *hostales* on the beach. **Poto Blanco (The White Ass Bar)** ★, Playa del Amor, s/n (☎ **073/706-320**) is a two-story bar at the party hostel The Point. A place to meet other young travelers and down innumerable tropical-themed drinks, it has great open-air views of the beach. On summer weekends, the hostel generally sponsors raucous parties. **Praia Bar** ★★, Av. Piura 336 (☎ **073/258-571**) is a sleek bar and restaurant behind a pull-down metal garage door, more upscale than the rowdier bars along the main drag. It has terrific nightly drink specials. Also on the main drag, **Iguana's Place,** Av. Piura 245 (☎ **01/9853-5099**) is a lively, rustic bar (restaurant and outdoors travel agency by day, rowdy by night) for beers and cocktails.

Where to Stay & Eat

While budget travelers and *surfistas* congregate in occasionally raucous Máncora, my favorite beaches for lodging are the peaceful enclaves of Las Pocitas and Vichayito. The beaches are wide and calm, and lining them is a mix of second homes and small inns and boutique hotels. The following boutique-style hotels along the beach are superb lodging options; the first two count distinguished restaurants as part of their appeal, while the third was in the process of a major property overhaul at press time that will undoubtedly have a significant impact on the hotel's restaurant as well.

EXPENSIVE

DCO Suites, Lounge & Spa ★★★   This chic and airy, upscale boutique hotel is unexpected in still rough-around-the-edges Máncora. The modern, multilevel hotel, built like an ingenious architect's town house, blends local stone and wood with stark white, silver, and turquoise retro accents and rises above the beach. You can see and hear the surf crashing below as you relax in luxury at the small infinity pool, lounge terrace, or the open-air, top-floor spa—one of the finest places you'll ever get a full-body rubdown and soak in a foamy Jacuzzi. The seven suites are hip and, while not huge, have extraordinary showers and sea views. Every detail, from iPods with special playlists given to you at check-in to colorful print robes and the gourmet menu, has been thought of. The hotel's name, by the way, is a play on the Spanish word *deseo*, or desire. Apt.

Las Pocitas, s/n (3km/2 miles south of Máncora). www.hoteldco.com. ⓒ **01/242-3961** for reservations, or **073/258-171.** 14 units. $180 double; $280 master suite. AE, DC, MC, V. Rate includes breakfast buffet. **Amenities:** Restaurant; bar; outdoor pool; spa. *In room:* A/C, TV, fridge, Wi-Fi (free).

Vichayito Bungalows & Carpas ★★★ ☺   A low-key beachside ecolodge has been wholly transformed by the Aranwa hotel group. Expanded and made more upscale and family-friendly, with paved pathways and landscaping, it fronts one of the prettiest and cleanest stretches of sandy beach in the entire region. The biggest change, though, has been the addition of unique luxury tents *(carpas)* to the already existing thatched-roof bungalows. The concept is something like "Out of Africa." The tents have handsome furnishings, poured concrete floors, headboards, king beds, LCD TVs, and porcelain sinks and, in some cases, deep clawfoot bathtubs; the only nod to "roughing it" is the tent itself, made of a tough French canvas, and the need to zip oneself in and out. Spread out over the large property, which has 270m (710 ft.) of beachfront, are a large pool, restaurant (with chandeliers under a thatched roof), games room, outdoor hot tub, and a brand-new luxury spa. Bungalows with capacity for six or eight people are great for families.

Antigua Panamericana Norte, Km 1211, Playa Vichayito (20 min southwest of Máncora). www.vichayito.com. ⓒ **01/434-1452.** Fax 01/ 434-6199. 35 units. $90–$135 bungalow double; $125–$165 carpa double. Rate includes breakfast. AE, DC, MC, V. **Amenities:** Restaurant; bar; outdoor pool; spa. *In room:* A/C, TV, fridge, Wi-Fi (free).

MODERATE

Costa Azul Hotel & Spa ★ ☺   The most upscale of places to stay on low-key Zorritos, this comfortable, thatched-roof spa-hotel is built around a pair of lush pools.

It has clean and cute rooms, an attractive open-air, beachside restaurant, and the only spa in the area, making it a nice little oasis way up north.

Antigua Panamericana Norte Km. 1229, Zorritos. www.costaazulperu.com/costaazul. © **072/544-135.** $85 double. Rate includes breakfast buffet. **Amenities:** Restaurant; bar; 2 outdoor pools; spa; gym. *In room:* A/C, TV, fridge, Wi-Fi (free).

Hotelier Arte y Cocina ★★

Just south of Máncora—walking distance or a short mototaxi ride—this small (nine-room) and unpretentious three-story place has stunning beach and sea views, friendly and knowledgeable young owners, a cool vibe, and an excellent little beachside restaurant. Rooms are minimalist and modern, with a comfortable, beachy feel enlivened by local art and poetic graphics on the walls. Named for the mother of one of the owners, Teresa Ocampo, who is a bit of a celebrity chef in Peru, with the country's first TV cooking show, the open-air restaurant "Donde Teresa" serves the finest local seafood and specialties like *"chancho al barril"* (wood-fired, slow-cooked pork).

Las Pocitas (1km/½ mile south of Máncora). www.hotelier.pe. © **073/258-702.** S/330–S/420 double. MC, V. Rate includes breakfast. **Amenities:** Restaurant; bar; outdoor pool. *In room:* A/C, TV, fridge, Wi-Fi (free).

INEXPENSIVE

Pink Parrot

This airy beachside place, previously (and often still) called Del Wawa, is one of the better inexpensive options in Máncora. It's got a funky, relaxed style (perhaps too relaxed: management can be lax), and some of the new rooms have high ceilings and loft spaces. On weekends, the bar is hopping, and loud.

Av. Piura s/n (facing el Point), Máncora. www.delwawa.com. © **073/258-427.** 10 units. S/65–S/95 double. No credit cards. **Amenities:** Bar. *In room:* No phone.

The Point Máncora Beach

If you've come north strictly for the party, this back-packers' resort on the beach should do the trick. It's got a large pool and a rocking bar, as well as a mix of two-story beachfront bungalows and shared hostel rooms, though sleep seems to be the last thing on anyone's mind. It has more amenities than most beach hostels.

Playa del Amor, s/n, Máncora. www.thepointhostels.com. © **073/706-320.** 30 units. S/50 private cabin double; S/22–S/28 shared dorm room per person. MC, V. **Amenities:** Restaurant; bar; outdoor pool. *In room:* TV; no phone.

HUARAZ & THE CORDILLERA BLANCA ★★

Rugged Peru is synonymous with the bold peaks of the Andes, and those mountains, particularly the spectacular Cordillera Blanca range 400km (250 miles) northeast of Lima, are a magnet for thousands of mountaineers and adventure-sports travelers every year. The string of dramatic snowcapped 5,000m (16,400-ft.) peaks east of the Callejón de Huaylas Valley, accessible from the main tourist hub of Huaraz (reached by bus in 7–8 hr. from Lima), is the premier spot in Peru—and perhaps the best in all of South America—for climbing and trekking. Nearly three dozen peaks soar to more than 6,000m (19,680 ft.); Huascarán, topping out at 6,768m (22,205 ft.), is Peru's highest mountain and the highest tropical mountain in the world. Nearly the entire chain is contained within the protected Huascarán National Park, a UNESCO Biosphere Reserve and World Heritage Trust site.

The Cordillera Blanca

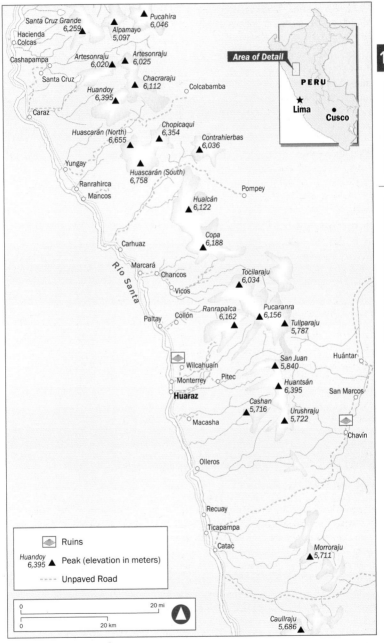

Área de Detalle

PERU

Lima ★ • Cusco

Santa Cruz Grande
6,259 ▲
Hacienda
Colcas ○
Cashapampa ○
Santa Cruz ○
Caraz ○

Pucahira
6,046 ▲
Alpamayo
5,097 ▲
Artesonraju
6,020 ▲
Artesonraju
6,025 ▲
Chacraraju
6,112 ▲   Colcabamba ○
Huandoy
6,395 ▲

Huascarán (North)
6,655 ▲
Yungay ○
Ranrahirca ○
Mancos ○

Chopicaqui
6,354 ▲
Contrahierbas
6,036 ▲

Huascarán (South)
6,758 ▲
Pompey ○
Hualcán
6,122 ▲

Carhuaz ○
Marcará ○
Chancos ○
Vicos ○
Paltay ○
Collón ○

Copa
6,188 ▲

Tocilaraju
6,034 ▲

Ranrapalca
6,162 ▲
Pucaranra
6,156 ▲
Tullparaju
5,787 ▲

Wilcahuaín ◇
Monterrey ○
Pitec ○
Huaraz

San Juan
5,840 ▲
Huántar ○
Huantsán
6,395 ▲
San Marcos ○
Cashan
5,716 ▲
Urushraju
5,722 ▲
Macasha ○
Chavín ◇

Olleros ○

Recuay ○
Ticapampa ○
Catac ○

Morroraju
5,711 ▲

Río Santa

Legend
◇ Ruins
Huandoy
6,395 ▲ Peak (elevation in meters)
--- Unpaved Road

0   20 mi
0   20 km

Caullraju
5,686 ▲

💬 "La" Huascarán?

The Cordillera Blanca's El Huascarán, the namesake of the mountainous National Park in Peru's central Andes, might seem to be an eminently macho mountain: At 6,768m (22,205 ft.), it's the highest peak in Peru, the fourth highest in the Americas, and the highest tropical-zone mountain in the world. But its north peak was first climbed in 1908 by a woman, the 58-year-old American Annie Smith Peck (who 3 years later climbed Peru's Mt. Coropuna, where she proudly displayed a women's suffrage banner that read "Votes for Women").

Not surprisingly, the region appeals above all to experienced, veteran mountaineers and adventurers. A burgeoning lineup of other adventure sports, from white-water rafting and mountain biking to hang-gliding and rock climbing, have lifted off in popularity in recent years. Above all, those kinds of adventure travelers, equipped and prepared for the rigors and thrill of roughing it outdoors, get the most out of the region.

The extraordinary mountain scenery of the region, however, also appeals to those with limited time and abilities, or only passing interest in testing their physical mettle in Peru. The valley, some 20km (12 miles) wide and 180km (112 miles) long, is a superb destination for those who are more interested in day walks and village markets, too. For those who would say all play and no culture makes for a dull adventure, visitors can marry interests in adventure sports and antiquity at the marvelous ruins of Chavín de Huántar, built about 1,500 years ago, a hearty journey about 4 hours from Huaraz. However, getting to the Cordillera Blanca still requires a considerable investment of time, even though one Peruvian airline (LC Busre) has finally begun to fly from Lima to Huaraz. Other outdoors areas in Peru (such as the Sacred Valley between Cusco and Machu Picchu, and the Colca Canyon beyond Arequipa) are easier to get to for most light adventurers.

The best months for climbing are the dry season, between May and October; of those, July and August are perhaps best. (Note that the traditional dry season has shifted a bit in recent years, with rains often lasting until the end of May but often not beginning until late November.) Mountain biking and trekking can be practiced other months as well, but the adventurous should be duly prepared for rain.

The small and bustling, ramshackle mountain city of Huaraz has few attractions besides its spectacular setting, but it serves as the base for most adventure-tour operators. With its roster of restaurants, bars, and small hotels, it's where most travelers gather to get acclimated to the altitude and get organized for their forays into the mountains. Besides Huaraz, several other small towns and villages at the

Acute Mountain Sickness

The usual warnings about altitude in the Peruvian Andes especially apply in Huaraz and the Cordillera Blanca. Headaches and nausea are common ailments. Take several days to adequately acclimatize to the high elevation of more than 3,000m (9,840 ft.), or up to a week if you're planning to attempt a serious ascent. In the early going, don't overextend yourself physically, and drink plenty of *mate de coca* (coca-leaf tea). If symptoms persist, see a doctor. Acute mountain sickness, known locally as *soroche*, is serious business.

base of the Cordillera mountains serve as starting points for trekking and climbing expeditions, but none is so well equipped as the capital of the Ancash department. Many expeditions to the scenic Llanganuco lakes in the Huascarán National Park begin at Yungay, while Caraz, a pleasant small mountain town known for its agreeable climate and flowers, serves as a quieter alternative to Huaraz and offers similar services required for ascents and other adventure activities.

HUARAZ

420km (261 miles) N of Lima

Huaraz is the primary base destination for most visitors keen on exploring the Callejón de Huaylas Valley that runs 200km (125 miles) right down the middle of Peru. At an altitude of 3,100m (10,170 ft.), Huaraz enjoys a spectacular setting at the foot of the Cordillera Blanca: The town is ringed by 20 snowcapped peaks, each higher than 6,000m (19,680 ft.), which rise in splendor just beyond reach of the city. Huaraz itself is a far cry from the postcard perfection of a picturesque alpine village, however. It is rough around the edges—as well as the center. Of course, it has a major earthquake to blame for its ragged look, a product of rapid and cheap concrete construction: The massive 1970 earthquake leveled nearly the entire city, eradicating half its population in the process.

Today Huaraz hums—albeit messily—with the business of mountain and adventure tourism. A wide range of facilities has sprung up to support outdoor travel; dozens of tour operators and travel agencies, restaurants and bars, and hotels and inns can be found in town, most clustered along the main drag, Avenida Luzuriaga.

Essentials

GETTING THERE

BY PLANE   To Huaraz, there are again daily afternoon flights (80 min.) from Lima on **LC Busre** (www.lcbusre.com.pe; ✆ 01/619-1313). Flights start at $119 one-way. Check the website for updates, as in recent years no Peruvian airline has consistently flown into Huaraz. Flights arrive at Aeropuerto de Anta, 23km (14 miles) north of Huaraz.

BY BUS   Traveling by arduous bus from Lima or from other points along the north coast or the northern Andes was, until recently, the only way to get to Huaraz, though travelers now have the more comfortable option of daily flights from Lima. Most of the individual bus company terminals are along Avenida Raymondi or Avenida Fitzcarrald. For the 7- to 8-hour journey to Huaraz from Lima, major companies offering daily service include **CIVA** (www.civa.com.pe; ✆ 01/418-1111), **Cruz del Sur** (www.cruzdelsur.com.pe; ✆ 01/311-5050), and **Móvil Tours** (www.moviltours.com.pe; ✆ 01/433-9000). Móvil Tours and **Transportes Línea** (www.transportes linea.com.pe; ✆ 01/424-836 or 044/297-000) are the principal carriers to and from Trujillo (8 hr.).

GETTING AROUND

The main axis in town is Avenida Luzuriaga, which is overrun with tourist agencies, outdoor outfitters, and nearly every strolling traveler who hits Huaraz. The easiest way to get around town is by taking an inexpensive taxi—the ones incessantly honking at every pedestrian hoping for a fare—or a colectivo. Myriad bus companies serve the Cordillera Blanca region, including Chavín, Caraz, and Yungay.

📎 **Safe Bus Travel**

Night bus trips departing Huaraz for Trujillo, Chiclayo, and other cities in northern Peru have earned bad reputations for theft. Some travelers have reported armed thieves boarding long-distance buses and forcibly relieving passengers of their valuables. Perhaps for this reason, the better "executive-level" services don't stop between Lima and their final destination. Be very careful with your belongings on board, even if it means threading your arms through the straps of your carry-on, if you plan to sleep.

BY TAXI   Taxis cruise Avenida Luzuriaga in search of travelers day and night. Rides in town cost S/2, and cabs can be safely and easily hailed on the street. One operator to call is **Radio Taxi** (📞 **043/721-482**).

BY BUS   Combis service towns in the Callejón de Huaylas around Huaraz: Chavín (4 hr.), Caraz (90 min.), and Yungay (90 min.). Most depart from the Quillcay Bridge on Alameda Fitzcarrald; others leave from Calle Caraz, a half-block east of Fitzcarrald. Fares are inexpensive, usually S/3 to S/10.

ORGANIZED TOURS

Guides and travel agencies are extremely useful, if not downright indispensable, for most adventure sports in the remote and often dangerous mountains. Like Cusco and Iquitos, Huaraz is chock-full of agencies and tour operators. Unfortunately, some of them are less than reliable; others are far worse. See "Trekking & Climbing in the Cordillera Blanca," later in this chapter, for a discussion of guides and agencies. It's best to check with fellow tourists (or, before arriving in Huaraz, with the South American Explorers clubs in either Lima or Cusco) to get recent reports about services.

VISITOR INFORMATION

The **iPerú** tourist office is at Av. Luzuriaga 734 (Pasaje Atusparía, Of. 1), across from the Plaza de Armas (📞 **043/428-812**); it's open Monday to Friday 8am to 1pm and 4 to 7pm. General tourist information is also available during the same hours from the **tourist police** office between City Hall and the Post Office on Avenida Luzuriaga (📞 **043/421-341**). For mountaineering and trekking information, though, you're best off consulting the **Casa de Guías,** Parque Ginebra 28 (📞 **043/421-811**). The office is open Monday through Friday from 9am to 6pm, and Saturday from 9am to 1pm. The friendly folks there have up-to-date information on trails, maps, lists of certified guides, and message-board postings for those looking to form trekking and climbing groups. Mostly, though, they're there to set you up with a guide. Basic information on visiting the Huascarán National Park can be obtained from the **Parque Nacional Huascarán** office, in the Ministerio de Agricultura building on Avenida Raymondi (📞 **043/422-086**). The website **www.huaraz.com** has pretty good information on the area.

FAST FACTS

Most banks and ATMs are found around the Plaza de Armas and along Avenida Luzuriaga. Among those that exchange traveler's checks and cash and have ATMs are **Banco de Crédito,** Av. Luzuriaga 669, at the corner of Sucre (📞 **043/421-170**); **Interbank,** Sucre 913 (📞 **044/423-015**); and **Banco Wiese,** Sucre 766 (no

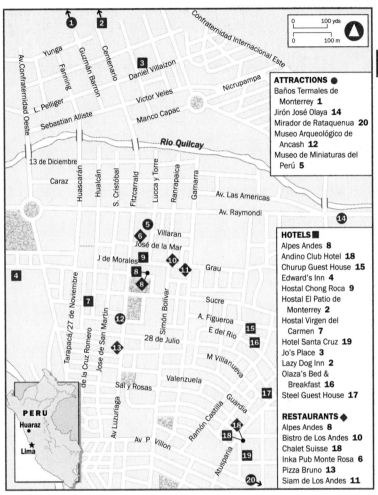

ATTRACTIONS ●
Baños Termales de
  Monterrey **1**
Jirón José Olaya **14**
Mirador de Rataquenua **20**
Museo Arqueológico de
  Ancash **12**
Museo de Miniaturas del
  Perú **5**

HOTELS ■
Alpes Andes **8**
Andino Club Hotel **18**
Churup Guest House **15**
Edward's Inn **4**
Hostal Chong Roca **9**
Hostal El Patio de
  Monterrey **2**
Hostal Virgen del
  Carmen **7**
Hotel Santa Cruz **19**
Jo's Place **3**
Lazy Dog Inn **2**
Olaza's Bed &
  Breakfast **16**
Steel Guest House **17**

RESTAURANTS ◆
Alpes Andes **8**
Bistro de Los Andes **10**
Chalet Suisse **18**
Inka Pub Monte Rosa **6**
Pizza Bruno **13**
Siam de Los Andes **11**

phone). Money-changers can usually be found hanging around outside banks around the Plaza de Armas.

In an **emergency,** call ℂ **105.** For climbing accidents and assistance, including evacuations, contact **Unidad de Salvamento de Alta Montaña (High Altitude Rescue),** Av. Arias Grazziani s/n, Yungay, at ℂ **043/493-333** or **043/493-327;** or **Casa de Guías,** Parque Ginebra 28 (ℂ **043/421-811**). If you need the police, the **tourist police** have an office just off the Plaza de Armas (ℂ **043/421-341**); see "Visitor Information," above. You can also contact the **national police,** Larrea y Loredo 720 (ℂ **043/421-461**). For medical attention, go to **Hospital de Apoyo Víctor Ramos Guardia,** Av. Luzuriaga s/n (ℂ **043/421-290**), or **Hospital**

Regional de Huaraz, Av. Luzuriaga s/n ((℄ **043/421-321**). There are **InkaPharma** locations at Av. Luzuriaga 435 and 488; **Botica Fasa** at Av. Luzuriaga 591.

There are a number of Internet *cabinas* dotting the downtown area. Try **Avance,** Av. Luzuriaga 672, 2nd Floor (℄ **043/426-736**), which has special deals for repeat visits and is open late. The main cafes, including **California Café** (p. 412) and **Café Andino** (p. 412), offer free Internet access.

The Huaraz **post office** is at Av. Luzuriaga 702 (℄ **043/421-030**), across the street from the Plaza de Armas. The **Telefónica del Perú** office is at Bolívar and Sucre, just east of the Plaza de Armas.

Exploring Huaraz

The emphasis on seeing and doing in Huaraz is definitely on the latter—most visitors are in town as long as it takes them to get acclimatized and organize an excursion into the mountains and valleys nearby or participate in some sort of adventure-sports activity. The town itself was hastily reconstructed after the devastating 1970 earthquake. A single street, **Jirón José Olaya** (to the right of Raymondi), gives a hint of what Huaraz looked like before it came crumbling down.

The **Museo Arqueológico de Ancash ★** is an interesting and well-organized small museum crammed with exhibits presenting the long history (more than 12,000 years) of the region through mummies, trepanned crania, and a terrific collection of monoliths from the Recuay and Huari cultures. There are textiles, ceramics, and other pieces from the Chavín, Huaraz, Moche, and Chimú cultures, as well as scale models of various ruins sites in the area. The museum, at Av. Luzuriaga 762 (℄ **043/ 421-551**), is open Monday through Saturday from 9am to 5pm, and Sunday from 9am to 2pm. Admission is S/10; the ticket is also good for same-day entrance to the ruins at Wilcahuaín (below).

Another diversion might be the **Museo de Miniaturas del Perú (Miniatures Museum).** It houses dolls in traditional Peruvian dress and scale models of the ruins at Chavín de Huántar, pre-earthquake Huaraz, and the city of Yungay. The museum is in the gardens of the Gran Hotel Huascarán, Jirón Lúcar y Torre 46 (℄ **043/421-466**). It's open Monday through Friday from 8am to 1pm and 3 to 6pm. Admission is S/3.

But because Huaraz is almost wholly about its stunning location and getting outdoors, visitors are usually more interested in the **Mirador de Rataquenua ★**, a lookout spot on a 3,650m (12,000-ft.) mountain pass with great panoramic views; it's just less than an hour's walk southeast of downtown. The direct trail is pretty steep; there's also a less demanding dirt road with plenty of switchbacks. Go with a group during the day because the area has experienced a spate of crime in recent years and become quite dangerous; locals warn that under no circumstances should a lone traveler walk there. To get there, head south on Luzuriaga to Villón and follow the road at the end, just beyond the cemetery. A round-trip taxi (S/25) is by far the safest way to go.

Located about 8km (5 miles) north of Huaraz, the **Monumento Arqueológico de Wilcahuaín** is a set of ruins from the Huari culture, which lived in the region around A.D. 1000. Two sites named for their relative size, Grande and Chico, were burial grounds and storage centers. The major temple was built around 1100. The ruins don't have established opening and closing hours, but it's certainly wisest to go during daylight. Admission is S/5 for adults and S/2 for students. To get there, take any combi marked "Wilcahuaín" from the Río Quillcay bridge. The trip takes about a

FESTIVAL calendar

Huaraz and the villages in the Callejón de Huaylas celebrate their Andean roots in traditional festivals that are among Peru's most spirited. If your visit coincides with a regional festival, you'll see a profusion of folk dances, costumed dances (some with extraordinary masks), and the stirring local music that accompanies them, played on exotic instruments such as *roncadoras, quenas,* and *zampoñas.* Carnaval, the Fiesta de Mayo, the Semana del Andinismo, the Patron Saint Festival, the Fiesta de las Luces, and Virgen de las Mercedes are among the most festive, but be warned that accommodations are at a premium, and prices skyrocket at these times.

Here's the complete list of regional festivals:

o **January 18 to January 21:** La Virgen de Chiquinquirá (Caraz)

o **February or March:** Carnaval Huaracino (Huaraz)

o **March or April:** Semana Santa and the steps of the pilgrimage (Huaraz and Callejón de Huaylas)

o **May 2 to May 10:** Fiesta de Mayo, celebrated with traditional dances, ski races, and a lantern procession (Huaraz)

o **June:** Semana del Andinismo, a celebration of outdoor adventure (Huaraz and Callejón de Huaylas)

o **June 22 to June 24:** San Juan Bautista, Day of the Indian (Pomabamba and the entire Sierra Andina)

o **July 6 to July 9:** La Virgen Santa Isabel (Callejón de Huaylas)

o **July 20 to July 30:** Independence Celebration (Huaraz and Caraz)

o **July 28 to July 29:** Fiestas Patrias

o **August 1 to August 6:** Patron Saint Festival (Coyllur and Huaraz)

o **August 13 to August 16:** Virgen de la Asunción (Huata and Chacas)

o **August 29 to August 30:** Fiesta Patrona (Chiquián and Santa Rosa)

o **September 14:** Fiesta de las Luces (Huaraz)

o **September 14 to September 27:** Señor de Burgos (Recuay)

o **September 23 to September 27:** Virgen de las Mercedes (Carhuaz)

o **October 5 to October 7:** Virgen del Rosario (Huari)

o **October 12:** Virgen del Pilar (Ticapampa)

o **October 28:** Fiesta Cívica (Yungay)

half-hour and costs S/3. After visiting Chico, walk down to Grande and catch a return combi to Huaraz.

A relaxing spot to visit, perhaps after you've indulged in some trekking or other adventure sports, is the thermal baths **Baños Termales de Monterrey** (*✆* **043/427-690**). A series of small wells and two large pools has mineral-rich waters that make the water look dark brown and rather unappealing, but your body might not be as picky as your eyes. The upper pool is the nicer of the two. The baths are open daily from 7am to 6pm, and they're usually very crowded on weekends and holidays. Admission is S/5. The baths are about 6km (3¾ miles) north of Huaraz along the road to Caraz; a colectivo from Avenida Luzuriaga drops passengers at the entrance.

Where to Eat

Huaraz has plenty of pretty good, informal restaurants serving the band of Gore-Tex gringos that come to town. The main drag, Avenida Luzuriaga, is thick with restaurants offering fixed-price menus and other cheap eats. The Andean cuisine of the Cordillera includes hearty items such as Huaracino *picante de cuy* (spicy roasted guinea pig), *jaca-chasqui* (spicy guinea pig soup), *charqui* (dried pork), and *trucha* (fried river trout). For the less adventurous, there are several *chifas* and pizzerias in town where you can get a filling, inexpensive meal.

Alpes Andes INTERNATIONAL/PIZZA   The food here might appear to take a back seat to the planning of mountain-climbing expeditions—as many mountain guides as eager tourists come through the doors—but this relaxing and informal cafe next door to the Casa de Guías (on Parque Ginebra) goes about its business of fortifying trekkers and adventurers for their trips to the Cordillera. Start with a breakfast of granola and yogurt, or chow down on the international trekkers' favorites: pizza and pasta (gotta load up on the carbs, you know).

Jr. Julián de Morales 753. ☎ **043/421-811.** Reservations not accepted. Main courses S/12–S/28. No credit cards. Daily 7am–11pm.

Bistro de Los Andes ★ INTERNATIONAL/PERUVIAN   This welcoming restaurant has long been one of the most popular places in town. It offers an interesting mix of French and Peruvian items for lunch and dinner and for Huaraz, a simple mountain town, it qualifies as upscale and almost elegant. The varied menu includes vegetarian dishes, pastas, and nicely done dishes such as *trucha a la almendra* (trout baked with almonds).

Jr. Julián de Morales 823. ☎ **043/426-249.** Reservations not accepted. Main courses S/14–S/32. DC, V. Daily 5–11pm.

Chalet Suisse ★ FONDUE/SWISS   This upscale restaurant has a pretty simple chalet decor, but the food is some of the city's best. The restaurant is primarily occupied by those staying in the attached Andino Club Hotel, so if you're not a guest, it's best to ring for a reservation. Dishes are generally hearty. The Swiss fondues, while not cheap, are delicious, as are steaks (such as the Argentine *bife angosto* and *asado al vino tinto*). The attractive dining room is the perfect subdued spot to celebrate your big climb (if you're too weary to hit the pubs).

Huaraz's Cafe Culture

A number of cafes around town are inviting spots for good, inexpensive meals in addition to getting your coffee fix. **Café California** ★★, Av. 28 de Julio 562 (☎ **043/428-354**), a favorite of gringos, has fresh-roasted coffee, a sitting lounge, fast Wi-Fi, and a book exchange. **Café Andino** ★, on Av. Lucar y Torre 530, 3rd floor (☎ **043/421-203**), is another popular hangout with good coffee (including cappuccinos and lattes) and breakfasts. It has a library book exchange with titles in several languages, board games, Wi-Fi, and a nice selection of tunes. Also worth a stop is **El Parque** (no phone), Figueroa 1025, an informal but clean and cute cafe with filling breakfasts and very cheap lunches as well as mixed drinks. Finally, the pub upstairs at the climbing agency **Monttrek**, Av. Luzuriaga 646 (☎ **043/421-121**), has tasty pizza, a roaring fireplace, and strong pisco sours.

Pedro Cochachín 357. ✆ **043/421-949.** Reservations recommended. Main courses S/26–S/38. AE, DC, MC, V. Daily noon–2pm and 7–10pm.

Inka Pub Monte Rosa ★ 🍴 INTERNATIONAL/PERUVIAN Probably Huaraz's best-looking restaurant, this two-level place with an inviting bar feels, appropriately, like a mountain lodge. It has an extensive menu that's all over the board but universally pretty good. Choose from traditional *criollo* cooking, *chifa*, or pizzas; there are steaks, fondues, and pastas, too. Service is friendly, and between regular dining hours, it's a fine place to linger over a book and a beer.

Jr. José de la Mar 661. ✆ **043/421-447.** Reservations not accepted. Main courses S/13–S/39. MC, V. Tues–Sun noon–3pm and 6:30–10:30pm.

Pizza Bruno ★ 🍴 INTERNATIONAL/PIZZA With a French chef but a largely Italian menu, this upscale but relaxed restaurant—with a family-run Mediterranean decor and large-format photos of Paris—might appear a little confused, but it's one of the best dining options in town. The pizzas are of the authentic thin-crust type, and the pastas are excellent. If you're in the mood for experimenting, try one of the chef's specialties, which includes *"plato del diablo"* (devil's plate, or sirloin flambéed with whiskey). A French touch is delivered in the desserts, which include a tarte tatin and profiteroles. Breakfast is also offered.

Av. Luzuriaga 834. ✆ **043/425-689.** Reservations recommended. Main courses S/14–S/35. AE, MC, V. Daily 6am–11pm.

Siam de Los Andes ★ THAI It's unusual to alight upon a Thai restaurant in Huaraz, but hungry trekkers looking for a taste of something different are really glad when they do—especially one with a fireplace. It's far from the cheapest restaurant in Huaraz, but the food is authentic and very well prepared. The stir-fries and curries are especially delicious. The amiable chef/owner Naresuan likes to greet diners, and, besides cooking, he knows a thing or two about trekking in the area.

Gamarra 419 (at the corner of Julián de Morales). ✆ **043/428-006.** Reservations not accepted. Main courses S/12–S/36. DC, V. Daily 5–10pm.

Shopping

Huaraz is recognized as an *artesanía* center, and all of the usual Andean handicrafts are available at markets targeting gringos. However, the city has none of the upscale, tourist-friendly shops found in Cusco and Lima. Some of the best items are custom-made and hand-tooled leather goods, wool sweaters, ponchos, and blankets. Open-air handicrafts markets are open daily along the covered walkway (Pasaje Cáceres) off Avenida Luzuriaga and along the streets Juan de la Cruz Romero, Avenida Raymondi, and Avenida Tarapacá. A *mercado callejero* (street market) is open Monday and Thursday on Avenida Bolognesi and Confraternidad Oeste.

PeruKraft, on Jirón 28 de Julio, stocks good-quality alpaca sweaters; **Andes Souvenirs,** Parque Ginebra next to the Casa de Guías, has handicrafts, textiles, and silver jewelry. **Andean Expressions,** Jr. Julio Arguedas 1246 (www.andeanexpressions. com; ✆ **043/422-529**) specializes in great-quality T-shirts with cool Andean designs; its products are found in several shops in town or its factory site.

But unless you're going on a trekking excursion with all your provisions included, shopping for foodstuffs might be more important. At the **Mercado de Huaraz (Mercado Modelo)** on Cruz Romero, just south of Raymondi, you can find most everything you'll need to sustain yourself for a mountain climb or a trek, including canned foods, nuts, and fresh fruits and vegetables. **Mercado Ortiz,** Av. Luzuriaga

401, is a good and well-stocked supermarket. Cheese and *manjar blanco* (a caramel-like sweet) are good local items to take along on an expedition.

Entertainment & Nightlife

It's not hard to find a nightspot in Huaraz. With all the gringos gearing up for or celebrating the completion of trekking expeditions, the place hops in high season.

Taverna El Tambo ★, José de la Mar 776, about 3 blocks from Avenida Luzuriaga (www.huaraz.com/tambo; ℂ 043/423-417), is the most happening disco in town. There's plenty of drinking, dancing, and smoking until the wee hours, and the music careens between international Top 40 and more homegrown Latin sounds. There's usually a pretty good mix of locals and gringos. The cover charge ranges from S/10 to S/20. **Makondo's** (ℂ 043/428-424), a full-throttle nightclub with food and dancing, is across from El Tambo on José de la Mar 812.

Other bars worth dropping in on include the intimate **Las Kenas,** Jr. Gabino Uribe 620 (ℂ 043/428-383), which features live and recorded (often Andean) music and good pisco sours; **La Cueva del Oso,** Av. Luzuriaga 674 (no phone), a lively peña with good music and dancing; and the laid-back **Monttrek Pub,** Av. Luzuriaga 646 (ℂ 043/421-121). Next door to Las Kenas is a slightly rowdier bar, **X-Treme,** Jr. Gabino Uribe 630 (www.huaraz.info/xtreme/index.html; ℂ 043/682-115), a place to drink, listen to classic rock, and meet trekkers from around the world. Popular with backpacking types—who must feel at home with all the maps on the walls—is **Vagamundo Travelbar & Maps,** Av. Julián de Morales 753 (ℂ 043/614-374), which has cool rock and blues music, a bar with couches, and frequent bonfires out on the patio.

Where to Stay

In addition to the inns and hotels below, **Alpes Andes** Parque Ginebra 28-G (casa_de_guias@hotmail.com; ℂ 043/421-811; S/25 per person in dorm), part of the Casa de Guías (guide headquarters), is the city's official youth hostel. It's well run, clean, and safe, with kitchen and laundry facilities. Independent trekkers and mountaineers frequently gather there to form groups.

EXPENSIVE

Andino Club Hotel ★   The top choice in town, this Swiss-owned, upscale alpine lodge is the favorite of well-equipped climbers and upscale business folks in town to visit the nearby mines. A modern, raked construction about a 10-minute uphill walk southeast of the Plaza de Armas, in the Pedregal district, it has the kind of comfort and amenities that are hard to come by in Huaraz. Accommodations are modern, spacious, and comfy, with beds with thick, striped Andean wool blankets. Some rooms have fireplaces. The best (but most expensive) rooms are on the second floor and have excellent panoramic views of the snowcapped Cordillera Blanca and Huascarán peaks from private balconies. With a friendly vibe and a good Swiss restaurant (p. 412), it's a fine place to prepare for or recover from rugged adventure travel. In high season, book well in advance because it's popular with trekking and climbing groups. There's climbing equipment rental, horseback riding, and free Internet access for guests.

Pedro Cochachín 357, Huaraz. www.hotelandino.com. ℂ 043/421-662 or ℂ/fax 01/241-5927 for reservations. 60 units. S/339–S/471 double; S/471 and up suites. Rates include buffet breakfast. AE, DC, MC, V. **Amenities:** Restaurant. *In room:* TV, Wi-Fi (free).

MODERATE

Hostal El Patio de Monterrey ★ 🎁 Although not inexpensive for the region, this handsome hacienda-style rustic hotel just 6 km (3½ miles) beyond Huaraz, near the thermal baths of Monterrey, is a very agreeable place. It has a country flavor, with red tile-roofed stucco buildings built around a stone patio and pleasant gardens; rooms are cheery and nicely maintained. Some have high ceilings and balconies. For couples or small families, there's a large cabaña with a fireplace.

Km. 206, Huaraz–Caras Hwy, Monterrey. www.elpatio.com.pe. 𝒞 **043/424-965.** 25 units. S/222 double, S/376 cabaña with chimney. Rate includes breakfast. AE, MC, V. **Amenities:** Restaurant; Wi-Fi (free). *In room:* TV.

Lazy Dog Inn ★★ 🎁☺ This spectacularly sited, eco-styled inn, run by a Canadian couple in the Cordillera Blanca, 8km (5 miles) east of Huaraz, is a great place to get away and get outdoors. The adobe lodge features a main lodge with two rooms and three private cabins with fireplaces and bathtubs. Rooms are stylish, cozy, and colorfully decorated; the Condor Suite has a private balcony and great mountain views, while the Rima Rima cabin has an outdoor deck and fireplace. Cabins are perfect for families, with either extra bunk beds or an extra double bed. The inn operates a small NGO, Andean Alliance, that works with local communities, and recycles 90% of its waste, grows most of its own vegetables, and features an adobe outdoor sauna, outside fire pit, and has horses available for local mountain rides. Full meal plans are also available.

Km 3.1, Marian-Cachipampa Rd. (Huaraz). www.thelazydoginn.com. 𝒞 **943/789-330.** 5 units. S/210–S/310 double. Rates include breakfast and dinner. AE, MC, V. **Amenities:** Horseback riding excursions; sauna. *In room:* Wi-Fi (free).

INEXPENSIVE

Churup Guest House ★ 🔥 One of the friendliest family-run inns in Huaraz, this low-key budget place plays happy host to lots of young gringo trekkers. In a quiet residential area just a short 5-block walk from the Plaza de Armas, Hostal Churup has good, clean rooms with private bathrooms for two to four people, and small dormitory rooms with shared bathrooms. The owners, the Quirós Romero family, are eager to share not only their knowledge of the area and trekking expeditions, but also their home (around the corner on Jirón Pedro Campos), where a filling and inexpensive breakfast is served with family members each morning. The lovely backyard is a good place to sit, read, and relax; the two double rooms there are the most private in the house. There's also a cool, brightly colored lounge, and guests can use the kitchen. It's a good idea to reserve in advance from June to September, when outdoors enthusiasts descend on Huaraz.

Jr. Amadeo Figueroa 1257 (near Iglesia Soledad), Huaraz. www.churup.com. 𝒞 **043/424-200.** 12 units. S/80–S/120 double with private bathroom; S/25–S/28 per person in dorm room with shared bathroom. Rates include breakfast and bus station pickup. MC, V. **Amenities:** Café; bar. *In room:* No phone, Wi-Fi.

Edward's Inn 🔥 One of Huaraz's most popular and longest-running inns, Edward's is an easygoing place that packs in trekkers during high season. Rooms are large and have good mountain views, although some detractors find the inn overpriced, given its fairly basic facilities. (The hot water, fueled by solar power, can be spotty.) The inn's also a bit removed from the action in town (about a 15-min. walk from the Plaza de Armas). Still, it's a good place to meet and hang out with fellow gringo trekkers and climbers. The eponymous owner, an experienced trekker and mountaineer, rents gear, speaks good English, and can provide good climbing and trekking information. He can also arrange tours, treks, and climbing trips. The rooftop patio is a good gathering spot.

Av. Bolognesi 121 (near the stadium), Huaraz. www.edwardsinn.com. *C*/fax **043/422-692.** 14 units. $35 double. DC, MC, V. **Amenities:** Cafe; dining room. *In room:* TV.

Hotel Santa Cruz A clean, modern, three-level boutique-style inn with panoramic mountain views from massive windows and room balconies (in half the accommodations), this easygoing, well-run place (owned by Norwegians, managed by an American) splits the difference between Huaraz's one upscale hotel and the city's numerous budget offerings. Rooms are cozy and comfortable, with a nod to Scandinavian simplicity (beds feature "eiderdown" comforters from Norway), and have clean private bathrooms. The public spaces, which include a nice terrace and dining room and lounge with large fireplaces, are great spots to relax after tiring treks and bike rides. The big breakfasts, including pancakes, eggs, fruits, and more, are quite fortifying.

Jr. Gabino Uribe 255. www.santacruzperu.com. *C***043/396-096.** 12 units. $50 double. AE, MC, V. **Amenities:** Library; TV lounge.

Olaza's Bed & Breakfast ★ This small, spotless, and friendly inn, owned by one of the Olaza brothers (who have their hands in everything from mountain biking to T-shirts), is one of the best values in town. Set back from the street in the Soledad district (a 10-min. walk from Avenida Luzuriaga), it is quiet and safe, as well as very comfortable for the price. Rooms are simply equipped but large and have thick wool blankets and 24-hour hot water (often a rare commodity at the budget level). Bathrooms are impeccable. On the top floor is a terrific, sunny terrace with excellent mountain views, and there's also a fourth-floor lounge with a fireplace, DVD player, and even a fridge full of beer.

MORE budget ACCOMMODATIONS

Huaraz can fill up with trekking groups and plenty of independent travelers between June and September. Many of the budget inns hawked by people who meet arriving buses are neither clean nor especially comfortable, though. If you arrive without a reservation and are looking for a solid, safe, and inexpensive inn, try one of the following hotels.

Hostal Chong Roca This plain *hostal* has large and decent rooms that have either a full private bathroom or a toilet and sink. It's okay in a pinch. Morales 687. *C* **043/421-154.** S/30 per person.

Hostal Virgen del Carmen This comfortable *hostal* is run by a warm older

couple who have converted their attractive house into an inn with very nice bedrooms. Cruz Romero 622. *C* **043/421-729.** S/35 double.

Jo's Place This relaxed, colorful and friendly inn has a cool garden terrace, excellent mountain views, and very well-maintained rooms. It's on the north side of the Río Quillcay, a 10- to 15-minute walk from the center of town, and is pretty popular with a steady stream of backpackers. Jr. Daniel Villayzán 276. www.huaraz.com/josplace. *C* **043/425-505.** S/20–S/40 double.

Julio Arguedas 1242 (La Soledad), Huaraz. www.andeanexplorer.com/olaza. © **043/422-529.** 9 units. S/80–S/90 double. Rates include breakfast and bus station pickup. No credit cards. *In room:* No phone, Wi-Fi (free).

Steel Guest House ★★ ✦ In the Pedregal district, near the more upscale and much more expensive Andino Club Hotel, this five-story hotel has a welcoming feel, with great amenities at this economical price level: a kitchen, sauna, DVD lounge, pool table, and terrace with great rooftop views. Rooms are spacious, very clean, and colorfully decorated.

Alejandro Maguina 1467. www.steelguest.com. © **043/429-709.** 15 units. $50 double. Rate includes breakfast. AE, MC, V. **Amenities:** Games room. *In-room:* TV, Wi-Fi (free).

Side Trips from Huaraz

Most folks who make it to Huaraz are understandably eager to get out into the countryside and up into the mountains. The point of a visit to Huaraz is really to explore some of the most stunning scenery on the planet; the entire valley is characterized by spectacular snowcapped mountains, stunning alpine lakes, and tranquil meadows. For information on trekking, climbing, and other adventure sports, see "Trekking & Climbing in the Cordillera Blanca," below. Less rigorous excursions by organized tour are also possible; the most popular are the spectacular Lagunas de Llanganuco and the ancient ruins at Chavín de Huántar. The small towns of the Callejón de Huaylas, the valley that splits the middle between the mountain ranges of the Cordillera Blanca and the Cordillera Negra north of Huaraz, make good bases for hikes and are worthwhile visits in themselves.

CHAVÍN DE HUÁNTAR ★★
110km (68 miles) E of Huaraz

East of the Cordillera Blanca, Chavín de Huántar, the nearly 3,000-year-old ruins of the Chavín culture, is some 4 long hours by a largely unpaved and twisting mountain road (which is very slowly being improved) from Huaraz. The ruins, a UNESCO World Heritage Site and the best-preserved ruins of the culture, consist of a U-shaped fortress-temple with excellent stonework constructed over several centuries. The Chavín, who thrived in the region from about 1200 to 300 B.C. and whose influence was felt from Ecuador all the way to southern Peru, were the most ancient of the major cultures known to exist in Peru, and certainly one of its most sophisticated. The Chavín are considered perhaps the most influential people to have existed in the Andes until the arrival of the dynasty-building Incas (who came along a mere 2,000 years later).

However, don't expect a stunning set of Machu Picchu-like ruins. The site's archaeological importance isn't nearly as transparently aesthetic. The temple comprises more than a dozen underground galleries or chambers; only a few are open to the public. Some appear as labyrinthine tunnels today because they were interred by a landslide in the 1940s. The main structure on the premises is a large pyramid, called the **Castillo,** built over well-constructed canals where water once flowed. A way away is a large, sunken central plaza, a ceremonial gathering place. The highlight of the ruins is the **Lanzón ★★★,** a remarkable cultist carving in white granite and shaped like a prism or dagger. The monolith is found in an underground passage behind the original temple, which is much smaller than the several-times-enlarged

Castillo. The huge 4.5m (15-ft.) carving depicts three figures worshiped by the Chavín culture: the serpent, the bird, and the feline, the principal deity. The Lanzón remains in its original location, at an underground crossroads, even though other important artifacts, including the famous Tello Obelisk and Raymondi Stela, were removed and are now housed at Museo de la Nación in Lima. A guide and a flashlight are needed to get the most out of the site. Once visitors could walk completely around and inspect the prized Lanzón; today, however, it can be viewed only from the side and at a distance, down a cramped corridor.

The **Monumento Arqueológico Chavín de Huántar** (© 044/754-042), which includes a small museum, is open daily from 8am to 4pm. The most convenient and fastest way to visit Chavín is by organized tour from Huaraz (Chavín Tours or Pablo Tours); most cost about S/50 per person (plus the S/11 entrance fee to the ruins). Virtually every agency offers the same program, a long day trip leaving Huaraz around 9am and returning around 8pm. **Chavín Express,** Mariscal Cáceres 338, Huaraz (© 043/424-652) also operates a couple of buses daily to Chavín.

Nearby, the village of Chavín de Huántar is a traditional settlement. Although very few tourists stay overnight, the Lanzón has been known to exert a mystical hold on some visitors. In case you want to make a second day's visit to the ruins, you could spend the night at the inexpensive **Hotel La Casona,** on the Plaza de Armas (© 044/754-020).

GLACIAR PASTORURI
70km (43 miles) S of Huaraz

The Cordillera Blanca is tightly packed with towering peaks that should be ascended only by skilled and properly outfitted climbers. If you're not in that camp, this relatively flat glacier, another popular day trip from Huaraz, might be a draw. Provided that you've already become acclimatized to the altitude of the area, the 45-minute trek up the glacier (5,240m/17,187 ft.) isn't difficult and can be done without special equipment, although horses and mules are frequently available to help those having a hard time trudging through the snow. Though Peruvians often ski and snowboard on the glacier, veteran skiers will be disappointed; the glacier is shrinking, the snow is icy, and the rope-tow seems to come and go. Bring sufficient cold-weather gear because it can get very frigid.

As an organized outing, the trip to Pastoruri is usually combined with a visit to the valley of **Pachacoto,** 57km (35 miles) south of Huaraz, an opportunity to see the Callejón de Huaylas's famous **Puya Raimondi** plants. The bizarre, spiky plants, like towering alien cacti, are the largest members of the bromeliad family (a relative of the pineapple). The species is thought to be one of the most ancient in the world, and it is found only in a few isolated, high-altitude parts of the Andes. The plant, which can reach a height of 12m (39 ft.), is like a tragic protagonist: It flowers but once in its life, and although it might live to be 100 years old, it dies immediately after flowering. Flowering usually happens in May, when tour groups make pilgrimages to witness the brief, beautiful sight, like a stage set against the snowy mountains. Organized Pastoruri/Puya Raimondi visits begin at about S/35 per person.

CARHUAZ
31km (19 miles) N of Huaraz

This quiet, rather plain Andean town stands in stark contrast to the tourism hustle of Huaraz. It's becoming better known as a base in its own right for mountain-adventure travel, but it doesn't have even a fraction of the tourism infrastructure found in Huaraz. Still, it has a couple of nice *hostales* and restaurants for people looking for a more serene atmosphere. Carhuaz is locally renowned for its Virgen de las Mercedes festival, which takes place for 10 days in mid-September and is perhaps the most raucous festival in the valley.

There aren't many actual sights in town, other than the bustling Sunday market, but a few places just outside Carhuaz are worth a look. Near the small town of Mancos (a half-hour from Carhuaz by combi) is the ancient cave Cueva de Guitarreros, which some anthropologists believe to be 12,000 years old. The cave, which contains primitive rock paintings, is a nice 30-minute walk from Mancos south across the river. There are good views of Huascarán. Near Marcará, about 6.5km (4 miles) south of Carhuaz, are the Baños Termales de Chancos (hot springs).

To get to Carhuaz, take a combi from Huaraz; the trip takes about an hour and costs S/4. Right on the plaza, **Café Heladería El Abuelo ★**, La Merced 727 (www. elabuelohostal.com/cafe_el_abuelo; ☎ 043/394-149), is a congenial spot (open daily for breakfast, lunch, and dinner) serving Peruvian specialties like *lomo saltado* and stuffed avocado, as well as sandwiches and salads. For dessert, don't miss the artisanal ice cream with funky flavors (like pisco sour). If you want to spend the night in Carhuaz, perhaps your best bet is one of the family-run guesthouses, or *casas de alojamiento.* Try **La Casa de Pocha** (☎ 043/943-613-058), an eco-ranch about a mile east of town, which positions itself as a retreat focusing on alternative living and health, social wellbeing, and harmony with nature. It has excellent views and opportunities for horseback riding and hiking in the forest. The adobe guesthouse has cozy rooms and excellent views of Hualcán, while the organic farm provides produce for meals. There are good hikes in the nearby forest, a wood sauna, and yoga studio. It runs to $80 for a double room including meals.

YUNGAY

54km (33 miles) N of Huaraz

This small town is permanently marked by tragedy: It was completely buried in just a matter of minutes in a 1970 landslide, which was precipitated by the massive earthquake (7.8 on the Richter scale) that loosened tons of granite and ice from the north peak of Huascarán. The hurtling mass killed at least 20,000 people, nearly the town's entire population. Only a few children and those who, ironically, scrambled to the higher grounds of the local cemetery, survived. The rubble, called **Campo Santo,** is now a macabre tourist attraction. The only reminders of the life that once existed there are four palm trees that graced the Plaza de Armas and rosebushes and monuments honoring the dead. A new settlement was established about a half-mile away. Predictably, the rebuilt town isn't too easy on the eyes, save its alpine location; it's mostly a functional transportation hub for those looking to approach the stunning lakes of Llanganuco (above). In town, there's a small museum, the **Museo de Arqueología e Historia Natural de Yungay,** Avenida Las Palmeras, Ranrahirca (☎ 043/682-322), which exhibits regional flora and fauna, ceramics, textiles, and other historical relics.

Combis leave from the Quillcay Bridge on Alameda Fitzcarrald Huaraz for Yungay. The trip, which takes about 1½ hours, costs S/3.

The best place to stay in the vicinity is **Llanganuco Lodge ★★★** (www.llanganuco lodge.com; ☎ 043/943-688-791; S/118–S/236 doubles, S/153–S/306 suites). On the edge of Huascarán National Park and adjacent to Keushu Lake, at an altitude of

3,500m (11,483 ft), this outdoorsman's lodge has a singular location—and some of the finest views a hotel could have in the Peruvian Andes, of the three highest peaks of the Cordillera Blanca. Within walking distance of Llanganuco gorge, it has excellent, well-equipped and spacious rooms, and a very nice restaurant. This inn, founded and run by Charlie, an expat Brit, is kind of complicated to get to (about a 30 min. taxi from Yungay), but for day treks or to recover after days in the mountains, it's ideal.

CARAZ ★★

68km (42 miles) N of Huaraz

Caraz is the farthest of the valley towns north of Huaraz that are accessible by public transportation. Much more charming and attractive than some of the other highland towns that suffered great natural disaster, and located at an elevation about 1,000m (3,280 ft.) lower than Huaraz, Caraz makes a good base for trekking and climbing in the Cordillera Blanca. The town has a pleasant, colonial-styled Plaza de Armas and a growing amount of infrastructure to serve trekkers and mountaineers, including one of the area's top outdoor-adventure agencies. Many people end up (and rest up) in Caraz after trekking the popular Llanganuco–Santa Cruz route, although nearly as many embark from here to remote treks into the northern Cordillera Blanca.

Caraz has a couple of small museums: a **Museo de Arqueología,** Esquina 1 de Mayo y Manuel Cáceres (✆ 043/791-029; Tues–Sun 9am–1pm and 2–5pm; admission S/3), which has some deformed skulls and artifacts uncovered at the Cueva de Guitarreros, and the **Museo Amauta de Arte Ancashino,** Av. Noe Bazán Peralta s/n (✆ 043/791-004; daily 9am–noon and 3–5pm; admission S/3), which contains some ethnographic exhibits representing villages of the Callejón de Huaylas. About 2 km. (1 mile) from the center of town across the Río Llullán, near the turn to Laguna Parón, are some pre-Chavín ruins, **Tunshucaiko,** Av. Noe Bazán Peralta s/n (✆ 043/791-004), about a half-mile from the center of town across the Río Llullán.

Although many people make their way to Caraz to begin some hard-core mountain excursions, several worthwhile and easier excursions make excellent day trips. Gorgeous **Laguna Parón** is a bold, bright blue lake that sits at an elevation of more than 4,000m (13,120 ft.) and is surrounded by a dozen snowcapped peaks, 30km (19 miles) east of town. Colectivos run from Santa Rosa in Caraz to Parón (90 min.), but they don't go all the way to the lake, requiring a lengthy hike. A taxi from Caraz (S/75 round trip) is a better, if much more expensive, option. The **Cañón del Pato** is a fantastic, sheer canyon formed by the Río Santa, dividing the Cordilleras Blanca and Negra. Although it is more than 1,000m (3,280 ft.) deep, it is only 15m (49 ft.) wide. The road that knifes through the canyon, from Caraz to Huallanca, is one of the most thrilling in the country; it penetrates more than three dozen tunnels. By colectivo, it's about 2 hours to Huallanca, the far end of the canyon, from Caraz.

Caraz is about a 2-hour combi ride from Huaraz. If you want to stay overnight in Caraz, try one of the following inexpensive inns that are popular with trekkers and backpackers: **Hostal Perla de los Andes,** Daniel Villar 179/Plaza de Armas (www. huaraz.com/perladelosandes; ✆ 043/392-007; $20 double) next to the cathedral, with simple rooms overlooking the handsome Plaza de Armas; **Los Piños Lodge,** Parque San Martín 103 (www.lospinoslodge.com; ✆ 043/391-130; $20 double), an attractive place with a nice cafe; or **Grand Hostal Caraz Dulzura,** Sáenz Peña 212 (www.hostalcarazdulzura.com; ✆ 043/391-523; S/60 double), a pleasant, modern hotel built around a patio.

In town are **Pony Expeditions,** one of the best trekking and mountaineering agencies in the valley, with equipment rental and good guides (see "Recommended Tour Companies," below), and **Apu Expeditions,** Villar 215 (© **043/392-159**). **Café de Rat** (© **043/291-642**), Jr. Sucre 1286, on the Plaza de Armas above Pony Expeditions, is the place for mountaineers to hang out and fortify themselves with pizzas, pastas, crepes, good vegetarian meals, and beer. (It also has Internet access, maps, and guidebooks.)

LAGUNAS DE LLANGANUCO ★★★

82km (51 miles) N of Huaraz

These two brilliant turquoise alpine lakes, at nearly 4,000m (13,120 ft.) above sea level, compose a dazzling vista at the base of the Cordillera Blanca's highest snow-capped summits. The views of Chopicalqui (6,354m/20,841 ft.), Huandoy (6,395m/20,976 ft.), and hulking Huascarán (6,768m/22,199 ft.) are simply mesmerizing. If possible, wait for a clear morning to go; the sun shining on the lakes makes them shimmer and their colors change. The glacier-fed lakes within the Huascarán National Park (entry fee S/5) are a popular day trip from Huaraz, and many tour companies in Huaraz offer Llanganuco as an organized tour for about S/35 per person. Those up for more of an adventure can also organize a day trek to the lagunas (those with more time on their hands might opt for the 4- to 5-day Llanganuco–Santa Cruz trek, one of the most beautiful and popular treks on the continent; see "Trekking & Climbing in the Cordillera Blanca," below). If you're traveling independently, the lakes are easiest to get to from Yungay, which is 26km (16 miles) away; it's simple to catch a combi or truck up to the lakes from the Plaza de Armas in Yungay, but the ride can take up to 90 minutes. From Huaraz, you'd have to take a Caraz-bound colectivo, get off in Yungay, and from there hop a combi from Av. 28 de Julio.

> ### Top of the Peaks
>
> Among the highest and best known of Peru's daunting pinnacles—trophies prized by climbers the world over—are Mount Huascarán, 6,768m (22,205 ft.); the Huandoy massif's three summits, all more than 6,000m (19,680 ft.) high; Chopicalqui, 6,354m (20,846 ft.); Chacraraju, 6,112m (20,052 ft.); Alpamayo, 5,957m (19,544 ft.); and Copa, 6,118m (20,072 ft.).

Trekking & Climbing in the Cordillera Blanca ★★★

The Cordillera Blanca, the highest tropical mountain chain in the world, is one of South America's most impressive ranges. Its glorious and imposing mountain peaks proclaim their beauty and power over a 180km (112-mile) stretch through the heart of Peru. Most visitors to the Cordillera Blanca mountain range want to view the stunning scenery of snowcapped peaks, glaciers, lakes, and rivers from up close and on high. They have one thing in mind: strapping on high-tech gear and embarking on trekking or climbing expeditions.

This section of Peru has become one of the world's mountaineering meccas. Fifty summits soar between 4,800 and 6,662m (15,748–21,857 ft.) high, and nearly the entire range forms part of the protected Parque Nacional Huascarán. Although the most challenging peaks are beacons to some of the most tested mountaineers in the world, there are plenty of trekking and climbing activities for those who haven't quite perfected their ascent techniques. And although some of the peaks are plenty daunting, access to the trail heads is fairly simple, reached by public transportation in just a few hours from Huaraz.

The 340,000-hectare (839,800-acre) Parque Nacional Huascarán was created in 1975 to protect the region's great natural resources. Within the park are the towns Recuay, Huaraz, Carhuaz, Yungay, Huaylas, Bolognesi, Huari, Asunción, Piscobamba, and Pomabamba, several of which serve as bases for explorers. The park counts 32 peaks higher than 6,000m (19,680 ft.) and includes Huascarán, Peru's highest summit, and Alpamayo, whose legendary fourth face is considered by many mountaineers as the most beautiful in the world, as well as 269 lakes and 41 rivers among its spectacular roster of natural blessings.

Most of the top climbs in the Cordillera Blanca are best done with the assistance of local guides and experts. Several climbs are not only arduous, but also extremely dangerous. Unless you're a certified member of the hard-core ilk, it's best to contract a guide or organized tour in Huaraz. There, you'll find a whole complement of services, including licensed guides, porters, climbing-gear rentals, and rescue teams. However, plenty of independent and self-reliant trekkers simply hire an *arriero* (muleteer) and set off without a proper guide.

In recent years, there has been a fair amount of grousing about the deteriorating state of the Parque Nacional Huascarán, from both trekkers and agencies; many complain that it is not being kept up as it should, with the most popular trails littered with refuse and bribes supplanting group payment of entry fees. If one of Peru's national treasures is being neglected, it will surely have a great impact not only on the local environment, but also on the local economy. So many individuals and communities depend upon the income produced by largely foreign adventure travelers who come to enjoy the remote beauty of the Peruvian Andes.

The fee to enter Huascarán National Park is S/5 for a single-day visit and S/65 for a multi-day pass (valid up to 1 month). The entrance ticket to Huascarán National Park can be purchased at the Llanganuco and other entrances. You should keep a copy of your passport ready when entering and leaving the park.

RECOMMENDED TOUR COMPANIES

In Peru, it's important to pick tour operators carefully to avoid being ripped off. A good guide from a respected agency knows the routes, the weather, and the risks, and can usually steer you away from the latter. In the event of an emergency, he or she will know how to get injured parties evacuated. If you're serious about adventure

 A Gear Checklist

Appropriate technical gear is required for nearly all treks and climbs in the Cordillera Blanca. If you're going with an organized group, you can rent anything you need that's not provided. Independent trekkers and climbers can also rent almost anything they need in Huaraz. Some equipment is invariably dated and in less than optimal condition, so experienced mountain climbers pursuing technical climbs will surely want to bring all their own equipment. At a minimum, you'll need cold-weather and water-repellent clothing; good backpacking or climbing boots; a tent, a sleeping bag, a camping stove, and cookware; a filter and/or water-purification tablets; a compass; and topographical maps of trails.

sports, you don't want to skimp when it comes to the people to whom you're entrusting your safety and well-being. Locals suggest that you demand a *factura* (receipt) with an "RUC" (taxpayer registration number) from any prospective agency or guide.

The following are all recommended agencies and guides with many years of experience and good reputations in the Huaraz/Cordillera Blanca region. Even so, ask around first. Talk to people who've recently returned from treks and climbing expeditions. Contact the **South American Explorers** either in Lima, at Av. Piura 135, Miraflores (www.saexplorers.org; ☎ **01/445-3306**) or Cusco, at Choquechaca 188, no. 4 (cuscoclub@saexplorers.org; ☎ **084/245-484**). Also speak to the **Casa de Guías de Huaraz,** Parque Ginebra 28 (www.casadeguias.com.pe; ☎ **043/421-811**), an excellent source of current information (although understand that its mission is primarily to hook you up with one of its guides—who generally charge about $50 per day). Don't overlook your guide's ability to speak English, which could be critical if your understanding of Spanish is poor. Even if the agency says that the guide speaks good English, don't automatically take its word for it.

Virtually every agency in town runs the basic and most popular little-to-no-difficulty programs to Lagunas de Llanganuco, Glaciar Pastoruri, and Chavín de Huántar (see "Side Trips from Huaraz," earlier in this chapter) for about $10 per person. Agencies often pool travelers when they can't round up enough on their own.

General Tours

o **Huaraz Chavín Tours,** Av. Luzuriaga 502, Huaraz (www.chavintours.com.pe; ☎ **043/421-578** or **01/447-0024**): A good company offering standard tours, including trips to Chavín de Huántar, Pastoruri Glacier, and Llanganuco lakes.

o **Pablo Tours,** Av. Luzuriaga 501, Huaraz (www.pablotours.com; ☎ **043/421-145**): A standard tour company, similar to Chavín Tours but offering a few more options. Also organizes good group treks.

Mountain Trekking & Climbing

o **Explorandes Peru ★★★,** Av. Centenario 489, Huaraz (www.explorandes.com; ☎ **043/421-960** or **01/715-2323**): This environmentally sensitive and serious agency is one of the big-name and longest-established adventure-tour operators in Peru, with fixed-departure treks in the Cordillera Blanca. It's expensive, but it's one of the best and most dependable. Explorandes offers both hard-core adventure and soft-adventure programs, and will custom-tailor a trip for small groups. Programs range from llama trekking to Chavín to 12-day treks in the Cordillera Huayhuash.

o **JM Expeditions,** Av. Luzuriaga 465, Of. 4, Huaraz (www.jmexpeditions.com; ☎ **043/428-017** or **01/426-0599**): Good mountain-climbing equipment and roster of guides.

o **Monttrek ★★★,** Av. Luzuriaga 646, 2nd Floor, Huaraz (☎ **043/421-124**): One of the climbing and trekking pioneers in Huaraz, now going on 20 years in the area, this serious agency organizes hard-core ascents and expeditions, including ice and rock climbing. The company also offers programs for budget-conscious trekkers, as well as camping- and climbing-equipment rental, guides, mountain- and ice-climbing classes, and horseback riding, mountain biking, river rafting, and hang-gliding. New programs include Overland Andino (aka World War II jeep) and excursions to Cañon del Pato and Lagunas Llanganuco. With its nice upstairs pub restaurant (which has an interior climbing wall), Monttrek is a good spot to put

The Cost of Trekking & Climbing

All multi-day excursions (up to 1 month) into the Huascarán National Park carry entrance fees of S/65. If you're going with a tour operator, ask whether this fee is included in your package cost. Single-day entry costs S/5.

Licensed climbing and trekking guides charge between $60 and $100 per day. *Arrieros*, local porters with mules who'll lead you on trails, charge about $15 per day, plus food. (*Arrieros* can be arranged at trail heads or at the Casa de Guías in Huaraz.) Organized treks with one of the firms listed earlier are generally around $35 to $50 per day, per person. A certified guide to lead technical mountain climbs can cost upwards of $90. Serious climbers should also factor in the cost of insurance (obtained at home) that protects against the prohibitive cost of rescue operations.

together a group of like-minded adventurers. Serious climbers will want to speak to the owner, Pocho, and check out his technical drawings of nearly every peak in the region.

o **Pony Expeditions ★★**, Jr. Sucre 1266, Plaza de Armas, Caraz (www.pony expeditions.com; ✆ **043/391-642**): This professional outfitter is run by a respected guide, Alberto Cafferata, with lots of different treks and climbs available. It offers an extensive program of trekking and climbing itineraries, mountain biking, and rock and ice climbing.

o **Pyramid Adventures,** Av. Luzuriaga 530, Huaraz (www.pyramidadventures.net; ✆ **043/421-864**): One of the better climbing agencies, run by a family of brothers, with good service and knowledge.

Guides & Equipment Rental

o **Galaxia Mountain Shop,** Leoniza y Lescano 603, Huaraz (✆ **043/422-792**), and **MountClimb,** Mariscal Cáceres 421, Huaraz (✆ **043/426-060**): Both have a full range of mountain-climbing gear, including boots, sleeping bags, and crampons, for rent (about S/30 per day for a full complement of equipment).

o **Montañero Aventura y Turismo,** Parque Ginebra 30B, Huaraz (✆ **043/726-386**): Climbing equipment, guides, mountain bikes, and standard tours—operated by the founder of the Casa de Guías.

o **Mountain Bike Adventures ★★**, Jirón Lúcar y Torre 530, Huaraz (www.chakinani peru.com; ✆ **043/424-259**): The top company for single-track riding in the Cordilleras Blanca and Negra, run by Julio Olaza. He has Trek front-suspension bikes for rent (including helmets) and offers several 4- to 7-day itineraries, as well as 1-day bike trips. The company also runs a small and enjoyable guesthouse.

TREKKING

The Cordillera Blanca is blessed with some of the greatest trails and most spectacular scenery in South America, and it draws trekkers from across the world. Across gorgeous valleys and mountain passes nearly 5,000m (16,400 ft.) high, past stunning lakes, waterfalls, and rivers, the region truly earns the cliché so often accorded it: It's a mountaineer and trekker's paradise. There are terrific campsites throughout the valley and excellent guides, porters, and mules to round out your expedition.

There are some three dozen well-established treks in the Cordillera Blanca (and many dozens more that draw few tourists). Of the many treks possible from Huaraz, the classic **Llanganuco–Santa Cruz** route, one of the most beautiful on the continent, is understandably the most popular. The route across the Santa Cruz gorge begins in the village of Cashapampa and makes its way to the emerald-green lakes at the Llanganuco ravine. The 45km (28-mile) trek usually takes 4 or 5 days. Other popular circuits include **Alpamayo,** a beautiful trek among snowcapped summits that takes about 12 days; **Cedros Gorge,** which takes in mountains in the northern sector of the Huascarán Park (4 days); and **Llanganuco** and **Portachuelo,** a less demanding trek through the Quillcayhuanca ravine (1–2 days).

Other well-known routes are:

○ **Cojup Valley** (Huaraz to Laguna Palcacucha), 20km (12 miles), 2 days (moderate)
○ **Laguna Churup,** 25km (16 miles), 1 to 2 days (difficult)
○ **Olleros to Chavín,** a pre-Columbian trail that ends at Chavín de Huántar, 40km (25 miles), 3 days (moderate)
○ **Quebrada Quillcayhuanca to Cayesh,** 25km (16 miles), 2 to 3 days (easy to moderate)

The Casa de Guías in Huaraz has detailed information about these and other treks, and South American Explorers produces a good map of various treks in the region. Another good resource is *Peru & Bolivia: Backpacking and Trekking* (Bradt Publications, 2002), by Hilary Bradt, with descriptions of a number of treks in the Cordillera Blanca.

Even more accessible hikes in this daunting region should be undertaken only by individuals in good physical shape; tackling a mountain pass at nearly 5,000m (16,400 ft.) with gear and food is not easy for those unaccustomed to high altitudes.

CORDILLERA HUAYHUASH: THE new "IT" RANGE

As the treks in the Cordillera Blanca have become more popular in recent years, intrepid trekkers who are determined to find yet more solitude and untrammeled scenery are now setting out on extended trekking circuits of the **Cordillera Huayhuash ★★★**, which is even more pristine and remote. Although it extends only 30km (19 miles) from north to south, it, too, has phenomenal mountain vistas and sparkling lagunas—perhaps more spectacular still than the Cordillera Blanca—but only a few very isolated and primitive mountain communities.

The range, which was made a natural preserve in 2002, comprises seven peaks more than 6,000m (19,680 ft.) high and seven additional peaks higher than 5,500m (18,040 ft.). The landscape is more wide-open than that of the Cordillera Blanca, which is characterized by deep canyons. The major trekking and climbing agencies in Huaraz and Caraz offer Huayhuash treks, which usually begin in the town of Chiquián at 3,400m (11,150 ft.), 110km (68 miles) south of Huaraz. Trekking in the range is difficult, with as many as eight passes higher than 4,500m (14,760 ft.), and two main circuits are popular: One is an 80km (50-mile) round-trip; the other, which covers the entire range, is as much as 165km (102 miles) and takes from 12 to 14 days.

Llanganuco–Santa Cruz Trek ★★★

Popularly called the Santa Cruz trek (4–5 days), this is the most famous route in the Cordillera Blanca, one of the most scenic on the continent, and probably second in terms of popularity in Peru after the Inca Trail. Touted as one of the top five treks in the world by several outdoors magazines, its beauty is extraordinary, taking in towering snowcapped peaks, brilliant lakes, glacier-fed rivers, waterfalls, and pretty meadows. The route across the Santa Cruz gorge usually begins in the village of Cashapampa; many trekkers eventually make their way to emerald-green Lagunas de Llanganuco by combi, while others choose to begin at the lakes, thus adding a day or two to the trek. Although the 45km (28-mile) trail ranges from 2,900 to 4,750m (9,512–15,580 ft.) in altitude, it is rated moderate to difficult and can be undertaken by anyone in good physical shape who has allowed for time to acclimatize in Huaraz. In peak season (July–August), the trail can be quite crowded and the campsites and pit toilets along the route taxed. Trekkers can walk the trail in either direction, starting at Cashapampa (2 hr. by bus from Caraz) or Vaquería (2½ hr. by bus from Carhuaz). Some independent travelers prefer to start the trail at Vaquería because the daily bus from Huaraz allows time to make it to the campsite on the first day and get a good jump on the high pass the following day. All-inclusive treks from Santa Cruz to Llanganuco in a "pooled" service start at about $175 per person.

MOUNTAIN CLIMBING

Climbing in the Cordillera Blanca ranges from highly technical, multipitch ascents to rigorous, but nontechnical, climbs. The optimal climbing season is May through September. Huaraz serves as the principal hub for contracting qualified guides and tour operators and renting gear, but some similar infrastructure, on a smaller scale, can also be found in Caraz. The **Casa de Guías** in Huaraz (www.casadeguias.com. pe; ✆ 043/421-811) is one of your best preclimb resources, with a list of registered guides.

For experienced climbers up to the challenge, the Cordillera Blanca is nirvana. The range includes 50 permanently snowcapped mountain peaks of more than 5,610m (18,400 ft.), amazingly packed into an area just 177km (110 miles) long and 19km (12 miles) wide. Tested mountaineers can hope to bag several 6,000m (19,680-ft.) summits in just a 2- or 3-week trip. Less experienced climbers can choose among several easier and more popular climbs. For anyone, though, acclimatization is paramount. Allow between 3 days and 1 week before attempting any serious ascent.

The snowy peaks of **Ishinca** (5,534m/18,156 ft.) and **Pisco** (5,752m/18,871 ft.)—essentially 3-day climbs—require appropriate gear, conditioning, and guides, but can be undertaken by inexperienced climbers. Peru's most beautiful mountain, **Alpamayo** (5,957m/19,544 ft.) is an appropriate climb for those with some experience. **Huascarán** (6,768m/22,205 ft.), the highest mountain in the Peruvian Andes and the tallest tropical mountain in the world, takes between 6 and 9 days and poses a very challenging climb, suitable only for those with technical knowledge and extensive experience.

OTHER ADVENTURE SPORTS

HANG-GLIDING   Yungay's hill Pan de Azúcar is the most common spot for hang-gliding. For more information, contact **Monttrek** (✆ 043/421-124).

ICE CLIMBING   The Cordillera Blanca is a great spot to give this serious sport a try. The best mountains for ice climbing are Pisco, Ishinca, Huascarán, Alpamayo, Chopicalqui, and Artesonraju. Contact **Pony Expeditions** (www.ponyexpeditions.com;

© 043/391-642) or **Monttrek** (www.monttrekperu.com; © 043/421-124) for more information.

MOUNTAIN BIKING   The Callejón de Huaylas is one of Peru's top destinations for mountain bikers, with hundreds of mountain and valley horse trails cutting across fields, bridges, and creeks, and past traditional Andean villages. Dedicated cyclists can also look forward to the thrill of climbing to 5,000m (16,400 ft.) through mountain passes.

In Huaraz, you can rent mountain bikes for an hour, a day, or a week. During the annual Semana del Andinismo in June, there's a mountain-bike competition. Two of Peru's best mountain-bike agencies operate in the area: **Mountain Bike Adventures** in Huaraz (www.chakinaniperu.com; © 043/424-259) and **Pony Expeditions** in Caraz (www.ponyexpeditions.com; © 043/391-642). Both have equipment rental and excellent biking itineraries.

RIVER RAFTING   Near Carhuaz, the Río Santa, which runs the length of the Callejón de Huaylas from Laguna Conococha, is where rafting in the area is practiced. Sections differ in degree of difficulty from easy (Classes II–III) to technical (Class V). The section that's most often rafted is between Jangas and Caraz. The season is May through September, when water levels are low. **Monttrek** (© 043/421-124) and a handful of other tour operators in Huaraz offer rafting.

ROCK CLIMBING   Several agencies in Huaraz offer full-day rock-climbing tours in Caraz and Yungay, ranging from easy to moderate. Monterrey's Rocódromo and Uquia are the most popular spots. For more information, contact **Monttrek** (www.monttrekperu.com; © 043/421-124); the agency even has an interior climbing wall at its headquarters in Huaraz.

PLANNING
YOUR TRIP
TO PERU

GETTING THERE

By Plane

All overseas flights from North America and Europe arrive at Lima's **Aeropuerto Internacional Jorge Chávez** (www.lap.com.pe; ✆ **01/ 517-3100;** airport code LIM). Major international airlines from North and South America, Europe, and Asia all fly to Lima. For more information on which airlines travel to Peru, please see "Airline, Hotel & Car-Rental Websites," p. 450.

Within Peru, it's very important to reconfirm airline tickets in advance. For domestic flights, reconfirm 48 hours in advance; for international flights, reconfirm 72 hours before traveling (and be sure to arrive at the airport a minimum of 2 hr. in advance). Airport taxes are now included in the fares of tickets on both domestic flights and international flights. For domestic and international flight information, visit www.lap.com.pe or call ✆ **01/511-6055.** Connecting flights to other cities in Peru depart from the same terminal.

By Bus

You can travel overland to Peru through Ecuador, Bolivia, or Chile. Although the journey isn't short, Lima can be reached from major neighboring cities. If traveling from Quito or Guayaquil, you'll pass through the major northern coastal cities on the way to Lima. From Bolivia, there is frequent service from La Paz and Copacabana to Puno and then on to Cusco. From Chile, most buses travel from Arica to Tacna, making connections to either Arequipa or Lima.

The most common overland trip to Peru from a neighboring country is from La Paz, Bolivia, to Puno, on the banks of Lake Titicaca (which is partly in Peru and partly in Bolivia). The trip is about a 5-hour direct ride. **Ormeño** (www.grupo-ormeno.com.pe; ✆ **01/472-5000**) travels to La Paz as well as Venezuela, Colombia, Ecuador, Chile, and Argentina.

GETTING AROUND

Because of its size and natural barriers, including difficult mountain terrain, long stretches of desert coast, and extensive rainforest, Peru is complicated to navigate. Train service is very limited, covering only a few principal tourist routes, and many trips take several days by land. Visitors with limited time tend to fly everywhere they can. Travel overland, though very inexpensive, can be extremely time-consuming and uncomfortable. However, for certain routes, inter-city buses are your only real option.

By Plane

Flying to major destinations within Peru is the only practical way around the country if you want to see several places in a couple of weeks or less. Peru is a deceptively large country, and natural barriers make getting around rather difficult. Most major Peruvian cities can be reached by air, although not always directly. Some places in the jungle, such as Iquitos, can be reached only by airplane (or a very long and arduous boat ride). Flying to major destinations, such as Lima, Cusco, Arequipa, Puerto Maldonado, and Iquitos, is simple and relatively inexpensive. One-way flights to most destinations are between $89 and $219. Prices fluctuate according to the season. There is no airport in Puno (Lake Titicaca), however, so passengers must fly to Juliaca and continue by land the rest of the way (45km/28 miles). For some, this inconvenience prompts them to choose a direct train or bus from Cusco to Puno instead.

Peru's carriers, some of which are small airlines with limited flight schedules, include **LAN** (www.lan.com; ✆ **212/582-3250** in the U.S., or **01/213-8200** in Lima), **LC Busre** (www.lcbusre.com.pe; ✆ **01/204-1313**), **Peruvian Airlines** (www. peruvianairlines.pe; ✆ **01/716-6000**), **Star Perú** (www.starperu.com; ✆ **01/705-9000**); and **TACA Airlines** (www.taca.com; ✆ **800/400-TACA [8222]** in the U.S., or **01/511-8222** in Lima). All airlines fly in and out of Lima. **LAN** is the only domestic airline that flies to most major destinations in Peru (Arequipa, Cajamarca, Chiclayo, Cusco, Iquitos, Lima, Piura, Pucallpa, Puerto Maldonado, Tacna, Tarapoto, Trujillo, and Tumbes). **Peruvian Airlines** travels to Arequipa, Cusco, Iquitos, Lima, Piura, and Tacna. **Star Perú** flies to Ayacucho, Arequipa, Cusco, Iquitos, Juliaca, Puerto Maldonado, Trujillo, and Tumbes. **LC Busre** flies to Ayacucho, Cajamarca, Cusco, Huaraz, and Lima; while **Taca** flies to Arequipa, Chiclayo, Cusco, Juliaca, Piura, Puerto Maldonado, Tarapoto, and Trujillo.

Connections through Lima are often necessary, although a few destinations are accessible directly from Arequipa, Cusco, and Juliaca, and some routes might be limited to only a couple of days a week. Both flight schedules and fares are apt to change frequently and without notice. One-way fares are generally half the round-trip fare. Flights should be booked several days in advance, especially in high season, and you should also make sure that you get to the airport at least 1 hr. in advance to avoid being bumped from a flight.

LAN has a somewhat complicated and inconvenient air pass program for those who fly to Peru on its airline; passengers may purchase a minimum of three flight coupons (purchase must be made prior to landing in Peru). Depending on your flight schedule, however, this program may not save you much money over purchasing flights once in Peru.

By Train

The four tourist or passenger train routes operated by **PeruRail** (a private company owned by Orient Express) are popular and scenic journeys. Because luggage theft has been a problem on Peruvian trains, it's probably wise to purchase a premium-class ticket that limits access to ticketed passengers.

By far the most popular train routes in Peru connect Cusco, the Sacred Valley, and Machu Picchu. The train to Machu Picchu from Cusco is a truly spectacular journey.

Two competing tourist train companies, **Inca Rail** and **Machu Picchu Train,** now travel from the Sacred Valley (Ollantaytambo) to Machu Picchu. For prices and schedules of these and all Cusco and Sacred Valley trains, see chapter 9. PeruRail's **Titicaca Route** journey from Cusco to Puno is one of the most scenic and popular in Peru, although it is rather slow and pricey; trains stop in Juliaca en route. There are no PeruRail train passes.

For additional information, contact **PeruRail** (www.perurail.com ✆ 01/612-6700 in Lima, or 084/581-414 in Cusco); **Inca Rail** (www.incarail.com; ✆ 084/233-030 in Cusco or 01/613-5272 in Lima); or **Machu Picchu Train** (www.machupicchutrain.com; ✆ 084/221-199).

The **Ferrocarril Central Andino S.A.,** the spectacular high-altitude journey from Lima to Huancayo in the central highlands—the world's highest passenger line—is again in service for passenger travel after being shut down until a few years ago, though its notoriously problematic history makes it very difficult to plan a trip around riding the train. As of this writing, it runs once a month between July and November. For additional information, see chapter 7, and check for updates before you arrive in Peru (www.ferrocarrilcentral.com.pe; ✆ 01/226-6363).

By Bus

Buses are the cheapest and most popular form of transportation in Peru—for many Peruvians, they are the only means of getting around—and they have by far the greatest reach. A complex network of private bus companies crisscrosses Peru, with many competing lines covering the most popular routes. Many companies operate their own bus stations, and their locations, dispersed across many cities, can be endlessly frustrating to travelers. Luggage theft is an issue on many buses; passengers should keep a watchful eye on carry-on items and pay close attention when bags are unloaded. Only a few long-distance companies have luxury buses comparable in comforts to European models (bathrooms, reclining seats, and movies). These premium-class ("Royal" or "Imperial" class) buses cost up to twice as much as regular-service buses, although for many travelers, the additional comfort and services are worth the difference in cost (which remains inexpensive).

For many short distances (such as Cusco to Pisac), *colectivos* (smaller buses without assigned seats) are the fastest and cheapest option.

Ormeño (www.grupo-ormeno.com.pe; ✆ 01/472-5000), **Cruz del Sur** (www.cruzdelsur.com.pe; ✆ 01/311-5050), **Oltursa** (www.oltursa.com.pe; ✆ 01/708-5000), and **Civa** (www.civa.com.pe; ✆ 01/418-1111) are the bus companies with the best reputations for long-distance treks. Given the extremely confusing nature of bus companies, terminals, and destinations—which makes it impossible to even begin to list every possible option here—it is best to approach a local tourism information office or travel agency (most of which sell long-distance bus tickets) with a destination in mind and let the office direct you to the terminal for the best service (and, if possible, book the ticket for you).

By Car

Getting around Peru by means of a rental car isn't the easiest or best option for the great majority of travelers. It is also far from the cheapest. Distances are long, the terrain is either difficult or unrelentingly boring for long stretches along the desert coast, roads are often not in very good condition, Peruvian drivers are aggressive, and accident rates are very high. The U.S. State Department warns against driving in

GETTING around IN & OUT OF TOWN

Getting around Peru demands a mastery of terms that designate varied modes of transportation and a bewildering array of vehicles that aren't always easy to distinguish.

Within cities, travelers have several options. The most convenient and expensive are **taxis**, which function, for the most part, like taxis elsewhere in the world. However, taxis in Peru are wholly unregulated; in addition to registered, licensed taxis, you'll find "taxi" drivers who are merely folks with access to a two-bit car—usually rented for the purpose—and a taxi sticker to plunk inside the windshield. In Lima, this is overwhelmingly the case, and unregistered taxi drivers can be difficult to negotiate with for a fair price. There are no meters, meaning that you have to negotiate a price before (not after) accepting a ride. In other cities, such as Cusco, taxis conform to standard pricing (S/3–S/4 within town), so taking cabs outside of Lima is a considerably less daunting proposition for most travelers.

Combis are vans that function as private bus services. They often race from one end of town to another, with fare collectors hanging out the door barking the name of the route. Combis also cover routes between towns. **Colectivos** are essentially indistinguishable from combis—they are vans that cover regular routes (such as between Cusco and Pisac), and they usually depart when they're full. Routes are often so popular, though, that colectivos leave regularly, as often as every 15 minutes, throughout the day.

For inter-city transport, there is a similar slate of options. **Micros** are small buses, often old and quite colorful, that travel between cities. Both colectivos and micros are quite crowded, have a reputation for pickpockets, and can be hailed at any place along the street without regard for bus stops. You pay a *cobrador* (money collector), who usually hangs out at the door barking destinations at would-be travelers, rather than the driver.

Autobuses (also called *buses* or *omnibuses*) are large coaches for long-distance travel on scheduled inter-city routes. Classes of buses are distinguished by price and comfort: *Económico* is a bare-bones bus with little more than a driver and an assigned seat; classes designated *especial* (or sometimes "Inka") have reclining seats, videos, refreshments, and bathrooms.

As if that complex web of terms wasn't enough to get a handle on, there's an additional warning to heed: It's not uncommon to hear locals refer—loosely and confusingly—to buses as *carros* (which normally just means "car") and to colectivos as *taxis*.

Peru, particularly at night or alone on rural roads at any time of day. A four-wheel-drive vehicle is the best option in many places, but trucks and jeeps are exceedingly expensive for most travelers.

However, if you want maximum flexibility and independence for travels in a particular region (say, to get around the Sacred Valley outside of Cusco, or to visit Colca Canyon beyond Arequipa) and you have several people to share the cost with you, a rental car could be a decent option. By no means should you plan to rent a car in Lima and head off for the major sights across the country; you'll spend all your time in the car. It is much more feasible to fly or take a bus to a given destination and rent a car there. The major international rental agencies are found in Lima, and a handful of international and local companies operate in other cities, such as Cusco and Arequipa. Costs average between $40 and $70 per day, plus 18% insurance, for an economy-size vehicle.

To rent a car, you need to be at least 25 years old and have a valid driver's license and passport. Deposit by credit card is usually required. Driving under the influence of alcohol or drugs is a criminal offense. Major rental companies in Peru include **Avis** (www.avis.com; ✆ 01/444-0450); **Budget** (www.budgetperu.com; ✆ 01/517-1890); **Dollar** (www.dollar-rentacar.com.pe; ✆ 01/517-2572); **Hertz** (www.hertz.com.pe; ✆ 01/517-2402); **InterService Rent a Car** (✆ 01/442-2256); **National Car Rental** (www.nationalcar.com.pe; ✆ 01/517-2555); and **Paz Rent a Car** (✆ 01/436-3941). Taxes are included in the price. One U.S. gallon equals 3.8 liters or .85 imperial gallons.

For mechanical assistance, contact the **Touring Automóvil Club del Perú** (Touring Club of Peru) in Lima at www.touringperu.com.pe or ✆ **01/611-9999.**

TIPS ON HOTELS

A wide range of places to stay—including world-class luxury hotels in modern high-rise buildings and 16th-century monasteries and manor houses, affordable small hotels in colonial houses, rustic rainforest lodges, and inexpensive budget inns—can be found in Peru. Midrange options have expanded in recent years, but the large majority of accommodations still court budget travelers and backpackers (outside Lima's hosting of international business travelers).

Those places go by many names in Peru. *Hotel* generally refers only to comfortable hotels with a range of services, but *hostal* (or *hostales,* plural) is used for a wide variety of smaller hotels, inns, and pensions. (Note that *hostal* is distinct from the English-language term "hostel.") At the lower end are mostly *hospedajes, pensiones,* and *residenciales.* However, these terms are often poor indicators—if they are indicators at all—of an establishment's quality or services. Required signs outside reflect these categories: H (hotel), HS *(hostal),* HR *(hotel residencial),* and P *(pensión).* As in most countries, the government's hotel-rating system means that establishments are awarded stars for the presence of certain criteria—a pool, restaurant, elevator, and so on—more than for standards of luxury. Thus, it is not always true that the hotel with the most stars is necessarily the most comfortable or elegant. Luxury hotels were once exceedingly rare outside Lima, Cusco, and Machu Picchu, but that is no longer the case; budget accommodations are plentiful across the country, and many of them are quite good for the price. Some represent amazing values at less than $50 a night for a double—with a dose of local character and breakfast, to boot.

The great majority of hotels in Peru are small and midsize independent inns; few international hotel chains operate in Peru. You'll find a handful of Marriott, Best Western, and Orient Express hotels here and there, but by and large the chains you'll come into contact with are Peruvian. The most prominent, although they have only a handful of hotels each, are Casa Andina, Sonesta, Aranwa, and Libertador. Casa Andina and Sonesta hotels are comfortable, decorated similarly, and generally good value. Casa Andina also has an upscale line of Private Collection hotels in a few choice spots. The Libertador hotels are elegant four- and five-star establishments, largely in historic buildings, as are Aranwa.

Breakfast

Most hotels in Peru include breakfast in their rates. Breakfast may range from a huge buffet breakfast (and not only at the largest and most luxurious hotels) to continental breakfasts or more austere, European-style breakfasts of bread, coffee and jam.

In-room air-conditioning isn't as common, especially in lower-priced and moderately priced inns and hotels, as it is in many countries. In highland towns, such as Cusco and Puno, that's not usually a problem, as even in warmer months it gets pretty cool at night. In coastal and jungle towns (and at jungle lodges), it gets considerably warmer, though most hotels that don't offer air-conditioning units have ceiling or other fans. If you're concerned about having air-conditioning in your room in a warmer destination, it may be necessary to bump up to a more expensive hotel.

Advance reservations are strongly recommended during high season (June–Oct) and during national holidays and important festivals. This is especially true of hotels in the middle and upper categories in popular places such as Cusco and Machu Picchu. Many hotels quote their rates in U.S. dollars. If you pay in cash, the price will be converted into *soles* at the going rate. Note that at most budget and many midrange hotels, credit cards are not accepted. Most published rates can be negotiated and travelers can often get greatly reduced rates outside of peak season simply by asking. This is especially true of jungle lodges, where published international prices differ greatly from the rate one might obtain on-site.

Hotel taxes and service charges are an issue that has caused some confusion in recent years. Most upper-level hotels add a 19% general sales tax (IGV) and a 10% service charge to the bill. However, foreigners who can demonstrate they live outside of Peru are not charged the 19% tax (though they are responsible for the 10% service charge). In practice, hotels sometimes either mistakenly or purposely include the IGV on everyone's bill; presentation of a passport is sufficient to have the tax deducted from your tab. Many hotels—usually those at the midlevel and lower ranges—simplify matters by including the tax in their rates; at these establishments, you cannot expect to have the tax removed from your charges. At high-end hotels, be sure to review your bill and ask for an explanation of additional taxes and charges. Prices in this book do not include taxes and service charges unless otherwise noted.

Breakfast is most often included in the price, and increasingly that is the case for Wi-Fi Internet access, too.

Safety can be an issue at some hotels, especially at the lower end, and extreme care should be taken with regard to personal belongings left in the hotel. Leaving valuables lying around is asking for trouble. Except for hotels at the lowest levels, most have safety deposit boxes. (Usually only luxury hotels have

 Where are you @?

The @ symbol is hard to find on a Latin American keyboard. You must keep your finger on the "Alt" key, and then press "6" and "4" on the number pad to the right. If you're still unsuccessful and at an Internet cafe, ask the assistant to help you type an *arroba*.

shopping **IN PERU**

Peru is one of the top shopping destinations in Latin America, with some of the finest and best-priced crafts anywhere. Its long traditions of textile weaving and colorful markets bursting with tourists have produced a dazzling display of alpaca-wool sweaters, blankets, ponchos, shawls, scarves, typical Peruvian hats, and other woven items. Peru's ancient indigenous civilizations were some of the world's greatest potters, and reproductions of Moche, Nasca, Paracas, and other ceramics are available. (Until recently, it was surprisingly easy to get your hands on the real thing, but that's no longer the case.) In some cities—especially Lima, Cusco, and Arequipa—antique textiles and ceramics are still available. Some dealers handle pieces that are 1,000 years old or more (and others simply claim their pieces are that old). However, exporting such pre-Columbian artifacts from Peru is illegal.

Lima and Cusco have the lion's share of tourist-oriented shops and markets—particularly in Lima, you can find items produced all over the country—but other places might be just as good for shopping. Locals in Puno and Taquile Island on Lake Titicaca produce spectacular textiles, and Arequipa is perhaps the best place in Peru to purchase very fine, extremely soft baby-alpaca items. Handcrafted *retablos* (altars) from Ayacucho, depicting weddings and other domestic scenes, are famous throughout Peru and are available across the country. The Shipibo tribe of the northern Amazon produces excellent hand-painted textiles and decorative pottery. You'll also see items in the jungle made from endangered species—alligator skins, turtle shells, and the like. Purchasing these items is illegal, and it only encourages locals to further harm the natural environment and its inhabitants.

Baby alpaca and very rare vicuña are the finest woolens and are amazingly soft. Although many merchants are happy to claim that every woven wool item in their possession is alpaca or baby alpaca, much of what is sold in many tourist centers is anything but. Most, if not all, of the inexpensive, look-alike (S/15–S/60) sweaters, shawls, hats, and gloves you'll see in countless markets and stalls are made of acrylic or acrylic blends, and some even are blends of natural fibers and fiberglass. (A trekking guide in Cusco recently told me only partly in jest that you have to listen closely to people hawking cheap alpaca goods; they aren't saying "baby alpaca," but "may be alpaca.") If your new "alpaca" sweater stinks when it gets wet, it's llama wool. If you want the real thing—which is not nearly as cheap but still much less expensive than what you'd pay for alpaca of such fine quality in other countries—visit one of the established chain stores in large cities (most have "alpaca" in the name). Arequipa is one of the finest centers for alpaca goods, though Cusco and Lima are also excellent places to shop for alpaca.

The *artesanía* (popular arts/handicrafts) center par excellence of Peru is the highlands city of Ayacucho. The distinctive ceramic churches and *retablos* that are mainstays of handicrafts shops across Peru all come from Ayacucho (and a couple of small towns nearby), although a number of artisans have relocated to larger cities to more effectively market their wares.

In Lima, Cusco, and most tourist centers, there are scores of general, look-alike *artesanía* shops, and prices might not be any higher than what you'd find at street markets. At stores and in open markets, bargaining—gentle, good-natured haggling over prices—is accepted and even expected. However, when it gets down to ridiculously small amounts of money, it's best to recognize that you are already getting a great deal on probably hand-made goods and you should relinquish the fight over a few *soles*.

Many prices for goods include a 19% sales tax, which, unfortunately, is refundable only on purchases made at the international departure lounge of Jorge Chávez International Airport.

FROMMERS.COM: THE COMPLETE travel RESOURCE

Planning a trip or just returned? Head to **Frommers.com,** voted Best Travel Site by *PC Magazine.* We think you'll find our site indispensable before, during, and after your travels—with expert advice and tips; independent reviews of hotels, restaurants, attractions, and preferred shopping and nightlife venues; vacation giveaways; and an online booking tool. We publish the complete contents of more than 135 travel guides in our **Destinations** section, covering more than 4,000 places worldwide. Each weekday, we publish original articles that report on **Deals and News** via our free **Frommers. com Newsletters.** What's more, **Arthur**

Frommer himself blogs 5 days a week, with strong opinions about the state of travel in the modern world. We're betting you'll find our **Events** listings an invaluable resource; it's an up-to-the-minute roster of what's happening in cities everywhere—including concerts, festivals, lectures, and more. We've also added weekly **podcasts, interactive maps,** and hundreds of new images across the site. Finally, don't forget to visit our **Message Boards,** where you can join in conversations with thousands of fellow Frommer's travelers and post your trip report once you return.

---

room safes.) Place your belongings in a carefully sealed envelope. If you arrive in a town without previously arranged accommodations, you should be at least minimally wary of taxi drivers and others who insist on showing you to a hotel. Occasionally, these will provide excellent tips, but, in general, they will merely be taking you to a place where they are confident they can earn a commission.

A final precaution worth mentioning is the electric heater found on many showerheads. These can be dangerous, and touching them while functioning can prompt an unwelcome electric jolt.

For tips on surfing for hotel deals online, visit www.frommers.com.

FAST FACTS

Addresses "Jr." doesn't mean "junior"; it is a designation meaning "Jirón," or street, just as "Av." (sometimes "Avda.") is an abbreviation for "Avenida," or avenue. "Ctra." is the abbreviation for *carretera,* or highway; cdra. means *cuadra,* or block; and "of." is used to designate office *(oficina)* number. Perhaps the most confusing element in Peruvian street addresses is "s/n," which frequently appears in place of a number after the name of the street; "s/n" means "sin número," or no number. The house or building with such an address simply is unnumbered. At other times, a building number may appear with a dash, such as "102–105," meaning that the building in question simply contains both address numbers (though usually only one main entrance).

Area Codes Even though many area codes across Peru were changed back in 2003, you many find that many published telephone numbers may still contain old area codes. The area codes for the regions covered in this book are: Lima, **01;** Ica, Nasca, and Pisco, **056;** Cusco and the Sacred Valley, **084;** Puerto Maldonado, **082;** Iquitos, **065;** Puno/Lake Titicaca, **051;** Arequipa, **054;** Trujillo, **044;** Chiclayo, **074;** Máncora, **073;** Cajamarca, **076;** and Huaraz, **043.**

Business Hours Most stores are open from 9 or 10am to 12:30pm, and from 3 to 5 or 8pm. Banks are generally open Monday through Friday from 9:30am to 4pm, although some stay open until 6pm. In major cities, most banks are also open Saturday from 9:30am to 12:30pm. Offices are open from 8:30am to 12:30pm and 3 to 6pm, although many operate continuously from 9am to 5pm. Government offices are open Monday through Friday from 9:30am to 12:30pm and 3 to 5pm. Nightclubs in large cities often don't get going until after midnight, and many stay open until dawn.

Car Rental See "Getting Around/By Car," above.

Cell Phones See "Mobile Phones," later in this section.

Crime See "Safety," later in this section.

Customs Exports of protected plant and endangered animal species—live or dead—are strictly prohibited by Peruvian law and should not be purchased. This includes head-pieces and necklaces made with macaw feathers, and even common "rain sticks," unless authorized by the Natural Resources Institute (INRENA). Vendors in jungle cities and air-ports sell live animals and birds, as well as handicrafts made from insects, feathers, or other natural products. Travelers have been detained and arrested by the Ecology Police for carrying such items. It is also illegal to take pre-Columbian archaeological items and antiques, including ceramics and textiles, and colonial-era art out of Peru. Reproductions of many such items are available, but even their export could cause difficulties at Customs or with overly cautious international courier services if you attempt to send them home. To be safe, look for the word "reproduction" or an artist's name stamped on reproduction ceramics, and keep business cards and receipts from shops where you have purchased them. Particularly fine items might require documentation from Peru's National Institute of Culture (INC) verifying that the object is a reproduction and may be exported. You might be able to obtain a certificate of authorization from the INC kiosk at Lima's Jorge Chávez International Airport or the **INC** office at the National Museum Building, Av. Javier Prado Este 2465, 6th Floor, San Borja (✆ **01/476-9900**).For information on what you're allowed to bring home, contact one of the following agencies:

U.S. citizens: U.S. Customs & Border Protection (CBP), 1300 Pennsylvania Ave., NW, Washington, DC 20229 (✆ **877/287-8667;** www.cbp.gov).

Canadian Citizens: Canada Border Services Agency (www.cbsa-asfc.gc.ca; ✆ **800/461-9999** in Canada, or **204/983-3500**).

U.K. Citizens: HM Customs & Excise at ✆ **0845/010-9000** (from outside the U.K., 020/8929-0152), or consult their website at **www.hmce.gov.uk**.

Australian Citizens: Australian Customs Service at ✆ **1300/363-263,** or log on to **www.customs.gov.au**.

New Zealand Citizens: New Zealand Customs, The Customhouse, 17–21 Whitmore St., Box 2218, Wellington (✆ **04/473-6099** or **0800/428-786; www.customs.govt.nz**).

Disabled Travelers Most disabilities shouldn't stop anyone from traveling. However, Peru is considerably less equipped for accessible travel than are most parts of North America and Europe. Comparatively few hotels are outfitted for travelers with disabilities, and only a few restaurants, museums, and means of public transportation make special accom-modations for such patrons. There are few ramps, very few wheelchair-accessible bath-rooms, and almost no telephones for the hearing-impaired. Though it continues to lag behind Europe and North America, Peru has been a perhaps unlikely leader in South America in terms of seeking to make its tourist infrastructure more accessible to people with disabilities. In 1998, Peru initiated a countrywide project targeting tourism establish-ments to improve facilities, and in the last decade, Peru was the only country in South America to attend a Society for Accessible Travel & Hospitality conference. Request a copy of "Tourism for the People with Disabilities: The First Evaluation of Accessibility to Peru's Tourist Infrastructure," available from the Peruvian embassy in your home country, before your visit to Peru. The 99-page report features evaluations of hotels, restaurants, museums, attractions, airports, and other services in Lima, Cusco, Aguas Calientes, Iquitos, and Trujillo.

A helpful website for accessible travel in Peru is **Access-Able Travel Source** (www.access-able.com), which offers detailed destination articles on accessible travel in Peru and a wealth of specific information about Aguas Calientes, Chiclayo, Cusco, Huanchaco, Iquitos, Lima, the Chicama and Moche valleys, Pisac, Trujillo, and Yucay. Within individual reviews, you'll find information on ramps, door sizes, room sizes, bathrooms, and wheelchair availability.

One Peruvian hotel chain, **Posadas del Inca** (www.sonesta.com), stands out in a country where few places are equipped for accessible travel. With properties in Lima, Cusco, Yucay, and Puno, it maintains rooms in every hotel that are accessible for travelers with disabilities. See individual destination chapters for full reviews. Many travel agencies offer customized tours and itineraries for travelers with disabilities. **Apumayo Expediciones** (www.apumayo.com; © **054/246-018**) is way out in front in Peru, offering tours specifically designed for travelers with physical disabilities. **Accessible Journeys** (www.disabilitytravel.com; © **800/846-4537** or **610/521-0339**) caters specifically to slow walkers and wheelchair travelers and their families and friends; the organization offers a 10-day "Peru Explorer" trip to Lima, Paracas, Cusco, the Sacred Valley, and Machu Picchu. **InkaNatura Travel** (www.inkanatura.com) is also particularly well equipped to deal with travelers with disabilities: Beyond the website's specifics on Peru, it is an excellent resource with all kinds of general information and answers to frequently asked questions about traveling with disabilities.

For visitors coming from North America, a number of travel agencies offer tours and itineraries for those with disabilities. **Flying Wheels Travel** (www.flyingwheelstravel.com; © **877/451-5006** or **507/451-5005**) offers independent trips. **Accessible Journeys** (www.disabilitytravel.com; © **800/846-4537** or **610/521-0339**) caters specifically for slow walkers and those in wheelchairs and their families and friends.

U.S. groups that offer assistance to people with disabilities include **MossRehab** (www.mossresourcenet.org; © **800/CALL-MOSS [2255-6677]**), which provides a library of accessible-travel resources online; the **American Foundation for the Blind** (**AFB**; www.afb.org; © **800/232-5463** or **212/502-7600**), a referral resource for the blind or visually impaired that includes information on traveling with Seeing Eye dogs; and **SATH** (**Society for Accessible Travel & Hospitality;** www.sath.org; © **212/447-7284**), which offers a wealth of travel resources for people with all types of disabilities and informed recommendations on destinations, access guides, travel agents, tour operators, vehicle rentals, and companion services. You can also connect with SATH on Twitter and Facebook. The "Accessible Travel" link at **Mobility-Advisor.com** (www.mobility-advisor.com) offers a variety of travel resources to persons with disabilities. **Access-Able Travel Source** (www.access-able.com) offers extensive access information and advice for traveling the world with a disability. The quarterly magazine *Emerging Horizons* (www.emerginghorizons.com) is another handy resource.

Doctors If you need a non-emergency doctor, your hotel can recommend one, or contact your embassy or consulate.

In any medical emergency, immediately call tel] **105.** See "Health," later in this section.

Drug & Drinking Laws Until recently, Peru was the world's largest producer of coca leaves, the base product that is mostly shipped to Colombia for processing into cocaine. Cocaine and other illegal substances are perhaps not as ubiquitous in Peru as some might think, although in Lima and Cusco, they are commonly offered to foreigners. (This is especially dangerous; many would-be dealers also operate as police informants, and some are said to be undercover narcotics officers themselves.) Penalties for the possession and use of or trafficking in illegal drugs in Peru are strict; convicted offenders can expect long jail sentences and substantial fines. Peruvian police routinely detain drug smugglers at Lima's international airport and land-border crossings. Since 1995, more than 40 U.S. citizens have been convicted of narcotics trafficking in Peru. If you are arrested on drug charges, you will face protracted pretrial detention in poor prison conditions. Coca leaves, either chewed or brewed for tea, are not illegal in Peru, where they're not considered a narcotic. The use of coca leaves is an ancient tradition dating back to pre-Columbian civilizations in Peru. You might very well find that *mate de coca* (coca-leaf tea) is very helpful in battling altitude sickness. However, if you attempt to take coca leaves back to your home country from Peru, you should expect them to be confiscated, and you could even find yourself prosecuted. The hallucinogenic plants consumed in *ayahuasca* ceremonies are legal in Peru.

A legal drinking age is not strictly enforced in Peru. Anyone over the age of 16 is unlikely to have any problems ordering liquor in any bar or other establishment. Wine, beer, and alcohol are widely available—sold daily at grocery stores, liquor stores, and in all cafes, bars, and restaurants—and consumed widely, especially in public during festivals. There appears to be very little taboo associated with public inebriation at festivals.

Electricity All outlets are 220 volts, 60 cycles AC (except in Arequipa, which operates on 50 cycles), with two-prong outlets that accept both flat and round prongs. Some large hotels also have 110-volt outlets.

Embassies & Consulates The following are all in Lima: **United States,** Avenida La Encalada, Block 17, Surco (☎ **01/434-3000**); **Australia,** Victor A. Belaúnde 147/Vía Principal 155, Bldg. 3, Of. 1301, San Isidro (☎ **01/222-8281**); **Canada,** Calle Bolognesi 228, Miraflores (☎ **01/319-3200**); **United Kingdom** and **New Zealand,** Av. Jose Larco 1301, 22nd Floor, Miraflores (☎ **01/617-3000**).

The U.S. consulate is located at Av. Pardo 845 (CoresES@state.gov; ☎ **084/231-474**). The honorary U.K. consulate is at Manu Expeditions, Urbanización Magisterial, G-5 Segunda Etap (bwalker@terra.com.pe; ☎ **084/239-974**). Both are open daily from 9am to noon and 3 to 5pm.

Emergencies In case of an emergency, call the 24-hour **traveler's hotline** at ☎ **01/574-8000,** the general police emergency number at ☎ **105,** or the **tourist police** (POLTUR; ☎ **01/460-1060**). The **Tourist Protection Service** can assist in contacting police to report a crime; call ☎ **01/224-7888** in Lima, or **0800/4-2579** toll-free from any private phone (the toll-free number cannot be dialed from a public pay phone).

Also see the "Fast Facts" in individual destination chapters for branch information.

Family Travel Peruvians are extremely family-oriented, and children arouse friendly interest in locals. Although there aren't many established conventions, accommodations, or discounts for families traveling with children, Peru can be an excellent country in which to travel, as long as families remain flexible and are able to surmount difficulties in transportation, food, and accommodations. Few hotels automatically offer discounts for children or allow children to stay free with their parents. Negotiation with hotels is required. On buses, children have to pay full fare if they occupy a seat (which is why you'll see most kids sitting on their parent's or sibling's lap). Many museums and other attractions offer discounts for children 5 and under. Children's meals are rarely found at restaurants in Peru, but sometimes it's possible to specially order smaller portions. Peruvian food might be very foreign to many children—how many kids, or adults, for that matter, will be keen on tasting roasted guinea pig?—but familiar foods, such as fried chicken, pizza, and spaghetti, are easy to find in almost all Peruvian towns.

For a list of family-friendly travel resources, turn to the experts at www.frommers.com.

The Web is chockfull of excellent family-travel resources. Recommended U.S. general family travel sites include **Family Travel Forum** (www.familytravelforum.com), a comprehensive site that offers customized trip planning; **Family Travel Network** (www.familytravelnetwork.com), an award-winning site that offers travel features, deals, and tips; and **Traveling Internationally with Your Kids** (www.travelwithyourkids.com), a comprehensive site offering sound advice for long-distance and international travel with children. The best family travel blogs with an international outlook are **Delicious Baby** (www.deliciousbaby.com) and **Travel Savvy Mom** (www.travelsavvymom.com). In the U.K., the mighty **Mumsnet** (www.mumsnet.com/travel) has plenty of holiday and travel advice and reviews. **Take the Family** (www.takethefamily.co.uk) has ideas and inspiration for England and Wales. For a list of more family-friendly travel resources, turn to the experts at **Frommers.com**.

To find hotels, restaurants, and attractions that are particularly child-friendly, refer to the "Kids" icon throughout this guide.

Guides Officially licensed guides are available on-site at many archaeological sites and other places of interest to foreigners. They can be contracted directly, although you should verify their ability to speak English if you do not comprehend Spanish well. Establish a price beforehand. Many cities are battling a scourge of unlicensed and unscrupulous guides who provide inferior services or, worse, cheat visitors. As a general rule, do not accept unsolicited offers to arrange excursions, transportation, or hotel accommodations. See "Tipping" below for advice on tipping guides.

Health No vaccinations are officially required of travelers to Peru, but you are wise to take certain precautions, especially if you are planning to travel to jungle regions. A yellow-fever vaccine is strongly recommended for trips to the Amazon. Peruvian authorities confirmed an outbreak of yellow fever in the northeastern Department of Amazonas, but that was back in 2005. The Pan American Health Organization reported an outbreak and 52 total cases of yellow fever in Peru during the first 6 months of 2004, with slightly more than half of those resulting in death. (However, just two of those occurred in areas covered in this book, Loreto and Madre de Dios.) The **Centers for Disease Control and Prevention** (www.cdc.gov; ✆ **800/311-3435**) warns that there is a risk of malaria and yellow fever in all areas except Arequipa, Moquegua, Puno, and Tacna; Lima and the highland tourist areas (Cusco, Machu Picchu, and Lake Titicaca) are also not at risk.

The Centers for Disease Control and Prevention also recommend taking anti-malarial drugs at least 1 week before arriving in the jungle, during your stay there, and for at least 4 weeks afterward. In addition, the CDC recommends vaccines for hepatitis A and B and typhoid, as well as booster doses for tetanus, diphtheria, and measles, although you might want to weigh your potential exposure before getting all these shots. For additional information on travel to tropical South America, including World Health Organization news of disease outbreaks in particular areas, see the CDC website at www.cdc.gov/travel/tropsam.htm. Also of interest is the WHO's informational page on Peru, www.who.int/countries/per/en.

Remember to carry your vaccination records with you if you are traveling to the jungle. It's wise to get all vaccinations and obtain malarial pills before arriving in Peru, but if you decide at the last minute to go to the jungle and need to get a vaccine in the country, you can go to the following **Oficinas de Vacunación** in Lima: Av. del Ejército 1756, San Isidro (✆ **01/264-6889**); Jorge Chávez International Airport, second floor; and the International Vaccination Center, Dos de Mayo National Hospital, Av. Grau, block 13. In the airport at Puerto Maldonado, in the southern jungle, public nurses are also frequently on hand to administer yellow-fever shots to travelers who have not received the vaccination.

Visitors should drink only bottled water, which is widely available. Do not drink tap water, even in major hotels. Try to avoid drinks with ice. *Agua con gas* is carbonated; *agua sin gas* is still.

As a tropical South American country, Peru presents certain health risks and issues, but major concerns are limited to those traveling outside urban areas and to the Amazon jungle. The most common ailments for visitors to Peru are common traveler's diarrhea and altitude sickness, or **acute mountain sickness (AMS),** called *soroche* locally; sun exposure; and dietary distress.

North American visitors can contact the **International Association for Medical Assistance to Travelers (IAMAT;** www.iamat.org; ✆ **716/754-4883,** or **416/652-0137** in Canada) for tips on travel and health concerns. The United States **Centers for Disease Control and Prevention** (www.cdc.gov; ✆ **888/232-6348**) provides up-to-date information on health hazards by region or country. If you suffer from a chronic illness, consult your doctor before your departure. All visitors with such conditions as epilepsy, diabetes, or heart problems should consider wearing a **MedicAlert Identification Tag** (www.medicalert.org; www.medicalert.org.uk in the U.K.; ✆ **888/633-4298** or **209/668-3333**), which will alert doctors to your condition should you become ill, and give them access to your records through MedicAlert's 24-hour hotline.

Deep vein thrombosis, or as it's known in the world of flying, "economy-class syndrome," is a blood clot that develops in a deep vein. It's a potentially deadly condition that can be caused by sitting in cramped conditions—such as an airplane cabin—for too long. During a flight (especially a long-haul flight), get up, walk around, and stretch your legs every 60 to 90 minutes to keep your blood flowing. Other preventative measures include frequent flexing of the legs while sitting, drinking lots of water, and avoiding alcohol and sleeping pills. If you have a history of deep vein thrombosis, heart disease, or another condition that puts you at high risk, some experts recommend wearing compression stockings or taking anticoagulants when you fly; always ask your family doctor about the best course for you. Symptoms of deep vein thrombosis include leg pain or swelling, or even shortness of breath.

It's always worth consulting the following official travel health websites before leaving home: In Australia, **www.smartraveller.gov.au**; in Canada, **www.hc-sc.gc.ca**; in the U.K., **www.nathnac.org**.

Insurance   U.S. visitors should note that most domestic health plans (including Medicare and Medicaid) do not provide coverage abroad, and the ones that do often require you to pay for services upfront and reimburse you only after you return home. Try **MEDEX** (www.medexassist.com; ✆ **410/453-6300**) or **Travel Assistance International** (www.travelassistance.com; ✆ **800/821-2828**) for overseas medical insurance coverage. **Canadians** should check with their provincial health plan offices or call **Health Canada** (www.hc-sc.gc.ca; ✆ **866/225-0709**) to find out the extent of their coverage and what documentation and receipts they must take home in case they are treated overseas.

For general travel insurance, it's wise to consult one of the price comparison websites before making a purchase. U.S. visitors can get estimates from various providers through **InsureMyTrip.com** (✆ **800/487-4722**). Enter your trip cost and dates, your age, and other information, for prices from several providers. For U.K. travelers, **Moneysupermarket** (www.moneysupermarket.com) compares prices and coverage across a bewildering range of single- and multi-trip options. For all visitors, it's also worth considering trip-cancellation insurance, which will help retrieve your money if you have to back out of a trip or depart early. Trip cancellation traditionally covers such events as sickness, natural disasters, and travel advisories.

For information on traveler's insurance, trip cancellation insurance, and medical insurance while traveling, please visit **www.frommers.com/planning**.

Internet & Wi-Fi   The availability of the Internet across Peru is in a constant state of development. How you access it depends on whether you've brought your own computer or smartphone, or if you're searching for a public terminal. Internet access is plentiful, both in cybercafes (*cafés Internet,* or *cabinas*) and frequently in hotels, several of which now offer Wi-Fi. More and more hotels, airports, cafes, and retailers are offering free high-speed **Wi-Fi.** To find public Wi-Fi hotspots in Peru and throughout South America, go to **www.jiwire.com**.

Many hotels have computers for guest use, although pricing can vary from gratis to extortionate. To find a local Internet cafe, start by checking **www.cybercaptive.com** or **www.easyinternetcafe.com**. Although such places have suffered due to the spread of smartphones and free Wi-Fi (see below), they do tend to be prevalent close to popular tourist spots, especially ones frequented by backpackers. Aside from formal cybercafes, most **hostels** have Internet access.

If you have your own computer or smartphone, **Wi-Fi** makes access much easier. Always check before using your hotel's network—many charge exorbitant rates, and free or cheap Wi-Fi isn't hard to find elsewhere, in urban locations at least. Ask locally, or even Google "free Wi-Fi + [town]" before you arrive.

Savvy smartphone users from overseas may call using Wi-Fi in combination with a **Skype** (www.skype.com) account and mobile app.

Language Spanish is the official language of Peru. The Amerindian languages Quechua (now given official status) and Aymara are spoken primarily in the highlands. (Aymara is mostly limited to the area around Lake Titicaca.) English is not widely spoken but is understood by those affiliated with the tourist industry in major cities and tourist destinations. Most people you meet on the street will have only a very rudimentary understanding of English, if that. Learning a few key phrases of Spanish will help immensely. Turn to chapter 14 for those, and consider picking up a copy of the *Frommer's Spanish PhraseFinder & Dictionary.*

Legal Aid If you need legal assistance, your best bets are your embassy (which, depending on the situation, might not be able to help you much) and the **Tourist Protection Service** (✆ **0800/4-2579** toll-free, or **01/574-8000** 24-hr.), which might be able to direct you to an English-speaking attorney or legal assistance organization. Note that bribing a police officer or public official is illegal in Peru, even if it is a relatively constant feature of traffic stops and the like. If a police officer claims to be an undercover cop, do not automatically assume that he is telling the truth. Do not get in any vehicle with such a person. Demand the assistance of your embassy or consulate, or of the Tourist Protection Service.

Your first move for any serious matter should be to contact your consulate or embassy (see "Embassies & Consulates," earlier in this section). They can advise you of your rights and will usually provide a list of local attorneys (for which you'll have to pay if services are used), but they cannot interfere on your behalf in the English legal process. For questions about American citizens who are arrested abroad, including ways of getting money to them, telephone the **Citizens Emergency Center** of the Office of Special Consulate Services in Washington, D.C. (✆ **202/647-5225**).

LGBT Travelers Although the Inca nation flag looks remarkably similar to the gay rainbow flag, Peru, a predominantly Catholic and socially conservative country, could not be considered among the world's most progressive in terms of societal freedoms for gays and lesbians. It remains a male-dominated, macho society where homosexuality is considered deviant. Across Peru, there is still considerable prejudice exhibited toward gays and lesbians who are out, or men—be they straight or gay—who are thought to be effeminate. The word *maricón* is, sadly, a commonly used derogatory term for homosexuals. In the larger cities, especially Lima and Cusco, there are a number of establishments—bars, discos, inns, and restaurants—that are either gay-friendly or predominantly gay. Outside those areas, and in the small towns and villages of rural Peru, openly gay behavior is unlikely to be tolerated by the general population.

There are a number of helpful websites for gay and lesbian travelers to Peru. **Gay Peru** (www.gayperu.com) includes gay-oriented package tours, news items, and nightclubs and hotels (with versions in both English and Spanish). **Purple Roofs** (www.purpleroofs.com/southamerica/peru.html) has a decent listing of gay and lesbian lodgings, restaurants, and nightclubs throughout Peru. **Gay Lima** (http://lima.queercity.info) covers Lima and other parts of Peru, with English-language information on nightclubs and gay-friendly establishments and activities. The site **www.decajon.com** lists events, restaurants, and bars, with a special category devoted to gay establishments throughout the country. If you can read Spanish, **www.deambiente.com** also has detailed listings and articles about gay life in Peru. **GlobalGayz** (www.globalgayz.com) includes a very interesting article on gay life in Peru.

If you're planning to visit from the U.S., the **International Gay and Lesbian Travel Association** (**IGLTA;** www.iglta.org; ✆ **800/448-8550** or **954/630-1637**) is the trade association for the gay and lesbian travel industry, and offers an online directory of gay- and lesbian-friendly travel businesses. Many agencies offer tours and travel itineraries specifically for gay and lesbian travelers. **Above and Beyond Tours** (www.abovebeyondtours.com; ✆ **800/397-2681**) is a gay and lesbian tour operator. **Now, Voyager** (www.nowvoyager.com; ✆ **800/255-6951**) is a well-known San Francisco-based gay-owned and operated travel service.

For more gay and lesbian travel resources, visit **Frommers.com**.

Mail Peru's postal service is reasonably efficient, especially now that it is managed by a private company **(Serpost S.A.).** Post offices are open Monday through Saturday from 8am to 8pm; some are also open Sunday from 9am to 1pm. Major cities have a main post office and often several smaller branch offices. Letters and postcards to North America take between 10 days and 2 weeks, and cost S/5.50 for postcards, S/7.20 for letters; to Europe either runs to S/7.80. If you are purchasing large quantities of textiles and other handicrafts, you can send packages home from post offices, but it is not inexpensive—more than $100 for 10kg (22 lb.), similar to what it costs to use DHL, where you're likely to have an easier time communicating. UPS is found in several cities, but for inexplicable reasons, its courier services cost nearly three times as much as those of DHL.

Medical Requirements No vaccinations are officially required of travelers to Peru, but you are wise to take certain precautions, especially if you are planning to travel to jungle regions. A yellow-fever vaccine is strongly recommended for trips to the Amazon. Also see "Health," earlier in this section.

Mobile Phones (Cell Phones) The three letters that define much of the world's wireless capabilities are **GSM** (Global System for Mobiles), a seamless satellite network that makes for easy cross-border cell phone use throughout most of the planet. If your cell phone is unlocked and on a GSM system, and you have a world-capable multiband phone, you can make and receive calls throughout much of Peru. (Mobile coverage in Peru, even in rural areas, is surprisingly good.) Just call your wireless operator and ask for "international roaming" to be activated on your account. Unfortunately, per-minute charges can be high.

There are other options if you're visiting from overseas but don't own an unlocked GSM phone. For a short visit, **renting** a phone may be a good idea, and we suggest renting the handset before you leave home. North Americans can rent from **InTouch USA** (www.intouchglobal.com; ✆ **800/872-7626** or **703/222-7161**) or **BrightRoam** (www.brightroam.com; ✆ **888/622-3393**). You can also rent an inexpensive cell phone once you touch down in Peru. In the International Arrivals terminal of Lima's Jorge Chávez International Airport (as you enter the baggage carousels area), you'll find young female representatives of **Peru Rent-a-Cell** (✆ **01/517-1856**) offering inexpensive cell phones and plans (just $10 for the phone, up to a month, and incoming calls are free).

Per-minute charges for international calls can be high whatever network you choose, so if you plan to do a lot of calling home, use a VoIP service like **Skype** (www.skype.com) or **Truphone** (www.truphone.com) in conjunction with a Web connection. See "Internet & Wi-Fi," above. For advice on making **international calls,** see "Telephones," later in this section.

Multicultural Travelers   On occasion, travelers of color have reported being sub-jected to discrimination and unwelcoming behavior, either on the street or occasionally at bars and nightclubs. If you are the victim of what appears to be discriminatory treatment based on your ethnicity or color of your skin, call the 24-hour **traveler's hotline** at © **01/574-8000,** or the **Tourist Protection Service,** © **01/224-7888.**

Newspapers & Magazines   In Lima (but to a much lesser extent anywhere else in the country), you will find copies (although rarely same-day publications) of the *International Herald Tribune,* the *Miami Herald,* and the odd European newspaper, as well as *Time, Newsweek,* and other special-interest publications. All might be at least several days old. Top-flight hotels sometimes offer free daily fax summations of the *New York Times* to their guests. Otherwise, your best source for timely news is likely to be checking in with news outlet websites. Outside Lima, international newspapers and magazines are hard to come by. Among local publications, look for *Rumbos,* a glossy Peruvian travel magazine in English and Spanish with excellent photography. If you read Spanish, *El Comercio* and *La República* are two of the best daily newspapers.

Packing   Outside of a few high-end restaurants and clubs in Lima, Peru is overwhelm-ingly casual. You should probably be more concerned about packing the proper outdoor gear than the best duds to go out and be seen in. If traveling in rainy season, you'll want to be extra prepared for deluges in the highlands and Amazon. For those headed to Peru's great outdoors, see "What to Bring" in chapter 3.

For more helpful information on packing for your trip, download our Travel Tools app for your mobile device. Go to **www.frommers.com/go/mobile** and click on the Travel Tools icon.

Passports   Citizens of the United States, Canada, Great Britain, South Africa, New Zea-land, and Australia do not require visas to enter Peru as tourists—only valid passports (your passport should be valid at least 6 months beyond your departure date from Peru, though in practice many travelers with as little as 3 months' validity are frequently permitted entry). Citizens of any of these countries conducting business or enrolled in formal educa-tional programs in Peru do require visas; contact the embassy or consulate in your home country for more information.

White tourist (or landing) cards, distributed on arriving international flights or at border crossings, are good for stays of up to 90 days. Keep a copy of the tourist card for presen-tation upon departure from Peru. (If you lose it, you'll have to pay a $4 fine.) A maximum of three extensions, at 30 days each for a total of 180 days, is allowed.

No immunizations are required for entry into Peru, although travelers planning to travel to jungle regions should see "Medical Requirements," above.

See www.frommers.com/planning for additional information on how to obtain a pass-port. See "Embassies & Consulates," above, for whom to contact if you lose yours while traveling in the U.S.

Passport Offices

o **Australia   Australian Passport Information Service** (www.passports.gov.au; © **131-232**).

o **Canada   Passport Office,** Department of Foreign Affairs and International Trade, Ottawa, ON K1A 0G3 (www.ppt.gc.ca; © **800/567-6868**).

○ **Ireland** **Passport Office,** Setanta Centre, Molesworth Street, Dublin 2 (www.foreign affairs.gov.ie; ✆ **01/671-1633**).

○ **New Zealand** **Passports Office,** Department of Internal Affairs, 47 Boulcott Street, Wellington, 6011 (www.passports.govt.nz; ✆ **0800/225-050** in New Zealand or **04/474-8100**).

○ **United Kingdom** Visit your nearest passport office, major post office, or travel agency or contact the **Identity and Passport Service (IPS),** 89 Eccleston Square, London, SW1V 1PN (www.ips.gov.uk; ✆ **0300/222-0000**).

○ **United States** To find your regional passport office, check the U.S. State Department website (travel.state.gov/passport) or call the **National Passport Information Center** (✆ **877/487-2778**) for automated information.

Pharmacies Prescriptions can be filled at *farmacias* and *boticas;* it's best to know the generic name of your drug. For most health matters that are not serious, a pharmacist will be able to help and prescribe something. In the case of more serious health issues, contact your hotel, the tourist information office, or, in the most extreme case, your consulate or embassy for a doctor referral. Two of the biggest pharmacy chains, with locations in most cities, are Botica Fasa and InkaFarma. Hospitals with English-speaking doctors are listed in individual destination chapters.

Police Losses, thefts, and other criminal matters should be reported at the nearest police station immediately. Peru has special tourist police forces (Policía Nacional de Turismo) with offices and personnel in all major tourist destinations, including Lima, Cusco, Arequipa, and Puno, as well as a dozen other cities. You are more likely to get a satisfactory response, not to mention someone who speaks at least some English, from the tourist police rather than from the regular national police (PNP). The number for the tourist police in Lima is ✆ **01/225-8698** or **01/225-8699.** For other cities, see "Emergencies" above and "Fast Facts" in individual destination chapters. Tourist police officers are distinguished by their white shirts.

Safety Peru's reputation for safety among travelers has greatly improved and the country is more stable and safer than at any time I can remember—and I've been traveling to Peru for two decades. While some general warnings are required, for the most part, the majority of travelers will find Peru a very safe country with few of the overt threats to belongings or one's person that are sadly common in many parts of the world. Hopefully, the following warnings will seem over-the-top to travelers who enjoy Peru without incident.

The most precautions, as in most countries, are required in the largest cities: principally Lima and, to a lesser extent, Arequipa and Cusco. In most heavily touristed places in Peru, though, a heightened police presence is noticeable. Simple theft and pickpocketing are not uncommon; assaults and robbery are rare. Most thieves look for moments when travelers, laden with bags and struggling with maps, are distracted. In downtown Lima and the city's residential and hotel areas, there is a risk of street crime. Occasional carjackings and armed attacks at ATMs have been reported, but they are very isolated incidents. Use ATMs during the day, with other people present. Street crime and pickpocketing are most likely to occur—when they do—at crowded public markets and bus and train stations. You should be vigilant with belongings in these places and should not walk alone late at night on deserted streets. In major cities, taxis hailed on the street can lead to assaults. (Use telephone-dispatched radio taxis, especially at night.) Ask your hotel or restaurant to call a cab, or call one from the list of recommended taxi companies in the individual city sections. Travelers should exercise caution on public city transportation, and on long-distance buses and trains (especially at night), where thieves have been known to employ any number of strategies to relieve passengers of their bags. You need to be vigilant, even to the extreme of locking backpacks and suitcases to luggage racks.

In general, do not wear expensive jewelry; keep expensive camera equipment out of view as much as possible; use a money belt worn inside your pants or shirt to safeguard cash, credit cards, and passport. Wear your daypack on your chest rather than your back when walking in crowded areas. The time to be most careful is when you have most of your belongings on your person—such as when you're in transit from airport or train or bus station to your hotel. At airports, it's best to spend a little more for official airport taxis; if in doubt, request the driver's official ID. Don't venture beyond airport grounds for a street taxi. Have your hotel call a taxi for your trip to the airport or bus station.

Peru's terrorist past seems to be behind it. The terrorist activities of the local insurgency groups Sendero Luminoso (Shining Path) and MRTA (Tupac Amaru Revolutionary Movement)—which together waged a 2-decade guerrilla war against the Peruvian state, killing more than 30,000 people—were effectively stamped out in the early 1990s. It has now been years since there were significant concerns about a possible resurgence of those groups. Though it remains a situation worth watching, to date the most populous (and traveled) regions of the country have not been affected, and neither group is currently active in any of the areas covered in this book.

Senior Travel   Discounts for seniors are not automatic across Peru, though many attractions do offer a senior rate. Mention the fact that you're a senior (and carry ID with your birth date) when you make travel reservations; many hotels still offer lower rates for seniors. Many museums and other attractions also offer discounts; if a senior rate (often expressed as *mayores de edad* or *jubilados* (retired) is not posted, inquire and show your passport).

Smoking   Smoking is still quite common in Peru, and it is rare to find restaurants or bars with nonsmoking rooms. However, there are now a few hotels (usually high-end) and restaurants with designated nonsmoking rooms, and the trend is growing. There are nonsmoking cars on trains, and most long-distance buses are also nonsmoking.

Student Travel   Never leave home without your student I.D. card. Visitors from overseas should arm themselves with an **International Student Identity Card (ISIC),** which offers local savings on rail passes, plane tickets, entrance fees, and much more. Each country's card offers slightly different benefits (in the U.S., for example, it provides you with basic health and life insurance and a 24-hour helpline). Apply before departing in your country of origin. In the U.S. or Canada, at **www.myisic.com**; in Australia, see **www.isic-card.com.au**; in New Zealand, visit **www.isiccard.co.nz**. U.K. students should carry their NUS card. If you're no longer a student but are still younger than 26, you can get an **International Youth Travel Card (IYTC),** which entitles you to a more limited range of discounts.

Taxes   A general sales tax (IGV) is added automatically to most consumer bills (19%). In some upmarket hotels or restaurants, service charges of 10% are often added. Foreigners who can demonstrate that they do not reside in Peru (generally all you need to do is show your passport) are exempt from having to pay the IGV tax at hotels. Some unscrupulous smaller hotels occasionally try to dupe guests into believing that they have to pay this 19% tax; this is flatly untrue.

Telephones   Your best bet for making international calls from Peru is to head to any Internet cafe with an international calling option. These cafes have connections to Skype, Net2Phone, or some other **VoIP service.** International calls made this way can range anywhere from 5¢ to $1 per minute—much cheaper than making direct international calls or using a phone card. If you have your own Skype or similar account, you just need to find an Internet cafe that provides a computer with a headset. The easiest way to make a long-distance call within the country is to purchase a phone card (maximum S/30). Many of these cards, purchased at newspaper kiosks and street vendors who sell nothing else, are called **Tarjeta 147.** To use such a card, rub off the secret number; dial the numbers 1-4-7 and then dial the 12-digit number on your card. A voice recording will tell you (in Spanish only) the value remaining on the card and instruct you to dial the desired telephone number. It will then tell you how many minutes you can expect to talk with the amount remaining. You can also make international calls from Telefónica offices and hotels, although surcharges levied at the latter can be extraordinarily expensive. **Toll-free numbers:** Numbers beginning with 0800 within Peru are toll-free when called from a private phone (not from a public pay phone).

Callers beware: Many hotels routinely add outrageous surcharges onto phone calls made from your room. Inquire before you call. It may be a lot cheaper to use your own calling-card number or to find a phone card.

See also "Mobile Phones" earlier in this section.

Time   Peru is 5 hours behind GMT (Greenwich Mean Time). Peru does not observe daylight saving time. For help with time translations, and more, download our convenient Travel Tools app for your mobile device. Go to **www.frommers.com/go/mobile** and click on the Travel Tools icon.

Tipping   Whether and how much to tip is not without controversy. Visitors from the U.S. in particular tend to be more generous than locals and European visitors. Most people leave about a 10% tip for waitstaff in restaurants. In nicer restaurants that add a 10% service charge, many patrons tip an additional 5% or 10% (because little, if any, of that service charge will ever make it to the waiter's pocket). Taxi drivers are not usually tipped unless they provide additional service. Bilingual tour guides on group tours should be tipped ($1–$2 per person for a short visit, and $5 or more per person for a full day). If you have a private guide, tip about $10 to $20. For help with tip calculations, and more, download our convenient Travel Tools app for your mobile device. Go to **www.frommers.com/go/mobile** and click on the Travel Tools icon.

Toilets   Public lavatories (*baños públicos*) are rarely available except in railway stations, restaurants, and theaters. Many Peruvian men choose to urinate in public, against a wall in full view, especially late at night; it's not recommended that you emulate them. Use the bathroom of a bar, cafe, or restaurant; if it feels uncomfortable to dart in and out, have a coffee at the bar. Public restrooms are labeled WC (water closet), DAMAS (Ladies), and CABALLEROS or HOMBRES (Men). Toilet paper is not always provided, and when it is, most establishments request that patrons throw it in the wastebasket rather than the toilet, to avoid clogging.

VAT   See "Taxes," above.

Visas   For information about visas, see "Passports," above. Citizens of countries not covered there should visit the website of Peru's Ministry of Foreign Relations: www.rree.gob.pe.

Visitor Information   Within Peru, there's a 24-hour tourist information line, **iPerú** (© **01/574-8000**). Peru doesn't maintain national tourism offices abroad, so your best official source of information before you go is **www.peru.info**, the website of Prom Perú (Commission for the Promotion of Peru). Other helpful trip-planning websites include **www.peruvianembassy.us**, the Embassy of Peru in Washington, D.C.; **www.traficoperu.com/english**, the site for Traficoperu, a travel agency with information about flights, hotels, and special deals; **www.enjoyperu.com**, a similar site with good background information on specific areas; **www.perurail.com**, the official PeruRail website with route and service information; and **www.saexplorers.org**, the South American Explorers website, which is especially good for trekking and adventure travel information. Sites with good information on specific places include **www.huaylas.com** and **www.andeanexplorer.com**, for trekking and other information on Huaraz and the Callejón de Huaylas; and **www.machupicchu.org**, for more information on the celebrated Inca ruins and other sights in the Sacred Valley of the Incas. **South American Explorers** (www.saexplorers.org), with clubhouses in Lima and Cusco, is an excellent source of information, particularly on trekking and mountaineering in Peru, with a good selection of guides, maps, and dossiers on travel and trails, which is available to members. You can contact the group in the United States at ℂ **800/274-0568** or **607/277-0488;** otherwise, visit its Lima office at Piura 135, Miraflores (ℂ **01/445-3306**), or the Cusco office at Choquechaca 188, no. 4 (ℂ **084/245-484**).

The **Tourist Protection Bureau (Servicio de Protección al Turista),** which handles complaints and questions about consumer rights, operates a 24-hour traveler's assistance line at ℂ **0800/42-579**, or **01/224-7888** in Lima. The Tourist Protection Bureau office is at La Prosa 138, San Borja, Lima (ℂ **01/224-7888**) or toll-free from cities other than Lima (ℂ **0800/42-579**). For local branch locations and telephone numbers of the Tourist Protection Bureau, see "Fast Facts" in individual destination chapters.

For domestic and international **flight information,** visit www.lap.com.pe or call ℂ **01/575-1712.**

And, of course, there's plenty more—including features and updates—at **www.frommers. com/destinations/peru**.

Wi-Fi   See "Internet & Wi-Fi," above.

Women Travelers   Peru continues to be a very macho, male-dominated society. Although women are a growing part of the professional workforce and a relatively recent feminist movement is evident in urban areas, women do not yet occupy the (still unequal) position they do in many Western societies. Still, women should not encounter any insurmountable difficulties traveling in Peru. However, women should not be surprised to encounter perhaps unwelcome attention from men, especially if traveling alone. Many Peruvian men consider *gringas*—essentially, any foreign women—to be more sexually open and permissive than Peruvian women; thus, foreigners are frequently the targets of their advances. Blonde women are frequently singled out. *Piropos,* come-ons that are usually meant as innocuous compliments rather than as crude assessments of a woman's physical attractiveness or sexuality, are common in Latin America. However, comments can occasionally be crude and demeaning, and groping is not unheard of in public places (such as on crowded buses). Sexual assaults are rare, but the threat felt by some women, especially if they do not comprehend the Spanish slang employed in come-ons, is understandable.

Many men, as well as Peruvian women, might be curious about why a woman isn't married or traveling with a boyfriend. A woman traveling alone could elicit comments of sympathy or even pity. Wearing a ring on your wedding finger and deflecting comments and advances with a story about your husband working in Lima and meeting you in 2 days (or something to that effect) could be a useful tactic. In general, the problem is much more pronounced in large cities than in small towns and the countryside. Amerindian populations are conservative and even shy in dealing with foreigners, including women.

Women on the receiving end of catcalls and aggressive come-ons should do what Peruvian women do: ignore them. Their advances can usually be warded off with a forceful "No!", simple *"Déjame en paz"* ("Leave me alone"), or claim that one is married and traveling with her husband (*"Estoy casada. Ya viene mi marido"*). If that doesn't succeed, contact the tourist police (see above). Although some Peruvian men might be innocently interested in meeting a foreign woman, it is not a good idea to accept an invitation to go anywhere alone with a man. Women traveling in a group with other females, or especially with a man, are less likely to attract unwanted attention from men. Although I would hesitate to tell a woman friend that she should not travel alone in Peru, traveling with even one other woman might feel like a safer situation for many women, at least psychologically. If you are traveling alone, never walk alone at night anywhere—always call for a registered taxi. It's also a good idea to have a whistle handy; a piercing sound blast will deter almost any aggressor.

Journeywoman (www.journeywoman.com) is the best source of tips and ideas for women travelers. For general travel resources for women, go to **Frommers.com**.

MONEY & COSTS

THE VALUE OF THE PERUVIAN NUEVO SOL (S/) VS. OTHER POPULAR CURRENCIES

S/	US$	Can$	UK£	Euro (€)	Aus$	NZ$
S/1	$0.36	C$0.38	£0.24	€0.29	A$0.37	NZ$0.48

Frommer's lists exact prices in local currency (and occasionally in dollars, principally with regard to hotels that list rates in U.S. dollars). The currency conversions quoted above were correct at press. However, rates fluctuate, so before departing consult a website such as **www.oanda.com/currency/converter** to check up-to-the-minute rates. At press time, US$1 equals S/2.66.

On the whole, though prices have risen in the past few years and Peru is slightly more expensive than its Andean neighbors Ecuador and Bolivia (but less expensive now than Argentina and especially Brazil), Peru remains relatively inexpensive by North American and European standards. To those with strong currencies, Peru (outside of top-end restaurants and hotels) is likely to seem comparatively cheap. Peruvians tend to haggle over prices and accept and even expect that others will (politely) haggle, except of course in major stores and restaurants. In the bigger cities, prices for virtually everything—but especially hotels and restaurants—are higher, particularly in Lima. In addition, prices can rise in the high season, such as the Independence Day holidays (late July), Easter week (Mar or Apr), or Christmas, due to heavy demand, especially for hotel rooms and bus and plane tickets.

Peru's official currency is the **nuevo sol (S/),** divided into 100 *centavos*. Coins are issued in denominations of 5, 10, 20, and 50 centavos, and 1, 2, and 5 *soles*; bank notes in denominations of 10, 20, 50, 100, and 200 *soles*. At press time, the rate of exchange had dipped quite a bit under 3 *soles* to the U.S. dollar (from a high a few years ago of about 3.5). The U.S. dollar is the second currency; some hotels post their rates in dollars, and plenty of shops, taxi drivers, restaurants, and hotels across Peru will also accept U.S. dollars for payment. **Note:** Because many Peruvian hotels, tour operators, and transportation vendors charge prices solely in dollars, U.S. dollar rates are often listed in this book.

For help with currency conversions, tip calculations, and more, download Frommer's convenient Travel Tools app for your mobile device. Go to **www.frommers.com/go/mobile** and click on the Travel Tools icon.

Peru is still largely a cash society. In villages and small towns, it could be impossible to cash traveler's checks or use credit cards. Make sure that you have cash (both *soles* and U.S. dollars) on hand. If you pay in dollars, you will likely receive change in *soles*, so be aware of the correct exchange rate. U.S. dollars are by far the easiest foreign currency to exchange. Currencies other than U.S. dollars receive very poor exchange rates.

Automated teller machines (ATMs) are the best way of getting cash in Peru; they're found in most towns and cities, although not on every street corner. ATMs

WHAT THINGS COST IN PERU	S/
Taxi from Lima airport to Miraflores	S/45
Short taxi ride in town	S/3–S/8
Double room, inexpensive hotel	S/60–S/120
Double room, moderate hotel	S/120–S/250
Double room, expensive hotel	S/250–S/600
Three-course dinner for one without wine, moderate	S/45–S/75
Cocktail	S/16–S/20
Cup of coffee or bottle of water	S/3
Museum admission	S/5–S/20

allow customers to withdraw money in either Peruvian *soles* or U.S. dollars. Screen instructions are in English as well as Spanish. Some bank ATMs dispense money only to those who hold accounts there. Most ATMs in Peru accept only one type of credit/debit card and international money network, either **Cirrus** (www.mastercard.com; ✆ 800/424-7787) or **PLUS** (www.visa.com; ✆ 800/843-7587). Visa and Master-Card ATM cards are the most widely accepted; Visa/PLUS is the most common.

Be sure you know your personal identification number (PIN) and daily withdrawal limit before you depart. At some ATMs, your personal identification number (PIN) must contain four digits.

Travelers should beware of hidden **credit- or debit-card fees.** Check with your card issuer to see what fees, if any, will be charged for overseas transactions. Recent reform legislation in the U.S., for example, has curbed some exploitative lending practices. But many banks have responded by increasing fees in other areas, including fees for customers who use credit and debit cards while out of the country—even if those charges were made in U.S. dollars. Fees can amount to 3% or more of the purchase price. Check with your bank before departing to avoid any surprise charges on your statement.

You'll avoid lines at airport ATMs by exchanging at least some money—just enough to cover airport incidentals and transportation to your hotel—before you leave home (though don't expect the exchange rate to be ideal). You can exchange money at your local American Express or Thomas Cook office or at your bank. American Express also dispenses traveler's checks and foreign currency via www.americanexpress.com or ✆ 800/807-6233, but they'll charge a $15 order fee and shipping costs.

Banks are no longer the place of choice in Peru for exchanging money: Lines are too long, the task is too time-consuming, and rates are often lower at *casas de cambio* (exchange houses) or by using credit or debit card ATMs or money-changers, which are legal in Peru. If you can't avoid banks, all cities and towns have branches of major international and local banks; see "Fast Facts" in individual destination chapters for locations. Money-changers, often wearing colored smocks with "$" insignias, can still be found on the street in many cities. They offer current rates of exchange, but count your money carefully (you can simplify this by exchanging easily calculable amounts, such as $10 or $100), and make sure you have not received any counterfeit bills.

Counterfeit bank notes and even coins are common, and merchants and consumers across Peru vigorously check the authenticity of money before accepting payment or change. (The simplest way: Hold the bank note up to the light to see the watermark.) Many people also refuse to accept bank notes that are not in good condition (including those with small tears, that have been written on, and even that are simply well worn), and visitors are wise to do the same when receiving change, to avoid problems with other payments. Do not accept bills with tears (no matter how small) or taped bills.

Making change in Peru can be a problem. You should carry small bills and even then be prepared to wait for change. At one bar in Iquitos, I once paid with a S/20 note (less than $7) and the waiter said, "Hold on, I'm going to get change"—and he hopped on a bicycle and took off, not reappearing with correct change for nearly a half-hour.

13 AIRLINE, HOTEL & CAR-RENTAL WEBSITES

MAJOR AIRLINES

Aeroméxico
www.aeromexico.com

Air France
www.airfrance.com

American Airlines
www.aa.com

Aviacsa (Mexico and southern U.S.)
www.aviacsa.com.mx

British Airways
www.british-airways.com

Continental Airlines
www.continental.com

Delta Air Lines
www.delta.com

Iberia Airlines
www.iberia.com

LAN Airlines
www.lan.com

TACA Airlines
www.taca.com

United Airlines
www.united.com

AIRLINES IN PERU

LAN Airlines
www.lan.com

LC Busre
www.lcbusre.com.pe

Peruvian Airlines
www.peruvianairlines.pe

Star Perú
www.starperu.com

TACA Airlines
www.taca.com

MAJOR HOTEL CHAINS

Best Western
www.bestwestern.com

Doubletree Hotels
www.doubletree.com

Hilton Hotels
www.hilton.com

Marriott
www.marriott.com

Orient Express Hotels
www.orient-express.com

Sheraton/Luxury Collection Hotels
www.starwoodhotels.com

Westin Hotels & Resorts
www.starwoodhotels.com/westin

PERUVIAN HOTEL CHAINS

Aranwa Hotels Resorts & Spas
www.aranwahotels.com

Casa Andina
www.casa-andina.com

Costa del Sol
www.costadelsolperu.com

Inkaterra
www.inkaterra.com

Libertador Hotels Resorts & Spas
www.libertador.com.pe

Sonesta Posadas del Inca
www.sonesta.com

Tierra Viva Hotels
tierravivahoteles.com

CAR-RENTAL AGENCIES

Avis
www.avis.com

Budget
www.budget.com

Dollar
www.dollar.com

Enterprise
www.enterprise.com

Hertz
www.hertz.com

National
www.nationalcar.com

Thrifty
www.thrifty.com

USEFUL TERMS & PHRASES

14

Peruvian Spanish is, for the most part, straightforward and fairly free of the quirks and national slang that force visitors to page through their dictionaries in desperation. But if you know Spanish, some of the terms you will hear people saying are *chibolo* for *muchacho* (boy); *churro* and *papasito* for *guapo* (good-looking); *jato* instead of *casa* (house); *chapar* (literally "to grab or get"), slangier than but with the same meaning as *besar* (to kiss); *¡que paja está!* (it's great); *mi pata* to connote a dude or chick from your posse; and *papi* (or *papito*) and *mami* (or *mamita*), affectionate terms for "father" and "mother" that are also used as endearments between relatives and lovers (which can get a little confusing to the untrained outsider). The inherited Amerindian respect for nature is evident; words such as *Pachamama* (Mother Earth) tend to make it into conversation remarkably frequently.

Spanish is but one official language of Peru, though. **Quechua** (the language of the Inca Empire) was recently given official status and is still widely spoken, especially in the highlands, and there's a movement afoot to include **Aymara** as a national language. (Aymara is spoken principally in the southern highlands area around Lake Titicaca.) A couple of dozen other native tongues are still spoken. A predominantly oral language (the Incas had no written texts), Quechua is full of glottal and magical, curious sounds. As it is written today, it is mystifyingly vowel-heavy and apostrophe-laden, full of q's, k's, and y's; try to wrap your tongue around *munayni-ykimanta* (excuse me) or *hayk' atan kubrawanki llamaykikunanmanta* (how much is it to hire a llama?). Very few people seem to agree on spellings of Quechua, as alluded to in chapter 7. Colorful phrases often mix and match Spanish and Amerindian languages: *Hacer la tutumeme* is the same as *ir a dormir,* or "to go to sleep."

In addition to these primary languages, there are dozens of Indian tongues and dialects in the Amazon region, many of which are in danger of extinction.

BASIC SPANISH VOCABULARY

English	Spanish	Pronunciation
Good day	**Buenos días**	*Bweh*-nohs *dee*-ahs
Hi/hello	**Hola**	*Oh*-lah
Pleasure to meet you	**Mucho gusto/Un placer**	*Moo*-choh *goos*-toh/Oon plah-*sehr*
How are you?	**¿Cómo está?**	*Koh*-moh es-*tah*
Very well	**Muy bien**	Mwee byehn
Thank you	**Gracias**	*Grah*-syahs
How's it going?	**¿Qué tal?**	Keh tahl
You're welcome	**De nada**	Deh *nah*-dah
Goodbye	**Adiós**	Ah-*dyohs*
Please	**Por favor**	Pohr fah-*bohr*
Yes	**Sí**	See
No	**No**	Noh
Excuse me (to get by someone)	**Perdóneme/Con permiso**	Pehr-*doh*-neh-meh/Kohn pehr-*mee*-soh
Excuse me (to begin a question)	**Disculpe**	Dees-*kool*-peh
Give me	**Déme**	*Deh*-meh
What time is it?	**¿Qué hora es?**	Keh *ohr*-ah ehs?
Where is . . . ?	**¿Dónde está . . . ?**	*Dohn*-deh eh-*stah*
the station	**la estación**	lah eh-stah-*syohn*
(bus/train)	**estación de ómnibus/tren**	eh-stah-*syohn* deh *ohm*-nee-boos/trehn
a hotel	**un hotel**	oon oh-*tel*
a gas station	**una estación de servicio**	*oo*-nah eh-stah-*syohn* deh sehr-*bee*-syoh
a restaurant	**un restaurante**	oon res-tow-*rahn*-teh
the toilet	**el baño** (or **servicios**)	el *bah*-nyoh (sehr-*bee*-syohs)
a good doctor	**un buen médico**	oon bwehn *meh*-dee-coh
the road to . . .	**el camino a/hacia . . .**	el cah-*mee*-noh ah/*ah*-syah
To the right	**A la derecha**	Ah lah deh-*reh*-chah
To the left	**A la izquierda**	Ah lah ee-*skyehr*-dah
Straight ahead	**Derecho**	Deh-*reh*-choh
Is it far?	**¿Está lejos?**	Eh-*stah leh*-hohs
It is close?	**¿Está cerca?**	Eh-*stah sehr*-kah
Open	**Abierto**	Ah-*byehr*-toh
Closed	**Cerrado**	Seh-*rah*-doh
North	**Norte**	*Nohr*-teh
South	**Sur**	Soor
East	**Este**	*Eh*-steh
West	**Oeste**	Oh-*eh*-steh
Expensive	**Caro**	*Cah*-roh

English	Spanish	Pronunciation
Cheap	**Barato**	Bah-*rah*-toh
I would like	**Quisiera**	Kee-*syeh*-rah
I want	**Quiero**	*Kyeh*-roh
to eat	**comer**	koh-*mehr*
a room	**una habitación**	oo-nah ah-bee-tah-*syohn*
Do you have . . . ?	**¿Tiene usted . . . ?**	*Tyeh*-neh oo-*stehd*
a book	**un libro**	oon *lee*-broh
a dictionary	**un diccionario**	oon deek-syoh-*na*-ryoh
change	**cambio**	kahm-byoh
How much is it?	**¿Cuánto cuesta?**	*Kwahn*-toh *kwes*-tah
When?	**¿Cuándo?**	*Kwahn*-doh
What?	**¿Qué?**	Keh
There is (Is/Are there . . . ?)	**(¿)Hay (. . . ?)**	eye
What is there?	**¿Qué hay?**	Keh eye
Yesterday	**Ayer**	Ah-*yehr*
Today	**Hoy**	Oy
Tomorrow	**Mañana**	Mah-*nyah*-nah
Good	**Bueno**	*Bweh*-noh
Bad	**Malo**	*Mah*-loh
Better (best)	**(Lo) Mejor**	(Loh) Meh-*hohr*
More	**Más**	Mahs
Less	**Menos**	*Meh*-nohs
No smoking	**Se prohibe fumar**	Seh proh-*ee*-beh foo-*mahr*
Postcard	**Tarjeta postal**	Tahr-*heh*-tah pohs-*tahl*
Insect repellent	**Repelente contra insectos**	Reh-peh-*lehn*-teh *cohn*-trah een-*sehk*-tohs
Now	**Ahora**	Ah-*ohr*-ah
Right now	**Ahora mismo (ahorita)**	Ah-*ohr*-ah *mees*-moh (ah-ohr-*ee*-tah)
Later	**Más tarde**	Mahs *tahr*-deh
Never	**Nunca**	*Noon*-kah
Guide	**Guía**	*Ghee*-ah
Heat	**Calor**	Kah-*lohr*
It's hot!	**¡Qué calor!**	Keh kah-*lohr*
Cold	**Frío**	*Free*-oh
Rain	**Lluvia**	*Yoo*-byah
It's cold!	**¡Qué frío!**	Keh *free*-oh
Wind	**Viento**	*Byehn*-toh
It's windy!	**¡Cuánto viento!**	*Kwahn*-toh *byehn*-toh
Money-changer	**Cambista**	Kahm-*bee*-stah
Bank	**Banco**	*Bahn*-koh
Money	**Dinero**	Dee-*neh*-roh

English	Spanish	Pronunciation
Small (correct) change	**Sencillo**	Sehn-*see*-yoh
Credit card	**Tarjeta de crédito**	Tahr-*heh*-tah deh *creh*-dee-toh
ATM	**Cajero automático**	Kah-*heh*-roh ow-toh-*mah*-tee-koh
Tourist information office	**Oficina de información turística**	Oh-fee-*see*-nah deh een-for-mah-*syohn* too-*ree*-stee-kah

NUMBERS

1	**uno** (*oo*-noh)
2	**dos** (dohs)
3	**tres** (trehs)
4	**cuatro** (*kwah*-troh)
5	**cinco** (*seen*-koh)
6	**seis** (sayss)
7	**siete** (*syeh*-teh)
8	**ocho** (*oh*-choh)
9	**nueve** (*nweh*-beh)
10	**diez** (dyehs)
11	**once** (*ohn*-seh)
12	**doce** (*doh*-seh)
13	**trece** (*treh*-seh)
14	**catorce** (kah-*tohr*-seh)
15	**quince** (*keen*-seh)
16	**dieciséis** (dyeh-see-*sayss*)
17	**diecisiete** (dyeh-see-*syeh*-teh)
18	**dieciocho** (dyeh-*syoh*-choh)
19	**diecinueve** (dyeh-see-*nweh*-beh)
20	**veinte** (*bayn*-teh)
30	**treinta** (*trayn*-tah)
40	**cuarenta** (kwah-*ren*-tah)
50	**cincuenta** (seen-*kwen*-tah)
60	**sesenta** (seh-*sehn*-tah)
70	**setenta** (seh-*tehn*-tah)
80	**ochenta** (oh-*chen*-tah)
90	**noventa** (noh-*ben*-tah)
100	**cien** (syehn)
200	**doscientos** (do-*syehn*-tohs)
500	**quinientos** (kee-*nyehn*-tohs)
1,000	**mil** (meel)

SPANISH MENU GLOSSARY

GENERAL TERMS

Beef/steak **Lomo**
Bread **Pan**
Chicken **Pollo**
Dessert **Postre**
Eggs **Huevos**
Fish **Pescado**
Fruit **Fruta**
Lamb **Cordero**
Meat **Carne**
Pork **Cerdo/puerco**
Potatoes **Papas**
French fries **Papas fritas**
Rice **Arroz**
Roast **Asado**
Salad **Ensalada**
Seafood **Mariscos**
Shrimp **Camarones**
Soup **Sopa (chupe)**
Sweet potato **Camote**
Vegetables **Verduras**

MEAT

Adobo Meat dish in a spicy chili sauce
Alpaca Alpaca steak
Anticuchos Shish kebab
Cabrito Goat
Carne de res Beef
Chicharrones Fried pork skins
Conejo Rabbit
Cordero Lamb
Empanada Pastry turnover filled with meat, vegetables, fruit, manjar blanco, or sometimes nothing at all
Estofado Stew
Lomo asado Roast beef
Parrillada Grilled meats
Pato Duck
Pollo a la brasa Spit-roasted chicken
Venado Venison

SEAFOOD

Corvina Sea bass
Langosta Lobster
Langostinos Prawns
Lenguado Sole
Mero Mediterranean grouper

Spanish Menu Glossary | USEFUL TERMS & PHRASES

Paiche   Large Amazon fish
Tollo   Spotted dogfish

BEVERAGES
Beer   **Cerveza**
Cocktail   **Cóctel/trago**
Juice   **Jugo**
Milk   **Leche**
Mixed fruit juice   **Refresco**
Soft drink   **Gaseosa**
Water   **Agua**
 carbonated   **con gas**
 still   **sin gas**
Wine   **Vino**

PREPARATION
Cold (temperature)   **Frío**
Cooked   **Cocido**
Fixed-price menu   **El menú**
Fried   **Frito**
Hot (temperature)   **Caliente**
Raw   **Crudo**
Spicy   **Picante**
Vegetarian   **Vegetariano**

PERUVIAN FAVORITES
Ají de gallina   Spicy/creamy chicken
Anticuchos   Beef-heart brochettes
Causa   Mashed potatoes with avocado, stuffed with chicken or tuna
Ceviche   Marinated raw fish
Chaufa   Chinese fried rice
Chicha   Fermented maize beer
Chicha morada   Blue-corn nonalcoholic beverage
Chifa   Peruvian–Chinese food
Choclo   Maize (large-kernel corn)
Chupe   Soup or chowder (chupe de camarones, prawn chowder, is the most common)
Cuy   Guinea pig
Flan   Caramel custard
Lomo saltado   Strips of beef with fried potatoes, onions, and tomatoes over rice
Manjar blanco   Sweetened condensed milk
Pachamanca   Roast meat and potatoes, prepared underground
Paiche   Amazon river fish
Palta   Avocado
Palta rellena (or palta a la Reina)   Stuffed avocado (with chicken or tuna salad)
Panqueque   Crepe
Papa a la huancaína   Boiled potatoes in a creamy and spicy cheese sauce
Papa rellena   Stuffed and fried potato
Quinua   Andean grain (quinoa), often in soup (sopa de quinua)

Rocoto relleno   Stuffed hot pepper

Sopa a la criolla   Creole soup (noodles or grain, often quinoa, vegetables, and meat)

Tamal   Ground corn cooked and stuffed with chicken or pork, wrapped in banana leaves or corn husks, and then steamed

Tiradito   Ceviche-like strips of raw fish, marinated with ají peppers and lime but without sweet potatoes or onions, akin to Peruvian sashimi or carpaccio

QUECHUA & QUECHUA-DERIVED TERMS

Quechua ("*Ketch*-u-wa") was the language of the Inca Empire, and it remains widely spoken in Peru and throughout Andean nations 5 centuries after the Spaniards did so much to impose their own culture, language, and religion upon the region. It is the most widely spoken Amerindian language. Called *Runasimi* (literally, "language of the people") by Quechua speakers, the language is spoken by more than 10 million people in the highlands of South America. As much as one-third of Peru's 28 million people speak Quechua. Quechua speakers call themselves Runa—simply translated, "the people."

Quechua is an agglutinative language, meaning that words are constructed from a root word and combined with a large number of suffixes and infixes, which are added to words to change meaning and add subtlety. Linguists consider Quechua unusually poetic and expressive. Quechua is not a monolithic language, though. More than two dozen dialects are currently spoken in Peru. The one of greatest reach, not surprisingly, is the one still spoken in Cusco. Though continually threatened by Spanish, Quechua remains a vital language in the Andes.

In recent decades, however, many Andean migrants to urban areas have tried to distance themselves from their Amerindian roots, fearful that they would be marginalized by the Spanish-speaking majority in cities—many of whom regard Quechua and other native languages as the domain of the poor and uneducated. (Parents often refuse to speak Quechua with their children.) In some ways the presidency of Alejandro Toledo, himself of Amerindian descent, has led to a new valuation of Quechua (and Aymara). Toledo said he hoped to spur new interest and pride in native culture in schools and among all Peruvians, and he made a point of having the Quechua language spoken at his 2001 inaugural ceremonies at Machu Picchu. (Even Toledo's Belgian-born wife addressed the crowd in Quechua.)

Quechua has made its influence felt on Peruvian Spanish, of course, which has hundreds of Quechua words, ranging from names of plants and animals (*papa,* potato; *cuy,* guinea pig) to food (*choclo,* corn on the cob; *pachamanca,* a type of earth oven) and clothing (*chompa,* sweater; *chullu,* knitted cap). Quechua has also made its way into English. Words commonly used in English that are derived from Quechua include coca, condor, guano, gaucho, lima (as in the bean), llama, and puma.

Common Terms

Altiplano   Plateau/high plains

Apu   Sacred summit/mountain spirit

Campesino   Rural worker/peasant
Chacra   Plot of land
Cocha   Lake
Huayno   Andean musical style
Inca   Inca ruler/emperor
Inti   Sun
Intiwatana   "Hitching post of the sun" (stone pillar at Inca ceremonial sites)
Mestizo   Person of mixed European and Amerindian lineage
Pachamama   Mother Earth
Pucara   Fortress
Runasimi   Quechua language
Soroche   Altitude sickness (hypoxia)
Tambo   In-transit checkpoint on Inca highway
Tawantinsuyu   Inca Empire
Tumi   Andean knife
Viracocha   Inca deity (creator god)

TRY A LITTLE QUECHUA

English	Quechua	Pronunciation
Yes	**Riki**	*Ree*-kee
No	**Mana**	*Mah*-nah
Madam	**Mama**	*Mah*-mah
Sir	**Tayta**	*Tahy*-tah
Thank you	**Añay**	*Ah*-nyahy

ETIQUETTE & CUSTOMS

APPROPRIATE ATTIRE   Many travelers to Peru are dressed head-to-toe in adventure or outdoor gear (parkas, fleece wear, hiking boots, and cargo pants). This is perfectly acceptable attire for all but the fanciest restaurants, where "neat casual" would be a better solution. In churches and monasteries, err on the side of discretion (low-rise pants, midriff shirts, peekaboo thongs, and anything else that reveals a lot of skin are not usually acceptable).

AVOIDING OFFENSE   In Peru, you should be tactful when discussing local politics, though open discussion of the corruption of past presidents and terrorism in Peru is perfectly acceptable and unlikely to engender heated debate. Discussion of drugs (and coca-plant cultivation) and religion should be handled with great tact. Visitors should understand that chewing coca leaves (or drinking coca tea) is not drug use but a long-standing cultural tradition in the Andes.

In a country in which nearly half the population is Amerindian, expressing respect for native peoples is important. Try to refer to them not as *indios,* which is a derogatory term, but as *indígenas.* Many Peruvians refer to foreigners as *gringos* (or *gringas*) or the generic "mister," pronounced "*mee*-ster." Neither is intended or should be received as an insult.

On the streets of Cusco and other towns across Peru, shoeshine boys and little girls selling cigarettes or postcards can be very persistent and persuasive. Others just ask directly for money (using the euphemism *propinita,* or little tip). The best way to give money to those who are obviously in need of it is to reward them for their work. I get my scruffy shoes shined on a daily basis in Peru, and I buy postcards I probably don't need. If you don't wish to be hassled, a polite but firm *"No, gracias"* is usually sufficient, but it's important to treat even these street kids with respect.

Queries about one's marital status and children are considered polite; indeed, women traveling alone or with other women should expect such questions. However, discussion of how much one earns is a generally touchy subject, especially in a poor country such as Peru. Although Peruvians might be curious and ask you directly how much you make, or how much your apartment or house or car or even clothes cost, I suggest that you deflect the question. At a minimum, explain how much higher the cost of living is in your home country, and how you're not as wealthy as you might seem. Ostentatious display of one's relative wealth is unseemly, even though Peru will be blissfully inexpensive to many budget travelers.

GESTURES   Peruvians are more formal in social relations than most North Americans and Europeans. Peruvians shake hands frequently and tirelessly, and although kissing on the cheek is a common greeting for acquaintances, it is not practiced among strangers (as it is in Spain, for example). Amerindian populations are more conservative and even shy. They don't kiss to greet one another, nor do they shake hands as frequently as other Peruvians; if they do, it is a light brush of the hand rather than a firm grip. Many Indians from small villages are reluctant to look a stranger in the eye.

Using your index finger to motion a person to approach you, as practiced in the United States and other places, is considered rude. A more polite way to beckon someone is to place the palm down and gently sweep your fingers toward you.

GREETINGS   When entering a shop or home, always use an appropriate oral greeting (*buenos días,* or good day; *buenas tardes,* or good afternoon; *buenas noches,* or good night). Similarly, upon leaving, it is polite to say goodbye (*Adios* or *Hasta luego*), even to shop owners with whom you've had minimal contact. Peruvians often shake hands upon leaving as well as greeting.

PHOTOGRAPHY   With their vibrant dress and expressive faces and festivals, Peruvians across the country make wonderful subjects for photographs. In some heavily touristed areas, such as the Sunday market in Pisac outside of Cusco, locals have learned to offer photo ops for a price at every turn. Some foreigners hand out money and candy indiscriminately, while others grapple with the unseemliness of paying for every photo. Asking for a tip in return for being the subject of a photograph is common in many parts of Peru; in fact, some locals patrol the streets with llamas and kids in tow to pose for photographs as their main source of income. Often it's more comfortable to photograph people you have made an effort to talk to, rather than responding to those who explicitly beg to be your subject. I usually give a small tip (50 centavos to S/1, or 35¢) if it appears that my camera has been an intrusion or nuisance, or especially if I've snapped several shots.

It's not common except in very touristed places (such as the Pisac market), but some young mothers carrying adorable children in knapsacks and with flowers in their hair (and outstretched hands requesting a *propinita,* or tip) aren't actually mothers (or at least, not the mothers of the children they're carrying around); to tug at your

Etiquette & Customs

USEFUL TERMS & PHRASES

tourist heartstrings and pockets, they have essentially "rented" the babies from real moms in remote villages. I don't think it's an especially good idea to reward this practice. If a very young woman has several children in tow, all dolled up for pictures and making the rounds all afternoon, she is very likely one of these rent-a-moms.

Photographing military, police, or airport installations is strictly forbidden. Many churches, convents, and museums also do not allow photography or video.

PUNCTUALITY   Punctuality is not one of the trademarks of Peru or Latin America in general. Peruvians are customarily a half-hour late to most personal appointments, and it is not considered very bad form to leave someone hanging in a cafe for up to an hour. It is expected, so if you have a meeting scheduled, unless a strict *hora inglesa* (English hour) is specified, be prepared to wait.

SHOPPING   Bargaining is considered acceptable in markets and with taxi drivers, and even hotels, but only up to a point—don't overdo it. Also bear in mind that many shops in large and small towns close at midday, from 1 to 3pm or 2 to 4pm.

14

USEFUL TERMS & PHRASES

Etiquette & Customs

Index